Practice, Engage, and Assess

- **Enhanced eText**—The Pearson eText gives students access to their textbook anytime, anywhere. In addition to note-taking, highlighting, and bookmarking, the Pearson eText offers interactive and sharing features. Students actively read and learn through embedded and auto-graded practice, real-time data-graphs, animations, author videos, and more. Instructors can share comments or highlights, and students can add their own, for a tight community of learners in any class.

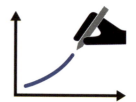

- **Practice**—Algorithmically generated homework and study plan exercises with instant feedback ensure varied and productive practice, helping students improve their understanding and prepare for quizzes and tests. Draw-graph exercises encourage students to practice the language of economics.

- **Learning Resources**—Personalized learning aids such as Help Me Solve This problem walkthroughs, Teach Me explanations of the underlying concepts, and Figure Animations provide on-demand help when students need it most.

- **Personalized Study Plan**—Assists students in monitoring their own progress by offering them a customized study plan based on Homework, Quiz, and Test results. Includes regenerated exercises with unlimited practice, as well as the opportunity to earn mastery points by completing quizzes on recommended learning objectives.

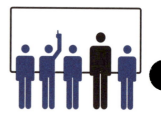

- **Digital Interactives**—Engaging assessment activities that promote critical thinking and application of key economic principles. Each Digital Interactive has progressive levels where students can explore, apply, compare, and analyze economic principles. Many Digital Interactives include real time data from FRED® that displays, in graph and table form, up-to-the-minute data on key macro variables. Digital Interactives can be assigned and graded within MyEconLab, or used as a lecture tool to encourage engagement, classroom conversation, and group work.

- **NEW: Math Review Exercises in MyEconLab**—MyEconLab now offers an array of assignable and auto-graded exercises that cover fundamental math concepts. Geared specifically toward principles and intermediate economics students, these exercises aim to increase student confidence and success in these courses. Our new Math Review is accessible from the assignment manager and contains over 150 graphing, algebra, and calculus exercises for homework, quiz, and test use.

$$P = c + dQ_S$$

with MyEconLab®

- **Real-Time Data Analysis Exercises**—Using current macro data to help students understand the impact of changes in economic variables, Real-Time Data Analysis Exercises communicate directly with the Federal Reserve Bank of St. Louis's FRED® site and update as new data are available.

- **Current News Exercises**—Every week, current microeconomic and macroeconomic news articles or videos, with accompanying exercises, are posted to MyEconLab. Assignable and auto-graded, these multi-part exercises ask students to recognize and apply economic concepts to real-world events.

- **Experiments**—Flexible, easy-to-assign, auto-graded, and available in Single Player and Multiplayer versions, Experiments in MyEconLab make learning fun and engaging.

- **Reporting Dashboard**—View, analyze, and report learning outcomes clearly and easily. Available via the Gradebook and fully mobile-ready, the Reporting Dashboard presents student performance data at the class, section, and program levels in an accessible, visual manner.

- **LMS Integration**—Link from any LMS platform to access assignments, rosters, and resources, and synchronize MyLab grades with your LMS gradebook. For students, new direct, single sign-on provides access to all the personalized learning MyLab resources that make studying more efficient and effective.

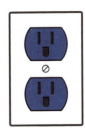

- **Mobile Ready**—Students and instructors can access multimedia resources and complete assessments right at their fingertips, on any mobile device.

International Economics

SEVENTH EDITION

The Pearson Series in Economics

Abel/Bernanke/Croushore
Macroeconomics*

Bade/Parkin
Foundations of Economics*

Berck/Helfand
*The Economics of the
Environment*

Bierman/Fernandez
*Game Theory with Economic
Applications*

Blanchard
Macroeconomics*

Blau/Ferber/Winkler
*The Economics of Women, Men
and Work*

**Boardman/Greenberg/Vining/
Weimer**
Cost-Benefit Analysis

Boyer
*Principles of Transportation
Economics*

Branson
*Macroeconomic Theory and
Policy*

Brock/Adams
*The Structure of American
Industry*

Bruce
*Public Finance and the Ameri-
can Economy*

Carlton/Perloff
Modern Industrial Organization

Case/Fair/Oster
Principles of Economics*

Caves/Frankel/Jones
*World Trade and Payments: An
Introduction*

Chapman
*Environmental Economics:
Theory, Application, and Policy*

Cooter/Ulen
Law & Economics

Downs
*An Economic Theory of
Democracy*

Ehrenberg/Smith
Modern Labor Economics

Farnham
Economics for Managers

Folland/Goodman/Stano
*The Economics of Health and
Health Care*

Fort
Sports Economics

Froyen
Macroeconomics

Fusfeld
The Age of the Economist

Gerber
International Economics*

González-Rivera
*Forecasting for Economics and
Business*

Gordon
Macroeconomics*

Greene
Econometric Analysis

Gregory
Essentials of Economics

Gregory/Stuart
*Russian and Soviet Economic
Performance and Structure*

Hartwick/Olewiler
*The Economics of Natural
Resource Use*

Heilbroner/Milberg
*The Making of the Economic
Society*

Heyne/Boettke/Prychitko
The Economic Way of Thinking

Hoffman/Averett
*Women and the Economy:
Family, Work, and Pay*

Holt
*Markets, Games, & Strategic
Behavior*

Hubbard/O'Brien
Economics*

*Money, Banking, and the
Financial System**

Hubbard/O'Brien/Rafferty
Macroeconomics*

Hughes/Cain
American Economic History

Husted/Melvin
International Economics

Jehle/Reny
*Advanced Microeconomic
Theory*

Johnson-Lans
A Health Economics Primer

Keat/Young
Managerial Economics

Klein
*Mathematical Methods for
Economics*

Krugman/Obstfeld/Melitz
*International Economics:
Theory and Policy**

Laidler
The Demand for Money

Leeds/von Allmen
The Economics of Sports

Leeds/von Allmen/Schiming
Economics*

Lipsey/Ragan/Storer
Economics*

Lynn
Economic Development: Theory and Practice for a Divided World

Miller
Economics Today*

Understanding Modern Economics

Miller/Benjamin
The Economics of Macro Issues

Miller/Benjamin/North
The Economics of Public Issues

Mills/Hamilton
Urban Economics

Mishkin
The Economics of Money, Banking, and Financial Markets*

The Economics of Money, Banking, and Financial Markets, Business School Edition*

Macroeconomics: Policy and Practice*

Murray
Econometrics: A Modern Introduction

Nafziger
The Economics of Developing Countries

O'Sullivan/Sheffrin/Perez
Economics: Principles, Applications and Tools*

Parkin
Economics*

Perloff
Microeconomics*

Microeconomics: Theory and Applications with Calculus*

Phelps
Health Economics

Pindyck/Rubinfeld
Microeconomics*

Riddell/Shackelford/Stamos/Schneider
Economics: A Tool for Critically Understanding Society

Ritter/Silber/Udell
Principles of Money, Banking & Financial Markets*

Roberts
The Choice: A Fable of Free Trade and Protection

Rohlf
Introduction to Economic Reasoning

Ruffin/Gregory
Principles of Economics

Sargent
Rational Expectations and Inflation

Sawyer/Sprinkle
International Economics

Scherer
Industry Structure, Strategy, and Public Policy

Schiller
The Economics of Poverty and Discrimination

Sherman
Market Regulation

Silberberg
Principles of Microeconomics

Stock/Watson
Introduction to Econometrics

Studenmund
Using Econometrics: A Practical Guide

Tietenberg/Lewis
Environmental and Natural Resource Economics

Environmental Economics and Policy

Todaro/Smith
Economic Development

Waldman
Microeconomics

Waldman/Jensen
Industrial Organization: Theory and Practice

Walters/Walters/Appel/Callahan/Centanni/Maex/O'Neill
Econversations: Today's Students Discuss Today's Issues

Weil
Economic Growth

Williamson
Macroeconomics

International Economics

James Gerber

San Diego State University

SEVENTH EDITION

New York, NY

For Monica and Elizabeth.

Vice President, Business Publishing: Donna Battista
Director of Portfolio Management: Adrienne D'Ambrosio
Director, Courseware Portfolio Management: Ashley Dodge
Editorial Assistant: Michelle Zeng
Senior Sponsoring Editor: Neeraj Bhalla
Vice President, Product Marketing: Roxanne McCarley
Director of Strategic Marketing: Brad Parkins
Strategic Marketing Manager: Deborah Strickland
Product Marketer: Tricia Murphy
Field Marketing Manager: Ramona Elmer
Product Marketing Assistant: Jessica Quazza
Vice President, Production and Digital Studio, Arts and Business: Etain O'Dea
Director of Production, Business: Jeff Holcomb
Managing Producer, Business: Alison Kalil

Operations Specialist: Carol Melville
Creative Director: Blair Brown
Manager, Learning Tools: Brian Surette
Content Developer, Learning Tools: Lindsey Sloan
Managing Producer, Digital Studio, Arts and Business: Diane Lombardo
Digital Studio Producer: Melissa Honig
Digital Studio Producer: Alana Coles
Digital Content Project Lead: Courtney Kamauf
Full-Service Project Management and Composition: SPi Global
Interior Design: SPi Global
Cover Design: SPi Global
Cover Art: Luciano Mortula/Shutterstock
Printer/Binder: LSC Communications Crawfordsville
Cover Printer: Phoenix

Library of Congress Cataloging-in-Publication Data

Names: Gerber, James, author.
Title: International economics / James Gerber, San Diego State University.
Description: Seventh edition. | Boston: Pearson Education, [2018]
Identifiers: LCCN 2016042070| ISBN 9780134472096 | ISBN 0134472098
Subjects: LCSH: International economic relations. | International economic integration. | International trade. | Commercial policy. | United States—Foreign economic relations.
Classification: LCC HF1359 .G474 2018 | DDC 337—dc23 LC record available at https://lccn.loc.gov/2016042070

4 17

ISBN 10: 0-13-447209-8
ISBN 13: 978-0-13-447209-6

BRIEF CONTENTS

Suggested Readings are available at www.pearsonhighered.com

CONTENTS

PREFACE

International Economics is designed for a one-semester course covering both the micro and macro components of international economics. The Seventh Edition continues the approach of the first six editions by offering a principles-level introduction to the core theories, together with policy analysis and the institutional and historical contexts of international economic relations. My goal is to make economic reasoning about the international economy accessible to a diverse group of students, including both economics majors and nonmajors. My intention is to present the consensus of economic opinion, when one exists, and to describe the differences when one does not. In general, however, economists are more often in agreement than not.

New to the Seventh Edition

This Seventh Edition of *International Economics* preserves the organization and coverage of the Sixth Edition and adds a number of updates and enhancements. New to this edition:

- All tables and graphs have been updated.
- New case studies are added in Chapter 2 on the Asian Infrastructure and Investment Bank; Chapter 5 on industrial policies targeting clean energy technology; and Chapter 16 on the Worldwide Governance Indicators.
- Chapter 9 on the balance of payments has incorporated the accounting revisions of the IMF and the implementation of the revisions by the U.S. Bureau of Economic Analysis. The changes recommended by the IMF are mostly terminology, but also in the presentation of debits and credits. Chapter 9 also adds a new appendix on the terminology of numbers: billions, thousands of millions, milliards, and trillions.
- The discussion of financial crises in Chapter 12 is presented in terms of vulnerabilities and triggers, following the terminology used by former Fed Chairman Ben Bernanke, among others.
- Chapter 16 has dropped the World Bank's now-dated terminology and focus on the High Performance Asian Economies in favor of a more empirically determined set of high growth, export oriented East Asian economies.
- Chapter 17 is focused on India and China, exclusively.

- The discussion of trade and jobs in Chapters 4, 13, and 17 is more nuanced and reflects the growing challenge to the consensus that trade is not the cause of manufacturing's decline in high-income countries.

Hallmarks of International Economics

Several features of *International Economics* distinguish it from the many excellent texts in the field:

- First, the approach is broader than the theoretical apparatus used by economists. Economic theory is covered and its mastery is essential, but most readers grasp theory more completely when it is presented along with real-world applications. To this end, I have supplemented economic theory with case studies and other content ranging from the role of economic institutions and the analysis of international economic policies to the recent history of the world economy and the challenges facing different geographical regions as they become more economically integrated internationally .

- Second, the objective of covering both the micro and macro sides in a one-semester course necessitates paring back the coverage of theory in order to focus on the central concepts. As all instructors are aware, many theoretical topics are of secondary or tertiary importance, which can pose a problem for students who may lack the needed breadth and depth of understanding to rank topics by their relative importance.

- Third, *International Economics* provides richer historical and institutional detail than most other texts. This material illuminates the relationships between economic theory and policy, and between economics and the other social sciences.

- Fourth, I have organized Part 4 of the book into five chapters, each focused on a geographic area as follows: North America with emphasis on the United States, the European Union, Latin America, East Asia, and India and China. These chapters offer students the chance to broaden their understanding of world trends and to observe the intellectual power of economic theory in practice.

Flexibility of Organization

A text requires a fixed topical sequence because it must order the chapters one after another. This is a potential problem for some instructors, as there is a wide variety of preferences for the order in which topics are taught. The Seventh Edition, like the previous editions, strives for flexibility in allowing instructors to find their own preferred sequence.

Part 1 includes two introductory chapters that are designed to build vocabulary, develop historical perspective, and provide background information about the different international organizations and the roles they play in the world economy. Some instructors prefer to delve into the theory chapters immediately, reserving this material for later in the course. There is no loss of continuity with this approach.

Part 2 presents the micro side of international economics, while Part 3 covers the macro side. These two parts can easily be reversed in sequence if desired.

Part 2 includes six chapters that cover trade models (Chapters 3–5) and commercial policy (Chapters 6–8). A condensed treatment of this section could focus on the Ricardian model in Chapter 3, and the analysis of tariffs and quotas in Chapters 6 and 7. Chapter 8 on labor and environmental standards can stand on its own, although the preceding chapters deepen student understanding of the trade-offs.

Part 3 covers the balance of payments, exchange rates, open-economy macroeconomics, and international financial crises. Chapter 11 on open economy macroeconomics is optional. It is intended for students and instructors who want a review of macroeconomics, including the concepts of fiscal and monetary policy, in a context that includes current accounts and exchange rates. If Chapter 11 is omitted, Chapter 12 (financial crises) remains accessible as long as students have an understanding of the basic concepts of fiscal and monetary policy. Chapter 12 relies most heavily on Chapters 9 (balance of payments) and 10 (exchange rates and exchange rate systems).

Part 4 presents five chapters, each focused on a geographic area. These chapters use theory presented in Chapters 3–12 in a similar fashion to the economics discussion that students find in the business press, congressional testimonies, speeches, and other sources intended for a broad civic audience. Where necessary, concepts such as the real rate of exchange are briefly reviewed. One or more of these chapters can be moved forward to fit the needs of a particular course.

Supplementary Materials

The following supplementary resources are available to support teaching and learning.

- In recognition of the importance of the Internet as a source of timely information, the MyEconLab offers Web links for each chapter of *International Economics*. These links, complete with descriptions of the content available at each site, provide easy access to relevant, current data sources.

Other Supplements

Leonie Stone of State University of New York (SUNY) at Geneseo, has revised the TestGen and Instructor's Manual to bring it up to date with the text. The TestGen is available for download on the Instructor's Resource website. The Instructor's Powerpoints are also available online as an additional resource.

MyEconLab

MyEconLab has been designed and refined with a single purpose in mind: to create those moments of understanding that transform the difficult into the clear and obvious. With comprehensive homework, quiz, test, and tutorial options, instructors can manage all their assessment needs in one program.

MyEconLab for *International Economics*, Seventh Edition offers the following resources for students and instructors:

- **All end-of-chapter questions** from the text are available in MyEconLab.
- **Personal study plans** are created for each individual student based on performance on assigned and sample exercises.
- **Instant tutorial feedback** on a student's problem and graphing responses to questions.
- **Interactive learning aids**, such as *Help Me Solve This* (a step-by-step tutorial), help the student right when they need it.
- **News articles** are available for classroom and assignment use. Up-to-date news articles and complementary discussion questions are posted weekly to bring today's news into the classroom and course.
- **Real-Time Data Analysis** These exercises allow instructors to assign problems that use up-to-the-minute data. Each RTDA exercise loads the appropriate and most currently available data from FRED, a comprehensive and up-to-date data set maintained by the Federal Reserve Bank of St. Louis. Exercises are graded based on that instance of data, and feedback is provided.
- **An enhanced Pearson eText** available within the online course materials and offline via an app. The enhanced eText allows instructors and students to highlight, bookmark, and take notes.
- **Prebuilt courses** offer a turn-key way for instructors to create a course that includes prebuilt assignments distributed by chapter.
- **Auto graded problems and graphs** for assignments.
- **A powerful gradebook,** flexible and rich with information, including student and class data on assignment performance and time on task.
- **Advanced communication tools** provides students and instructors the capability to communicate through e-mail, discussion board, chat, and ClassLive.
- **Customization options** provide new and enhanced ways to share documents, add content, and rename menu items.
- **Temporary access** for students who are awaiting financial aid; a seventeen-day grace period of temporary access.
- **One place for students to access all of their MyLab courses**. Students and instructors can register, create, and access all of their MyLab courses, regardless of discipline, from one convenient online location: www.pearsonmylab.com.

For more information, please visit www.myeconlab.com.

Acknowledgments

All texts are team efforts, even single-author texts. I owe a debt of gratitude to a large number of people. At San Diego State University, I have benefited from the opportunity to teach and converse with a wide range of students. My colleagues in San Diego and across the border in Mexico have been extremely helpful. Their comments and our conversations constantly push me to think about the core economic ideas that should be a part of a college student's education, and to search for ways to explain the relevance and importance of those ideas with greater clarity and precision. Any failure in this regard is, of course, mine alone.

I am deeply grateful to Neeraj Bhalla, Nicole Suddeth, Sree Meenakshi R, and the MyEconLab team.

Finally, my gratitude goes to the numerous reviewers who have played an essential role in the development of *International Economics*. Each of the following individuals reviewed the manuscript, many of them several times, and provided useful commentary. I cannot express how much the text has benefited from their comments.

Mary Acker
Iona College

Jeff Ankrom
Wittenberg University

David Aschauer
Bates College

H. Somnez Atesoglu
Clarkson University

Titus Awokuse
University of Delaware

Mohsen Bahmani-Oskooee
University of Wisconsin, Milwaukee

Richard T. Baillie
Michigan State University

Mina Baliamoune-Lutz,
University of North Florida

Eugene Beaulieu
University of Calgary

Ted Black
Towson University

Bruce Blonigen
University of Oregon

Lee Bour
Florida State University

Byron Brown
Southern Oregon University

Laura Brown
University of Manitoba

Albert Callewaert
Walsh College

Tom Carter
Oklahoma City University

Srikanta Chatterjee
Massey University, New Zealand

Jen-Chi Cheng
Wichita State University

Don Clark
University of Tennessee

Raymond Cohn
Illinois State University

Peter Crabb
Northwest Nazarene University

David Crary
Eastern Michigan University

Al Culver
California State University, Chico

Joseph Daniels
Marquette University

Alan Deardorff
University of Michigan

Craig Depken II
University of North Carolina, Charlotte

John Devereaux
University of Miami

K. Doroodian
Ohio University

Carolyn Evans,
Santa Clara University

Noel J. J. Farley
Bryn Mawr College

Ora Freedman
Stevenson University

Lewis R. Gale IV
University of Southwest Louisiana

Kevin Gallagher
Boston University

Ira Gang
Rutgers University

John Gilbert
Utah State University

James Giordano
Villanova University

Amy Jocelyn Glass
Texas A&M University

Joanne Gowa
Princeton University

Gregory Green
Idaho State University

Thomas Grennes
North Carolina State University

Winston Griffith
Bucknell University

Jane Hall
California State University, Fullerton

Seid Hassan
Murray State University

F. Steb Hipple
East Tennessee State University

Paul Jensen
Drexel University

Ghassan Karam
Pace University

George Karras
University of Illinois at Chicago

Kathy Kelly
University of Texas, Arlington

Abdul Khandker
University of Wisconsin, La Crosse

Jacqueline Khorassani
Marietta College

Sunghyun Henry Kim
Brandeis University

Vani Kotcherlakota
University of Nebraska at Kearney

Corrine Krupp
Michigan State University

Kishore Kulkarni
Metropolitan State College of Denver

Farrokh Langdana
Rutgers University

Daniel Y. Lee
Shippensburg University

Mary Lesser
Iona College

Benjamin H. Liebman
Saint Joseph's University

Susan Linz
Michigan State University

Marc Lombard
Macquarie University, Australia

Thomas Lowinger
Washington State University

Nicolas Magud
University of Oregon

Bala Maniam
Sam Houston State University

Mary McGlasson
Arizona State University

Joseph McKinney
Baylor University

Judith McKinney
Hobart & William Smith Colleges

Howard McNier
San Francisco State University

Michael O. Moore
George Washington University

Stephan Norribin
Florida State University

William H. Phillips
University of South Carolina

Frank Raymond
Bellarmine University

Donald Richards
Indiana State University

John Robertson
University of Kentucky Community College System

Jeffrey Rosensweig
Emory University

Marina Rosser
James Madison University

Raj Roy
University of Toledo

Michael Ryan
Western Michigan University

George Samuels
Sam Houston State University

Craig Schulman
University of Arizona

William Seyfried
Winthrop University

Eckhard Siggel
Concordia University

David Spiro
Columbia University

Richard Sprinkle
University of Texas, El Paso

Ann Sternlicht
Virginia Commonwealth University

Leonie Stone
State University of New York at Geneseo

Carolyn Fabian Stumph
Indiana University, Purdue University, Fort Wayne

Rebecca Summary
Southeast Missouri State University

Jack Suyderhoud
University of Hawaii

Kishor Thanawala
Villanova University

Henry Thompson
Auburn University

Cynthia Tori
Valdosta State University

Edward Tower
Duke University

Ross vanWassenhove
University of Houston

Jose Ventura
Sacred Heart University

PART 1

Introduction and Institutions

An Introduction to the World Economy

Learning Objectives

After studying this chapter, students will be able to:

1.1 Discuss historical measures of international economic integration with data on trade, capital flows, and migration.

1.2 Compute the trade-to-GDP ratio and explain its significance.

1.3 Describe three factors in the world economy today that are different from the economy at the end of the first wave of globalization.

1.4 List the three types of evidence that trade supports economic growth.

INTRODUCTION: INTERNATIONAL ECONOMIC INTEGRATION

In August of 2007, a crisis erupted in the housing sector of the United States. At the time, few people realized that the subprime mortgage crisis would become a demonstration of international economic integration or that it would push the world economy to the brink of collapse. The crisis grew through the remainder of 2007 and into 2008, so that by the summer nearly all high-income economies were in deep distress. Contagion from the crisis spread like an epidemic as banks and other financial firms collapsed and solvent firms stopped lending. The scarcity of credit caused difficulties for businesses that could not find financing for their day-to-day operations while, at the same time, consumers cut back on their spending and businesses cut back on new investment. By the end of 2008, economies around the world were in recession, with the notable exceptions of China, India, and the major oil producers.

This episode is the most dramatic instance since the Great Depression of the 1930s of a crisis leading to severe economic recession in many countries around the world. It is, however, only one of several recent examples of crises spilling across national borders. The Russian Crisis of 1998–99, the Asian Crisis of 1997–98, the Mexican Crisis of 1994–95, the Latin American Debt Crisis of 1982–89, and a number of others caused major damage to financial systems, businesses, and households, both in the places where they originated and in many other countries.

The international integration of national economies has brought many benefits to nations across the globe, including technological innovation, less expensive products, and greater investment in regions where local capital is scarce, to name a few. But it has also made countries vulnerable to economic problems that have become more easily transmitted from one place to another. Given that the benefits and costs of international economic integration are surrounded by controversy, it is worth clarifying what we mean by the term *international economic integration*, or *globalization in the economic sphere*. To help us understand these forces better, a historical perspective is also useful.

ELEMENTS OF INTERNATIONAL ECONOMIC INTEGRATION

LO 1.1 **Discuss historical measures of international economic integration with data on trade, capital flows, and migration.**

LO 1.2 **Compute the trade-to-GDP ratio and explain its significance.**

LO 1.3 **Describe three factors in the world economy today that are different from the economy at the end of the first wave of globalization.**

LO 1.4 **List the three types of evidence that trade supports economic growth.**

Most people would agree that the major economies of the world are more integrated than at any time in history. Given our instantaneous communications, modern transportation, and relatively open trading systems, most goods can move from one country to another without major obstacles and at relatively low cost. For example, most cars today are made in fifteen or more countries after you consider where each part is made, where the advertising originates, who does the accounting, and who transports the components and the final product. Nevertheless, the proposition that today's economies are more integrated than at any other time in history is not simple to demonstrate. It is clear that our current wave of economic integration began in the 1950s, with the reduction of trade barriers after World War II. In the 1970s, many countries began to encourage financial integration by increasing the openness of their capital markets. The advent of the Internet in the 1990s, along with the other elements of the telecommunications revolution, pushed economic integration to new levels as multinational firms developed international production networks and markets became ever more tightly linked.

Today's global economy is not the first instance of a dramatic growth in economic ties between nations, however, as there was another important period between approximately 1870 and 1913. New technologies such as transatlantic cables, steam-powered ships, railroads, and many others led the way, much as they do today. For example, when the first permanent transatlantic cable was completed in 1866, the time it took for a New York businessperson to complete a financial transaction in London fell from approximately three weeks to one day, and by 1914 it had fallen to one minute as radio telephony became possible.

We have mostly forgotten about this earlier period of economic integration, and that makes it easier to overestimate integration today. Instantaneous communications and rapid transportation, together with the easy availability of foreign products, often cause us to lose sight of the fact that most of what we buy and sell never makes it out of our local or national markets. We rarely pause to think that haircuts, restaurant meals, gardens, health care, education, utilities, and many other goods and services are partially or wholly domestic products. In the United States, for example, about 83.4 percent of goods and services are produced domestically, with imports (16.6 percent) making up the remainder of what we consume (2014). By comparison, in 1890 the United States made about 92 percent of its goods and services, a larger share than today, but not radically different.

The question as to whether we are more economically integrated today or some period in the past is not academic. Between the onset of World War I in 1914 and the end of World War II in 1945, the world economy suffered a series of human-made catastrophes that de-integrated national economies. Two world wars and a global depression caused most countries to close their borders to foreign goods, foreign capital, and foreign people. Since the end of World War II, many of the economic linkages between nations have served to repair the damage done during the first half of the twentieth century, but there is no reason to think that events might not cause a similar decoupling in the future.

Understanding international economic integration requires us to define what we mean by the term. Economists usually point to four criteria or measures for judging the degree of integration, which are trade flows, capital flows, people flows, and the similarity of prices in separate markets. The first three points are relatively self-explanatory, while the similarity of prices refers to the fact that integrated economies have price differences that are relatively small and are due mainly to differences in transportation costs. Goods that can move freely from a low-cost to a high-cost region should experience price convergence as goods move from where they are plentiful and cheap to where they are relatively scarcer and more expensive. All of these indicators—trade flows, factor (labor and capital) movements, and similarity of prices—are measures of the degree of international economic integration.

The Growth of World Trade

Since the end of World War II, world trade has grown much faster than world output. One way to show this is to estimate the ratio of exports by all countries to total production by all countries. In 1950, total world exports—which are the same as world imports—are estimated to have been 5.5 percent of world **gross domestic product (GDP)**, a measure of total production. Sixty-three years later, in 2013, they were approximately 30 percent of world GDP, nearly six times more important relative to the size of the world economy. One important measure of international trade in a nation's economy is the sum of exports plus imports, divided by the GDP. Specifically, it is the value of all final goods and services produced inside a nation during some period, usually one year. The **trade-to-GDP ratio** is represented as follows:

$$\text{Trade to GDP ratio} = (\text{Exports} + \text{Imports}) \div \text{GDP}$$

The ratio does not tell us about a country's trade policies and countries with higher ratios do not necessarily have lower barriers to trade, although that is one possibility. In general, large countries are less dependent on international trade because their firms can reach an optimal production size without having to sell to foreign markets. Consequently, smaller countries tend to have higher ratios of trade-to-GDP.

Figure 1.1 shows the trade-to-GDP ratio for four countries between 1913 and 2013. The decline in trade between the onset of World War I and 1950 is clearly visible in each country, as is the subsequent increase after 1950. Another pattern shown in Figure 1.1 is the smaller ratios for the United States and Japan, which have the largest populations, and the much higher ratio for the Netherlands, which has the smallest population in the sample. In general, smaller countries trade more than larger ones since they cannot efficiently produce a wide range of goods and must depend on trade to a greater extent. For example, if the Netherlands were to produce autos solely for its own market, it would lack economies of scale and could not produce at a competitive cost, whereas the U.S. market can absorb a large share of U.S. output. Hence, the trade-to-GDP ratio measures the relative

FIGURE 1.1   Trade-to-GDP Ratios for Four Countries, 1913–2013

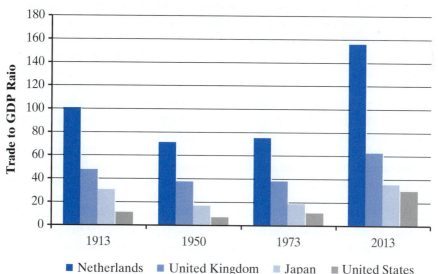

Data from Maddison, A. (1991). "Dynamic Forces in Capitalist Development" and The World Bank, *World Integrated Trade Solution*, © James Gerber.

importance of international trade in a nation's economy, but it does not provide any direct information about trade policy or trade barriers.

Figure 1.1 gives a historical overview of the decline and subsequent return of international trade after World War II, but it obscures important changes in the composition of trade flows from early in the twentieth century to those at the end of the century. Before World War I most trade consisted of agricultural commodities and raw materials, while current trade is primarily manufactured consumer goods and producer goods (machinery and equipment). Consequently, today's manufacturers are much more exposed to international competition than was the case in 1900. In addition, much of the growth of world trade since 1950 has been accomplished by multinational corporations. With production sites in multiple countries and inputs that pass back and forth between affiliates, multinational corporations have become dramatically important. This trend has been supported and encouraged by the telecommunications revolution and transportation improvements that have lowered the costs of coordinating operations physically separated by oceans and continents. And finally, it has also become possible to coordinate service operations such as accounting and data processing from a great distance. In sum, trade today is qualitatively different than in 1913, and the growth of the trade-to-GDP ratio since 1950 does not tell the whole story.

Capital and Labor Mobility

In addition to exports and imports, factor movements also are an indicator of economic integration. As national economies become more interdependent, labor and capital should move more easily across international boundaries. Labor, however, is less mobile internationally than it was in 1900. Consider, for example, that in 1890 approximately 14.5 percent of the U.S. population was foreign born, while in 2010, the figure was 12.9 percent. In 1900, many nations had open door immigration policies, and passport controls, immigration visas, and work permits were exceptions rather than rules. The movement of people was severely restricted by the two world wars and the Great Depression of the 1930s. In the 1920s, during the interwar period, the United States sharply restricted immigration with policies that lasted until the 1960s, when changes in immigration laws once again encouraged foreigners to migrate to the United States.

On the capital side, measurement is more difficult, since there are several ways to measure capital flows. The most basic distinction is between flows of financial capital representing paper assets such as stocks, bonds, currencies, bank accounts, and flows of capital representing physical assets such as real estate, factories, and businesses. The latter type of capital flow is called **foreign direct investment (FDI)**. To some extent, the distinction between the two types of capital flows is immaterial because both represent shifts in wealth across national boundaries and both make one nation's savings available to another.

When we compare international capital flows today to a century ago, there are two points to keep in mind. First, savings and investment are highly correlated. That is, countries with high savings tend to have high rates of investment, and low savings is correlated with low investment. If there were a single world market in which capital flowed freely and easily, this would not necessarily be the case. Capital would flow from countries with abundant savings and capital to countries with low savings and capital, where it would find its highest returns. Second, a variety of technological improvements increased capital flows in the 1800s, as they are doing today. Transoceanic cables and radio telephony have already been mentioned, but capital flows also increased in the late 1800s because there were new investment opportunities such as national railroad networks and other infrastructure, both at home and abroad.

If we compare the size of capital flows today to the previous era of globalization, flows today are much larger but mainly because economies are larger. Relative to the size of economies, the differences are not great and may even favor the 1870 to 1913 period, depending on what is measured. Great Britain routinely invested 9 percent of its GDP abroad in the decades before 1913, and France, Germany, and the Netherlands were as high at times. For significant periods, Canada, Australia, and Argentina borrowed amounts that exceeded 10 percent of their GDP, a level of borrowing that sends up danger signals in the world economy today. In other words, it is hard to make the argument that national economies have a historically unprecedented level of international capital flows today.

While the relative quantity of capital flows today may not be that much different for many countries, there are some important qualitative differences. First, there are many more financial instruments available now than there were a century ago. These range from relatively mundane stocks and bonds to relatively exotic instruments such as derivatives, currency swaps, and others. By contrast, at the turn of the twentieth century, there were many fewer companies listed on the world's stock exchanges and most international financial transactions involved the buying and selling of bonds.

A second difference today is the role of foreign exchange transactions. In 1900, countries had fixed exchange rates and firms in international trade or finance had less day-to-day risk from a sudden change in the value of a foreign currency. Many firms today spend significant resources to protect themselves from sudden shifts in currency values. Consequently, buying and selling assets denominated in foreign currencies is the largest component of international capital movements. For example, according to the Bank for International Settlements in Geneva, Switzerland, *daily* foreign exchange transactions in 2013 were equal to $5.3 *trillion*. In 1973, at the end of the last era of fixed exchange rates, they were $15 billion.

The third major difference in capital flows is that the costs of foreign financial transactions have fallen significantly. Economists refer to the costs of obtaining market information, negotiating an agreement, and enforcing the agreement as **transaction costs**. They are an important part of any business's costs, whether it is a purely domestic enterprise or a company involved in foreign markets. Due to sheer distance, as well as differences in culture, laws, and languages, transaction costs are often higher in international markets than in domestic ones. Today's lower transaction costs for foreign investment mean that it is less expensive to move capital across international boundaries.

The volatile movement of financial capital across international boundaries is often mistakenly regarded as a new feature of the international economy. Speculative excesses and overinvestment, followed by capital flight and bankruptcies, have occurred throughout the modern era, going back at least to the 1600s and probably earlier. U.S. and world history show a number of such cases. Financial crises are not a new phenomenon, nor have we learned how to avoid them—a fact driven home by the recent subprime mortgage crisis.

Features of Contemporary International Economic Relations

While international economic integration has been rapid, it does not appear to be historically unprecedented. The trade-to-GDP ratio is about 50 percent higher in the U.S. economy than it was in 1890, and manufacturers and service providers are more exposed to international forces. Labor is less mobile than in 1900 due to passport controls and work permits, but capital is more mobile and encompasses a larger variety of financial forms. Prices in many U.S. and foreign markets tend to be similar, although there are still significant differences. In quantitative terms, the differences between today and a hundred years ago may not be as great as many people imagine, but qualitatively, a number of additional features of the world economy separate the first decade of the twenty-first century from the first decade of the twentieth.

Deeper Integration   High-income countries have low barriers to imports of manufactured goods. There are some exceptions (processed foodstuffs and apparel), but as a general rule import **tariffs** (taxes on imports) and other barriers such as **quotas** (quantitative restrictions on imports) are much less restrictive than they were in the middle of the twentieth century. As trade barriers came down during the second half of the twentieth century, two other trends began to intensify economic integration between countries. First, lower trade barriers exposed the fact that most countries have domestic policies that are obstacles to international trade. National regulations governing labor, environmental, and consumer safety standards; rules governing investment location and performance; rules defining fair and unfair competition; rules on government "buy-national" programs; and government support policies for specific industries—all have little impact on trade until formal trade barriers start to fall and trade volume increases. These policies were not implemented to protect domestic industries from foreign competition, and as long as tariffs were high and trade flows were limited, they did not matter much to trade relations. Once tariffs fell, however, many forms of domestic policies began to be viewed as barriers to increased trade. Economists sometimes refer to the reduction of tariffs and the elimination of quotas as **shallow integration** and negotiations over domestic policies that impact international trade as **deep integration**. Deep integration is much more contentious than shallow integration and much more difficult to accomplish since it involves domestic policy changes that align a country with rules that are created abroad, or at least negotiated with foreign powers.

A second noticeable trend over the last few decades is that technologically complicated goods such as smart phones and automobiles are made of components produced in more than one country and, consequently, labels such as "Made in China" or "Made in the USA" are less and less meaningful. Low tariffs along with innovations in transportation and communication technologies have enabled firms to locate production of the different components of a sophisticated product in different countries. For example, the hardware for a 3G iPhone is produced in Germany, Korea, Japan, and the United States, and then it is assembled in China. The most valuable share of the hardware is made in Japan, but no one thinks of this device as a Japanese phone. In this case, as in many others, it is not accurate to say the product is made in one particular country since the parts come from all over, and the product is the result of a multinational effort involving firms and workers from many different countries.

These two trends raise new issues that are shaping the world economy in the twenty-first century. The first trend, greater interest in the consequences of different domestic policies, makes trade negotiations more difficult and creates widespread discussion of labor, environmental, and other standards that may affect trade flows. The second trend, greater participation in the production of a single product by firms in multiple countries, leads to concerns about the impact of trade on national economies, employment, and working conditions. National and international dialogues on these issues are a key feature of international economics in the twenty-first century.

Multilateral Organizations   At the end of World War II, the United States, Great Britain, and their allies created a number of international organizations to maintain international economic and political stability. Although the architects of these organizations could not envision the challenges and issues they would confront over the next fifty years, the organizations were given significant flexibility, and they continue to play an important and growing role in managing the issues of shallow and deeper integration.

The International Monetary Fund (IMF), the World Bank, the General Agreement on Tariffs and Trade (GATT), the United Nations (UN), the World Trade Organization (the WTO began operation in 1995, but grew out of the GATT), and a host of smaller organizations have broad international participation. They serve as forums for discussing and establishing rules, as mediators of disputes, and as organizers of actions to resolve problems. All of these organizations are controversial and have come under increasing fire from critics who charge that they promote unsustainable economic policies or that they protect the interests of wealthy countries. Others argue that they are unnecessary foreign entanglements that severely limit the scope for national action (Chapter 2 examines this issue in detail). These organizations are attempts to create internationally acceptable rules for trade and commerce and to deal with potential disputes before they spill across international borders; they are an entirely new element in the international economy.

Regional Trade Agreements   Agreements between groups of nations are not new. Free-trade agreements and other forms of preferential trade have existed throughout history. What is new is the significant increase in the number of **regional trade agreements (RTAs)** that have been signed in the last twenty years.

The formation of preferential trade agreements is controversial. Trade opponents dislike the provisions that expose more of the national economy to international competition, whereas some trade proponents dislike preferences that favor countries included in the agreement at the expense of countries outside the agreement. The North American Free Trade Agreement (NAFTA), the European Union (EU), the Mercado Común del Sur (MERCOSUR), and the Asia Pacific Economic Cooperation (APEC) are examples of RTAs, but more than 417 have been recorded by the World Trade Organization (2016).

Trade and Economic Growth

Many people are more than a little apprehensive about increased international economic integration. The list of potential problems is a long one. More trade may give consumers lower prices and greater choices, but it also means more competition for firms and workers. Capital flows make more funds available for investment purposes, but they also increase the risk of spreading financial crises internationally. Rising immigration means higher incomes for migrants and lower labor costs or a better pool of skills for firms, but it also means more competition in labor markets and, inevitably, greater social tensions. International organizations may help resolve disputes, but they may also reduce national sovereignty by putting pressure on countries to make operational changes. Free-trade agreements may increase trade flows, but again, that means more competition and more pressure on domestic workers and firms.

In general, economists remain firmly convinced that the benefits of trade outweigh the costs. There is disagreement over the best way to achieve different goals (for example, how to protect against the harmful effects of sudden flows of capital), but the general belief that openness to the world economy is a superior policy to closing off a country is quite strong. To support this stance, economists can point to the following kinds of evidence:

- Casual empirical evidence of historical experience
- Evidence based on economic models and deductive reasoning
- Evidence from statistical comparisons of countries

While none of these is conclusive by itself, together they provide solid support for the idea that open economies generally grow faster and prosper more than closed ones.

The historical evidence examines the experiences of countries that tried to isolate themselves from the world economy. There are the experiences of the 1930s, when most countries tried to protect themselves from world events by shutting out flows of goods, capital, and labor. This did not cause the Great Depression of the 1930s, but it did worsen it, and ultimately it led to the misery and tragedy of World War II. There are also the parallel experiences of countries that were divided by war, with one side becoming closed to the world economy, and the other side open. Germany (East versus West), Korea (North versus South), and China (mainland China before the 1980s versus Taiwan and Hong Kong) are the best examples.

Economic theory generally supports these examples by suggesting the causal mechanisms that lead from trade to faster growth. Generally, the benefits of increased innovation, competitive pressure to raise productivity levels, and access to new technologies and ideas that are fostered by trade are positive factors. On the consumer side, trade provides a greater variety of goods and offers them at lower prices.

The statistical evidence of the benefits of more open economies comes from comparisons of large samples of countries over different periods. While the statistical tests of the relationship between trade policy and economic growth suffer from their own technical shortcomings, the results consistently show that more open economies grow faster. These results cannot be viewed as absolutely conclusive, but together with trade theory and the casual empirical evidence drawn from historical experiences, the available statistical analysis provides additional support for the notion that trade is usually beneficial.

TWELVE THEMES IN INTERNATIONAL ECONOMICS

Each of the twelve themes discussed next are examined in the chapters that follow. These themes are overlapping, multidimensional, and often go beyond pure economics. International economic analysis cannot claim the final word, but it is hoped that it will provide you an analytically powerful and logically consistent approach for thinking about the issues raised by these themes.

The Gains from Trade and New Trade Theory (Chapters 3, 4, and 5)

Why is international trade desirable? We have briefly addressed this issue, and we will consider additional points as we continue. Given that economic analysis clearly demonstrates that the benefits of international trade outweigh the costs, it is not surprising that virtually all economists generally support open markets and increased trade. The benefits of international trade were first analyzed in the late 1700s and are perhaps the oldest and strongest finding in all of economics. More recently, economists have begun to analyze returns to scale within firms and industries. Under the label "New Trade Theory," economists have demonstrated a number of new sources of national welfare improvements due to international trade and added greater sophistication to our understanding of market structure and trade effects.

Wages, Jobs, and Protection (Chapters 3, 6, 7, and 8)

International trade raises national welfare, but it does not benefit every member of society. Workers in firms that cannot compete may be forced to find new jobs or take pay cuts. The fact that consumers pay less for the goods they buy, or that exporters hire more workers, may not help laid off workers. Increased awareness of the international economy has heightened the fears of people who feel vulnerable to change. They are concerned that wages in high-income countries must fall in order to compete with workers in low-wage countries, and that their jobs may be moved overseas. One of the key challenges for policymakers is to find the right mix of domestic policies so that the nation benefits from trade without creating a backlash from those individuals and industries that are hurt.

Trade Deficits (Chapters 9, 11, and 12)

In 1980, a comprehensive measure of trade accounts in the United States showed that there was a slight surplus. Every year since then, the United States has had a trade deficit and the sum of the deficits since 2000 is more than $7.9 trillion (2001 through 2010). The United States was not the only country running deficits, but each year a country runs a deficit in its trade accounts, it must borrow from abroad, essentially selling a piece of its future output in order to obtain more goods and services today. As the United States and other countries borrowed, China, Germany, Japan, and oil producers like Saudi Arabia and Russia lent. These large imbalances in lending and borrowing played a key role in the crisis that began in 2007.

Regional Trade Agreements (Chapters 2, 13, and 14)

As the world economy becomes more integrated, some regions are running ahead of the general trend. Western Europeans, for example, have eliminated many of the economic barriers separating their nations, and are creating a broad political and economic union. With implementation of NAFTA in 1994, the United States, Canada, and Mexico became a free-trade area. All three countries have signed individual agreements with most of Central America and recently negotiated a trade pact (yet to be implemented as of 2016) with nine other Pacific-region countries. The United States continues to negotiate with countries in South America and Asia, including China, and more than 400 regional trade agreements have been negotiated world-wide. Since 2004, ten Central and Eastern European countries have joined the EU, along with two small Mediterranean states. The ten members of the Association of South East Asian Nations (ASEAN) have moved to create a free-trade zone, and China has become an active participant in trade agreements, along with a number of other countries. The pros and cons of these and other agreements is an active area of economic interest and will be considered in several chapters.

The Resolution of Trade Conflicts (Chapters 2, 7, and 8)

Commercial conflicts between nations cover a wide variety of issues and complaints. In one sense these conflicts are routine, as the WTO provides a formal dispute resolution procedure that has the assent of most of the world's nations. The WTO process does not cover all goods and services, however, nor does it say much about a large number of practices that some nations find objectionable. The ability of nations to resolve conflicts without resorting to protectionist measures is one key to maintaining a healthy international economic environment. Disputes can become acrimonious, so it is imperative that differences of opinion are not permitted to escalate into a wider disagreement. Trade wars are not real wars, but they are harmful nonetheless.

The Role of International Institutions (Chapters 2, 8, and 12)

The organization with the greatest responsibility for resolving trade disagreements is the WTO. The WTO came into existence in 1995 and was an adaptation of the GATT, which was created shortly after World War II. Resolving trade disputes is only one of the new roles played by international organizations. Various organizations offer development support, technical economic advice, emergency loans in a crisis situation, and other services and assistance. These organizations perform services that were not offered before World War II (development support), or that were done by a single country (lending in a crisis)—usually the world's greatest military power. They exist today only through the mutual consent and cooperation of participating nations; without that cooperation, they would dissolve. Their abilities are limited, however. They cannot prevent crises, and they cannot make poor countries rich. They are also controversial and are viewed by some as tools of the United States or as a threat to national independence. They are very likely to grow in function, however, as many international problems cannot be solved by individual nations alone.

Exchange Rates and the Macroeconomy (Chapters 10 and 11)

Seventeen of the twenty-seven members of the EU have adopted the euro as a common currency, and several more are preparing to join them in spite of the euro crisis that began in 2011. Panama, El Salvador, and Ecuador use the U.S. dollar. Some members of the U.S. Congress and some economists think that China artificially manipulates its currency to gain commercial advantages, and China's leaders worry that the United States might let the dollar sink in value to depreciate its foreign debt. Exchange rate systems come in a variety of forms and link the domestic economy to the rest of the world. They can help protect a country against harmful developments outside its borders, but they can also magnify and transmit those developments to the domestic economy. Exchange rates play a key role in the international economy.

Financial Crises and Global Contagion (Chapter 12)

As international trade and investment barriers declined, and as new communications and transportation systems developed, increasing quantities of capital flowed across national borders. These flows were encouraged by financial innovation and a general spirit of deregulation that held sway in much of the world from the late 1970s forward. Capital flows brought many desirable things, such as investment, new technology, and higher consumption, but they also often outpaced our ability to monitor and supervise, and were frequently at the root of financial crises, including the severe global crisis that began in 2007. Economists are engaged in a broad discussion today, aimed at finding techniques for reducing the macroeconomic and financial volatility caused by capital flows without hampering the new investment and lending that they provide.

Capital Flows and the Debt of Developing Countries (Chapters 2, 9, and 12)

In 1996, the World Bank and the IMF began a debt relief program for a group of forty-two countries labeled the *Highly Indebted Poor Countries (HIPC)*. Thirty-four of these countries are in Africa. At the same time, non-governmental groups and celebrities, such as Bono, began to lobby successfully for a reduction in the debts of poor countries and for changes in the lending policies of rich countries. In many parts of the world, problems of extreme poverty are compounded by large foreign debts that are unlikely to be repaid and often require a constant supply of new loans to pay interest on the old ones. The search for workable solutions is complicated in the borrowing countries by economic shocks, corruption, and unsustainable economic policies. Common problems in the lending countries include unwise loans to corrupt dictators and loans for some expensive and unnecessary goods sold by rich countries.

Latin America and the World Economy (Chapter 15)

In Latin America, the 1980s are known as the *Lost Decade.* High levels of debt, deep recessions, and hyperinflation caused the region to lose a decade of growth and development. In response, many countries embarked on a profound shift in their economic policies. They opened markets, allowed increased foreign investment, signed trade agreements, and ended a long period of relative isolation from the world economy. These policy changes became known as the Washington Consensus and helped to bring an end to the Lost Decade, but few economists think the policies were successful. Growth remained relatively low in many places, financial crises continued to undermine economic gains, and traditional issues of economic fairness were largely ignored. Latin American countries have developed a wide variety of new policies and experiments as they try to reduce poverty, generate prosperity, and provide opportunity for all their citizens.

Export-Led Growth in East Asia (Chapter 16)

Throughout the late 1980s and into the 1990s, it was hard to ignore the East Asian "miracle." While some economists point out that it was not really a miracle—just a lot of hard work and sound economic policies—the growth rates of the "high-performance Asian economies" were unique in human history. Rates of growth of real GDP *per person* commonly reached 4 to 5 percent per year, with 6 to 8 percent not unusual. In 1997, an economic and financial crisis hit the region hard. Although there were lingering effects, by 2000 the economies of the region's developing countries were growing at more than 7 percent a year. One of the dominant traits of the countries in East Asia is the extent to which they are outward looking and dependent on the growth of their manufactured exports.

China and India in the World Economy (Chapter 17)

China and India are the most populous countries in the world. In 2016, China's 1.37 billion people plus India's 1.25 billion accounted for nearly 36 percent of the world's population of 7.30 billion. Throughout much of the twentieth century, neither country had deep economic ties with nations other than India's tie to its colonial power, and neither had much impact on the world economy. Change began in 1978, when China started its dramatic shift away from isolationism. Chinese reforms led to an ever-growing presence of foreign investment, more exports and imports, fewer restrictions on privately owned enterprises, rapid urbanization, and in 2001, membership in the WTO. India's transformation from a relatively closed economy toward greater openness began later, in 1991, and has proceeded at a slower pace. Nevertheless, its sheer population size coupled with the technical excellence of its scientists and engineers and its developing high technology sector have turned it into a growing force in the world economy. Low wages and competitive firms and technologies in China and India have caught the attention of nearly all developing and developed nations, and have generated a variety of fears and opportunities, both realistic and unrealistic.

Vocabulary

deep integration	shallow integration
foreign direct investment (FDI)	tariffs
gross domestic product (GDP)	trade-to-GDP ratio
quotas	transaction costs
regional trade agreement (RTA)	

Study Questions

All problems are assignable in My EconLab.

1.1 How can globalization and international economic integration be measured?

1.2 How is the U.S. economy more integrated with the world today than it was a century ago? How is it less integrated?

1.3 What does the trade-to-GDP ratio measure? Does a low value indicate that a country is closed to trade with the outside world?

1.4 Describe the pattern over the last century shown by the trade-to-GDP ratio for leading industrial economies.

1.5 Trade and capital flows were described and measured in relative terms rather than absolute terms. Explain the difference. Which terms seem more valid—*relative* or *absolute*? Why?

1.6 In relative terms, international capital flows may not be much greater today than they were a hundred years ago, although they are certainly greater than they were fifty years ago. Qualitatively, however, capital flows are different today. Explain.

1.7 What are the new issues in international trade and investment? In what sense do they expose national economies to outside influences?

1.8 Describe the three kinds of evidence that economists use to support the assertion that economies open to the world economy grow faster than economies that are closed.

CHAPTER 2

International Economic Institutions Since World War II

Learning Objectives

After studying this chapter, students will be able to:

2.1 Classify with examples the main types of international economic organizations.

2.2 Identify economic circumstances in which the IMF, the World Bank, and the WTO are active.

2.3 Compare the different levels of integration found in regional trade agreements with examples.

2.4 Analyze the roles of international economic organizations.

2.5 Debate the pros and cons of international economic organizations.

INTRODUCTION: INTERNATIONAL INSTITUTIONS AND ISSUES SINCE WORLD WAR II

LO 2.1 Classify with examples the main types of international economic organizations.

As World War II was drawing to a close, representatives from the United States, Great Britain, and other Allied nations met in the small New Hampshire town of Bretton Woods. The outcome of these meetings was a series of agreements that created an exchange rate system (which lasted until 1971); the International Bank for Reconstruction and Development (IBRD), also known as the **World Bank**; and the **International Monetary Fund (IMF)**. In 1946, two years after Bretton Woods, twenty-three nations including the United States and Great Britain began talks on reducing their trade barriers, leading to the **General Agreement on Tariffs and Trade (GATT)**, which began operation in 1948. This chapter focuses on these global economic institutions, their history, their role in the world economy, and controversies surrounding their activities.

International Institutions

International economic institutions are an important feature of the world economy. When social scientists try to explain the increasing integration of national economies after World War II, one of the key explanations must be the increased stability and reduced uncertainty that these institutions help to create. Nevertheless, as international economic integration has increased, these organizations have come under more scrutiny and received much criticism. Before we look at their impact and some of the criticisms levied at them, we should define what we mean by an *institution*.

When most people hear the word **institution**, they probably think of a formal organization. However, economists tend to define institutions more abstractly. For example, the "New Institutionalists," led by economist Douglas North, have argued that organizations are not institutions in themselves, but are rather the rules that govern behavior—telling us what is permissible and what is not and acting as constraints that limit our actions.

Institutions can be formal or informal. A formal institution is a written set of rules that explicitly state what is and is not allowed. The rules may be embodied in a club, an association, or a legal system. An informal institution is a custom or tradition that tells people how to act in different situations but without legal enforcement. For example, informal institutions include the rules of socializing, gift exchange, table manners, e-mail etiquette, and so on. In this chapter, the term *institution* refers to both rules and organizations.

A Taxonomy of International Economic Institutions

International economic institutions come in many shapes and sizes. They can be lobbying groups for a particular commodity or an international producer's association, the joint management by several nations of a common resource, trade agreements or development funds for a select group of nations, or even global associations. Although this chapter's focus is on global economic institutions, it is useful to look at a taxonomy of international economic institutions, from the most limited and specific, to the most general. Table 2.1 shows five main types.

TABLE 2.1   **A Taxonomy of International Economic Institutions, with Examples**

Type	Examples
Commodity- or industry-specific organizations: These range from trade associations, to international standards-setting bodies, to powerful cartels	■ Oil Producing and Exporting Countries (OPEC) ■ International Telecommunications Union (ITU)
Commissions and agencies for managing shared resources	■ International Boundary and Water Commission (IBWC) ■ Mekong River Commission
Development funds and banks	■ Asian Development Bank ■ Islamic Development Bank
International trade agreements involving a few nations (regional trade alliances or trade blocs)	■ North American Free Trade Agreement (NAFTA) ■ European Union
Global organizations for trade, development, and macroeconomic stability	■ International Monetary Fund (IMF) ■ World Bank ■ World Trade Organization (WTO)

THE IMF, THE WORLD BANK, AND THE WTO

LO 2.2   Identify economic circumstances in which the IMF, the World Bank, and the WTO are active.

Three global organizations play a major role in international economic relations and are central to this book: the International Monetary Fund (IMF), the World Bank, and the **World Trade Organization (WTO)**. The IMF and the World Bank date from the end of World War II; the WTO began in 1995 and grew out of the GATT, which it deepens and broadens. Accordingly, it is useful to know the history and function of the GATT as well as the WTO.

The IMF and World Bank

During World War II, the United States, Great Britain, and several other nations held regular discussions about the shape of the postwar international economic order. They wanted to avoid the mistakes of the 1920s and 1930s, when a lack of international cooperation led to the complete collapse of economic relations. The culmination of these talks was the **Bretton Woods conference** held in July 1944, in Bretton Woods, New Hampshire. The agreement was largely a result of negotiations between the United States and the United Kingdom, and led directly to the creation of the IMF and the IBRD, which later became the World Bank.

The IMF began operation on December 27, 1945, with a membership of twenty-nine countries. Over time, it added new members and is currently at 188 countries. The IMF provides loans to its members under different programs for the short, medium, and long term. Each member is charged a fee, or **quota**, as the price of membership. The size of the quota varies with the size of the nation's economy and the importance of its currency in world trade and payments. Important decisions within the IMF are made by vote with the weight of each nation's vote proportional to its quota. This gives the high-income countries of the world a voting power that is disproportionate to their population. For example, the United States alone controls nearly 17 percent of the total votes, and the seven largest high-income industrial economies (Canada, Italy, France, Germany, Japan, the United Kingdom, and the United States) control almost 45 percent. Some votes on IMF policy require a "super majority" of 85 percent, giving the United States a veto power on those particular issues. In 2008, the asymmetry in quotas and votes came under pressure from dynamic emerging economies that wanted more say in IMF policies and from advanced economies that wanted to increase quotas paid by other members. In 2010, a reform of votes and quotas was agreed upon but has not yet been implemented as of 2012.

The most visible role for the IMF is to intercede, by invitation, whenever a nation experiences a crisis in its international payments. For example, if a country imports more than it exports, then it may run out of foreign exchange reserves. **Foreign exchange reserves** are dollars, yen, pounds, euros, or another currency (or gold) that is accepted internationally. In addition, the IMF has its own currency, called an *SDR,* or *special drawing right.* SDRs are based on a country's quota and are a part of its international reserves. If a country lacks reserves, it cannot pay for its imports, nor can it pay the interest and principal it owes on its international borrowings. This is one scenario that warrants a call to the IMF. The IMF makes loans to its members, but it usually extracts a price above and beyond the interest it charges. The price is an agreement by the borrower to change its policies so that the problem cannot recur. If simple economic reforms such as a cut in the value of the currency, or limits on the central bank's creation of credit, are insufficient to solve the problem permanently, then the IMF usually requires a borrower to make fundamental changes in the relationship between government and markets in order to qualify for IMF funds. These requirements are known as **IMF conditionality**. For example, during the crisis of 1997–1998, the IMF was the main provider of funds and expertise to East Asia, again, with a great deal of controversy over the advice it gave and the conditions it imposed.

The IMF's resources for dealing with crises are limited. When the United States and other large economies experienced the crisis that began in 2007, IMF resources were far from adequate for addressing the issues. In 2009, the largest member countries voted to increase its resources to $750 billion, still far below the amount necessary to stem a crisis in the United States or in other large economies. In part, this reflects the institution's asymmetry, as high-income countries are generally unwilling to give the IMF either the funds or the power to allow it to intervene effectively in their economies.

The World Bank is the other major organization that emerged from the Bretton Woods Conference. It has the same membership and a similar structure. Members buy shares that convey voting rights on policy proportional to the shares. The original purpose of the World Bank was to provide financing mechanisms for rebuilding Europe at the end of World War II; however, it was soon apparent that its capital reserves were inadequate to the task. In addition, the United States found it politically preferable to have more direct control over the reconstruction funds, rather than routing them through an international organization. Hence, the job of reconstruction was directed toward the newly created Marshall Plan, and the World Bank moved toward assisting development in non-industrial economies.

The GATT, the Uruguay Round, and the WTO

At the end of World War II, a third global economic organization, the International Trade Organization (ITO), was proposed. If it had been created, the ITO's job would have been to establish rules relating to world trade, business practices, and international investment. U.S. opposition killed the idea of the ITO, however, and no such organization was created until 1995. Nevertheless, in 1946, while they were still considering the idea of the ITO, twenty-three countries opened negotiations over tariff reductions. These negotiations led to about 45,000 tariff reductions affecting $10 billion, or one-fifth of world trade. In addition, a number of agreements were made on rules for trade, with the expectation that the rules would become a part of the ITO. Both the tariff reductions and the rules were implemented in 1948; when the possibility of an ITO died in 1950, the agreements on tariffs and trade rules remained in force as a separate agreement, known as the *General Agreement on Tariffs and Trade (GATT)*. The GATT has been very successful in bringing down trade barriers gradually. One indicator is that international trade has grown over the last fifty years from 5 percent of world gross domestic product (GDP) to over 31 percent in 2011.

The GATT functions through a series of **trade rounds** in which countries periodically negotiate a set of incremental tariff reductions. Gradually, through the Kennedy Round in the mid-1960s and the Tokyo Round of the 1970s, trade rules other than tariffs began to be addressed, including the problems of dumping (selling in a foreign market below cost or below a fair price), subsidies to industry, and nontariff barriers to trade.

The GATT intentionally ignored the extremely contentious sectors of agriculture, textiles, and apparel. In addition, trade in services was ignored because it was not important. The accumulation of unresolved issues in these sectors, however, along with the increased importance of nontariff trade barriers, led to the demand for a new, more extensive set of negotiations. These demands culminated in the **Uruguay Round** of trade negotiations that began in 1986. Among other outcomes, the Uruguay Round created the World Trade Organization (1995). In 2016, there are 162 members and 22 other governments with observer status.

The WTO continues trade talks and sector-specific discussions between comprehensive rounds of negotiations. For example, in 1997, sixty-nine countries signed an agreement to open their telecommunication sectors, and another seventy agreed to significant opening in their financial services sectors. In addition, every two years, trade ministers from the member countries meet to set the WTO's policy objectives. In 2001, trade ministers meeting in Doha, Qatar, agreed to launch a new round of trade negotiations emphasizing issues of developing countries. The **Doha Round** proposed a **Doha Development Agenda** to consider trade issues of importance to developing countries. The key issues are farm subsidies and agricultural protection and trade in services. These issues are contentious and progress has been stalled. In all likelihood, the Doha Round will be the first round of GATT or WTO sponsored negotiations to fail. As of 2016, the negotiations are fifteen years old and show no sign of success. Nevertheless, while a comprehensive agreement on all the issues under discussion seems unlikely, member countries continue to negotiate on specific issues, such as trade and food security, and special safeguards to protect developing countries from sudden surges in imports that threaten a particular industry. Even with a failed Doha Round, the agreements and rules negotiated under the auspices of the GATT and the WTO remain the core set of international trade rules.

The foundation of all WTO and GATT agreements are the principles of **national treatment** and **nondiscrimination**. *National treatment* is the requirement that foreign goods are treated similarly to the same domestic goods once they enter a nation's markets. *Nondiscrimination* is embodied in the concept of **most-favored nation (MFN) status**. MFN requires all WTO members to treat each other as they treat their most-favored trading partner. In effect, this is a prohibition against discrimination. Somewhat contradictorily, MFN allows trade agreements such as the North American Free Trade Agreement (NAFTA) and the European Union (EU) even though every trade agreement causes countries to discriminate in favor of each other and implicitly against nonmembers. In theory, the WTO permits such agreements as long as they do not harm the overall level of international trade, and in practice, the WTO has never challenged the validity of a trade agreement between member countries.

CASE STUDY

The GATT Rounds

Agreements in the GATT forum to reduce trade barriers take place in rounds of negotiations. Counting the first round, there have been nine rounds of negotiations, with the Doha Round still in progress. Originally, the GATT was an international agreement and not an organization. The failure to create the International Trade Organization in 1950, however, resulted in the gradual conversion of the GATT into a *de facto* organization by 1960, with a permanent secretariat to manage it from Geneva. Table 2.2 lists the various rounds of negotiations.

The first five rounds were organized around product-by-product negotiations in which countries mutually cut their tariffs on specific products. Beginning with the Kennedy Round, negotiations were simplified as countries negotiated an across-the-board percentage reduction in all tariffs for a range of industrial products. One effect is that tariffs have never been uniform across countries. The goal has been to bring them all down, but not to create the same tariff for all countries.

The Tokyo Round is notable because it was the first round to begin to establish rules regarding subsidies. Subsidies give an industry a competitive

TABLE 2.2   The GATT Rounds

Round	Year	Number of Participants
Geneva I	1947	23
Annecy	1949	13
Torquay	1951	38
Geneva II	1956	26
Dillon	1960–1961	26
Kennedy	1964–1967	62
Tokyo	1973–1979	102
Uruguay	1986–1993	105
Doha (WTO)	2001–	162

advantage, since the national government pays part of the cost of production, either through direct payment or indirectly through subsidized interest rates, artificially cheap access to foreign currency, or some other way. The Tokyo Round began the laborious process of creating rules in this area, one of the most important being the agreement to prohibit subsidies for exports of industrial goods (but not agricultural goods or textiles and apparel).

The subsidy issue of the Tokyo Round was carried forward into the Uruguay Round, where subsidies were defined in greater detail. The Uruguay Round accomplished many other things as well, not the least of which was the creation of the WTO as a formal organization to oversee and administer the GATT. Additional accomplishments are described in Chapter 7, which explores trade policy and trade barriers in more detail.

REGIONAL TRADE AGREEMENTS

LO 2.3   Compare the different levels of integration found in regional trade agreements with examples.

Regional trade agreements (RTAs) between two or more countries are another important institution in the world economy. Many of these have familiar names, such as NAFTA and the EU. Regional agreements can be classified into one of five categories, although they often combine elements from a couple of the categories.

Five Types of Regional Trade Agreements

RTAs are bilateral (two countries) or plurilateral (several countries). The WTO is not an RTA because it is worldwide in scope and not just regional. In trade jargon it is called a *multilateral* agreement because it includes, potentially, all the countries of the world. Some plurilateral agreements are quite large, such as the EU, which has twenty-eight members, or the proposed free-trade area of the Pacific, called the Asia Pacific Economic Cooperation group, which has twenty-one. Table 2.3 lists five types of trade agreements and their characteristics.

TABLE 2.3   Five Types of Regional Trade Agreements

Type of Agreement	Characteristics
■ Partial trade agreement	■ Free trade in the outputs of one or a few industries
■ Free-trade area	■ Free trade in outputs (goods and services)
■ Customs union	■ Free trade in outputs plus a common external tariff
■ Common market	■ Custom union plus free movement of inputs (capital and labor)
■ Economic union	■ Common market plus substantial harmonization of economic policies, including a common currency

CASE STUDY

Prominent Regional Trade Agreements

Each of the five levels of integration is an example of a different kind of **regional trade agreement (RTA)**, or **trade bloc**. The question naturally arises as to how many agreements there are and whether they are beneficial or harmful for the world economy. The simple question of how many is difficult to answer precisely. Many of the agreements do not fit neatly into any of the five categories, so it is not clear they should be counted. That is, should all partial agreements be counted when they are not quite free-trade areas, yet they have elements of free trade, customs unions, and even common markets? In addition, many of the agreements exist either on paper only (have no real effect), or have yet to be fully negotiated and/or implemented. Until there is substantial implementation, there is always the possibility that the agreement will collapse, because opening an economy inevitably generates opposition from uncompetitive sectors.

Countries that have signed the GATT are obligated to notify the GATT secretariat when they form an RTA. According to the WTO, since the implementation of the GATT in 1948 they have been notified of more than 500 RTAs. Some of these are defunct, but 417 were active in 2016. Most of the functioning agreements were started in the 1990s or 2000s.

The answer to the second question posited earlier—are agreements beneficial or harmful?—is even more difficult to answer. A 1995 study by the WTO concluded that in most cases "regional and multilateral integration initiatives are complements rather than alternatives."[*] Broadly speaking, the WTO sees these agreements as helping it to further reduce trade barriers. This view is not shared by all economists, however, as any regional agreement must favor the interests of its members over the interests of outsiders. In other words, there is an element of discrimination that goes against the WTO's fundamental principle of equal treatment (most favored nation). Preferential treatment for members of the trade agreement causes most regional trade agreements to destroy some of the trade between their members and nonmembers. The WTO recognizes this problem, but argues that as long as a regional agreement creates more new trade than it destroys, the net result is beneficial. In addition, the WTO sees the regional trade agreements as places where countries can try out new arrangements, some of which will be eventually incorporated into the larger, global agreement.

Nearly all WTO members belong to at least one RTA, and many countries belong to several. For example, Mexico is a member of NAFTA (Canada-Mexico-United States) but in 2000 it entered a free-trade agreement with the EU. It has also signed free trade and other agreements with other countries, including Chile, Japan, Israel, and Costa Rica, among others. Table 2.4 lists

[*]© 1995 World Trade Organization.

some of the RTAs currently in force. Among the best known are the EU, the EFTA, the NAFTA, MERCOSUR in South America, the ASEAN Free Trade Area in Southeast Asia, and COMESA in Eastern and Southern Africa. There are many more, however, ranging from tariff agreements on a subset of output, to common markets and economic unions. The dates in parentheses are the dates of implementation of the agreements.

TABLE 2.4   Prominent Regional Trade Blocs

Region/Trade Bloc	Objective
Africa	
COMESA—Common Market for Eastern and Southern Africa (1993)	Common market
ECOWAS—Economic Community of West African States (1975)	Common market
Asia	
AFTA—ASEAN Free Trade Arrangement (1992)	Free-trade area
APEC—Asia-Pacific Economic Cooperation (1989)	Free-trade area
Europe	
EFTA—European Free Trade Association (1960)	Free-trade area
EU—European Union (1957)	Economic union
Middle East	
ACM—Arab Common Market (1964)	Customs union
GCC—Gulf Cooperation Council (1981)	Common market
Western Hemisphere	
MERCOSUR—Southern Cone Common Market (1991)	Common market
NAFTA—North American Free Trade Area (1994)	Free-trade area

Sources: Data from Harmsen and Leidy, "Regional Trading Arrangements," in *International Trade Policies: The Uruguay Round and Beyond. Volume II: Background Papers*. Washington, DC: IMF, 1994. The WTO, "Regionalism." Geneva: The World Trade Organization, © James Gerber.

A **partial trade agreement** is the least comprehensive RTA. It occurs when two or more countries agree to drop trade barriers in one or a few economic sectors, such as steel, autos, or any other line of production. Partial trade agreements are used when countries are reluctant to open all sectors, but they desire free trade for a limited set of goods.

As more goods are included in the partial trade agreement, it begins to look more like a **free-trade area**. One example is NAFTA, but there are many others, such as the European Free Trade Area (EFTA) and the U.S.-Israel Free Trade Agreement. In a free-trade area, nations trade goods and services across international boundaries without paying a tariff and without the limitations imposed by quotas, which are direct limits on imports. In reality, however, most free-trade areas such as NAFTA do not allow completely free trade. Nations usually reserve some restrictions for particularly sensitive items. For example, as part of its efforts to protect its culture, Canada limits the number of U.S. television programs that Canadian television stations may purchase. With a free-trade area, nations usually keep their own health, safety, and technical standards, and may deny entry of imports if they do not meet national standards.

The next level of integration is called a **customs union**. A customs union is a free-trade area plus a **common external tariff** toward nonmembers. By 1968, the EU (then called the European Economic Community) had become a customs union, and in today's economy, MERCOSUR (Brazil, Argentina, Uruguay, Paraguay, and Venezuela) aspire to become one. As with free-trade areas, many items are usually left out of the agreement. In the European case, for example, each nation retained its own tariffs and quotas with respect to Japanese autos. Common markets are the next level beyond customs unions. A **common market** is a customs union plus an agreement to allow the free mobility of inputs, such as labor and capital. The clearest example is the EU in the 1990s. The three NAFTA countries have elements of a common market (without the common external tariff) because they allow capital to move freely around the region. NAFTA also grants relatively free movement to certain types of white-collar labor, such as architects, business consultants, and others.

The final level of economic integration is an **economic union**. An economic union is a common market with substantial coordination of macroeconomic policies, including a common currency, and harmonization of many standards and regulations. The clearest examples are the states of the United States or the provinces of Canada. The BENELUX Union of Belgium, the Netherlands, and Luxembourg is an example of separate nations that have formed a union, and the EU is in the process of becoming an economic union, with the euro as its common currency, and at some point, with a common defense policy, common citizenship rights, and a common fiscal policy.

Regional Trade Agreements and the WTO

When a WTO member signs an RTA, it is obligated to notify the WTO. Since 1948, over 500 agreements have been listed with the WTO, with a majority of the notifications having occurred since 1990. Not all of these agreements are still active, but 338 were considered active at the start of 2012.

RTAs are inherently discriminatory since countries in an RTA discriminate in favor of each other and thereby deny most-favored nation treatment to non-RTA members. Nevertheless, the GATT and the WTO have allowed RTAs under the assumption that they create more new trade than they destroy with their discriminatory practices. In economic terms, **trade creation** must exceed **trade diversion**. An example will clarify these two concepts.

Suppose that the United States imports apparel from a wide variety of locales, including Haiti. Further, suppose that the United States has high tariffs on apparel, but the tariffs are nondiscriminatory and therefore in compliance with the WTO rules. If Haiti is a low-cost producer, then after paying the same tariff that all exporters to the United States face, its goods will be competitive in the U.S. market. One last assumption is that Mexico also produces apparel, but its costs are above Haiti's, so most U.S. imports come from Haiti, not Mexico. In this hypothetical example, when the United States signs a free-trade agreement with Mexico, Mexican apparel can enter the United States without paying a tariff, while Haiti continues to pay. As a result, even though Mexico has higher costs of production than Haiti, its goods could become cheaper in the U.S. market. In that case, trade is diverted from Haiti to Mexico, even though Haiti is the low-cost producer. This would be a backward step in world production since resources would be allocated from the lower-cost producer to the higher-cost one, and it is precisely this type of change the WTO rules are meant to guard against.

The GATT/WTO agreement recognizes that most RTAs create some trade diversion, but the goal is to create more new trade, due to the dropping of barriers between trading partners, so that new trade outweighs the value of trade that is diverted. Something very close to the hypothetical scenario just described, however, occurred throughout many parts of the Caribbean Basin and Central America when the United States, Mexico, and Canada became a free-trade area in 1995. In response, the United States provided financial assistance and relaxed its trade barriers for countries in Central America and the Caribbean.

For and Against RTAs

The arguments for and against RTAs involve more than pure economics. Politics, international relations, and national security also play a role. The central economic question is whether they are supportive of a gradual, long-run increase in world trade, or whether they tend to become obstacles to further relaxation of trade barriers. In trade jargon, the issue is whether they are building blocks or stumbling blocks.

Proponents of trade agreements view them as building blocks toward freer, more open world trade. They have several arguments on their side. First, it is easier for a few countries to reach agreement than it is for all the countries in the WTO. Therefore, RTAs create conditions where countries can lower their barriers without having to negotiate an agreement with all 162 members. Second, the domestic effects of a reduction of trade barriers are less dramatic since an RTA covers less than the world economy, and thereby limits the sudden surge of competition that might occur if all the WTO nations adopted the same policies. This also allows members to go further and to potentially open more than they would under a multilateral agreement. Third, RTA member countries can experiment with new agreements that are impossible among a large number of countries, such as the opening of certain types of services that have been traditionally closed. Insurance and telecommunications are examples. And fourth, RTAs can be used as a political and economic threat to encourage agreements in the WTO forum. For example, some argue that the U.S.-Mexico-Canada agreement helped push countries toward conclusion of the Uruguay Round agreement, as they feared the United States might develop its own regional bloc and abandon its multilateral commitments.

Opponents of RTAs question many of these assumptions. Their greatest criticism is that RTAs undermine progress toward multilateral (worldwide) agreements. Pro-trade opponents of RTAs do not believe that they encourage agreements through the WTO, but instead they believe that they polarize countries and draw energy away from the work of reaching agreement. Opponents point out that RTAs are often discriminatory against poor and less-developed countries, particularly when they involve a rich giant like the United States and small, developing countries such as Guatemala and El Salvador. Not only are low-income countries unable to negotiate forcefully, they often lack the resources and infrastructure that will be needed to take advantage of a market opening. Further, in their view, rich countries like the United States have no need of trade barriers against products from small developing countries.

THE ROLE OF INTERNATIONAL ECONOMIC INSTITUTIONS

LO 2.4 **Analyze the roles of international economic organizations.**

People rely on institutions to create order and reduce uncertainty. By defining the constraints or limits on economic, political, and social interactions, institutions define the incentive system of a society and help to create stability. The provision of order and the reduction of uncertainty are so important that when they are absent, economies cannot grow. Within a nation, the formal rules of behavior are defined by the various levels of government. In the United States, for example, these include cities, counties, special districts, states, and the federal government. In the international sphere, however, there are no corresponding levels of government. The establishment of rules for international trade and international macroeconomic relations are dependent on the voluntary associations of nations in international economic organizations.

The primary difference between international economic organizations and the government of a single nation is that the former have limited enforcement power. National and local governments have police powers they can use to enforce their rules; international organizations have no police power, but they do have more subtle powers for encouraging cooperation. For example, the IMF and World Bank can withdraw lines of credit to developing countries. The withdrawal of IMF credit raises a red flag for private lenders and makes it more costly for uncooperative nations to gain access to private capital markets. Likewise, the WTO can legitimize retaliatory sanctions against nations that fail to honor their trade obligations. Basically, however, international organizations rely on moral persuasion and the commitments of individual nations to remain effective. If individual nations choose not to join or decide to withdraw their support, there is nothing the IMF, World Bank, or WTO can do.

The provision of order and the reduction of uncertainty are services that everyone values. This is why we pay police officers, judges, and legislators. Although public order and the lessening of uncertainty are intangibles, they are desired and valued in the same sense as more tangible material objects. Their economic characteristics are different from those of most goods and services, however, and they fall into the category known as **public goods**.

The Definition of Public Goods

By definition, public goods are **nonexcludable** and **nonrival** or **nondiminishable**. *Nonexcludability* means that the normal price mechanism does not work as a way of regulating access. For example, when a signal is broadcast on the airwaves by a television station, anyone with a TV set who lives in its range can pick it up. (Of course, this is not the case with cable stations, which are granted permission to scramble their signals. Signal scrambling is a clever technological solution to the problem of nonexcludability.)

The second characteristic of public goods is that they are nonrival or nondiminishable. This refers to the attribute of not being diminished by consumption. For example, if I tune in to the broadcast signal of a local TV station, my neighbors will have the same signal amount available to them. Most goods get smaller, or diminish, when they are consumed, but public goods do not.

Private markets often fail to supply optimal levels of public goods because of the problem of **free riding**. Free riding means that there is no incentive to pay for public goods because people cannot be excluded from consumption. Given this characteristic, public goods will not be produced optimally by free markets unless institutional arrangements can somehow overcome the free riding. In most cases, governments step in as providers and use their powers to tax as a means to force people to pay for the goods.

Maintaining Order and Reducing Uncertainty

Two of the most important functions of international economic institutions are to maintain order in international economic relations and to reduce uncertainty. Together, these functions are often instrumental in the avoidance of a global economic crisis. Furthermore, if a national crisis threatens to become global, international institutions often help to bring it to a less costly end and to prevent nations from shifting the cost of national problems to other countries.

The maintenance of order and the reduction of uncertainty are general tasks that require specific rules in a number of areas of international economic interaction, although economists do not completely agree on the specific rules or the specific types of cooperation that should be provided. Nevertheless, the proponents of international institutions, such as economist Charles Kindleberger, have noted several areas where institutions are needed in order to strengthen cooperation and prevent free riding in the provision of international public goods. Among these items are the four public goods listed in Table 2.5.

Kindleberger and others have argued that the absence of a set of rules for providing one or more of these public goods is usually part of the explanation of historical crises such as the worldwide Great Depression of the 1930s. If no international institutions are available to help nations overcome the tendency to free ride, then international economic stability grows more fragile. As an illustration, consider the first item listed in Table 2.5. During recessions, politicians begin to feel enormous pressure to close markets in order to protect jobs at home. During the 1930s, for example, most nations enacted high tariffs and restrictive quotas on imports. This set in motion waves of retaliation as other nations followed suit and imposed their own tariffs and quotas. In the end, no one benefited and international trade collapsed. By comparison, during the worldwide recession of 2008 and 2009, national commitments to maintain open markets as agreed under the rules of the WTO prevented individual countries from raising tariffs or implementing quotas even when there were strong domestic political pressures for closing markets.

In a recession, free riders want to close their markets to reduce imports and create more jobs. At the same time, however, they want all other nations to stay open so that they do not lose any export markets. These motives are inconsistent, and the effect of free riding behavior is that all countries retaliate by closing their markets, international trade collapses, and everyone is worse off than before. Kindleberger shows that the shift in trade policies toward high tariffs and restrictive quotas helped to intensify and spread the Great Depression of the 1930s.

Kindleberger also argues that the sudden decline in capital flows to developing countries in the 1930s and the complete absence of a **lender of last resort** deepened the Great Depression and provides further historical evidence for the importance of international institutions. The lack of a lender of last resort was particularly critical because a number of countries with temporary financial problems soon passed into full-blown financial collapse. As it became impossible for countries to

TABLE 2.5 **Four Examples of International Public Goods**

Public Good	Purpose
Open markets in a recession	To prevent a fall in exports from magnifying the effects of a recession
Capital flows to less-developed countries (LDCs)	To assist economic development in poor countries
International money for settlement of international debts	To maintain a globally accepted system for paying debts
Last-resort lending	To prevent the spread of some types of financial crises

pay their foreign debts, the crisis spread from the indebted nations to the lending nations. In 2009, during the recent crisis, the world's largest economies approved an increase in funding for the IMF so that it would be able to continue its role as a lender of last resort.

International economic crises, such as the Mexican peso crisis of 1994–1995, the Asian Crisis of 1997–1998, and the more recent and very severe subprime mortgage crisis of 2007–2009, are relatively frequent occurrences. In each crisis or potential crisis, international institutions play an important role by preventing free riding. Lacking much in the way of formal enforcement mechanisms, they overcome the free rider problem by changing each nation's expectations about every other nation. For example, if all countries are committed to open markets in good times and bad, then during a worldwide recession no country expects its trading partners to close their markets. Or, if each country pays a share of the IMF's operating funds, then it overcomes the problems that arise when every country waits for the others to make risky loans during a crisis. The effectiveness of international institutions depends on the credible commitment of the world's nations. If a country agrees to a set of rules, but has a reputation for breaking its agreements, then its commitment is not credible. Institutions cannot overcome the free rider problem under those circumstances.

CASE STUDY

Bretton Woods

After World War I, the United States retreated into a relative isolationism under the mistaken belief that noninvolvement in European affairs would protect the country from entanglement in disastrous European conflicts such as World War I. The rise of Hitler, Japanese aggression in the Pacific, and the start of World War II showed that this policy would not work.

The United States began to realize its mistake in the 1930s as it watched Hitler take over a large part of the European continent. U.S. and British cooperation and planning for the postwar era began before the United States entered the war in December 1941, and long before the outcome was known. President Roosevelt and Prime Minister Churchill met on a battleship off the coast of Newfoundland in August 1941. Soon after, they announced the Atlantic Charter, a program for postwar reconstruction that committed both nations to working for the fullest possible economic collaboration among all nations after the war. Concurrent with the Atlantic Charter, the United States and Britain began discussing the kinds of international institutions that might be proposed.

All parties agreed that in any postwar order the United States would have to be the political, military, and economic leader. The United States had surpassed

(continued)

Great Britain in wealth and size several decades earlier, and its leadership during the war gave it prestige and credibility. In addition, the physical infrastructure of the United States was not damaged by the war, and it was the only industrial nation able to provide the financial capital and physical material needed to repair the war damage.

Looking back to the 1920s and 1930s, the postwar planners recognized four serious problems that they should guard against (1) the worldwide depression; (2) the collapse of international trade; (3) the collapse of the international monetary system; and (4) the collapse of international lending. Discussions during World War II were mainly devoted to rules, agreements, and organizations that could be created to avoid these problems. The following international institutions were viewed as central for the achievement of these goals:

- An international organization to help stabilize exchange rates and to assist nations that are unable to pay their international debts
- Agreements to reduce trade barriers
- An international organization for providing relief to the war-damaged nations, and to assist with reconstruction

Plans for the postwar period were finalized at a conference held in July 1944, in Bretton Woods, New Hampshire. The Bretton Woods institutions include the IMF, the World Bank, and the Bretton Woods exchange rate system. Although it was conceived separately, the GATT is sometimes included because it embodies the goals and ideas of the Bretton Woods planners with respect to international trade. Together, these institutions are a historically unique set of international economic institutions, and each, in its own area, has played a key role in the history of the international economy since 1945.

The founding principles of the Bretton Woods institutions are relatively simple. First, trade should open in all countries, not just in the United States alone, or in the United States and the United Kingdom together. In economic terms, this was a call for multilateral opening as opposed to unilateralism (one-sided opening) or bilateralism (two-sided opening). Second, nations should not discriminate against other nations. Whatever tariffs and quotas the United Kingdom or the United States might levy against another country, they should be the same ones imposed on everyone. Third, in order to ensure the ability of importers to purchase goods abroad, countries should not limit the buying and selling of currency when its purpose is to pay for imports. Fourth, exchange rates should be fixed but with the possibility for periodic adjustment. These principles formed the cornerstones of the institutions.

CRITICISM OF INTERNATIONAL INSTITUTIONS

LO 2.5 Debate the pros and cons of international economic organizations.

The World Bank, IMF, WTO, and various regional trade agreements have provided financial resources for development, technical assistance for crisis management, and mechanisms for opening markets. Not everyone agrees that these efforts are positive on balance, however, and even those who view their actions favorably would agree that there is room for improvement. The range of criticism covers a wide spectrum, from public demonstrations against trade ministers meeting under the auspices of the WTO to well-informed criticisms by leading economists such as Nobel Laureate Joseph Stiglitz. The underlying question is whether the IMF, World Bank, and WTO are fostering development and economic security, or generating greater economic inequality and compounding the risks to vulnerable groups.

In general, most analysts probably agree that some types of international institutions are necessary due to the international public goods discussed earlier. The IMF, World Bank, and WTO were created in response to real historical events and for the explicit purposes of avoiding crises and promoting growth. Economic changes such as transportation and communication revolutions; the integration of new markets in Africa, Europe, Asia, and Latin America; and technological innovations have increased the need for institutions by reducing the isolation of nations and creating more interactions and spillovers among them. While there is a widely recognized need for a set of agreements covering the international economic policies practiced by individual nations, there is less consensus regarding the content of the agreements and how they should be implemented.

Sovereignty and Transparency

Sovereignty refers to the rights of nations to be free from unwanted foreign interference in their affairs. One of the strongest complaints about international institutions is that they violate national sovereignty by imposing unwanted economic policies. For example, when a country experiences a financial crisis, the IMF is often the only potential source of outside help. Once engaged, however, the IMF imposes conditions that sometimes amount to a complete rearrangement of national economic policies. Specific examples include IMF requirements that countries cut government spending, privatize their publicly owned enterprises, and open their financial sector to the free movement of capital. Each of these may go against public preferences. For example, when a country is in the midst of a financial crisis, cuts in government spending can increase the depth of a recession and often have a disproportionately large impact on the middle class and the poor. Aside from the potential benefits or costs, it often appears that governments are coerced by the international financial community. In response to this perception, some argue that if countries avoid financial crises, they do not need to ask for help. Furthermore, it would be harmful to everyone if the IMF lent money unconditionally. Still, the issue of how hard international institutions should be allowed to push countries to change their policies is an open debate.

Closely related to the issue of sovereignty is the issue of transparency. Transparency concerns are based on questions about the decision-making that occurs within international institutions. As noted earlier, the IMF and the World Bank have voting structures based on the size of the quotas or dues paid by each country. This gives the United States in particular, and developed country interests in general, control over these bodies and makes it difficult for them to differentiate U.S. or EU interests from the interests of client countries. For example, a client country may be told to open its financial markets because it will increase foreign capital inflows and investment, but the main beneficiaries are banks and financial firms in the United States or the EU. Some critics conclude that IMF and World Bank policies are explicitly designed to benefit special interests in developed countries and do not serve the interests of the world economy.

The governing structure of the WTO is not based on quotas or dues, but developing countries are at a disadvantage because they lack the armies of lawyers, trade association lobbyists, and industry specialists that the United States and the EU can muster during a round of negotiations. A specific example is the Uruguay Round deal on agriculture and intellectual property rights. Developed countries pushed a comprehensive and strict set of enforcement policies for protecting intellectual property rights (copyrights, trademarks, patents, brand names, and so on). In return, developing countries thought that they would face fewer barriers to selling agricultural products in industrial country markets. In fact, their access to developed country agricultural markets was much less than anticipated, and the costs of enforcing intellectual property rights turned out to be higher than expected.

Ideology

Issues of sovereignty and transparency are compounded by questions about the value of the technical economic advice given by the IMF and other institutions. Some of the sharpest criticisms come from economists who strongly favor international economic integration but argue that the advice and technical assistance provided to developing countries reflect the biases and wishes of developed countries' interests. These economists think the IMF and World Bank have been too insistent in their demands that countries open their financial markets to capital flows (something the IMF itself reconsidered after the financial crisis of 2007–2009), that they privatize government-owned firms, and that they cut government programs in times of crisis. These critics share a deep skepticism about grand schemes to "fix a country" with a universal set of policies that are applicable everywhere and at all times, although the IMF and World Bank would argue that their advice and conditions for assistance are more nuanced than the critics acknowledge.

The Chinese government has voiced similar criticism repeatedly, and has recently gone so far as to create an alternative to the World Bank and the IMF, called the **Asian Infrastructure Investment Bank (AIIB)**. The AIIB began operation in 2016, amid promises that it would respond to developing countries more quickly, with fewer conditions, and with fewer layers of oversight and review than the World Bank or the IMF. It is too soon to know whether the AIIB will succeed or not, but it is certain that it represents a new development in China's growing importance to the world economy.

Implementation and Adjustment Costs

Trade agreements and the WTO are a major focus of complaints by the critics of economic integration. In particular, when agreements combine developing and developed countries, asymmetries in negotiating skills and the ability to absorb the costs of implementation and adjustment are singled out for criticism. An often cited example is the previously mentioned case of the Uruguay Round agreement on intellectual property rights. In order to implement this part of the agreement, developing countries have to create or improve their patent systems and copyright and trademark enforcement mechanisms. The latter step would entail cutting down on pirated drugs, videos, CDs, software, and so on. The opportunity cost of implementing this part of the agreement is substantial, particularly for a developing country with very limited resources.

Once in place, trade agreements always impose costs in the form of adjustments to the new opportunities and challenges. Some markets will expand while others will contract. In general, the costs of adjusting to the new incentives are less significant than the benefits, but for some developing countries the adjustment costs may be quite large. Developing countries tend to have higher unemployment (often disguised or hidden in the informal sector), so that workers laid off in a contracting industry may spend more time looking for work. Their economies are also less diversified, and sudden shocks such as a surge of imports can have large effects. These problems are made more severe by the lack of social safety nets to protect unemployed workers and their families. In order to take advantage of the opportunities presented by greater access to foreign markets, countries may need to construct new infrastructures, for example, roads and ports for moving fresh produce. The ability of developing countries to build infrastructures is more limited than for developed countries, as is the access to credit.

Issues of sovereignty and transparency, ideological biases, and the costs of implementation and adjustment are only a partial catalog of the concerns raised by the critics of international institutions. In general, however, there is widespread agreement among professional economists that there are theoretical and practical reasons for their existence. Nevertheless, beyond a basic consensus about need, many issues remain subject to debate, particularly issues of governance and the amount of authority that should be vested in international organizations. In spite of these uncertainties, it is safe to say that if these international institutions did not exist, we would create them.

CASE STUDY

China's alternative to the IMF and World Bank: The AIIB

The first meeting of the directors of the newly created AIIB took place in Beijing, China, during January 2016 (see www.aiib.org). This was the culmination of several years of planning and negotiations by the Chinese government and was one more sign that China is reclaiming a leading role in international economic and political affairs.

The Chinese government has tried to change the voting structure and leadership of the IMF and the World Bank but met with little success. Both institutions were created during the years of China's revolution, and operated for decades during the period of China's greatest isolation. As China began major economic reforms in 1978, it began to look for ways to have a stronger voice in international institutions that help set the rules of trade and investment. Along the way, China became a leading voice for low-income and middle-income countries that were asking for a larger role in decision-making in international bodies.

The IMF is dominated by Western Europe, Japan, and the United States. As explained in the text, countries vote on issues in proportion to the size of the quota they pay into the IMF, and the quota is determined by the size of their GDP, their openness to trade, the variability of their economic growth, and other factors. China has 3.8 percent of the weighted votes, while the U.S. has just under 17 percent and the G7 almost 45 percent. China's push to have a greater say in rule-making and policy implementation reflects its belief that it deserves a larger role, given its size and its importance to the world economy.

When China first proposed an alternative to the IMF, the United States opposed the idea, and was successful for some years in forestalling its creation. Ultimately, however, China proposed the Asian Infrastructure Investment Bank in 2013 and began to recruit member countries. The United States opposed this initiative and for awhile was successful in persuading its closest allies to refrain from joining. By January 2016, at the inaugural meeting of its Board of Directors, China had recruited 56 other nations as founding members, including important allies of the United States such as Australia, France, Germany, and the United Kingdom.

China proposes to operate a "lean, clean, and green" organization, with few layers of bureaucracy ("lean"), no tolerance for corruption ("clean"), and sensitivity to environmental sustainability ("green"). Its focus is the financing of infrastructure in Asia, including power supplies, transportation and telecommunication systems, water supplies and sanitation, and agricultural development, among others. It has capital equivalent to $US 100 billion.

Will the AIIB undermine the effectiveness of the IMF by enabling countries to avoid its surveillance and oversight? Will it replace the World Bank in Asia? And how will its sponsorship by China shape future relations between that country, Asia, and the United States? It may take some years to begin to see an answer to these questions.

Summary

- Institutions are the "rules of the game." They can be formal, as in a nation's constitution, or informal, as in a custom or tradition. In both cases, we depend on institutions as mechanisms for creating order and reducing uncertainty. Global institutions have played an important role in fostering the growth of international trade and investment during the last fifty years. They have defined a set of rules that have helped avoid trade wars and the problems of the 1930s.

- The "Big 3" of international economic organizations are the International Monetary Fund (IMF), the World Bank, and the World Trade Organization (WTO). The latter grew out of the General Agreement on Tariffs and Trade (GATT). The IMF, World Bank, and the GATT were created at the end of World War II with the purpose of avoiding a return to the destructive economic conditions of the interwar years.

- Regional trade agreements are another important type of international institution, although they are not global in scope. Formally, there are five types of regional trade agreements. In order, from less integrated to more integrated, they are partial trade agreements, free-trade areas, customs unions, common markets, and economic unions. Each level is cumulative and incorporates the features of the previous level. In reality, however, actual trade agreements usually combine features from two or more types.

- Many economists favor regional trade agreements as building blocks for more open world trade, but some pro-free-trade economists are opposed on the grounds that they are harmful to multilateral WTO agreements and are discriminatory. In general, the WTO allows regional trade agreements (RTAs) as long as they create more trade than they divert.

- International economic institutions are an attempt to overcome the problem of free riding by individual nations in the sphere of providing international public goods. The most important public goods are order and a reduction in uncertainty. Some economists believe that these goods are best provided when there are agreements that help keep markets open in recessions and in boom periods, when there is an international lender of last resort, when there are sufficient lenders of capital to developing nations, and when there is an adequate supply of money for international payment.

■ Most analysts agree that some forms of international institutions are necessary as a precaution against crises and to promote growth, but there is significant disagreement over the design of governance structures and the scope of their responsibilities.

■ Primary areas of criticism are in sovereignty, transparency, ideological bias, and implementation and adjustment costs.

Vocabulary

Asian Infrastructure Investment Bank (AIIB)

Bretton Woods conference

common external tariff

common market

customs union

Doha Development Agenda

Doha Round

economic union

foreign exchange reserves

free riding

free-trade area

General Agreement on Tariffs and Trade (GATT)

IMF conditionality

institution

International Monetary Fund (IMF)

lender of last resort

most-favored nation (MFN) status

national treatment

nondiminishable

nondiscrimination

nonexcludable

nonrival

partial trade agreement

public goods

quota

regional trade agreement (RTA)

sovereignty

trade bloc

trade creation

trade diversion

trade rounds

Uruguay Round

World Bank

World Trade Organization (WTO)

Study Questions

All problems are assignable in MyEconLab.

2.1 What is an institution? Give examples of formal and informal institutions. Explain how they differ from organizations.

2.2 What are the arguments in favor of international organizations? What are the arguments against them? Which do you think are stronger?

2.3 Give the arguments for and against free-trade agreements. How might the signing of a free-trade agreement between the United States, Central America, and the Dominican Republic have harmed Bangladesh?

2.4 What are public goods and how do they differ from private ones? Give examples of each.

2.5 Describe the main tasks or functions of each of the following:

- The IMF
- The World Bank
- The GATT
- The WTO

2.6 When nations sign the GATT, they bind their tariffs at their current level, or lower. *Tariff binding* means that they agree not to raise the tariffs except under unusual circumstances. Explain how tariff binding in the GATT prevents free riding during a global slowdown.

2.7 Kindleberger's study of the Great Depression of the 1930s led him to believe that market economies are sometimes unstable and that nations can get locked into prolonged downturns. Other economists are not convinced. Suppose that you disagree with Kindleberger and that you believe that market-based economies are inherently stable. How would you view the need for international institutions to address the provision of each of the public goods listed in Table 2.5?

2.8 What are the five main types of regional trade agreements and what are their primary characteristics?

2.9 Critics of global institutions have a variety of complaints about the WTO, the IMF, and the World Bank. Explain the main categories of complaints.

PART 2

International Trade

Comparative Advantage and the Gains from Trade

INTRODUCTION: THE GAINS FROM TRADE

LO 3.1 **Analyze numerical examples of absolute and comparative advantage.**

This chapter introduces the theory of comparative advantage. A simple model is used to show how nations maximize their material welfare by specializing in goods and services that have the lowest relative costs of production. The improvement in national welfare is known as the **gains from trade**. The concepts of comparative advantage and the gains from trade are two of the oldest and most widely held ideas in all of economics, yet they are often misunderstood and misinterpreted. Therefore, it is worth the effort to develop a clear understanding of both.

Adam Smith and the Attack on Economic Nationalism

The development of modern economic theory is intimately linked to the birth of international economics. In 1776, Adam Smith published *An Inquiry into the Nature and Causes of the Wealth of Nations*, a work that became the first modern statement of economic theory. In the process of laying out the basic ground rules for the efficient allocation of resources, Smith initiated a general attack on **mercantilism**, the system of nationalistic economics that dominated economic thought in the 1700s. Mercantilism stressed exports over imports, primarily as a way to obtain revenues for building armies and national construction projects.

The key mistake in mercantilist thinking was the belief that trade was a **zero sum** activity. In the eighteenth century the term *zero sum* did not exist, but it is a convenient expression for the concept that one nation's gain is another nation's loss. A moment's reflection should be enough to see the mistake in this belief, at least as it applies to voluntary exchange. When a grocery store sells a gallon of milk or a loaf of bread, both the store and the consumer are better off. If that were not the case, the store would not sell or the consumer would not buy. Voluntary exchanges such as this are positive sum, not zero sum. In this sense, sports metaphors that have a winner and loser are usually not an apt description of trade relations. Trade is more dance than football, more rock climbing than bicycle racing.

No one in the 1770s thought that they were living in the midst of an industrial revolution, but Smith was observant enough to perceive that many improvements in the standard of living had occurred during his lifetime as a result of increasing specialization in production. When he analyzed specialization, he made one of his most important contributions to economics: the discovery that specialization depends on the size of the market.

A contemporary example may be helpful. If a car company were permitted to sell its cars and trucks only in Michigan, it would have much less revenue and would sell many fewer vehicles. It would hire fewer employees, and each person would be less specialized. As it is, the market is so large (essentially, the world) that car companies can hire engineers who completely specialize in small, even minuscule, parts of a car—door locks, for example. Your door lock engineer will know everything there is to know about the design, production, and assembly of door locks and will be able to put them into cars most efficiently. A firm that was limited to the Michigan market could never afford to hire such specialized skills and could never be as efficient.

One of the keys to Smith's story of wealth creation is access to foreign markets. If no one is willing to import, then every company is limited by the size of the national market. In some cases, that may be large enough (the United States or China), but in most cases, it is not. Small- and medium-sized countries cannot efficiently produce every item they consume. Holland, for example, has always imported a large share of its goods and has depended on access to foreign markets in order to earn export revenues to pay for imports.

Smith was highly critical of trade barriers because they decrease specialization, technological progress, and wealth creation. He also recognized that imports enable a country to obtain goods that it cannot make or cannot make as cheaply, while exports are made for someone else and are useful only if they lead to imports. The modern view of trade shares Smith's dislike of trade barriers for mostly the same reasons. Although international economists recognize that there are limitations to the application of theory, in most cases a majority of economists share a preference for open markets. In Chapters 6 and 7 we will examine trade barriers in greater detail, but at this point we will develop a deeper understanding of the gains from trade by means of a simple algebraic and graphical model.

A Simple Model of Production and Trade

We will begin with one of the simplest models in economics. The conclusion of this analysis is that a policy of free trade maximizes a nation's material well-being. Later, we will examine some of the cases where real-world conditions do not conform to the assumptions of the model and where the optimality of free trade is questionable.

The basic model is often referred to as a *Ricardian model,* since it first took form in the analysis of David Ricardo. The model begins by assuming that there are only two countries, producing two goods, using one input (labor). The Ricardian model assumes that firms are price takers, or, in other words, markets are competitive, and no firm has market power. The model is static in the sense that it assumes that technology is constant and there are no learning effects of production that might make firms and industries more productive over time. Ricardo also assumed that labor is perfectly mobile between industries but perfectly immobile across national borders. Table 3.1 lists the main assumptions of the model; many of these will be relaxed in later chapters.

Absolute Productivity Advantage and the Gains from Trade

To begin, we define *productivity* in the Ricardian model. Productivity is the amount of output obtained from a unit of input. Since labor is the only input, we can define **labor productivity** as follows:

$$(\text{units of output})/(\text{hours worked})$$

If, for example, 2 loaves of bread can be produced in one hour, then productivity is as follows:

$$(2 \text{ loaves})/(1 \text{ hour})$$

or 2 loaves per hour. If four loaves are produced in two hours, then productivity is still as follows:

$$(4 \text{ loaves})/(2 \text{ hours}) = 2 \text{ loaves per hour}$$

TABLE 3.1   **Assumptions of the Simple Ricardian Trade Model**

Labor	■ The only input
	■ Cannot migrate across borders
	■ Is completely mobile between sectors
	■ Fully employed
Markets	■ Two outputs
	■ Perfect competition
	■ No transportation or trade costs
Technology	■ Constant returns to scale
	■ No changes in technology or skills

TABLE 3.2　Output per Hour Worked

	United States	Canada
Bread	2 loaves	3 loaves
Steel	3 tons	1 ton

Canada is more productive than the United States in bread production, but the United States is more productive in steel production.

Suppose that there are two goods, bread and steel, and two countries, the United States and Canada. Suppose also that each produces according to the productivities shown in Table 3.2.

The values in Table 3.2 show that productivity in the making of bread is greater in Canada than in the United States, and that productivity in steel is greater in the United States. Canada has an **absolute productivity advantage** in bread because it produces more loaves per hour worked (three versus two in the United States). Using the same logic, the United States has an absolute productivity advantage in steel production.

The basis of Adam Smith's support for free trade was the belief that every country would have an absolute advantage in something, and that the source of the advantage did not matter. Whether it was due to special skills in the labor force, climate and soil characteristics of the country, or the temperament of its people, there would be goods that each country could manufacture, grow, or dig out of the ground more efficiently than its trading partner. Consequently, every country could benefit from trade.

In the numerical example outlined in Table 3.2, each loaf of bread costs the United States 1.5 tons of steel. Put another way, the **opportunity cost** of bread is 1.5 tons of steel, since each unit of bread produced requires the economy to move labor out of steel production, forfeiting 1.5 tons of steel that it could have produced instead. This follows from the fact that each hour of labor can produce either 2 loaves of bread or 3 tons of steel. We can write this ratio as the barter price of bread as follows:

$$P_{us}^b = \frac{3 \text{ tons}}{2 \text{ loaves}} = 1.5 \left(\frac{\text{tons}}{\text{loaves}} \right),$$

where b is bread and us is the country. Similarly, we can write the U.S. price of steel as the inverse as follows:

$$P_{us}^s = \frac{2 \text{ loaves}}{3 \text{ tons}} = 0.67 \left(\frac{\text{loaves}}{\text{tons}} \right).$$

You should be able to verify that the Canadian price of bread will be 0.33 (tons/loaf) and that steel will cost 3 (loaves/ton).

If the United States can sell a ton of steel for more than 0.67 loaves of bread, it is better off. Similarly, if Canadians can obtain a ton of steel for fewer than 3 loaves of bread, they are better off. Each country will gain from trade if there is agreement to sell steel for fewer than 3 loaves of bread but more than 0.67 loaves. Anywhere in that range, both Canadians and Americans will benefit. In the end, trade will occur at a price somewhere between these two limits as follows:

$$3.0\left(\frac{\text{loaves}}{\text{tons}}\right) > P_w^s > 0.67\left(\frac{\text{loaves}}{\text{tons}}\right),$$

where P_w^s = the world price of steel (the trade price). Without knowing more details about the demand side of the market, it is impossible to say whether the price will settle closer to 3.0 (the Canadian opportunity cost of steel) or 0.67 (the U.S. opportunity cost). The closer the price is to 0.67, the more Canada benefits from trade, and the closer it is to 3.0, the more the United States benefits. Regardless of which country benefits more, as long as the price is between these two limits, both countries benefit from trade.

CASE STUDY

Gains from Trade in Nineteenth-Century Japan

A fundamental result from international economics is that nations gain from trade. We have just shown this in a simple theoretical framework by illustrating how trade enables countries to consume a bundle of goods that is of greater value than what they can produce on their own. The key to this result is that the two trading partners have different productivities, which lead to different prices in autarky.

One question economists have struggled to answer is, "How large are the gains from trade?" Does trade create a relatively small gain, or a relatively large one? The answer is complicated for a couple of reasons. First, there are gains from trade opening that occur immediately and are called *static gains from trade*. But there are also gains that occur over time, called *dynamic gains from trade,* that are difficult to predict since they depend on changes in innovation and productivity. A second reason why it is hard to measure gains from trade is that all countries already trade, so most of what is measured are the potential gains from some additional amount of trade and not the benefits or gains that a country currently has from participating in trade. In our simple model, we went from no trade to some trade, but in the real world, when countries reduce their trade barriers, they go from some trade to some more trade.

Two economists (Bernhofen and Brown, *American Economic Review*, 95(1), 2005) tackled this problem in an original way by looking at the case of Japan. Japan's rulers closed their market to outsiders in 1639 when it felt threatened by

Christian missionaries and their Portuguese supporters. From that time on, only the Dutch and the Chinese were permitted to trade with Japan, and each was limited to just a handful of ships per year. In the Dutch case, by the mid-1800s, only one ship per year was allowed to trade, while the Chinese were limited to three or four junks per year. Bernhofen and Brown estimated that Japan exported goods worth about 1.2 cents per person and imported even less, around 0.4 cents per person, by the mid-1800s. Essentially, trade was nil and Japan lived in autarky.

As most Americans know from their history books, the United States decided to force open the Japanese market in the early 1850s and sent Admiral Matthew Perry to accomplish the task. Perry made first contact with Japanese officials in 1853 and signed a limited agreement in 1854. The United States continued to request further opening until a full commercial treaty was signed in 1858 and took effect on July 4, 1859. Following close on the heels of the Americans were the Dutch, Russians, British, and French, and by the mid-1860s, Japan was living under a regime of nearly free trade since its ability to limit imports with tariffs was curtailed by the foreign powers.

The Japanese case is an excellent one for measuring the static gains from trade. Japan had closed markets before it was forced to open, and after opening it was forced to practice more or less free trade. Our simple theoretical model of trade predicts that Japan should have shifted its domestic production to take advantage of the higher prices offered for its exports, and that its national income should have grown in value since its export goods are worth more and its import goods cost less. Both effects seem to have occurred.

After trade began, Japanese production of silk and tea increased dramatically and these products became major export items. Imported goods included woolen textiles (Japan had no sheep industry) and a variety of manufactured goods, such as weapons, that it did not make itself. National income seems to have grown as well. Bernhofen and Brown estimated that an upper bound on the increase was 8–9 percent of gross domestic product (GDP). This is not a huge amount, but it is not inconsequential either, and represents only the static gains from trade. Over time, as Japanese producers adjusted to a larger market and as new technologies and products were introduced, additional gains would accrue from increased productivity and innovation.

COMPARATIVE PRODUCTIVITY ADVANTAGE AND THE GAINS FROM TRADE

LO 3.2 **Draw a diagram showing gains from trade.**

At this point, the obvious question to ask is what happens if a country does not have an absolute productivity advantage in anything. It is not hard to imagine an extremely poor, resource-deficient nation with low literacy and scarce capital.

What can these countries produce more efficiently than the United States or Germany? Why would a rich country want to trade with them when they are inefficient at everything? The answer is that even if a country lacks a single good in which it has an absolute productivity advantage, it can still benefit from trade. Perhaps even more surprising, high-income countries also benefit from the trade. In other words, the idea that nations benefit from trade has nothing to do with whether a country has an absolute advantage in producing a particular good. In order to see this, first we must develop a few more basic concepts.

The Production Possibilities Curve

The **production possibilities curve (PPC)** shows the trade-offs a country faces when it chooses its combination of bread and steel output. Figure 3.1 illustrates a hypothetical PPC for the United States. Point B on the PPC is an efficient point of production because it utilizes existing resources to obtain the maximum possible level of output. The assumption of full employment is equivalent to assuming that the United States is operating at a point like B that lies on its PPC. At point A, the economy is inside its production curve and is operating at an inefficient and wasteful level of output because it is not obtaining the maximum possible output from its available inputs. Point C is infeasible because resources do not permit the production of bread and steel in the combination indicated.

The PPC shown in Figure 3.1 is a straight line because it is assumed that the trade-off between bread and steel does not change. This follows from the assumption that labor is homogeneous and that no group of workers is more skilled than another group. The trade-off between bread and steel is another way to refer to the opportunity cost of steel. This follows from the definition of opportunity cost as the best forgone alternative: In order to produce a ton of steel, the United

FIGURE 3.1   A PPC for the United States

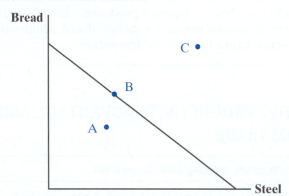

In a model with only two goods, the production possibilities curve shows the trade-offs.

FIGURE 3.2   Opportunity Costs and the Slope of the PPC

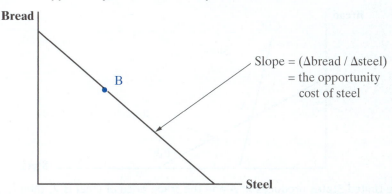

The slope of the PPC is the opportunity cost of the good on the horizontal axis. This follows from the definition of the slope as the ratio of the vertical change to the horizontal change moving along the PPC.

States gives up two-thirds of a loaf of bread. In Figure 3.2, the slope of the PPC is −0.67, the number of loaves of bread forgone (Δbread) divided by the quantity of steel obtained (Δsteel)—written as follows:

$$\text{Slope of the PPC} = (\Delta\text{bread output})/(\Delta\text{steel output})$$
$$= \text{opportunity cost of steel}$$

Relative Prices

Suppose that the slope of the PPC is −0.67, as shown in Figure 3.2. If the United States does not trade, it gives up 0.67 loaves of bread for an additional ton of steel. This trade-off is called the **relative price** of steel or the opportunity cost of steel. The term *relative price* follows from the fact that it is not in monetary units, but rather in units of the other good. If no trade takes place, then the relative price of a good must be equal to its opportunity cost in production.

It is easy to convert the relative price of steel into the relative price of bread: Simply take the inverse of the price of steel. In other words, if 0.67 loaves of bread is the price of 1 ton of steel in the United States, then 1.5 tons of steel is the price of 1 loaf of bread. By the same reasoning, 1.5 tons of steel is the opportunity cost of 1 loaf of bread in the United States when production is at point B or at any other point along the PPC in Figure 3.2.

The Consumption Possibilities Curve

The complete absence of trade is called **autarky**, and in this situation both the United States and Canada are limited in their consumption to the goods that they produce at home. Suppose that autarky prevails initially and the opportunity cost

FIGURE 3.3   Production and Trade Before Specialization

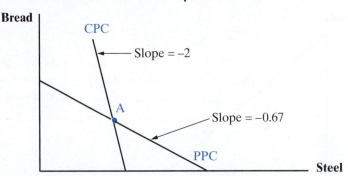

If the United States produces at A and the trade price of steel is 2, then it can trade steel for bread and move its consumption bundle outside its PPC.

of steel in Canada is 3 loaves of bread per ton, and in the United States, it is 0.67 loaves per ton (as given in Table 3.1). In this case, both countries can raise their consumption levels if they trade. In particular there will be gains from trade if the price settles somewhere between the opportunity costs in Canada and in the United States. That is, the countries benefit if the following is true:

$$3.0 \ (\text{loaves/ton}) > P_w^s > 0.67 \ (\text{loaves/ton})$$

Suppose that the price settles at 2 loaves per ton. In the United States, the pre-trade price was 0.67 loaves per ton. This is illustrated in Figure 3.3, where the PPC for the United States is shown with the production point at A. The trading possibilities for the United States are illustrated by the **consumption possibilities curve (CPC)**. The slope of the CPC is −2, which is the relative price of steel, or the rate at which bread and steel can be traded for each other. The CPC passes through point A because this is the combination of steel and bread that is available to trade if the United States produces at A. If the United States chooses to trade, it could move up the CPC, trading each ton of steel for 2 loaves of bread. This is a better trade-off than it gets if it tries to make more bread, since along its PPC each ton brings only two-thirds more loaves of bread. While it is always impossible to produce outside the PPC, in effect, the United States can consume outside it by trading steel for bread.

The Gains from Trade

You should wonder why the United States would choose to make bread at all, since a ton of steel not produced brings in only two-thirds of a loaf of bread. If the United States were to specialize in steel production and trade for bread, it could do much better, since it would get 2 loaves for each ton. This possibility is shown in Figure 3.4. Here, the pre-trade production point for the United States is at A. This is also its consumption point, since in the absence of trade, consumption must

FIGURE 3.4   Production to Maximize Income

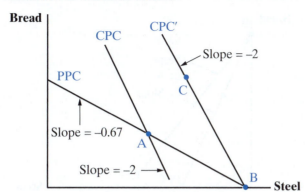

By specializing production at B and trading for bread, the United States obtains the largest possible consumption bundle.

equal production. Point B in Figure 3.4 represents production that is completely specialized in steel. With the opening of trade, production could occur at B, and the United States could trade up along CPC′, which has a slope of −2, the same as the CPC. If the United States produces at B and moves up CPC′, it can reach a point like C, which is unambiguously superior to the consumption bundle available when production is at point A because it represents more of both bread and steel. Similarly, for any combination of bread and steel that is available along the PPC or CPC if the United States produces at A and trades, there is a consumption bundle on CPC′, which represents more of both goods.

The most important thing to note about production point B is that it maximizes U.S. income. This follows from the fact that it makes available the greatest combinations of bread and steel. To see this, consider that no other point of production puts the United States on a price line that lies farther out from the origin. Every other production point on the United States' PPC lies below the CPC′, and every CPC with a slope of −2 that passes through the PPC at a point other than B also lies below CPC′. In other words, given the United States' PPC and a relative steel price of 2, the largest bundle of consumption goods is obtained when the United States specializes in steel and trades for its bread.

The United States benefits from trade, but does Canada? Unequivocally, the answer is yes. Consider Figure 3.5 where point A is Canada's pre-trade production point. Along Canada's PPC, the opportunity cost of steel is 3 loaves of bread per ton. After trade, the price settles at 2 loaves per ton. With a trade price of 2, Canada maximizes its income by moving along its PPC to where it is completely specialized in bread production. Then it can trade bread for steel at a trade price that is more favorable than its domestic trade-off of 3 loaves per ton. Canada, too, can consume at a point on CPC that is outside its PPC and above and to the right of its pre-trade equilibrium at point A. Canada, like the United States, is better off because with trade it gets a larger combination of both goods than it can produce for itself.

FIGURE 3.5   **Canada's Gains from Trade**

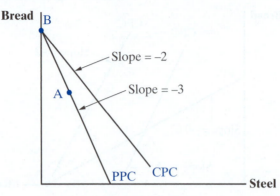

By specializing production at B and trading for steel, Canada obtains the largest possible consumption bundle.

A numerical example will help clarify the existence of gains from trade. Suppose the relative price of steel is 2 loaves per ton. When the United States increases its steel output by 1 ton, it gives up 0.67 loaves of bread output, but it can trade the steel for 2 loaves, leaving a net gain of 1.33 loaves ($2 - 0.67 = 1.33$). In order to meet U.S. demand for 2 more loaves of bread, Canada must give up 0.67 ton of steel production. It trades the 2 loaves for 1 ton of steel, however, leaving a net gain of 0.33 ton ($1 - 0.67 = 0.33$). Hence, both countries benefit from the trade.

Domestic Prices and the Trade Price

Now we know that as long as the trade price is between the pre-trade domestic prices in Canada and the United States, both countries can gain from trade. What ensures that the trade price actually settles within this range, 3.0 (loaves/ton) $> P_w^s > 0.67$ (loaves/ton)? What would happen if, for example, P_w^s were equal to 4, or 0.5?

Consider the first case when the trade price is 4 loaves per ton of steel. At $P_w^s = 4$, the trade price of steel is greater than the production cost in each country. Clearly, the United States would want to continue to specialize in steel and trade it for bread. Nothing has changed with regard to the U.S. strategy for maximizing its consumption bundle, or income. The only difference now is that the United States gets 4 units of bread for each unit of steel, instead of 2 as before. In Canada's case, the higher price of steel makes it profitable for Canadian producers to switch to steel production. This follows because the production opportunity cost of steel is 3 loaves of bread, but each ton produced can trade for 4 loaves. By specializing in steel production and trading for bread, Canada maximizes its consumption bundle.

Finally, it should be obvious that both countries are specialized in steel production and that no one is producing bread. There is a bread shortage and a glut of steel. Consequently, bread prices rise, and steel prices fall. This goes on at least until the trade price of steel falls below the opportunity cost of production in Canada, the higher cost country. Once P_w^s is less than 3, Canadian producers switch back to bread, steel production goes down, bread is up, and trade can resume.

In the second case, where P_w^s is less than 0.67, Canada continues to specialize in bread, and the United States switches. Bread is the surplus good, steel is in short supply, and a similar dynamic causes the price to move in order to ensure that both goods are produced. The equilibrium trade price, then, has to be within the range we specified earlier, between the opportunity costs in the two countries. In our case, this is between 0.67 and 3.0 loaves per ton.

At the extreme, the trade price could be equal to the opportunity cost in one country; for example, if the trade price of steel is 0.67 loaves per ton, then the United States is indifferent about trading. It cannot be hurt by trading, but it does not gain either, since all the gains go to Canada. Similarly, if the trade price is equal to Canada's opportunity cost, then Canada is indifferent and all the gains accrue to the United States.

Without more information we cannot say much more about the trade price. Will it be close to 0.67 or to 3.0? The answer depends on the strength of demand for each good in both countries, but we have not explicitly included demand in our model, so we cannot say. We do know that if the price is closer to 0.67, then the gains from trade are larger for Canada, and if it is closer to 3.0, the United States benefits more. Nevertheless, both countries gain as long as the price is between the two opportunity costs, and economic forces determine that the price must be in that range.

ABSOLUTE AND COMPARATIVE PRODUCTIVITY ADVANTAGE CONTRASTED

LO 3.3 Numerically compare and contrast absolute and comparative advantage.

Absolute productivity advantage is defined as having higher labor productivity. We saw that if each country has an absolute productivity advantage in one of the goods, they can both benefit by specializing in that good and trading it for the other good. Note, however, that the gains from trade did not depend in any way on each country having an absolute advantage. In fact, it was the pre-trade opportunity costs of bread and steel in each country that mattered. Opportunity costs were derived from the productivities, but since they are a ratio, vastly different levels of productivity can lead to the same trade-off.

A country has a **comparative productivity advantage** in a good, or simply a comparative advantage, if its opportunity costs of producing a good are lower than those of its trading partners. The concept of comparative advantage is based on the idea that nations maximize their material well-being when they use their resources where they have their highest value. In order to know the highest-valued usage for any resource, we must compare alternative uses. If, by comparison to that of the United States, Canada's opportunity cost of bread is lower, then it should produce more bread and trade for steel.

The distinction between absolute and comparative productivity advantages is one of the most important in economics. It is also one of the least understood, in spite of the fact that it is relatively simple. For example, it is common to read or hear comments about competitiveness that assume that if a country does not have an absolute advantage, it will not be able to sell its products abroad. Our model explains why this logic is erroneous and why even the least productive nations export some goods.

GAINS FROM TRADE WITH NO ABSOLUTE ADVANTAGE

LO 3.4 Explain how a country with no absolute advantage can still gain from trade.

Consider the case shown in Table 3.3. Japan has an absolute advantage in both cars $(2 > 0.5)$ and steel $(2 > 1)$, yet it can still gain from trade, as can Malaysia, even though it lacks an absolute advantage in either good. If Japan does not trade, it is limited to its own production possibilities, which require it to give up 1 ton of steel for each car it produces. In Malaysia, each car costs 2 tons of steel. Hence, there is scope for a mutually beneficial exchange.

Japan's opportunity cost of steel production is greater than Malaysia's even though it has a higher absolute rate of productivity in steel. Therefore, if it follows its comparative advantage and maximizes its income, it will specialize in cars, the sector where its opportunity cost is lower than Malaysia's. Once trade opens, the world price of cars will be between 1 and 2 tons of steel per car, the opportunity costs of production in Japan and Malaysia, as follows:

$$1\left(\frac{\text{tons}}{\text{car}}\right) < P_W^c < 2\left(\frac{\text{tons}}{\text{car}}\right)$$

Let the price be 1.5 tons of steel per car. If Japan moves to specialize in cars with the opening of trade, it gives up 1 ton of steel for each additional car it produces. With the additional car, it can trade for 1.5 tons of steel, which is a net gain of 0.5 tons over its own production. Similarly, Malaysia gives up 0.5 cars produced for each additional ton of steel it manufactures, but it gains 0.67 cars from each ton of steel traded. Both countries benefit and are able to consume a greater amount of both goods than they could if they relied on their national production alone.

TABLE 3.3 Output per Hour Worked

	Japan	Malaysia
Cars	2	0.5
Steel	2 tons	1 ton

This is a very simplified example of the gains from trade, but it illustrates a fundamental principle. What matters most for the purposes of trade is not a country's absolute advantage, but rather its comparative advantage. This is a central point of international economics: Differences in absolute advantage do not eliminate gains from trade. Furthermore, although both countries gain from trade, it does not imply that their living standards or incomes are equal. Malaysia's income will be less than Japan's because it produces less per hour. In effect, an hour of work in Malaysia returns the equivalent of 1 ton of steel or, through trade, 0.67 cars. Japanese workers produce 2 cars per hour worked, which is equivalent to 3 tons of steel through trade. As a result of higher absolute productivity, incomes in Japan are quite a bit higher, with or without trade.

CASE STUDY

Changing Comparative Advantage in the Republic of Korea, 1960–2010

Few countries began life with a more limited set of possibilities than the Republic of Korea (South Korea). Liberated from its forty years of colonial status (1905–1945) by the defeat of Japan in World War II, Korea was soon wracked by civil war (1950–1953) and divided into two nations. Many observers were pessimistic about the future of noncommunist South Korea. The industrial capacity of the country was mostly located in communist-controlled North Korea, and South Korea had little to offer besides the dedication and hard work of its people. Yet, over the following fifty years, few countries have grown faster.

From 1960 to 2010, per capita income in the Republic of Korea grew at the rate of 5.4 percent per year, in real terms (Table 3.4). At this rate, per capita income doubles every thirteen years.

Korea's economic strategy for the first few years after the Korean War was to limit imports and concentrate on producing import substitutes, a common strategy for developing countries in the 1950s. Korea was one of the first to recognize its limitations and to change its policies. In 1960 and 1961, political changes led to a change in economic policies and a more aggressive engagement

TABLE 3.4   Indicators of the Korean Economy

	1960	1980	2000	2010
GDP per capita ($US, 2000)	1,154	3,358	11,347	16,372
Trade-to-GDP ratio	15.8	72.0	74.3	102.0

(continued)

with the world economy. Korea removed many of its restrictions on imports and began to promote export-oriented industries. Between 1960 and 2010, its trade-to-GDP ratio increased from 15.8 to 102.

Initially, Korea's export efforts were limited to the commodities on hand, mostly minerals, a few agricultural and marine products (for example, seaweed), and very simple consumer goods. Over several decades after 1960, its export industries evolved several times, from simple products requiring few skills and little capital to products that required more skills and greater capital. After its first few years of exploring its comparative advantage, Korea developed competitive sectors in wigs, textiles, shoes, and plywood. With the increase in income came increases in skills and financial capital. This permitted the development of more skill- and capital-intensive industries such as steel, shipbuilding, household appliances, and electronic subassemblies. Eventually, these were followed by cars, computers, and electronics. By the first decade of the new millennium, Korea was a high-income industrial economy capable of exporting the most technologically advanced products available in several fields. Clearly, its history demonstrates that comparative advantage is not unchangeable, and that it can be a vehicle for raising incomes and promoting development.

An increasing share of Korea's output was sold in world markets. Consequently, production was not limited to the growth in its own domestic market. In addition, its goods had to be competitive in quality and price. Its ability to obtain imports at world prices was also important, but standing behind Korea's competitiveness was its rapid increases in productivity. Without more output per hour of work, incomes could not have risen as fast as they did, and Korea's ability to shift its comparative advantage from low-skill to increasingly higher-skill products could not have gone forward. In turn, productivity increases require a host of complementary changes, ranging from the development of universities and research institutes to organizational changes and the raising of financial capital for investing in new machinery and equipment.

In the process of promoting exports and raising productivity, Korea encountered a number of obstacles including its own bureaucratic inflexibility, problems in marketing to foreign markets that are radically different from Korea's, and a shortage of technical management and industrial expertise. It met and overcame these obstacles, and today Korea is an example of a country that used its comparative advantage to develop its economy. At the same time, it also used the pressure of foreign competition to raise its own productivity and quality standards, which in turn raised the incomes of its citizens. Korea's success was a joint product of efforts by its government, the private sector, and a number of public-private organizations. It is an open question whether each of these played a similar role: Is Korea's success due to the wise guidance of government policies, or did those policies play a secondary (or even negative) role compared to markets and competition?

COMPARATIVE ADVANTAGE AND "COMPETITIVENESS"

LO 3.5   Contrast the concepts of comparative advantage and competitiveness.

The rhetoric of "competitiveness" is so common in our public discourse that it is useful to consider its relationship to comparative advantage. In the analysis so far, comparative advantage resulted from productivity differences between nations in autarky. In our simple model of a barter economy, wages, prices, and exchange rates were omitted. Real businesses do not barter steel for bread, however, and they cannot pay their workers by dividing up the firm's output.

In general, by ignoring money wages, money prices, and exchange rates, we assumed that all goods and labor were correctly priced. In other words, we assumed that the prices of outputs and inputs are an accurate indication of their relative scarcity. In this case, there is no difference between a nation's comparative advantage and the ability of its firms to sell goods at prices that are competitive. That is, if all markets correctly value the price of inputs and outputs, then a nation's commercial advantage is determined by its comparative advantage.

Unfortunately, markets sometimes fail to produce optimal outcomes, and at times, outputs and inputs are incorrectly priced. Sometimes, undervaluation or overvaluation of a good stems from inherent difficulties in measuring its true value or in measuring its true cost of production. For example, we usually ignore the costs of air pollution when we measure the costs of driving a car. Other times, undervaluation or overvaluation may result from government policies, as when prices are maintained at an artificially high or low level. In either case, the fact that a market price may not accurately reflect the economic value of an input or an output means that a wedge is driven between commercial or **competitive advantage** and comparative advantage.

It is often (incorrectly) argued that nations should pursue commercial advantages for their firms even if it means a misallocation of resources. In effect, this means that a country follows policies that lower living standards by failing to maximize the value of national output. In terms of Figure 3.4 and Figure 3.5, this is equivalent to asserting that the United States and Canada should each remain at a point like A, where the United States overestimates the value of producing its own bread and Canada overestimates the value of steel. Both countries end up with consumption bundles that are suboptimal from the standpoint of national welfare.

Consider a real-world example. Indonesia tried to develop an aircraft industry in spite of the fact that it lacks a comparative advantage in aircraft production. Nevertheless, through a combination of government policies (some of which paid people to buy the planes!), the price to foreigners was competitive at times. From the perspective of Indonesian national welfare and the optimal use of scarce Indonesian resources, this was a mistake. From the perspective of a business, however, Indonesian policies made it profitable to make airplanes, even though it meant using resources in ways that were suboptimal from the national perspective.

This case illustrates the common mistake of equating nations with business enterprises. Indonesian plane manufacturers care about their subsidies and any other policy that makes them profitable. The national interest, however, is to achieve the most efficient allocation of resources possible within the framework of the nation's laws and values. It is possible to make individual firms highly profitable through subsidies or protection from international competition, while at the same time and through the same policies cause the nation's overall standard of living to be lower than it would be otherwise. Businesses are not designed to ensure that resources are efficiently allocated at the national level. If they can legally tip the playing field in their direction, they will not hesitate.

Another important distinction between nations and business enterprises is that nations do not compete with each other in any normal sense of the word. Economic relations between the United States and Canada, or any pair of nations, are not equivalent to the commercial competition that exists between companies such as Coke and Pepsi. If Canada grows, the United States does not go out of business or suffer in any identifiable way. In fact, Canadian growth would be a stimulus to U.S. growth and would create spillover benefits for Americans. Cola companies fight over a relatively static market size, but nations can all simultaneously increase their incomes.

ECONOMIC RESTRUCTURING

LO 3.6 **Discuss the economic and ethical considerations of economic restructuring caused by international trade.**

Economic restructuring refers to changes in the economy that may require some industries to grow and others to shrink or disappear altogether. For example, the United States has seen a dramatic decrease in the size of its steel industry and, some years later, a rebirth of a new industry based around smaller, more specialized steel mills. The car industry has been through several periods of decline and recovery and has unknown long-term prospects. In any dynamic economy, some types of economic activity will be growing, and others will be scaling back or dying. In some cases, these changes are a direct consequence of increased openness to foreign competition. For example, the influx of Japanese cars has played a major role in the reorganization and restructuring of the U.S. auto industry.

In our simple Ricardian model, after the opening of trade, the United States was able to maximize its well-being by shifting workers out of bread production and into steel production. Even though this restructuring of the economy improved overall economic welfare, it does not mean that it benefited every individual—a nation's gains from trade may be divided in different ways, and it is usually the case that some individuals benefit while others are hurt by trade. If there are net gains from opening trade (which are measured by an increase in the consumption bundle), then it means that the economic gains of the winners are greater than the economic losses of the losers, and therefore the nation as a whole is better off. Nevertheless, opening an economy to increased foreign competition is rarely painless and usually generates a number of new problems. In the model used in this chapter, it was assumed that workers can effortlessly and without costs move back and forth between industries as one expands and the other shrinks. In reality, this is not an option. While some laid-off workers in a declining industry may quickly find new jobs, many do not. They may not know which companies need workers, or their skills may not match those that are in demand.

The model of comparative advantage does not offer a set of policies for addressing the problems of dislocated workers. Those policies have to come from another branch of economic analysis, such as labor economics, and from outside economics. It is widely recognized, however, that changes in trade patterns, whether they are due to trade agreements, a unilateral reduction in trade barriers, technological breakthroughs, or any other cause, will result in some dislocation of firms and workers. Most economists continue to support more open trading arrangements, however, because foreign trade increases our choices as consumers, it lowers the costs of inputs for producers, it increases competition and innovation, and it leads to a greater diffusion of technological change. Nevertheless, it is important to keep in mind that the gains from trade do not mean that every worker or every firm benefits.

To a large extent, political assumptions about the way the world works will color the solutions to the problem of worker dislocation offered by economists, political scientists, and other social scientists. For example, believers in less government intervention in the economy would argue that government should not have any policies for handling unemployment caused by the rapid growth of imports. They maintain that unemployment is a self-correcting problem; laid-off workers will look for new jobs and will, if necessary, accept lower wages. Others make a value judgment that this sort of social problem should not be a governmental concern, and that it should be left up to the private economy and individual initiative.

An alternative to the "do nothing" approach is for the government to look for ways to compensate the losers. The proponents of this view justify it on several grounds. First, the nation as a whole benefits from trade, so there are newly added resources to the economy that make compensation possible. Second, many people believe that they have an ethical obligation to assist people hurt by economic change. And third, compensation reduces the incentives to oppose foreign trade.

The practice of offering **trade adjustment assistance (TAA)** is common in many countries, including the United States. Usually these programs take the form of extended unemployment benefits and worker re-training. For example, the U.S. government created a special program of benefits for workers who are hurt by trade with Mexico due to the North American Free Trade Agreement (NAFTA). In 1994, the first year of NAFTA, 17,000 workers qualified for TAA under the NAFTA provision. Generally, in order to qualify for the benefits, workers must demonstrate that they were laid off as a result of imports from Mexico or Canada or because their firm relocated to one of those countries. Needless to say, it is sometimes difficult to establish a direct link between imports and job loss; a poorly managed firm may have been on its way out of business with or without imports.

The important point is that trade creates change, and it may be difficult for some people, industries, or communities to deal with it. When a nation moves along its PPC toward a different mix of industries, there is a period of transition that is painful for some. Economic restructuring does not happen overnight, and although it is desirable for the higher living standard it brings, change and transformation cost time and money.

CASE STUDY

Losing Comparative Advantage

The case study on Korea shows that comparative advantage is not fixed in time but changes as countries develop their economies. Changing comparative advantage cuts two ways, however, and some production stops being an efficient use of a country's capital and labor. In the Korean case, there are products that it exported early in its development that are no longer cost efficient to make.

Agriculture is an area where many countries experience a declining comparative advantage over time. Some agricultural crops tend to be very labor intensive, and the cost of labor rises as an economy develops. Technology may solve some of the problems of rising wages by reducing the need for labor, but other crops resist an efficient technological solution. In an ideal world, workers in industries that lose their comparative advantage would easily and quickly move to an industry where new opportunities appear.

Comparative advantage in agriculture is not the only concern countries have when thinking about their agricultural sector. Issues of food safety, food independence, and support for rural culture and society are all concerns to one degree or another, more in some countries than others.

One of the objectives of the nearly defunct Doha Round of the WTO was to create an economic environment in which low-cost agricultural producers have access to other countries' markets. The goal was to increase efficiency in the world economy by locating production where the opportunity costs are lowest, while at the same time creating opportunities for developing countries. If a developing country has a comparative advantage in, say, cotton, but foreign markets are not open, it cannot fully obtain the benefits of its comparative advantage.

Cotton is not a food crop, and its treatment highlights some of the fundamental difficulties involved in persuading countries to drop trade barriers, as well as the fundamental reasons why it is desirable to see barriers fall. According to the International Cotton Advisory Committee, the highest cost producers in the world include Greece, Spain, and the United States, all of which are countries classified as high-income by the World Bank. Lowest-cost producers are in sub-Saharan western Africa (for example, Burkina Faso, Mali, Benin) and central Asia (for example, Uzbekistan and Tajikistan).

Cotton is not a major item in world trade and is significantly less than one-half of one percent of total merchandise trade. Nevertheless, it is important since as many as one hundred million households depend on income earned growing cotton, and several of the low-cost producers depend on their cotton export earnings to buy essential imports such as grain. Table 3.5 compares cotton production, its share of trade, and income per person in a few of the low-cost and high-cost producers. As shown, low-cost countries produce less but depend more on cotton exports, as their very low levels of income put them close to the edge of survival and they have fewer goods to export. High-cost producers depend much less on their cotton exports and have much higher incomes.

High-cost producers like the United States and Greece depend on a variety of government interventions to keep their cotton producers in business. In Greece, direct and indirect payments, along with tariffs on imports of cotton, are administered through the European Union's Common Agricultural Program. In the United States, the Department of Agriculture administers a number of farm support programs, including payments to farmers, subsidized loans, revenue guarantees, subsidized insurance, marketing and promotion assistance, and others, while the Department of Commerce administers a set of tariffs on foreign cotton entering the U.S. market.

Rich countries that try to keep their high-cost producers in business do more than keep production going where it is less efficient. They also have the potential to harm the living standards of some of the world's poorest countries and to block one of their paths to higher incomes. By using their wealth to subsidize production, high-cost producers increase world supply and limit the ability of low-cost producers to fully exploit their comparative advantage in cotton. In sum, high-income countries find it politically difficult to give up their support for older, less efficient sectors.

TABLE 3.5 **Low-Cost and High-Cost Cotton Producers**

Country	Cotton Exports, 2014 (millions $)	Percent of Total Exports, 2014	Income per Person, 2014
Low-cost producers			
Western Africa			
Benin	475.3	23.6	890
Burkina Faso	575.3	23.1	700
Mali	639.9	30.5	650
Central Asia			
Tajikistan	154.9	14.6	1,080
Uzbekistan	840.5	6.3	2,090
High-cost producers			
Greece	418.1	1.2	22,680*
United States	4,516.1	0.3	55,200

*2013
Sources: Data from United Nations Conference on Trade and Development; World Bank, © James Gerber.

Summary

- The single most important determinant of trade patterns is the opportunity cost of producing traded goods. Countries that sacrifice the least amount of alternative production when producing a particular good have the lowest opportunity cost, or a comparative advantage. The idea of comparative advantage has been one of the most enduring concepts of economic thought and has been a central theme in international economic policy since the mid-1800s.

- Nations that produce according to their comparative advantage are maximizing the benefits they receive from trade and, consequently, their national welfare. This is the same as maximizing their gains from trade.

- Comparative advantage is often confused with absolute advantage. The latter refers to the advantage a nation has if its absolute productivity in a particular product is greater than that of its trading partners. It is not necessary to have an absolute advantage in order to have a comparative advantage.

- One common fallacious argument against following comparative advantage is that workers in other countries are paid less than workers at home. This argument neglects the issue of productivity. Developing countries' wages are lower because the value of output from one hour of labor is less. Labor productivity is less because workers are generally less skilled, they have less capital on the job, and they have less capital in the surrounding economy to support their on-the-job productivity.

- Businesspeople look at the issue of trade differently than economists do because they have different objectives in mind. Businesspeople are often concerned about their ability to compete—that is, to sell a particular item in a given market at the lowest price. Their perspective is that of the firm. Economists focus on the efficient use of resources at the national or global level. The perspective is that of all firms taken together.

Vocabulary

absolute productivity advantage	labor productivity
autarky	mercantilism
comparative productivity advantage	opportunity cost
competitive advantage	production possibilities curve (PPC)
consumption possibilities curve (CPC)	relative price
economic restructuring	trade adjustment assistance (TAA)
gains from trade	zero sum

Study Questions

All problems are assignable in MyEconLab.

3.1 Use the information in the following table on labor productivities in France and Germany to answer questions a through f.

Output per Hour Worked

	France	Germany
Cheese	2 kilograms	1 kilogram
Cars	0.25	0.5

a. Which country has an absolute advantage in cheese? In cars?

b. What is the relative price of cheese in France if it does not trade? In Germany?

c. What is the opportunity cost of cheese in France? In Germany?

d. Which country has a comparative advantage in cheese? In cars? Explain your answer.

e. What are the upper and lower bounds for the trade price of cheese?

f. Draw a hypothetical PPC for France and label its slope. Suppose that France follows its comparative advantage in deciding where to produce on its PPC. Label its production point. If the trade price of cars is 5 kilograms of cheese per car, draw a trade line (CPC) showing how France can gain from trade.

3.2 Suppose that the table in Study Question 3.1 looks as follows. Use the information to answer questions a through f.

Output per Hour Worked

	France	Germany
Cheese	1 kilogram	2 kilograms
Cars	0.25 car	2 cars

a. Which country has an absolute advantage in cheese? In cars?

b. What is the relative price of cheese in France if it does not trade? In Germany?

c. What is the opportunity cost of cheese in France? In Germany?

d. Which country has a comparative advantage in cheese? In cars? Explain your answer.

e. What are the upper and lower bounds for the trade price of cheese?

f. Draw a hypothetical PPC for France and label its slope. Suppose that France follows its comparative advantage in deciding where to produce on its PPC. Label its production point. If the trade price of cars is 5 kilograms of cheese per car, draw a trade line (CPC) showing how France can gain from trade.

3.3 Explain how a nation can gain from trade even though as a result not everyone is better off. Is this a contradiction?

3.4 Economic nationalists in developed countries worry that international trade is destroying the national economy. A common complaint is that trade agreements open the economy to increased trade with countries where workers are paid a fraction of what they earn at home. Explain the faulty logic of this argument.

3.5 Many people believe that the goal of international trade should be to create jobs. Consequently, when they see workers laid off due to a firm's inability to compete against cheaper and better imports, they assume that trade must be bad for the economy. Is this assumption correct? Why, or why not?

3.6 Suppose that Germany decides to become self-sufficient in bananas and even to export them. In order to accomplish these goals, large tax incentives are granted to companies that will invest in banana production. Soon, the German industry is competitive and able to sell bananas at the lowest price anywhere. Does Germany have a comparative advantage? Why, or why not? What are the consequences for the overall economy?

Comparative Advantage and Factor Endowments

Learning Objectives

After studying this chapter, students will be able to:

4.1 Use the Heckscher-Ohlin Trade Model to analyze trade patterns between two countries with two inputs and two outputs.

4.2 Predict the impacts on different factors of production of trade-opening.

4.3 Discuss the limits of the HO model.

4.4 Explain the trade-offs for firms between trading and investing internationally.

4.5 Give examples of the determinants of international migration and its impact on comparative advantage.

4.6 Describe the controversies surrounding the impact of international trade on wages and jobs.

INTRODUCTION: THE DETERMINANTS OF COMPARATIVE ADVANTAGE

The theory of comparative advantage presented in the previous chapter assumed that countries have different levels of productivity without going into the reasons behind the differences. In this chapter, the emphasis is on the factor endowments of labor, capital, and resources found inside a country. We hypothesize that these factor endowments determine a country's opportunity costs of production and its comparative advantage. We also look more closely at the role of trade in causing changes in production and the consequent impacts on wages earned by workers and profits and rents earned by owners of capital and resources. This analysis helps clarify the opposition to expanded trade that comes from people who fear that it will reduce the demand for their labor or capital and lead to a decline in income.

MODERN TRADE THEORY

LO 4.1   Use the Heckscher-Ohlin Trade Model to analyze trade patterns between two countries with two inputs and two outputs.

In Chapter 3, comparative advantage depended on each country's relative productivity, which was given by assumption at the start of the discussion. Smith and Ricardo thought that each country would have its own technology, its own climate, and its own resources, and that differences among nations would give rise to productivity differences. In the twentieth century, several economists developed a more detailed explanation of trade in which the comparative advantage of a country depends on its endowments of the inputs (called *factors of production,* or simply, *factors*) that are used to produce each good. The theory has various names: the Heckscher-Ohlin theory (HO), the Heckscher-Ohlin-Samuelson theory, or the Factor Proportions theory. They all refer to the same set of ideas.

The HO Trade Model

The HO trade model begins with the observation that nations are endowed with different levels of each input (factors). Furthermore, each output has a different technology for its production and requires different combinations and levels of the various inputs. Steel production, for example, requires a lot of iron ore, coking material, semiskilled labor, and some expensive capital equipment. Clothing production requires unskilled and semiskilled workers with rudimentary capital equipment in the form of sewing machines.

In order to analyze how the availability of inputs creates productivity differences, we first define **factor abundance** and **factor scarcity**. Table 4.1 illustrates the concepts with a numerical example. The capital-labor ratio of the United States (K_{us}/L_{us}) is $^{50}/_{150}$, or $^1/_3$. Canada's (K_{can}/L_{can}) is $^2/_{10}$, or $^1/_5$. Because the United States' capital-labor ratio is higher than Canada's ($K_{us}/L_{us} > K_{can}/L_{can}$), the United States is the relatively capital-abundant country and Canada is the relatively labor-abundant country. Note that Canada's absolute labor endowment is less than that of the United States, but Canada is still considered labor-abundant because it has more labor relative to its capital.

Relative abundance of a factor implies that in autarky its relative cost is less than in countries where it is relatively scarcer. Conversely, relatively scarce resources are more expensive. Consequently, capital is relatively cheap and labor is relatively expensive in the United States, and vice versa for Canada. It follows

TABLE 4.1   An Example of Factor Abundance

	United States	Canada
Capital	50 machines	2 machines
Labor	150 workers	10 workers

The United States is capital abundant and Canada is labor abundant.

that economies have relatively lower costs in the production of goods where the technology calls for greater quantities of the abundant factor and smaller quantities of the scarce factor. In this example, Canada will have a lower opportunity cost in production that uses relatively more labor and relatively less capital, while the United States will have a lower opportunity cost in production that uses relatively more capital and less labor.

The **HO trade theory** makes this point. It asserts that a country's comparative advantage lies in the production of goods that intensively use relatively abundant factors. To clarify, consider the United States. It is richly endowed with a wide variety of factors. It has natural resources in the form of rich farmland and extensive forests. It has highly skilled labor, such as scientists, engineers, and managers. The wealth of the nation has enabled it to create an abundance of physical capital, both public and private. Its exports, therefore, should include agricultural products, particularly those requiring skilled labor and physical capital, and all sorts of machinery and industrial goods that require intensive input of physical capital and scientific and engineering skills.

One leading U.S. export is commercial jet aircraft—a product that requires a vast array of physical capital and scientific, engineering, and managerial talent. The United States is also a major exporter of grains and grain products, such as vegetable oils. These are produced with relatively small labor inputs, very large capital inputs (combines, tractors, and so on), farmland, and a great deal of scientific research and development that has produced hybrid seeds, pesticides, herbicides, and other agricultural inputs.

Gains from Trade in the HO Model

In the Ricardian model we assume that each country faces a constant set of trade-offs: two loaves of bread for three tons of steel (United States) or three loaves of bread for one ton of steel (Canada). The constant costs of the Ricardian model stem from the fact that there is one homogeneous input—labor, which can be used to make bread or steel. Workers do not vary in their skills, and since there is no capital input, each worker is as productive as the next. Consequently, when labor is reallocated from bread to steel, or vice versa, the trade-off is always at a constant rate.

In the HO model, we have a multiplicity of inputs—labor, capital, farmland—so each worker may be equipped with a different quantity of supporting inputs, such as capital. Obviously, at the end of the day a worker with a $5 shovel will have dug a smaller hole than one equipped with a $150,000 earth-moving machine. Furthermore, the quality of labor and capital can vary. Some labor is skilled, and some is unskilled. Certain jobs require scientific or other technical training, while others require basic literacy or even less. Similarly, capital can be low- or high-tech, and resources such as farmland have different fertility and climate characteristics. In effect, each important qualitative difference can be treated as a key characteristic of a separate input, so unskilled and skilled labor can be considered different factors.

If a country has multiple inputs with various suitabilities for different tasks, we can no longer assume a production possibilities curve (PPC) with constant costs.

Rather, the economy is assumed to have increasing costs, which implies that each country has a rising opportunity cost for each type of production. Consequently, as the United States or Canada moves labor, capital, and land into bread production, each additional unit of bread leads to a greater loss of steel output than the one before. The reason is straightforward: If more bread is wanted, resources must be taken out of steel. The optimal strategy is to move resources that are relatively good at bread production, but poor at steel production. This leads to the greatest gain in bread with the smallest loss of steel. The next shift in production, toward more bread, cuts deeper into the stock of resources used for steel production, and in all likelihood there will not be resources to move that are as good at bread and as poor at steel as the previous production shift. Consequently, in order to get the same increase in bread, more steel must be given up than before. This result is symmetric, so shifts going the other way, toward more steel, cause the opportunity cost of steel to rise with each shift. Figure 4.1 illustrates a PPC with increasing costs.

As with constant costs, the trade-off between bread and steel is equal to the slope of the PPC. Since the PPC is curved, its slope changes at every point, and we must measure the trade-off at the point of production. For example, in Figure 4.2, if the United States is producing at point A, then the opportunity cost of an additional ton of steel is equivalent to the slope of the PPC at point A. Since the PPC is a curve rather than a straight line, the slope is measured by drawing a tangent line at the point of production and measuring its slope.

Most of the analysis of the gains from trade discussed in Chapter 3 carries over into the HO model. In order to demonstrate this, assume that point A is the U.S. production point in autarky and that at point A the opportunity cost of steel is 0.67 loaves of bread. This means that the slope of the tangent at A is −0.67. Also assume that Canada's opportunity cost of steel is above that of the United States at 3 loaves of bread per ton, the same as before and that after trade begins, the world price, or trade price, is 2 loaves of bread per ton of steel, the same as the example shown in Chapter 3. After trade opens, the United States can continue to produce at A and not trade, or it can produce at A and move along its consumption possibilities curve (CPC), trading steel for bread. As before, line CPC is both

FIGURE 4.1  **The United States' PPC with Increasing Costs**

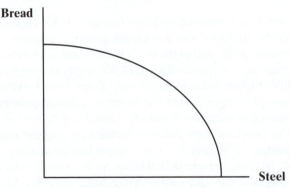

Moving from left to right, the opportunity cost of another unit of steel increases.

FIGURE 4.2   Opportunity Costs and the Slope of the PPC

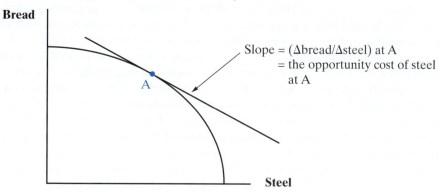

The opportunity cost of steel is measured by the slope of the tangent at the point of production.

the trade line showing the rate at which bread and steel exchange for each other, and it is the CPC since it shows the possible consumption bundles when production is at A and trade occurs.

In Figure 4.3, CPC' is a trade line that is tangent to the PPC at point B, an alternative production point to the right of A and closer to the steel axis. If the United States exploits its comparative advantage and shifts toward increased steel production, increasing costs come into play. Moving towards the steel axis raises the marginal cost of steel output. As production rises, the gap between the opportunity cost of production and the trade price narrows until, finally, they are equal at point B. Further increases in steel production would push the cost above its value in trade; therefore, they are not warranted.

At point B, the opportunity cost of steel equals its trade price. Since the model is symmetric and the opportunity cost and trade price of bread are the inverse of the

FIGURE 4.3   Gains from Trade in the HO Model

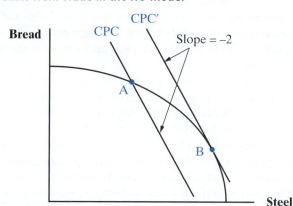

CPC is the trade line if production is at A. Production at B maximizes income.

steel, the same equivalency holds for bread. To the left of B, the opportunity cost of steel (bread) is less (greater) than the trade price, so more (less) production is warranted. To the right of B, the opportunity cost of steel (bread) is greater (less) than the trade price, so less (more) production is warranted. Only at point B does the opportunity cost equal the trade price. Since no other changes can make the United States better off, point B is the production combination that maximizes income.

Graphically, the superiority of point B can be seen by first comparing B to A. Point B is clearly superior to A in terms of the consumption possibilities because for every point along CPC there is another point on CPC' that offers more of both goods. That is, CPC' lies above and to the right of CPC. Since a greater combination of both goods is available if the United States produces at B and trades, B is superior to A. Furthermore, when the trade price is 2, every other production point along the PPC leads to smaller consumption bundles. That is, at any other production point, a trade line with a slope of -2 that passes through the point will lie below and to the left of CPC', representing smaller combinations of steel and bread. Consequently, point B maximizes income by creating the largest possible consumption bundle.

The notion of gains from trade in the HO model is nearly the same as in the Ricardian model. The only significant difference is that specialization is not complete in the HO model. The United States continues to make some bread, and Canada makes some steel.

TRADE AND INCOME DISTRIBUTION

LO 4.2 **Predict the impacts on different factors of production of trade-opening.**

Recall that in the Ricardian model of comparative advantage, the nation as a whole gained from trade, and, by assumption, we ruled out the potentially harmful effects of trade on some members of society. When trade began, the economy shifted from one point on its production frontier to a different point. Workers that were affected by the production shift simply moved out of the declining industry and into the expanding one. Everyone had the same skills, and each type of production required only labor, so everyone had access to a job, and everyone benefited from both the fall in the price of the imported good and the rise in the price of the exported one.

The HO trade model is a more sophisticated way to analyze the gains and losses from trade because it drops these unrealistic assumptions. Labor can be divided into two or more skill categories, other types of inputs can be included, and industries can require different mixes of the various inputs. Under these more realistic assumptions, it can be shown that while trade benefits the nation as a whole, some groups within the nation benefit more than others, and some will actually be harmed. Furthermore, it can be shown that there is a systematic relationship between the factor endowments of a country and the winners and losers from trade. Opening the discussion to an analysis of winners and losers adds an important and necessary element of realism. We are all aware that not everyone favors increased trade, and without an analysis of trade's income distribution effects, we have no basis for understanding the opposition to increased trade.

The Stolper-Samuelson Theorem

Everyone's income depends on the inputs that he or she supplies to the economy. Labor earns wages that may be high or low, depending on the skill level; owners of capital earn profits; landowners earn rents. The amount of income earned per unit of input depends on the demand for the inputs as well as their supply. The demand for a particular input is sometimes referred to as a **derived demand** because it is derived indirectly from the demand for the output that it is used to produce. If the output is in high demand, and consequently its price is high, then the inputs that are used to produce it will benefit by receiving higher returns.

In general, any change in the economy that alters the price of outputs will have a direct impact on incomes. We have seen that trade causes output prices to change by causing an increase in export prices and a decrease in import prices. The movement of prices causes a change in the demand for each factor and leads to a change in the returns paid to each factor. Hence, trade affects income distribution.

When trade begins and output prices change, some resources leave the sector that produces imported goods and move into the sector that produces exports. In the HO model, unlike the simple Ricardian model, different goods are produced with different combinations of inputs, so the movement along the production possibilities frontier causes a change in the demand for each input. Factors that are used intensively in the imported goods sector will find that the demand for their services has shrunk—and so has their income. Conversely, factors used intensively in the export sector will experience an increase in the demand for their services and in their incomes. In sum, when trade begins, incomes of the factors used intensively in the import sector fall, and incomes of the factors used intensively in the export sector rise.

These effects are summarized in the **Stolper-Samuelson theorem**, which is derived from the HO theory. The Stolper-Samuelson theorem says that an increase in the price of a good raises the income earned by factors that are used intensively in its production. Conversely, a fall in the price of a good lowers the income of the factors that it uses intensively.

Figure 4.4 illustrates these tendencies. Suppose that the United States and Canada can make bread or steel, using capital and labor. Also suppose that bread is the labor-intensive product, shown as follows:

$$K^b/L^b < K^s/L^s$$

and that the United States is relatively well endowed with capital, compared to Canada, as follows:

$$K_{can}/L_{can} < K_{us}/L_{us}.$$

FIGURE 4.4   The Stolper-Samuelson Theorem

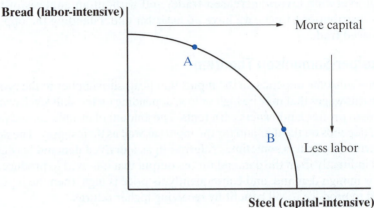

Movement along the PPC from A to B reduces the economy's demand for labor and increases its demand for capital.

According to the HO theory, the United States will have a comparative advantage in steel, which it will export in return for Canadian bread. In Figure 4.4, after trade begins, the United States moves along its PPC toward the steel axis from point A to point B.

As the United States shifts along its PPC, the change in the mix of goods produced leads to lower demands for labor and higher demands for capital. The steel industry will pick up some of the labor laid off in the bread industry, but since it is not as labor intensive as bread, its increase in labor demand is less than the fall in labor demand in the bread industry. The net result is that labor experiences a fall in demand, leading to a fall in wages and income earned. Note that Stolper-Samuelson does not state that all factors used in the export industries are better off, or that all factors used in the import competing industry get hurt. Rather, the abundant factor that is used to determine comparative advantage and exports is favored, and the scarce factor sees a decline in its income, regardless of industry.

The Stolper-Samuelson theorem is a starting point for understanding the income distribution effects of trade, but it tells only part of the story. An extension of the theorem, called the **magnification effect**, shows that the change in output prices has a magnified effect on factor incomes. For example, if after opening trade bread prices decline by 75 percent, then the fall in labor income will be greater than 75 percent. Similarly, if the price of an export good (steel) rises by 50 percent, for example, incomes earned by the intensively used factors in the export sector (capital) rise more than 50 percent.

The ultimate effects on income of an opening of trade depend on the flexibility of the affected factors. If labor is stuck in bread production and unable to move to the steel sector, it could be hurt much worse than if it were completely flexible to move. Another example illustrates this point: Within the debate over U.S.-Mexico free trade, there was a small, but intense, controversy surrounding avocado production. Mexico has a comparative advantage in avocados because it is well endowed with the necessary inputs (a particular quality of land and climate, together with unskilled labor and a little capital). If free trade were to open in the avocado market, the owners of avocado orchards in California argued that they would find their investments in land, equipment, and avocado trees worthless. Why would anyone pay $1 or more per avocado when Mexican ones cost 25¢ or less? However, many of the California avocado groves are located in the suburbs of sprawling metropolitan regions, and presumably, if the land were worthless for avocado production, it could be put to valuable use in another line of production—for example, as housing developments. Consequently, the income of the landowners may not decline in the long run, although in the short run landowners may be unable to put their land to an alternative use. In order to build these considerations into a trade model, we must turn to a short-run version of the HO model.

The Specific Factors Model

In the short run, the ability of factors to move between different output sectors is more limited. For example, suppose stiffer competition in the world steel industry causes American steelworkers to take pay cuts, and perhaps some to lose their jobs. In the long run, most of the laid-off steelworkers will find jobs outside the steel sector, but in the short run, they are stuck with cuts in pay and layoffs. Similarly, physical capital is usually dedicated to a particular use and cannot be converted to producing a different product, and, as we have seen, land is usually tied up in a particular use and cannot be switched to something else instantaneously. In the long run, however, plants and equipment can be redirected to a different line of production, land can be put to different uses, and workers find jobs doing something else.

In order to highlight the ability of labor and other factors to find alternative employment in the long run but not in the short run, economists sometimes add conditions to the HO model. Suppose there are three factors—land, labor, and capital—and two goods—steel and bread. Assume that the production of steel takes capital and labor, while bread takes land and labor. In this version of the HO model, labor is the variable factor because its use varies between both goods. Land and capital are the specific factors because their use is specific to bread and steel, respectively.

The model just described is an example of the **specific factors model**, a special case of the HO model. The HO model assumes that factors migrate easily from one sector to another—from steel to bread, for example. In the specific factors model (Table 4.2), each good is produced with a specific factor that is used only in the production of that good, and a variable factor that is used to produce both goods. The specific factors (land and capital) are immobile and cannot move

TABLE 4.2   A Specific Factors Model

Inputs	Outputs	
	Bread	Steel
Specific factors	Land	Capital
Variable factors	Labor	Labor

The specific factors of land and capital can be used to produce only one good. The variable factor of labor is used in both bread and steel production.

between bread and steel, while the variable factor (labor) is completely mobile between industries.

The determinants of comparative advantage with a specific factors model are similar to the analysis with an HO model. As with HO, comparative advantage depends on factor endowments. The main difference in the two models is that the specific factor plays a critical role. Suppose that Canada is relatively well endowed with land and that the United States is relatively well endowed with capital. Then Canada exports bread, and the United States exports steel. The reasoning is the same as with the HO model. Since Canada is well endowed with the specific factor used to make bread, its opportunity cost of bread production is lower than it is in the United States, where land is relatively less abundant. Similarly, steel uses capital, which is abundant in the United States and relatively scarce in Canada.

The analysis of the income distribution effects of trade is straightforward. When trade opens, each country follows its comparative advantage and moves toward greater specialization. The shift in production reduces the demand for the specific factor that is used in the industry that shrinks and the income of the factor declines. For example, Canada cuts back on steel production in order to concentrate on bread. Canadian owners of capital are hurt, since the structure of the economy moves away from the production of capital-intensive steel, while Canadian landowners experience precisely the opposite effect. Their incomes rise as the demand for land to produce bread exports rises. In the United States, landowners lose and capital owners win.

In this example, the income distribution effects of trade on labor, the variable factor, are indeterminate. Since labor is mobile, workers laid off in the declining sector find employment in the expanding sector. Canadian workers find that steel is cheaper, so they are better off to the extent that they consume products that embody steel. On the other hand, the fact that the world price of bread is above the price that Canadians paid in autarky means that they are worse off to the extent that their income goes to buy bread. The net effect on Canadian labor depends on which effect is strongest, rising bread prices or falling steel prices. U.S. workers face rising steel prices and falling bread prices, and, again, the net effect is ambiguous and depends on their consumption patterns.

CASE STUDY

Comparative Advantage in a Single Natural Resource

Natural resources are a source of comparative advantage in many countries. Chile has copper, Botswana has diamonds, and Saudi Arabia has oil. Crude oil is probably the most important geopolitical resource today, and it is certainly the largest resource market. In fact, other than currency trading, international trade in crude oil exceeds the volume and value of any other good or service. According to the United Nation's Commission on Trade and Development and the U.S. Energy Information Administration, worldwide daily exports of crude oil in 2014 were approximately 88 million barrels. At an average price of around $48 per barrel, this is equivalent to more than $4.2 billion per day.

Comparative advantage in crude oil production depends largely on a country's endowment of oil, and as everyone is aware, countries in the Middle East have a majority of the world's proven reserves of crude oil. Table 4.3 shows the ten countries with the world's largest reserves and the share of fuel products in their total exports.

Oil is valuable. Consequently, when countries are endowed with crude oil reserves, capital and labor are pulled into the sector because it is the most valuable use of inputs. It is also a clear example of following comparative advantage based on resource endowments. There is a downside, however, as the potential returns

TABLE 4.3   Ten Largest Oil Reserves

Country	Reserves*(2015)	(Fuel Exports/Total Exports) $\times$ 100 (2013)
Venezuela	298	96.7
Saudi Arabia	268	80.6
Canada	172	27.0
Iran	158	60.4
Iraq	144	99.6
Kuwait	104	90.7
UAE	98	30.0
Russia	80	63.6
Libya	48	96.3
Nigeria	37	79.3

*Billions (thousands of millions) of barrels, given current technology.

Data from U.S. Energy Information Administration; World Trade Organization, © James Gerber.

(continued)

from developing an oil industry can make it difficult to develop other economic activities. This is evident in Table 4.3, which shows that oil's share of total exports is high for most countries. Most of the economies listed are one-product economies.

The problem of a single, valuable resource that crowds out the development of other economic activities is called a **resource curse**. The resource curse is not inevitable for economies with large endowments of oil or some other valuable mineral—Canada, for instance, has overcome it—but it poses a challenge and it gives caution to the idea that resources are always a path to prosperity. Other types of resource curses have been noted when a country has a sudden discovery of gold or another valuable mineral. Regardless of the resource behind the curse, in all cases where it is not overcome, labor and capital are concentrated in the extraction of one natural resource and it becomes difficult to develop a diversified economy. When the price of the dominant commodity fluctuates, national income is altered in a very short amount of time and can result in severe macroeconomic instability and alternating boom and bust cycles.

A further problem of a large endowment of a single resource is that it often causes political turmoil. There are strong incentives to try to gain control of the resource, leading to factions in leadership and political strife as different groups struggle with each other. The promise of significant wealth can easily lead to corruption in countries with weak governments, as politicians buy the political support they need. In the worse cases, civil war is a possibility.

Not every country with resources suffers from a resource curse. Strong institutions to guard against corruption, and commitment to education, skills, and savings can develop the human capital and financial capital that a country needs in order to diversify its economy and provide for the inevitable day when the resource is no longer as valuable. Canada has done this, and the United Arab Emirates (UAE) is following a similar path.

EMPIRICAL TESTS OF THE THEORY OF COMPARATIVE ADVANTAGE

LO 4.3   Discuss the limits of the HO model.

All the popular theories of trade are variations on the idea of comparative advantage, and each theory makes predictions about the goods that a country will export and import. Therefore, it should be relatively straightforward to test each theory by holding its predictions up to actual trade flows and seeing if the two match. Unfortunately, empirical tests of trade theories are more difficult to conduct than they are to describe. Part of the problem is that it is difficult to measure variables such as factor endowments and prices in autarky.

The trade theories presented here and in Chapter 3 are the two most widely accepted by economists—the Ricardian theory of trade, based on relative productivities, and the HO theory, based on factor endowments. In the Ricardian theory discussed in Chapter 3, comparative advantage depended on relative productivity. This model is easier to test because it is easier to measure labor productivity than factor endowments. Consequently, it is not surprising that statistical tests of the Ricardian theory have been more successful. In general, they have confirmed the hypothesis that trade patterns between pairs of countries are determined to a significant degree by the relative differences in their labor productivities. More specifically, as labor productivity in a particular industry increases, the greater the likelihood the country becomes a net exporter of the good.

Tests of the HO theory of trade have been mixed. One of the problems for researchers in this area is that it is difficult to obtain a uniform set of measurements of factor endowments. In the presentation of the model in this chapter, only two inputs were considered, although we expanded that to three when we covered the specific factors model. In reality, there are many more than three factors. There are different kinds of labor (unskilled, semiskilled, managerial, technical, and so on), and there are many varieties of natural resources and capital. None of these categories has standardized definitions, and consequently each type of labor, capital, and natural resource is measured differently in each country. As a result, formal statistical analyses of tests of the HO theory have concluded that measurement errors in the data are a major problem.

Nevertheless, the consensus among economists seems to be that endowments matter, although they are far from the whole story. Even if it were possible to measure factor endowments accurately, technological differences between countries would not be captured, and these can be a significant source of productivity differences. In addition to technology, other important determinants of trade patterns not considered by the factor endowment theory are economies of scale, corporate structure, and economic policy.

While the theory of trade based on factor endowments receives mixed empirical support, it nevertheless remains the foundation of most economists' thinking about trade. This may seem curious, but there is actually a good reason for it. While factor endowments cannot explain all of the world's trade patterns, they do explain a significant part of them. Therefore, it is useful to begin with factor endowments and to supplement this view with other ideas. Perhaps most importantly, the factor endowment schema is a useful way to categorize the income distribution effects of trade. For both of these reasons, the HO model and its variations remain at the core of international economics.

EXTENSION OF THE HO MODEL

LO 4.4   **Explain the trade-offs for firms between trading and investing internationally.**

LO 4.5   **Give examples of the determinants of international migration and its impact on comparative advantage.**

Several alternative trade models are popular in the literature. Both of the models presented next focus on an attribute of production in an industry or group of industries that makes them unlike the simple models assumed by the Ricardian and HO models. Both, however, are elaborations of the theory of comparative advantage. In Chapter 5, we will leave the comparative advantage framework and look at cases where trade is not determined by productivity differences or factor endowments.

The Product Cycle

The **product cycle** model of trade was developed by Raymond Vernon. The model is an insightful analysis that incorporates ideas about the evolution of manufactured goods and technology. One of its greatest strengths is that it can explain exports of sophisticated manufactured goods from countries that have shortages of skilled labor and capital.

Vernon pointed out that many manufactured products, such as automobiles, electronic devices, and new appliances, go through a product cycle in which the inputs change over time. Initially, when these goods are brand new, there is a great deal of experimentation in both the characteristics of the final product and its manufacturing process. For example, when computer tablets were first developed, there was a wide variety of different forms to choose from. Each had different sets of options—often even within the same technology—and the size of the device, memory capacity, connectability, and other features were not standardized.

In this early stage of production, manufacturers need to be near a high-income market, where consumer feedback is greatest. Experimentation with basic design features requires information about the market's reaction. Consequently, there must be a consumer base with substantial income and skilled marketing to advertise information about the product. In addition, on the input side, experimentation and improvement in design and manufacturing require scientific and engineering inputs, along with capital that is willing to risk failure and an initial period of little or no profits. Both the consumption side and the production side necessitate that product research, development, and initial production take place in industrial countries.

Over time, however, the product begins to leave the early phase of its development and production and enters the middle phase (see Figure 4.5 and Figure 4.6). The product itself begins to be standardized in size, features, and manufacturing process. Experimentation with fundamentally new designs begins to wane as product development shifts toward incremental improvements in a basic design. In the middle phase, production begins to shift to countries with low labor costs. Standardized manufacturing routines are increasingly common, using low-skilled and semiskilled labor in assembly-type operations.

Countries reach the late phase of the product cycle when consumption in high-income nations begins to exceed production. At this point, an increasing share of the world's output is moving to developing countries where abundant unskilled and semiskilled labor keeps labor costs low. The pressure on high-income countries in the late phase is to turn toward innovation of new products, which starts the cycle over again.

The product cycle is a more elaborate story about technology than either the Ricardian or HO models. It may seem to differ fundamentally from those models,

FIGURE 4.5   The Product Cycle in High-Income Countries

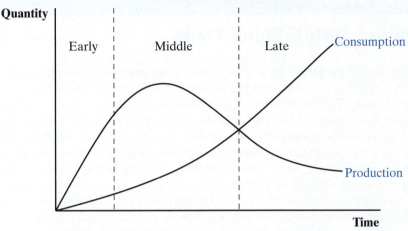

Many manufactured goods experience a product cycle of innovation, stabilization, and standardization.

but in fact it is very similar. At its core is a story about opportunity costs. As manufacturing processes become standardized, they can be performed by relatively unskilled labor. In effect, the blend of inputs changes over time, from highly skilled scientific, engineering, and marketing elements to basic unskilled and semiskilled labor. Consequently, the opportunity cost of production in developing countries becomes lower than the cost in high-income countries. In essence, it's the Ricardian story once again.

FIGURE 4.6   The Product Cycle in Low-Income Countries

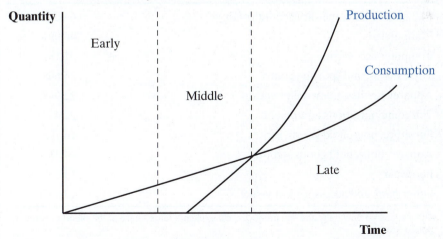

Low-income countries begin producing during the middle period when product design and production techniques begin to stabilize.

CASE STUDY

United States–China Trade

According to the IMF, China is the world's most populous country, with more than 1.37 billion people, and the second largest economy after the United States, with GDP equivalent to 10.98 trillion U.S. dollars in 2015. China's economy was substantially closed to the outside until 1978, when it began significant economic reforms. Initially, the reforms were limited to agriculture, but they quickly incorporated a number of special economic zones in the coastal regions (see Chapter 17). China's proximity to Hong Kong, along with large populations of Chinese in Taiwan, Hong Kong, Singapore, and other regions of East Asia, enabled it to attract huge amounts of foreign investment once it became receptive to capital inflows. The net result is that its economy and, especially, its exports have grown rapidly over the last two decades.

China's resource endowment includes a huge population of unskilled and semiskilled labor and a relative scarcity of scientific and engineering talent. It is not surprising, therefore, that its exports are heavily weighted toward labor-intensive manufactured goods. Table 4.4 lists the top ten Chinese exports to the United States in 2014. Six of the top ten items are simple manufactured goods that use China's abundant labor together with a small amount of capital: household goods, toys and sporting goods, apparel, footwear, and furniture.

TABLE 4.4 Top Ten Chinese Exports to the United States, 2014

Item	Millions of $U.S.
Cell phones and other household goods	64,074
Computers	46,091
Computer accessories	31,181
Toys, games, and sporting goods	25,608
Apparel, textiles, nonwool or cotton	22,957
Telecommunications equipment	22,454
Furniture, household goods, etc.	16,705
Apparel, household goods—cotton	14,413
Footwear	14,294
Other parts and accessories of vehicles	13,392

China's labor endowment and the product cycle explain a large share of its exports to the United States.

U.S. Imports from China by 5-digit End-Use Code 2006 - 2015, Foreign Trade (2014) , U.S. Census Bureau.

The remaining items give the appearance that China is upgrading its technological sophistication by making cell phones, computers, and computer accessories. While no one should doubt the fact of technological upgrade, China's exports of computers, telecommunications equipment, and other items do not reflect a high level of overall sophistication. Mostly, they illustrate the product cycle and the way multinational firms have cut up the value chain. Some of the goods are simple, standardized products, but others are assembled in China from parts that are imported. The next two case studies in this chapter explore this issue in more detail.

Foreign Trade versus Foreign Investment

In the product cycle, firms invest abroad instead of exporting, and some of the output may be imported back into the home country. This pattern is very different from the simple HO model where countries export one good and import another. First, it implies that under the conditions outlined in the product cycle, firms prefer to invest abroad rather than to export. That is, they substitute foreign investment for foreign trade. Second, the part of the output that they ship from their foreign operation back into the home country is international trade, but it is handled entirely within a single firm. That is, they engage in **intrafirm trade**: international trade between a parent company and a foreign-owned affiliate.

Intrafirm trade is difficult to measure, but in the mid-1990s, it was estimated that about one-third of U.S. merchandise exports and two-fifths of merchandise imports were intrafirm. Most foreign investment, however, is not for the purpose of exporting, but rather is intended to supply the market where the foreign investment is located. Whether for trade purposes or not, the selection of foreign investment instead of foreign trade poses a number of questions for economists and business scholars. Why do firms sometimes prefer to set up foreign-based operations instead of buying imports directly from a separate company located overseas? Or, if the foreign investment is for the purpose of selling in the foreign market, why don't companies export directly to the market instead of producing there? In essence, the questions are the same because both ask about the circumstances that cause foreign investment rather than foreign trade.

The product cycle provides one answer to these questions, but it is an incomplete answer, because it does not explain why a firm would invest in China instead of in Mexico. If labor costs are the only reason, then Africa would have the most foreign investment instead of the least of any continent. Furthermore, the product cycle is unable to explain why the greatest proportion of foreign investment goes to developed, industrial countries in Europe and North America where the comparative advantages are the same as or similar to those of the countries that supply the most foreign investment. According to United Nations data, high-income countries normally provide and receive the vast bulk of foreign investment; since the financial crisis, they have received "only" 65 percent of foreign investment (while making over 80 percent), which is down from a more normal 75 percent received before the crisis, but is still nearly two-thirds of all foreign direct investment.

Research into the trade-offs between investing abroad versus exporting from a home base acknowledges the importance of both the microeconomic characteristics of firms and the macroeconomic characteristics of countries that attract foreign investment. Microeconomic factors look at the internal constraints and opportunities of individual firms, while macroeconomic factors take into account the conditions inside countries that cause them to be suitable locations for a foreign firm to invest. The analytical framework that combines both sets of characteristics is known as the **OLI theory** of foreign direct investment. Its founder, John Dunning, offered it as an eclectic theory combining many different microeconomic and macroeconomic elements.

OLI is an acronym for *ownership-location-internalization*. In Dunning's analysis, firms investing abroad own an asset that gives them a competitive advantage in the world market (ownership). The asset may be something tangible, such as a patent, an innovation, a blueprint, or a trade secret; or it may be something intangible, such as a trademark or the firm's reputation. In either case, ownership of a valuable asset confers a potential advantage on the firm. Second, the firm will seek a production location that offers advantages (location). These may be in the form of low input costs, a large customer base, or an ability to produce a better product more efficiently due to the surrounding economic environment. Cheap labor is only one possibility, and if it does not come with a good infrastructure of roads and utilities, does not supply the skills that employers need, or is too far from the product's final market, then the fact that wages are low will not overcome the country's disadvantages.

Third, and most abstractly, the firm that invests abroad tries to capture within itself all the advantages that ownership of its asset confers (internalization). A firm that invests abroad can, if it chooses, simply sell the rights to its asset and let a foreign firm do the production—and in fact, many firms operate this way. That is, as an alternative, the investing firm can sell a license to its technology or its trademark or its trade secrets. Some firms, however, choose to take on the added costs of setting up production in a foreign location. There are many potential reasons for this choice, including the fear of theft or copy of its technology, the problem of monitoring and enforcing a contract with a foreign firm, and the concern that production mistakes by the foreign firm may hurt the reputation or trademark of the home country firm. Whatever the reason, the investing firm decides that it benefits more if it internalizes the advantages of asset ownership within itself rather than sells those advantages to another firm.

Dunning's analysis has been added to and extended by a large number of scholars who have found it to be a robust and adaptable description of the behavior of many firms. It is not a theory of trade, because it describes the circumstances that motivate firms to invest abroad rather than to engage in trade, but it does not contradict trade theory. Rather, it simply states that firms are internationally mobile and will use the comparative advantages they find in different locations.

In this sense, it demonstrates how those advantages motivate individual firms to adapt their own behavior.

Off-Shoring and Outsourcing

Off-shoring and **outsourcing** are frequently used terms, but with varying definitions. In this text, off-shoring is defined as the movement of some or all of a firm's activities to a location outside the home country; outsourcing is the reassignment of activities to another firm, either inside or outside the home country. All combinations of off-shoring and outsourcing are possibilities and exist in the world economy. Some firms off-shore but do not outsource, choosing to use a **foreign affiliate**, which is defined as a foreign-based operation owned by the firm in the home country. For example, a great deal of U.S.-Mexico trade is intrafirm, with car parts and electronic components going back and forth between parent companies in the United States and their foreign affiliates in Mexico. The parent companies have off-shored some production to Mexico, while choosing not to outsource. Others outsource, but do not off-shore; for example, if they subcontract activities with a domestic provider. A car company might decide to buy parts from a local firm rather than make them or have them made in Mexico. Finally, a firm may off-shore and outsource when it relocates production to a foreign location and signs a contract for delivery of services or goods with a firm that is not owned by the parent company.

Off-shoring became a concern in the 1980s when modern communications and transportation technology made it possible for firms to relocate production abroad. Initially, off-shoring was of greatest concern to workers in manufacturing industries, but by the 1990s, as advancements continued in information technologies, it became possible to off-shore some services. This created concerns for workers in service sectors outside of manufacturing. Historically, most services have been consumed at the point of production, but more recently it has become possible to relocate some service production away from the point of consumption. For example, a doctor in the United States or Europe might consult a colleague in India who is specialized in reading a particular type of x-ray. The Internet and increased efficiencies in telecommunications make it possible for doctors in both places to see the same image and to inexpensively communicate with each other.

The effects and extent of off-shoring of services are not well understood since most countries do not collect the necessary types of data. Nevertheless, the first generation of research and analysis points toward a conclusion that is consistent with our traditional understanding of trade and comparative advantage—there is no obvious reason why trade in services should be different from trade in goods. An import that arrives by truck or ship is not conceptually different from one that arrives over the Internet. Services imports and exports should not be any different in this regard, and specialization and trade should provide the same or similar gains for services as they do for goods.

The main focus of debate about off-shoring, whether in services or manufacturing, is the effect that it has on the home country, and in particular, the issue of job loss. Off-shoring is particularly unsettling for workers who felt immune from international trade, such as service workers, and it seems to be another instance of creeping globalization making life less certain. Research, however, shows that off-shoring has a variety of possible patterns. In some cases it leads to job losses in the home country, while in others it is complementary to home production rather than a substitute, and leads to an expansion of jobs and production rather than a contraction.

CASE STUDY

Off-Shoring by U.S. Multinational Corporations

As technology makes communications easier and as economies become more open to foreign investments, firms have responded by shifting production overseas. National statistical agencies such as the Bureau of Economic Analysis (BEA) in the United States have increased their efforts over the years so that economists and policymakers might better understand the extent of the phenomenon and the reasons behind it.

Table 4.5 shows two pictures of U.S. multinational corporations, one in 1989 and the other in 2013. The table shows the percent of multinational activities that are performed off-shore, through a foreign affiliate. **Value added** is a measure of the total value of production minus the value of purchased intermediate inputs. Capital expenditures include machines, laboratories, and buildings, and employment is the number of workers. As shown in the table, the share of multinationals' value added created abroad rose from 23 percent in 1989 to 28.5 percent in 2013. Employment grew from 21 percent of total workers off-shore in 1989 to 34.7 percent in 2013.

TABLE 4.5   U.S. Multinational Corporations and Production Outside the United States (Percent of total production)

	1989	2013
Value added	23.1	28.5
Capital expenditures	22.4	26.9
Employment	21.0	34.7

The share of multinational employment outside the United States rose approximately 50 percent from 1989 to 2013.

Source: Barefoot and Mataloni (November, 2011), "Operations of U.S. Multinational Companies in the United States and Abroad," *Survey of Current Business* (Bureau of Economic Analysis); and Scott (August 2015), "Activities of U.S. Multinational Enterprises in 2013," *Survey of Current Business*, Bureau of Economic Analysis.

As shown in the OLI model, several factors motivate firms to locate off-shore or to move some of their production there. Most importantly, firms locate production off-shore in order to obtain access to a market and to produce specialized products that fit a particular market's need. This finding runs counter to the conventional wisdom that says that firms locate abroad in order to find low wages or to escape environmental or labor regulations. The conventional wisdom is not wrong, but describes a minority of off-shoring since two-thirds is in high-income, high-wage economies.

Most production abroad by U.S.-controlled firms is primarily for serving foreign markets and not the U.S. market. The vast majority of the production of U.S.-owned affiliates is sold in the host country of the affiliate, while about one-third is exported to another foreign market. Less than 5 percent of their production was exported back to the United States in 2013. These patterns are largely determined by economies of scale and transportation costs: Firms find it cost effective to locate production next to the market where they intend to sell their products. Labor costs, like all costs of production, are important, but they are often outweighed by transportation costs and considerations of infrastructure and efficiency. Some firms do indeed move in order to find lower wages and to cut production costs, but that is less common than supposed and is far from the primary consideration of firms that off-shore.

Note that off-shoring is only one mechanism through which the international economy affects wages and jobs in the domestic economy. Firms might also choose to off-shore and outsource, so that imported goods are not produced by a foreign affiliate. That situation would not show up in the statistics in this case study.

Migration and Trade

According to the Migration Policy Institute and the World Bank, in 2013 there were more than 231 million international migrants spread across the globe. Nearly two-thirds were living in high-income countries, and almost 20 percent were in the United States alone. In our presentation of the HO model, international migration was not taken into account. Workers are allowed to move between sectors in the model, but not between countries. This is an important consideration since international migration alters the labor endowments that the model assumes to be fixed.

Economists have long studied migration, as have sociologists, demographers, political scientists, and other social scientists. Each discipline brings its own tools of analysis and contributes another piece to our understanding of the determinants and effects of migration. Sociologists and anthropologists, for example, have helped to clarify that the decision to migrate is often a family decision or, in some cases, a community decision to send one of its members abroad. Political scientists have helped to clarify how migration policies are set and enforced, or not enforced, as the case may be. The economic view of migration tends to understand it in terms of the individual migrant and the underlying incentives to migrate. In this view, economic incentives play a major role by determining the factors that cause migrants to leave and the factors that attract them to a particular destination.

Economists refer to **supply-push factors** as the forces inside a country that cause people to think about leaving. Push factors include recessions, long-run structural changes that cause job dislocations, wars, natural disasters, and anything else that makes life difficult at home. Examples of structural changes include the transformations of Central European economies from socialism to capitalism, or Latin American economic reforms, or industrial development in Asia and Africa. In the near future, we can expect large migrations from changing agricultural patterns and the inundation of coastal areas as a result of climate change.

Demand-pull factors are the forces that pull migrants to a particular country or place within a country. Key factors include the cost of reaching a particular destination, the probability of finding a job, and the wage that will be earned. The wage gap between developed countries and developing countries explains a large share of the flow of migrants, but other factors are important as well. The business cycle in the receiving country, its migration policies, and the overall set of opportunities encountered by foreign workers are all important demand-pull factors.

A third factor determining migration is the existence of **social networks**. Migrants do not scatter randomly around a desirable destination, but instead congregate in certain places. This is partly due to job opportunities, but it also reflects the fact that migration is hard and expensive and the presence of family or community members makes it a little easier. The supply of information about the new locale is better if there are already migrants who can report home on conditions, and who can help newcomers become established with a place to live, a job, and familiar faces to ward off loneliness.

In theory, if the endowment of a particular factor increases, then the relative abundance of the factor and, potentially, its comparative advantage also change. In practice, labor inflows are often used to produce services that are not traded. For example, two countries with large percentages of foreigners in their population are Qatar (86.5 percent of residents are immigrants) and the United Arab Emirates (70.0 percent of residents are immigrants). A large share of the foreign workers in those countries are Filipinos, Palestinians, and other migrants who work as domestics, providing cleaning, cooking, day care, and other services that cannot be traded. These migrants do not have a direct impact on the host country's comparative advantage since the labor is not used to produce tradable goods (although they free up citizens to work in the export sector). However, many migrant workers are also engineers and business specialists who provide technical expertise to the oil and gas industry. Without some high-skilled migrant labor, it is possible that production in these oil- and gas-producing countries would be much more limited.

Most international migration is from developing to developed countries. For example, in the 1980s and 1990s, civil wars in Central America produced large outflows of Salvadorian and Guatemalan immigrants to the United States, many of whom settled in California where some found employment in apparel manufacturing. California's apparel sector added over 40,000 jobs between 1983 and 1997 (a growth of almost 50 percent), largely based on the availability of low-wage, unskilled immigrant workers. Given that apparel is a declining sector in the United States, immigrant labor appears to have postponed the decline of the industry in California for about a decade. Other U.S. examples of where immigration influences comparative advantage include certain agricultural crops that depend on abundant supplies of immigrant labor and the tourism industry. In these cases, increases in the supply of unskilled labor shifted production towards industries that intensely use that factor of production.

THE IMPACT OF TRADE ON WAGES AND JOBS

LO 4.6 Describe the controversies surrounding the impact of international trade on wages and jobs.

Manufacturing in North America and Europe has struggled for decades. As a share of GDP and as a share of overall employment, it has been on a long, downward trend. At the same time, wage inequality has increased, rather slowly at first, then more rapidly in the 1980s. Wage inequality has been particularly severe in the United States and has primarily affected younger workers and workers with less education or fewer skills. These trends in manufacturing employment and wages raise a couple of questions about trade. Are industrialized countries losing jobs to developing countries? Does trade with low-wage countries cause wages to fall in high-wage countries?

Economic theory offers insight into the issue of the overall number of jobs in the economy. In the medium-run and long-run, the absolute number of jobs depends mainly on factors such as the age and size of the population, labor market policies, and the business cycle. While trade may have a short-run effect as well, particularly if firms cannot compete against imports, or if sudden opportunities for export expansion appear, these impacts are outweighed by macroeconomic policies affecting the entire domestic economy over the medium and long runs. By comparison, changes in trade flows usually affect one or two manufacturing industries and a small share of overall GDP.

While trade is not the main determinant of the number of jobs in most economies, it might affect the kinds of jobs or the sectors of the economy where jobs are available. For example, manufacturing employment in the United States and most high-income countries has been falling for quite awhile. Throughout the 1980s and 1990s, most economists thought that the reductions in manufacturing employment in all industrial countries resulted from productivity gains, not trade. Manufacturing is easier to automate than services and as a consequence has much faster rates of productivity growth than services. Many services, on the other hand, have stagnant or very slow rates of productivity growth. Often, the same number of workers is required today as a century ago; one haircut, for example, still takes one barber, and modern musicians are no more "productive" at playing

Bach's *Brandenburg Concertos* than they were in the 1700s. When incomes rise, we consume more services and more manufactured goods, but because the services require more-or-less the same number of workers per unit of output, and manufactured goods can be made with fewer workers per unit, a growing share of our total employment ends up in services.

More recently, some economists have seriously questioned the idea that manufacturing is shrinking because productivity in that sector is increasing more rapidly. For example, an influential study has shown that communities in the United States that have industries that compete with Chinese-made products, have experienced a number of negative effects, including higher unemployment rates, lower labor force participation, and reduced wages. The authors of the study believe that exposure to competition with China may explain as much as one-fourth of the overall decline in manufacturing employment in the United States. Another influential study by a Nobel Prize winning economist and his co-author, points out that nearly all of the growth in the number of jobs has been in services and other sectors that do not produce tradable goods. They argue that many U.S. businesses have outsourced their inputs to firms in foreign countries so that middle-skill manufacturing is disappearing while very high-skill manufacturing jobs remain. Both of these studies support the idea that trade may have changed the composition of jobs in the United States in a way that does not favor manufacturing, even if the total number of jobs in all other sectors of the economy has grown significantly.

The second issue concerns the impact of trade with less-developed countries (LDCs) on the wages of workers in the advanced industrial economies. This question has been studied by many economists, and the general consensus until relatively recently was that trade may have caused some of the decline in wages for the less skilled (and, hence, some of the increase in wage inequality), but it was responsible for only a small share of the overall changes. Most economists thought that technological changes that reduced the role of unskilled and semiskilled labor in manufacturing were the primary causes of the increasing gap in wages between the skilled and the unskilled. In the late 1990s, however, the gap in wages between the skilled and unskilled stopped increasing and after approximately 2000, everyone's wages stagnated except the top 1 percent of the income distribution.

The consensus among economists is that there is no consensus about the impact of trade on wages. We know that export industries tend to pay more, but we do not know if trade is responsible for the stagnation in wages, or if it is but one of many factors, or perhaps has no impact at all on wages. This is an area of very active research as economists try to understand how trade might cause the wage stagnation and decline that we observe in many parts of the U.S. economy. If trade has played a far larger role in the growth of wage inequality or wage stagnation than is generally recognized, then the policy conclusions about trade are not likely to change much. In either case, where trade is responsible for inequality or lower wages and where it is not, there is a need for education and training programs targeted at the less skilled. Chapters 6 and 7 will show that blocking trade to protect jobs is extraordinarily expensive, and doing so to protect wages could make things worse in the long run.

CASE STUDY

Do Trade Statistics Give a Distorted Picture of Trade Relations? The Case of the iPhone 3G

Off-shoring enables firms to cut-up their production chain and move different parts of the production process to different global locations. We know that car parts come from around the globe and any vehicle labeled "Made in America" or any other country is likely to have components from a wide range of countries. Modern production processes span the globe, particularly when we examine sophisticated high technology products. Firms find it advantageous to off-shore and to outsource different pieces of the production process, and then bring the parts together for assembly in a completely different country. The iPhone is a case in point.

A 2009 investigation of the cost of components for an iPhone 3G revealed that four countries produced the majority of the value of the phone: Japan, Korea, Germany, and the United States. Since Apple is not a manufacturer, it outsources all of its production and off-shores a large part as well. When assembled, the cost of assembly and of materials for the iPhone3 was $178.96. This price is not the retail price since it does not include additional costs such as marketing, royalties, transportation, and insurance, and it omits the dealer mark-up. The $178.96 price tag can be thought of as the price of the materials and components that go into the iPhone, plus assembly costs. China's contribution to the value added is $6.50, which is the value of the assembly of components coming from Japan, Korea, Germany, and the United States. After the iPhone is assembled, it is ready for shipping. If it is sold in the United States, then U.S. import statistics will record a $178.96 import from China (not counting insurance and transportation). The U.S.' contribution to the cell phone's manufacture was $10.75, so trade statistics will record the iPhone 3G as a net deficit for the U.S., equal to $178.96 minus $10.75, or $168.21. This is odd if you consider that China's contribution to the iPhone's manufacture was only $6.50. If we re-examine the situation by looking only at value added in each country, the U.S. "iPhone trade balance with China" was actually in surplus: $10.75 minus $6.50 or $4.25. Correspondingly, U.S. actual trade deficits with Japan, Korea, and Germany are larger than official statistics indicate since most of its value was created in Japan (33 percent), Germany (17 percent), Korea (13 percent), and a host of other countries.

Analysis of China's production reveals systematic patterns in the share of export value added created in China. The WTO estimates that 32 percent of the value of China's exports was value created outside China in 2011, but the pattern varies by industry. Exports of goods produced with large amounts of unskilled and semiskilled labor such as apparel, footwear, or toys, have most

(continued)

of their value added from Chinese inputs of labor and capital, while exports of sophisticated electronics draw much more of their value from outside the country. Looking at many countries worldwide, natural resource products like oil or iron ore are almost entirely produced in the exporting country, while final products with many parts, such as consumer electronics or automobiles, are more likely to be produced in many countries, leaving the final exporter of the finished product with a smaller share of the overall value creation.

Some economists, including a previous Director General of the WTO, think that this type of mis-characterization of trade flows inadvertently contributes to greater trade tensions. Accordingly, the WTO began an initiative some years ago to measure trade flows in terms of value added rather than total value in the hopes that this would bring greater clarity to the actual source of the value of exports, and help reduce trade tensions between low-wage exporting countries and high-wage importing ones. Additional reasons for trying to understand which countries contribute to the production of a product are that it tells us whether firms in developing countries are participating in the value chains of multinational companies, and whether they are moving up into areas of increasing technological sophistication.

Summary

- The Heckscher-Ohlin (HO) model hypothesizes that comparative advantage is based on national differences in factor endowments. Countries export goods that have production requirements that are intensive in the nation's relatively abundant factors. They import goods that require intensive input from the nation's relatively scarce factors.

- The HO model has implications for the income distribution effects of trade. The opening of trade favors the abundant factor and reduces the use of the scarce factor. Consequently, the income or returns earned by the abundant factor rises, while it falls for the scarce factor. A corollary to the HO model, called the *Stolper-Samuelson theorem*, describes these effects.

- In the specific factors model, some factors of production are assumed to be immobile between different outputs. Consequently, when trade expands the production of a good, the specific factor used to produce it experiences a rise in the demand for its services and an increase in its income. The specific factor used to produce the imported good experiences a fall in the demand for its services, and its income declines. The specific factors model can be viewed as a short- to medium-run version of the HO model.

- Empirical tests of the theory of comparative advantage give mixed results. While underlying productivity differences explain a significant share of trade, national differences in factor endowments are less successful at explaining trade patterns.

■ Several alternative trade models have been hypothesized. Most are elaborations of the theory of comparative advantage. Two of the most popular alternative trade theories are the theory of the product cycle and the theory of intrafirm trade. The product cycle focuses on the speed of technological change and the life history of many manufactured items through periods of innovation, stabilization, and standardization. The theory of intrafirm trade allows a role for comparative advantage but also has industrial organization elements. It is impossible to state a general rule about the determinants of intrafirm trade.

■ Off-shoring is the movement of some or all of a firm's activities to another country. Outsourcing is the reassignment of activities to another firm, in either a domestic or a foreign location. Off-shoring has been advanced by the telecommunications revolution and is a relatively new phenomenon. Nevertheless, traditional trade models are useful in its analysis.

■ International migration can alter a country's comparative advantage, although in practice most countries do not receive enough migrants or a sufficiently long enough flow of migrants to cause long-run changes. Migrants are motivated by supply-push factors in their home country, demand-pull factors in the receiving country, and social networks that provide information and resources for settling in the new country.

■ In the medium to long run, trade has little or no effect on the total number of jobs in a country. The abundance or scarcity of jobs is a function of labor market policies, incentives to work, and the macroeconomic policies of the central bank and government. In the short run, trade may reduce jobs in an industry that suffers a loss in its competitiveness, just as it may increase jobs in an industry with growing competitiveness. Trade may also affect the kinds of jobs and the economic sectors that grow or shrink.

■ There is no consensus among economists about the impact of trade on wages. Recent research seems to point toward the possibility trade plays some role in the pattern of wage stagnation and the decline of recent years, but it is uncertain if its role is direct or indirect, and if it is large or small. This question is not settled and is an area of very active research.

Vocabulary

demand-pull factors	Heckscher-Ohlin (HO) trade theory
derived demand	intrafirm trade
factor abundance	magnification effect
factor scarcity	off-shoring
foreign affiliate	OLI theory

outsourcing   specific factors model

product cycle   Stolper-Samuelson theorem

resource curse   supply-push factors

social networks   value added

Study Questions

All problems are assignable in MyEconLab

4.1 According to the following table, which country is relatively more labor-abundant? Explain your answer. Which country is relatively more capital-abundant?

	United States	Canada
Capital	40 machines	10 machines
Labor	200 workers	60 workers

4.2 Suppose that the United States and Canada have the factor endowments in the preceding table. Suppose further that the production requirements for a unit of steel are 2 machines and 8 workers, and the requirement for a unit of bread is 1 machine and 8 workers.

a.   Which good, bread or steel, is relatively capital-intensive? Labor-intensive? Explain your answer.

b.   Which country would export bread? Why?

4.3 Suppose that before trade takes place, the United States is at a point on its PPC where it produces 20 loaves of bread and 20 units of steel. Once trade becomes possible, the price of a unit of steel is 2 units of bread. In response, the United States moves along its PPC to a new point where it produces 30 units of steel and 10 units of bread. Is the country better off? How do you know?

4.4 Given the information in Study Questions 4.1 and 4.2, explain what happens to the returns to capital and labor after trade begins.

4.5 Suppose that there are three factors: capital, labor, and land. Bread requires inputs of land and labor, and steel requires capital and labor.

a.   Which factors are variable, and which are specific?

b.   Suppose Canada's endowments are 10 capital and 100 land and the United States' are 50 capital and 100 land. Which good does each country export?

c.   How does trade affect the returns to land, labor, and capital in the United States and in Canada?

4.6 Describe the changes in production requirements and location of production that take place over the three phases of the product cycle.

4.7 Does intrafirm trade contradict the theory of comparative advantage? Why or why not?

4.8 General Motors is a U.S.-based multinational, but it is also one of the largest car manufacturers in Europe and South America. How might Dunning's OLI theory explain the trade-offs GM faced as it decided whether to export to those two markets or to produce in them?

4.9 Many domestically owned apparel manufacturers buy their garments overseas, sew their labels into them, and then sell them abroad or back into the home market. What are some of the considerations that a clothing manufacturer might go through to choose this strategy instead of producing at home and exporting?

4.10 Suppose Spain were to open its borders to the large number of unskilled Africans seeking to immigrate. In general, what effects would you expect to see in Spain's trade patterns and its comparative advantage?

5

Beyond Comparative Advantage

Learning Objectives

After studying this Chapter, students will be able to:

5.1 Give examples of interindustry and intraindustry trade.

5.2 Compare and contrast internal and external economies of scale.

5.3 Analyze the effects of international trade in a monopolistically competitive market.

5.4 Describe the gains from intraindustry trade.

5.5 Explain how transportation costs and internal economies of scale help determine firm location decisions.

5.6 Present the pros and cons of industrial policies.

INTRODUCTION: MORE REASONS TO TRADE

Comparative advantage is the foundation of our understanding of the gains from trade and the potential income distribution effects of trade. Unfortunately, trade models built exclusively on the idea of comparative advantage have a mixed record when it comes to predicting a country's trade patterns. This is an important failure since we tend to think that if we accurately measure a country's comparative advantage we should be able to predict import and export patterns. The problem, however, is that it is exceedingly difficult to precisely measure a country's comparative advantage. This problem is compounded by the fact that there are many potential products an economy might export that use the same comparative advantage, and there is no way to determine which specific products will dominate. Furthermore, and perhaps most seriously, a large share of international trade is not based on comparative advantage. This chapter takes up two important exceptions to the models of the previous chapters, and examines how and why many countries try to select and plan the development of their export industries.

The first section of this chapter explains why an important share of world trade consists of countries exporting the same thing they import. Canada and the United States, for example, have the largest trade relationship in the world, and a large share of it consists of exporting cars and car parts to each other. This pattern is clearly at odds with the bread-for-steel examples shown in Chapters 3 and 4. In the second section of the chapter, we examine industrial clustering. Many traded goods and services that are essential parts of a country's exports are produced in regional clusters. For example, the U.S. advantage in entertainment products (music, television programming, and movies) largely reflects the output of a handful of regions such as Hollywood and Nashville. Software reflects clusters in Silicon Valley, Seattle, and a few other spots; biotechnology is in San Francisco, San Diego, and a handful of other places. Surprisingly, international trade can play an important role in this type of clustering and may, under certain conditions, prevent new clusters from forming.

The issue of regional clusters leads directly into a discussion of industrial policies in the third section of the chapter. Industrial policies are used to address the challenge of trying to plan an advantage in a particular industry or a group of products. Can countries pick the items they will export and successfully build a strong export industry? What are the costs and benefits of the policies they follow? Basically, we are asking how nations can use policies to shape their economic development.

INTRAINDUSTRY TRADE

LO 5.1 Give examples of interindustry and intraindustry trade.

LO 5.2 Compare and contrast internal and external economies of scale.

LO 5.3 Analyze the effects of international trade in a monopolistically competitive market.

LO 5.4 Describe the gains from intraindustry trade.

The models of comparative advantage developed in Chapters 3 and 4 are built on the foundation of country differences. In those models, differences in productivity (Chapter 3) or factor endowments (Chapter 4) enable countries to raise their living standards by specializing their production and trading. The point of these models is not to paint a detailed portrait of economic life, but rather to create a simplified abstract model of the economy that focuses on key economic relations in the area of trade. To that end, unnecessary details are omitted, and rare or exceptional cases are ignored.

Sometimes rare or exceptional cases become more important over time. An example of this phenomenon is the increasing importance of **intraindustry trade** (the prefix "intra" means *within*). Intraindustry trade is the international trade of products made within the same industry, for example steel-for-steel or bread-for-bread. The opposite of intraindustry trade is **interindustry trade** (the prefix "inter" means *between*). Interindustry trade is international trade of products between two different industries (for example, bread-for-steel). The growing importance of intraindustry trade has forced economists to develop new models to explain why countries often export the same goods they import, and the benefits from this type of trade.

Characteristics of Intraindustry Trade

Intraindustry trade between industrial countries is common. Empirical measures of the importance of intraindustry trade vary, however, because of the fundamental problem of defining an industry. For example, if computers are defined as office machinery, then computers and pencil sharpeners are in the same industry, and a country that exports computers and imports pencil sharpeners would engage in intraindustry trade. In general, the more broadly an industry is defined, the more trade appears to be intraindustry. Conversely, the more detailed the definition, the less trade is defined as intraindustry. Evidence suggests that intraindustry trade is greater in high-technology industries (where there is more scope for product differentiation), in countries that are more open to trade, and in nations that have received larger amounts of foreign direct investment.

In the models of comparative advantage–based trade presented in Chapters 3 and 4, production costs are either constant (Chapter 3) or increasing (Chapter 4). Accordingly, each additional unit of bread produced led to the loss of a fixed or increasing amount of steel. The production of many goods, however, is characterized by economies of scale, or decreasing costs, over a relatively large range of output. The creation of new models of international trade based on economies of scale is one of the newest and most significant developments in trade theory over the last several decades and has increased our understanding of intraindustry trade. In the economics literature, this body of work is known as **New Trade Theory**, since it moves beyond traditional trade theory based on models with constant returns or decreasing returns to scale.

In New Trade Theory, economies of scale can be either **internal economies of scale** or **external economies of scale**. Internal economies are defined as falling average costs over a relatively large range of output. In practice, this leads to larger firms because size confers a competitive advantage in the form of lower average costs. One of the distinguishing features of intraindustry trade is the presence of internal economies of scale.

Table 5.1 illustrates a firm's cost structure when it experiences increasing returns to scale. Typically, there is a threshold level of production above which the average cost per good begins to increase rather than continuing to fall. Increasing returns are usually based on the inherent development, engineering, or marketing aspects of production and are associated with products that have a large fixed cost component. Car companies, software, and popular household brand name products, to name a few, tend to have large fixed costs. These occur for various reasons, such as the cost of constructing a large production plant, large R&D budgets, or large marketing expenditures. Software, for example, requires large up-front expenditures on R&D to develop a product, and the more units a firm can sell, the more it can spread out those fixed R&D costs.

Internal economies of scale have important implications for the type of market that prevails. In Chapters 3 and 4, it is assumed that firms operate in competitive markets where no one firm can influence prices or overall industry output. When larger firms are more competitive, however, it reduces the number of firms in a

TABLE 5.1   Increasing Returns to Scale for a Single Firm

Output	Total Cost	Average Cost
100	1000	10
200	1400	7
300	1500	5
400	1600	4
500	1650	3.5
600	1950	3.25

As production increases, total costs rise, but the cost per unit falls. Bigger firms are more efficient than smaller firms.

market and leads to one of several types of market structures. In an **oligopoly**, a handful of firms produce the entire market output. In this case, the pattern of production and trade is very difficult to predict because each firm uses predictions about the actions of its competitors as it formulates its own profit-maximizing strategy. This type of response means that each firm alters its output level as it sees what its competitors are doing, and production levels and trade become less predictable.

Often, internal economies lead to the relatively common market structure called **monopolistic competition**. Recall that in a pure monopoly, one firm produces the entire industry output. In monopolistic competition, there is competition among many firms, but their competition is attenuated by the practice of **product differentiation**. With product differentiation, each firm produces a slightly different product. This gives rise to the monopoly element of monopolistic competition, in that each firm is the sole producer of its products. For example, only Ford can sell the Ford Focus. Unlike a pure monopoly, however, every other firm produces a close substitute, and this introduces a real element of competition.

In monopolistic competition, the level of competition among firms increases whenever new firms enter the market. This has two effects. On the one hand, heightened competition will lead to lower prices because products are substitutes for each other and in the struggle to capture sales, downward pressure is placed on prices. On the other hand, when more firms divide the market, each firm sells fewer units of output on average, and so costs rise. This follows directly from the internal economies of each firm. As long as prices are above costs, more firms will enter the market, and whenever prices are below costs, firms exit.

The presence of internal economies of scale is the reason why firms want to enter export markets. Any firm that exports has a competitive advantage since it will have higher sales and be able to take advantage of the cost-reducing effects of its internal economies of scale. For any given number of firms, average costs are lower in a larger market. This follows from the economies of scale that each firm experiences and the fact that if the number of firms is held constant, each firm sells more as the size of the market expands.

Figure 5.1 illustrates the relationship between (1) the number of firms in the industry, (2) average costs, and (3) output prices. The horizontal axis measures the number of firms in the industry, while the vertical axis measures average cost and price. Line segment P shows the relationship between the number of firms and prices. It slopes downward to the right because more firms entering the market put downward pressure on prices. Line segment AC shows the relationship between the average cost for each individual firm and the total number of firms in the market. It slopes upward because as more firms enter the market, the quantity each existing firm sells is reduced and the average cost of production increases. At prices above P_1, new firms have an incentive to enter the market since price exceeds average cost. At prices below P_1, just the opposite occurs and some firms will leave the market because their costs are greater than the market price.

Figure 5.1 also makes obvious the reason why firms want to export. Any firm that exports is at a competitive advantage since it will have the greater sales it needs to drive down its costs. This idea is illustrated in Figure 5.2, where the alternative cost curve, AC*, is identical to AC except that it belongs to a larger market. For any given number of firms, AC* shows that average costs are lower in a larger market. This follows from the economies of scale that each firm experiences and the fact that if the number of firms is held constant, each firm sells more when the size of the market expands.

The Gains from Intraindustry Trade

Intraindustry trade also creates gains from trade. While the increased size of the market leads to lower costs through the effect of scale economies, competition among firms forces them to pass on their lower costs to consumers in the form of

FIGURE 5.1   Monopolistic Competition

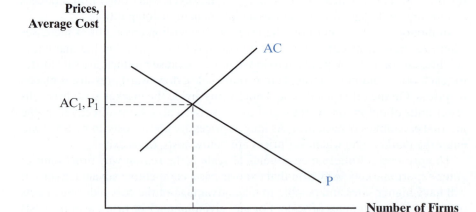

In monopolistic competition, an increase in the number of firms drives down prices and drives up each firm's average costs. Equilibrium occurs when price equals average cost.

FIGURE 5.2   An Increase in Market Size

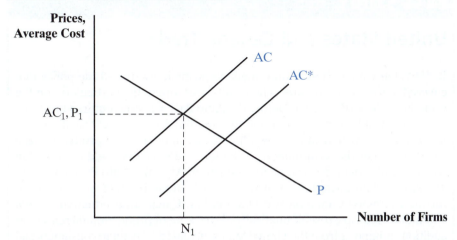

For any given number of firms, an increase in the size of the market through the creation of foreign sales allows economies of scale to be realized and pushes down average costs.

lower prices. Lower prices for exports and imports stands in marked contrast to the case of comparative advantage-based trade. Recall that in the trade models of Chapters 3 and 4, each country's consumers benefit from a reduction in the price of the good it imports, but at the same time, the price of the export rises. With intraindustry trade, however, prices for both imports and exports decline, leading to unambiguous benefits for consumers in both countries. Trade enables firms to produce for a larger market and at a higher level of efficiency. That raises everyone's real income through the reduction in prices.

The expansion of the market that occurs with trade ultimately leads to an increase in the number of firms. This follows from the fact that exports costs are below the selling price, and new firms are attracted into the market until excess profits are competed away. While it is safe to say that the combined foreign and domestic industry will expand, the location of the expansion is indeterminate and depends on the individual firm characteristics. Some firms may be more efficient than others and a larger market via international trade will give them an opportunity to expand their production. Less efficient firms are likely to suffer from the increased competition, but there is no way to predict if they are mostly home-grown firms or foreign firms. Hence, there is no way to determine in advance which firms survive and expand and which ones fall by the wayside.

In addition to lower prices (higher real income) and the potential expansion of production, another benefit from intraindustry trade is that it increases consumer choices. Without trade, consumers are limited to the goods produced in the domestic market. This is not necessarily a limitation for some people, but a scan of the highways should be enough to convince anyone that many consumers prefer foreign-made goods over their domestic substitutes. The value of added choices is not easy to measure in dollar terms, but it is clearly a significant benefit for most people.

CASE STUDY

United States and Canada Trade

In 1965, the United States and Canada implemented a free-trade policy that covered autos and auto parts. The results were dramatic, particularly on the Canadian side of the border. Before the Auto Pact, Canada required most cars sold domestically to be made inside the country. The relatively small market in Canada meant that only a few different car models were produced, each in small batches that cost more to make since automakers could not take full advantage of economies of scale in production. After the Auto Pact, automakers refocused production on a smaller number of models that were produced for the combined Canadian and U.S. market. Canadian productivity in the automobile industry rose dramatically as the scale of production increased. In addition, as imports from the United States increased, Canadian consumers had many more models from which to choose.

The automobile industry integrated production in the United States and Canada completely. Trade between the two countries rose dramatically and eventually grew into the largest bilateral trade relationship of any two countries in the world. Table 5.2 illustrates the importance of intraindustry trade.

Three of the top five U.S. exports, and two of the top five imports, are motor vehicles or related products. In terms of value, an overwhelming share of the top five exports and imports are car related. Clearly, intraindustry trade is fundamental to the U.S.-Canadian trade pattern.

Note that the top five U.S. imports include three Canadian exports that take advantage of its natural resource endowment. This part of the trade relationship illustrates comparative advantage–based trade built around differing factor endowments. As a result, U.S.-Canadian trade is partly intraindustry, partly interindustry comparative advantage–based.

TABLE 5.2   **U.S.-Canadian Merchandise Trade, 2014 (Billions of US$)**

Top Five U.S. Exports	Value	Top Five U.S. Imports	Value
Vehicle parts, not engines*	23.2	Crude oil	83.1
Busses, trucks, other vehicles*	15.0	Passenger cars*	42.7
Passenger cars*	14.6	Natural gas	12.6
Other petroleum products	12.9	Vehicle parts, not engines*	11.9
Industrial machines	10.9	Other petroleum products	8.8

*Vehicles and vehicle parts are the largest component of U.S.-Canadian trade.
Source: U.S. Census Bureau, "End-Use Data," Country and Product Trade Data, 2014.

TRADE AND GEOGRAPHY

LO 5.5 Explain how transportation costs and internal economies of scale help determine firm location decisions.

Paul Krugman, winner of the 2008 Nobel Prize in Economics, has stated that international trade is really about geography and the decision every firm must make about the location of its activities. Produce at home or abroad? If abroad, then in which country? If at home, in what part of the country? Produce close to a city, or in the countryside where land is cheaper? In many cases the choices are obvious, and the factors that make them obvious are related to the characteristics of a particular place. For example, availability of labor or energy resources, or proximity to a market or specialized input suppliers may determine a firm's choices. Geography, which is the study of the characteristics of places, is an important consideration for firms, and in turn has significant effects on trade.

Trade and geography are linked in two fundamental ways. First, a place such as a major city may pull in economic activity because it is a large market. Second, a place may offer firms the opportunity to find critical inputs, including skilled labor, and to stay abreast of current developments. For both of these reasons, on the output side and the input side the characteristics of places are an important part of firm decision making. As a result, geography plays a key role in some trade.

Geography, Transportation Costs, and Internal Economics of Scale

For most manufactured goods, it is not practical to produce next to each market because there are economies of scale. For example, it would not make sense to locate car assembly firms next to every car dealership. Production would be at too small a scale, and costs would be extremely high. Instead, car production tends to be concentrated in a few areas, and the final product is shipped to the markets where it is sold. As a result, there are significant transportation costs, both in bringing in the parts that are assembled into the final car and in shipping the car to its final market. Accordingly, car companies think carefully about the location of their activities and try to mitigate their high transportation costs by locating near their markets.

Not all types of manufacturing have the same level of transportation costs, and services have few or none, but to one degree or another, the cost of bringing parts to the assembler and then shipping the final product to market are important considerations for many firms. If there were no internal economies of scale, it would be possible to locate production next to the market where the good will be sold, but the presence of scale economies makes that impractical for most production. Milk and eggs tend to be produced locally because there are more limited scale economies and higher transportation costs, while aircraft are highly concentrated in their production because there are large scale economies and relatively smaller transportation costs.

Transportation costs and scale economies are characteristics of manufacturing that help explain several patterns observed in the global economy. For example, it was noted in Chapter 4 that most foreign investment in the world today is directed toward high-income countries, not toward developing countries. Largely this is because high-income countries have larger markets, and firms find it convenient to locate next to the market. All other factors being equal, the lower transportation costs often outweigh other costs that might be higher. It also explains the southward shift of U.S. car manufacturing in the 1990s, as firms in Michigan and Ohio moved to Texas in order to be closer to the new final assemblers springing up in Mexico. The cost of transporting the many parts that are assembled into a car or truck requires that assemblers and parts suppliers be in close proximity to one another.

CASE STUDY

The Shifting Geography of Mexico's Manufacturing

Approximately two-thirds of the trade between the United States and Mexico is intrafirm. Most of this occurs within the context of Mexico's special export processing sector, called the **maquiladora** industry. Originally limited to its border with the United States but later expanded to the whole country, the maquiladora industry began in 1965. The original purpose of the government was to generate employment along Mexico's northern border. In the long run, the maquiladora industry became a major source of manufacturing activity, a major employer, and one of the country's main sources of exports.

The maquiladora industry is an example of an **export processing zone (EPZ)**. In EPZs, both domestic and foreign firms produce goods for export without paying tariffs on the parts and materials they import. This allows firms such as General Motors and Sony to set up in Mexico and pay no tariffs on the inputs they bring into the country from abroad, as long as they export the output. (Note that the rules for maquiladoras changed under NAFTA and export requirements are no longer in place.)

The number of firms in the export processing industry grew slowly but steadily, and by 1980, fifteen years after the initial legislation, there were 620 plants with 120,000 workers. Nevertheless, the export processing industry was an exception to the dominant trend in Mexico, as manufacturing remained firmly focused on production for the domestic market. Until the middle of the 1980s, Mexico's development strategy was inward looking, and most firms found that it was less profitable to export than to produce for the home market since goods sold domestically were protected from competition and goods sold abroad were not.

In 1982, a financial crisis struck Mexico and policymakers began to rethink the country's development model. Until then, the focus on production for the domestic market caused most firms to locate near Mexico City or one or two other major urban areas such as Monterrey or Guadalajara. The choice of locations reduced their transportation costs by locating production near their final market, and allowed them to take advantage of their internal economies of scale since they operated out of only one or a few plants. In an unforeseen way, Mexico's development model during the 1950s, 1960s, and 1970s caused Mexico City to grow into one of the world's largest cities and resulted in a very high proportion of the population becoming concentrated in the country's largest urban centers.

In the middle of the 1980s, Mexican policymakers shifted toward a more neutral policy with respect to production for domestic or foreign markets. They did this by removing many of the tariffs and other protections that had kept domestic firms free from foreign competition. By reducing and in some cases eliminating tariffs and other measures that limited imports, policymakers created a more level playing field for exports producers. In effect, this made it relatively more profitable to produce goods for sale in foreign markets since it took away the advantages of producing for the domestic market.

Partly as a consequence of these policy changes, the export processing industry along Mexico's northern border took off. By the middle of 2000, the maquiladora industry employed more than 1.3 million workers in more than 3,700 firms and was responsible for more than half of Mexico's total exports. The maquiladora industry grew rapidly because the new incentives caused both Mexican and non-Mexican firms to locate near the border with the United States, rather than in Mexico City. Under the new rules, the largest profitable market is the United States rather than Mexico City. Given internal economies of scale and transportation costs, location as close as possible to the U.S. market made a great deal of sense, and cities on Mexico's northern border, such as Tijuana, Ciudad Juarez, and others, began to grow rapidly almost a decade before the free-trade agreement between the United States, Mexico, and Canada.

External Economies of Scale

External economies of scale occur when firms become more productive as the number of firms in the industry increases, but individual firms may or may not have an economic incentive to increase in size. External economies may occur for several reasons. First, if the firms in a region produce similar products, there are likely to be knowledge spillovers that help keep all firms abreast of the latest technology and newest developments. Close physical proximity enhances knowledge spillovers because it creates more opportunities for information exchange through formal and informal networks of people. Regional industry associations can be important, but so can soccer teams, churches, Girl Scouts, and other civic organizations that bring together people who work in different firms. Knowledge spillovers are particularly important in frontier industries undergoing rapid technological change, and they seem to be very sensitive to the face-to-face contact that is impaired by geographical distance.

A second form of external economies of scale occurs when the presence of a large number of producers in one area helps to create a deep labor market for specialized skills. If an industry is large enough to attract a steady stream of potential employees with specialized skills, it reduces the search costs of firms and also offers them the best available skills. This advantage is particularly important in industries that demand highly technical or scarce skills.

A third potential advantage to a large geographical concentration is that it can lead to a dense network of input suppliers. Manufacturers of intermediate inputs prefer to locate near the market for their products since it holds down transportation costs and may keep them better informed. In high-tech sectors, a large number of nearby supplier firms will lower the cost of finding a producer of a specialized input and will also create a wider and deeper selection of input goods and services. All of these effects hold down producer costs. The linkage from producers back to their suppliers can also occur in the other direction. If the concentrated industry manufactures intermediate goods or services, it may attract firms that use its products to make a final good or service. This gives firms more information about their market and may also lead to closer collaboration between suppliers and purchasers of intermediate inputs.

Trade and External Economies

One of the essential features of geographical concentration is that it is self-reinforcing. For example, as firms attract skilled workers or specialized input suppliers, the increased availability of high-quality inputs creates feedback leading to more firms in the same industry locating in the area. In turn, this leads to a stronger pull for workers and input suppliers. In effect, each of the elements acts on each other to propel the system forward.

One implication of these features is that small differences in initial conditions may lead to large differences in outcome. That is, a region with a small head start or other small initial advantage in attracting firms may develop significant scale economies before other regions. Once the scale advantages become significant, the gap between the lead region and its competitors can widen, and may turn into a permanent competitive advantage. The source of the initial advantage can be anything, including historical accidents. For example, during World War II, as jet engines were being developed in Great Britain, the Allies decided to locate production in the United States on the West Coast, minimizing the probability that the Axis powers could destroy the factories with air raids. Ultimately, this led to a supplier industry around the major jet aircraft manufacturers (Boeing, Lockheed, and McDonnell-Douglas), and helped in the development of specialized labor skills such as aerospace engineering. As a result of a historical accident and the Allies' decisions during the war, the United States dominated the commercial jet aircraft industry for several decades, until a consortium of European governments used large subsidies and other interventions to foster a European competitor, Airbus.

Once the U.S. lead was established, other countries with essentially the same technological ability as the United States could never catch up, even though in theory they had the capacity to achieve the same level of efficiency. The development of U.S. regional agglomerations (for example, the concentration of specialized aerospace manufacturing firms in the Seattle and Southern California regions) gave the United States a head start and a competitive advantage that could not be easily overcome. U.S. planes were always available at lower prices than a newer, less developed, industry could offer. In this instance, trade stifles the development of an industry that may be as competitive as existing producers.

In theory, trade could stifle the development of a new industry that is more efficient than the existing one. Suppose, for example, that Europeans are potentially more efficient at making commercial aircraft than Americans. Their potential can only be realized, however, after a period of experimentation and development. The initial problem they face is that the efficiency advantage goes to the United States because of its better developed linkages between suppliers and producers. In this case, trade and the initial availability of U.S. planes at a lower cost remove the incentive for Europeans to invest in their industry and prevent the development of what might ultimately be a more efficient industry. As long as U.S. planes are available at a lower price than European planes, there is no economic reason why anyone would buy European, and the lack of an initial market for their planes guarantees the Europeans a period of financial losses, thereby discouraging investment. In effect, the historical accident of locating jet aircraft production in the United States in order to avoid Hitler's bombers is locked in by trade.

The aircraft example is instructive because it illustrates a case in which trade may not be beneficial. In every other case we've examined so far, trade is beneficial. Under the circumstances outlined earlier, however, it is potentially harmful since it reduces global efficiency by concentrating world production in the less-efficient producer. The aircraft example also illustrates how small initial differences can cascade into large differences in outcome and how with external economies, trade patterns can be a result of completely unpredictable accidents of history.

INDUSTRIAL POLICY

LO 5.6 Present the pros and cons of industrial policies.

Faced with a more competitive U.S. aircraft industry, what can Europeans do to get their own industry off the ground? This was the question asked several decades ago by the governments of Britain, France, Germany, and Spain. Their answer was to pool the resources of their domestic aircraft and aerospace firms and to provide generous subsidies from the four governments to help the consortium absorb the initial losses and to develop their own industry. The result was Airbus, the large European challenger to the U.S.-based Boeing company. The creation of Airbus is an example of governments using **industrial policies** to explicitly direct economic activity. As the name and example imply, industrial policies are government policies designed to create new industries or to support existing ones.

Not surprisingly, industrial policies are controversial; so much so, that recent international agreements limit the scope of action that countries can take to support their industries. In some cases, they end up wasting large sums of money. Brazil and Indonesia, for example, have used industrial policies to develop regional commercial jet aircraft industries, targeted at the 20- to 100-passenger plane market. While Brazil has had commercial success (Embraer), the Indonesian industry spent billions of dollars and used many engineers and other skilled workers whose talents could have been put to work developing the Indonesian economy. No doubt, comparative advantage can change, but was it counter-productive for Indonesia to try to speed along the development process by promoting a specific industry? How can a country know which industries to promote? Will doing so lead to better outcomes than simply providing the basic components of a well-functioning economy, including education, stable institutions, and sound macroeconomic policies?

Industrial Policies and Market Failure

When the private market economy fails to deliver an optimal quantity of goods and services, it is called a **market failure**. An optimal quantity is one where the full value of the goods to private consumers and society is equal to its full cost of production. It follows that too little or too much of a good is a market failure. Market failures are a divergence between **private returns** and **social returns**. A frequent cause of this divergence is that some of the costs or benefits of an activity are externalized, or outside the area of concern of the economic agents engaged in the activity. For obvious reasons, economists refer to the market failure that results from the externalization of costs or benefits as an **externality**. Externalities cause some of the costs or benefits of an action to go to people or firms other than those engaged in the economic activity. For example, a steel mill that pollutes a river imposes a cost on inhabitants downstream, and parents who vaccinate their children create a benefit for their neighbor's children. In an accounting sense, the private returns are the cost and benefits to the steel mill or to the parents with the vaccinated child, while the social returns include the private costs or benefits, but also take into account the costs and benefits to the rest of society—the downstream inhabitants or the neighbor's children. Note that externalized costs or benefits do not mean that they disappear and are of no consequence. From an economic viewpoint, they are as important as any other costs or benefits even though they do not fall on the individuals or firms that created them.

There are two simple rules for analyzing cases of market failure. First, when social returns are greater than private returns, a free-market economy produces less than the optimal amount. This occurs because some of the benefits are captured by individuals or firms other than those that produce the benefits, so naturally they do not consider the entire set of benefits when they decide how much to produce. The second rule is that when social returns are less than private returns, a free-market economy produces more than the optimal amount. In this case, economic agents do not take into account the costs that spill over onto others and that reduce the value to society of the good or service.

The divergence between private and social returns is shown in Figure 5.3. Supply and demand are plotted for a competitively produced good that generates external benefits when it is produced. The supply curve S_{priv} is a normal market supply curve, embodying all of the private costs encountered by firms. It is labeled with the subscript "priv" to indicate that only the private costs, the costs paid by the firms producing the good, are taken into account. Since production entails some external benefits to members of the society (who are not specified in this model), we can offset some of the costs of production with the external benefits. These are subtracted from the supply curve to derive the social supply curve, S_{soc}, which embodies the private costs minus the external benefits. The supply curve S_{soc} is more comprehensive than S_{priv} since it takes into consideration all of the costs and benefits to society, not simply the private ones.

As can be seen in Figure 5.3, private markets lead to output Q_1 at price P_1. From the standpoint of the social optimum, however, the price is too high and the quantity is too low. The social optimum, at P_2 and Q_2, takes into account the costs and benefits that are external to the producing firms and their internal costs and

FIGURE 5.3   Market Failure: Externalities

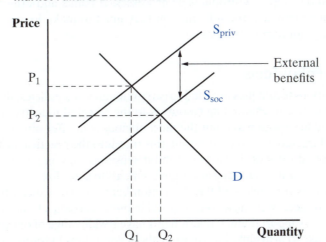

When social returns exceed private returns, markets produce less than the optimum and sell it at too high a price.

benefits. In effect, private agents earn less than the social return, which includes the external benefit that firms cannot capture. As a result, there is less than the socially optimal amount of investment in the activity generating the returns. For advocates of industrial policies, the solution is activist government intervention to increase the level of the desirable activity.

There are many reasons why social returns and private returns may differ. Knowledge spillovers are a common example and are often cited as a reason for industrial policies. In this case, the social return to the new knowledge is greater than the private return because some of the value of the knowledge spills over from the firm that created it into other firms. An important case of knowledge spillovers comes from the first entrant into a particular industry since they show others the possibilities in a new industry or market. A related knowledge spillover occurs in the area of research and development since firms that create new technologies often generate benefits for competitors who copy their breakthroughs, make slight improvements, and introduce a new product of their own.

Coordination problems are another source of divergence between social and private returns. Individual projects, for example, may require complementary actions by other firms. Chile's successful development of a fruit and vegetable export industry required simultaneous investment in transportation and port facilities, as well as infrastructure to deliver cleaner water. A fruit producer, on its own, could not provide all the needed components; and without coordination between agricultural interests, infrastructure investors, and local water utilities, the fruit and vegetable export industry might never have taken off.

Another source of divergence between private and social returns is capital market imperfections. According to this argument, new firms may have difficulty attracting sufficient start-up capital. The same applies to existing firms that need to borrow to develop new products or processes. If banks and other lenders in the financial system lack the information they need to make loans, many solid prospects may not receive funding.

Industrial Policy Tools

Although various techniques are used to carry out industrial policies, they all share the same objective of channeling resources to the targeted industry. This can be accomplished in various ways, but the most obvious is to offer direct subsidies to firms in the targeted industry. As noted, this runs into the practical difficulty that Uruguay Round rules of the WTO prohibit subsidies for competitive products. Nevertheless, the rules generally allow governments to subsidize "precompetitive" activities such as research, and the distinction between the two can be blurry at times. It is not necessary, however, to provide direct subsidies to targeted indus-tries in order to support them. Governments have a wide range of options, ranging from tax breaks to providing information about conditions in foreign markets, to lobbying foreign governments to adopt home country technical standards, or tying foreign aid to purchases from home country firms.

CASE STUDY

Clean Energy and Industrial Policy

Power generation is one of the foundations of a modern, high-income economy and it is not an exaggeration to say that without energy, there is very little GDP. At the same time, energy production and consumption are dramatically altering the planet and making life much more precarious in many places, but especially low-lying coastal areas and areas subject to extreme weather events. We need energy, but the forms we produce and consume are harming the planet. One central part of a solution to the problems created by global climate change is to transition to clean energy sources that do not put carbon and other greenhouse gases into the environment.

Carbon pollution is a classic case of a negative externality. A significant part of the cost of burning fossil fuels is not included in the price of the fuels since producers and consumers of electricity from coal fired plants, or producers and consumers of transportation that uses gas powered internal combustion engines, do not pay the full cost of the environmental damage that results from burning coal and gasoline.

Along with this externality, another characteristic of our energy production and consumption is a very strong movement toward research, development, and deployment of investments in low-carbon energy sources in general, and wind and solar power in particular. In 2015, for example, new investments in solar and wind and other forms of clean energy outpaced investments in oil and gas and coal, even though the latter are more than 80 percent of all energy production today and solar and wind are a very small percentage of the world's energy supply. The World Bank, for example, estimates that only 1 percent of the total energy supply in the United States was from solar and wind in 2012.

Such a momentous shift in world energy production and consumption will create enormous disruptions but also fantastic opportunities for any producer able to bring clean energy costs down quickly and commercialize the new technology. Governments across the globe are aware of this potential for clean energy to create new industries and many have formulated industrial policies to try to make their firms world leaders. Winning the clean energy race will avoid environmental catastrophe and it promises to be extremely lucrative for whichever country or firms develop the most widely used technologies.

Leaders in the race include China, the United States, Japan, Germany, and the United Kingdom. Their tools for promoting their industries include subsidies in the form of direct payments to producers and consumers, tax breaks for businesses and households that produce or adopt clean energy, and the funding of research and development. Each of these forms of support—subsidies, tax breaks, and direct support for R&D—have multiple subcategories. In the United States, wind and solar received the most support, with approximately 18 percent and 20 percent, respectively, of the $29.3 billion in total financial

(continued)

support offered by the federal government in 2013. In addition to financial supports, governments at the national and sub-national levels also offer support in the form of regulations that push producers and consumers towards cleaner energy. Examples include the carbon emissions targets such as those agreed at the UN Conference on Climate Change held in Paris in December 2015, or Germany's Renewable Energy Act of 2000.

As governments have made clearer their intentions to support new energy sources, the private sector has jumped into the market with large investments and new research and development. In the final analysis, it is difficult to say how important a role governments played in encouraging the private sector to get serious about climate change, or in helping firms to reach the technological frontiers where they can begin to sell their products internationally, but it seems likely that many new developments would not have been realized without these industrial policies. Financially, some countries are likely to realize very sizable gains from trade as they become global producers of clean energy technology.

Source: Based on Direct Federal Financial Interventions and Subsidies in Energy in Fiscal Year 2013,U.S. Energy Information Administration,March 12, 2015 and Sustainable Energy for All Database by World Bank,February, 2016, © James Gerber

World Bank, *Sustainable Energy for All Database*. February, 2016.

Problems with Industrial Policies

While every economist recognizes that markets do not always produce the optimal outcome, many are skeptical about the practicality of using industrial policies to solve problems of market failure. Furthermore, many of the practices described are considered harmful to the interests of foreign firms, and new rules introduced by the WTO as part of the Uruguay Round limit the ability of countries to employ policies that were once relatively common (see the case study at the end of the chapter).

One problem is that it is difficult to obtain the information necessary to measure the extent of market failure. For example, an efficient industrial policy requires governments to provide precisely the right amount of additional resources to the targeted industry. This implies that governments should keep adding resources as long as the external benefits are greater than the cost of the resources; but in many cases it is difficult to measure the benefits, particularly if they are spread throughout the economy and if they are only realized over a long period of time. Without the advantage of hard numbers, it is easy to imagine a situation where a government program spends $100 million to capture $50 million of external benefits.

A second problem is determining which industry to target. If everyone acknowledges that a particular industry has a bright future, then entrepreneurs and investors will jump on it and government support is unnecessary. On the other hand, we know that external benefits cause markets to underinvest. Consequently, one possibility for choosing industries to target is to pick the ones that have the largest external benefits. One potential problem with this strategy is that the positive externalities that develop out of new technologies and inventions are often a surprise to everyone involved and it is impossible to know beforehand that they will occur. In 1990, for example, almost no one foresaw the advent of the Internet.

Another problem with industrial policies is that they encourage **rent seeking**, which is any activity by firms, individuals, or special interests that is designed to alter the distribution of income in their favor without adding to the amount of total income in the economy. If firms know that governments are willing to use industrial policies, they will spend resources to obtain some of the subsidies. This may require the hiring of lobbyists, economists, or engineers who will work to persuade the legislature or some other rule makers. The downside is that it uses resources but does not add to total output. The extent to which industrial policies encourage resources to be wasted in lobbying and other non-economically productive activities partly depends on the administrative process through which targeted industries are chosen, and the political culture of the country enacting the industrial policy. Countries that have a greater degree of corruption in their political system are likely to have a much harder time choosing between industries on the basis of scientific, technological, or economic criteria.

Another problem with industrial policies is that it is impossible to contain the external benefits of R&D spending within national boundaries. New technologies soon spread to every nation that has the technological sophistication to take advantage of them. One set of estimates puts the benefits to foreigners of R&D spending by the home country at around one-fourth of the total benefits. The fact that many U.S. firms have separate joint ventures in research and production with European and Japanese firms increases the chances that a new breakthrough will spread to firms in other countries.

Despite these obstacles, industrial policies remain an intensely debated topic, particularly in the arena of economic development. Japan and South Korea used them extensively and are frequently cited as models for developing countries. Opponents of industrial policies continue to argue that sound macroeconomic policies, high rates of saving and investment, and high levels of schooling were the keys to success in those two countries, and that industrial policies were a distraction at best. Given the difficulties of determining cause and effect in economic development, an active debate between opponents and proponents will probably continue for some time. We will examine the East Asian case in greater detail in Chapter 16.

CASE STUDY

Do the WTO Rules Against Industrial Policies Hurt Developing Countries?

The Uruguay Round of the General Agreement on Tariffs and Trade (GATT) accomplished more than the creation of the WTO and the lowering of tariffs. It created new agreements in a range of areas, including trade in services, investment rules, intellectual property protection, and limits to industrial subsidies.

(continued)

All economists agree that one effect of the new agreements is that countries are much more limited in their ability to implement industrial policies that target an enterprise, an industry, groups of enterprises, or groups of industries. There is much less consensus on whether these limits on industrial policies are harmful to developing countries. Economists that favor industrial policies as a tool for development see the limits imposed by the WTO as potentially harmful constraints on national development policies, while economists that view industrial policies as unhelpful see the limits on them as beneficial and useful for avoiding trade disputes.

Two agreements in particular are singled out as creating limits on the deployment of industrial policies by national governments. These are the **TRIMs (Trade-Related Investment Measures)** and **SCM (Subsidies and Countervailing Measures)** agreements. A third agreement, **TRIPS (Trade-Related Aspects of Intellectual Property Rights)**, is also blamed for limiting access to new knowledge and technology, and for causing potential harm to developing countries.

TRIMs Agreement

The TRIMs agreement is designed to ensure that national governments do not favor domestic investment over foreign investment (national treatment). It does not define trade-related investment measures in general but it gives an illustrative list of prohibited actions. Two areas of TRIMs' prohibitions are most important. Nations are not allowed to condition the permission they grant to foreign investment on the use of local inputs or on export performance. Historically, many countries used performance requirements to link foreign investors with local manufacturers. For example, they required a certain percentage of domestic content to be used in the plants built by foreign investors in order to increase domestic value added, to strengthen linkages within an industry, and to increase the transfer of technology from the foreign firm to domestic firms. This technique was used often in the auto industry. Nations also often imposed trade balancing requirements on foreign investment and required exports to match imports or foreign exchange earnings to be equal to foreign exchange used to buy imported inputs.

SCM Agreement

The SCM defines prohibited subsidies and "actionable" subsidies. Prohibited subsidies are ones that require a firm to use domestic inputs or to meet export targets; in a sense the SCM is parallel to the TRIMs in the limits it places on national policies. Actionable subsidies are any financial benefit given to a firm that harms firms or industries in another country. If, for example, a government gives special tax incentives to its auto industry and this hurts sales by auto companies located in another WTO member, then that member may file a grievance with the WTO, or it may do its own investigation leading to taxes on imports from the country with the subsidized firms.

TRIPS Agreement

The third agreement, TRIPS, which many view as harmful to the interests of developing countries, is argued to limit their access to new technology and to knowledge. It does this by requiring a much more rigorous enforcement of intellectual property rights such as patents and copyrights. Those who oppose the TRIPS agreement argue that many rich countries had weak intellectual property rights early in their period of industrial development. This enabled them to take products apart, see how they are designed, and then copy them, a process known as *reverse engineering.* TRIPS restricts reverse engineering and places many new fields of technology under its jurisdiction, where previously countries could make some fields of technology off-limits to patents and copyrights. TRIPS also extends the duration of patent rights, and parallel to the SCM and TRIMs agreements, it limits the ability of governments to regulate patent holders by imposing local production or technology transfer requirements.

Summary

- Comparative advantage cannot account for a significant part of world trade. In many countries, well over 50 percent of the merchandise trade is intraindustry, and for the United States and a number of other large economies, it is over two-thirds.

- Intraindustry trade is not based on comparative advantage since it consists of the export and import of similar products and occurs mostly between countries that have similar productivity, technology, and factor endowments. Intraindustry trade is based on economies of scale and product differentiation.

- Economies of scale occur whenever average costs decrease as production increases. Economies of scale are an important determinant of trade patterns because they form a separate basis for trade that is in addition to comparative advantage–based trade.

- Economies of scale can be internal, external, or both. With internal economies of scale, the gains from trade include a wider selection of consumer choices and lower prices. With external economies of scale, the gains from trade are less certain since, in theory, they can lock in production in a less efficient country and prevent the development of production in a more efficient country.

- External economies of scale lead to regional agglomerations of firms. Firms are attracted by several positive factors derived from operating in close geographical proximity to each other. The three main factors are large pools of skilled labor, specialized suppliers of inputs, and knowledge spillovers.

■ Industrial policies are premised on the idea that markets may fail to develop an industry that is essential for future prosperity, or that there will be less development than is optimal if many of the benefits of an industry are external to the firms in the industry.

■ Historically, governments have used a number of tools to foster the development of industries that they thought were essential to future prosperity. These tools included a number of different types of direct and indirect subsidies. The Uruguay Round of the GATT agreement has made it illegal to subsidize a commercial product and much more difficult to target specific firms and industries.

■ Problems with industrial policies include the absence of a reliable method for selecting the industry to target, rent seeking, international spillovers, and the difficulty of correctly estimating the optimal amount of support to provide.

Vocabulary

export processing zone (EPZ)

external economies of scale

externality

industrial policy

interindustry trade

internal economies of scale

intraindustry trade

maquiladora

market failure

monopolistic competition

New Trade Theory

oligopoly

private returns

product differentiation

rent seeking

social returns

Subsidies and Countervailing Measures (SCM)

Trade-Related Investment Measures (TRIMs)

Trade-Related Aspects of Intellectual Property Rights (TRIPS)

Study Questions

All problems are assignable in MyEconLab

5.1 What is intraindustry trade, how is it measured, and how does it differ from interindustry trade? Are the gains from trade similar?

5.2 Comparing U.S. trade with Germany and Brazil, is trade with Germany more likely to be based on comparative advantage or economies of scale? Why?

5.3 What are the differences between external and internal economies of scale with respect to the size of firms, market structure, and gains from trade?

5.4 What are three key incentives for firms in a particular industry to cluster together in a geographical region?

5.5 How might trade hurt a country if it imports goods that are produced under conditions of external economies of scale?

5.6 When the United States signed a free-trade agreement with Canada (1989), no one thought twice about it. When the agreement with Mexico was signed (1994), there was significant opposition. Use the concepts of interindustry and intraindustry trade to explain the differences in opposition to the two trade agreements.

5.7 What are the theoretical justifications for targeting the development of specific industries?

5.8 What are some common problems in implementing industrial policies?

5.9 Figure 5.3 illustrates the case of an industry that generates external social benefits with its production. Draw a supply and demand graph for an industry that creates external costs with its production. Compare and contrast the market-determined price and output level with the socially optimal price and output levels.

CHAPTER 6

The Theory of Tariffs and Quotas

Learning Objectives

After studying this chapter, students will be able to:

6.1 Use supply and demand analysis to explain and illustrate consumer and producer surplus.

6.2 Graphically demonstrate the effects of tariffs and quotas on prices, output, and consumption for small and large countries.

6.3 Differentiate and explain the resource allocation and income distribution effects of tariffs and quotas.

6.4 Use tariff data on inputs and outputs to compare effective and nominal rates of protection.

6.5 Compare and contrast quotas and tariffs.

INTRODUCTION: TARIFFS AND QUOTAS

LO 6.1 **Use supply and demand analysis to explain and illustrate consumer and producer surplus.**

Chapters 6 and 7 are an introduction to the theory and policy of tariffs and quotas. In the economics literature, this analysis is called commercial policy. Chapter 6 is an introduction to tariff theory and Chapter 7 focuses on an empirical estimate of the direct costs of protectionism and the arguments used by proponents of restricted trade. The inefficiency and expense of tariffs and quotas as a means to protect industries and jobs will be apparent after measuring their direct costs.

Analysis of a Tariff

Barriers to trade come in all shapes and sizes. Some are obvious or **transparent**, whereas others are hidden or **nontransparent**. Quotas directly limit the quantity of imports, while tariffs indirectly limit imports by taxing them. Tariffs and quotas cause consumers to switch to relatively cheaper domestic goods or to drop out of the market altogether. They also encourage domestic producers to increase their output because demand switches from foreign to domestic goods.

In the analysis that follows we will look only at the effects of tariffs and quotas on the industry in which they are imposed. For example, the economy-wide effect of a tariff in, say, the steel industry will not be analyzed. In the language of economics, the analysis in Chapter 6 is known as *partial equilibrium analysis* because it considers the effects of tariffs and quotas on only a part of the economy—the market in which the trade barrier is erected. Before we turn to tariff analysis, however, we must introduce two important concepts: consumer and producer surplus.

Consumer and Producer Surplus

What is the maximum price you would be willing to pay for a gallon of milk? The answer is likely to be different for each consumer, depending on income, how much he or she likes milk, whether he or she has kids who need it, whether he or she can tolerate lactose or not, and a number of other factors, many of which are subjective. The subjective value that consumers place on milk is contained in the market demand curve for milk, which describes the total quantity of a good that consumers are willing and able to buy at each and every price. As the market price falls, a greater quantity is purchased because more consumers will feel that the lower price is equal to or below the value they place on the milk.

Suppose, for example, that you are willing to pay $3.50 for a gallon of milk, but the price is only $3.20. In essence, each gallon of milk provides $0.30 of value that is "free" in the sense that it is over and above what you must pay. This excess value, called **consumer surplus**, is the value received by consumers that is in excess of the price they pay. It occurs because everyone values each good differently, yet for most goods there is only one price. Consumer surplus can be measured if the demand curve is known. Since the demand curve is a summary of the value that each consumer places on a particular good, the area between the demand curve and the price line is a measurement of consumer surplus.

Figure 6.1 shows hypothetical market demand and supply curves for milk. At the market equilibrium price of $3.20 per gallon, 10,000 gallons will be supplied and demanded. Many people value milk at a higher price, however, and the value they receive in consuming milk is greater than $3.20. In Figure 6.1, consumer surplus is the area below the demand curve and above the price line of $3.20. The size or value of consumer surplus is the area of the triangle given by the formula $(\frac{1}{2}) \times$ (height) $\times$ (width), or $(\frac{1}{2}) \times$ (1.30) $\times$ (10,000), which is equal to $6,500. This equals the difference between the subjective value of the milk consumed and the total amount that consumers spent for it.

Consumer surplus is a real savings to consumers. If firms had a way to determine the maximum price that each consumer was willing to pay, then theoretically they could charge every individual a different price and thus reduce consumer surplus to zero. Luckily for those of us not in the milk business, firms usually cannot get this information without going through a long and costly interview procedure. As a result, it is usually impractical (and in some cases, illegal) for firms to charge different customers different prices. Nevertheless, some firms such as car dealers manage to charge different prices for the same goods. The easiest strategy for most

FIGURE 6.1   Consumer and Producer Surplus

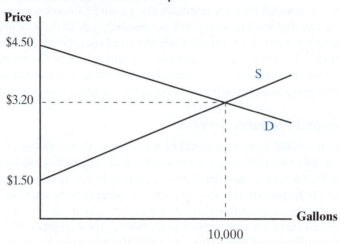

Consumer surplus is the area below the demand curve and above the price line.
Producer surplus is the area above the supply curve and below the price line.

firms is simply to charge everyone the same price, so consumer surplus is a real savings for most consumers in most markets.

On the production side, the analogous concept is called **producer surplus**. In our hypothetical milk example, if you owned a dairy farm and were willing and able to produce milk at $3.00 per gallon, you would receive producer surplus of $0.20 per gallon if you sold milk at $3.20. Recall that the supply curve for a market is the sum of supply curves for the firms in the market and that it reflects the minimum price firms will accept to produce a given amount. In Figure 6.1, some firms are willing to produce at $2.00 per gallon, and at every price above $1.50 at least some firms will have output to sell. Every firm that is willing to sell for less than the equilibrium price of $3.20 earns revenue that is above the minimum it needs. This excess or surplus revenue is a firm's producer surplus.

As in the case of consumer surplus, we can measure producer surplus. Measurement in this case depends on knowing the parameters of the supply curve (where it crosses the price axis and its slope) because producer surplus is the area above the supply curve and below the price line. In our example, it is equal in value to the triangle given by the formula $(^1/_2) \times (\$1.70) \times (10{,}000)$, which equals $8,500. This is the revenue received by producers that is in excess of the minimum amount of revenue that would be required to get them to produce 10,000 gallons of milk.

Prices, Output, and Consumption

We will use the concepts of producer and consumer surplus when we discuss the income distribution effects of tariffs and quotas. Before we analyze those effects, however, we must begin with a description of the effects of tariffs on prices, domestic output, and domestic consumption.

Figure 6.2 shows the domestic or national supply and demand for an imported good. We are assuming that there is one price for the good, which we will call the world price, or P_w, and that foreign producers are willing to supply us with all of the units of the good that we want at that price. This is equivalent to assuming that foreign supply is perfectly elastic, or that the United States does not consume a large enough quantity to affect the price. We will drop this assumption when we discuss the case of a large country. Note that the world price is below the domestic equilibrium price. This means that domestic producers are not able to satisfy all domestic demand at the market price of P_w and that consumers depend on foreign producers for some of their consumption. Specifically, at price P_w, consumers demand Q_2, but domestic producers supply only Q_1. The difference, $Q_2 - Q_1$, or line segment Q_1Q_2, is made up by imports.

Now suppose that the government imposes a tariff of amount "t." Importers will still be able to buy the good from foreign producers for amount P_w, but they will have to pay the import tax of "t," which they tack onto the price to domestic consumers. In other words, the price to consumers rises to $P_w + t = P_t$, as shown in Figure 6.3. The price increase in the domestic market has effects on domestic consumption, domestic production, and imports. First, the price increase squeezes some people out of the market, and domestic consumption falls from Q_2 to Q_2^*. Next, on the production side, the higher price encourages domestic production to increase from Q_1 to Q_1^*. The increase in domestic production occurs because domestic firms are able to charge a slightly higher price ($P_w + t$) to cover their increasing costs while remaining competitive with foreign firms. Finally, imports

FIGURE 6.2   Domestic Supply and Demand for an Imported Good

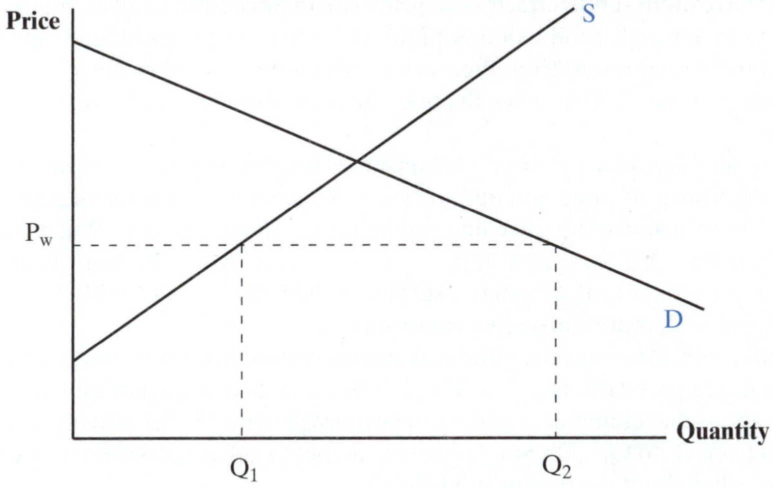

The difference between domestic demand and domestic supply, $Q_2 - Q_1$, is the quantity of imports at price P_w.

FIGURE 6.3   The Effects of a Tariff

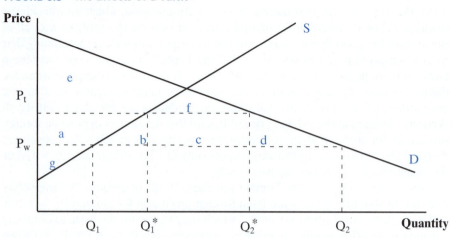

Tariffs cause an increase in domestic prices and domestic production, and a fall in domestic consumption. They increase producer surplus and government revenue, but decrease consumer surplus.

decrease from Q_1Q_2 to $Q_1^*Q_2^*$. To summarize, tariffs cause the domestic price to rise by the amount of the tariff, domestic consumption falls, domestic production rises, and imports fall.

Resource Allocation and Income Distribution

Tariffs have more subtle effects than just a rise in prices and a fall in imports. The increase in domestic production requires additional resources of land, labor, and capital to be reallocated from their prior uses into the industry receiving protection under the tariff. Also, when the price changes, consumer and producer surplus do too.

First, let's consider the effect on consumer surplus. Figure 6.3 shows both the pre- and post-tariff price and output levels. Remember that consumer surplus is the entire area above the price line and below the demand curve. When consumers pay price P_w, it is areas a + b + c + d + e + f. After the tariff is imposed and the price rises to P_t, consumer surplus shrinks to e + f. The difference, area a + b + c + d, represents a loss to consumers.

Unlike consumer surplus, producer surplus grows. Pre-tariff producer surplus is area g, and post-tariff is g + a. The difference, area a, is the additional revenue that is above the minimum necessary to encourage domestic firms to increase their output from Q_1 to Q_1^*. On net, producers are better off, and consumers are worse off, but what about the nation as a whole?

If we consider the whole loss to consumers, areas a + b + c + d, we see that it can be subdivided into several different areas. Part of the loss, area a, is a transfer from consumer surplus to producer surplus. Although the loss makes consumers worse off, it makes producers better off by the same amount. Therefore, the nation as a whole is neither better nor worse off unless it can be established that giving the resources to producers somehow benefits or harms national welfare. This part of the lost consumer surplus is an income distribution effect of the tariff, since it rearranges national income by transferring resources from one group (consumers) to another group (producers).

Another income distribution effect of the tariff is represented by area c. Note that the height of this area is equal to the tariff, and the width is the amount of imports after the tariff is imposed. Therefore, this part of lost consumer surplus is equal to (tariff) × (imports), which is the amount of revenue collected by the government when it enacts the tariff. In this case, the income distribution effect is a transfer from consumers to the government. Again, it is assumed that there is no net effect on national welfare since the loss by consumers is exactly matched by the gain of government. As long as this transfer does not change national welfare, there is no net effect.

The two remaining areas of lost consumer surplus are b and d. Both represent net national losses, and both involve a misallocation of resources. Consider area d first. Along the demand curve between Q_2^* and Q_2, there are consumers that value the good above the cost of purchasing it at the world price. As a result of the tariff, however, they have been squeezed out of the market and are not willing or able to pay price P_t. The fact that consumers value the good above the cost of obtaining it in the world market but cannot purchase it is a net loss to the nation. Economists refer to the destruction of value that is not compensated by a gain somewhere else as a **deadweight loss**. Area d is this type of loss.

The final area to consider is b. Along the domestic supply curve between Q_1 and Q_1^*, output is increased at existing plants. Given that the supply curve slopes upward, firms can only increase their output if the price is allowed to rise. In other words, in order to obtain the additional output, domestic producers must be able to charge a higher price that will cover their rising costs for each additional unit. At the pre-tariff price of P_w, the total cost of imports $Q_1 Q_1^*$ would have been the price times the quantity, or $(P_w) \times (Q_1 Q_1^*)$. The cost of producing the same goods at home is equal to the cost of the imports plus area b. In other words, the triangle b is the additional cost to the nation when it tries to make the extra output $Q_1 Q_1^*$ at home instead of buying it in the world market at price P_w. Area b is a resource misallocation and a net loss to the nation because the same goods $(Q_1 Q_1^*)$ could have been acquired without giving up this amount. Area b is another deadweight loss, sometimes referred to as an **efficiency loss** because it occurs on the production side.

We can summarize the net effect of the tariff on the nation's welfare by subtracting the gains of producers and government from the losses of consumers: $(a + b + c + d - a - c) = b + d$. The two triangular areas are losses for which there are no compensating gains; therefore, they represent real losses to the nation as a whole. Table 6.1 summarizes the effects of tariffs that we have noted.

TABLE 6.1   Economic Effects of the Tariff in Figure 6.3

Variable	Free Trade	Post-Tariff
Price to consumers	P_w	P_t
Domestic consumption	Q_2	Q_2*
Domestic production	Q_1	Q_1*
Imports	Q_1Q_2	Q_1*Q_2*
Consumer surplus	$a + b + c + d + e + f$	$e + f$
Producer surplus	g	$g + a$
Government revenue	0	c
Deadweight consumption loss	0	d
Deadweight production (efficiency) loss	0	b

Tariffs reallocate income from consumers to producers and government. They also create deadweight losses, one on the consumption side and one on the production side.

CASE STUDY

A Comparison of Tariff Rates

The Doha Development Agenda of the World Trade Organization (WTO) is focused on the trade problems of developing countries. One impetus for the start of the Doha negotiations, and a factor behind the emphasis on economic development issues, is the complaint by many developing countries that they did not derive sufficient benefits from the Uruguay Round of trade negotiations that concluded in 1993. At issue for many developing countries are the levels of tariffs and other industrial country barriers that block access to agriculture, clothing, and textile markets. These product lines tend to be areas where developing countries have comparative advantage, particularly in cases where climate is a factor or where production uses abundant labor but requires little capital.

For their part, many industrial countries, the World Bank, and the WTO have argued that a major part of the problem faced by developing countries is the relatively high level of protection among developing countries themselves. High tariffs limit these countries' ability to sell into each other's markets—and consequently their ability to follow their comparative advantage.

Figure 6.4 shows trends and levels of tariff rates in three groups of countries that are arranged according to their income levels. In 2010 U.S. dollars, low-income countries have per capita income levels below $1,005, middle income ranges from $1,005 to $12,275, and high income is anything above the middle group.

Although the numbers in Figure 6.4 should be treated with caution since the year-to-year data in each group varies in the number of countries included, two patterns are visible in Figure 6.4 and are widely accepted as qualitatively accurate. First, the higher a country's income, the lower its tariffs are likely to be. There are exceptions, of course, and one can point to low- and middle-income countries with low tariffs (Albania and El Salvador) and high-income countries with relatively high tariffs (Bermuda and Bahrain), but in general, low income implies relatively higher tariffs, and high income implies the opposite. Second, tariffs have come down over time. In each of the three groups mentioned, the average tariff fell by about 50 percent between 1986 and 2003.

Why then, if trade is beneficial for growth, do low-income countries tend to have higher tariff rates? Although the complete answer varies by country circumstances, one of the most important reasons is that tariffs are a relatively easy tax to administer and often form an important part of government revenue. Taxes on income, sales, and property require more complex accounting systems and formal markets through which a large share of economic activity passes. In countries with large informal markets, where sales of goods and services are not recorded, it is difficult to apply many kinds of taxes. In addition, taxes on income and property run into powerful interest groups that have the power to prevent the creation or payment of taxes. Consequently, tariff revenue is an important source of operating revenue for governments in many developing countries.

FIGURE 6.4   Average Tariff Rates, 1997–2012

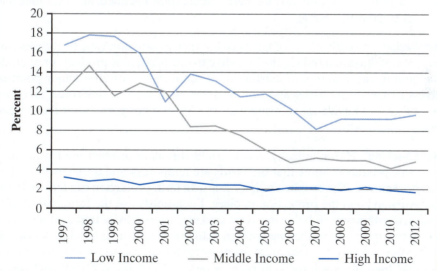

Tariff rates tend to be higher in countries with lower incomes, and nearly all countries have seen a decline in their rates over a long period of time.

Source: Data from World Bank, World Development Indicators, © James Gerber.

Other Potential Costs

These effects of tariffs are the ones that are most predictable and quantifiable. In Chapter 7 there are some actual estimates of the production and income distribution effects of tariffs and quotas for a number of industries in the United States, Europe, and Japan. These are not the only effects of tariffs, however—three others should be noted: the effects if trading partners retaliate, the impact of protection on domestic innovation and productivity, and the incentive for firms to engage in rent-seeking behavior. Each of these effects broadens our focus to a consideration of more than the directly affected industry.

Retaliation   Retaliation can add to the net loss of a tariff by hurting the export markets of other industries. For example, in 1995, the United States imposed a tariff on European (mainly Italian) pasta because of some trade practices that the United States felt discriminated against its pasta manufacturers. In return, the European Community retaliated by imposing tariffs on U.S. manufacturers of vegetable oils—corn, soybean, safflower, and other cooking oils. The cost of the U.S.-imposed tariff not only affected U.S. consumers of Italian pasta, who were forced to pay higher prices, but also affected workers and owners of capital in the U.S. vegetable oil industry. In essence, in addition to the deadweight losses brought on by the tariff, the vegetable oil industry lost export markets. A further problem is that retaliation can quickly escalate. For example, in the 1930s, many depressed nations reduced imports through tariffs. The result was that they gained jobs in industries that competed with imports but lost jobs in industries that produced exports. In the end, no jobs were gained, trade declined, and everyone had a lower standard of living.

Innovation   A costly effect of tariffs is that they isolate domestic firms from foreign competition and reduce the incentive to introduce new products or upgrade the quality and features of existing ones. Imports are often a major point of access to new technologies and new products. As Chapter 1 described, there are several types of evidence showing that open economies grow faster than closed ones.

Rent Seeking   Hypothetically, tariffs could stimulate product improvement if domestic producers know that the tariffs are temporary and if they believe they will be removed. The problem is that firms with tariff protection can hire lobbyists and work to keep the protection in place. Economists use the term *rent seeking* to describe this type of behavior. Rent seeking is any activity that uses resources to try to capture more income without actually producing a good or service. If it is easier to lobby a government for protection than it is to become more competitive, then firms will use rent seeking tactics. If, on the contrary, lobbying is not likely to succeed in gaining protection, then firms are less likely to engage in that particular form of rent seeking. For this reason, political systems that do not easily provide protective tariffs are much more likely to avoid one source of wasted resources.

The Large Country Case

Economists distinguish between large and small countries when it comes to tariff analysis. As a practical matter there may not be much difference between the two, but in theory it is possible for large countries to actually improve their national welfare with a tariff as long as their trading partners do not retaliate. In economic terms, a large country is one that imports enough of a particular product so that if it imposes a tariff, the exporting country will reduce its price in order to keep some of the market it might otherwise lose.

An example of the **large country case** tariff is shown in Figure 6.5. Suppose that the United States, a large country, imposes a tariff of size t on its imports of oil. The fall in U.S. demand brought on by the tariff causes P_w, the world price, to fall to P_w^*, offsetting some or all of the deadweight loss from the tariff.

Looking more closely at Figure 6.5, we can compare the large and small country cases. The situation before the tariff is the same as the one shown in Figure 6.3. The main difference between the two cases stems from the fact that foreign suppliers cut the price to P_w^* after the tariff is levied. Consequently, less additional domestic production occurs, and fewer consumers are squeezed out of the market. In other words, areas b and d in Figure 6.5 are smaller than they would be in the small country case where there is no price drop. A smaller deadweight loss is not the only effect, however. In Figure 6.5, area g represents tariff revenue, which together with area c is the total tariff revenue collected. Compared to the pre-tariff situation, however, area g is a net gain to the importing nation. Pre-tariff, area g was part of the money paid for imports. After the tariff, and due to the price decline, it is part of the revenue collected by the government and, hence, stays within the nation.

FIGURE 6.5   Tariffs in the Large Country Case

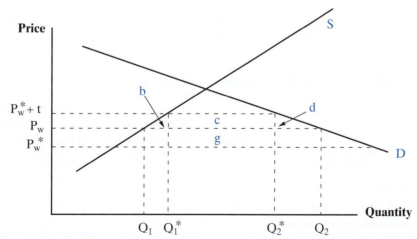

A tariff in a large country reduces demand so much that foreign producers cut their prices.

As long as g > b + d, a large country can improve its welfare by imposing a tariff. This outcome, however, assumes that there is no retaliation, rent seeking, or harmful effects on innovation.

Effective Versus Nominal Rates of Protection

One of the ironies of tariff protection is that often it is not what it seems. In fact, the amount of protection given to any one product depends not only on the tariff rate but also on whether there are tariffs on the inputs used to produce it. Suppose, for example, that the United States decided to impose a tariff on imports of laptop computers. If American-made laptops have foreign parts in them, then the amount of protection they receive from a U.S. tariff depends also on whether there are tariffs on their imported inputs. It is conceivable, in other words, that the protection given by a tariff on laptops could be completely undone by forcing laptop manufacturers to pay tariffs on their imported inputs.

Economists distinguish between the **effective rate of protection** and the **nominal rate of protection**. The nominal rate is what we have discussed so far in this chapter—the rate that is levied on a given product. The effective rate of protection takes into account the nominal rate and any tariffs on intermediate inputs. Consequently, it gives a clearer picture of the overall amount of protection that any given product receives. The effective rate of protection is related to the concept of value added. Value added is the price of a good minus the costs of the intermediate goods used to produce it. Value added measures the contributions of capital and labor at a given stage of production. The effective rate of protection is defined as follows:

$$(VA^* - VA)/VA$$

where VA is the amount of domestic value added under free trade, and VA* is the amount of domestic value added after taking into account all tariffs, both on final goods and intermediate inputs.

Consider the example shown in Table 6.2. Suppose that laptop computers sell for $1,000, and foreign producers are willing to sell to the United States all it wants at that

TABLE 6.2   Nominal and Effective Rates of Protection

Variable	No Tariff	A 20% Tariff on the Final Product	A 20% Tariff Plus a 50% Tariff on Imported Inputs
Price of a laptop computer	$1,000	$1,200	$1,200
Value of foreign inputs	$600	$600	$900
Domestic value added	$400	$600	$300
Effective rate of protection	0	50%	−25%

Effective rates of protection are higher than nominal rates if intermediate inputs are imported tariff free. If intermediate inputs are subject to tariffs, it reduces the effective rate of protection and can even turn it negative.

price. In order to make a laptop, American manufacturers must import $600 worth of parts, so that a domestic laptop actually has $400 of value added in the United States ($1,000 − $600 = $400). If the United States imposes a 20 percent tariff, then the price rises to $1,200. Value added in the United States is now $600 ($1,200 − $600), and the effective rate of protection is 50 percent (($600 − $400)/$400). That is, a 20 percent tariff provides 50 percent protection! This happens because a large share of the value of the final product is produced elsewhere, so all of the domestic protection falls on the share produced in the United States.

Now consider what happens if the United States decides also to protect domestic component manufacturers and levies a large tariff on intermediate inputs. If the tariff on foreign parts is 50 percent, then the cost of intermediate inputs rises from $600 to $900. With a 20 percent tariff on the value of the final product, the price of imports stays at $1,200, which is the price American laptop makers must meet. Value added with the tariff on intermediate inputs is $300 ($1,200 − $900), and the effective rate of protection is now −25 percent (($300 − $400)/$400). That is, even with a 20 percent tariff on foreign laptops, American laptop makers receive *negative* protection. The tariff on the final product is more than offset by the tariffs on the intermediate products, so that the overall situation leaves producers more exposed to foreign competition than if there were no tariffs levied at all.

Negative rates of effective protection are not uncommon. Part of the reason stems from the fact that tariffs are enacted in a piecemeal fashion over long periods and are not constructed in a planned and coherent way. Pressures from domestic lobbyists, considerations of strategic interests, and numerous other forces go into the shaping of national tariff systems. Consequently, it is not surprising to find contradictory tariff policies where newer tariffs undo the effects of older ones.

This discussion should add a note of caution to attempts to determine exactly which industries are protected. Clearly, the notion of effective rates of protection is more relevant than nominal rates. With tariff rates, what you see may not always be what you get.

CASE STUDY

The Uruguay and Doha Rounds

The Uruguay Round concluded in 1993 after seven years of negotiations. It took three years longer than planned, and included one complete breakdown in the talks. The agreement was ratified by most of its 123 participating countries in 1994, and implemented in 1995.

Table 6.3 summarizes the four main outcomes of the negotiations. Trade barriers were reduced through several mechanisms, including tariff reductions, clarification of the rules on subsidies, a number of new areas of agreement, and institutional reforms within the framework of the existing General Agreement on Tariffs and Trade (GATT). Most notably, the Uruguay Round created the

(continued)

TABLE 6.3   The Uruguay Round

Category	Results
Tariffs	■ Most industrial product tariffs cut by 40 percent ■ Conversion of some agricultural quotas to tariffs
Subsidies	■ Subsidies defined ■ Classifies prohibited and actionable subsidies
New agreements	■ Agreement on Textiles and Clothing (ATC) ■ Trade-Related Aspects of Intellectual Property Rights (TRIPS) ■ Trade-Related Investment Measures (TRIMs) ■ General Agreement on Trade in Services (GATS)
Institutional	■ Creates the World Trade Organization (WTO) ■ Refines the dispute settlement process ■ Implements periodic trade policy reviews

The Uruguay Round included far more than tariff cuts.

WTO as a body to oversee the implementation and further refinement of the various agreements.

One of the main effects on world trade patterns of the Uruguay Round was the negotiation of a separate Agreement on Textiles and Clothing (ATC). Until 1994, textiles and clothing had a separate international agreement, called the *Multi-Fiber Arrangement,* which was a system of quotas and tariffs. Under the ATC, textiles and clothing were integrated into the WTO system, with a complete phase-out of all quotas.

Other notable accomplishments of the Uruguay Round include an extension of rules governing services trade, the General Agreement on Trade in Services (GATS); an agreement on intellectual property enforcement, called Trade-Related Aspects of Intellectual Property Rights (TRIPS); and an agreement on investment, the Trade-Related Investment Measures (TRIMs)(see the Case Study in Chapter 5 for a discussion of the TRIPS and TRIMS agreements). The Uruguay Round also created the WTO to administer all of the agreements (ATC, GATS, TRIPS, TRIMs, GATT), and initiated a more efficient dispute settlement process. In addition, the WTO conducts periodic reviews of individual country trade policies, which it publishes online.

The Doha Round was launched in 2001 in Doha, Qatar. Although the goal was to reach an agreement by the end of 2005, the talks collapsed in July 2006. They were later restarted, collapsed again, and as of 2016, there is no further progress. Most countries have abandoned the effort to conclude the talks. Not surprisingly, the biggest areas of disagreement were trade barriers and subsidies in agriculture and market access for services. In addition, high income countries pushed middle income ones to further reduce their barriers to imports of manufactured goods.

Doha is the first set of trade talks to fail since the signing of the GATT agreement in 1947. Its failure has caused some observers to question the future relevance of the WTO, but as a dispute settlement body it is invaluable. In retrospect, it is not a surprise that it failed to achieve the original goals. Many quotas have been converted to tariff equivalents, and tariffs have fallen, more or less constantly since the signing of the GATT agreement in 1947. As a consequence, issues of deep integration and issue affecting sensitive production sectors such as agriculture have come to the forefront of negotiations. Many of these issues are too contentious for easy resolution, especially in the context of a negotiation by all 162 members. Countries continue to negotiate outside the WTO, but now the focus is often on investor protections, patent issues, and services, and the negotiations are bilateral or plurilateral, rather than multilateral through the WTO. These new issues reflect the fact of already low tariffs for many items, and the goal of multinational companies to protect their investments in production centers across the globe. There may not be another WTO negotiation to match the previous rounds, but there are continuing commitments and ongoing negotiations between groups of countries.

ANALYSIS OF QUOTAS

LO 6.2   **Graphically demonstrate the effects of tariffs and quotas on prices, output, and consumption for small and large countries.**

LO 6.3   **Differentiate and explain the resource allocation and income distribution effects of tariffs and quotas.**

LO 6.4   **Use tariff data on inputs and outputs to compare effective and nominal rates of protection.**

LO 6.5   **Compare and contrast quotas and tariffs.**

The economic analysis of quotas is nearly identical to that of tariffs. Quotas are quantitative restrictions that specify a limit on the quantity of imports rather than a tax. The net result is much the same: tariffs and quotas lead to a reduction in imports, a fall in total domestic consumption, and an increase in domestic production. The main difference between quotas and tariffs is that quotas that are not followed up with additional policy actions do not generate tariff revenue for the government. The lost tariff revenue can end up in the hands of foreign producers as they raise their prices to match demand to supply. Hence, the net loss from quotas can exceed that from tariffs.

In terms of Figure 6.3, consumers still lose area a + b + c + d, but the government does not collect area c as a tax. (We will examine what happens to area c, but try to reason it out for yourself first.)

Types of Quotas

The most transparent type of quota is an outright limitation on the quantity of imports. Limitations are sometimes specified in terms of the quantity of a product coming from a particular country, and at other times there is an overall limit set without regard to which country supplies the product. For example, in the apparel sector, until 2005, the United States set quotas for imports of each type of garment (men's suits, boys' shirts, socks, and so on). The quota for each good was further divided by country; so, for example, Hong Kong and Haiti had different limits on each type of apparel that they could export to the United States.

Another type of quota is an import licensing requirement. The United States uses this form infrequently, but many other nations have relied on these quotas for the bulk of their protection. For example, until 1989, they were the main form of protection in Mexico. As the name implies, import licensing requirements force importers to obtain government licenses for their imports. By regulating the number of licenses granted and the quantity permitted under each license, import licenses are essentially the same as quotas. They are less transparent than quotas because governments usually do not publish information on the total allowable quantity of imports, and foreign firms are left in the dark about the specific limits to their exports.

A third form of quota, and the one that has been common in U.S. commercial policy, is the **voluntary export restraint (VER)**, also known as the *voluntary restraint agreement* (VRA). Under a VER, the exporting country "voluntarily" agrees to limit its exports for some period. The agreement usually occurs after a series of negotiations in which the exporter may be threatened with much more severe restrictions if they do not agree to limit exports in a specific market. Given that there is usually more than a hint of coercion, it may be a misnomer to call these restrictions "voluntary."

VERs were popular forms of protection in the 1970s and 1980s, but new limits on their use were implemented under the Uruguay Round agreement. In 2005, however, both the United States and the European Union (EU) negotiated export restraints in textiles and apparel with China.

The Effect on the Profits of Foreign Producers

The main difference between tariffs and quotas is that there is no government revenue from quotas. In place of tariff revenue, there are greater profits for foreign producers, called **quota rents**.

In Figure 6.6, the world price is set at P_w, domestic production is Q_1, and imports are Q_1Q_2. Suppose that the government decides to set a quota on imports of quantity $Q_1Q_2^*$. At price P_w, demand exceeds supply, which is equal to Q_1 domestic plus $Q_1Q_2^*$ imports. Consequently, the price rises until supply equals demand when the gap between the domestic supply curve and the domestic demand curve

FIGURE 6.6   Analysis of a Quota: 1

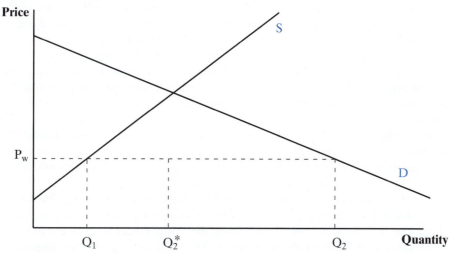

A quota restricts imports to line segment $Q_1Q_2^*$ and creates excess demand equal to $Q_2^*Q_2$.

is equal to $Q_1Q_2^*$. This is illustrated in Figure 6.7, where domestic supply is shown as having grown to Q_1^*, and the domestic price is P_q, which is above P_w. $Q_1^*Q_2^*$ is equal to $Q_1Q_2^*$ in Figure 6.6.

Figure 6.7 looks the same as Figure 6.3, which shows a tariff in a small country case, because they have nearly identical effects on production, consumption, and prices paid by consumers. Indeed, for any given quota there is some tariff that will accomplish the

FIGURE 6.7   Analysis of a Quota: 2

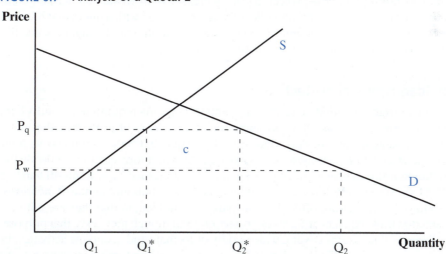

The quota generates extra revenue for foreign producers in area c.

identical import restriction. One difference stands out, however. In the tariff case, the government earned revenue from imports—area c in Figures 6.3 and 6.7. In the quota case, no revenue is earned unless the government auctions the quota. Instead, area c represents the extra profits of foreign producers due to the higher prices.

A second important difference between tariffs and quotas relates to their effect on producer surplus over time, as demand for the good increases. If a quota remains fixed, an increase in consumer demand also increases the price paid by consumers and the quantity of producer surplus garnered by domestic firms. In contrast, an increase in consumer demand for an item that has an import tariff increases the quantity of imports and leaves the price intact. This assumes that the country is relatively small and the increase in its demand does not alter the world (pre-tariff) price. Given this difference, it is not surprising that domestic firms prefer quotas over tariffs as a form of protection for their industry.

Two circumstances can mitigate or limit the ability of foreign suppliers to earn extra profits. First, if there is a large number of foreign suppliers, then competitive conditions may prevent them from raising their prices. Second, a clever government can extract the extra profits from foreign producers and domestic importers through the implementation of an auction for import licenses.

Suppose that the country imposing the quota decides to auction off the right to import. How much would a domestic importer be willing to pay? In Figures 6.6 and 6.7, foreign suppliers are willing to sell the amount of the quota ($Q_1Q_2^*$ in Figure 6.6, or $Q_1^*Q_2^*$ in Figure 6.7) at price P_w. A domestic importer, recognizing that he or she can sell the good at price P_q, should be willing to pay an amount equal to something slightly less than the difference P_q minus P_w. In other words, he or she pays P_w for the good that sells for P_q. If he or she pays anything less than $P_q - P_w$ for the right to sell in the market with the quota, he or she makes a profit. In equilibrium, an auction market should lead to bids for the right to sell that are more or less equal to the projected price increase. With an auction market, then, the government can potentially collect the same revenue with a quota that it would with a tariff. Of course, administrative costs of a quota may be higher, since the government must implement its auction market.

Hidden Forms of Protection

While outright quantitative restrictions, import licensing requirements, and VERs are all forms of quotas, there are numerous other forms of protection that function the same as quotas. Any kind of trade barrier that reduces imports without imposing a tax functions more or less like a quota. Therefore, economists divide the different forms of protection into two main categories: tariffs and **nontariff barriers (NTBs)**. Nontariff barriers can be subdivided into quotas and **nontariff measures**. Nontariff measures are often nontransparent, or hidden, in that they are not presented as trade barriers or forms of protection even though they serve that purpose.

Nontariff measures cover a wide variety of formats and economic activities. In many cases, it is difficult to decide if they are directly intended as trade-related measures, or if they exist for some other purpose, but have impacts on trade flows.

They include excessively complicated customs procedures, environmental and consumer health and safety precautions, technical standards, government procurement rules, limits imposed by state trading companies, and others. In general, nontariff measures include any regulatory or policy rule other than tariffs and quotas that limits imports. Often, it is difficult for nonspecialists to determine whether a nontariff measure is imposed in order to protect an industry, or out of some other concern. For example, the United States and the EU have a long-running disagreement over the EU's prohibition of imports of beef and pork from livestock that is fed growth hormones. The EU claims that this is to protect the health of its consumers, while the United States argues that there is no scientific evidence to support the ban. The WTO agrees with the United States, but the EU insists that the meat has long-run health effects. Does the EU continue to ban imports in order to protect its beef and pork producers, or is it simply exercising a reasonable level of caution?

While there is no consensus about the dollar value of economic losses due to nontariff measures, there is a consensus among economists that the world economy would be better off if they were reduced. Research indicates that benefits would accrue through the lowering of prices for many goods, increases in export and import volumes, increases in production levels, and overall economic welfare. In this respect, they are not much different from tariffs or quotas. They are generally much more difficult to eliminate, however, as they are embedded more deeply in national economic policies.

CASE STUDY

Intellectual Property Rights and Trade

Intellectual property is usually divided into copyrights and related rights for literary and artistic work, and industrial property rights for trademarks, patents, industrial designs, geographical indications, and the layout of integrated circuits. Books, music, movies, logos, pharmaceuticals, car parts, designer clothing, software, computer chips, and much, much more are all subject to intellectual property rights protection and, unfortunately, to counterfeiting and piracy. The rules for respecting **intellectual property rights** as they relate to trade were negotiated during the Uruguay Round (1986–1994), and culminated in the TRIPS agreement.

The growth of world trade over the last half of the twentieth century led to a greater awareness of the importance of intellectual property. Over time, more traded goods and services incorporated specialized knowledge and unique ideas. Pharmaceuticals, telecommunications equipment, and other high technology products are valuable because of the innovation and research they incorporate, while software, movies, music, and other artistic expressions are valued for their creativity. The protection given to creators and innovators varied greatly until standardization began with the signing of the TRIPS agreement.

(continued)

The lack of intellectual property protection is viewed as a nontariff measure since the failure or inability to protect intellectual property restricts trade flows. Exporters are reluctant to sell products into a market if they know that their ideas or brands will be stolen and copied by local producers. Hence, there were strong pressures by high-income countries to reach an agreement on enforcement of protections for intellectual property. Since the implementation of the Uruguay Round in 1995, there have been thirty-four intellectual property disputes brought to the WTO, most having to do with patents, and a large share of those related to pharmaceuticals.

It is probably impossible to prevent copyright infringements that happen through informal networks of families and friends. For example, friends copying each other's music or sharing software cannot be easily stopped when it is done outside a formal market. By contrast, the market for counterfeit and pirated goods in many countries is relatively visible. Car parts, electronics, pharmaceuticals, and other counterfeit and pirated goods pass through established market places where, in theory, they can be stopped. Many of these markets are controlled by international criminal syndicates and everyone would benefit from their suppression. Estimates of the size of counterfeited and pirated products sold in international markets was several hundred billion dollars in 2005, and there is no reason to believe it has not grown since then.

A key question for trade economists is whether the TRIPS agreement provides the right strategy for controlling these illegal markets. The fundamental economic rationale for the TRIPS agreement is that it protects innovation and gives a financial incentive to firms and individuals for their efforts. Some economists do not see the lengthening of patent rights and spending large sums on enforcement efforts as the best strategy. Critics have argued that it imposes significant costs on middle-income countries such as China, Mexico, and others because they must devote scarce resources to the enforcement of rules that protect businesses in high-income countries. Empirically, it is not well established that the benefits of innovation outweigh the costs associated with limiting access for those low- and middle-income countries that cannot pay.

Pharmaceuticals are a case in point. Access to drugs that combat HIV and AIDS is critical. If patent enforcement under the TRIPS agreement prevents the production of inexpensive copies, then it is harmful to world prosperity. Although a number of exceptions were written into the agreement to allow access to life-saving medicines and other critical technologies, it is difficult for many developing countries to take advantage of the exceptions because they lack the technical know-how to make generic versions of expensive and sophisticated drugs. In addition, the United States and other governments put pressure on developing countries' governments to respect patent rights, even in cases where the rules permit a developing country to break a patent. In the end, many countries simply lack the resources to fully implement the TRIPS agreement. Nevertheless, it remains an area of active interest, and has become a key focus of U.S. trade policy.

Summary

- Tariffs increase domestic production and employment at the cost of greater inefficiency and higher prices. Production and distribution effects are measured by estimating the changes in producer surplus and consumer surplus.

- In addition to short-run welfare and efficiency effects, tariffs have long-run costs of increased rent seeking, slower innovation, and the loss of export markets through the retaliation of trading partners.

- In theory, a large country can improve its welfare with tariffs. In general, welfare-improving tariffs tend to be small, and they improve welfare only if there is no retaliation by supplying nations and no external costs such as increased rent seeking.

- Economists distinguish between nominal and effective rates of protection. The effective rate is the difference in domestic value added with and without tariffs, expressed in percentage terms.

- Quotas have similar effects as tariffs, although the overall national losses are greater due to the transfer of quota rents to foreign producers. Auction markets, in which governments auction the right to import an item under a quota, can reduce the amount of quota rents and, in the limit, provide the same revenue as an equivalent tariff.

- Administratively, quotas take many forms. They can be well-specified quantitative restrictions on imports, negotiated limits on a trading partner's exports, or requirements to obtain a license to import.

- Nontariff measures include a wide variety of regulations and policies that effectively reduce the volume of international trade. They often act as hidden forms of protection and are commonly embedded deeply in a country's rules and institutions. Together with quotas, they make up nontariff barriers to trade.

Vocabulary

consumer surplus	nontariff barrier (NTB)
deadweight loss	nontariff measure
effective rate of protection	nontransparent
efficiency loss	producer surplus
intellectual property rights	quota rents
large country case	transparent
nominal rate of protection	voluntary export restraint (VER)

Study Questions

All problems are assignable in My EconLab

6.1 Graph the supply and demand of a good that is produced domestically and imported. Assume that the country is not large enough to affect the world price. Illustrate the effects that a tariff on imports has. Discuss the following:

    a.   Income distribution effects

    b.   Resource allocation effects

    c.   Domestic production and consumption effects

    d.   Government revenue effects

    e.   Price of the good effects

6.2 Suppose that the world price for a good is 40 and the domestic demand-and-supply curves are given by the following equations:

Demand: $P = 80 - 2Q$

Supply: $P = 5 + 3Q$

    a.   How much is consumed?

    b.   How much is produced at home?

    c.   What are the values of consumer and producer surplus?

    d.   If a tariff of 10 percent is imposed, by how much do consumption and domestic production change?

    e.   What is the change in consumer and producer surplus?

    f.   How much revenue does the government earn from the tariff?

    g.   What is the net national cost of the tariff?

6.3 Under what conditions may a tariff actually make a country better off?

6.4 In addition to the production and consumption side deadweight losses, what are some of the other potential costs of tariffs?

6.5 The Uruguay Round of the GATT began a process of phasing out the use of voluntary export restraints. Why did they come into widespread use in the 1980s? For example, given that VERs are a form of quotas, and that they create quota rents and a larger reduction in national welfare than tariffs, why did nations use them instead of tariffs?

6.6 The GATT strongly favors tariffs as a protective measure over quotas or other nontariff measures. It encourages new members to convert quotas to their tariff equivalents. One of the main reasons that tariffs are preferred is because they are more transparent, particularly by comparison to nontariff measures. Explain the idea of transparency, and how nontariff measures may be nontransparent.

6.7 Suppose that in the United States bikes are built from a combination of domestic and foreign parts.

    a. If a bike sells for $500 but requires $300 of imported parts, what is the domestic value added?

    b. If a 20 percent tariff is levied on bikes of the same quality and with the same features, how do the price and the domestic value added change? (Assume that the United States cannot cause the world price to change.)

    c. What is the effective rate of protection?

    d. If, in addition to the 20 percent tariff on the final good, a 20 percent tariff on imported parts is levied, what is the effective rate of protection for U.S. bike manufacturers?

CHAPTER 7

Commercial Policy

Learning Objectives

After studying this chapter, students will be able to:

7.1 Describe the differences in tariffs across economic sectors and over time.

7.2 Cite at least three reasons why economists favor trade openings.

7.3 Explain why costs to consumers of a tariff or quota are greater than the net welfare costs to a nation.

7.4 Analyze the economic validity of common justifications for protectionism.

7.5 Define each form of legal protection granted by the U.S. government.

INTRODUCTION: COMMERCIAL POLICY, TARIFFS, AND ARGUMENTS FOR PROTECTION

Tariffs around the world have come down significantly in the last few decades, leading to rapid increases in the volume of world trade. Countries have converted many of their quotas into tariff-equivalents, and new agreements on subsidies, foreign investment, and intellectual property have been signed. In 2001, the World Trade Organization (WTO) launched the Doha Round of negotiations to bring agriculture and services into the system of trade agreements and to facilitate trade through infrastructure improvements and new market access agreements. More than sixty years after the signing of the General Agreement on Tariffs and Trade (GATT) and eight completed rounds of trade negotiations, tariffs are low for most of the nonagricultural goods that make up the largest share of international trade. By nearly any standard, the system of trade rounds under the auspices of the GATT and the WTO has been successful at creating trade rules and reducing trade barriers.

In this chapter, we look at the data on tariff levels and consider the most frequently given arguments for protection. Given that tariffs are relatively low and that nontariff barriers have been significantly reduced in the world's major trading nations, diminishing returns to trade negotiations implies that the remaining gains from trade due to further tariff reductions are also relatively small in terms of world gross domestic product (GDP). Chapter 7 looks at these numbers and asks why economists still favor further reductions in trade barriers if the gains are not great. There are several reasons to pursue further market openings, not the least of which is that the direct gains from trade are not the only way to judge the cost of protectionist policies. Tariffs and other barriers are usually implemented for a specific purpose, such as to protect jobs or to protect an industry, and if we want to know the opportunity costs of tariffs we need to consider the reasons given for their use. This naturally leads to a question as to whether or not there are better policies for achieving the same outcome. This chapter offers a deeper look into the reasons given for protection and sets forth criteria showing that trade barriers are not usually an optimal policy tool for achieving those goals.

TARIFF RATES IN THE WORLD'S MAJOR TRADERS

LO 7.1   **Describe the differences in tariffs across economic sectors and over time.**

Figure 6.4 in the previous chapter shows that tariff rates have declined significantly since the mid-1980s. If we extended the data back further, we would see that the decline has been underway since the end of World War II and especially since the signing of the GATT in 1947. Table 7.1 illustrates the current situation for three major trading countries and one region. The European Union (EU) is treated as a single country for purposes of comparing trade and trade policies since it negotiates and acts as a single entity in the WTO and in its trade relations with individual nations. The countries and region in Table 7.1 have about 66 percent of world GDP and account for 39 percent and 41 percent of world merchandise exports and imports, respectively.

Table 7.1 shows several patterns. First, tariffs are higher in agriculture than in other sectors of the economy. This is well known and applies to most but not all countries. Exceptions to this pattern are usually countries such as Argentina and Australia, which have robust, highly productive agricultural sectors and a comparative advantage in agricultural products. In general, however, most countries impose more barriers on agricultural trade. Reasons usually include considerations of food security (to ensure a local capacity for food production), a desire to transfer income to farmers as a policy to support the countryside and rural citizens, and the ability of agricultural interests to shape national policies.

A second pattern in Table 7.1 is that there is overlap between countries in the sectors they protect most rigorously. Within agriculture, for example, dairy, sugar and confectionary, and beverages and tobacco receive the strongest levels of protection, while the nonagricultural sector is most protective of clothing, textiles, and leather goods and footwear. These tend to be labor-intensive sectors where high-income countries have lost comparative advantage.

TABLE 7.1   Applied Tariffs for Major World Traders

	Average Applied Tariffs	
	Agriculture	Nonagricultural
EU	12.2	4.2
China	15.2	8.6
Japan	14.3	2.5
United States	5.1	3.2

	Products with Highest Average Applied Tariffs*	
	Agriculture	Nonagricultural
EU	■ Dairy products (42.1) ■ Sugars and confectionary (25.2)	■ Clothing (11.4) ■ Textiles (6.5)
China	■ Sugars and confectionary (28.7) ■ Beverages and tobacco (22.8)	■ Clothing (16.0) ■ Leather goods and footwear (12.8)
Japan	■ Dairy products (76.3) ■ Cereals and preparations (34.7)	■ Leather goods and footwear (9.4) ■ Clothing (9.0)
United States	■ Beverages and tobacco (18.6) ■ Dairy products (17.2)	■ Clothing (12.0) ■ Textiles (7.9)

Tariffs (and nontariff barriers) are higher for agricultural products than nonagricultural. A handful of sectors account for the highest barriers.

Source: World Trade Organization, *Tariff Profiles*, 2015

A third pattern in Table 7.1 is that overall levels of tariff rates (top part of the table) are relatively low, particularly for nonagricultural goods and especially in high-income countries. If tariff cuts have diminishing marginal returns, so that each successive round of cuts leads to a smaller gain than the cuts before, it is reasonable to guess that future cuts are not likely to have a large impact on world trade and income. Large is relative, but thinking back to the case study of Japan in Chapter 3, two economists estimated that Japan's GDP rose as much as 8 or 9 percent when it moved from completely closed to nearly free trade in the 1860s. By comparison, the value of the now moribund Doha Round of trade negotiations were estimated to in the range of 0.1 percent to 0.5 percent of world GDP, with most estimates falling about mid-range at 0.3 percent. A potential gain of 0.5 percent is not trivial when it comes to world GDP, but it is far different from the gains that accrue when countries go from relatively closed to open.

THE COSTS OF PROTECTIONISM

LO 7.2 **Cite at least three reasons why economists favor trade openings.**

LO 7.3 **Explain why costs to consumers of a tariff or quota are greater than the net welfare costs to a nation.**

There are several reasons why further trade opening is beneficial even if the dollar values of the gains are not that high. Some economists argue that the failure of the Doha Round of negotiations undermines the legitimacy of the world trading system, with potentially severe consequences in the future. Recall that one of the public goods of international agreements on trade is the commitment that countries keep their markets open when there is a severe downturn. This prevents conditions such as those in the 1930s when each country individually decided to close its markets to protect import competing producers and, in the end, every country's export industries suffered. During the global recession of 2007–2009, countries kept their markets open, and while world trade declined due to the decline in overall economic activity, it picked up again as soon as GDP growth returned.

Other economists argue that the usual way to estimate the gains from trade leaves out so many of the benefits that the numbers are not to be trusted. For example, some of the effects of trade that are difficult to put into monetary terms are the effects of economies of scale that drive down costs, the benefits of increased product differentiation, the impact of intensified competition, and the benefits of spreading risks by, for example, diversifying food sources. Ultimately, trade increases exposure of countries to each other, and in the process, it leads to new knowledge. All of these benefits are difficult to quantify, and many of them are extremely dependent on context. Nevertheless, it is a mistake to think that they are not real gains, even if our economic models cannot measure them precisely.

A third reason to consider further opening as desirable is that in most cases, trade protection is grossly inefficient in achieving the goals it seeks. Table 7.2 illustrates this point with estimates of the costs to consumers and net national welfare loss (deadweight losses) *per job saved* in the mid-1990s. The table compares the EU, Japan, and the United States in clothing, textiles, and agriculture. The estimates are the dollar value (mid-1990s prices) of areas a, b, c, and d in Figure 6.3 in Chapter 6, divided by a separate estimate of the number of jobs saved. As shown, the total cost to consumers in each sector is significant. This cost is equivalent to a tax since it raises the domestic price of the goods with tariffs (and/or quotas) and redistributes the income to producers and government.

The net national welfare loss per job saved is smaller since it is a subset of the impacts of tariffs and quotas on consumers. It is still high in a few areas, however, such as clothing in the United States. Given that a full-time garment worker in the U.S. apparel industry averaged around $15,000 per year in the mid-1990s, a net welfare loss to the nation of $55,615 per job saved is a very inefficient way to protect employment. Furthermore, the cost to consumers of $138,666 to save a job that pays $15,000 is so exorbitantly expensive that it could only be tolerated when

TABLE 7.2   Costs of Tariffs and Quotas in High-Income Countries (Current U.S. dollars, circa mid-1990s)

	Per Job Saved	
	Cost to Consumers	National Welfare Loss
European Union		
Agriculture	149,820	34,835
Clothing	248,204	12,735
Textiles	252,036	9,078
Japan		
Agriculture	945,979	14,897
Clothing	778,406	5,620
Textiles	503,333	309
United States		
Agriculture	486,866	2,045
Clothing	138,666	55,615
Textiles	202,123	4,423

Three sectors account for a large share of the remaining protectionism found in most high-income countries.

Sources: Data from Messerlin (2001) *Measuring the Costs of Protection in Europe*; Sazanami, Urata, and Kawai (1995) *Measuring the Costs of Protection in Japan*; Hufbauer and Elliott (1994) *Measuring the Costs of Protection in the United States*. Estimates are based on data from the mid-1990s, © James Gerber.

consumers are unaware of the price tag. Fortunately, since the period covered by the data in Table 7.2, tariffs have come down significantly and many quotas have been eliminated.

This exercise is not useful for understanding the role of agriculture in national culture, nor the effects of keeping strong garment and textile manufacturing sectors. It is useful, however, for uncovering some of the hidden costs of tariffs and quotas and it adds to our understanding of the real tradeoffs we face when we turn to protectionism. Agriculture, clothing, and textiles are singled out because they have higher levels of protectionism and because they are sectors that many developing countries use to start their own development process. In the final analysis, Table 7.2 simply says that trade protectionism is a very expensive policy for protecting jobs.

The Logic of Collective Action

Given that the costs to consumers are so high for each job saved, why do people tolerate tariffs and quotas? Ignorance is certainly the case for some goods, but for others, the costs of protectionism have been relatively well publicized. For example, many people are aware that quotas on sugar imports cost each man, woman, and child in the United States between $5 and $10 per year. The costs are in the form of higher prices on candy bars, soft drinks, and other products containing sugar. Few of us work in the sugar industry, so the argument that our jobs depend on keeping tariffs in place is not valid for most people.

In a surprising way, however, we probably permit our tariffs and quotas because of a version of the jobs argument. The economist Mancur Olson studied this problem and similar ones and noticed two important points about tariffs and quotas. First, the costs of the policy are spread over a great many people. Second, the benefits are concentrated. For example, we all pay a little more for sweets and soft drinks, but a few sugar producers reap large benefits from our restrictions on sugar imports. Olson found that in cases such as this, there is an asymmetry in the incentives to support and to oppose the policy. With trade protection, the benefits are concentrated in a single industry and, consequently, it pays for the industry to commit resources to obtaining or maintaining its protection. The industry will hire lobbyists and perhaps participate directly in the political process through running candidates or supporting friendly candidates. If people in the industry think their entire livelihood depends on their ability to limit foreign competition, they have a very large incentive to become involved in setting policy.

The costs of protection are nowhere near as concentrated as the benefits because they are spread over all consumers of a product. The $5 to $10 per year that sugar quotas cost each of us is hardly worth hiring a lobbyist or protesting in Washington. Thus, one side pushes hard to obtain or keep protection, and the other side is silent on the matter. Given this imbalance, it is a wonder that there are not more trade barriers.

CASE STUDY

Agricultural Subsidies

Agricultural issues have long sparked conflict among the members of the WTO. Some cases have pitted high-income countries against each other, among them are disputes between the United States and Japan over apples and EU-U.S. disputes over bananas. More recently, the WTO's Doha Development Agenda has tried to address agricultural issues that are central to relations between developing and industrial countries. In particular, three issues are on the table: tariffs and quotas (market access), export subsidies given by countries to encourage farm exports, and production subsidies granted directly to farmers.

Direct subsidies are viewed as harmful because they lead to overproduction, squeeze out imports, and in some cases result in the dumping of the surplus product in foreign markets. The original GATT included language on agriculture, but there were so many loopholes that it had little impact. Not until the Uruguay Round was finalized in 1993, nearly **fifty** years after the signing of the original GATT, were significant changes made in the rules for agricultural trade. Many quotas were converted to tariffs, and industrial countries agreed

(continued)

to reduce their direct support for the farm sector by 20 percent. Indirect supports such as research and development and infrastructure construction were recognized as necessary, desirable, and permissible.

While direct-support payments were reduced, the Uruguay Round left intact direct payments to farmers that theoretically do not increase production, are part of a country's environmental or regional development plan, or are intended to limit production. If you think these are a lot of loopholes, you are right. Consequently, the current round of trade negotiations, the Doha Development Agenda, has taken up the issue of agriculture again, and developing countries in particular are pushing to limit government practices that block their access to markets in high-income countries or that subsidize production by industrial countries.

Table 7.3 shows the range of direct-support payments to agricultural producers in several industrial nations. The **twenty-seven** members of the EU are grouped together because their trade and agricultural policies are formulated at the EU level, not at the national level. In terms of absolute support, the EU spends the most, but Japan's farmers depend more on subsidies since 49.2 percent of farm receipts are from government support programs. Not all countries subsidize agriculture, however. As a share of GDP, Australia's supports are less than one-fourth those of the United States, and despite its lower support levels, Australia uses its comparative advantages to be among the top **fifteen** agricultural exporting countries in the world.

The impact of these subsidies on developing countries is not easy to generalize as it depends on the individual country and its factor endowments. In the case of sub-Saharan cotton producers such as Mali and Benin, subsidies given by high-income governments to cotton farmers increase the world's supply of cotton and reduce its price, so the subsidies are clearly harmful. (See the case study in Chapter 3.) Similarly, subsidies to U.S. corn producers have

TABLE 7.3   Agricultural Subsidies, 2009

	Agricultural Subsidies (Millions of US$)	As a Percent of Farm Receipts
Australia	1,070	2.3
Canada	4,618	9.0
European Union	106,902	18.4
Japan	44,256	49.2
United States	41,461	9.8

The EU provides the largest subsidies, but Japanese farmers are more dependent on agricultural subsidies.

Source: Data from OECD, *Producer Support Estimate by Country*, © James Gerber.

increased the supply of corn in Mexico and driven down the prices received by that country's small farmers, who operate near subsistence levels. This has contributed to a crisis in the rural sector of Mexico and reduces the demand for agricultural implements and household items that a prosperous rural class might otherwise buy from local producers.

On the other hand, subsidies given by high-income countries to support their farmers will lead to cheaper world food prices, all other factors being equal. This benefits some countries where there is a large urban working class. For example, many young Chinese farmers have migrated to the cities where they work in factories. Given that the productivity of these individuals in agriculture is very low, the country as a whole gains when they become city dwellers and factory workers, while cheaper food makes life easier and raises living standards. As a result, agricultural subsidies in high-income countries benefit China and some other developing countries.

WHY NATIONS PROTECT THEIR INDUSTRIES

LO 7.4   Analyze the economic validity of common justifications for protectionism.

Trade protectionism is used in different times and places to achieve a variety of potential goals. Very few countries have zero tariffs across all industries (Hong Kong is the only country, although some others such as Singapore have very few and very low tariffs), but many countries have low tariffs, as shown in Table 7.1 and Figure 6.4. Other countries have tariffs but do not use them to achieve any goal besides adding to government revenue. Chile, for example, decided not to use the tariff for commercial policy reasons and has a uniform tariff of **6** percent across all sectors. Uniformity means that no sector is favored more than another and resources are not drawn to any particular sector due to a tariff. In general, the reasons given for using trade protectionism can be grouped into **six** categories: revenue, jobs, industrial targeting, cultural protection, national security, and retaliation against unfair trade practices.

Revenue

In a developing country's economy, a large percentage of economic activity is unrecorded. Subsistence farmers sell their surplus in the town market, and repairmen and craftsmen take on jobs without leaving a paper trail of work orders or receipts. In this environment, income taxes and sales taxes are difficult if not impossible to impose. Tariffs, on the other hand, can be relatively easily collected by inspectors at the ports and border crossings. They simply have to value the goods coming in and levy a fee (the tariff) on the person transporting the goods. The United States is a case in point, as tariff revenues were the single greatest source of income for the U.S. government until well into the twentieth century.

TABLE 7.4   Tariffs as a Share of Government Revenue, by Region

Income and Country	Tariffs as a Share of Total Taxes
Low income	
■ Afghanistan	■ 36.4
■ Ethiopia	■ 45.2
Lower middle income	
■ Bangladesh	■ 30.3
■ Philippines	■ 21.3
Upper middle income	
■ China	■ 5.14
■ Brazil	■ 4.58
High income	
■ New Zealand	■ 3.29
■ United States	■ 1.99

Source: Data from World Bank, World Development Indicators Database, © James Gerber.

Table 7.4 shows the percent of government revenue that is provided by tariffs. The data are arranged by income level, with two examples for each income category. Table 7.4 shows the general pattern that tariffs become less important as a source of government revenue as income grows and other sources become available. The worldwide pattern is much more variable than shown in the table, but the general point about the diminishing importance of tariffs for revenue is valid.

The Labor Argument

The labor argument is a perennial justification for trade barriers. It was used throughout the nineteenth century, and recently it has been resurrected by many opponents of expanded trade agreements. The argument states that nations must protect their markets against imports from countries where wages are much lower because otherwise the advantage of lower wages will either wreck the domestic industry or force it to match the lower wages. For example, in the debate leading up to the ratification of North American Free Trade Agreement, opponents argued that Mexico would have an unfair advantage in trade with the United States because Mexican firms pay their workers a fraction (on average, about one-eighth) of the wages paid to American workers.

The labor argument fails to consider productivity differences. Mexican workers, for example, earn about one-eighth of the salary of U.S. workers because their productivity, on average, is about one-eighth of the level of U.S. workers. Mexico has lower productivity because the education and skill levels of its workforce are less than in the United States, Mexican workers have less capital at work than U.S. workers, and the infrastructure of the Mexican economy is not as developed as the U.S. infrastructure. As Mexican workers gain more skills and education, and as the capital available on the job and in the surrounding economy increases, their productivity will rise, and so will their wages.

If the goal is an adequate number of jobs to reach full employment, then appropriate macroeconomic and labor market policies are better instruments. Monetary and fiscal policies (see Chapter 11) that maintain economic growth, and labor market policies that provide adjustment assistance to dislocated workers and incentives for employers to hire them are far less expensive than trade policy for this purpose. If the goal is to keep a particular sector alive, then direct subsidies to the producers are preferable because they do not have the distortions that result from forcing consumers out of the market.

The Infant Industry Argument

A much more sophisticated argument for protection is the **infant industry** argument. The argument is mainly associated with the tariff policies of developing nations that protect their "infant" industries against the competition of more mature firms in industrial countries.The infant industry argument for protection is very similar to the arguments for industrial policy that were given in Chapter 5. Two beliefs lie at the root of the infant industry argument. The first is that market forces will not support the development of a particular industry, usually because foreign competition is too well established, but also possibly because the industry is too risky. The second belief is that the industry in question has some spillover benefits, or positive externalities, that make the industry more valuable to the national economy than simply the wages and profits it might generate. Whenever there are spillover benefits, the market may not support the development of an industry to the optimum level. With positive externalities, many of the benefits of production are captured by other firms or individuals outside the producing firm. Since the producers do not get the full benefit of their own production, they produce less than the amount that is most beneficial for society.

Positive externalities are usually argued to be in the form of linkages to other industries or of a technological nature. As an example of the linkage case, many nations have attempted to start their own steel industries because they assumed it would create a cheaper source of steel for other industries, such as cars. The problem with this argument is that it does not demonstrate that there is some inherent advantage in making something as opposed to buying it, or in other words, that the car industry will have a special advantage if it can buy steel from local producers. If the car industry is forced to buy locally at prices above world levels, protection of the domestic steel industry may actually harm the car industry. This is what happened to firms in Brazil when the government tried to start a domestic computer industry by keeping out foreign producers. The policy had negative linkage effects on Brazilian businesses because they had to pay higher prices for computers that were of lower quality. Brazil would have been better off importing its computers, as it does now.

Even if externalities are present, it is not enough to establish the validity of the infant industry argument. Two more conditions must hold. First, the protection that is offered must be limited in time, and second, the protected industry must experience falling costs. The time limits on protection ensure that the industry does not become a permanent recipient of transfers from consumers, while the presence of falling costs ensures that the policy will eventually pay for itself and that the industry will become competitive.

The National Security Argument

Every nation protects some industries as a way to guard its national security. The most obvious examples include weapons industries, and somewhat more broadly, strategic technologies. Most countries refuse to trade military technologies or weapons with potential adversaries, and some nations also include strategic minerals that have specialized uses in military hardware such as jet aircraft. Prohibitions imposed on exports or tariffs on imports to develop domestic mineral or other resources are often not an optimal policy. Usually it is more efficient to build stockpiles of minerals and other materials by buying large quantities in peacetime when they are less expensive.

The Cultural Protection Argument

The cultural industries include movies, television programming, music, print media, theater, and art. Some nations worry that if they allow completely free trade in the cultural industries, then the most commercially viable firms will dominate, and the cultural values of the home country will be obscured and forgotten. Since the United States has the strongest presence in much of the entertainment industry, the goal of protecting national cultural values is usually an argument in favor of protecting a nation's filmmaking, television programming, and music production against domination by its U.S. counterparts. For example, the precursor to the North American Free Trade Agreement, called the *Canadian-United States Free Trade Agreement* (signed in 1988), established Canada's right to require its television and radio stations to broadcast a certain proportion of Canadian-produced programs. There are similar requirements in music, theater, and the print media. U.S. television and movie producers naturally opposed this limitation on free trade and demanded the right to sell an unlimited amount of U.S.-produced entertainment. They lost this argument, however, and they lost again when the Uruguay Round of the GATT was signed. It allows all nations to place similar restrictions on their film, television, and other cultural industries.

A more complicated assessment involves protection of noncultural industries for cultural reasons. An example illustrates this point. France and some other EU members argue that their high levels of agricultural protection are justified as a rural development and maintenance policy. Without barriers on agricultural imports, parts of the countryside would go into economic decline since many farms would be unprofitable, rural communities would be abandoned, and the cultural heritage of the nation would be injured. Is this a clever protectionist argument, or a valid, noneconomic reason for trade barriers? It is hard to tell.

The Retaliation Argument

A final category of reasons given by nations to justify trade barriers is retaliation for unfair trade practices. When a country decides that another country's trade practices unfairly discriminate against it, a common response is to impose a trade barrier. Retaliatory tariffs and quotas can provide an incentive for negotiations, but they can also lead to escalating trade wars.

Economic analysis is of limited utility in understanding this situation, since the outcome depends on political processes that determine how nations respond to pressure, their willingness to negotiate, and the outcome of negotiations. There are three camps of economists on this issue. One camp argues that free trade is beneficial regardless of the actions of a country's trading partners. If other countries choose to protect their markets, this argument goes, then it lowers their standard of living, and it would be foolish to do the same by imposing trade barriers in retaliation. Another camp argues that since free trade is beneficial, it is in everyone's interest to see it followed as widely as possible. Therefore, if a tariff today causes other nations to open their markets tomorrow, the world economy will benefit in the long run.

A third group argues that countries that have a closed market or that restrict market access by imposing barriers to trade have an unfair advantage, particularly in high-technology products. They have a domestic market all to themselves, and they can compete freely in other markets that are more open than their own. In cases where the size of the market is important, the ability to sell to a larger market (home plus foreign) than a competitor's may give the firms in the protected markets a competitive advantage. If firms in the open market are forced out of business, then the technology, skills, and expertise that go with them will exist only in the firms from the country that adopted the strategy of protecting its market. To ensure that this scenario does not play out and to avoid losing critical technologies, some would argue that the threat of retaliation should be used to force open markets that currently are closed.

CASE STUDY

Traditional Knowledge and Intellectual Property

Traditional knowledge forms part of the cultural heritage of traditional societies and indigenous communities. This knowledge, often embedded in cultural practices and everyday activities as a part of a world view and cultural life, can also embody intellectual knowledge of plants, animals, and the natural world, gathered over generations. Those who practice Chinese traditional medicine, traditional healers in indigenous cultures, small-scale farmers, and hunters and gatherers have knowledge of plants and animals that has commercial potential. When that knowledge is expropriated and used by outsiders without recognition of its origin, it is not only unfair to the originators of the knowledge but also could harm them.

For example, U.S. researchers asked for a patent on turmeric, a spice that is effective in healing skin cuts and lesions. Turmeric is the bright yellow ingredient

(continued)

used in curries and other dishes, and it has been used for over four thousand years in traditional Indian medicine. Nevertheless, Patent No. 5,401,504 was granted by the U.S. Patent Office to the University of Mississippi for its use as a healing agent. As a practical matter, the patent probably would have been unenforceable, but it might have imposed a legal requirement on users to pay royalties. The Indian government protested, arguing that it was a part of their traditional knowledge base and that it had long been used as a healing agent in India. After they produced ancient Sanskrit texts describing its use, the patent was overturned.

Brazil and India are foremost among a group of tropical countries working to protect their traditional knowledge and their biodiversity. One fear is that "bio-prospectors" will collect plant samples shown to them by traditional healers in indigenous communities, isolate the key compounds in their laboratories, patent new pharmaceuticals, and ignore the interests of the traditional community or the nation where they live.

Traditional healers in Samoa use the bark of the mamala tree for a variety of medicinal purposes, including combating hepatitis. After observing this practice, researchers discovered that it was an effective agent for making prostratin, an anti-AIDS compound. This story appears to end well since revenue from the development of the drug is expected to be shared with the village and the families that assisted in its discovery and used for further AIDS research. Without aggressive enforcement and vigilance, it is feared that traditional knowledge will not be recognized and respected.

In another example, new plant varieties are adapted from traditional ones and patented by a seed company. In the African nation of Mali, the Bela community uses a wild rice that is more resistant to blight and other crop-destroying diseases. Researchers from the University of California, Davis, were able to clone the gene responsible and use it to strengthen some varieties of rice. They patented this gene, which raises the question of the connection between the new, genetically modified rice with the blight-resistant gene, and the interests of the Bela people. In the end, a Genetic Resource Recognition Fund was created to pay for fellowships for agricultural students from Mali and other countries where the wild rice grows.

Given the potential stakes, both monetary and cultural, many international organizations take an active interest in these issues. Among the most visible are the World Intellectual Property Organization (WIPO), the International Union for the Protection of New Plant Varieties (UPOV), the Food and Agriculture Organization (FAO), the WTO, the United Nations Development Program (UNDP), the World Health Organization (WHO), and the United Nations Environmental Program (UNEP). There are many international agreements, but the issues are relatively new, and it is an area of international law that will continue to evolve over time.

Source: Based on World *Intellectual Property Organization, Intellectual Property and Traditional Knowledge*, © James Gerber.

THE POLITICS OF PROTECTION IN THE UNITED STATES

LO 7.5   Define each form of legal protection granted by the U.S. government.

Although U.S. trade with the rest of the world has grown, political pressures to protect domestic industries have frequently been intense. One reason for this is that Congressional reforms removed some of the insulation from industry lobbyists that Congress enjoyed in the 1950s and 1960s. Another reason stems from the end of the Cold War and the lessening of U.S. willingness to sacrifice trade issues for the sake of maintaining close geopolitical alliances. A third reason is the rise of the export-oriented East Asian newly industrializing countries (NICs), including China, and the pressure they have put on a number of domestic U.S. industries. Finally, the growth of the U.S. trade deficit and the widespread fear in the 1980s that the United States had lost its competitive edge also contributed to a greater reluctance to open U.S. markets without reciprocity by other countries. More recently, the rapid increase of the U.S. trade deficit and the loss of manufacturing jobs since 2000 are conditions likely to bring back the competition fears of the 1980s. For each of these reasons, trade conflicts have intensified.

Protection in the United States is usually obtained through direct action by the president (for example, the Voluntary Export Restraints [VERs] on Japanese autos in the 1980s) or through one of the following different legal procedures:

- Antidumping duties
- Countervailing duties
- Escape clause relief
- Section 301 retaliation

In each case, a firm, an industry trade association, or a government agency may petition the federal government to initiate an investigation into a foreign country's or foreign firm's practices.

Antidumping Duties

An **antidumping duty (ADD)** is a tariff levied on an import that is selling at a price below the product's **fair value**. This is the most common form of protection used by countries, including the United Sates, in part because the determination of fair value introduces an element of subjectivity into the process of justifying an antidumping duty and it makes it easier for a firm or an industry to justify a complaint against a foreign firm or industry. Since 1985, the United States has imposed an average of twenty-one new antidumping duties per year. Consequently, antidumping duties have become a source of significant trade tension between countries; unsurprisingly, many countries would like to strengthen the WTO's rules regarding antidumping duties by making them harder to apply.

The WTO does not regulate dumping or antidumping duties, but it does try to establish what countries can and cannot do when they retaliate against dumping.

According to the WTO rules, **dumping** occurs when an exporter sells a product at a price below what it charges in its home market. It is not always possible to compare the home market and foreign market prices, however, and wholesalers, transportation costs, and other price add-ons may limit the comparison's usefulness. Therefore, two other methods may be used to determine whether a good is being dumped. Comparisons can be made between the price in the import market and either the price charged in third-country markets, or to an estimate of the cost of production. Comparison to prices in third-country markets is similar to that between prices in the exporter's home market and the importer's market, and it may be uninformative for the same reasons. A comparison of the import price and the estimated cost of production, including a normal rate of return on invested capital, assumes that production costs in an exporting country can be measured with accuracy.

One final criterion must be met before antidumping duties are allowed. The country claiming dumping must also be able to show that the dumping has caused material injury to its firms. If dumping occurs, but there are no harmful effects on domestic firms, then antidumping duties are not allowed. This would happen if the dumping margin is too small to matter.

At their most basic level, antidumping duties are a tool of commercial policy that protects against predatory pricing by foreign firms. Selling below cost as a strategy to drive the competition out of business is widely perceived as unfair, and allowing it to happen can harm the economic interest of a country. This is particularly likely if it results in higher prices after the domestic producers have been driven out of the market.

Problems arise, however, because the economic theory and the legal definition are not completely in agreement. First, in order for a firm to sell in a foreign market at a price below its cost of production, it must have market power at home that allows it to earn higher-than-normal profits so it can subsidize its foreign sales. A firm that is not earning above-average profits somewhere cannot maintain a price that is below its cost somewhere else. Yet, when countries investigate a dumping complaint, market structure is rarely considered. This problem is compounded by the use of estimated production costs to determine dumping, since estimated values require some guesswork about technology and other inputs, and this creates a significant margin of error.

Second, within the scope of normal commercial operations, firms often sell below cost. The most obvious case is that of goods that are likely to spoil. A fresh fish exporter with a load sitting on a dock is likely to lower the price progressively as time passes. In this case, the cost of producing the shipment of fish represents sunk costs that have already been incurred, and the only option is to sell the goods for whatever is possible. Firms also sell selected items below cost as a technique for penetrating markets. This is similar to the behavior of large retail chains that offer some goods at an extremely low price to create a reputation as a value-oriented retailer. Finally, firms will sell for extended periods at prices that do not cover the cost of their capital and other fixed costs as long as the costs of their variable inputs such as labor and materials are covered. Since capital costs such as interest on loans have to be paid no matter what is produced, in the short run, the chief consideration is whether the price is high enough to cover labor and material input costs. In the long run, a firm that cannot sell at a high enough price to meet its capital costs will have to shut down; in the short run, however, it continues to produce.

The increasing use of antidumping duties has generated much interest in defining their usage more carefully. As things now stand, countries vary widely in their application of these duties and their willingness to negotiate their usage. Some countries rarely apply them, and some trade agreements, such as the one between Canada and Chile, ban their usage except under exceptional circumstances. Other countries use them frequently—often it seems, as a politically expedient way to satisfy an important industry lobbying group.

In the United States, the procedure for firms to obtain protection requires filing a petition with the International Trade Administration (ITA) in the Department of Commerce. The ITA investigates whether dumping (or subsidization in the case of a petition for countervailing duties) has occurred. If its finding is positive (dumping has occurred), the case is turned over to the United States International Trade Commission (USITC), an independent regulatory commission. The USITC conducts an additional investigation to determine whether substantial harm has been done to the domestic industry and so an antidumping or countervailing duty is warranted. The relative success of U.S. firms in proving that foreign companies are dumping has encouraged a growing number of antidumping petitions in recent years.

Countervailing Duties

A **countervailing duty (CVD)** is a tariff that is granted to an industry that has been hurt by foreign country **subsidies** of its national firms. Since subsidies permit a firm to sell its goods at a lower price and still make a profit, an effect of subsidies is to make firms more competitive. The goal of a CVD is to raise the price of the foreign good enough to countervail the effect of the subsidy. The idea is to level the playing field between domestic firms that receive no subsidies and foreign ones that do.

CVDs are used less often than antidumping duties. In the United States, there have been, on average, four to five cases per year since 1985. CVDs require a clear definition of a subsidy since they are intended to counteract the effects of subsidies. One of the benefits of the Uruguay Round is that it standardized the definition as a financial contribution by a government (national or local) or public agency that confers a benefit. Subsidies take on a variety of forms, including grants, low-interest loans, preferential tax treatments, provision of goods or services for free or below cost, or any of a number of other financial benefits.

Escape Clause Relief

Escape clause relief is so named because it refers to a clause in the U.S. and GATT trade rules that permits an industry to escape the pressure of imports by temporarily imposing a tariff. Escape clause relief is a temporary tariff imposed on imports to provide a period of adjustment to a domestic industry. It is initiated when an industry or firm petitions the USITC directly for relief from a sudden surge of imports. The burden of escape clause relief is on the firm; it must establish that it has been harmed by imports and not by some other factor, such as bad management decisions. In practice, it has become so difficult to obtain relief from import competition under this procedure that few cases are filed.

Section 301 and Special 301

Section 301 of the U.S. Trade Act of 1974 requires the president's chief trade negotiator, the United States Trade Representative (USTR), to take action against any nation that persistently engages in unfair trade practices. The action usually begins with a request for negotiations with the targeted country. The goal of the negotiations is to change the policies of countries that restrict U.S. commerce unreasonably or unjustifiably. Note that it is left to the United States to define unreasonable and unjustifiable restrictions on U.S. commerce.

The types of trade practices that the USTR is required to investigate are quite broad. Recent cases have included an investigation of China's management of its exchange rate, Ukraine's actions to enforce intellectual property rights, and the EU's lack of compliance with a WTO ruling against its blockage of imports of hormone-fed beef.

A similar program to Section 301 is known as **Special 301**. This part of U.S. trade law requires the USTR to monitor property rights enforcement around the globe. In 2005, the USTR surveyed ninety countries and identified fifty-two as lacking adequate enforcement or as denying market access to U.S. artists and industries that rely on intellectual property enforcement. Inclusion on this list means that the USTR has some concerns and will continue to monitor the situation.

CASE STUDY

Economic Sanctions

Economic sanctions are a form of trade restriction. Unlike tariffs and quotas, which affect imports alone, sanctions are often put on exports as well as imports and may include financial components as well. Access to international credit through privately owned banks or international lending agencies may be limited or blocked, as may investment by domestic firms in the country singled out for sanctions. The international sanctions against Iran, which ended in 2016, is the best known recent example. There are many other examples, including export prohibitions by the United States during the Cold War that limited computer sales to the Soviet Union, and the continuing prohibitions on selling goods or services to Cuba and North Korea. The world community's boycott of investment in South Africa before the ending of apartheid is another example of a comprehensive investment and trade sanction, similar to the recently dismantled sanctions against Iran.

Economic sanctions go beyond simple trade or investment measures. In most cases, they are used as one of several tactics aimed at achieving a broader policy objective—the ending of Soviet expansion, Iranian nuclear weapons ambitions, or South African apartheid. Another feature of sanctions is that they are often accompanied by additional measures, ranging from diplomatic pressure to military invasion.

The logical question to ask about sanctions is "Do they work?" In an important two-volume study of this question, three economists analyzed 120 episodes of economic sanctions throughout the world between World War I and 1990; Table 7.5 summarizes their findings. The economists found it useful to categorize the goals of sanctions into five separate groups: those designed to create a relatively modest policy change (for example, to free a political prisoner or to limit nuclear proliferation); those intended to destabilize a government; those aimed at disrupting a military adventure of another nation (for example, stopping Iraq's invasion of Kuwait); those designed to impair another nation's military potential; and a fifth category of other goals, such as stopping apartheid, or the Arab League's boycott of oil sales to the United States in retaliation for support of Israel.

To be classified as a success, the policy outcome must have been the one desired by the country imposing the sanctions, and the sanctions must have been a contributor to the policy outcome. Hufbauer, Schott, and Elliott find 41 successes in the 120 cases they examined, but they report a drop in the number of successes after about 1973. They determined that sanctions are more effective when the target country is small, economically weak, and politically unstable. Also, success is more likely when the target country is an ally; sanctions are imposed quickly and decisively; the costs to the sending country are small; and the goal is a relatively small change.

The more difficult the goal, the more likely military force is needed to back up the sanctions. The U.S. invasion of Iraq in 2003 is a case in point. United

TABLE 7.5 **Economic Sanctions Since World War I**

Goal	Number of Cases	Successes
Modest policy change	51	17
Destabilize a government	21	11
Disrupt a military adventure	18	6
Impair military potential	10	2
Other	20	5

Sanctions imposed between World War I and 1990 had about a 38 percent success rate.

Source: From *Economic Sanctions Reconsidered*: History and current policy, Volume 1 by Gary Clyde Hufbauer, Jeffrey J. Schott, Kimberly Ann Elliott, © 1990 Peterson Institute for International Economics.

(*continued*)

Nations sanctions against Iraq undoubtedly helped to cripple its economy, even though the sanctions were never enforced completely. In that sense, they contributed to the success of U.S. policy in replacing Iraq's government. Still, without a military invasion, it seems unlikely that the sanctions alone would have led to a change of government.

Summary

- Regardless of their cost or their ability to achieve a desired objective, every nation uses trade barriers. In most industrial nations, they are not used to develop comparative advantage in new industries, but rather to protect old industries that can no longer compete or to temporarily protect industries that are under pressure from new competitors. Agriculture, clothing, and textiles are the most protected sectors in many industrial countries.

- Tariffs and quotas are inefficient mechanisms for creating (or keeping) jobs. Because the costs are hidden in the prices consumers pay for foreign and domestic goods, few people realize how inefficient they are.

- The primary beneficiaries of trade barriers are producers who receive protection and governments that receive tariff revenue. The losers are consumers. Because the gains are concentrated among a relatively few people, and the losses are dispersed across many, there is usually a small economic incentive to oppose trade barriers but a large incentive to seek them.

- The valid arguments in favor of protection involve economic returns to society that are undervalued or not counted by markets. That is, it must be the case that the market does not take into consideration the gains that spill over from production. The total value of producing a good, including any spillovers, is extremely difficult to measure, however, and it is often impossible to know the future value of the skills or technology that an industry will create.

- In addition to presidential action, there are several forms of protection in the United States: countervailing duties to counter a foreign subsidy, antidumping duties to counter dumping of foreign goods, escape clause relief to counter an import surge, and Section 301 actions to retaliate against foreign trade practices that have been labeled as unfair. Except for escape clause relief, each type of tariff requires a demonstration that foreign products are competing unfairly in the U.S. market and that they have harmed domestic producers. The most common form of tariff imposition is an antidumping duty.

Vocabulary

antidumping duty (ADD)

countervailing duty (CVD)

dumping

escape clause relief

fair value

infant industry

Section 301

Special 301

subsidies

Study Questions

All problems are assignable in MyEconLab

7.1 Which industries are more heavily protected in the United States and Japan? Are high-income or low-income nations more affected by American and Japanese trade barriers? Explain.

7.2 What new areas of trade and investment received coverage under the agreement signed after the Uruguay Round of the General Agreement on Tariffs and Trade?

7.3 Given that tariffs and quotas cost consumers and that they are grossly inefficient means for creating or preserving jobs, why do citizens allow these policies to exist?

7.4 What four main groups of arguments do nations use to justify protection for particular industries? Which are economic, and which are noneconomic?

7.5 Evaluate the labor and infant industry arguments for protection.

7.6 Are tariffs justified as a retaliatory measure against other nations? Justify your answer.

7.7 What are the four legal procedures that American firms have at their disposal for seeking protection? What are the conditions that would generate a request for each kind of protection?

CHAPTER 8

International Trade and Labor and Environmental Standards

INTRODUCTION: INCOME AND STANDARDS

Since the end of World War II, many of the formal barriers to international trade have been removed. This was accomplished through the sustained efforts of the world's trading nations, often working through the negotiating frameworks provided by the General Agreement on Tariffs and Trade (GATT), the World Trade Organization (WTO), and more recently, the regional trade agreements around the globe.

As trade barriers are removed, however, new obstacles to increased international economic integration begin to appear. In Chapter 1, this was described as obstacles to deep integration. These obstacles are driven by two distinct but equally important forces. First, it sometimes happens that national laws and regulations adopted for strictly domestic reasons unintentionally limit international commerce in a more integrated economic environment. For example, a law designed to capture economies of scale by giving one company a monopoly in telephone services makes it impossible for foreign telephone companies to enter the market.

A second obstacle to increased international economic integration is the conflict over standards. These include differences in technical product standards, health and safety standards, labor and environmental standards, and legal systems. For example, the adoption of a common set of product standards gives a significant commercial advantage to firms already producing to the standard, and hence, each country would like to see wider application of its own standards. In addition to commercial incentives, many of the conflicts over standards result from the wide variation in world income levels. Trade between high- and low-income countries is usually based on comparative advantage that moves countries along their production possibility curves, causing greater specialization in production. Although each nation's gains from trade may be large, greater specialization creates winners and losers inside each country and raises questions of fairness.

Economic conditions and living standards inside low-income countries are vastly different from conditions inside middle- or high-income economies and, in particular, lower wages, longer hours, less safe working conditions, dirtier industries, and less regard for environmental degradation are relatively more common in low-income economies than in high-income ones. When trade occurs between countries with different living standards, people begin to wonder about the inexpensive goods they import from low-income countries. Does their production exploit children, are working conditions safe and healthy, do workers have political and civil rights, and are the methods employed environmentally friendly? If not, can trade barriers such as tariffs, quotas, or complete prohibition of imports effectively pressure the exporting country into changing its practices?

SETTING STANDARDS: HARMONIZATION, MUTUAL RECOGNITION, OR SEPARATE?

LO 8.1 **Compare and contrast the three options for setting standards in trade rules.**

LO 8.2 **Give examples of the relationship between income levels and environmental and labor problems.**

Two or more economies can be deeply integrated even if they have different rules, regulations, and standards governing their individual economies. The United States is an obvious example, since individual states impose different standards on vehicle emissions, minimum wages, teacher training, food safety, construction codes, and product availability, to name just a few. Lesser forms of integration between sovereign nations, such as partial trade agreements, free-trade areas, customs unions, and common markets, are likely to vary even more with respect to rules, regulations, and standards.

Harmonization of product and process standards is one of the three options for countries seeking to expand their commercial ties. **Harmonization of standards** refers to the case where two or more countries share a common set of standards in an area of concern, such as product safety, labor, environment, fair competition, and so on. Another option is **mutual recognition of standards**, in which countries keep their own product and process standards, but accept the standards of others as equally valid and sufficient. For example, a physician trained in a foreign country may not receive the same training as physicians in the home country, but under a system of mutual recognition he or she would be certified to practice in either country. A third option is **separate standards**. In this case, countries keep their own standards and refuse to recognize those of anyone else. For example, if the home country has a more stringent rule for pesticide residue on vegetables after harvest, separate standards might prohibit imports that are considered unsafe. Most regional trade agreements and the WTO agreements practice a combination of harmonization, mutual recognition, and separate standards.

There are no general rules to determine which approach is most efficient or fairest in all cases. Often, the harmonization of technical standards having to do with product design or performance is useful since it leads to a larger, more unified market and creates greater efficiency since firms have to consider only one set of standards. Simple examples such as vehicle emissions or the definition of organic produce illustrate cases where harmonization unifies a market and creates efficiency gains in production for the economy. In other cases, harmonization of standards may conceivably freeze into a set of inferior standards. New technologies are a prime example, since the evolution of new products and processes is impossible to forecast, and freezing technical standards into legal requirements may have a harmful effect on future developments. In addition, there are many areas such as labor or environmental legislation where it is unclear which country has the "best" rules. Mutual recognition is a superior option under these conditions, as it allows competition between different standards and may help clarify the costs and benefits of each one.

Harmonization of standards sometimes poses an additional problem in its failure to take into account the differences between countries. Generally speaking, the lower a country's average income, the less administrative, scientific, and technical capacity it has to design and enforce standards. In addition, national priorities change as income levels change, and there is no reason why the priorities of one group of countries should dominate. Differences in income levels are not always an obstacle to the harmonization of standards, however, because many product standards are technical considerations where adopting a common set of rules makes a great deal of sense if it widens the market and lowers the prices.

When countries vary significantly in their income levels, it is generally better to mutually recognize each other's standards, or if that is not possible for safety or other reasons, to maintain separate standards. While trade theory is clear on this point, many people living in high-income countries find it hard to accept, particularly with respect to labor and environmental standards. Many fear that in the absence of a common set of labor and environmental standards, low standards abroad create competitive pressures for domestic firms to lower their standards, or to move to a foreign location in order to reduce their costs. This possibility has been labeled as **race to the bottom**, where the bottom is the lowest possible level of standards. In the following sections, we examine this issue and others in the context of labor and environmental standards.

CASE STUDY

Income, Environment, and Society

The World Bank uses four categories to classify the countries of the world according to their income levels. **High-income** countries have per capita incomes (2014, U.S. dollars) of $12,736 or more, **upper-middle-income** countries range between $4,126 and $12,735 per person, **lower-middle-income** countries range between $1,046 and $4,125 per person, and **low-income** countries have per capita incomes of $1,045 or less.

Table 8.1 shows the number of countries, population, and average income per person for each of the four categories of income. In 2014, just under one-half of the world's population was low- or lower- middle-income. Income differences of the magnitude shown in Table 8.1 inevitably create significant differences in social and environmental indicators, as shown in Table 8.2.

Table 8.2 displays four indicators that are important to the economy, society, and the environment. The first variable, infant mortality, is a key measurement of health conditions. It shows a strong and consistent decline as income growth brings improved sanitation and nutrition, wider access to health care, and improvements in the quality of health care. The second variable, access to safe drinking water, is one of the most significant public health problems in the world and can also be considered an environmental problem with direct health effects. As incomes rise, the percentage of the population with access to safe water increases significantly until nearly all citizens in high-income countries are covered. This should not be interpreted to mean that high-income countries do not have water problems; it simply means that all or nearly all their citizens have access to safe drinking water.

The other two indicators show a mixed pattern. In the case of a major contributor to global climate change, carbon dioxide emissions, large increases occur as higher income countries burn more fossil fuels than lower income ones. The high-income countries of Table 8.2 produce 37 times more carbon

TABLE 8.1   **Income and Population by World Bank Categories, 2014**

Income Category	Number of Countries	Population (Millions)	Average Income per Person (US$)
Low	27	622.0	641
Lower middle	52	2,879.1	2,003
Upper middle	50	2,360.8	8,000
High	54	1,398.8	37,755

Most of the world's population lives in countries classified as lower- or upper-middle income.

Source: Data from World Bank, World Development Indicators, © James Gerber.

(*continued*)

TABLE 8.2   Income Levels, Society, and the Environment

Income Category	Under 5 Mortality, per 1000, 2014	Population (%) with Treated Water, 2014	CO$_2$ Emissions, Metric Tons per Person, 2011	Change (%) in Forest Reserves, 2000–2012
Low	78.8	65.0	0.3	−0.60
Lower middle	54.7	88.9	1.5	−15.86
Upper middle	19.8	94.5	5.7	−7.08
High	7.0	99.0	11.1	−0.01

Some conditions improve with income growth, some worsen, and some vary widely.

Source: Data from World Bank, World Development Indicators, © James Gerber.

dioxide per person than low-income countries, and each successive income group emits more carbon dioxide than the income group below it. The final column of Table 8.2 shows that forest reserves are depleted at an expanding rate as income grows, but depletion begins to taper off eventually. High-income countries use much less wood for fuel and replace it with metal, plastic, and other materials in manufacturing.

In sum, when thinking about labor and environmental standards, it is useful to keep in mind the potential effects of highly different income levels.

LABOR STANDARDS

LO 8.3   **Define labor standards.**

LO 8.4   **State four potential problems with using trade sanctions to enforce labor standards.**

Since the signing of the North American Free Trade Agreement in 1993, the United States and other countries included labor and environmental standards as part of the regional trade agreements they negotiate. This is a politically charged issue that reflects domestic politics but also rising worldwide interests in issues related to human rights and the environment. To date, the United States' trade agreements with Canada and Mexico (the North American Free Trade Agreement), Jordan, and Chile contain language on labor and environmental standards, either in the treaty itself or as a side agreement. In each case, the language specifies that each country must enforce its own standards or face monetary fines. Many labor and environmental activists view this as inadequate and are pushing to include trade sanctions as part of the enforcement mechanism, both in existing agreements and in future agreements, including those reached by the WTO.

The complaints against trade by labor and environmental interests are relatively similar. In both cases, it is alleged that trade with countries that have lower standards creates a race to the bottom in standards, and that countries with high standards are forced to lower their standards or experience a loss of jobs and industry. Furthermore, it is alleged that this type of trade is unfair, since the failure to enact or to enforce standards gives firms in countries with lower standards a commercial advantage. Before addressing these issues, it is useful to clarify what is meant by standards, particularly labor standards.

Defining Labor Standards

The concept of labor standards is multifaceted, since it covers many potential rights, from basic rights such as the right to be free from forced labor, to civic rights such as the right to representation in a union. Currently, there is no core set of work-related rights that everyone views as universal human rights.

As a starting point, we take the following five labor standards proposed as basic rights by the **International Labour Organization (ILO)** (see the ILO case study later in this chapter) and revised by the Organization for Economic Cooperation and Development (OECD):

- Prohibition of forced labor
- Freedom of association
- The right to organize and bargain collectively
- An end to the exploitation of child labor
- Nondiscrimination in employment

Most people would probably agree to these rights, although there is a fair amount of ambiguity attached to each of them. For example, conditions considered exploitative in a high-income country might seem acceptable in a poor one, or cultural or religious values regarding employment opportunities for men and women may be at odds with the idea of nondiscrimination.

Other potential standards are significantly more contentious. For example, universal standards for minimum wages, limits on the number of hours someone can work in a day, and health and safety issues in the workplace are difficult to define given the wide variation in incomes and living conditions around the world. High-income countries, where unskilled labor is relatively scarce, face an entirely different set of economic constraints compared to those faced by low-income countries where unskilled labor is relatively abundant. For example, if low-income countries are forced to pay a minimum wage high enough to satisfy critics in high-income countries, many people fear that the result would be the closing down of production and a rise in unemployment rather than an increase in living standards. In other words, too high a minimum wage may be well intentioned, but it may reduce living standards in low-income countries. Even this is ambiguous, however, since it is no easy matter to determine how high is too high.

CASE STUDY

Child Labor

The most common definition of a *child* is a person under 18 years of age. This is the definition set forth by the United Nations and the International Labour Organization (ILO; see the next case study) and accepted by most countries. Many children are economically active without falling into the negative category of child labor because their work is light, their hours are not long, and they work to supplement their studies or to learn a skill.

It is easy to be opposed to the evils of child labor, particularly when it is hazardous to the physical and psychological well-being of children. Opposition becomes more complicated, however, when schools do not exist and impoverished families depend on the few cents their children can bring home. In these cases, children and their work contribute to family survival and a humane policy requires more than a simple prohibition of work by children.

Child labor appears to be in decline worldwide, having fallen from an estimated 215.3 million in 2008 to 167.9 million in 2012, but it is still common in some parts of the world. Using 75 national surveys, the ILO estimated that the number of children, ages 5–17, that were employed in 2012 was 264.4 million. A subcategory of this group, numbering 167.9 million, are considered child laborers. The difference between children in employment and child laborers is that the latter category does not count children who work within legal frameworks agreed by most nations and that serve to protect children from physically or psychologically harmful work as well as school absences. A working child who has access to schooling and is not subjected to long hours or dangerous work is considered to be employed, but not a child laborer. For example, family businesses or farms where children work limited hours are not considered to be using child labor. Of the 167.9 million child laborers, slightly more than one-half (85.3 million) were engaged in hazardous work. Child labor disproportionately affects boys more than girls, and geographically it is most numerous in the Asia-Pacific region, largely because there are more children (Figure 8.1).

Sub-Saharan Africa has fewer child laborers than the Asia-Pacific region, but a larger percentage of its children are pressed into labor. In 2012, more than one in five children in the 5–17 age group were child labors (Figure 8.2), although this was down from one in four in the ILO's previous survey for 2008. Poverty, a lack of educational opportunities, and agriculture are the main causes. Agriculture is the primary user of child labor (58.6 percent of all child labor), with services second (32.3 percent) and industry (manufacturing, construction, mining, and utilities) third (7 percent of all child laborers). Very few children work in export-oriented sectors and, in general, the incidence of child labor declines as gross domestic product (GDP) increases. It also decreases as opportunities for schooling become available. The ILO and others argue that child labor is most effectively combated by supporting the expansion of schooling.

FIGURE 8.1   **Child Labor, Ages 5–17, by Region, 2012 (millions)**

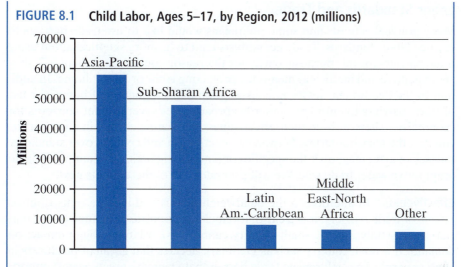

Asia has the most child labor, followed by sub-Saharan Africa.

Source: Data from *Global Child Labor Trends, 2008 to 2012.* International Labour Office, (2013), © James Gerber.

FIGURE 8.2   **Percent of Children Working, Ages 5–17, 2012**

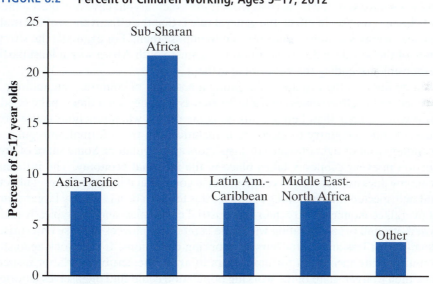

Sub-Saharan Africa has the highest proportion of children working, followed by the Asia-Pacific region.

Source: Data from *Global Child Labor Trends, 2008 to 2012.* International Labour Office, (2013), © James Gerber.

Labor Standards and Trade

Many political activists and some politicians would like to use trade barriers to enforce labor standards. Trade economists tend to be more skeptical about using trade barriers for this purpose, partly for the reasons outlined in Chapter 7: they are expensive and inefficient means for protecting labor or jobs at home. In addition to the deadweight losses in consumption and production at home, the use of trade barriers to enforce standards abroad raises several other concerns for economists. These include their effectiveness in creating change in an exporting country, the hazy borderline between protectionism and concern over standards, the lack of agreement over the specific content of standards, and their potential to erupt into a wider trade war. We will examine each of these points next.

Effectiveness   In addition to the deadweight losses and income redistribution effects of trade barriers, it is clear that only large countries can hope to use barriers successfully, since a small country cannot have a large enough impact on demand. If a small country such as Denmark decides that garment producers in Haiti are exploiting children, no trade barrier that Denmark erects against imports from Haiti is likely to reduce demand enough to change Haitian practices. Only countries that constitute a significant share of the Haitian market could erect barriers that would impose costs on Haitian producers, and even then only if there are no alternative markets for Haitian goods. Nor would this necessarily lead to changes, since there are numerous examples (Cuba, Myanmar, and others) where countries have suffered large costs from trade sanctions but have not altered their policies in response. In effect, the general rule is that the effectiveness of the trade barrier increases as more countries join to impose them. For example, the strong unity of the world's industrial economies against South Africa was at least partly responsible for ending the policy of apartheid.

In addition to the problem of creating a coalition of countries, an additional obstacle to the effectiveness of trade barriers is that they sometimes make conditions worse rather than better. This outcome occurs when sanctions cause producers inside a country to move their facilities into the informal, unregulated economy—out of sight of domestic inspectors and regulators. Some share of production in every economy takes place in the **informal economy**. The informal economy does not necessarily produce illegal goods, but it is untaxed, unregulated, and uninspected. In developing countries this tends to be a relatively larger share of overall economic activity than in industrial economies, and it is typically composed of small firms operating with little capital. Employees in these enterprises usually earn less and suffer harsher working conditions. If sanctions against a country create incentives for employers to avoid the scrutiny of labor inspectors, then a larger share of the working population could find themselves laboring under worse conditions.

Hazy Borderline between Protectionism and Concern   When does concern over foreign labor practices justify protectionism? There is no definitive answer to this question, although special interests certainly sometimes use the issue of labor standards as a means to justify their real goal—protection against foreign competition. Indeed, this is the fear of many low- and middle-income countries, which explains why their governments resist negotiating labor standards. Low- and middle-income countries tend to have abundant supplies of unskilled labor and they depend on low-wage, low-productivity jobs for a large share of their employment. In these countries, proposals to set labor standards and to use trade barriers as an enforcement mechanism are widely viewed as a form of protectionism on the part of high-income countries. Given that most high-income countries continue to protect their markets in key areas of developing country activity—agriculture, clothing, and textiles—there is a strong suspicion that calls for labor standards are a way to undermine the comparative advantage of low-income countries and to close the markets of high-income countries in selected areas.

The Specific Content of Labor Standards   The problem of reaching agreement on the specific content of standards has yet to be resolved. We have seen how child labor varies by income, and that even the definition of a child varies across countries. For example, disputes over the minimum age at which someone may legally enter the labor force have so far blocked international agreement on child labor, other than vague condemnations of the practice. Other standards are equally contentious, although it is always conceivable that an international consensus may develop in the long run. Currently, however, the lack of international agreement on the specific content of labor standards, other than the relatively vague proposals from the OECD and ILO, means that trade sanctions are unilateral measures with a large potential for creating conflict and undermining international economic relations.

The Potential to Set Off a Trade War   One primary obligation of countries in the WTO is to treat other members the same. That is, discrimination by one WTO member against another is not allowed. There are exceptions, as in the case of national security, or in the case of the special benefits given to members of a free-trade area. In general, however, discriminatory trade practices are not allowed. Consequently, the use of trade sanctions to enforce labor standards places a country out of compliance with its WTO obligations and opens it to the risk of retaliation by the targeted country. Where this ends is indeterminate.

Evidence on Low Standards as a Predatory Practice

One concern expressed by the proponents of trade sanctions is that low standards may reflect a deliberate policy to capture markets and foreign investment; that is, a country may use its coercive power to hold down or repress labor standards, thereby reducing the costs of producing goods. While theoretically possible, this too has many issues that must be examined empirically.

In practice, there is little or no support for the view that countries use low labor standards to attract foreign investment. While evidence indicates that a country can reduce production costs by outlawing unions or by some other repressive practice, there is no evidence that this type of policy has given any country a comparative advantage in lines of production that it did not already have. In other words, low standards can reduce production costs, but they do not change a country's comparative advantage.

This result does not affect competition between countries with the same or similar comparative advantages. Within a particular line of production, such as the clothing industry, countries may compete by lowering labor standards; but in that case, the low standards have harmful competitive effects on other countries with low standards, not on countries with high standards and an entirely different comparative advantage.

While low labor standards may help a country compete against another country with low labor standards, there is clear evidence that low labor standards are not a successful strategy for attracting foreign investment. The reason is simple. Low labor standards are highly correlated with a labor force that has an abundance of illiterate and unskilled workers. Furthermore, it is a sign that the nation's infrastructure of roads, ports, power supply, telecommunications, schools, and sanitation are also undeveloped. Hence, the labor cost savings of low labor standards is more than likely to be offset by higher costs everywhere else in production. Consequently, empirical studies show that countries with low labor standards are less successful at attracting foreign investment.

Finally, there is the case of intolerable situations, such as the practice of apartheid in South Africa till 1994, the gulags of the former Soviet Union, and slavery in Sudan and elsewhere. These types of practices raise multiple moral issues, which make it unreasonable to rely solely on economic analysis. Clearly, however, the more united the world is against a particular inhumane labor practice, the more likely sanctions are to succeed. For example, the United States is isolated in imposing sanctions on Cuba, and although it has imposed significant costs on Cuba's economy, the lack of international support for U.S. policies has prevented the sanctions from successfully changing Cuban policies.

CASE STUDY

The International Labour Organization

The International Labour Organization (ILO) "seeks the promotion of social justice and internationally recognized human and labour rights."[*] The ILO began in 1919 and is the only surviving element of the League of Nations, which was founded after World War I and was the precursor of the United Nations (UN). In 1946, the ILO was incorporated into the United Nations and since then, most of the world's countries have become members.

The ILO uses several tools to attain its goals. Most prominently, it develops labor standards that are embodied in specific Conventions and Recommendations. Individual countries are encouraged but not required to ratify the ILO Conventions. Currently, there are 183 conventions, about 26 of which have been shelved and are no longer proposed, leaving 157 in force.

*From About the International Labour Organization, © International Labour Organization.

On June 18, 1998, the ILO adopted the "Declaration on Fundamental Principles and Rights at Work and its Follow-up." This document specifies the eight **core labor standards** that it believes all countries should respect regardless of which conventions they ratified. The ILO groups the eight core standards into four areas:[*]

- Freedom of association and recognition of the right to collective bargaining
- Elimination of all forms of forced labor
- Effective abolition of child labor
- Elimination of discrimination in employment and occupations

The most serious type of complaint handled by the ILO concerns cases where worker's organizations, firms, or governments file a formal complaint that a member government is not enforcing core labor rights. The process for handling such complaints begins with a consultation with the alleged offender, followed by an official investigation if the consultation does not resolve the issue. The investigating committee may make recommendations, which the target country may appeal to the International Court of Justice. If there is an appeal, afterward the ILO can propose actions against the offending country. Economic actions such as trade sanctions are within the legal framework of options available to the ILO. It should be noted, however, that throughout its lengthy history, the ILO has recommended actions against only one country.

The ILO's reluctance to use the full extent of its power, along with the failure of some of its members to support it, results in a fairly weak organization. For example, in 1998, it began an investigation of Myanmar for using forced labor to fill the ranks of its military. When it proposed trade sanctions in 2000, Myanmar quickly assured the ILO that it was addressing the problem and the ILO withdrew the proposal for trade sanctions in 2001. While most national governments probably agreed with the implicit criticisms of Myanmar that follow from the ILO's proposed sanctions, they also are reluctant to set a precedent allowing an international organization to impose sanctions based on labor practices. Hence, the ILO has more authority on paper than it has in reality. Further, it illustrates the political obstacles to an international agreement with the authority to impose sanctions for labor or environmental policies.

The fact that the ILO has no enforcement authority does not mean that it is not a useful organization. Perhaps its most important function is that it provides technical assistance in all aspects of labor policy, including labor law, worker benefit programs, vocational training, development and administration of cooperatives, and many other areas.

Sources: Based on "The ILO and Enforcement of Core Labor Standards." by Kimberly Ann Elliott,Institute for International Economics,July 2000 and "Gathering Mild Rebuke: Myanmar," *The Economist*. September 2, 2006, © James Gerber.

---

*From the text of the Declaration and its follow-up, © 18 June 1998 International Labour Organization.

TRADE AND THE ENVIRONMENT

LO 8.5 Compare and contrast transboundary and nontransboundary environmental problems.

Over the last forty years, the realization has grown that our activities profoundly affect the natural environment. Unfortunately, our production and consumption choices do not always reflect the environmental costs of our decisions, and in the short run, our economies too often perform as if environmental costs and limits are irrelevant. When economic agents are allowed to ignore the environmental costs of their actions, then conflict between financial and environmental interests is inevitable. Most high-income countries have a significant amount of such conflict, and trade, along with other economic activities, has received its share of environmental criticism.

Transboundary and NonTransboundary Effects

There is a considerable overlap between environmental standards and labor standards. For example, many proponents of putting environmental standards into trade agreements believe that trade sanctions—tariffs, quotas, prohibitions on imports—should be used as enforcement mechanisms, while the critics of trade sanctions have the same concerns raised earlier: They are relatively ineffective, there is a hazy borderline between protectionism and concern for the environment, there is a lack of international agreement, and there is a potential to start trade wars.

Some differences exist between labor and environmental standards, however, beginning with the fact that some, but not all environmental impacts are transboundary. In other words, low standards in one country can degrade the environment in other countries. When it comes to trade policy, the distinction between **transboundary and nontransboundary environmental impacts** is an important one. We will look at nontransboundary, or exclusively national impacts, first.

Trade and Environmental Impacts That Do Not Cross Borders   Proponents of trade barriers to enforce environmental standards base their analysis on two types of claims. First, they argue that environmental standards reduce industrial competitiveness. This induces an environmental race to the bottom where countries are forced to rescind standards to stay competitive. Second, they argue that standards in high-income countries cause them to "export pollution" to low- and middle-income countries by relocating their dirty industries there. Both effects are harmful to the environment, as they lead to downward pressures on environmental standards and the concentration of dirty industries in a few countries with lower incomes.

The first claim, that environmental standards reduce industrial competitiveness, is theoretically valid since standards must raise the costs of production. Essentially, environmental standards prohibit the shifting of environmental costs to the public at large and thereby force firms to take a more complete measure of all their costs of production. If the standards are correctly implemented, they raise national well-being and lead to an economically optimal level of production. This implies that the argument against standards by firms that are subject to them is an argument between their interests and the nation's interests. Clearly, the nation is better off if the production of dirty industries is curtailed somewhat, even though the workers and firms in the shrinking industry may be worse off in the short-to-medium runs. The idea that the sectional interests are so politically strong that they can force environmental deregulation (race to the bottom) or prevent the introduction of new standards altogether may have some merit; but in general, environmental standards in most countries have gotten tougher over time, not more lax.

Countries that compete by offering foreign firms a reduced set of environmental compliance requirements are known as **pollution havens**. Note the essential similarity between the pollution haven concept and the claim that countries compete for foreign investment by lowering their labor standards. Empirically, there is evidence that some dirty industries from high-income industrial economies moved to low- and middle-income countries in the 1970s when the industrial economies first began cracking down on environmental polluters. Steel and chemical industries fall into this pattern, although it is possible that the developing countries were gaining a comparative advantage in these areas as high-income countries were losing theirs. Regardless, there is strong evidence showing that the idea of pollution havens is invalid; that is, it is impossible to identify any country that successfully competes for new investment on the basis of low environmental standards. The fact that there are no pollution havens is good news, but it does not mean that individual firms cannot move to escape the environmental regulations of a high-standards country. Undoubtedly, there are cases of this, although numbers and overall importance are uncertain.

From a trade perspective, the issue is complicated by the fact that differences in income and preferences make the optimal set of environmental standards variable by country. An optimal set of standards in Europe, for example, might be entirely different from the optimal set in North Africa or Central Asia. The fact that budgets and regulatory abilities are limited implies that countries cannot do everything and that they must prioritize their efforts. Biodiversity and habitat preservation may receive top priority in one place, while clean water and soil conservation are first in another. When the optimality of standards varies across countries, introducing trade barriers to enforce one country's standards in another country's production system would actually lower global welfare rather than raise it.

Trade and Transboundary Environmental Problems   Transboundary environmental impacts happen when one country's pollution spills over into a second country; for example, when a shared watershed is polluted by an upstream user, or industrial production in one country creates acid rain in another country. It can also happen in a mutual way; for example, when heavy truck traffic between two countries creates air pollution in both. Finally, transboundary environmental impacts can occur as the result of similar activities in many countries, leading to global impacts such as global warming and ozone depletion. There are a variety of potential corrective actions that countries may contemplate, from tariffs on the output of the polluting industries, to embargoes, to multicountry or global negotiations.

The analysis of labor standards applies here, as unilateral actions by one country are unlikely to have any effect whatsoever except in the large country case. Even then, the more isolated the sanctions-imposing country is, the lower the probability that its actions will successfully alter the policies of the offending countries.

CASE STUDY

Trade Barriers and Endangered Species

The connection between trade and endangered species protection is an area where the environmental movement has been critical of the WTO. The original precedent-setting case began with the U.S. ban on imports of tuna caught with nets that were particularly harmful to dolphins. Under the terms of its Endangered Species Act of 1973, the United States imposed a ban on tuna imports that were not certified as "dolphin-safe." Mexico lodged a complaint, and the outcome of the investigation was a GATT ruling that countries cannot prohibit imports based on the method of production, as long as the goods are legal. Because the United States allowed tuna to be sold in its market, it could not keep out tuna harvested in a way that hurt dolphins.

The U.S. prohibition on certain shrimp imports was the next important case to draw attention to the conflict between trade and the protection of endangered species. The United States sought to protect endangered sea turtles from being harmed by shrimp trawlers that do not use turtle excluder devices (TEDs) on their nets. In 1987, it issued guidelines requiring shrimp trawlers to use TEDs, and in 1989, it announced that beginning in May of 1991, it would ban shrimp from countries that were not certified. The guidelines applied only to the Caribbean and the Western Atlantic, and the countries were given three years to come into compliance. In 1996, a number of additional conditions were placed on shrimp imports, the guidelines were extended worldwide, and countries were given four months to come into compliance.

India, Malaysia, Pakistan, and Thailand immediately protested to the WTO. The primary basis of the protest was that they were given four months to comply with the U.S. rules, while countries in the Caribbean were given three years and technical assistance. In addition, they cited the dolphin-tuna case and argued that the GATT rules forbid discrimination against imports based on the process of production. After the United States and the Asian nations failed to resolve their dispute through informal consultations, the Asian nations asked the WTO's Dispute Settlement Body to establish a panel to resolve the issue. The issue wound its way through the dispute resolution process of rulings and appeals and finally culminated in a decision acknowledging the right of countries to impose import barriers to protect endangered species and over-turning the basis of the previous ruling on tuna imports. However, the final decision also stated that the United States' failure to negotiate or confer with the affected countries put it in violation of WTO rules. Furthermore, by treating the Asian nations differently, the United States acted in a discriminatory manner. In response, the United States began a series of negotiations with the countries that filed the complaint. In the end, it revised its timetable and procedures for certification and agreed to provide technical assistance in the use of TEDs.

This case is important because, in the words of the WTO, "We have not decided that the sovereign nations that are Members of the WTO cannot adopt effective measures to protect endangered species, such as sea turtles. Clearly, they can and should."[*] In effect, the WTO forced a multilateral solution by arranging for the United States—which places a relatively high value on sea turtles—to assist a number of less well-off countries—which place a relatively higher value on their commercial fishing industries—in acquiring the technology they needed. This enabled the United States to extend its protection of an endangered species worldwide, while the fishing fleets of South Asia remained commercially viable.

The WTO also clarified the controversial issue of products versus processes that first began with the dolphin-tuna dispute. In its ruling, the WTO states that trade measures are permitted to protect endangered species. At the same time, the ruling stressed the need to negotiate a solution and disallowed uni-lateral action.

Source: Based on United States-Import Prohibition of Certain Shrimp and Shrimp Products Product by World Bank © James Gerber.

―――――――――――
*From United States - Import Prohibition Of Certain Shrimp And Shrimp Products,
© 12 October 1998 World Trade Organization.

ALTERNATIVES TO TRADE MEASURES

LO 8.6   **Explain three alternatives to trade measures for enforcing labor and environmental standards.**

Currently, it is impossible to predict how, or even if, trade rules might eventually change to accommodate labor and environmental standards. These are new issues for the world trading system, and it is possible that they will become a permanent source of tension in international economic relations. As long as there are large income gaps between rich and poor countries, it seems unlikely that differences in standards will disappear. If trade tensions over standards are likely to continue in one form or another, then it is important to look for ways to preserve the benefits created by world trade while simultaneously resolving the conflicts over standards.

In the search for alternatives to trade measures, it is useful to recognize the general economic principle that efficient policies go directly to the root of the problem they are designed to correct. This was illustrated in Chapter 7, where it was demonstrated that trade barriers are an expensive way to solve the problem of job shortages in a particular industry. In the cases of environmental degradation and the exploitation of labor, the root of the problem lies in the production and/or consumption of particular goods, not in their trade. If a steel mill pollutes a river or exploits children, the direct cause of the environmental and human harm is the set of production standards employed by the mill, not the fact that the steel is exported. In some cases of negative environmental effects (for example, air pollution caused by gas-burning cars) the root of the problem is consumption, not production. Given that environmental degradation and labor exploitation are by-products of production and consumption decisions, the optimal policies for addressing them are at the level of production and consumption, not at the level of trade measures, since the latter create production and consumption inefficiencies in the country that imposes them. In some cases, such as countries that still allow slavery, trade measures may be the only available option short of military intervention; but in most international conflicts over labor and environmental standards, there are policies that are more efficient than trade measures.

Labels for Exports

The idea of labeling is widespread and has been implemented with mixed success. This idea is a certification process producing a label that is attached to the good when it is exported. The label tells consumers that the good was produced under conditions that are humane or environmentally sustainable. This method is already in place, although not always successful, and it seems to be growing as a strategy for telling consumers about the products they buy. For example, in 1999, the United States and Cambodia agreed that the United States would increase its quota of Cambodian textiles and garments if the country allowed foreign observers to visit its factories. Cambodia agreed to the intrusion of labor inspectors because it was desperate for the export business. The initial result was a heightening of conflict between Cambodian unions and employers, and a threat by producers to move elsewhere. Coffee is a somewhat more successful example, where retailers have used independent inspection agencies that offer services to firms that import coffee and other tropical products. This allows retailers to advertise that they sell one or more types of coffee certified as beneficial to small farmers. Similarly, some cosmetic brands and retailers certify that their products are not tested on animals.

Labeling probably has an important role to play in resolving conflicts, despite the several obstacles to its expanded use. Two main obstacles are that some countries resist what they consider an infringement of their sovereignty when foreign inspectors are allowed to probe into the details of labor and environmental conditions, and consumers have to be convinced that the label provides reliable information. If a sweater made in Cambodia has a label saying it was made under humane conditions, what degree of confidence should you put on that information? As the procedure of labeling becomes more widespread, it is possible that the true information value of labels will decrease, or that the labeling organizations become better at what they do and the labels carry more reliable information.

Requiring Home Country Standards

A second alternative to trade measures is to require home country firms to follow home country standards whenever they open foreign operations. An example is the Sullivan Principles, which asked multinationals operating in South Africa during the apartheid era (pre-1994) to practice nondiscrimination. In the case of labor standards, a domestic firm in a high-standards country that wants to open a plant in a lower-standards country would be required by law to adhere to the same labor standards as the ones it must follow at home. This does not mean that wages and benefits must be the same, since the cost of labor varies; but minimum wages might be included, along with some benefits, workplace health and safety standards, child labor standards, hours of work standards, and so on. In the environmental sphere, firms often adopt the same standards abroad as they use at home, since environmental control is often built into the technology and a least-cost strategy usually involves the adoption of one set of standards rather than multiple standards.

The advantage of this approach is that it addresses the issue of a race to the bottom by making it impossible for a home-based company to exploit low labor or environmental standards abroad, while, at the same time, preserving access to the low-wage labor of labor-abundant countries. Furthermore, this technique shifts the costs of improved standards to firms and consumers in high-income countries—which is where much of the concern originates. It might seem strange to regulate companies operating outside the nation, but it is well within the legal right of nations to impose standards on domestic firms that operate abroad, as long as the standards do not conflict with the laws of the host country. Given that the required standards are meant to be more stringent than those in the host country, this should not be a problem.

One weakness of this approach, however, is that it addresses only the problem of firms in high-standards countries that go abroad, not that of foreign-owned and foreign-operated firms that export into the domestic market. In other words, firms based in countries with low standards are untouched by this type of rule. More problematically, a clothing manufacturer based in a high-standards country might outsource its production through contracts with firms based in low-standards countries. This puts part of the production at arm's length and makes it more difficult to ensure that working conditions are satisfactory. Since the firms doing the actual cutting and sewing are foreign-owned, they may lie completely outside the reach of the regulations governing the clothing manufacturer located in the high-standards country.

Nevertheless, regulations placed on domestic firms operating abroad address a significant share of the fears of a race to the bottom. In particular, they remove the threat by domestic firms to relocate abroad if standards are not reduced at home, and ensure that the attraction of foreign-based production is the foreign comparative advantage, not the ability to lower labor standards or ignore the environment. In addition, they help avoid the problems created when high-income countries appear to be dictating labor and environmental standards for low- and middle-income countries. Each country sets its own standards, but when firms cross national boundaries, they must conform to whichever standards are higher—those in the sending country, or those in the receiving country.

Increasing International Negotiations

A third alternative to trade measures is to increase the level of international negotiations, either using existing international organizations such as the ILO for labor, or creating new agreements and organizations for the environment. In the labor standards arena, proponents of increased negotiations would like to see the ILO publicize examples of countries that are out of compliance with core labor rights. It could do this with the information it already gathers on the labor practices of its member countries. An expanded role for the ILO is supported by the growing recognition that it has the technical capability to assess labor policies, whereas the WTO does not.

In the environmental arena, the WTO maintains an environmental database that reports all environmental agreements with potential trade impacts and that have been reported to the WTO. As of 2012, there were 569 reported environmental agreements. These range in scope and include important global agreements such as the Montreal Protocol regulating the use of chlorofluorocarbons, the Basel Convention regulating the transportation of hazardous waste, and the Convention on International Trade in Endangered Species. In cases where two or more countries have signed an agreement and the agreement allows trade sanctions as part of its enforcement mechanism, the WTO's position is that disputes should be resolved within the environmental agreement and not within the WTO. In cases where there are no environmental agreements, however, as with the United States' shrimp import ban, the WTO rules of nondiscrimination apply.

It is significant that the WTO has staked out a position on the issue of multilateral environmental agreements. The WTO recognizes explicitly that it is not an environmental organization and that it has no expertise in this area. However, it has left room for environmental agreements to develop their own enforcement mechanisms. This does not change the fact that trade sanctions are unlikely to be the least expensive technique for resolving environmental disputes, but it does leave it up to the nations involved to decide on their own methods of enforcement.

CASE STUDY

Global Climate Change

A consensus of climate scientists tell us that global warming is happening and that it is caused by human activity. This view was reflected in the United Nations Conference on Climate Change, held in Paris during late November and December, 2015. One hundred ninety-five nations signed pledges to reduce their emission of carbon dioxide and other gasses responsible for the bulk of the world's human-caused climate change. Global warming is clearly a transboundary environmental problem; no matter how far you live from places where greenhouse gases (GHG) are produced, it will affect everyone on the planet.

Most human activity involves the burning of fossil fuels, either directly as when we drive cars, or indirectly as when we use electricity generated by oil or coal fired power plants, or when we consume goods and services produced with fossil fuels. Emissions of the gases generated by the burning of fossil fuels exceeds the earth's ability to absorb them, and over the decades they build up in the atmosphere where they trap more of the infrared energy reflected off the earth's surface and cause an increase in temperatures. Economists examining this problem usually focus on the policy aspect, not the science of global warming, since the discipline of economics does not lead to expertise in areas needed to do research on atmospheric chemistry and physics. Economics does lead to a set of tools and analyses that help society understand the net value of remediation efforts, however, and is essential for evaluating the different policy proposals for addressing the problems of climate change. Economics can evaluate the costs and benefits along the entire spectrum of choices, from doing nothing all the way to very aggressive actions to cut fossil fuel use and emissions.

The first generation of coordinated global action against climate change resulted in the Kyoto Protocol of 1997. The Kyoto agreement set strict targets on greenhouse gases produced by high-income countries but did not try to limit emissions by low- and middle-income countries. The reasoning is that high-income countries can afford to make the necessary changes, while other countries cannot, and in the 1990s most GHG originated in industrial, high-income countries. The United States did not ratify the Kyoto Protocol, nor did it make commitments at a follow-up summit in Copenhagen in 2010. Nevertheless, both the U.S. and China—another large emitter of GHG—made strong commitments to reduce emissions at the Paris Summit in 2015.

Two layers of problems make it difficult to address the problem of climate change. One, science can only provide probabilities and likelihoods, not certainties. That complicates the effort to understand the right level of response,

(continued)

and it also opens the door to greater confusion in the public's mind when energy companies and others with a financial stake in fossil fuels try to discredit the science of climate change. The right level of response depends on how much damage might be averted, how much the prevention efforts cost today, and how far into the future the benefits occur. The best that economists can do is to take the various estimates of the future consequences of climate change given by scientists and then see how much reduction in emissions would avert or reduce the damage, while measuring the costs in terms of lost output, environmental damage, and the purchase of new technologies. Economists have run numerous scenarios, based on different estimates of future damages and with different policy responses. A key problem is how to take into account that we are spending money today to protect the incomes of people in the future who, judging by the last 200 years of world history, are likely to be much better off than we are.

A central result of this modeling is that we should pay more for carbon. This follows from the fact that each of us imposes a negative externality on the rest of world when we consume carbon-based fuels. As with any negative externality, the solution is to incorporate the full cost of its consumption into its price. The Yale University economist William Nordhaus points out that a carbon tax tells consumers which goods use a lot of fossil fuel energy in their production, it tells producers which methods are intensive in the use of fossil fuels, and it sends a signal to innovators and entrepreneurs to look for alternatives. He estimates that a tax of \$30–\$50 per ton of carbon emission would raise electrical bills for the average American household approximately \$90 per year, from around \$1,200 to \$1,290.

For a carbon tax to work with maximum effect, it has to be a global tax, and this brings up the second layer of problems for addressing climate change: How do the world's nation's organize a coordinated global response? A harmonized global carbon tax could be adjusted up when estimates of future damage increase in severity and adjusted down if the damage is understood to be less than previously thought. As with all transboundary problems, this would require coordination. Unlike most environmental problems, however, which affect only two countries or a handful of countries, climate change is global, and even though most GHG emissions have historically been from high-income countries, large amounts of emissions today also come from middle-income countries such as China, India, Brazil, and Russia. In the final analysis, unless there is a grand technological fix that no one currently foresees, increased international negotiations, such as the Paris conference in late 2015, are essential for an effective response to the problem of climate change.

Summary

- The increase in world trade over the last fifty years has reduced tariffs and eliminated quotas, but as a result, many domestic policies have become unintentional barriers to trade. Examples include competition policies, product standards, health and safety standards, and labor and environmental standards.

- Countries do not need to harmonize standards in order to trade. In many cases, harmonization would remove some of the differences between countries and eliminate the gains from trade. Alternative treatment of standards includes mutual recognition and maintaining completely separate standards.

- Differing labor and environmental standards have become a point of significant conflict between high-income and low-income countries. Standards differ primarily because of differences in income and factor endowments.

- Core labor standards defined by the OECD and the ILO include prohibitions against forced labor, freedom of association and collective bargaining, the elimination of child labor, and nondiscrimination in employment.

- Child labor is most common in Africa and Asia. Asia has the most children working, but a larger proportion of African children under age fourteen are at work. Child labor is most common in agriculture and in small-scale, family-operated businesses.

- Proponents of using trade barriers to enforce labor and environmental standards abroad argue that differences in standards are an unfair competitive advantage for the low-standards countries. They also fear that trade and foreign investment cause a race to the bottom in standards and that low environmental standards make some countries "pollution havens."

- Evidence is scarce that countries use low standards to attract industry. In practice, low standards are associated with low levels of foreign investment. In addition, there is no evidence of pollution havens.

- Most economists oppose the use of trade measures to enforce standards because they are relatively ineffective, do not go to the root of the problem, are not based on an agreement regarding the content of standards, encourage protectionism in the guise of support for standards, and can lead to wider trade conflict.

- Environmental problems can be transboundary or nontransboundary. International conflicts over both types of problems are similar to conflicts over labor standards. Transboundary problems, in particular, require international negotiations.

- Alternatives to trade measures include labeling, enforcement of home country standards on home country firms operating abroad, and increased international negotiations. Greater support for the ILO and increasing support for international environmental agreements are also more efficient alternatives to trade measures.

Vocabulary

core labor standards

harmonization of standards

high-income

upper-middle-income

lower-middle-income

and low-income countries

informal economy

International Labour Organization
(ILO)

mutual recognition of standards

pollution havens

race to the bottom

separate standards

transboundary and nontransboundary environmental impacts

Study Questions

All problems are assignable in MyEconLab

8.1   What are the three ways for countries to handle different standards
abroad? Do standards have to be the same for countries to be integrated?

8.2   What are the advantages and disadvantages for countries that adopt the
same standards?

8.3   When high-definition television (HDTV) was first considered a possibility
in the United States, the U.S. government held a competition to select the
technical standards that would be used nationwide. Why would the government see an advantage to setting one standard, and what are the pros and
cons for the private businesses that were interested in producing for the
U.S. market?

8.4   Why do standards vary across countries? Illustrate your answer with examples in the area of labor standards.

8.5   What are labor standards, and why are arguments about labor standards
confined primarily to arguments between high-income countries on the one
hand, and low- and middle-income countries on the other?

8.6   Discuss the reasons why using trade barriers to enforce labor or environmental standards may be less efficient than other measures.

8.7   What are the arguments in favor of using trade barriers to enforce labor
and environmental standards? Assess each argument.

8.8 One common critique of the WTO is that it overturns national environmental protections and forces countries to lower their standards. For example, when the United States tried to protect endangered sea turtles, the WTO prevented it. Assess this claim.

8.9 What are the alternatives to trade measures for raising labor and environmental standards? What are the strengths and weaknesses of each one?

International Finance

9 Trade and the Balance of Payments

Learning Objectives

After studying this chapter, students will be able to:

9.1 Define the current, capital, and financial accounts of a country's balance of payments.

9.2 Explain the importance of the three main components of the current account.

9.3 Describe three types of international capital flows.

9.4 Use a simple algebraic model to relate the current account to savings, investment, and the general government budget balance.

9.5 Discuss the pros and cons of current account deficits.

9.6 Show the relationship between a country's balance of payments and its international investment position.

INTRODUCTION: THE CURRENT ACCOUNT

LO 9.1 **Define the current, capital, and financial accounts of a country's balance of payments.**

LO 9.2 **Explain the importance of the three main components of the current account.**

The international transactions of a nation are divided into three separate accounts: the *current account*, the *capital account*, and the *financial account*. For most countries, the capital account is relatively minor, and the two most important accounts are the current and financial accounts. The **current account** tracks the flow of goods and services into and out of the country, while the **financial account** is the record of financial transactions occurring between one country and the rest of the world, such as foreign investment, purchases, or sales of foreign stocks and bonds, and international bank lending. The **capital account** is by far the smallest of the three and is a record of transfers of specialized types of capital, such as the gift of an embassy building or the land it is on, from residents of one country to residents in another. This chapter examines the accounting system used to keep track of a country's international transactions. One of its primary goals is to understand the accounting relationships among domestic investment, domestic savings, and international flows of goods, services, and financial assets. In addition, we will use the international accounts to examine the meaning of international indebtedness and to discuss its consequences.

The Trade Balance

In 2014, the United States imported goods and services worth $2,851 billion. The composition of the purchases included a wide array of tangibles and intangibles, from Japanese cars to Venezuelan oil, and from luxury Mexican vacations to tickets on the European rail system. In the same year, U.S. firms exported $2,344 billion worth of aircraft, software, grain, trips to Disneyworld, and other goods and services. The difference between exports and imports of goods and services is called the **trade balance**. For the United States, the 2014 trade balance was $2,344 billion minus $2,851 billion, or −$507 billion. Because the number is negative, the United States had a trade deficit.

Exports and imports include both goods and services, so the trade balance can be decomposed into the balance on goods and the balance on services. In the case of the United States, the goods balance was in deficit by $741 billion, while the services balance was in surplus by $232 billion. In 2014, services were 30 percent of total exports, and for many years they have been a growing part of U.S. and world trade. The main items in services trade include travel and passenger fares; transportation services; royalties and license fees; and education, financial, business, and technical services. Although the U.S. trade balance for services is in surplus, total trade in services is still too small a share of overall trade to counteract the very large deficit in the merchandise goods trade balance.

The Current and Capital Account Balances

The merchandise goods trade balance is the most commonly cited measurement of a nation's transactions with the rest of the world. The widespread dissemination of the monthly merchandise trade balance statistics through press releases and news articles makes it the most familiar concept in international economics and the basis of most people's understanding of U.S. international economic relations.

A more comprehensive statistic is the **current account balance**, which measures all current, nonfinancial transactions between a nation and the rest of the world. It has three main items: (1) goods and services trade; (2) earned income paid abroad and received from abroad, called **primary income**; and (3) transfer payments made abroad and received from abroad, called **secondary income**. All three of these items have credit and debit components in the balance of payments and in the construction of the current account balance. The simplest framework for conceptualizing these three components is in terms of credits and debits, as portrayed in Table 9.1.

The investment income items in Table 9.1 should not be confused with the flow of investment capital that is used to buy a business or invest in another country's stock market. Investment income is the income received or paid on the

TABLE 9.1   Components of the Current Account

	Credit	Debit
1. Goods and services	Exports	Imports
2. Primary income	Investment earnings income received from foreigners and compensation of employees	Investment earning income paid to foreigners and compensation of employees
3. Secondary income	Transfers received from abroad	Transfers made to foreigners

There are three main components to the current account. Each component is divided into debit and credit elements.

existing investments. For example, financial capital sent to another country with the purpose of buying a bond would not be included, but the interest received on the bond would be. The purchase or sale of assets are counted in the financial accounts of buying and selling countries, and are discussed below. It is useful to think of primary income in the current account as the payments or receipts for the use of financial capital or for use of labor. For example, if a U.S. company invests in Mexico's stock market, the initial investment will not show up in the current account but will be included in the financial account. The subsequent flow of dividends back to the U.S. company will be counted in the United States as income received and in Mexico as income paid. Conceptually, it is as if U.S. investors are receiving payment for the rental of U.S. capital to Mexican firms, which makes it similar to payments for a service. Similarly, if a U.S. company operating in Mexico pays wages from its home in the U.S., the wages are included in the primary income category of the current account and are recorded as a receipt by Mexico and a payment by the U.S.

The third item in the current account balance, secondary income, includes payments made that are not in exchange for a good or service, such as foreign aid, or the **remittances** (the transfer of wages earned in one country to residents of another country) of immigrants temporarily residing in another country. In the U.S. case, these payments are large in absolute amounts but small relative to the U.S. current account. Transfers are sometimes very important to the current account balances of developing countries receiving either substantial foreign aid or large remittances from their citizens working abroad.

Table 9.2 gives a picture of the U.S. current account in 2014. The $390 billion deficit is part of the long-term persistence of U.S. current account deficits, as shown in Figure 9.1. Large deficits in the current account began around 1982, and have been more or less a constant feature of the U.S. economy since then. Although the deficit turned into a small surplus of $6.6 billion in 1991, due in part to the large flows of secondary income (transfers) received by the United States as payment for Operation Desert Storm, the pattern has been one of persistent deficits in the current account.

MyEconLab Real-time Data

TABLE 9.2 The U.S. Current Account Balance, 2014

	Billions of Dollars
1. Goods and services exports (credit) (Lines 1a + 1b)	2,343
1a. Goods exports	1,633
1b. Services exports	711
2. Primary income receipts (credit) (Lines 2a + 2b)	823
2a. Investment income received	816
2b. Compensation of employees received	7
3. Secondary income receipts (transfers) (credit)	140
4. Goods and services imports (debit) (Lines 4a + 4b)	2,852
4a. Goods imports	2,374
4b. Services imports	477
5. Primary income payments (debit) (Lines 5a + 5b)	585
5a. Investment income paid	569
5b. Compensation of employees paid	16
6. Secondary income payments (transfers) (debit)	259
7. Current account balance (Lines 1 + 2 + 3 − 4 − 5 − 6)	−390

The U.S. current account balance was in deficit in 2014. The deficit is largely the result of goods imports greater than exports. The U.S. has surpluses in services trade and primary income flows.
Source: U.S. Department of Commerce, Bureau of Economic Analysis

We will explore the causes and consequences of large current account deficits later, but here it should be noted that a current account deficit is not simply a sign of weakness. On the contrary, through much of the 1990s, rapid economic growth in the United States raised incomes and created a voracious appetite for imports. Meanwhile, economic growth among the United States' main trading partners ranged between negative and sluggish, so foreign incomes did not rise as rapidly. Consequently, foreign demand for U.S. exports grew less rapidly than the U.S. demand for imports. Therefore, it can be argued that the current account deficit in the 1990s was a sign of relative U.S. economic strength. It would be a mistake to carry this argument too far, however, since everyone agrees that the deficit is not sustainable in the long run and that it could create serious future problems. We will look at this issue later in the chapter after we introduce a few more concepts.

The **capital account** of the balance of payments is the record of specialized capital transfers. Because it is a measure of transfers and not purchases or sales, it is somewhat similar to the category of secondary income of the current account, but with the major distinction that it applies to capital transfers and not income transfers. Normally, this is a small item and includes relatively infrequent activities such as the transfer of military bases or embassies between countries, debt forgiveness, and the personal assets that migrants carry with them when they cross borders.

FIGURE 9.1   **U.S. Current Account Balances, 1960–2014**

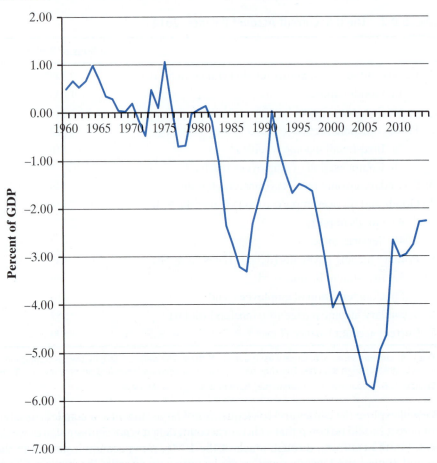

There are two periods of large current account deficits in the United States. The first lasted through most of the 1980s, while the second began in the early 1990s and continues today, although it has been moderated by the financial crisis of 2007–2009 which led to fewer imports.

Source: Data from Organization for Economic Co-operation and Development, Total Current Account Bal-ance for the United States, © James Gerber.

INTRODUCTION TO THE FINANCIAL ACCOUNT

Types of Financial Flows

LO 9.3   **Describe three types of international capital flows.**

The financial account is the main record of financial flows between countries. In its 2014 revision of the international accounts, the U.S. Bureau of Economic Analysis (BEA) brought U.S. accounting procedures into alignment with the recent revisions

MyEconLab Real-time Data

TABLE 9.3   The U.S. Balance of Payments, 2014

	Billions of Dollars
1. **Current Account Balance** (See Table 9.2.)	−390
2. **Capital Account Balance**	0
3. **Financial Account**	
3a. Net U.S. acquisition of financial assets, excluding financial derivatives (increase/outflow (+))	792
3b. Net U.S. incurrence of liabilities, excluding financial derivatives (increase/inflow (+))	977
3c. Net change in financial derivatives	−54
4. **Statistical Discrepancy**	151
5. **Memoranda**	
5a. Balance on current and capital accounts (lines 1 + 2)	−390
5b. Balance on financial account (lines 3a − 3b + 3c)	−239

The financial account measures capital inflows and outflows. A positive value for the net acquisition of assets is net lending abroad while a positive value for net incurrence of liabilities is net borrowing from abroad. The financial account balance (5b) indicates net lending (positive) or net borrowing (negative). The statistical discrepancy is the difference between net lending and borrowing on financial account and the current plus capital accounts (line 5b minus line 5a).

Source: U.S. Department of Commerce, Bureau of Economic Analysis

in methods and concepts made by the International Monetary Fund (IMF). Under the new system, the BEA emphasizes the terminology shown in Table 9.3 and uses "net acquisition of financial assets" and "net incurrence of liabilities" to categorize the bulk of financial flows. Following the new BEA and IMF terminology, these are the main categories we will use in this chapter when discussing the financial account.

Unlike the current account which deals with goods and services and income flows, the financial account covers all types of financial assets that can be bought and sold internationally. It is divided into three main categories, each with many subcomponents. The three main categories are (1) the net acquisition of financial assets, (2) the net incurrence of liabilities, and (3) changes in financial derivatives. Financial assets include bank accounts, stocks and bonds, real property such as factories, businesses, real estate, and monetary gold and foreign currencies that can be used to settle international payments. A positive net acquisition of financial assets implies that the country's residents are buying more foreign assets than they are selling. A positive net incurrence of liabilities means that foreigners are purchasing more of the home country's assets than they are selling. Seen another way, the acquisition of financial assets is a form of lending by the home country that takes place through the purchase of foreign owned real estate, stocks, bonds, or some other asset form. The net incurrence of liabilities is symmetrical in the sense that it is a form of borrowing by the home country that takes place through the sale of home country assets to foreigners.

The third category of the financial account is financial derivatives. These are assets with a value that is derived from the value of some other asset, such as commodity prices or exchange rates, or one of many other possibilities. They are complex financial contracts that are traded in a variety of forms, and until recently were not included in the balance of payments. Their inclusion in 2006 is thought to have eliminated a growing source of measurement error, as derivatives have become increasingly important in global finance.

Table 9.3 shows the financial account in relation to the current and capital accounts. Two points about the financial account should be kept in mind. First, it presents the flow of assets during the year and not the stock of assets that have accumulated over time. Second, all flows are "net" changes rather than "gross" changes. Net changes are the differences between assets sold and assets bought, as when U.S. residents purchase shares in the Mexican stock market while simultaneously selling Mexican bonds. The net change in U.S.-owned assets is the difference between the value of the shares purchased and the bonds sold. If the stocks and bonds are equal in value, then the net change is zero. Net changes are informative because they measure the monetary value of the change in a country's financial stake in foreign economies.

Under the accounting procedure used to tabulate credits and debits in the financial account, payments made abroad to buy financial assets are a debit, while payments received from abroad for selling home country assets (net incurrence of liabilities) are a credit. In this sense, credits can be viewed as the inflow received when assets are sold to foreigners and debits are the payment outflow when financial assets are purchased by home country residents. This way of looking at it makes the credits and debits of asset flows conceptually similar to the credits and debits of exports and imports.

The current, capital, and financial accounts are interdependent. The current and capital accounts measure the flows of goods, services, and transfers between a country and the rest of the world, and the financial account measures the net flows of asset purchases and sales. Because each element in the current account must include a financial transaction that is a payment or receipt, the current plus capital account must equal the financial account. A negative value in the current plus capital account implies net borrowing by the home country. This must show up in the financial account as net borrowing as well. The financial account of the United States shows it lends as well as borrows, but on net, it borrows. Table 9.3 shows that the U.S. lent abroad through the net acquisition of financial assets worth $792 billion. At the same time, the United States incurred liabilities or borrowed $977 billion from foreigners. Its balance on financial account is the amount lent minus the amount borrowed, or $792 billion minus $977 billion plus the net change in financial derivatives (−$54), or −$239.

The last item to discuss in Table 9.3 is the **statistical discrepancy** on line 4. Since it is impossible to record all transactions and to ensure they are accurately measured, the amount of net lending or borrowing on the current and capital accounts rarely matches the amount implied by the financial account balance. The statistical discrepancy is calculated as the residual difference between the financial account balance minus the current plus capital account balances $(-239 - (-390) = 151)$. In a sense, it is the size of the measurement error.

While the current and financial accounts are mirror images of each other, a large share of a nation's gross financial account transactions is not in response to the current account flows of goods, services, or income. For example, a London-based investment company may buy stock in a Chilean firm, lend money to the government of Thailand, and engage in any number of financial transactions that have nothing to do with the movements of goods and services on the current account. In an accounting sense, these purely financial transactions must have a net value of zero. The reason is that the purchase of an asset is simultaneously the sale of an asset of equal value. For example, if you buy a share of stock, you obtain an asset that is partial ownership of a company while the person selling the share obtains your cash. It is the same internationally. If a Canadian citizen buys shares in the Mexican stock market (capital outflow), he or she must sell Canadian dollars or some other asset (capital inflow). (If he or she pays for the shares by writing a check drawn on a Mexican bank, then it does not enter the financial account since it is a change of one foreign asset for another.) As a result, the financial account is a complete picture of net flows of financial assets during the year.

One of the primary concerns of most governments is the form of financial flows entering and leaving the country. Some financial flows are very mobile and represent short-run tendencies. These flows are often vehicles for transmitting a financial crisis from one country to another or for generating sudden responses to changes in investor expectations about the short-run prospects of an economy. The degree of mobility of financial flows and the potential of some flows to introduce a large element of volatility into an economy have turned the type of flows that a country receives into a major issue.

As a first approach to a more detailed representation of the financial account, it is useful to subdivide the financial flows in Table 9.3 into more specific subcategories. Table 9.4 shows the 2014 financial account for the United States, divided into seven subcategories representing the main components of outflows and inflows, or net assets acquired (outflow) and net liabilities incurred (inflow).

Line 1a in Table 9.4 shows a net acquisition of $357 billion of direct investments outside the United States, while line 2a shows a net incurrence of $132 billion in direct investment liabilities. The first number (1a) represents the purchase of factories, businesses, real estate, office buildings, and other forms of real property outside the United States by U.S. residents and businesses. The second item (2a) is symmetrical in that it represents the purchase in the United States of a similar category of items by foreign residents and businesses. **Foreign direct investment** (FDI) was discussed in Chapter 4 where Dunning's OLI theory was presented. In general, FDI varies considerably from year to year

TABLE 9.4   Components of the U.S. Financial Account, 2014

	Billions of Dollars
1. Net U.S. acquisition of financial assets (net increase in assets/ financial outflow (+))	792
1a. Direct investment assets	357
1b. Portfolio investment assets	538
1c. Other investment assets	−99
1d. Reserve assets	−4
2. Net U.S. incurrence of liabilities, excluding financial derivatives (net increase in liabilities/financial inflows (+))	977
2a. Direct investment liabilities	132
2b. Portfolio investment liabilities	705
2c. Other investment liabilities	140
3. Net change in financial derivatives	−54

Financial outflows and inflows can be subdivided into main categories of direct investment (businesses, real estate, or other physical assets), portfolio investment (stocks, bonds, and other financial instruments), and other investment assets (primarily international bank loans). In addition, every country buys and sells reserve assets which are monetary gold and foreign currencies used for international payments.

Source: U.S. Department of Commerce, Bureau of Economic Analysis

since it depends on the number of purchases and sales by foreigners, and is often linked to mergers. Once made, however, FDI is probably less likely to leave a country, particularly when compared to the next category of items in lines 1b and 1c and 2b and 2c.

Portfolio investments (1b and 2b) and the other investments (1c and 2c) are paper assets and liabilities. The main portfolio items are stocks and bonds, while the other investment category mainly includes currencies, bank deposits and loans, and insurance contracts. FDI, portfolio investments, and other investments assets all give their holders a claim on a country's future output, but they are very different in their time horizons. FDI which represents real assets as opposed to paper assets tends to have a longer time-horizon and is much less liquid than most of the items in the other two categories. As such, FDI represents a longer term position in the country. Portfolio investments and most other investments, by contrast, can be long- or short-term, but they are far more liquid and easier to dispose of in the event of a sudden change in the economy or in investor expectations. This poses a significant challenge for economic policymakers.

When investor expectations change, it can cause a **sudden stop** in inflows, followed by large destabilizing outflows. The economist Guillermo Calvo coined the term sudden stop to describe a quick reversal of portfolio or other assets and notes that they have been involved in most recent financial crises. In terms of Table 9.4, a sudden stop would appear as a shift from one period to the next in categories 2b and 2c. Specifically, there would be a drop in the net incurrence of liabilities as capital inflows ceased. In a severe crisis, net incurrence of liabilities might turn negative, implying that foreigners are selling off their holdings of home country assets. Categories 1b and 1c might drop as well, as home country residents stop acquiring foreign assets so that they can pay-off foreigners who are converting assets in the home country into cash and repatriating to their own country or to a third party country. If home country residents are forced to sell off foreign assets in order to obtain the liquidity they need to pay-off investors, categories 1b and 1c can become negative, representing a net reduction in the home country's holding of foreign portfolio and other financial assets.

Reserve assets are shown in category 1d. These are mainly the currencies of the largest and most stable economies in the world: U.S. dollars, European Union (EU) euros, British pounds, the Japanese yen, and recently the Chinese yuan (November 2015). In addition to key currencies, reserve assets also include monetary gold and special drawing rights (SDR), the artificial currency of the IMF. Since the financial account reports financial flows, it does not indicate the stock, or total supply, of assets available. From Table 9.4, we see that the United States had a net change of −$4 billion in official reserve assets. This represents payment for the purchase of official reserve assets, but does not indicate the total amount of reserve assets available to the United States. Since all forms of international debts can be settled with reserve assets, especially key currencies, these assets play a prominent role in international finance. When they become scarce in a country, it signals that potentially serious problems are arising. For example, when Mexico's economy collapsed in late 1994 and early 1995, it was because Mexicans owed dollars to various international investors but lacked dollars to pay them. The outflow of dollars from Mexico during 1994 severely reduced the supply of dollars and, in the short run, made it impossible for firms and the government to pay their dollar-denominated debts. Relief came when Mexico was able to arrange several loans from the IMF, the United States, and Canada, which replenished its supply of official reserve assets. (See the case study in Chapter 12.)

Reserve assets are used to settle international debts; consequently, central banks and treasury ministries use them as a store of value. For example, when an importer in a small country such as Chile purchases goods from Europe, payment may be in dollars or another reserve currency, but the supplier probably would not accept Chilean pesos from the purchaser. The importer must convert some pesos into a reserve currency which it can use to pay for its imports. If the Chilean Central Bank cannot provide dollars or another reserve currency to Chilean banks and importers, then the import business grinds to a halt unless the importer can secure some form of credit from the seller.

Limits on Financial Flows

Throughout the second half of the twentieth century, many nations limited the movement of financial flows across their national borders. A typical pattern was to allow financial flows related to transactions on the current account, but to limit and regulate financial account transactions. If an importer needed a foreign loan to purchase goods abroad, or if an exporter needed foreign financing to buy materials to make goods for export, the financial flows were regulated but generally allowed. Conversely, if a bank wanted to borrow abroad to make loans at home, then the inflow of financial capital to the bank was prohibited or subjected to such onerous terms and conditions that it was undesirable. These types of restrictions on financial flows were a normal part of the international economic landscape, even in many high-income industrial economies, until the 1980s and 1990s. For example, the members of the EU did not completely liberalize financial flows between member countries until 1993.

A movement toward more open financial markets over the last several decades included a significant lifting of controls on financial flows across international boundaries. This change in international economic policy was seen as desirable because restrictions on financial flows limit the availability of financial capital. Low- and middle-income countries, in particular, were thought to benefit from the liberalization of capital markets since they have the greatest scarcity of financial capital. Frequently, the quantity of investment in low- and medium-income countries depends on their access to the financial capital of high-income countries.

In addition to the positive benefits for growth, it is sometimes impossible for regulators to identify and separate financial flows that occur for reasons of financial transactions from those that are related to transactions on the current account. Consequently, it can be difficult to regulate or control international financial flows and the attempt to do so can lead to red tape, bureaucratic delay, and arbitrariness, all of which can reduce economic efficiency. For over two decades, from the 1980s until the crisis of 2007–2009, many economists argued that it is better to allow financial capital to move freely across international borders.

More recently, the extreme volatility in some financial markets and the severe damage it has caused to many countries has revived interest in regulations to limit the damage caused by unexpectedly large financial outflows. As the pendulum has swung back toward seeing benefits in more regulation of financial flows, it has generated a certain amount of tension between policymakers, politicians, and business people. It is easy to understand why. On the one hand, foreign capital inflows are beneficial because they enable countries to increase their investments in factories, ports, and other physical assets that help raise living standards and incomes. On the other hand, the sudden outward flight of foreign financial capital can generate a debt crisis and throw a country into deep depression. The key is to capture the benefits of increased investment while minimizing the risks of capital flight. At this point there is not much consensus among economists about the best policies. We will look at this issue in more detail in Chapter 12 after we introduce several more concepts.

CASE STUDY

The Crisis of 2007–2009 and the Balance of Payments

The global financial crisis that began in 2007 had both medium-run and short-run impacts on the balance of payments. In the United States and elsewhere, the first stages of the crisis began in the late summer of 2007 with severe strains in financial markets. Throughout late 2007 and into 2008, banks and other financial services firms such as insurance companies and securities dealers reassessed their portfolios and tried to reduce their risk exposure by selling their foreign assets in large quantities. The goal was to build reserves of short-term, highly liquid, and secure assets such as cash and U.S. Treasury securities. These strains continued into 2008 and then intensified with the bankruptcy of several large financial services firms that had significant international business.

Banks and financial firms knew that some of the assets they held were "toxic" and unlikely to maintain their value or any value at all in some cases. As the crisis progressed, problems grew more intractable as it became increasingly difficult to determine a market value for assets that had stopped trading and had no reference prices available. If banks could not sell their assets, then they could not build their cash reserves for handling their potential losses. The consequences would be disastrous, since they would lack the liquidity to pay their own debts. The shifts in financial markets that began in late summer and early fall of 2007 were sudden, and continued throughout 2008. The reversal in the normal pattern of global finance is illustrated in Table 9.5, which shows the main components of the financial account of the United States for 2007 and 2008.

Table 9.5 shows that both foreign and U.S. domestic interests shifted toward a defensive stance from 2007 to 2008 as they stopped accumulating each other's assets altogether, or greatly reduced their purchases. In 2007, the US acquired over $1.5 *trillion* in financial assets ($1,572,509,000,000). The crisis year of 2008 was entirely different, however, and U.S. interests were net sellers of financial assets. The negative value of −$309 billion represented a selling off of foreign financial assets, as opposed to the normal pattern in which U.S. interests are net purchasers. All of the subcategories under Line 1 declined in value, but the primary causes of the net sell-off were declines in portfolio holdings abroad (stocks and bonds) and other investments, which is mostly bank lending. In other words, U.S. households and businesses sold their foreign stocks and bonds and they reduced the loans they were making abroad. Net purchases of businesses, real estate, and other forms of foreign direct investment remained positive, illustrating the less volatile nature of that type of foreign capital flow.

(continued)

TABLE 9.5   The U.S. Financial Accounts, 2007–2008 (Billions of Dollars)

	2007	2008
1. Net U.S. acquisition of financial assets excluding financial derivatives (net increase in assets/financial outflow (+))	1,573	−309
1a. Direct investment assets	533	351
1b. Portfolio investment assets	381	−284
1c. Other investment assets	659	−381
1d. Reserve assets	0	5
2. Net U.S. incurrence of liabilities, excluding financial derivatives (net increase in liabilities. financial inflows (+))	2,182	454
2a. Direct investment liabilities	340	333
2b. Portfolio investment liabilities	1,157	524
2c. Other investment liabilities	687	−402

Source: U.S. Department of Commerce, Bureau of Economic Analysis

Line 2 shows that foreigners accumulated far fewer U.S. assets in 2008 than they did in 2007 ($2,182 trillion vs $454 billion). The biggest change occurred in the area of loans to U.S. banks and nonfinancial firms, which moved from a net inflow to the United States of nearly $687 billion to a net outflow of −402 billion (line 2c). At the same time, foreign purchases of securities fell by over $600 billion.

In general, Table 9.5 illustrates how firms in both the United States and abroad sought to protect themselves against the spreading crisis by reducing new investments outside their home country and by bringing liquid assets home.

THE CURRENT ACCOUNT AND THE MACROECONOMY

LO 9.4   **Use a simple algebraic model to relate the current account to savings, investment, and the general government budget balance.**

LO 9.5   **Discuss the pros and cons of current account deficits.**

There are two important practical reasons for learning about the balance of payments. One is to understand the broader implications of current account imbalances and to analyze the policies that might be used to tame a current account deficit. This is particularly important for small countries that are easily buffeted about by changes in the global economy, but it is also of interest to a big economy such as the United States, where very large current account deficits have been the norm for several years. The second practical reason for studying the balance of payments is to understand how countries might avoid a crisis brought on by volatile financial flows, and what policies will minimize the harmful effects of a crisis if it occurs. Economic analysis is still in its infancy when it comes to the problem of volatile financial flows, and there is some distance to travel before there is likely to be a consensus agreement on issues such as free versus restricted capital mobility, or the links from financial flows to economic growth. Nevertheless, there are some basic points of agreement among economists, and we will discuss them in Chapters 10 and 12. Before then, we must examine the relationship of the current account to the macroeconomy, which requires a brief review of basic concepts from the principles of macroeconomics.

The National Income and Product Accounts

The internal, domestic accounting systems that countries use to keep track of total production and total income are called the **national income and product accounts (NIPA)**. These accounts are very detailed presentations of income, output, and other measures of a nation's macroeconomy. We will use the most fundamental concepts from this accounting system, beginning with the concept of **gross domestic product (GDP)**. Recall from the principles of economics that a nation's gross domestic product is the market value of all final goods and services produced inside its borders during some time period, usually a year. GDP is the most common measure of the size of an economy, although it is widely recognized that it ignores some important considerations, such as the value of leisure time and environmental degradation that takes place during the process of producing the nation's output. In addition, GDP includes only goods that pass through organized markets, so household production (cooking, sewing, landscaping, childcare, and so on) and other nonmarket-oriented production are left out. For these and other reasons, economists caution against using GDP as the sole determinant of the well-being of a society. In spite of these limitations, however, it provides a starting point for understanding different economies.

To avoid the problem of double counting, GDP includes only the value of *final* goods and services. This is actually a strength of the measure, since if we added the value of steel sold to a car maker and the value of the cars, we would be counting the steel twice: once as steel, and a second time as part of the value of the car. The final part of the definition states that GDP must be measured over some time period, usually a year. Most countries measure GDP every 3 months, but for most purposes, including ours, the most useful time period to consider is one year.

An alternative concept for measuring a nation's output is **gross national product (GNP)**. For most countries, the difference between the two concepts is very small, because GNP is the value of all final goods and services produced by the labor, capital, and other resources of a country, regardless of where production occurred. In an accounting sense, GNP is equal to GDP plus investment income and unilateral transfers received from foreigners minus investment income and unilateral transfers paid to foreigners:

$$\text{GDP + foreign income received}$$

$$- \text{ income paid to foreigners}$$

$$+ \text{ foreign transfers received}$$

$$- \text{ transfers paid to foreigners} = \text{GNP}$$

Note that the difference between GNP and GDP is precisely equal to the credits minus debits in lines 2 and 3 in Table 9.1, which is the same as net primary income plus net secondary income. This fact is useful because GDP includes exports minus imports and it enables us to bring the entire current account concept into the picture.

The usefulness of adding net primary foreign income plus net secondary income is apparent when we look at the definition of GDP based on its four main components. Table 9.6 defines the necessary variables. GDP is equal to the sum of consumer expenditures plus investment expenditures plus government expenditures on goods and services plus exports of goods and services minus imports of goods and services:

$$\text{GDP} = \text{C} + \text{I} + \text{G} + \text{X} - \text{M} \tag{9.1}$$

Given that GNP is equal to GDP plus net primary income and net secondary income:

$$\text{GNP} = \text{GDP} + (\text{Net primary income} + \text{net secondary incomes}) \tag{9.2}$$

Or

$$\text{GNP} = (\text{C} + \text{I} + \text{G}) + (\text{X} - \text{M} + \text{Net primary income} + \text{net secondary income}) \tag{9.3}$$

TABLE 9.6 **Variable Definitions**

Variable	Definition
GDP	Gross domestic product
GNP	Gross national product
C	Consumption expenditures
I	Investment expenditures
G	Government expenditures on goods and services
X	Exports of goods and services
M	Imports of goods and services
CA	Current account balance
S	Private savings (savings of households and firms)
T	Net taxes, or taxes paid minus transfer payments received

we can write the definition of GNP in terms of the current account balance. Rewriting Equation (9.3) in a simpler form gives us the following:

$$GNP = C + I + G + CA \qquad (9.4)$$

Equation (9.4) explicitly shows the relationship between the current account and the main macroeconomic variables such as consumer spending, investment, and government purchases.

As the total value of goods and services produced by the labor, capital, and other resources of a country, GNP is also the value of income received. This follows from the fact that the production of final goods and services generates incomes equal in value to output and is embodied in the basic macroeconomic accounting identity stating that every economy's income must equal its output. From the point of view of the income recipients, there are three choices or obligations: They may consume their income (C), save it (S), or use it to pay taxes (T). In reality, all of us do a combination of the three. This permits us to rewrite the definition of GNP in terms of income and its uses as follows:

$$GNP = C + S + T \qquad (9.5)$$

Since Equations (9.4) and (9.5) are equivalent definitions of GNP—one in terms of the components of output, the other in terms of the uses of income—we can set them equal to each other as follows:

$$C + I + G + CA = C + S + T \qquad (9.6)$$

Subtracting consumption from both sides and rearranging terms gives us the following:

$$I + G + CA = S + T \qquad (9.7)$$

or

$$S + (T - G) = I + CA \qquad (9.8)$$

Equation (9.8) is an accounting identity, or something that is true by definition. It is worth memorizing because it summarizes the important relationship between the current account balance, investment, and public and private savings in the economy. Equation (9.8) does not reveal any of the causal mechanisms through which changes in savings or investment are connected to the current account balance, but it does provide insight into the economy. For example, if total savings remains unchanged while investment increases, then the current account balance must move toward, or deeper into, deficit.

To see this, be sure that you understand the term on the left side, $(T - G)$. This is the combined (federal, state, and local) budget balances of all levels of government, or, put another way, government savings. It is savings because (T) is government revenue (or income) and (G) is government expenditure. A positive $(T - G)$ states that the combined government budgets are in surplus, which in the governmental sector is equivalent to savings. Conversely, a negative $(T - G)$ is a deficit, or dissavings. Placing governmental budget balances on the left-hand side emphasizes that there are two sources of savings in an economy: the private sector (S) and the public or governmental sector (T − G). If governments dissave (run deficits), then they must borrow from the private sector, which reduces total national savings on the left-hand side.

From Equation (9.8) we see that a nation's savings (private plus public) is divided into two uses. First, it is a source of funds for domestic investment (I). This role is crucial because new investments in machinery and equipment are a source of economic growth. Investment is essential to upgrade the skills of the labor force, to provide more capital on the job, and to improve the quality of capital by introducing new technology. According to Equation (9.8), if government budgets are in deficit, the total supply of national savings is reduced, and, all else being equal, investment will be less than it might otherwise have been. Conversely, a surplus in government budgets will augment private savings and increase the funds available for investment, all else being equal.

The second use for national savings is as a source of funds for foreign investment. If the current account is in surplus, national savings finances the purchase of domestic goods by foreign users of those goods. In return, or as payment, the domestic economy acquires foreign financial assets. Recall from the discussion of the relationship between the current and financial accounts that the financial account reflects the same amount of lending or borrowing as the current account. If the current account is negative, there is net borrowing that will also be visible in the financial account as net borrowing, or in the terminology of Tables 9.3 and 9.4, a net incurrence of liabilities (borrowing, or financial inflows) that is greater than the net acquisition of financial assets (lending, or financial outflows). In other words, a negative current account is associated with net borrowing in the financial account, which is an inflow of financial capital. Equivalence between the inflow's magnitude and the current account surplus (other than the statistical discrepancy) ensures that home country businesses, households, and governments, obtain the financial resources they need to buy more goods and services than they sell in world markets. In a sense, surplus countries provides savings to the rest of the world, thereby making it possible for them to sell more goods abroad than they buy. For a surplus country, a financial capital outflow is an investment because it involves the acquisition of assets that are expected to pay a future return. It is not the same as domestic investment, however, because the assets are outside the country. Hence, another name for the current account balance is *net foreign investment*. A positive balance implies positive foreign investment, while a negative balance implies that foreigners accumulate more home country assets than the home country accumulates abroad.

The United States has had a current account deficit every year since 1981 with the exception of 1991, when it received large income payments in compensation for the Gulf War (see Figure 9.1). In 2010, the deficit was 3.2 percent of GNP. Figure 9.2 shows the current account balance since 2001 and the three related macroeconomic variables from Equation (9.8). As shown, the financial crisis and recession of 2007–2009 had a dramatic effect on savings, investment, and government budgets, and a smaller effect on the current account. Savings rose as households and businesses cut back on purchases, and investment fell as businesses saw fewer opportunities for expansion. Balances of combined state, local, and federal budgets fell into large deficits as tax payments declined and government assistance programs spent more on social benefits for the unemployed and struggling households. In addition, there was an improvement in the current account balance as falling U.S. incomes resulted in fewer imports.

The four macroeconomic variables in Figure 9.2 demonstrate that there is not a fixed relationship between current account balances and government budget balances, or between savings and investment. Each of the four variables is determined by the other three, and a change in any one of them influences all of the others. For example, during an economic recession, most countries experience government budget deficits. As noted, state, local, and federal governments all saw dramatic increases in their deficits from 2007 to 2010 as unemployment rose and tax collections fell. Nevertheless, the U.S. current account balance improved slightly due to the fall in consumption and the decline in spending on imports. Some other countries experienced the same pattern as the U.S. of increasing government budget deficits and falling current account deficits, (e.g., Spain) while still others watched as their budget deficits increased but the current account balances had little or no change (e.g., Germany). The link from any one of the four macroeconomic variables to any of the others is mediated by the other two, and changes in one variable can be amplified or offset by changes elsewhere.

FIGURE 9.2   Savings and Investment, 2001–2015

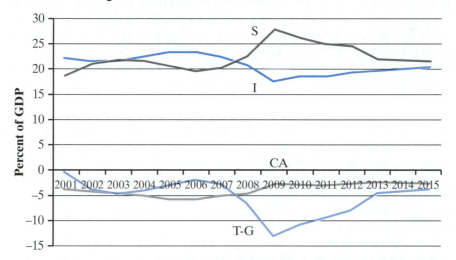

During the financial crisis and recession of 2007–2009, government budget deficits grew dramatically and private investment declined. The fall in consumption caused an increase in private savings and a decline in imports.

Source: Data from IMF, *World Economic Outlook Database*, © James Gerber.

The availability of global financial flows has made it easier for current account deficit countries to obtain the outside financing they need when their domestic savings is inadequate. Global capital flows have not completely broken the link between domestic savings and domestic investment, as most countries have savings and investment levels that are roughly similar. This is not true for every country, however, and in recent years it has been less and less true overall. For example, developing countries with relatively low savings such as Honduras, Ethiopia, and Kenya have managed to invest much larger shares of their GDP than they could if they relied on their domestic savings alone. This is possible because capital inflows are available to finance their current account deficits and to provide an additional source of funding for investment.

Are Current Account Deficits Harmful?

The relationship between the current account balance, investment, and total national savings is an identity. Consequently, it does not tell us why an economy runs a current account deficit or surplus. In Equation (9.8), the left and right sides are equal by definition. Consequently, we cannot say that the current account is in deficit because saving is too low any more than we can say it is because investment is too high.

There is a general tendency in the media and the public to interpret a current account deficit as a sign of weakness and as harmful to the nation's welfare. Another interpretation is that the deficit enables more investment than would be possible otherwise, and since higher investment is correlated with higher living standards, the current account deficit might be interpreted as beneficial. In addition, the capital inflows associated with current account deficits are an implicit vote of confidence by foreigners. For example, between 1980 and 1991, Japan invested more than $25 billion of its trade surplus in U.S. manufacturing. By the start of the 1990s, the Japanese owned 66 steel works, 20 rubber and tire factories, 8 major car assembly plants, and 270 auto parts suppliers, employing more than 100,000 workers. Furthermore, the investment came at a time when the three major U.S.-based auto manufacturers (Chrysler, Ford, and GM) were laying off workers and relocating production abroad. Some of the Japanese firms were acquisitions (which may have closed if they had not been bought), and many were new plants built with Japanese savings. During the U.S. current account deficits of the 1990s, foreign investors continued to pour in capital, enabling the United States to raise its level of investment and increase its productivity in spite of its declining savings rate. In this particular case, the current account deficit has been beneficial because, all else being equal, it enabled more investment than was possible otherwise, given the savings rate.

Current account deficits can also generate problems, however. The capital inflows that occur with a current account deficit increase the stock of foreign-owned assets inside the home country, raising the possibility that a change in investor expectations about the economy's future can lead to a sudden surge in capital outflows. In the worst case scenario, capital flight is followed by a depletion of international reserves and a financial crisis. This is an experience shared by a number of developing countries since the 1980s, but it should not lead you to believe that the optimal policy for a country is to avoid current account deficits. As we have just seen, such deficits allow countries to invest more than they could otherwise, and this is particularly important for developing countries where investment capital is especially scarce. Furthermore, current account surpluses are no guarantee that a country will be able to avoid a crisis if one develops among its trading partners. International financial crises, like some biological diseases, tend to be contagious. When Mexico slipped into the peso crisis in late 1994 and early 1995, for example, economists and journalists began to write about the "Tequila effect" on Latin America. Similarly, when Thailand's currency lost a large share of its value in July of 1997, the media reported stories of crisis spreading across East Asia and the rest of the developing world. In both cases, the size of a country's current account balances was not a good predictor of whether it was drawn into the crisis. (See Chapter 12 for a more detailed discussion of financial crises.)

The experiences of countries in the 1980s and 1990s has taught economists that financial crises are determined by more than the size of the current account deficit, and that there are no absolute thresholds between safe and dangerous levels of a deficit. While deficits of 3 to 4 percent of GDP begin to raise red flags, and deficits of 7 to 9 percent are considered extremely risky, too many other factors must be taken into consideration before the probability of a crisis can be determined.

CASE STUDY

Current Account Deficits in the United States

Figures 9.1and 9.2 illustrate the growing problem of the U.S. current account deficit. In 2015, the deficit was over $460 billion and more than 2.5 percent of GDP. As high as it was, the deficit in 2015 was significantly smaller than it had been in the first years of the twenty-first century, when it was often above 4 and even 5 percent of GDP (Figure 9.1). For most developed countries, current account deficits in the range of 4 to 5 percent of GDP usually trigger adjustments that force a reduction in their size. It seems only natural to ask whether the crisis that began in 2007 is related to the size of the U.S. current account deficit.

In Figure 9.1, there are two periods of widening current account deficits. In the 1980s, the deficit widened, then closed. The second episode began in the early 1990s with a deficit that continued to expand until very recently. While the current account deficits look similar in these two episodes, the movements of the other variables in Equation (9.8) were significantly different.

(continued)

Beginning around 1981, the budget of the federal government turned the combined federal, state, and local government balance (T − G), into a large negative number. Given the lack of private savings to finance both domestic investment (I) and public sector dissaving, foreign finance filled the gap and the current account turned negative. The 1990s story is different in several ways, but perhaps most importantly, in that over the course of the decade, the federal budget moved from a large deficit to a small surplus. If everything had remained the same, this would have reduced the need for foreign savings and pushed the current account in the direction of surplus, but (S) and (I) were not constant. The decade saw sharp increases in investment spending as corporations bought new computer technology and telecommunications equipment they needed to stay competitive. In addition, a stock market boom followed by a housing market boom made consumers much wealthier, with the result that households rapidly increased their consumption and decreased their personal savings. Therefore, the changes in the government budget were overwhelmed by the increases in investment and by the decline in savings, resulting in a large and growing current account deficit. In 2002, large federal budget deficits returned and put additional pressure on the United States to seek foreign financing for its domestic and foreign investment.

Before the crisis that began in 2007, a central concern of some observers was whether or not the U.S. current account deficit posed a danger to the U.S. economy. After the crisis began, a separate set of questions surfaced about the role of the deficit in creating the crisis itself. While no one argued that the current account deficits caused the crisis, there is perhaps a significant relationship between the crisis and the current account. In order for the United States to run a significant current account deficit over many years, it had to be financed by countries with surpluses that collectively matched it. In terms of the balance of payments, U.S. current account deficits were financed by capital inflows in its financial account. These net capital inflows represented the trade surpluses of countries such as Germany, Japan, Saudi Arabia, Russia, and China, which were invested in the United States. In other words, the counterpart to U.S. deficits was a series of surpluses elsewhere in the global economy.

In effect, the willingness of governments and firms outside the United States to invest their earnings inside the United States enabled it to run large current account deficits over a long period while maintaining a low level of public and private savings. This had a number of consequences, including the provision of financing for the housing boom of the 2000s and the consumption spree (low savings rates) of many Americans. Housing finance was awash in funds to lend, consumer credit was extremely easy to get, and many Americans had lifestyles supported by their indirect access to the savings of households, firms, and governments abroad. In Germany, Japan, China, and other surplus countries, savings rates were high, consumption ran well below incomes, and trade surpluses grew larger and larger, particularly after 2000.

If these global imbalances were short run, or if they were used to make a series of investments that raised productivity (which they did, in part), then the problems they caused would not be severe. However, some economists argue that the global imbalances were at the root of the crisis that began in 2007 because they persisted for a long time and encouraged the gradual accumulation of problems, such as risky lending, that eventually became extremely severe. Financial market regulators were not prepared for large inflows of foreign capital and lacked sufficient experience to understand the hidden dangers if the inflows persisted over a long period. Banks and securities firms that received deposits felt pressure to make loans so they would have earnings to cover the interest on their deposits. Over a period of many years, the steady availability of funds from surplus countries helped hold interest rates down and encouraged borrowing, especially for big-ticket items such as houses and cars. Easy money for home loans raised the demand for housing and pushed up home prices. Rising prices made homes seem like a safe investment, which only encouraged more borrowing and further building. When home prices began to fall, the entire system unraveled, causing enormous losses for the banks and others tied up in the home loan market.

INTERNATIONAL DEBT

Current account deficits must be financed through inflows of financial capital. Recall from Table 9.5 and the previous discussion that capital inflows take different forms, from direct investment to purchases of stocks, bonds, and currency, to loans. Loans from abroad add to a country's stock of **external debt** and generate **debt service** obligations requiring interest payments and repayment of the principal. External debt is defined as a debt that must be paid in a foreign currency. It includes the debts on borrowings by both governments and the private sector, and long- and short-term debt, where short term is anything under a year. Theoretically, foreign loans are no more harmful than any other type of debt. That is, as long as the borrowed funds are used to increase skills and production levels, the borrower will be able to service the debt without difficulty. In practice, however, it is not uncommon for borrowed funds to be used in a manner that does not contribute to the expansion of the country's productive capacity, and often debt service becomes an unsustainable burden that holds back economic development.

Most countries, rich and poor, have external debt. In high-income countries, debt service is rarely an issue, because the amount of debt is usually relatively small compared to the size of the economy. Furthermore, many high-income countries are able to borrow in their own currencies. Countries such as the United States, Japan, Switzerland, the United Kingdom, and others have all their debt denominated in their own currencies and are relieved of the pressure of having to run large trade surpluses in order to make payments on the principal and interest of their debt. Low- and middle-income countries are another matter. In a number of cases, the size of the external debt burden is unsustainable, given the economy's ability to make interest payments and to repay the principal.

Unsustainable debt occurs for many reasons. Sometimes, countries are dependent on exports of one or two basic commodities such as copper or coffee. The shock of a sudden drop in world commodity prices reduces the value of exports and sometimes generates unexpectedly large current account deficits. In other cases, countries experience natural disasters, such as hurricanes and earthquakes, that create a need for relief and foreign assistance, or civil conflicts that fuel a demand for arms purchases. Corruption, too, can play a role, as described later in the case of the Democratic Republic of the Congo (DRC). Even electoral politics may be a factor, as when officials try to gain support through unsustainable expenditures targeted at important constituents. Finally, the behavior of foreign lenders also plays a role, as described in the DRC case study in the next section.

Debt is a serious problem. In 2014, the world's low- and middle-income countries had total debt obligations over $5.3 trillion, which required more than $600 billion a year in interest and principal repayment. Debt burdens worsen the budget position of central governments by adding payments that must be made to outsiders, and they reduce the availability of funds for important domestic needs such as infrastructure projects, schools, and health care. In addition, there are many examples of excessive debt burdens that have intensified and spread economic crises.

Debt problems of developing countries have received considerable attention in recent years from multilateral organizations such as the World Bank, from governments of high-income governments, and from private organizations that have argued for debt relief. One notable movement is the Highly Indebted Poor Country (HIPC) program, which is a joint venture of the World Bank, the IMF, and high-income-country governments. The goal of the HIPC program is to provide debt forgiveness for a select group of countries that must qualify based on high levels of poverty and debt and a track record of economic reform. As of 2013, the thirty-five of the thirty-nine HIPC countries had received debt forgiveness.

CASE STUDY

Odious Debt

Countries classified as HIPC are some of the poorest in the world. Their average income per capita in 2014 was $899 and life expectancy at birth was 60.3 years (2013). Given the countries' conditions of extreme poverty, it is hard to argue against debt relief, yet some people question its value. Their primary argument is that it would be wasted money since the conditions that created debt are likely to persist, leading to a new round of borrowing and a return to previous levels of debt. Others worry that debt relief might cause some countries to borrow excessively in the belief that their debt burden will be forgiven later.

Economists do not have a single point of view on this issue, although many favor some sort of debt relief despite the arguments just made. The cost of debt forgiveness for the most severely indebted poor countries is inconsequential compared to the economies of the high-income countries, which are the ones that would be called upon to forgive the debts. In addition, some share of the debt is classified as odious debt, and in those cases the arguments in favor of debt relief are impossible to ignore. **Odious debt** is legally defined as debt incurred without the consent of the people and that is not used for their benefit. It is associated with corrupt governments and countries where freedom is severely limited.

Many cases of odious debt can be found among the thirty-nine countries that qualify for the HIPC initiative. For example, in sub-Saharan Africa, the DRC (formerly Zaire), Kenya, and Uganda almost certainly fall into this category, while at least part of the debt of many other countries would qualify them as well. Between 1972 and 1999, about 60 percent of the loans to HIPC went to regimes considered "not free" by Freedom House, an international organization that ranks countries as free, partly free, or not free; and between 1985 and 1995, about 67 percent of the loans made to HIPC went to places considered corrupt by the *International Country Risk Guide*, a risk analysis service.

The DRC is a clear-cut case. From 1965 to 1997, the DRC was ruled by the dictator Mobutu Sese Seko. During Mobutu's reign, real GDP, measured in the equivalent of U.S. dollars at 2000 prices, fell from $317 per person to $110 per person, while the regime amassed billions of dollars in foreign aid and loans. Mobutu's personal fortune was estimated to have reached $4 to $6 billion, most of which was deposited in Swiss bank accounts. In 2004, per capita income was at $88 and international debts were around $12 billion. The latter was equivalent to about 225 percent of GDP and 1,280 percent of a year's exports.

Given the continued decline in incomes and the large number of unfinished projects financed by various governments and multilateral agencies, there is little evidence that the borrowed money was successfully used for development purposes. Furthermore, lenders knew the situation when they made their loans, but they went ahead anyway since they wanted to secure access to the DRC's mineral deposits of cobalt and other strategic metals. In cases like the DRC, it is difficult to argue that citizens should be forced to pay off the debt. In 2003, the DRC was admitted to the HIPC program and qualified for up to 80 percent debt forgiveness, and by 2010, more than half of its debt had been forgiven.

Sources: Based on Birdsall and Williamson, *Delivering on Debt Relief*, 2002, Center for Global Development and Institute for International Economics, Washington, DC; World Bank, *Global Development Finance*, 2003, World Bank, Washington, DC, © James Gerber.

THE INTERNATIONAL INVESTMENT POSITION

LO 9.6 Show the relationship between a country's balance of payments and its international investment position.

Each year that a nation runs a current account deficit, it borrows from abroad and adds to its indebtedness to foreigners. Each year that it runs a current account surplus, it lends to foreigners and reduces its overall indebtedness. If the total of all domestic assets owned by foreigners is subtracted from the total of all foreign assets owned by residents of the home country, the result is the **international investment position**. If the international investment position is positive, then the home country could sell all its foreign assets and have more than enough revenue to purchase all the domestic assets owned by foreigners. If it is negative, then selling all foreign assets would not provide enough revenue to buy all the domestic assets owned by foreigners.

Consider the international investment position of the United States at the end of 2014. The market value of all assets outside the United States and owned by governments, businesses, and residents of the United States was $24,595 billion. Among other things, these assets included factories, shares of stock, bonds, foreign currency, and bank loans. At the same time, the market value of assets located in the United States and owned by governments, businesses, and residents abroad was $31,615 billion. As a result, the international investment position of the United States at the end of 2014 was −$7,020 billion. To summarize:

International investment position

= domestically owned foreign assets − foreign owned domestic assets
= $24,595 billion − $31,615 billion
= −$7,020 billion

The large current account deficits of the 1980s, 1990s, and 2000s have eroded the United States' investment position from a positive $288.6 billion in 1983 to zero in 1989, and negative since then. Each year a country experiences a current account deficit, foreigners acquire more assets inside its boundaries than its residents acquire abroad, and the international investment position shrinks further.

We have considered many of the costs and benefits of capital inflows. They enable countries to invest more than would otherwise be the case, but they also make it possible for governments and consumers to spend more (save less). One of the benefits not discussed so far is the possibility of **technology transfer**. When capital inflows take the form of direct investment, they may bring new technologies, new management techniques, and new ideas to the host country. This transfer is particularly important for developing countries that lack access or information about newer technologies, but it is also important for high-income countries. Technology transfer is by no means an inevitable outcome of foreign direct investment, and much of the current research on this type of capital flow seeks to understand the conditions that encourage or discourage it.

One of the costs of capital inflows is their potential to provide access to political power. Much depends on the political culture of the host country receiving the capital inflows, but large direct investment flows, as well as portfolio investment flows, are likely to provide access to politically significant people. This is the case in large and small countries, but it is particularly important in low- and middle-income countries, where wealth encounters fewer countervailing powers or contending interests.

Summary

- Every nation's transactions with the rest of the world are summarized in its balance of payments. The balance of payments has three components: the current account, the capital account, and the financial account. The two most important components are the current and financial accounts.

- The current account is a record of a nation's trade, income, and transfers between it and the rest of the world.

- The financial account is a record of financial capital flows between a country and the rest of the world. It is measured as net acquisition of foreign assets and net incurrence of foreign liabilities.

- Capital flows in the financial account are categorized as direct investment, portfolio investment, other investment, which includes mostly bank loans, and reserve assets. In general, direct investment is longer term and, therefore, less volatile.

- Large, sudden outflows of financial capital have created economic instability in many countries, particularly during the 1990s. This has created an active debate over the merits of restricting foreign capital flows. Economists are divided on this point, with some favoring restrictions and some favoring free capital mobility.

- There is a fundamental economic identity that total private and public saving in an economy must be equal to domestic investment plus net foreign investment. The current account balance is equal to net foreign investment, and a negative balance is equivalent to disinvestment abroad.

- Current account deficits enable a country to invest more than it could otherwise, which has a beneficial effect on national income. If deficits are too large, however, they increase the vulnerability of a country to sudden outflows of financial capital.

- Thirty-nine low-income countries are classified as highly indebted poor countries (HIPC). All have unsustainable debt levels, some of which may be considered odious debt because it is incurred without the consent of the country's citizens and is not used for their benefit.

- The international investment position is the difference between foreign-based assets owned by residents in the home country and home-based assets owned by residents of foreign countries.
- Foreign investment has costs and benefits for the host country. While it may lead to technology transfer and higher investment levels, it can also become a mechanism for spreading a crisis and give foreigners a voice in the nation's internal political affairs.

Vocabulary

capital account

current account

current account balance

debt service

external debt

financial account

foreign direct investment (FDI)

foreign portfolio investment

goods and services

gross domestic product (GDP)

gross national product (GNP)

international investment position

investment income

national income and product accounts (NIPA)

net acquisition of financial assets

net incurrence of liabilities

odious debt

official reserve assets

remittances

statistical discrepancy

sudden stop

technology transfer

trade balance

unilateral transfers

Study Questions

All problems are assignable in MyEconLab

9.1 Use the following information to answer the questions below. Assume that the capital account is equal to 0.

Exports of goods and services	500
Primary income received	200
Secondary income received	300
Imports of goods and services	700
Primary income paid abroad	300
Secondary income paid	100
Net acquisition of financial assets	300
Net incurrence of liabilities	400
Net change in financial derivatives	−100

    a.   What is the trade balance?

    b.   What is the current account balance?

    c.   Does the financial account balance equal the current plus capital account balance?

    d.   What is the statistical discrepancy?

9.2 Look at each of the following cases from the point of view of the balance of payments for the United States. Determine the subcategory of the current account or financial account that each transaction would be classified in, and state whether it would enter as a credit or debit.

    a.   The U.S. government sells gold for dollars.

    b.   A migrant worker in California sends $500 home to his village in Mexico.

    c.   An American mutual fund manager uses the deposits of his fund investors to buy Brazilian telecommunication stocks.

    d.   A Japanese firm in Tennessee buys car parts from a subsidiary in Malaysia.

    e.   An American church donates five tons of rice to the Sudan to help with famine relief.

    f.   An American retired couple flies from Seattle to Tokyo on Japan Airlines.

    g.   The Mexican government sells pesos to the United States Treasury and buys dollars.

9.3 Weigh the pros and cons of a large trade deficit.

9.4 Is the government budget deficit of a country linked to its current account balance? How so? Explain how it is possible for the United States' current account deficit to grow while the budget deficit has disappeared, as happened in the 1990s.

9.5 Compare and contrast portfolio capital flows with direct investment capital flows.

9.6 Why is a current account surplus equivalent to foreign investment?

APPENDIX A

Measuring the International Investment Position

It may seem like a straightforward job to add up the value of assets, but nothing could be further from the truth. Consider the following problem: The United States ran trade surpluses in the 1950s and 1960s and accumulated large holdings of foreign assets. In the 1980s and 1990s, the United States ran trade deficits and foreigners accumulated large holdings inside the United States. By 2014, a sizable proportion of U.S.-owned assets had been purchased decades ago when prices were much lower, and foreign-owned assets were purchased recently, after the worldwide inflation of the 1970s and the early 1980s. If asset values are tallied using their historical costs (the price at the time of purchase), then foreign-owned assets appear more valuable because they were acquired more recently when world prices were higher.

It seems logical to expect that the reporting of asset values would be done on a current cost basis rather than a historical cost basis, where current cost is the cost of purchasing the asset in the current period. Until 1991, the United States calculated only the historical cost of U.S.-owned foreign assets. As a result, the U.S. international investment position appeared to become negative very rapidly as large trade deficits in the mid-1980s led to a rapid accumulation of new assets in the United States by foreign interests. In the 1990s, the United States began to report all assets on a current value basis. The primary deficiency in this data as it now stands is that it cannot be broken down into country-specific or industry-specific data. Therefore, we know the overall international investment position for the United States, but we cannot accurately examine the U.S.-Japan bilateral investment position, since we have U.S. assets in Japan only on a historical cost basis.

APPENDIX B

Balance of Payments Data

Current account and international investment data are readily available for most nations of the world.

Bureau of Economic Analysis

The Bureau of Economic Analysis is the official source of national income and product and international accounts data for the United States. It has an easy-to-use Web site with a complete set of data for both the current and historical periods. It is located at http://www.bea.gov.

International Financial Statistics

International Financial Statistics (IFS) is a regular publication of the International Monetary Fund (IMF). A hardcopy appears monthly, with an annual *Yearbook* at the year's end, and online access is available through the IMF's website at http://www.imf.org. As the name implies, the *IFS* focuses on financial data, but it also contains information on current accounts and international capital flows. Coverage is of most of the world's nations, and the most recent *Yearbook* usually contains a decade of data for each country. IMF publications are one of the sources used by many international agencies and private enterprises. Nearly all university libraries and many city libraries will have the hardcopy version of the *IFS*.

Balance of Payments Statistics

Balance of Payments Statistics (BOPS) is a sister publication of the IMF that complements the data in the *IFS*. The *BOPS* has the most up-to-date and detailed current account statistics of any international data source. In addition, it contains detailed breakdowns of capital flows.

APPENDIX C

A Note on Numbers

The United States uses a numbering system that refers to a thousand million (1,000,000,000) as one billion, and a million million (1,000,000,000,000) as one trillion. Most of the rest of the world has a slightly different terminology. In many countries, the term billion is reserved for the value that is called a trillion in the United States, and what the United States calls a billion is called a thousand million or a milliard. For example, the number 15,000,000,000 would be fifteen billion in the United States, and 15 thousand millions or 15 milliards elsewhere. The numbers in this chapter use the conventional usage of the United States.

Exchange Rates and Exchange Rate Systems

INTRODUCTION: FIXED, FLEXIBLE, OR IN-BETWEEN?

Every country must choose an exchange rate system to determine how prices in the home country currency are converted into prices in another country's currency. Some countries peg their exchange rate to a fixed level while others let market forces determine its value. Both approaches have advantages and disadvantages. The choice of an exchange rate system varies along the continuum from completely fixed with no variation to completely flexible with variation determined by supply and demand for the country's currency on a minute-by-minute basis. Between these two extremes are several other exchange rate systems with semi-fixed or semi-flexible rates.

Each exchange rate system requires that governments and central banks have credible policies to support the selected system as trade, capital flows, and other pressures from the world economy push exchange rates up and down. In this chapter we define the actors in currency markets, analyze the basic mechanisms that determine the value of a country's currency, and discuss the considerations that countries should make in selecting their exchange rate system. Each of these elements is an important determinant of a country's exchange rate system and the value of its currency.

EXCHANGE RATES AND CURRENCY TRADING

LO 10.1   List the reasons for holding foreign exchange and the main institutions in the foreign exchange market.

The **exchange rate** is the price of one currency stated in terms of a second currency. An exchange rate can be given in one of two ways, either as units of domestic currency per unit of foreign currency or vice versa. For example, we might give the U.S.–Mexico exchange rate as dollars per peso (0.057 dollars) or pesos per dollar (17.5 pesos). The custom varies with the currency. For example, the U.S. dollar–British pound exchange rate is usually quoted in terms of dollars per pound, but the U.S. dollar–Mexican peso exchange rate is usually pesos per dollar. In this chapter and the rest of the book, the exchange rate is always given as the number of units of domestic currency per unit of foreign currency. For the United States, this means it is dollars per peso and dollars per pound.

Exchange rates are reported in every newspaper with a business section and on numerous Web sites. Figure 10.1 shows several years of U.S. dollar values for three of the most frequently traded currencies: the European Union's euro, the Japanese yen, and the British pound. The rates are taken from the U.S. Federal Reserve Bank's Web site, and are the interbank rates that one bank charges another when buying large amounts of currency. Tourists and individuals purchasing relatively small amounts would have paid more.

All three are flexible exchange rates and subject to constant fluctuations up and down in value, as shown in Figure 10.1. In the years leading up to the financial crisis and recession of 2007–2009, the pound and the euro appreciated against the dollar. When the crisis began in late 2007, world demand for dollars rose and it appreciated in value, or to say the same thing another way, the pound and euro depreciated. The most dramatic depreciation began in the middle of 2008 and lasted for approximately a year, until mid-2009, reflecting the flight of capital into dollars. The pound lost approximately 25 percent of its value in dollar terms and the euro lost approximately 15 percent. In contrast, the Japanese yen continued to appreciate until late 2012, gaining over 40 percent in value against the dollar, and then quickly reversed and lost all of its appreciated value by the middle of 2013. Considering that the changes in the real economies of each country were not nearly as large, Figure 10.1 gives an idea of the variability of exchange rates.

By March, 2016, which is the end of the series in Figure 10.1, the yen was worth $0.0088, or less than 1 cent. The euro stood at $1.10 and the pound was worth $1.42. It might be tempting to conclude that the yen is weak and the pound and euro are strong given that the yen is not worth 1 cent and other two are well over 1 dollar. This would be a mistake, however, because currencies are scales, just like Fahrenheit and centigrade, or miles and kilometers. No matter how many of one it takes to equal another, we cannot conclude that the scale implies strength or weakness. Until it began to lose some of its value in 2013, the yen appreciated against all three and was clearly the strongest currency. Generally speaking, the strength or

FIGURE 10.1   Dollar Exchange Rates for Three Main Currencies, 2006–2016

Euro and pound exchange rates are on the left scale; yen are on the right. Float-ing exchange rates can vary significantly, in both the short and the long run.

Source: Data from Board of Governors of the Federal Reserve System, © James Gerber.

weakness of a currency is related to the direction of change in its value and not its value at one point in time or the number of units it takes to buy a different currency.

Reasons for Holding Foreign Currencies

Economists identify three reasons for holding foreign currency. The first is for trade and investment purposes. Traders (importers and exporters) and investors routinely transact in foreign currencies, either receiving or making payments in another country's money. Tourists are included in this category because they hold foreign exchange in order to buy foreign goods and services.

The second reason for holding foreign exchange is to take advantage of interest rate differentials, or **interest rate arbitrage**. Arbitrage conveys the idea of buying something where it is relatively cheap and selling it where it is relatively expen-sive. Interest rate arbitrage is similar in that arbitrageurs borrow money where interest rates are relatively low and lend it where rates are relatively high. By moving financial capital in this way, interest rate arbitrage keeps interest rates from diverging too far, and also constitutes one of the primary linkages between national economies. Over the last several years interest arbitrageurs have played a major role in keeping the Japanese yen strong by borrowing in Japan where interest rates are very low and lending where they are high. Various other factors, such as perceptions of risk, are important, but in general, interest rate arbitrage is a powerful force in the world economy and tends to be one of the main reasons for holding foreign currency.

The third reason for holding foreign exchange is to speculate. Speculators are businesses that buy or sell a currency because they expect its price to rise or fall. They have no need for foreign exchange to buy goods or services or financial assets; rather, they hope to realize profits or avoid losses through correctly anticipating changes in a currency's market value. Speculators are often reviled in the popular press, but in fact they help to bring currencies into equilibrium after they have become over- or undervalued. If speculators view a currency as overvalued, they will sell it and drive down its value. If they guess wrong, however, they can lose a lot of money. For this reason, some economists have argued that speculation either serves the useful function of bringing currency values into proper alignment, or its practitioners lose money and go out of business. Not everyone agrees with this view, however, and some economists think that speculation against a currency can be destabilizing in the sense that it does not always push an exchange rate to its equilibrium value, but instead sometimes leads to a grossly over- or undervalued currency, which is a major problem for the country involved.

Institutions

There are four main participants in foreign currency markets: retail customers, commercial banks, foreign exchange brokers, and central banks. Of these four, commercial banks are the most important. Retail customers include firms and individuals that hold foreign exchange for any of the three reasons given in the previous section—to engage in purchases, to adjust their portfolios, or to profit from expected future currency movements. In most cases, they buy and sell through a commercial bank. Commercial banks in many parts of the world hold inventories of foreign currencies as part of the services offered to customers. Not all banks provide this service, but those that do usually have a relationship with several foreign banks where they hold their balances of foreign currencies. When a surplus accumulates, or a shortage develops, the banks trade with each other to adjust their holdings.

In the United States, foreign exchange brokers also play an important role. It is not very common for U.S. banks to trade currency with foreign banks. Instead, U.S. banks tend to go through foreign exchange brokers, who act as middlemen between buyers and sellers that do not usually hold foreign exchange. Brokers can also serve as agents for central banks. The market, then, works as follows. An individual or firm that needs foreign exchange calls its bank. The bank quotes a price at which it will sell the currency. The price is based on one of two possible sources of supply: The bank may have an account with another bank in the country where the currency is used, or it may call a foreign exchange broker. The broker keeps track of buyers and sellers of currencies and acts as a deal maker by bringing together a seller and a bank that is buying for its customer.

In most cases, currency trades take the form of credits and debits to a firm's bank accounts. For example, a local U.S. importer that must make payment in yen can call and tell its bank to transfer yen to the Japanese bank of the firm that supplies the importer with goods. The importer will have a debit to its local bank account that is equivalent to the cost of the yen. If the U.S. bank has a branch or correspondence bank in Japan, it can electronically notify the branch to debit the yen from the account of the U.S. bank and credit it to the Japanese bank of the supplier. If the U.S. bank goes through a currency trader instead of dealing directly with a Japanese bank, it first buys yen that are in an account with a Japanese bank. Next, it requests that some or all of its yen assets be transferred to the bank of the Japanese supplier of the U.S. importer.

Exchange Rate Risk

Firms that do business in more than one country are subject to **exchange rate risks**. These risks stem from the fact that currencies are constantly changing in value and, as a result, expected future payments that will be made or received in a foreign currency will be a different domestic currency amount from when the contract was signed.

Suppose, for example, that a U.S. semiconductor manufacturer signs a contract to send a British computer manufacturer a shipment of microprocessors in six months. If the U.S. manufacturer agrees on a price in British pounds, it must know the value of the pound six months from now in order to know the dollar equivalent of its future revenue. If the U.S. manufacturer specifies that the microprocessors be paid for in dollars, then it shifts the exchange rate risk to the British firm. The U.S. company knows the exact dollar amount it will receive in six months, but the British firm is uncertain of the price of the dollar and therefore the pound price of microprocessors.

Financial markets recognized this problem long ago and, in the nineteenth century, they created mechanisms for dealing with it. The mechanisms are the forward exchange rate and the forward market. The **forward exchange rate** is the price of a currency that will be delivered in the future; the **forward market** refers to the market in which the buying and selling of currencies for future delivery takes place. Forward markets for currencies are an everyday tool for international traders, investors, and speculators because they are a way to eliminate the exchange rate risk associated with future payments and receipts. Forward foreign exchange markets allow an exporter or importer to sign a currency contract on the day they sign an agreement to ship or receive goods. The currency contract guarantees a set price for the foreign currency, usually 30, 90, or 180 days into the future. By contrast, the market for buying and selling in the present is called a **spot market**. The prices of foreign currencies quoted in Figure 10.1 are "spot prices."

Suppose the U.S. semiconductor manufacturer signs a contract to deliver the microprocessors to the British firm in six months. Suppose also that the price is stated in British pounds. The manufacturer knows precisely how many pounds it will earn six months from now, but it does not know whether the pound will rise or fall in value, so it does not know what it will earn in dollar terms. The solution is to sign a forward contract to sell British pounds six months from now in exchange for U.S. dollars at a price agreed upon today. Using the forward market, the U.S. manufacturer avoids the risk that comes from exchange rate fluctuations.

Forward markets are important to financial investors and speculators as well as exporters and importers. For example, bondholders and other interest rate arbitrageurs often use forward markets to protect themselves against the foreign exchange risk incurred while holding foreign bonds and other financial assets. This is called **hedging** and it is accomplished by buying a forward contract to sell foreign currency at the same time that the bond or other interest-earning asset matures. When interest rate arbitrageurs use the forward market to insure against exchange rate risk, it is called **covered interest arbitrage**.

THE SUPPLY AND DEMAND FOR FOREIGN EXCHANGE

LO 10.2 **Diagram the effects on the home currency of a change in supply or demand for foreign currency.**

LO 10.3 **Differentiate short-run, medium-run, and long-run forces that help determine the value of a currency.**

LO 10.4 **Calculate a currency's forward premium or discount based on interest rate differentials.**

The value of one nation's money, like most things, can be analyzed by looking at its supply and demand. Under a system of flexible, or floating, exchange rates, an increase in the demand for the dollar will raise its price (cause an **appreciation** in its value), while an increase in its supply will lower its price (cause a **depreciation**). Under a fixed exchange rate system, the value of the dollar is held constant through the actions of the central bank that counteract the market forces of supply and demand. Consequently, supply and demand analysis is a useful tool for understanding the pressures on a currency regardless of the type of exchange rate system adopted. For this reason, we begin with the assumption that exchange rates are completely flexible. After examining the usefulness of supply and demand analysis, we will turn to alternative systems, including gold standards and other variations on fixed exchange rates.

Supply and Demand with Flexible Exchange Rates

Figure 10.2 shows the supply and demand for British pounds in the United States. The demand curve is a normal, downward sloping curve, indicating that as the pound depreciates relative to the dollar, the quantity of pounds demanded by Americans increases. Note also that we are measuring the price of the pound—the exchange rate—on the vertical axis. Because it is dollars per pound ($£), it is the price of a pound in terms of dollars, and an increase in the exchange rate (R) is a decline in the value of the dollar. Movements up the vertical axis represent an increase in the price of the pound, which is equivalent to a fall in the price of the dollar. Similarly, movements down the vertical axis represent a decrease in the price of the pound.

British goods are less expensive for Americans when the pound is cheaper and the dollar is stronger. Hence, at depreciated values for the pound, Americans

FIGURE 10.2   Supply and Demand in the Foreign Exchange Market

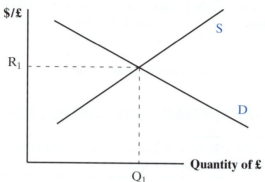

The intersection of the supply of British pounds to the U.S. market and the U.S. demand for British pounds determines the quantity of pounds available in the United States (Q_1) and their dollar price (exchange rate R_1).

will switch from U.S. or third-party suppliers of goods and services to British suppliers. However, before they can purchase goods made in Britain, first they must exchange dollars for British pounds. Consequently, the increased demand for British goods is simultaneously an increase in the quantity of British pounds demanded.

The supply curve in Figure 10.2 slopes up because British firms and consumers are willing to buy a greater quantity of American goods as the dollar becomes cheaper. That is, they receive more dollars per pound. However, before British customers can buy American goods, first they must convert pounds into dollars, so the increase in the quantity of American goods demanded is simultaneously an increase in the quantity of foreign currency supplied to the United States. The intersection of supply and demand determines the market exchange rate and the quantity of pounds supplied to the United States. At exchange rate R_1, the demand and supply of British pounds to the United States is Q_1.

Exchange Rates in the Long Run

We have determined that the supply curve slopes up to the right and the demand curve slopes down. The next step in supply and demand analysis is to consider the factors that determine the intersection of supply and demand and the actual exchange rate. We will continue to assume that the exchange rate is completely flexible. Later in the chapter we look at exchange rates that are fixed, and at intermediate rates between fixed and flexible.

In Figure 10.3, an increase in the U.S. demand for the pound (rightward shift of the demand curve) causes a rise in the exchange rate, an appreciation in the pound, and a depreciation in the dollar. Conversely, a fall in demand would shift the demand curve left and lead to a falling pound and a rising dollar. On the supply side, an increase in the supply of pounds to the U.S. market (supply curve

FIGURE 10.3   An Increase in Demand for British Pounds

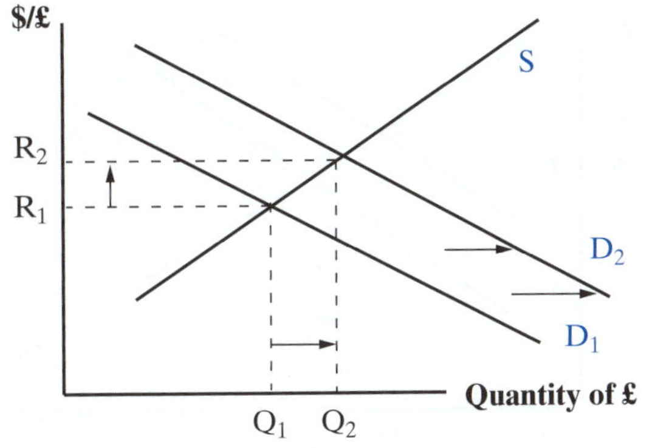

An increase in the U.S. demand for British pounds (rightward shift of the curve) causes the dollar to depreciate.

shifts right) is illustrated in Figure 10.4, where a new intersection for supply and demand occurs at a lower exchange rate and an appreciated dollar. A decrease in the supply of pounds shifts the curve leftward, causing the exchange rate to rise and the dollar to depreciate.

The causal factors behind the shifts in the supply and demand are easier to conceptualize if we divide the determinants of exchange rates into three periods: long run, medium run, and short run. This seems to be accurate empirically, as not all the factors that determine an exchange rate show up instantaneously. In fact, some causal factors take a very long time—a decade or more—to exert their full influence, and in the meantime, a number of short-run or medium-run factors may push in a completely opposite direction.

Looking at the long run first, **purchasing power parity** states that the equilibrium value of an exchange rate is at the level that allows a given amount of money to buy the same quantity of goods abroad that it will buy at home. By this criterion, the equilibrium exchange rate is the point where the dollar buys pounds at a rate that keeps its purchasing power over goods and services constant. That is, in equilibrium $100 is equivalent to the number of pounds needed to buy the same basket of goods and services in Britain that $100 buys in the United States. Table 10.1 illustrates this idea.

In Table 10.1, a hypothetical basket of goods costs $1,000 or £500, depending on the country where it is purchased. Accordingly, the long-run tendency is for the exchange rate to move to $2 per pound. If it is above that, the pound is overvalued and the dollar is undervalued. An overvalued pound buys more in the United States than in Britain since it would be possible to convert £500 to more than $1,000 and buy a larger basket of goods than can be bought in Britain. Exchange rates less than $2 would imply the opposite—the pound is undervalued and the dollar overvalued.

FIGURE 10.4 **An Increase in the Supply of British Pounds**

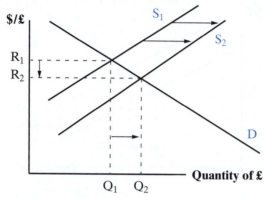

An increase in the supply of British pounds to the U.S. market (rightward shift of the curve) causes the dollar to appreciate.

TABLE 10.1 **A Hypothetical Example of the Exchange Rate in the Long Run**

	Cost of the Same Basket of Goods in Each Country
Price in dollars	$1,000
Price in pounds	£500
Long-run equilibrium exchange rate	($1,000/£ 500) = $2/£

Purchasing power parity states that dollars will tend to exchange for pounds at a rate that maintains a constant purchasing power of a given quantity of currency.

It should be stressed that this is an underlying tendency and not a description of actual exchange rates at any point in time. Over the long run, purchasing power parity exerts influence over exchange rates, but in the short to medium run, there are significant deviations from this pattern. If you have traveled outside your home country, you are probably aware of cases where your domestic currency buys you so much foreign currency that your standard of living is higher when you travel. You might be able to stay in a better class of hotel, eat in better restaurants, and shop for items that you cannot afford at home; or you may be familiar with the opposite scenario, where your standard of living declines because you get so little foreign currency in exchange for your domestic currency that everything seems inordinately expensive.

Purchasing power parity influences currency values indirectly. When a currency is overvalued or undervalued, it creates profit-making opportunities for merchants that can move goods across international borders. Suppose, for example, that the dollar is overvalued and that instead of $2 per pound, the exchange rate is $1.75 per pound. Prices are assumed to be the same as those shown in Table 10.1. In this case, $1,000 buys £571.43 ($1,000/$1.75 per pound). If merchants take the £571.43

and buy British goods and then ship the goods to the United States, they can earn more than $1,000. (They earn $1,142.86 since goods prices are 2 to 1.) In the long run, the demand for British pounds increases and, as shown in Figure 10.3, the exchange rate rises. The process will continue until the exchange rate hits $2 per pound and there are no more profit-making opportunities from shipping goods from Britain to the United States.

The process just described is reinforced by the flow of goods from Britain to the United States. The supply of goods shrinks in Britain, leading to rising prices there. In the United States, supply rises and, under normal competitive conditions, prices will fall. These effects will take a while to exert themselves, but they are another factor reinforcing purchasing power parity. In this case, however, prices are moving in the direction that equalizes the purchasing power of the two currencies instead of equalization through exchange rate movement as in the previous example. In theory, it does not matter which changes—prices or exchange rates—but given that prices in many countries tend not to fall easily, while exchange rates are relatively easily moved, most of the equalization probably occurs through exchange rate movements.

The story of goods arbitrage—buying where the goods are cheaper and selling where they are more expensive—which stands behind purchasing power parity, obviously has a few unrealistic assumptions. In particular, it requires that goods flow costlessly across international borders and that all goods and services can be traded. In reality, there are transportation costs involved with moving goods and some goods and services are not traded. This means that our merchant who buys £571.43 of goods in Britain and sells them for $1,142.86 in the United States loses some of his or her $142.86 profit to shipping, insurance, and other transaction costs. In addition, he or she pays a fee to a bank or a currency broker when buying the needed pounds. And finally, some of the goods and services bought and sold—haircuts for example—are never traded and arbitrage is not possible.

Finally, it is also the case that few nations have eliminated all their barriers to the entry of foreign goods and services. The merchant may face a tariff, import license fees, inspection fees, or some other barrier at the border that adds to his or her cost. In the limit, imports of the goods in question may be prohibited and goods arbitrage may be impossible at any price differential. In addition, some goods and many services are not traded. For example, restaurant meals, haircuts, landscape maintenance, and a host of other services that must be consumed on the spot are rarely, if ever, traded.

Once the assumptions of purchasing power parity are examined, it is not surprising that it exerts its influence over exchange rates only in the long run. If there are significant profit-making opportunities through goods arbitrage, then in spite of today's obstacles, entrepreneurs will work to create the conditions that will allow them to take advantage of the price differentials across markets. They will look for ways to lower transport costs, to minimize the costs of compliance with import rules and regulations, and to change the rules where it is feasible. All of these steps take time, but in spite of the real obstacles to its operation, purchasing power parity remains a significant long-run force in the determination of exchange rates.

Exchange Rates in the Medium Run and Short Run

While purchasing power parity is working slowly in the background, other forces have more immediate impacts on the position of the supply and demand curves for foreign exchange. We turn first to the forces that are correlated with the business cycle, the natural but irregular rhythms of expansion and recession that every country undergoes. Given that the time period from the peak of one expansion to the next is usually several years in duration, the forces that are tied to the business cycle can be considered medium run. That is, they are pressures on an exchange rate that may last for several years, but almost always less than a decade and usually less than five to seven years.

The most important medium-run force is the strength of a country's economic growth. Rapid growth implies rising incomes and increased consumption. When consumers feel secure in their jobs and at the same time experience a rapid growth in their incomes, they spend more, some of which will be on imports and travel abroad. As a result, rapid economic growth at home is translated into increased imports and an outward shift in the demand for foreign currency, as shown in Figure 10.3. Holding constant a host of short-run forces that may be in play at the same time, the effect of rapid economic growth at home is a depreciating currency.

The effect of growth is symmetrical, both with respect to slower growth at home, and with respect to the rate of economic growth abroad. Slower growth, such as a recession during which output declines (negative economic growth), raises consumer uncertainty about jobs and reduces many people's incomes. For the economy as a whole, as consumption expenditures fall, expenditures on imports decline as well, and the demand for foreign exchange falls. A leftward shift of the demand curve reduces the exchange rate and appreciates the currency. In other words, just as more rapid economic growth can cause a depreciation in a country's currency, slower growth sets forces in motion that lead to an appreciation.

Growth abroad does not have a direct effect on the home country's demand for foreign exchange (although it may have an indirect effect through its stimulation of the home economy), but it will directly affect the supply curve. More rapid foreign growth leads to more exports from the home country, and slower foreign growth results in fewer exports. More exports to foreigners increase the supply of foreign currency and shift the supply curve rightward, as shown in Figure 10.4. Fewer exports have the opposite effect. You should practice drawing the effects of changes in the rates of home and foreign economic growth on the supply and demand curves for foreign exchange.

Turning from the medium run of the business cycle to short-run periods of a year or less, a number of forces are constantly at work shaping currency values. The foremost short-run force is the flow of financial capital. The effects of financial flows range from minor and subtle to dramatic and, at times, catastrophic. They are as capable of creating slight day-to-day variations in the value of a currency as they are of creating complete financial chaos and bringing down governments. The degree of volatility in financial flows varies greatly and is highly responsive to governmental policies and conditions in the world economy. The impact on exchange rates of large-scale, short-run movements in financial capital has become one of the most serious issues in international economics.

Two variables in particular are responsible for a large share of short-run capital flows: interest rates and expectations about future exchange rates. These two forces often influence each other and are capable of creating unpredictable interactions, as when a change in interest rates reshapes investor confidence or catalyzes speculative actions in currency markets.

The role of interest rates in the short-run determination of exchange rates is crucial. The interest rate–exchange rate relationship is summed up in the **interest parity** condition, which states that the difference between any pair of countries' interest rates is approximately equal to the expected change in the exchange rate:

$$i - i^* \approx (F - R)/R,$$

where home and foreign interest rates are given by i and i*, and F and R are the expected future current exchange rates, respectively. The appendix at the end of this chapter develops the algebra of this relationship, but the intuition is not difficult to grasp. Suppose an investor has a choice between investing at home and earning interest rate/ i, or investing abroad and earning interest rate i*. If foreign interest rates are higher than domestic ones, it may seem advantageous to invest abroad, but this is not necessarily the case. The best choice is also determined by exchange rate movements during the investment period. If investors want to convert their future earnings back into their home currency, then exchange rate movements must be taken into account during the investment period. To protect against unanticipated losses due to currency fluctuations, cross border investors can sign a forward contract to sell the foreign exchange from their future earnings. This is known as covered interest arbitrage and is a common way to take advantage of interest differentials while guarding against the risk of exchange rate losses.

A simple example will help clarify. Suppose a U.S.-based investor has a choice between one-year bonds issued by U.S. and German banks. For the sake of simplicity, assume that the bonds are similar with respect to risk, transaction costs, and other characteristics. The U.S. investment is denominated in dollars and pays 3 percent (i) while the German investment is in euros and pays 2 percent (i*). In one year, $1,000 invested in the United States will pay $1,000 × 1.03, or $1,030, while the return on the German bond depends on the fixed interest rate and the exchange rate a year from now. If the dollar-euro spot rate is 1.2 today, then the investor can use the $1,000 to buy €833.33 (1,000/1.2) and invest it at 2 percent in Germany. In one year, the investor will have €833.33 × 1.02, or €850. If the exchange rate is 1.3 a year from now, then the $1,000 converted to euros and invested in Germany at 2 percent will be worth €850 × $1.3 per euro, or $1,105. That is, a dollar invested today in a German bond at 2 percent will earn the investor F/R × 1.02 in one year, where F is the future exchange rate and R is today's spot rate of exchange.

The problem for the investor is that he or she cannot know what the exchange rate will be one year from now. Our example fudged this point by assuming that the rate was 1.3 dollars per euro in one year's time, but in fact we cannot know what the spot exchange rate will be in a year. Given this uncertainty, investors turn to the forward market where they can sign a contract guaranteeing them a fixed amount of dollars for the euros they will have in one year when the bond matures.

The difference between the spot rate of exchange, R, and the forward rate, F, is the expected appreciation or depreciation. If F > R, then the dollar is expected to depreciate, and is said to be selling at a discount. If F < R, then the dollar is expected to appreciate and is selling at a premium. Given information about F and R, our investor is prepared to select between the dollar and euro bonds.

In our previous example, R is 1.2 and F is 1.3, implying that the dollar is at a discount in the forward market and people expect it to depreciate over the next year. The choices are as follows. An investor with $1,000 can earn $1,000 × 1.03, or $1,030 in the United States, or she can earn (1.3/1.2) × 1.02 × $1,000, or $1,105 in Germany. Clearly the German investment is better and will attract capital. Money flowing into German bonds will push down German interest rates (i* falls) and increase the spot price of the euro (R rises). Both changes reduce earnings on the German bond until, in the end, we reach the interest parity condition

$$i - i^* \approx (F - R)/R$$

where interest rate differences are approximately equal to the expected change in the exchange rate.

The utility of the interest parity condition is that it brings together capital flows, domestic interest rate policy, and exchange rate expectations. Suppose, for example, that domestic interest rates are above foreign rates, so that i > i*. In that case, investors expect a discount in the forward market, so that F > R. If the expected depreciation in the domestic currency is not sufficient to compensate for higher interest rates at home, then capital flows into the home country and increases demand for domestic currency, pushing down domestic interest rates until the difference between i and i* is approximately equal to the percentage difference between the forward and spot exchange rates.

Consider another example. Suppose that home interest rates are less than foreign rates (i < i*) and that forward rates are less than spot rates (F < R) by an appropriate amount so that the interest parity condition holds. Beginning at this point, home policymakers decide for some reason to raise their interest rates to the same level as foreign rates: i = i*. Now, investors in both home and foreign markets will invest more in the home country because they earn the same rate of interest, and they expect domestic currency to appreciate in value (since F < R). Figure 10.5 illustrates these shifts. Note that both the demand curve for foreign currency and the supply curve of foreign currency shift, with demand moving in and supply moving out. Taken together, both shifts reinforce a downward movement in the spot rate. As R falls, domestic currency appreciates and the gap between F and R closes. If i = i*, the process ends when F = R.

In addition to their impact on the forward-spot rate differential, expectations play a crucial role in the determination of exchange rates in another way. A sudden change in the expected future value of an exchange rate can have a dramatic and often self-fulfilling impact on a country's currency. For example, if investors

FIGURE 10.5   The Effects of an Increase in Home's Interest Rate

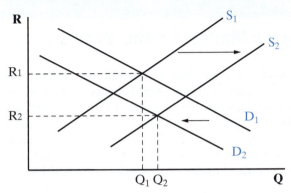

An increase in domestic interest rates causes a decrease in demand and an increase in supply of the foreign currency. Both effects cause an appreciation in the exchange rate from R_1 to R_2.

suddenly come to believe that a currency must depreciate more than they had anticipated, it lowers the expected value of assets denominated in that currency. This can create a sudden exodus of financial capital and put enormous pressure on the country's supply of foreign exchange reserves. To a significant extent, episodes of capital flight can be self-fulfilling in their expectations about an exchange rate. If investors expect depreciation, they try to convert their assets to another currency. This raises the demand for foreign exchange and depresses the supply, fulfilling the expectation of a depreciation.

There are numerous potential causes of this type of volatility in financial capital flows and exchange rate shifts. It also seems likely that technological changes in telecommunications have altered the sensitivity of markets toward changes in expectations, although this is yet to be established definitively. Nevertheless, it is certain that a frequent cause of sudden shifts in expectations is the realization that a particular government is practicing economic policies that are internally inconsistent and unsustainable. We will examine this in more detail in Chapters 11 and 12, but it is relatively easy to get a sense of the meaning of inconsistent policies. An example is policies that are designed to stimulate the economy strongly (more growth → more imports → more demand for foreign exchange) when the supply of foreign exchange is severely limited (not enough exports, very low interest rates).

The mechanisms from inconsistent policy to exchange rate crisis and collapse are fairly well understood, but this begs the question about the cause of a sudden shift in expectations. Many recent episodes of sudden exchange rate shifts have occurred when investors lost confidence in a particular currency. Yet why the sudden change in investor confidence? Government policies are often in place for years before they become unsustainable. Quite frequently, an external shock such as a sudden shift in the price of a key input such as oil, or a sudden change in policy by an important trade partner, are the tipping point.

CASE STUDY

The Largest Market in the World

In 2013, the world's foreign exchange markets traded an estimated $5,345 billion worth of currency per day. Another way to look at this is that every 3.1 days, currency trades equaled the value of U.S. annual gross domestic product (GDP). These estimates come from a survey of fifty-three central banks conducted every three years by the Bank for International Settlements (BIS), a "central bank for central banks." The BIS survey is the *Triennial Central Bank Survey,* conducted in April 2013 and available from the BIS at http://www.bis.org.

Between 1992 and 2013, the volume of exchange rate transactions grew from $880 billion per day to $5,345 billion. In 2013, the top four currencies traded around the world were the U.S. dollar (87 percent of all trades), the EU euro (33.4 percent), the Japanese yen (23 percent), and the British pound (11.8 percent). (See Table 10.2.) Not surprisingly, the U.S. dollar/euro exchange was the most common, with 24.1 percent of all transactions, followed by the U.S. dollar/yen (18.3 percent), and the U.S. dollar/U.K. pound (8.8 percent).

Note that the total in Table 10.2 is 200 percent rather than 100 percent because every sale is simultaneously a purchase. The dollar is so often traded because it is used as an international medium of exchange and because of the cross-trading that occurs between pairs of currencies. That is, a Chilean importer may pay his or her Mexican supplier in U.S. dollars, or he or she may use Chilean pesos to buy dollars and use the dollars to buy Mexican pesos. It

TABLE 10.2   Composition of Currency Trades, April 2013

Currency	Percent of Total Trades
U.S. dollar	87.0
EU euro	33.4
Japanese yen	23.0
U.K. pound	11.8
Australian dollar	8.6
Swiss franc	5.2
Canadian dollar	4.6
Mexican peso	2.5
Chinese yuan	2.2
Other	21.7

Source: Data from Bank for International Settlements, © James Gerber.

is unlikely that the Mexican exporter would accept Chilean pesos, so one way or another the importer has to come up with dollars.

Currency trading is concentrated in just a few financial centers. London is by far the largest center of foreign exchange trading, as is illustrated by the BIS survey's finding that more U.S. dollars are traded in London than in New York (see Table 10.3). Given the preponderance of the U.S. dollar in currency trades and the importance of London as a trading center, it follows that most of the trades in London do not involve the British pound.

TABLE 10.3   Currency Trading Centers

Location	Percent of World Currency Trading
United Kingdom	40.9
United States	18.9
Singapore	5.7
Japan	5.6
Hong Kong	4.1
Switzerland	3.2
France	2.8
Australia	2.7
Other	16.1

Source: Data from Bank for International Settlements, © James Gerber.

Table 10.4 summarizes the long-, medium-, and short-run factors that have been discussed. The list is not exhaustive, but the main elements are included.

TABLE 10.4   Major Determinants of an Appreciation or Depreciation

	R Falls: An Appreciation in the Domestic Currency	R Rises: A Depreciation in the Domestic Currency
Long run: Purchasing Power Parity	Home goods are less expensive than foreign goods	Home goods are more expensive than foreign goods
Medium run: The Business Cycle	Domestic economy grows more slowly than foreign	Domestic economy grows faster than foreign
Short run (1): Interest Parity	Home interest rates rise, or foreign rates fall	Home interest rates fall, or foreign rates rise
Short run (2): Speculation	Expectations of a future appreciation	Expectations of a future depreciation

THE REAL EXCHANGE RATE

LO 10.5 **Explain in words and with an equation the relationship between price changes and the real exchange rates.**

The concept of the exchange rate that has been used so far and that is exemplified by the values shown in Table 10.2 does not really tell us what a foreign currency is worth. Exchange rates tell us how many units of domestic currency we give up for one unit of foreign currency, but unless we know what foreign prices are, we still do not know the purchasing power of our domestic money when it is converted to a foreign currency. As an illustration of this problem, suppose that the U.S. dollar–Malaysian ringgit exchange rate is $0.25 and that it stays constant over the year. However, suppose also that Malaysian inflation is 4 percent while U.S. inflation is 1 percent. After one year, the four ringgits that cost one dollar will buy 3 percent less in Malaysia than the dollar buys in the United States. The relatively higher inflation in Malaysia erodes the value of a dollar's worth of ringgits more rapidly than the dollar loses value at home. Consequently, when converted to ringgits, the real purchasing power of the dollar has declined even though the exchange rate is still $0.25 per ringgit.

From the point of view of tourists and business people who use foreign exchange, the key item of interest is the purchasing power they get when they convert their dollars, not the number of units of a foreign currency. An American importer trying to decide between Malaysian and Chinese textiles does not really care if he or she gets four ringgits per dollar or eight Chinese yuan per dollar. The biggest concern is the volume of textiles that can be purchased in Malaysia with four ringgits and in China with eight yuan.

The **real exchange rate** is the market exchange rate (or **nominal exchange rate**) adjusted for price differences. The two are closely connected. By way of illustration, let's consider the case of a wine merchant who is trying to decide whether to stock his or her shop with American or French wine. Let's say that French wine of a given quality costs €200 and American wine of the same quality costs $180. Suppose that the nominal rate is $1.20 per euro so that $180 is equivalent to €150 in the currency market. In this case, French wine costs one-third more than American wine, and the real exchange rate is 1.33 cases of American wine per case of French wine. The algebra is straightforward:

Real exchange rate
$$= [(\text{Nominal exchange rate}) \times (\text{Foreign price})]/(\text{Domestic price})$$
$$= [(\$1.20 \text{ per euro}) \times (€200 \text{ per case})]/(\$180 \text{ per case})$$
$$= (\$240 \text{ per case of French wine})/(\$180 \text{ per case of American wine})$$
$$= 1\tfrac{1}{3} \text{ cases of American wine per one case of French wine}$$

Because the real purchasing power of the dollar is much less in France than in the United States, the choice facing the wine merchant is obvious.

In this example, the main lesson is clear. What matters most to exporters and importers is not the nominal exchange rate, but the real exchange rate—in other words, how much purchasing power they have in the countries under comparison. Let R_r symbolize the real exchange rate, R_n the nominal rate. Since we are interested in the whole economy rather than just one market such as the market for wine, we will use a price index to measure overall prices in the two countries. Price indexes are equivalent to the average price of a basket of goods and services in each economy. Let P stand for the home country price index, and P^* represent foreign prices. Then, following the algebra of the wine merchant's calculation:

> Real exchange rate
> = Nominal exchange rate $\times$ (Foreign prices)/(Domestic prices),

or, more compactly,

$$R_r = R_n(P^*/P).$$

Suppose, for example, that the U.S. dollar–EU euro nominal exchange rate is $1.20 per euro and that both price levels are initially set at 100. In this case, the cost of a basket of goods and services is the same in real terms in both countries and

$$R_r = R_n(P^*/P) = R_n(100/100) = R_n.$$

The real rate equals the nominal rate when the purchasing power is the same in both countries. Note that purchasing power parity indicates that this is the long-run equilibrium. Over time, however, if inflation is higher at home than in the foreign country, P rises more than P^*, and R_r falls, meaning the domestic currency appreciates in real terms.

By way of illustration, suppose that the United States has 10 percent inflation while the EU has 0 percent. Then, the real U.S.-EU exchange rate (in terms of dollars per euro) would be as follows:

$$R_r = (\$1.20 \text{ per euro}) \times (100/110) = \$1.0909 \text{ per euro.}$$

Tourists, investors, and businesspeople can still trade dollars and euros at the nominal rate of $1.20 per euro (plus whatever commissions they pay to the seller), but the real purchasing power of the U.S. dollar has risen in the EU compared to what it buys at home. The real exchange rate of $1.0909 per euro tells us that EU goods are now 9 percent cheaper than the U.S. goods that have risen in price. As a result, unless the nominal rate changes, the dollar goes further in the EU than at home. In real terms, the euro has depreciated and the dollar has appreciated.

Changes in the value of real exchange rates play an important role in international macroeconomic relations. When countries control the value of their nominal exchange rate, for example, they must be certain that their prices do not change in relation to the prices of their trading partners. If inflation runs higher at home, then the real value of their currency appreciates. Over a period of time, if uncorrected, this can lead to a build-up in the current account deficit as imports increase and exports decrease. In a number of cases, the end result has been currency crises and the collapse of nominal exchange rates. (For example, Mexico in December 1994 and Thailand in July 1997.)

ALTERNATIVES TO FLEXIBLE EXCHANGE RATES

Fixed exchange rate systems are also called **pegged exchange rate** systems. In these types of systems, there are several possibilities for setting the value of the country's currency. At one extreme, a few (mostly very small) countries give up their currency altogether and adopt the currency of another country, usually the dollar or the euro. More commonly, the value of a nation's money is set equal to a fixed amount of another country's currency, or less commonly to a basket of several currencies. If the exchange rate is not allowed to vary, then it is called a **hard peg**. Fixed exchange rates that fluctuate within a set band are **soft pegs** and these, in turn, can take several forms depending on the amount of variation allowed. Table 10.5 shows that in 2014, there were 25 countries with hard pegs and 101 with soft pegs in which the currency is fixed, but allowed to vary within set limits. Table 10.5 also shows that 65 countries have floating exchange rates. Of these, 36 intervene in currency markets when their currencies rise or fall too much in value, while 29 countries let their currencies float independently and usually without intervention.

Through the first seventy years of the twentieth century, fixed exchange rates were the norm, often within a framework that defined the value of a country's currency in terms of a fixed amount of gold. After World War II, many nations shifted away from gold and pegged the value of their currencies to the U.S. dollar or to the currency of another country with which they had strong historical ties. Beginning in the 1970s, the use of flexible exchange rate systems began to increase, first in the high-income industrial economies, and then in many developing countries in the 1980s and 1990s. By the end of the twentieth century, **flexible exchange rate systems** were common.

There is no best exchange rate system. Individual country conditions are unique and no single type of exchange rate system can be appropriate for every country. While the number of countries using flexible exchange rate systems grew rapidly after the early 1970s, it began to decline after 2001. Currently, less than half of the world's nations have flexible rates.

TABLE 10.5   Types of Exchange Rate Systems, 2014

Currency Regime	Countries
Hard pegs	25
Soft pegs	101
Managed floating	36
Independently floating	29
Total	191
More countries have fixed exchange rates than floating.	

Source: Data from International Monetary Fund, © James Gerber.

Fixed Exchange Rate Systems

Gold standards are one type of fixed exchange rate. The gold standard was abandoned nearly everywhere in the 1930s during the Great Depression, then was restored in a modified form after World War II, but has completely disappeared since the 1970s. Professional economists are overwhelmingly opposed to a return to the gold standard, and recent research shows that the first countries to end the gold standard were the first ones to escape the Great Depression. After World War II, Western economies adopted a modified gold standard under the **Bretton Woods exchange rate system** (1947–1971), but this too was abandoned in the early 1970s. While mainly of historical interest, gold standards highlight a pure form of fixed exchange rate with a hard peg. Under a pure gold standard, nations keep gold as their international reserve. Gold is used to settle most international obligations and nations must be prepared to trade it for their own currency whenever foreigners attempt to "redeem" the home currency they have earned by selling goods and services. In this sense, the nation's money is backed by gold.

There are essentially three rules that countries must follow in order to maintain a gold exchange standard. First, they must fix the value of their currency unit (the dollar, the pound, the yen, and so on) in terms of gold. This fixes the exchange rate. For example, under the modified gold standard of the Bretton Woods exchange rate system, the U.S. dollar was fixed at $35 per ounce and the British pound was set at £12.5 per ounce. Since both currencies were fixed in terms of gold, they were implicitly set in terms of each other: $35 = one ounce of gold = £12.5, or 2.80 dollars per pound (2.80 = 35/12.5).

The second rule of the gold standard is that nations keep the supply of their domestic money fixed in some constant proportion to their supply of gold. This requirement is an informal one, but is necessary to ensure that the domestic money supply does not grow beyond the capacity of the gold supply to support it. The third rule of a gold standard is that nations must stand ready and willing to provide gold in exchange for their home country currency.

Consider what would happen if a country decided to print large quantities of money for which there is no gold backing. In the short run, purchases of domestically produced goods would rise, causing domestic prices to rise as well. As domestic prices rise, foreign goods become more attractive, since a fixed exchange rate means that they have not increased in price. As imports in the home country increase, foreigners accumulate an unwanted supply of the home country's currency. This is the point at which the gold standard would begin to become unhinged. If gold supplies are low in relation to the supply of domestic currency, the gold reserves will begin to run out at some point as the country pays out gold in exchange for its currency. This spells crisis and a possible end to the gold standard.

Under a fixed exchange rate system, the national supply and demand for foreign currencies may vary but the nominal exchange rate does not. It is the responsibility of the monetary authorities (the central bank or treasury department) to keep the exchange rate fixed. Figure 10.6 illustrates the task before a national government when it wishes to keep its currency fixed. Suppose that the United States

FIGURE 10.6   Fixed Exchange Rates and Changes in Demand

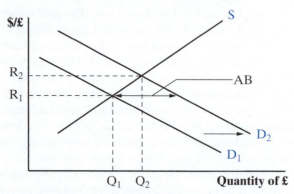

An increase in the demand for British pounds puts pressure on the exchange rate and will cause the dollar to depreciate to R_2 unless the increase in demand is countered by an increase in supply equal to line segment AB.

and the United Kingdom are both on the gold standard and the U.S. demand for British pounds increases.

In the short run or medium run, a rise in demand for pounds from D_1 to D_2 is caused by one of the factors listed in Table 10.4: increased U.S. demand for U.K. goods, higher U.K. or lower U.S. interest rates, or speculation that the value of the dollar might not remain fixed for much longer. If R_1 is the fixed U.S.–U.K. exchange rate, then the United States must counter the weakening dollar and prevent the rate from depreciating to R_2. One option is to sell the United States' gold reserves in exchange for dollars. This puts gold in the hands of merchants, investors, or speculators who are trying to obtain British pounds. The quantity of gold that must be sold is equivalent to the value of the pounds represented by line segment AB. In effect, the United States meets the increased demand for British pounds by supplying international money—gold—to the market through a sale of some of its gold stock. Since gold and pounds are interchangeable, an increase in the supply of gold is equivalent to an increase in the supply of pounds, as shown in Figure 10.7, and the exchange rate stays at R_1.

Under a pure gold standard, countries hold gold as a reserve instead of foreign currencies and sell their gold reserves in exchange for their own currency. This action increases the supply of gold—which is international money—and offsets the pressure on the home currency to depreciate. There are two possibilities for the home country as it sells its gold reserves. Either the demand for gold is satisfied and the pressure on its currency eases, or it begins to run out of gold. If the latter happens, the home country may be forced into a devaluation that is accomplished by changing the gold price of its currency. As an illustration, if the dollar is fixed at $35 per ounce of gold, a devaluation would shift the price of gold to something more than $35, say $50, and each ounce of gold sold by the United States buys back a greater quantity of dollars.

FIGURE 10.7   Selling Reserves of Pounds to Counter a Weakening Dollar

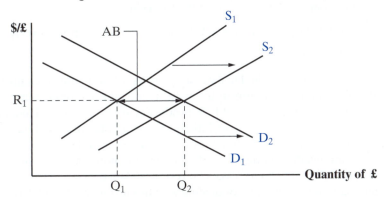

By selling gold equal in value to AB pounds, the United States prevents a depreciation in the dollar–pound exchange rate.

Pure gold standards have been rare since the 1930s. More commonly, countries have adopted modified gold standards, such as the Bretton Woods system (see the Case Study), or fixed exchange rate systems called *pegged exchange rates.* Pegged exchange rate systems operate similarly to a gold standard except that instead of gold, another currency is used to "anchor" the value of the home currency.

One potential source of problems with a pegged currency is that the home currency's value is synchronized with its peg, so changes between the peg and a third-party currency are identical for the home currency and the third party. An example will clarify. Suppose that Thailand decides to peg its currency to the U.S. dollar at the rate of 25 Thai baht per U.S. dollar. The goal of Thailand's central bank must be to supply dollars whenever it is asked to redeem its own baht. If the dollar appreciates against the Japanese yen, then so does the Thai baht, and at the same rate. Appreciation against the Japanese yen may or may not be a problem for Thailand's producers, depending on the importance of the Japan–Thailand trade relationship. In 1997, it turned out to be very important, and declining Thai competitiveness from its appreciating currency played a prominent role in triggering the Asian financial crisis of 1997–1998.

The simplest way to avoid this type of problem is to peg the currency not to one single currency, but to a group of currencies. This is, in fact, closer to Thailand's actual policy in 1997. While this is slightly more complex arithmetically, it reduces the importance of any single country's currency in the determination of the home country's currency value. Typically, countries that adopt this strategy select the currencies of their most important trading partners as elements of the basket.

Pegged exchange rates can work very well under many circumstances, but another factor that can cause them to unravel is a significant difference in inflation rates between the home country and its peg. We saw previously that real exchange rates play a greater role in determining trade patterns than nominal rates. Using the United States–Thailand example, and looking at the equation that describes the relationship between real and nominal exchange rates from Thailand's point of view (as the home country), we have the following:

$$R_r = (25 \text{ baht per dollar}) \times [(\text{U.S. price level})/(\text{Thai price level})]$$

$$= R_n(P^*/P)$$

Relatively high inflation in Thailand appears as a faster rate of change in P, and leads to a real appreciation in the baht. Under these circumstances, Thai producers are less competitive and U.S. producers are more so (in Thailand). If the situation persists, speculators will likely step in and begin to sell baht in the expectation that the pegged nominal rate of 25 baht per dollar will be devalued to offset the appreciation in the real rate. Moving the nominal peg from 25 to 30 or 40 baht per dollar may be necessary to restore balance.

The most common technique for dealing with this problem is through the adoption of a **crawling peg**. Crawling pegs are soft pegs that are fixed but periodically adjusted. The idea is to offset any differences in inflation (changes in P) through regular adjustments in R_n. If correctly handled, the real exchange rate remains constant and the impact of inflation differences never shows up as a change in competitiveness.

There are several other variations on the theme of fixed exchange rates. One of the key points to keep in mind is that purely fixed or purely flexible exchange rate arrangements are rare. When a currency is fixed in value, it is still subject to market pressures of supply and demand, which, at times, can force the government to alter the currency's value. Similarly, when countries adopt a flexible exchange rate system, there is frequently some degree of government intervention in currency markets to try to shape its value.

CASE STUDY

The End of the Bretton Woods System

The Bretton Woods system of exchange rates was enacted at the end of World War II. It included most nations outside the former Soviet Union and its allies. The exchange rate system was a major component of the institutions designed to manage international economic conflict and to support international economic cooperation. In addition to the exchange rate system, the other institutions created at the same time included the International Monetary Fund (IMF), the International Bank for Reconstruction and Development (IBRD) or World Bank, and the General Agreement on Tariffs and Trade (GATT). (See Chapter 2.)

Each institution had its own role in the management of world economic affairs. The roles of the exchange rate were to provide stability by eliminating excess currency fluctuations, to prevent nations from using exchange rate devaluations as a tactic for gaining markets for their goods, and to ensure an adequate supply of internationally accepted reserves so that nations could meet their international obligations.

In the Bretton Woods exchange rate system, the dollar was fixed to gold at the rate of $1 equaling $^1/_{35}$ ounce of gold, or $35 per ounce. Every other currency within the system was fixed to the dollar and, therefore, indirectly to gold. Unlike a pure gold standard, however, countries could use U.S. dollars as their international reserve and did not have to accumulate gold or tie their money supply to their gold reserves.

The Bretton Woods exchange rate system had one fatal flaw—the dollar. The United States was in a privileged position since its currency was treated the same as gold. This meant that the United States could simply increase its money supply (the supply of dollars) and gain increased purchasing power over European, Japanese, and other countries' goods. Other nations preferred the United States to maintain a relatively robust supply of dollars, since this ensured that there was an adequate supply of international reserves for the world economy.

Problems with this arrangement began when the U.S. economy expanded at a different rate than the economies of its trading partners. In the mid-to-late 1960s, the United States deepened its involvement in the Vietnam War while it simultaneously created the "War on Poverty" at home. Both policies generated large fiscal expenditures that stimulated the economy. While U.S. expansion raced ahead of expansion elsewhere, Europeans found themselves accumulating dollars more rapidly than they desired. The dollars were a by-product of U.S. economic expansion and partially reflected the price increases accompanying the expansion.

Under a different type of exchange rate system, it would have been appropriate for the United States to devalue its currency. U.S. prices had risen relative to foreign prices, the real exchange rate had appreciated as a consequence, and trade deficits were beginning to become a permanent feature of the U.S. economy.

One policy would have been to devalue the nominal dollar exchange rate, but this was not an option. Since every currency was tied to the dollar, there was no way for the United States to devalue against a group of other currencies selectively. An alternative was for the United States to devalue against all currencies by changing the gold value of the dollar. By the late 1960s, it was becoming apparent that this would be necessary.

Persistent U.S. deficits had led to an accumulation of dollars outside the United States, which greatly exceeded the United States' supply of gold. In other words, the United States lacked the gold reserves to back all of the dollars in circulation. Official recognition of this fact led to the **Smithsonian Agreement** of December 1971, in which the major industrialized countries agreed to devalue the gold content of the dollar by around 8 percent, from

(continued)

$35 per ounce to $38.02. In addition, Japan, Germany, and other trade surplus countries increased the value of their currencies.

Although the Smithsonian Agreement was hailed by President Nixon as a fundamental reorganization of international monetary affairs, it quickly proved to be too little and of only temporary benefit. The gold value of the dollar was realigned again in early 1973, from $38.02 to $42.22. In addition, further devaluation occurred against other European currencies. The end of the system came in March of 1973 when the major currencies began to float against each other. A few currencies, such as the British pound, had begun to float earlier.

In each case, the strategy of allowing the exchange rate to float in response to supply and demand conditions was adopted as a means of coping with speculation. When speculators had perceived that the dollar was overvalued at $38 per ounce or $42 per ounce, they sold dollars in anticipation of a future devaluation. Nor was the dollar the only currency speculated against. Other weak currencies such as the pound and the Italian lira had also been correctly perceived as overvalued and had been sold off by speculators. In the end, the central banks of the weak-currency countries found it impossible to support an unrealistically high value of their currency. The costs of buying up the excess supply of their currencies at overvalued prices proved to be too great. The simplest solution was to let the currencies float.

CHOOSING THE RIGHT EXCHANGE RATE SYSTEM

LO 10.6 **State the necessary conditions for two or more countries to form a successful single currency area.**

Given the menu of choices for exchange rate systems, an active area of economic research has focused on the performance characteristics of systems under different economic conditions and institutional arrangements. For many years, economists debated the pros and cons of fixed and flexible rates, but as the variety of exchange rate options has grown, as capital mobility has increased, and as international trade and investment relations have deepened, researchers have become more concerned with understanding how varying degrees of flexibility or fixity might best serve the interests of individual countries. In particular, economists have tried to learn how different exchange rate systems might influence the core elements of a country's macroeconomy such as the rate of economic growth, the rate of inflation, and the frequency of currency crises.

Traditional views held that countries with fixed exchange rate systems were better at controlling inflation, but that they paid a price in the form of slower economic growth. The reasoning behind this view was that in order to maintain a fixed rate, governments have to be very careful about issuing new money. Since most of the episodes of hyperinflation during the second half of the twentieth century resulted from overexpanding the money supply, it seems reasonable that an exchange rate policy that limits the supply of money would also help avoid inflation. In the view of some economists, however, the limits placed on the ability of a country to manipulate its money supply also remove an important tool that governments use to help manage the rate of economic growth. Therefore, the tradeoff was lower growth for lower inflation.

More recent research, particularly with data from the 1990s, has failed to demonstrate a strong relationship between the type of exchange rate system and either inflation or economic growth. Before the 1990s, countries with fixed or pegged exchange rates tended to have lower rates of inflation, but during the 1990s the differences disappeared. Similarly, there is evidence that countries with more flexible rates tend to have higher average rates of economic growth, but this result depends on the classification of the fastest growing Asian economies. Technically, many of these countries have flexible exchange rates, but at the same time they manage them very closely. When they are omitted from the analysis, there is no significant difference in the rate of growth between countries with relatively fixed and relatively flexible rates. And finally, neither fixed nor flexible rates seem to offer superior protection against a currency crisis. As a result, no particular system seems to rank above any other in its ability to provide superior macroeconomic performance.

Insofar as economists have been able to devise a set of rules for selecting an exchange rate system, they are very general and very basic. If the goal is to find the system that helps minimize negative shocks to an economy, then the source of the shock determines whether a more flexible or more fixed system should be adopted. When the shocks originate in the monetary sector—for example, a central bank that goes overboard in printing new money—a fixed rate is better since it imposes discipline on the central bank. On the other hand, if the shocks to an economy originate in the external environment—for example, a sudden change in the price of imported oil—then relatively more flexibility in the exchange rate enables the country to adapt to the changes more easily. The general argument here is that individual country characteristics matter a great deal. The problem with these rules, however, is that the source of the shocks to an economy are likely to vary from episode to episode and, as a consequence, the basic rules outlined above provide less practical guidance than desired.

Exchange rate pegs are popular, particularly with many developing countries. There are a couple of reasons for this. First, all economists agree that one of the most important elements of an exchange rate system is its credibility. That is, no matter what type of exchange rate is adopted, a successful system must generate confidence and the widespread belief that it is sustainable. Exchange rate systems that lack credibility are guaranteed to fail in their basic job of providing a smooth and reliable conversion between domestic and foreign money. Under some conditions, exchange rate pegs may offer greater credibility. One of the conditions, and the second reason why some countries continue to peg their currencies, is a relatively high degree of trade dependence on a single, major economy. Consider the case of Mexico, with about 80 percent of its trade with the United States.

Because of its trade dependence on the United States, Mexico pegged its peso to the U.S. dollar for many years. Because Mexican inflation ran higher than the U.S. rate, a crawling peg was favored as the means of keeping the real exchange rate relatively constant. The purpose of the dollar peg was to provide benefits to Mexican businesses and consumers by eliminating some of the price variation in Mexican imports and exports. The rule seems to be that when a country is closely tied to the economy of a large, industrial country such as the United States, pegging to its currency may provide additional stability and help businesses plan their futures with greater confidence.

This view is shared by many, but at the same time it is widely accepted that, in Mexico's case, a flexible exchange rate has served it better than the pegged rates it used before 1994. The reason for the discrepancy between what might work in theory and what has worked in practice highlights the complexity of choosing an exchange rate system when every country has unique economic factors and its own set of institutions shaping its economic outcomes. Mexico, due to a set of agreements between the business sector, organized labor, and government, was unable to make the periodic adjustments to its nominal exchange rate that are required with a crawling peg. In effect, Mexico's institutional inability to adjust its nominal exchange rate undermined the credibility of the exchange rate system. The lack of credibility led to periodic bouts of speculation against the peso whenever it was perceived to be overvalued and vulnerable. Several of these speculative bouts were followed by a peso collapse and economic recession. The lesson, in the end, seems to be that the first criterion for choosing an exchange rate system is that it must have credibility in currency and financial markets.

CASE STUDY

Monetary Unions

Some countries prefer not to have their own currency. Nineteen of the twenty-eight countries of the EU use a common currency, the euro, and more are expected to join. Panama adopted the dollar as a legal tender alongside its own currency, called the *cordoba*, in the early twentieth century, and in 2000 Ecuador and El Salvador eliminated their currencies altogether and adopted the dollar.

Dollarization is the term given to the adoption of another country's currency. Dollarization differs from a monetary union, such as the Eurozone, because a union has a common central bank that issues the currency and carries out monetary policy. By contrast, the central banks of El Salvador and Ecuador have no ability to issue money, and no control over monetary policy because they cannot expand or contract the money supply. There is no barrier in international law to using another country's money, but in doing so, a country becomes powerless to influence its exchange rate or the quantity of money in circulation.

There are currently four monetary unions in the world (Table 10.6). They are the European Monetary Union (EMU, or Eurozone is discussed in Chapter 14), the Eastern Caribbean Currency Union (ECCU), the West African Economic and Monetary Union (WAEMU), and the Central African Economic and Monetary Community, which is known by its French acronym, CEMAC.

The two African unions, WAEMU and CEMAC, are the oldest of the monetary unions. Both were formed out of former French colonies in Western Africa and both use the CFA franc as their currency. (CFA stands for Communauté; Française Africaine, or French African Community.) Both the WAEMU and the CEMAC have central banks that issue their currencies and both fix it to the euro at approximately 656 CFA francs per euro, and the two currencies are interchangeable. The French Treasury Department backs both currencies and stands ready to provide currency reserves if either of the two central banks of the monetary unions runs short.

According to most observers, the advantages of CFA francs over independent currencies is that they have lowered inflation in the participating countries and reduced macroeconomic instability. Since the central banks are responsible for more than one economy, it has probably reduced the political influence of individual governments and led to a steadier, less volatile monetary policy. The disadvantages are the same as those for a fixed exchange rate: Changes in the value of the currency cannot be used to protect the domestic economy against shocks that begin outside the country. For example, as the euro gained value against the dollar after 2000, the CFA franc also appreciated against the dollar and goods produced in the CFA franc zone became more expensive

TABLE 10.6   Monetary Unions

Monetary Union	Members	Exchange Rate System
European Monetary Union (EMU)	Nineteen of twenty-eight EU countries	Flexible
West African Economic and Monetary Union (WAEMU)	Eight countries in sub-Saharan West Africa	Fixed to euro
Central African Economic and Monetary Community (CEMAC)	Six countries in West-Central Africa	Fixed to euro
Eastern Caribbean Currency Union (ECCU)	Six island countries	Fixed to dollar

(continued)

when priced in dollars. This particularly affected the WAEMU, which mainly exports cotton and other agricultural products.

All of the monetary unions are also economic unions (for example, the EU), common markets (ECCU is the basis for the Caribbean Common Market), or customs unions (WAEMU and CEMAC). Monetary union implies a high level of integration and coordination and is only worthwhile if other elements of the economy are also integrated. There is not a great deal of agreement as to the value or necessity of monetary unions, but without additional economic integration they make little sense.

Single Currency Areas

On January 1, 1999 eleven members of the EU adopted the euro as their official currency. As the EU added new members in the first decade of the new century, several chose to use the euro, and as of 2016, nineteen of the EU's twenty-eight members had replaced their national currencies with the euro. This was the result of a shared vision developed over many decades of deeper economic, monetary, and political integration. Given that a nation's currency is one of its strongest symbols of national sovereignty, the fact that so many countries have decided to give up their currencies and their ability to set monetary policy is a remarkable set of events.

There are at least four potential reasons why a group of countries might want to share a common currency. First, a single currency eliminates the need to convert each other's money and thereby reduces transaction costs in a number of ways. It eliminates fees paid to the banks or to the currency brokers that arrange the conversion, it simplifies accounting and bookkeeping, and it enables consumers and investors to compare prices across international boundaries more accurately. Each of these advantages provides some gain in efficiency and a reduction in business costs. Second, a single currency eliminates price fluctuations caused by changes in the exchange rate. When speculators move their money into or out of a country, or when temporary interest rate changes in one country alter the supply and demand for foreign exchange, one country may become (temporarily) cheaper or more expensive for business. As a result, business decisions may reflect temporary shifts in currency values rather than underlying issues of economic efficiency. The elimination of misleading price signals that result from exchange rate fluctuations is also a potential gain in efficiency.

Third, the elimination of exchange rates through the adoption of a single currency can help increase political trust between countries seeking to increase their integration. A single currency removes some of the friction between integrating nations by eliminating the problems that are caused by exchange rate misalignments. Fourth, in some developing countries the adoption of a common currency may give their exchange rate system greater credibility. Use of such a currency can reduce exchange rate fluctuations and create greater confidence in the financial system of the adopting country, possibly leading to lower interest rates and increased availability of credit, although this depends on the overall soundness of the financial system.

Nations that give up their national money do not do so without cost. In addition to its political symbolism, the adoption of a common currency also means that the country no longer has its own money supply as a tool for managing its economic growth. The topic of monetary policy is taken up in more detail in Chapter 11, but the basic point is easy to grasp. Countries with their own currency can influence the rate of growth of the economy in the short run (but not in the long run) through a change in the supply of money. When a country adopts a common currency with one or more other countries, it gives up this tool. After the introduction of the common currency, there is only one money supply and, consequently, one rate of growth of the money supply. New York, for example, shares a common currency with California, and, as a consequence, both states experience the same changes in the money supply. If New York is growing fast and California is growing slowly, it would be impossible for the Federal Reserve to alter the money supply in a way that would speed up growth in California and slow it down in New York. With a single currency, there is a "one-size-fits-all" monetary policy.

A second potential cost to adopting a single currency is that countries give up their ability to alter their exchange rates. Exchange rate adjustments are sometimes the least costly way to restore competitiveness after a round of price increases. For example, during the years leading up to the financial crisis of 2007–2009, a number of Eurozone countries in the Mediterranean region experienced housing and construction bubbles which pushed up their prices and wages. Once the crisis began, they were less competitive against northern European nations where prices had not increased as much. In order to restore competitiveness, they were expected to implement policies aimed at pushing down prices and wages inside their countries and did not have the option to devalue their currencies to make their goods cheaper. Policies that attempt to create deflation are usually very painful to implement since they entail lower demand and slower or negative growth.

Conditions for Adopting a Single Currency

The starting point for analyzing the costs and benefits of a single currency area is the work of Robert Mundell on the theory of **optimal currency areas**. Mundell developed the first set of criteria to determine whether two or more countries are better off sharing a currency instead of using their separate national moneys. Mundell and subsequent research points to four conditions for deciding whether the gains are greater than the costs.

The first condition is that the business cycle must be synchronized and national economies must enter recessions and expansions at more or less the same time.

In this case, a single monetary policy is appropriate since each country is individually at the same point in the business cycle and there is no cost associated with the loss of national monetary policy and its replacement with a single policy for all member states. In fact, however, few countries are that well synchronized in their business cycles. Even the states of the United States enter and leave recessions at different points in time, and the national figures on growth only reflect an average across all fifty states.

The second condition is a high degree of labor and capital mobility between the member countries. This allows workers and capital to leave countries or regions where work is scarce and to join the supply of labor and capital in booming regions. In effect, free migration of the factors of production smooths out some of the differences in the business cycle by taking unemployed inputs and moving them to where they are needed. This is how the fifty states of the United States compensate for a lack of complete synchronization in the business cycles of individual states. When conditions are bad in one region, workers and investors move their labor and capital to another region, freeing inputs from areas where they are not needed and providing them to areas where they are.

While capital tends to be relatively mobile, labor is less so, even within countries. Therefore, a third condition is that there are regional policies capable of addressing the imbalances that may develop. Depressed areas may remain depressed if people cannot move or choose not to move because the psychological or other costs are too high or resources outside the region are not available. In the United States, federal taxes and transfer payments help depressed regions adjust and limit some of the shock. When a state is in recession, for example, people still receive their social security checks, Medicare, and other federal transfers. Federal taxes and payments spread the adjustment across the nation and ensure that it is not left up to the state alone. Insofar as the economics of regional policies are concerned, they may be determined at any level, from the currency area (multicountry), to individual nation-states, to subnational units (provinces or cities). The key point is not the agency responsible, but that there are effective policies for assisting regions that may not be synchronized with the majority of the currency area's economy.

Finally, the first three conditions point to the fourth: The nations involved must be seeking a level of integration that goes beyond simple free trade. Free trade requires that nations remove their tariffs, quotas, and other border barriers that inhibit the flow of goods. If this is the goal, a common currency is unnecessary. If something much deeper is sought, however, such as a greater harmonization of national economies and much closer economic and political ties, then a single currency can be helpful, provided the other three conditions are observed. This condition is admittedly ambiguous and is part of the reason why policymakers do not always agree in their analysis. It is somewhat circular reasoning, but true nevertheless, that the desirability of a single currency partly depends on the goals of the countries involved.

CASE STUDY

Is the NAFTA Region an Optimal Currency Area?

The EU is one model for the creation of a single currency. In the EU model, an entirely new currency is created, and each country gives up its national money. The on and off discussion of a single currency in the NAFTA countries has favored a different model. So far, discussion has centered on the adoption of the U.S. dollar by all three countries instead of the creation of an entirely new currency. Either model leads to the same outcome: a single currency area. Is the discussion realistic? That is, are the proponents of a single currency dreaming or is there something to be gained in such a move?

It is clear that whatever the long-run advantages or disadvantages of a single currency might be, the NAFTA countries have a long way to go before they meet the four conditions necessary for a single currency area to be an optimal policy. First, the business cycles of the three countries have not been synchronized, at least historically. While the macroeconomies of Canada and the United States have often moved together, Mexico has historically had a very different pattern of business cycles. This may be changing, however, since the Mexican cycle appears to be much closer to that of the United States since 1994. Second, given the legal restrictions on labor movement and the political obstacles to opening a North American labor market, labor flows cannot be counted on to help synchronize national business cycles. Third, there are no regional policies within the NAFTA framework and no way to create transfers from one country to another to compensate for slower growth or recession in one area while other places are expanding. Finally, NAFTA was originally conceived as a means to reduce border barriers. While its ultimate goal will surely evolve over time, currently there does not appear to be a consensus that it should be something more than a free-trade area.

As it is now constituted, the NAFTA region is clearly not an optimal currency area. Nevertheless, it is a safe bet that dollarization will continue to be explored, particularly in Mexico. In part, this is because there are counter-arguments to each of the above objections: A single currency will help synchronize the three economies; it is possible to formulate an agreement that allows a guest worker program such as the United States and Mexico had in the 1940s, 1950s, and 1960s; regional policies are simply a matter of political will and financial means, but they would not require huge expenditures; and closer integration of the NAFTA partners is inevitable. Nevertheless, given the problems of the euro zone countries beginning in 2011, it is highly unlikely that any serious analyst might try to push a single currency agenda in the NAFTA region.

Summary

- People hold foreign currency to buy goods and services, to take advantage of interest rate differentials, and to speculate. The primary institutions in the exchange-rate market are commercial banks and foreign exchange brokers.

- Exchange rates can be analyzed with supply and demand analysis, as if they are just another commodity in the economy. Increases (decreases) in the supply of foreign exchange cause the domestic currency to appreciate (depreciate). Increases (decreases) in the demand for foreign exchange cause the domestic currency to depreciate (appreciate).

- Exchange rates are unpredictable because they are simultaneously influenced by long-run, medium-run, and short-run factors. In the long run, purchasing power parity is important. In the medium run, the business cycle is important, and in the short run, interest-rate differentials and speculation are important.

- The interest parity condition says that the interest rate differential between two countries is approximately equal to the percentage difference between the forward and spot exchange rates.

- Firms use forward exchange rate markets to protect against exchange rate risk.

- Real exchange rates are equal to nominal or market exchange rates adjusted for inflation. They give a better picture of the purchasing power of a nation's currency.

- Fixed exchange rate systems were thought to help limit the growth of inflation, but there is little evidence of this over the last two decades. Fixed exchange rates eliminate the ability of governments to use monetary policies to regulate the macroeconomy.

- Flexible exchange rate systems were thought to help increase growth, but there is little evidence of this over the last two decades. Flexible exchange rates free a nation's macroeconomic policies from the priority of maintaining a fixed exchange rate and allow for a greater use of monetary and fiscal policies to achieve economic growth goals.

- All exchange rate systems are on a continuum between fixed and flexible rates. Crawling pegs and managed floating rates are examples of intermediate systems between absolutely fixed and completely flexible systems. The most important rule for countries is that their exchange rate system is credible.

- Optimal currency areas are geographical regions within which it is optimal for countries to adopt the same currency. The criteria for an optimal currency area are a synchronized business cycle, complete factor mobility, regional programs for lagging areas, and a desire to achieve a higher level of economic and political integration.

Vocabulary

appreciation

Bretton Woods exchange rate system

covered interest arbitrage

crawling peg

depreciation

dollarization

exchange rate

exchange rate risk

fixed exchange rate system

flexible (floating) exchange rate system

forward exchange rate

forward market

gold standard

hard peg

hedging

interest parity

interest rate arbitrage

nominal exchange rate

optimal currency area

pegged exchange rate

purchasing power parity

real exchange rate

Smithsonian Agreement

soft peg

spot market

Study Questions

All problems are assignable in My EconLab
Exercises that update with real-time data are marked with.

10.1   Draw a graph of the supply of and demand for the Canadian dollar by the U.S. market. Diagram the effect of each of the following on the exchange rate; state in words whether the effect is long, medium, or short run; and explain your reasoning.

    a.   More rapid growth in Canada than in the United States

    b.   A rise in U.S. interest rates

    c.   Goods are more expensive in Canada than in the United States

    d.   A recession in the United States

    e.   Expectations of a future depreciation in the Canadian dollar

10.2   Suppose the U.S. dollar–euro exchange rate is 1.20 dollars per euro, and the U.S. dollar–Mexican peso rate is 0.10 dollars per peso. What is the euro–peso rate?

10.3   Suppose the U.S. dollar–yen exchange rate is 0.01 dollars per yen. Since the base year, inflation has been 2 percent in Japan and 10 percent in the United States. What is the real exchange rate? In real terms, has the dollar appreciated or depreciated against the yen?

10.4 Which of the three motives for holding foreign exchange are applicable to each of the following?

   a. A tourist

   b. A bond trader

   c. A portfolio manager

   d. A manufacturer

10.5 If U.S. visitors to Mexico can buy more goods in Mexico than they can in the United States when they convert their dollars to pesos, is the dollar undervalued or overvalued? Explain.

10.6 In a fixed exchange rate system, how do countries address the problem of currency market pressures that threaten to lower or raise the value of their currency?

10.7 In the debate on fixed versus floating exchange rates, the strongest argument for a floating rate is that it frees macroeconomic policy from taking care of the exchange rate. This is also the weakest argument. Explain.

10.8 Brazil, Argentina, Paraguay, Uruguay, Venezuela, and Bolivia are members of the Common Market of the South (Mercado Común del Sur, or MERCOSUR), a regional trade area that is trying to become a common market. What issues should they consider before they accept or reject a common currency?

10.9 Suppose that U.S. interest rates are 4 percent more than rates in the EU.

   a. Would you expect the dollar to appreciate or depreciate against the euro, and by how much?

   b. If, contrary to your expectations, the forward and spot rates are the same, in which direction would you expect financial capital to flow? Why?

10.10 Why do some economists claim that the most important feature of any exchange rate system is its credibility?

APPENDIX

The Interest Rate Parity Condition

The following variables are defined as in the chapter:

i = home country interest rate, i^* = foreign interest rate, R = the nominal exchange rate in units of home country currency per unit of foreign currency, F = the forward exchange rate

The forward rate and the interest rates have the same term to maturity.

An investor has a choice between i and i^*. Letting the dollar be the home currency, $1 invested today will return $1(1 + i)$ next period if invested at home.

To make the comparison with a foreign investment, the dollar first has to be converted into the foreign currency, then invested, and the earnings must be converted back into dollars. The equivalent of $1 in foreign currency is 1/R. If 1/R is invested abroad, at the end of the next period it returns $(1/R)(1 + i^*)$, which is in units of foreign currency. The reconversion to dollars can be done in the forward market where the exchange rate for a forward contract is F. Therefore, in dollars, $1 invested abroad will return $(1/R)(1 + i^*)F$ in the next period.

The interest parity condition states that investors will be indifferent between home and foreign investments (of similar risk), implying that they will move their funds around and cause interest rates and exchange rates to change until the returns are the same in the two cases:

$$1 + i = (1/R)(1 + i^*)F = (1 + i^*)(F/R)$$

Divide by $(1 + i^*)$:

$$(1 + i)/(1 + i^*) = F/R$$

Subtract 1 from both sides:

$$[(1 + i)/(1 + i^*)] - [(1 + i^*)/(1 + i^*)] = F/R - R/R$$
$$[(1 + i) - (1 + i^*)]/[(1 + i^*)] = (F - R)/R$$
$$(i - i^*)/(1 + i^*) = (F - R)/R.$$

The left-hand side denominator is close to 1 for small values of i^* (this is why we state the interest parity condition as an approximation). The right-hand side is the percentage difference between the forward and spot rates. If it is negative, markets expect an appreciation in the home currency. Rewriting the last equation,

$$i - i^* \approx (F - R)/R,$$

which says that the difference between home country and foreign interest rates is approximately equal to the expected depreciation in the home country currency.

CHAPTER 11

An Introduction to Open Economy Macroeconomics

Learning Objectives

After studying this chapter, students will be able to:

11.1 Diagram a shift in aggregate demand or supply and explain the impact on the price level and GDP.

11.2 Diagram the effects on GDP and the price level of expansionary and contractionary fiscal and monetary policies.

11.3 Analyze the effects of fiscal and monetary policies on the current account and the exchange rate.

11.4 Explain how expenditure switching and expenditure reducing policies can be used to reduce a current account deficit.

11.5 Draw a J-curve and use it to show how exchange rate depreciation does not lead to an immediate reduction in the current account deficit.

INTRODUCTION: THE MACROECONOMY IN A GLOBAL SETTING

Chapters 9 and 10 introduced the concepts of the balance of payments and the exchange rate. In this chapter we look more closely at their relationship to each other and to the overall national economy. After a brief review of a few key macroeconomic concepts, the chapter focuses on the interactions among the current account, exchange rates, and key components of the macroeconomy—consumption, investment, and government spending. National governments are important to this chapter since they rarely take a passive role in the economy. Indeed, since the worldwide Great Depression of the 1930s, and especially since the end of World War II, national governments have shouldered a significant share of the responsibility for keeping the growth of the economy on track, the unemployment rate low, and prices stable. This role is particularly evident in the crisis that began in 2007 and the recession that followed. Therefore, a major focus of this chapter is the impact of macroeconomic policies on the exchange rate and current account.

The impacts of activist macroeconomic policies are one focus of this chapter, but it is also important to recognize that these are not the only links between a nation's macroeconomy and the rest of the world. Governments control a significant share of the national product and as a consequence, their normal, day-to-day operating decisions affect exchange rates and the current account. The same is true for consumers and businesses, both of which have significant macroeconomic impacts and can alter exchange rates, current account balances, and capital flows through their spending and saving.

AGGREGATE DEMAND AND AGGREGATE SUPPLY

LO 11.1   **Diagram a shift in aggregate demand or supply and explain the impact on the price level and GDP.**

Table 11.1 shows the four main economic agents in the macroeconomy: households, businesses, government, and foreigners. In our simplified model of the macroeconomy, households supply all the factors of production (land, labor, and capital) that businesses need to produce the nation's output. In return, the revenue that businesses earn when they sell their goods is used to pay for the factors supplied by households. Accordingly, all of the income generated in the economy accrues to households since they supply all of the factor inputs. This is a fundamental identity in the macroeconomy: The income for the economy as a whole equals the value of its output.

When we track income and output, it is important to understand the position of **intermediate inputs**—goods purchased by one business from another to use in production. For example, a car manufacturer not only hires labor, land, and capital (for which it pays wages and salaries, rents, interest, and dividends) but also purchases glass, tires, steel, and so on. The payment for auto glass is not directly income to households because it is paid to another business; but if we

TABLE 11.1   The Main Economic Agents in the Macroeconomy

Agent	Function
Households	■ Supply factors (land, labor, capital) to business ■ Purchase consumer goods and services (C) ■ Save ■ Pay taxes
Businesses	■ Use the factors supplied by households to produce the nation's output ■ Purchase investment goods (I)
Government	■ Purchase government goods and services (G) ■ Collect taxes (T)
Foreigners	■ Purchase exports (EX) ■ Supply imports (IM)

There are four main agents in the macroeconomy. Each one is a different source of demand for goods and services.

trace it back, it ultimately becomes income. For example, the glass manufacturer receives payment from the car company, and it uses the payment to pay wages, rent, interest, and dividends, as well as its suppliers. We can keep following the flow of payments through the suppliers to the glass firms, or more simply, we can recognize that all of the payments are incorporated into the value of the car. That is, the purchase price of the car ultimately generates an equivalent amount of income. As a result, the fundamental identity holds between income and output.

The identity between total expenditures on final goods and services and the value of total output in an economy can be looked at in another way that is similar to a graph of supply and demand in a single market, except that the demand curve is total demand for all final goods and services and the supply curve is total output. In other words, the curve with a negative slope is **aggregate demand (AD)**, and the curve with a positive slope is **aggregate supply (AS)**. In a simple supply and demand graph, the horizontal axis measures quantity and the vertical axis measures price; but in the AD/AS graph shown in Figure 11.1, all final goods gross domestic product (GDP) are included on the horizontal axis, and the price level (P) is shown on the vertical axis. The price level is equivalent to the consumer price index or another measure of economy-wide prices. Points along the AD curve show the equilibrium levels of output and prices that are consistent on the demand side of the economy, while the AS curve shows the points that

FIGURE 11.1   Aggregate Demand (AD) and Aggregate Supply (AS)

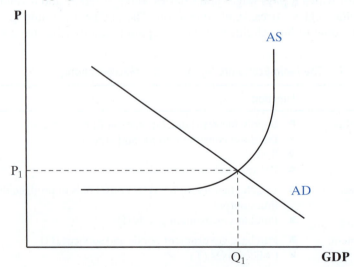

The aggregate demand (AD) curve shows the levels of output (GDP) and price (P) where expenditure decisions and prices match; aggregate supply (AS) shows the levels of output and prices where output and prices match. Together they show the levels of equilibrium output (Q_1) and prices (P_1).

are consistent from a supply-side point of view. Together, they show the levels of equilibrium output (Q_1) and prices (P_1) at a given point in time.

The shape of the aggregate supply curve is designed to call attention to three regions of GDP. On the horizontal part of the AS curve, the economy is operating below full employment. Theoretically, the availability of unemployed workers and other idle resources allows an increase in output to occur without putting upward pressure on prices. Workers and the owners of other factors cannot demand higher wages or other payments in return for more inputs of labor and capital because there are plenty of idle workers and other resources willing and able to contribute at the going rate. Hence, an increase in production can be relatively easily achieved without causing shortages of inputs or increases in prices. The middle, upward-sloping part of the AS curve symbolizes the range of GDP where inputs begin to become scarce. Some wage increases or other factor price increases are necessary to obtain more inputs and to produce more output. In the vertical region of the AS curve, the economy is at full employment and no more output is possible until new workers enter the labor force or new factories and machines are built. Figure 11.1 portrays this region as an absolute limit to production. In fact, it is possible to exceed this level for short periods of time, for example, during wars or other extraordinary events that cause people to work longer hours or at a faster pace than they are willing to maintain over the long run. Given that output levels beyond the vertical region can be sustained only for a short period, it is useful to think of the vertical portion of the AS curve as signifying the full-employment level of GDP.

In the short run and medium run, the focus is on changes in aggregate demand that are initiated by one or more of the economic agents listed in Table 11.1. Significant changes in expenditures are not at all uncommon over the course of a year or more. For example, as an economy goes into recession, consumers and businesses may quickly alter their expectations and their spending (C and I) as they reassess their economic circumstances. Similarly, recessions, wars, natural disasters, and other factors can cause large shifts in government tax (T) and expenditure (G) policies, as well as changes in other policies that directly affect consumer and business spending. Finally, economic booms or depressions abroad sometimes cause a rapid change in foreign purchases of products exported (EX) from the home country.

Figure 11.2 illustrates the case of an increase in aggregate demand. The source of the change could be an increase in expenditures by any one of the economic agents listed in Table 11.1. That is, it could be due to an increase in consumption expenditures (C), business investment (I), government purchases of final goods and services (G), government tax cuts that stimulate consumer or business spending, or exports (EX) purchased by foreigners. The net result of any of the changes is qualitatively the same. Prices rise slightly from P_1 to P_2 as factor inputs become scarcer, and GDP rises from Q_1 to Q_2. If the economy initially happened to be on the horizontal part of the AS curve, then prices would not have risen, but output would still have gone up. If the changes commenced from a position of full employment on the vertical part of the AS curve, then all of the change

FIGURE 11.2   A Shift in the AD Curve

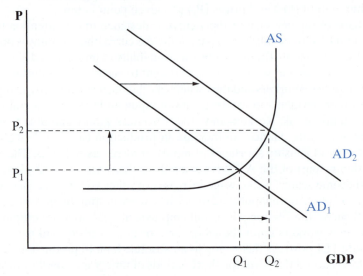

An increase in aggregate demand will cause an increase in GDP and a rise in the price level.

would have been in the price level, and no increase in output would occur. If AD falls instead of rising, the effects are symmetrical and in the opposite direction of the changes caused by an increase in AD.

Although the simple relationships between AD, AS, P, and GDP portrayed in Figures 11.1 and 11.2 are a useful way to conceptualize the interactions of a number of key macroeconomic variables, the graphs and the description hide a great deal of complexity. For example, the graphs illustrate only one point in time, and they do not show what happens as the economy grows over time. If an economy grows, it must have more labor or more physical capital or natural resources and be capable of producing more output. Hence, economic growth could be added by shifting the whole AS curve rightward. Consequently, the changes in Figure 11.2 must be viewed as short-run or medium-run changes that take effect separately from economic growth.

Another factor that is hiding behind Figure 11.2 is the actual mechanism that moves the economy from one level of GDP (Q_1) to a higher level (Q_2). Suppose, for example, that AD begins to shift rightward due to rising business optimism that prompts many firms to increase their investment spending. Firms order new machines or start new construction projects, and total spending in the economy goes up. This is not the end of the story, however, as the firms that supply the machines or do the construction will have to increase their output levels, and that will put additional income in the hands of their owners and workers. Those suppliers and their workers are likely to spend at least part of their additional income. Statistical analysis over long periods of time has shown that there is a very close quantitative relationship between income received by households and household consumption patterns. That is, as income rises, so do expenditures. Consequently, the workers and business owners who supply goods and services to the investing firms increase their own expenditures as well. They buy houses, furniture, cars, college education, medical care, and all the other things that households spend money on, thus creating another round of income increases and expenditures.

In effect, the original increase in investment spending causes an increase in production. Because output equals income in the macroeconomy, incomes go up by an amount equal to the value of the increased production. In turn, higher incomes lead to another set of expenditures and production increases and another round of income increases, and so on. When a new equilibrium is eventually reached and the effect of the original change in spending has completely worked its way through the economy, the total increase in GDP is greater than the original increase in spending. This is the **multiplier effect** of an increase in aggregate demand. There is no consensus among economists about the size of the multiplier effect, although there is a consensus that it varies quite a bit and depends on a number of factors. Some of the factors are whether an economy is in recession or near full employment, what sectors receive the initial increase in spending, and how the spending is financed. For example, if the economy is at full employment and has no idle resources, increases in government spending will crowd- out private spending and the net effect is likely to be zero. On the other hand, an economy in recession has many idle resources and increases in government spending are likely to lead to the re-employment of some of them and a net increase in output. After the United States implemented a stimulus package in 2009 to combat the recession, the politically independent Congressional Budget Office estimated a range of multipliers that reflected the views of most economists. In their analysis, spending multipliers for the purchase of goods and services during the recession were between 1.0 and 2.5, multipliers from transfers ranged between 0.8 and 2.5, and tax cut multipliers were between 0.2 and 1.5.

The multiplier process of spending-production-income-spending and so on might seem as if it could go on forever, but in fact the impact of the original expenditure gets smaller and smaller, rather like the waves that radiate out from a rock thrown into a pond. There are several forces that dampen the impact over time and bring GDP to a new equilibrium level. Three of the dampening forces are taxes, saving, and imports. In most countries, each successive increase in income will lead to additional taxes and saving, as well as additional spending. On average, when incomes rise, people spend part of the increase, pay taxes with part, and save part. Taxes vary by country, and as we saw in Chapter 9, the amount saved varies as well. The larger the part taken by government or saved by households, the faster the impact of the original expenditure dissipates.

Each successive increase in income in the spending-production-income-spending cycle will also trigger an increase in imports. We can be certain of this effect because part of what households buy is imported, so if they increase their purchases, they will also be buying more imported goods. All three of the variables—taxes, savings, and imports—cause the next round of spending on goods that are domestically produced to be less than the first round; therefore, they ensure that the income and spending effects moving through the economy are becoming smaller and smaller in each successive round. In addition, the three variables also show why the multiplier varies from country to country. The greater imports are as a share of spending, savings, and taxes, the more each successive round of spending is reduced from the previous. That is, countries with larger propensities to import, higher saving rates, or higher tax rates will have smaller multipliers.

FISCAL AND MONETARY POLICIES

LO 11.2 **Diagram the effects on GDP and the price level of expansionary and contractionary fiscal and monetary policies.**

The discussion of aggregate demand, aggregate supply, and the multiplier is background for the analysis of the effects of fiscal and monetary policies on GDP and prices. **Fiscal policy** includes government taxation and expenditures, while **monetary policy** covers the money supply and interest rates. The institutions that enact fiscal and monetary policy vary across countries; but generally the legislative and executive branches are responsible for tax policy and for determining spending priorities, and the central bank and the finance ministry set monetary policy, sometimes with direct input from the executive branch of government if the central bank is not independent of the government. During the last two decades, there has been a trend toward granting central banks complete independence in setting monetary policy, as has historically been the case in several countries, including the United States.

Fiscal Policy

Government's fiscal policies of expenditure and taxation are an important element of every country's macroeconomy, because they are a major determinant of the total demand for goods and services. All else being equal, when a government increases its spending, the increase ripples through the economy as a series of production-income-spending increases that lead to higher levels of equilibrium GDP. The same effect occurs when governments cut their expenditures, but in the opposite direction as production, income, and spending all decrease.

Changes in tax levels are similar in their analysis. A decrease in taxes will raise household income—what is available to save or spend—because fewer taxes are withdrawn from paychecks. The increase in after-tax income in turn will lead to increases in spending, production, and income again. Figure 11.2 can be interpreted as either an increase in government spending or a cut in taxes. In both cases, the AD curve shifts rightward, and both GDP and the price level rise.

For obvious reasons, cuts in taxes and increases in government spending are referred to as **expansionary fiscal policy**. The opposite, **contractionary fiscal policy**, or **austerity,** is a tax increase or a cut in government spending, both of which reduce the level of equilibrium GDP by shifting the AD curve to the left. Contractionary policy is symmetrical with expansionary policy, so that tax increases and government spending cuts have a negative multiplier effect on total output, while tax cuts and government spending increases have a positive multiplier effect. It is important to note that we are assuming that nothing else changes other than the single change in fiscal policy. For example, there is no assumption that government budgets are balanced, and an increase in government spending does not imply a simultaneous increase in taxes. Similarly, cuts in taxes are not countered by cuts in spending, nor are tax increases balanced by government spending increases.

For many macroeconomists of the 1940s and 1950s, the discovery of the multiplier effect of fiscal policy was like finding the holy grail of macroeconomics. It seemed to offer a technique for managing the economy and, most importantly, for avoiding disasters such as the Great Depression of the 1930s. Needless to say, most economists today are much more cautious about the use of fiscal policy. The reasons are not hard to understand. First, expansionary policies tend to cause inflation, which offsets some of the increased consumer spending by absorbing it into higher prices instead of higher output. Second, there is a substantial margin of error in the estimation of the size of the multiplier. Does a $50 billion tax cut lead to a $50 billion, $75 billion, or $100 billion increase in income? Third, the use of fiscal policy is complicated by the variation in effects stemming from the different possibilities for financing an expansionary policy. If governments accommodate the expansionary fiscal policy with an expansion of the money supply, the multiplier is larger if there is no accommodation. Taken together, the three technical problems of inflation, the margin for error in measuring the multiplier, and variation in the multiplier's size depending on the means of paying for the expansion make it difficult to use fiscal policy precisely.

But this is not all. The politics of turning government spending off and on, or turning taxes off and on, is a long, drawn-out, and complicated process. By the time the legislation is passed, the purpose for which it was originally intended may have disappeared entirely. In other words, fiscal policy as a tool for managing the economy to avoid recessions and curtail inflation is politically cumbersome. Taken together, the political problem plus the technical problem of measuring its precise effects make fiscal policy a less used tool for managing the economy. Nevertheless, it is still important to study, since government spending and taxation policies have significant impacts on the macroeconomy and the current account, regardless of whether they are implemented to achieve a particular macroeconomic objective. Furthermore, in times of extreme stress, such as the aftermath of the subprime crisis of 2007–2009, many economists argue that fiscal policy can be very effective in countering a deep recession.

Monetary Policy

Monetary policy is the other main category of policies that national governments use to influence the macroeconomy. As noted, in the United States, the European Union (EU), and a growing number of other nations, monetary policy is determined by an independent central bank. Therefore, it reflects the views of the central bank and its responses to economic conditions rather than the views of a particular political party or the executive branch of government.

Monetary policy works through a combination of changes to the supply of money and changes to interest rates. When the central bank changes the supply of money, it does so by changing the quantity of funds in financial institutions that are available for lending. The most frequently used technique for accomplishing this is called **open market operations**. Open market operations are simply the buying and selling of bonds in the open market. When a central bank sells bonds, banks and other financial institutions give up some of their cash. Consequently, cash reserves shrink throughout the financial system. Buying bonds has the opposite effect on the financial system's reserves of cash and is the primary technique for expanding the money supply.

As cash reserves in the financial system increase, there is likely to be more investment. That is, financial institutions such as banks need to generate revenue by making loans. Money sitting in the vaults earns the bank no revenue, so an increase in bank reserves leads banks to make more loans. To encourage businesses to borrow additional funds, however, interest rates must fall.

Figure 11.3 illustrates the process of a fall in interest rates with a simple supply and demand diagram showing an increase in the supply of money. The horizontal axis measures the quantity of money in the system, where money is defined to be cash, checking accounts, and other easily spendable assets such as money market accounts that allow check writing. The easier it is to spend an asset, the more *liquid* it is considered to be. Cash is the most liquid asset, while checking accounts are slightly less so, but still highly liquid compared to, say, stocks or bonds.

The supply curve is represented with a vertical line instead of the more common upward sloping supply curve because we are assuming that the central bank fixes the quantity of money at a given level, and that the quantity does not vary with the level of interest rates, measured on the vertical axis. The interest rate can be considered similar to the price of money. There are two reasons for this: It is the price you pay to borrow money, and it is the opportunity cost of holding your assets

FIGURE 11.3 Money Supply and Demand

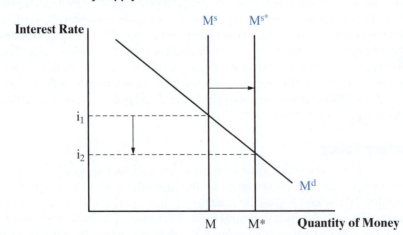

An increase in the supply of money reduces the rate of interest.

in the form of money instead of some other, interest-earning, form. This is admittedly a simplification, since borrowing costs and the return on savings are always different, and since some types of money earn interest (for example, money market accounts). Still, it is a simplification that is useful and one that captures the essential relationship between interest rates and the quantity of money in the economy.

The fall in interest rates shown in Figure 11.3 is the key to the increase in investment that comes about as a result of an expansionary monetary policy. Once investment increases, the expenditure multiplier takes over and the production-income-spending cycle is set in motion. Hence, an increase in the money supply will expand the economy and increase incomes. Not surprisingly, monetary policy is also symmetrical with respect to its contractionary and expansionary impacts, so a decrease in the money supply will result in a decline in production and incomes.

Expansionary monetary policy involves an increase in the money supply and a fall in interest rates, leading to a positive expansion in income. **Contractionary monetary policy** is exactly the reverse, and involves a decrease in the money supply and a rise in interest rates, leading to a contraction in income. As with fiscal policies, both expansionary and contractionary monetary policies work through the multiplier process to raise or lower income, depending on whether the policy is expansionary or contractionary.

CASE STUDY

Fiscal and Monetary Policy during the Great Depression

The Great Depression is the name Americans give to the worst economic period in modern American history. It was a worldwide phenomenon, however, and most countries experienced recessions which, in many cases, were quite severe. The onset of the crisis varied from country to country, but in the United States, it started in August 1929, with an unnoticed modest decline in economic activity. Stock prices continued to rise through the summer of 1929, in spite of the overall decline in output and income. September and October were bad months for the market, culminating in the panic of Black Thursday on October 24, when the market fell by more than one-third. Most people thought that the worst was over and many argued that the stock market collapse was good for the economy since it squeezed out excess speculation.

The small recession that began during the summer of 1929 grew into one of the worst decades in American history. By 1933, over 25 percent of the labor force was unemployed and real GDP had fallen by nearly 26 percent. Out of the cauldron of the Great Depression came Social Security, the Fair Labor Standards Act to regulate working conditions and wages, the Securities and Exchange Commission to oversee stock trading, the Federal Deposit Insurance

(continued)

Corporation to protect bank deposits, the Tennessee Valley Authority, and a host of other programs that inserted the federal government much deeper into American economic life.

Most Americans probably think of the 1930s and the Great Depression as synonymous, but there were two separate recessions in the United States during the decade. The first, and most severe, one began in 1929 and lasted until 1933. The second one began in 1937 and lasted into 1938. Between these two downturns in economic activity, there was a strong recovery, and by 1936, real GDP was above where it had been in 1929, the last year of overall positive growth until 1934. Figure 11.4 illustrates the annual rate of growth, 1930–1941.

In hindsight, it is easy to see the policy mistakes that prolonged the recession and made it far more severe than it needed to be. Based on what we know today about expansionary fiscal and monetary policy, the federal government should have done one or more of the following: raise government spending for goods and services, cut taxes, or increase the money supply to lower interest rates. The problem in the 1930s was that no one was aware of the relations discussed in this chapter. In a very real sense, if you read the first part of this chapter, then you know more about fiscal policy than presidents Roosevelt and Hoover and all of their advisers knew.

Instead of using increases in government spending and cuts in taxes to stimulate the economy, presidents Hoover (1929–1933) and Roosevelt (1933–1945) worried about the federal budget deficits that emerged during the 1930s. Both Roosevelt and Hoover thought that budget deficits undermined business confidence and were a major reason for the recession. Consequently, the budget deficit became a major issue of the 1932 presidential election, in which Roosevelt successfully campaigned on the platform of a balanced federal budget. As it turned out, however, the federal budget was in deficit during every year of Roosevelt's presidency.

Both Hoover and Roosevelt tried to balance the budget. Both presidents unsuccessfully opposed legislation to offer war veterans early payment of the

FIGURE 11.4   **Real GDP Growth in the United States, 1930–1941**

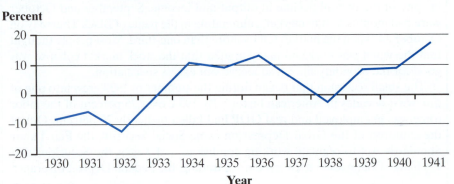

Source: Bureau of Economic Analysis.

retirement money they were owed, and both presidents supported tax increases when deficits began to appear after 1929. Hoover introduced a dramatic tax increase in 1932, while Roosevelt increased taxes at several points in time, most dramatically with the beginning of social security taxes in 1937. Given the contractionary impact of tax increases, it is not surprising that 1932 was the worst year of the depression, nor that the economy slipped back into recession in 1938 after the implementation of the new social security tax.

If fiscal policy was not helpful during the 1930s, monetary policy was a disaster in the early years. Between 1929 and 1933, the money supply (currency, checking accounts, and savings deposits) fell by nearly 31 percent. Credit became scarce and investment disappeared. In other words, if fiscal policy could be considered more or less neutral during most years of the Great Depression (neither expansionary nor contractionary), then monetary policy was contractionary.

In retrospect, it is easy to understand the failure to use expansionary fiscal policy. No one in the 1930s understood the macroeconomy well enough to discern how to use fiscal policy to fight the recession. It is more difficult to justify the misuse of monetary policy, however, because more was known about the relationships between the money supply, bank reserves, and investment. For many years after the Great Depression, prominent economists such as Nobel Prize winner Milton Friedman argued that the Federal Reserve was simply incompetent. This view cannot be ruled out, but more recent scholarship has shed new light on this historic episode. Rather than incompetence, the Fed's actions reflected a different set of priorities. In particular, it may have been acting responsibly if its first priority was to protect the gold standard.

Under the rules of the gold standard, central banks are required to use interest rates and monetary policy to attract gold whenever gold reserves run low. This usually means an interest rate hike in order to increase the demand for the domestic currency and to reduce the demand for foreign currencies.

In 1928, U.S. monetary policy turned contractionary as the Fed was worried about speculation in the stock market and wanted to make it more difficult for brokers to borrow from banks. The Fed raised interest rates and, unintentionally, created an inflow of gold to the United States. U.S. policy put pressure on European countries, which began to lose their gold reserves. Consequently, the contractionary policy in the United States spread across the Atlantic as countries began to raise their interest rates and slow their rate of money growth in order to stop the outflow of gold. The irony is that each country was acting responsibly according to the dictates of the gold standard, but they were following polices that resulted in a worldwide economic catastrophe.

At several points during the years that followed, U.S. and foreign policies turned even more contractionary. In 1931, it was widely expected that the United Kingdom would leave the gold standard altogether, and speculation turned against the pound. In September 1931, Britain left the gold standard and speculators immediately shifted their attention to the dollar. Expecting a

(continued)

similar decline in the value of the dollar, they began to sell dollars and dollar-denominated assets, all of which resulted in gold outflows. Once again, the Fed responded by raising interest rates in September and October 1931, and the U.S. economy continued its downward spiral.

It is no coincidence that the first countries to leave the gold standard (the United Kingdom and the countries that followed it in September 1931) were the first to experience recovery. Once their policies were freed from the constraint of supporting a fixed rate of exchange, they could turn them toward economic expansion. In the United States, Roosevelt's first act after taking office in March 1933 was to suspend the gold standard. It seems unlikely that he completely understood the relationship of gold to the depression, but it was a good move, as the economy began its recovery from the worst economic crisis of the twentieth century.

CURRENT ACCOUNT BALANCES REVISITED

LO 11.3 Analyze the effects of fiscal and monetary policies on the current account and the exchange rate.

Chapter 9 described the identity between private savings, government budget balances, investment, and the current account as follows: The identity between private savings, government budget balances, investment, and the current account is described as follows:

$$S + (T - G) = I + CA.$$

Now we are ready to look more closely at this identity and to incorporate the links among monetary and fiscal policies, income, and the current account. The goal is to analyze how a change in income caused by a change in monetary or fiscal policy influences the country's current account. We will do this in two steps. In the first step we will explore the links between changes in monetary and fiscal policies, interest rates, and exchange rates. The link from monetary policy to interest rates has already been described, but as we will see, fiscal policies have interest rate effects as well. In the second step we will put together policy changes, interest rates, exchange rates, and the current account balance. Once we have done this, we will have a much clearer understanding of the policies that a country must follow if it needs to eliminate a trade imbalance in its current account.

It is important to emphasize that we are looking at changes in income and other macroeconomic variables that are likely to take place over the span of a few years or less, while ignoring long-run impacts that may take many years, perhaps even a decade or longer, to materialize. We will return to this point later in the chapter when we try to distinguish long-run, permanent changes from short-run changes.

Fiscal and Monetary Policies, Interest Rates, and Exchange Rates

From Chapter 10 and the interest parity condition, we know that interest rate increases lead to an appreciation of the domestic currency (the exchange rate, (R), falls) and interest rate decreases lead to a depreciation (the exchange rate rises). Recall that this occurs through changes in the demand and supply of foreign currency. As interest rates rise, they increase the supply of foreign currency since interest arbitrageurs are constantly searching for the highest possible rate of interest. Similarly, a decline in interest rates reduces the inflow of foreign financial capital, decreasing the supply of foreign currency. Demand side effects are present in both cases as well, since home country interest arbitrageurs have the same motivation to move their capital in and out of the country.

The exchange rate effects of monetary policy are easily identified. We have already seen how an expansion of the money supply increases bank reserves and pushes down interest rates. Consequently, in addition to increasing income, expansionary monetary policy must also cause a depreciation of the exchange rate. Given the symmetry between expansionary and contractionary policies, monetary contraction reduces bank reserves and drives up interest rates, leading to an appreciation of the exchange rate.

Since a rapidly depreciating currency is a feature of most international financial crises, contractionary monetary policy is a very commonly adopted technique to stop a depreciation. This technique is discussed more fully in Chapter 12, but it should be noted that the downside of using monetary policy this way is a contraction in income and possibly even a recession. This illustrates once again that it is not unusual for a trade-off to exist between a country's exchange rate goal and its goals for income growth and employment. The Fed's action to raise interest rates to protect the dollar in 1931 is a classic example of a conflict between the needs of the domestic economy and the desire to protect the exchange rate.

The interest rate effects of fiscal policy are less easily identified, but they are present nonetheless. The key to understanding these links lies in the behavior of households and the changes they make when their incomes rise or fall. Looking first at the case of a rise in household income, we know that consumption expenditures will also rise. Furthermore—and this is key—rising incomes cause households to reevaluate the division of their assets between liquid forms such as money, and relatively less liquid forms such as stocks and bonds. When income rises, the average household will hold more money. In economic terms, the demand for money increases, as shown in Figure 11.5.

Why do households increase their demand for money when their incomes increase? The reasons are straightforward. First, at higher levels of income, they consume more. That is, they need a higher level of money holdings to pay for their purchases. Second, the opportunity cost of the interest they lose on holding money

FIGURE 11.5   **An Increase in the Demand for Money**

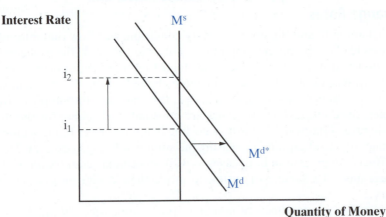

An increase in income causes households to increase their money holdings. As a consequence, interest rates rise.

instead of an interest-paying asset becomes less burdensome. In other words, when households have more income, they can "afford" to hold more money.

Lest this seem too abstract and immaterial to your personal situation, think about what you might do if your income doubled. Most likely, you would increase the amount of money in your wallet and checking account. You would also probably put aside some of your increased income into long-term savings. The point is that if you are more or less average in your spending behavior, an increase in income would cause you to spend more and you would facilitate your increased spending by carrying around more cash and larger balances in your checking account.

Now we have all of the pieces to analyze the exchange rate effects of fiscal policy. Expansionary fiscal policy will raise incomes and consumption. One outcome of these effects is an increase in the demand for money, which, as shown in Figure 11.5, leads to higher interest rates. Given the relationship between interest rates and exchange rates, we know that higher interest rates, all else being equal, lead to an inflow of foreign capital and a fall in the exchange rate (an appreciation). As usual, the effects of contractionary policy are symmetrical. A cut in government spending or an increase in taxes will cause income and money demand to fall, followed by a drop in interest rates and a rise in the exchange rate (depreciation).

Fiscal and Monetary Policy and the Current Account

Once the exchange rate effects of monetary and fiscal policies have been identified, it is relatively easy to describe their effects on the current account. As we will see, the effect of fiscal policy on the current account is definite, while the effect of monetary policy is ambiguous. We turn now to the analysis of these impacts.

Taking the case of expansionary monetary policy first, we have seen that an increase in the money supply reduces interest rates and causes a depreciation in the domestic currency. Exchange rate depreciation switches some consumer spending from foreign goods (imports) to domestic goods, because foreign goods become relatively expensive. The effect of **expenditure switching** is to partially or completely offset the increase in imports caused by rising incomes. As a result, there is a more robust expansion of the domestic economy because less of the expansion of demand leaks out of the economy as an increase in imports. In other words, expansionary monetary policy is reinforced by the changes in the exchange rate.

Contractionary monetary policy has the opposite effect. Interest rates rise, causing an appreciation of the domestic currency, which makes imports relatively cheaper. As a consequence, consumers switch some of their expenditures away from domestic goods toward foreign ones. The reduction in demand for domestic goods reinforces the impact of contractionary monetary policy on income, consumption, and investment, and leads to a more vigorous decline in economic activity than would occur in a closed economy.

To summarize, the impact of monetary policy on income is magnified by its exchange rate effects. We cannot definitely say, however, what the effects are on the current account balance because the income effect of monetary policy on the current account is the opposite of the exchange rate effect. The current account balance could rise or fall with either expansionary or contractionary policy. However, a key idea in the chain of causation is the notion of expenditure switching. This refers to switching back and forth between domestic and foreign goods, which, in this case, is in response to a change in the exchange rate. Expenditure switching magnifies the effects of monetary policy. Note, however, that this result depends on exchange rate flexibility. In an economy with a fixed exchange rate, changes in the money supply will not cause expenditure switching.

The effect of fiscal policy on the current account is more certain. As shown, expansionary fiscal policy increases interest rates, causing an exchange rate appreciation. Appreciation switches expenditures toward foreign goods because it makes them relatively cheaper, thereby increasing imports and reducing the current account balance. The expansionary fiscal policy leads to more imports, both from the rise in income and from exchange rate appreciation, which creates a feedback effect on domestic income. The shift in expenditures toward foreign goods offsets some of the increase in the demand for domestic goods and diminishes the impact of expansionary fiscal policy. Similarly, the exchange rate effect of contractionary fiscal policy switches expenditures away from foreign goods and toward domestic goods, diluting some of the contractionary effects of the policy.

The major short-run to medium-run effects of fiscal and monetary policy are summarized in Table 11.2. The differences between the two begin with their interest rate effects and carry over to exchange rates and current accounts. In the case of monetary policy, changes in the exchange rate and income have offsetting effects on the current account; but with fiscal policy, changes in the exchange rate and income have reinforcing effects on the current account. As a result, the impact of monetary policy on the current account is indeterminate, while the impact of fiscal policy is definite.

TABLE 11.2   The Main Effects of Fiscal and Monetary Policies

	Monetary Policy		Fiscal Policy	
	Contractionary	Expansionary	Contractionary	Expansionary
Y and C	⇓	⇑	⇓	⇑
i	⇑	⇓	⇓	⇑
R*	⇓	⇑	⇑	⇓
CA	⇑ or ⇓	⇑ or ⇓	⇑	⇓

Monetary and fiscal policies have different impacts on interest rates, exchange rates, and the current account. Monetary policy's impact on exchange rates and income partially offset each other's impact on the current account.

* A fall in R is an appreciation, while a rise is a depreciation.

The Long Run

How permanent are the effects? Economists more or less agree that in the long run, the level of output in an economy tends to fluctuate around a level that is consistent with full employment. Note that full employment does not mean that everyone has a job. No matter how strong the economy is, there is always some unemployment from the entry of new workers into the labor force, or the return of workers after an absence from work. While searching for their jobs, both groups are considered unemployed. In addition, there are always people who have voluntarily quit their jobs to look for better ones, and people who lack the job skills needed to find a job.

In a strong economy, unemployment may temporarily fall to a very low level, but this tends to resolve itself. Initially, employers may grab whoever is available to fill their job vacancies, but as the pool of the unemployed dries up, they raise wages and look for ways to get by with fewer workers. Ultimately, this returns the unemployment rate to its normal level. Conversely, in a weak economy unemployed workers put downward pressure on wages, which ultimately resolves the problem of unemployment, since employers hire more workers when wages fall. The most controversial issue is how long these changes might take. Some observers believe they happen fast, while others are skeptical, particularly about the speed at which wages fall. In one sense, the debate over the amount of time it takes an economy to reach its long-run equilibrium at full employment is a debate over the meaning of the long run. Is it two years, five years, or ten?

In Chapter 10, we saw that in the long run, purchasing power parity determines exchange rates. Fiscal and monetary policy may cause deviations from purchasing power parity, but in the long run, a combination of exchange rate changes and changes in domestic prices will restore balance to the purchasing power of national currencies.

The current account must also tend toward balance in the long run. No nation can run deficits forever, nor can it run surpluses forever. Since deficits are equivalent to foreign borrowing and surpluses equivalent to foreign lending, there are limits in each direction. The limits are not well defined, however, and countries such as the United States have been able to run enormous deficits for long periods, while countries such as Japan have run surpluses.

CASE STUDY

Argentina and the Limits to Macroeconomic Policy

In 1900, Argentina was among the richest countries in the world. Its good fortune was not to last, however, and by mid-century its per capita income had fallen behind. Although it still had the highest per capita income in Latin America, the gap with Western Europe and North America was substantial, and it was not getting smaller when it was hit by the Latin American debt crisis and the Lost Decade of the 1980s (see Chapter 15). The debt crisis was vicious and hard to shake off. In 1989, seven years after it began, Argentina was still caught in it, and its GDP fell 7 percent while inflation hit 3,080 percent. Politicians tried a variety of experiments to get out of the recession and hyperinflation, but none of them led to sustained growth or brought down the inflation rate. In 1991, a radical experiment was tried. The country fixed its currency to the dollar at a 1:1 rate and dramatically restricted the creation of new money. For every new Argentine peso put into circulation, the central bank was required to have a dollar to back it up, and a newly created **currency board** was there to oversee the exchange rate system and enforce the rules.

   The currency board worked extremely well through most of the 1990s. Argentina was back on a strong growth path with low inflation and was widely viewed as a successful model for other countries. Problems began to develop in 1998, however, when the global fallout from a crisis in East Asia spread to Latin America. Argentina's main trading partner, Brazil, devalued its currency in early 1999, giving Brazilian firms an advantage and putting Argentine firms at a disadvantage since goods valued in pesos were now more expensive. Argentina's current account balance developed a relatively large deficit of 4–5 percent of its GDP, and the loss of exports led to a recession in 1999.

   At this point, conventional economic theory prescribed a demand-side stimulus for Argentina. Total expenditures in the economy were down, in part because it was more difficult to export, so the country should have cut taxes, raised government spending, increased the money supply, or some combination of those policies. There were a few obstacles, though. First, anything that might upset the 1:1 exchange rate was viewed as a potential problem. All else being equal, expansionary macroeconomic policies cause prices to rise, and it was feared that deliberately increased government deficits might undermine confidence in the anti-inflation commitment of the government. Argentina was already running a budget deficit that was hard to control, and increased spending and tax cuts were not an option. Monetary expansion was also out since that would undermine the peg to the dollar by increasing the circulation of pesos beyond the level of dollars available to back them up.

   Second, a currency devaluation, whether intentional or not, would be a problem. During the growth years of the 1990s, Argentine firms and Argentina's

(continued)

government had borrowed dollars in international capital markets. There was nothing particularly unusual about Argentina's borrowing, except that its ability to raise revenue to service its debts was constrained by domestic political factors. Taking on debt denominated in dollars is common, but it imposes a high price when there is a currency devaluation, since the dollar value of the debt does not change, but the domestic currency value of debt rises. Given that the government and most firms earned revenues in pesos, but that their international debts were in dollars, anything that caused the value of the peso to decline would increase the burden of debt.

The debate over policy was intense: Should Argentina devalue and increase the debt burden, or maintain the exchange rate and continue to watch the current account deficit grow and the economy shrink? Cut government spending to create confidence in the fiscal soundness of the government, or use expansionary fiscal policy to address the recession while undermining confidence in the government's commitment to the 1:1 exchange rate? In effect, there were two choices. On the one hand, the government could use expansionary macroeconomic policies to try to combat the recession, but at the cost of a probable devaluation of the peso since no one would believe that it was still committed to anti-inflation policy and fiscal prudence. On the other hand, it could maintain the peso's link to the dollar at the 1:1 ratio, but at the cost of ignoring the recession.

Argentina's recession began in 1999. Two years later, in 2001, the country was still in recession, and prospects seemed to be getting worse. As people lost confidence in the government's ability to maintain the 1:1 exchange rate, they decided that a devaluation was coming and began to take their money out of banks. After enormous losses in the banking sector, the government closed all banks in early December 2001. When they reopened in January 2002, the peso's link to the dollar had been cut. The peso began a steady decline, dropping from 1 peso per dollar to 2.0 pesos in February 2002, and 3.8 pesos per dollar by June. After that, it recovered slightly and stabilized around 3 pesos per dollar, where it remained for several years.

Some observers argue that Argentina should have sought more flexibility in its policies by severing the one-to-one relationship between the peso and the dollar much earlier—in 1997 or 1998. Others argue that it should have made deeper cuts in its budgets, because that was the only way to maintain confidence in its currency. At first, the government tried the latter approach, but political and institutional obstacles prevented the budget cuts from being large enough.

The Argentine case still poses questions for economists. Recessions caused by a decline in demand are most effectively fought by increasing demand through government spending, tax policy, or monetary policy. If a country needs to demonstrate to the world that it is fiscally prudent, however, because doing so will prevent speculation against its own currency and maintain the inflow of foreign currency, then expansionary macroeconomic policies may be impossible. Does this mean that developing countries cannot use expansionary macroeconomic policies?

MACRO POLICIES FOR CURRENT ACCOUNT IMBALANCES

LO 11.4   **Explain how expenditure switching and expenditure reducing policies can be used to reduce a current account deficit.**

LO 11.5   **Draw a J-curve and use it to show how exchange rate depreciation does not lead to an immediate reduction in the current account deficit.**

Fiscal, monetary, and exchange rate policies are essential tools for eliminating a current account imbalance. While any persistent imbalance can be portrayed as a problem, in practice the most dangerous imbalances are large current account deficits. Persistently large surpluses may bother a country's trading partners, but they rarely threaten a national economy the way that large deficits sometimes do. The macro policies for addressing a current account deficit are a combination of fiscal, monetary, and exchange rate policies, often collectively called **expenditure switching policies** and **expenditure reducing policies**. Both are essential.

We have already seen one type of expenditure switching policy when we talked about the exchange rate effects of fiscal and monetary policy. In general, an appropriate expenditure switching policy for eliminating a current account deficit is one that turns domestic expenditures away from foreign-produced goods and toward domestic goods. As discussed, an exchange rate depreciation is one way to do this. Recall that a depreciation raises the domestic price of foreign goods. An alternative type of expenditure switching policy is a trade barrier, such as a temporary tariff to make foreign goods more expensive.

Expenditure reducing policies are simply contractionary fiscal or monetary policies that cut the overall level of demand in the economy. In most cases, they are necessary along with expenditure switching policies because without overall expenditure reductions, inflation ensues as home country domestic expenditures switch away from foreign producers and toward domestic producers. For this reason, expenditure switching policies must be accompanied by reductions in overall expenditures.

While expenditure shifts without expenditure reductions are inflationary, expenditure reductions without shifts toward domestic producers are recessionary. This makes the expenditure shifts necessary, since a shift in spending toward domestic producers offsets the decline in demand and leaves the economy with the same level of output but without a current account deficit. Given the need to use both types of policies simultaneously, expenditure reductions and expenditure shifts are not viewed as alternatives to each other but rather as two equally essential components of a macroeconomic policy designed to address a current account deficit.

The Adjustment Process

The term **adjustment process** is used to describe changes in the trade deficit that are caused by a change in the exchange rate. We have already seen that a depreciation raises the real price of foreign goods, making domestic substitutes relatively more attractive. While this is an accurate description of the general pattern, depreciations often have delayed effects. In the United States, for example, there is a median average lag of about nine and a half months between a change in the exchange rate and an impact on U.S. exports. The median average lag for import responses is slightly less, but still more than seven months. Consequently, it is a mistake to think that exchange rate changes will affect trade flows overnight.

In addition to the lag effects, the first impact of a depreciation on the current account may be a further deterioration rather than an improvement. This deterioration is known as the **J-curve** and is shown in Figure 11.6.

After a depreciation, there is usually a short period of no noticeable impact on the flow of goods and services. When imports and exports begin to respond, the immediate change is an increase in the value of imports, pushing the current account balance deeper into deficit. The size of the deterioration and the length of time before there is an actual improvement varies from country to country. In the United States, a depreciation results in an improvement in the trade balance only after a year or more. The reasons are straightforward. A depreciation makes foreign goods immediately more expensive, but it takes time for households and businesses to find substitutes. In the short run they lack information, and it takes time to find new suppliers in the domestic economy, to check the quality of their products, and to negotiate contracts. Meanwhile, until the alternative suppliers are found, foreign goods continue to be used even though they cost more.

FIGURE 11.6   The J-Curve

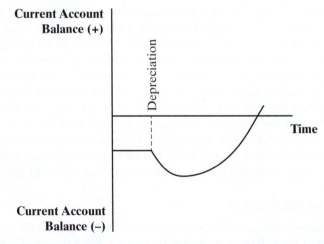

Initially, depreciations often cause the current account balance to deteriorate further. With time, substitutions of domestic goods for foreign goods lead to an improvement in the balance.

CASE STUDY

The Adjustment Process in the United States

Between 1981 and 1985, the U.S. current account balance moved from a small surplus to a deficit greater than 3 percent of GDP. In 1985, the Plaza Accord among the G5 (France, Germany, Japan, the United States, and the United Kingdom) created a cooperative effort to bring down the value of the dollar, partly as a means to shrink the U.S. current account deficit. The dollar started depreciating in early 1985, and from the first quarter of 1985 to the beginning of 1988, the dollar index fell nearly 37 percent.

While the dollar was falling, the trade deficit continued to widen. This was unsettling to a number of politicians, economists, and others, who had predicted a significant decline in the U.S. trade deficit as a result of the depreciation. Some journalists and politicians began to argue that the trade deficit would never respond to a change in the value of the dollar, that foreign trade barriers would make it impossible for the United States to substantially expand exports, and that our own open market would ensure a growing volume of imports regardless of the dollar's value.

Nevertheless, after a little more than two years, the trade balance began to respond to the fall in the dollar. Figure 11.7 shows the change in the value of

FIGURE 11.7   The U.S. Trade Balance and the Exchange Rate, 1980–1988

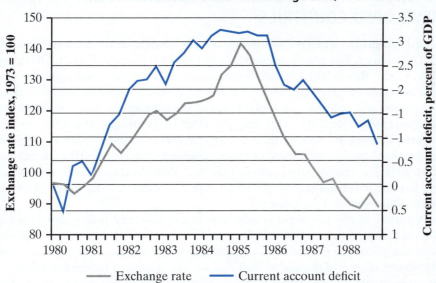

In the 1980s, changes in the U.S. trade balance mirrored changes in the exchange rate with a lag of two years.

Source: Data from U.S. Bureau of Economic Analysis, © James Gerber.

(continued)

the dollar and the current account balance over this time period. Figure 11.7 offsets the current account balance by two years in order to reflect the long lag in the adjustment process so that 1985 on the graph is the 1987 current account balance and the 1985 exchange rate index. It is apparent that there is a striking similarity in their movement, once adjustment is made for the two-year lag.

The question that economists have debated since this episode is why it took so long for trade balances to respond to the decline in the value of the dollar. There are several possible explanations. One is that the prior increase in the dollar's value had padded the profit margins of foreign producers. From 1980 to 1985, their exports to the United States rose in terms of their domestic prices even though they sold in the United States for the same dollar prices. Consequently, when the dollar began to fall, foreign producers were initially able to keep dollar prices constant and absorb the decline in its value by realizing lower profits in terms of their domestic currency.

Another possible reason for the long lag is that there were still impacts from earlier appreciations working through the system. A third reason for the long lag is that exports began to increase from a much lower base than imports and needed to increase much more rapidly in percentage terms in order for the trade deficit to begin to close.

MACROECONOMIC POLICY COORDINATION IN DEVELOPED COUNTRIES

Coordination of macroeconomic policies is a frequent issue for the leading industrial economies. The annual meetings of the old G8 (Canada, France, Germany, Italy, Japan, Russia, the United Kingdom, and the United States) and the new G20 are often an extended discussion of shared macroeconomic issues, international economic relations, and relations with developing countries. When global economic imbalances arise—for example, large U.S. current account deficits and growing Chinese surpluses—macroeconomic coordination becomes a topic of discussion. Actual coordination of macroeconomic policies is fairly rare, but not impossible. For example, the previous case study describes the agreement between five leading industrial economies to arrange a coordinated depreciation of the dollar, known as the *Plaza Accord*.

A variety of objectives are sought with macroeconomic policy coordination, from achieving a desirable level of world economic growth to avoiding a global economic crisis. The purpose of coordination is to avoid imposing a disproportionate burden on one of the major world economies. Unequal burdens result when one country pays a large share of the costs of economic adjustment. As an illustration, suppose that the world economy is in a period of relatively slow growth. Not every economy will experience this, but occasionally enough economies are in recession or growing so slowly that the average rate of growth throughout the world is too slow to raise living standards or to pull people out of poverty. If a group of industrial economies decide jointly to expand their economies with fiscal and monetary policies, then growth in their incomes raises incomes around the world as their demand for imports stimulates production in other countries. If all economies expand simultaneously, then no country is burdened by a sudden excess of imports over exports—their exports grow along with their imports and with the growth in demand in their trading partners' economies. For a variety of reasons, such as existing large budget deficits, or fear of the inflationary effects of expansionary policy, some countries may choose not to expand their economies. In this case, the effectiveness of the expanding economies as engines of growth across the globe is reduced. Furthermore, the country or countries using expansionary policy will probably experience a deterioration in their current accounts since their trading partners are not growing at the same rate. If expansionary fiscal policies cause interest rates to rise, then a further deterioration in the current account is likely due to the appreciation of the currency resulting from the inflow of foreign capital.

The way out of this dilemma is a coordinated effort at macroeconomic expansion. There are both political and economic problems with coordination, however. The political problem is that there is no international organization capable of arranging a multilateral agreement among nations, nor is one possible without a significant sacrifice of national sovereignty. The economic problem is that the only period in which nations find it in their own interest to pursue the same policies as their trading partners is when many countries face a similar crisis. For example, during the worldwide recession of 2007–2009, both the European Union and the United States implemented expansionary fiscal policies, and cooperation between the European Central Bank and the U.S. Federal Reserve Bank was extensive, even though it stopped short of a complete coordination of monetary policies.

Summary

- Households supply all the factors of production (land, labor, and capital) that businesses need to produce the nation's output. In return, they receive all the income, or factor payments, which are payments for the use of their land (rents), labor (wages and salaries), and capital (dividends, profits, and interest). The income received by households is equivalent to the value of the output produced by businesses.

- Businesses use financial institutions to borrow household savings. They use the savings to invest. Businesses also produce the nation's output. Governments spend on goods and services, using tax revenues from the income flow going to households. The foreign sector supplies imports and demands exports.

- Fiscal policies are government tax and expenditure policies. Monetary policies are for interest rates and the money supply. Expansionary policies raise GDP and national income, while contractionary policies do the opposite.

- Fiscal and monetary policies work by changing total demand. Fiscal policies either change government spending on goods and services, which is a direct change in demand, or they change household income through a change in taxes. This is an indirect change in total demand. Monetary policies work through a change in interest rates, which changes investment.

- The multiplier explains how an initial change in spending (demand) is multiplied through the economy into a larger change in spending.

- Fiscal policy is considered more difficult to implement than monetary policy because it requires Congress to pass legislation that must be signed by the president. Monetary policy is easier because it is conducted by the Federal Reserve.

- Both fiscal and monetary policy influence exchange rates and the current account balance. In each case, the effect is through a change in interest rates brought on by the fiscal or monetary policy. Neither policy is likely to have long-run effects on income.

- To reduce or eliminate a current account deficit, countries must practice expenditure switching and expenditure reducing policies. Expenditure switching policies turn demand away from the foreign sector and toward domestic production. Expenditure reducing policies cut back on the overall level of demand.

- The J-curve describes how a policy designed to eliminate a current account deficit may initially make it larger before reducing it. The lag between a depreciation and a reduction in the size of a current account deficit is one to two years in the United States.

Vocabulary

adjustment process

aggregate demand (AD)

aggregate supply (AS)

austerity

contractionary fiscal policy

contractionary monetary policy

currency board

expansionary fiscal policy

expansionary monetary policy

expenditure reducing policy

expenditure switching

expenditure switching policy

fiscal policy

intermediate inputs

J-curve

monetary policy

multiplier effect

open market operations

Study Questions

All problems are assignable in MyEconLab

11.1 Using aggregate demand and aggregate supply, graph the effects on the price level and GDP of each of the following:

   a. A cut in income taxes

   b. An increase in military spending

   c. A drop in export demand by foreign purchasers

   d. An increase in imports

   e. A decline in business investment spending

11.2 Explain the concepts of fiscal and monetary policy. Who conducts them and how do they work their way through the economy?

11.3 What are some of the problems in trying to use fiscal and monetary policies? Why can't economists and politicians make precise predictions about the effects of a policy change on income and output?

11.4 Describe the mechanism that leads from a change in fiscal policy to changes in interest rates, the exchange rate, and the current account balance. Do the same for monetary policy.

11.5 Some countries have fixed exchange rate systems instead of flexible systems. How does the exchange rate system limit their ability to use monetary policy?

11.6 The United States is currently running a large current account deficit. If Congress and the White House decide to enact policies to reduce or eliminate the deficit, what actions should they take? Describe the set of policy options available to them.

11.7 Describe the larger economic effects of the policies in the previous question. That is, what would be the effects on income, consumption, employment, interest rates, and real exchange rates of policies designed to reduce or eliminate a current account deficit?

11.8 During the second half of the 1980s, the United States depreciated the dollar in hopes that it would reduce the current account deficit. After a year, the deficit was actually larger and newspaper editorialists were writing columns claiming that there is no link between the exchange rate and the current account. Explain why they got this wrong.

11.9 Suppose the United States, Japan, and many other places around the world go into recession, but growth remains strong in Europe. Why would macroeconomic policy coordination help, who should coordinate, and what are some of the obstacles to coordination?

CHAPTER 12

International Financial Crises

Learning Objectives

After studying this chapter, students will be able to:

12.1 Define three types of crises.

12.2 Distinguish a crisis caused by economic imbalances from one caused by volatile capital flows.

12.3 List and explain three measures countries can take to reduce their exposure to financial crises.

12.4 Explain the need for reforms in the architecture of international finance and international financial institutions.

12.5 Describe the main forces behind the global financial crisis that began in 2007.

INTRODUCTION: THE CHALLENGE TO FINANCIAL INTEGRATION

Increasing international economic integration has created opportunities for growth and development, but it has also made it easier for crises to spread from one country to another. The worldwide recession that began in 2008 was triggered by a financial crisis that started in 2007, and while it is perhaps the most severe example of a crisis since the 1930s, there are several other recent examples. In 1992, before the advent of the euro, currency speculation against the British pound and other European currencies nearly caused the collapse of monetary arrangements in Europe and inflicted high costs on a number of countries in the European Union (EU). In late 1994, speculation against the Mexican peso led to its collapse and spread a "Tequila effect" through South America. In 1997, several East Asian economies were thrown into steep recession by a wave of sudden capital outflows, and in 1998, Russia's default on its international debt sent shockwaves as far as Latin America.

Financial crises are not new, but the way they develop and spread continues to evolve with the world's financial and economic integration. In some instances, they are an almost predictable result of inconsistent or unrealistic macroeconomic policies; but in other cases, countries with fundamentally sound macroeconomic policies have been pulled into a currency or **financial crisis** for no obvious reason. This makes financial crises difficult to predict, but it also increases the value of a set of early warning indicators. The **contagion effects** of a crisis do not conform to a single pattern, and they reinforce the idea that there are different types of crises with their own rules of behavior.

Financial crises have brought down governments, ruined economies, and destroyed individual lives. Their enormous costs have created an intense amount of research into causes, prevention, and treatment. This chapter reviews some of the basic themes of this literature. It begins by describing two types of crises that have been observed during the last twenty years. Then it turns to a discussion of several key issues, including the steps that a country might take to avoid or minimize a crisis, and the policy choices that it faces once one begins.

Much of the research in this area is designed to formulate sound principles for international financial reforms. The many reform proposals that have appeared in recent years are usually referred to as proposals for reform of the **international financial architecture**. Often their contents revolve around a set of proposed changes to the International Monetary Fund (IMF) and other multilateral institutions with a role in international financial relations. The final section of this chapter looks at two of the main questions in that discussion: Does the world economy need a **lender of last resort**, and what type of conditions should a lender impose on the recipients of its assistance?

DEFINITION OF A FINANCIAL CRISIS

LO 12.1 Define three types of crises.

Financial crises have a variety of potential characteristics, but they usually involve an exchange rate crisis, a banking crisis, a debt crisis, or some combination of the three. Exchange rates, banking systems, and debt are not the only components, but in recent crises they have been points of vulnerability—partly because they are often the variables through which the contagion effects of a crisis are spread from one country to another, and between the financial system and the rest of the economy.

A **banking crisis** occurs when the banking system becomes unable to perform its normal lending functions, and some or all of a nation's banks are threatened with insolvency. A bank, like any other business, is considered insolvent or bankrupt if its assets are less than its liabilities, or, to put it another way, if its net worth is negative. The recession that began in December 2007 is part of the fallout from a banking crisis that started earlier in the same year. A variety of financial institutions, including banks, were involved.

The primary role of banks is **intermediation** between savers and borrowers. Simply put, banks and other financial institutions pool the savings of households and make them available to businesses that want to invest. If the businesses that borrow from a bank go under, then the bank cannot repay its depositors, and the bank may go out of business as well. **Disintermediation** occurs when banks are unable to act as intermediaries between savers and investors—it is a serious problem with negative economic consequences.

When a bank or other financial institution fails, the investors that purchased its financial products lose some or all of their savings. Bank depositors in many countries are covered by deposit insurance, but holders of other types of financial products rarely are. The loss of savings causes households to cut back on consumption and spreads the recessionary effect wider and wider through the economy. This is one way in which a crisis is transmitted within an economy. Unaffected banks may stop making new loans as they take a cautious approach, new investment slows or stops altogether, layoffs occur, and the economy falls deeper into the vicious circle of a downward spiraling recession.

An **exchange rate crisis** is caused by a sudden and unexpected collapse in the value of a nation's currency. This can happen under a fixed, flexible, or intermediate type of exchange rate. If the exchange rate system is some form of a fixed exchange rate, the crisis entails a loss of international reserves, followed by a sudden devaluation once it appears that the reserves will run out. Devaluation is intended to accumulate reserves or to conserve existing reserves by making the rate of exchange less favorable to people trying to convert their domestic currency to dollars or another international reserve currency. If a country uses some form of flexible exchange rate, an exchange rate crisis involves a rapid and uncontrolled depreciation of the currency. While no type of exchange rate system guarantees safety, current research favors the idea that countries that adopt a pegged exchange rate may be more vulnerable to an exchange rate crisis.

Similar to the effects of a banking crisis, an exchange rate crisis often results in a steep recession. There are several channels through which recessionary effects may be transmitted, but one of the most common channels is the banking system. For example, before the Asian crisis of 1997 and 1998, banks borrowed dollars in international capital markets. When their home country currencies collapsed, the dollar value of their debt increased enormously. Consequently, many banks failed, disintermediation took place, new investment stopped, and the economies slid into a deep recession.

A **debt crisis** occurs when debtors cannot pay and must restructure their debt. It is somewhat rare that debtors completely repudiate their debt, and in most cases restructuring involves lowering the rate of interest, lengthening the payback period, partial forgiveness, or some combination. Debtors can be public or private, or some combination, and the debt may be external or domestic. External debt refers to debt owed in a foreign currency, regardless of the nationality of the party that is owed repayment, while domestic debt is denominated in the home country's currency. In addition, the rules governing external debt are set in a foreign legal system, while domestic debt uses the laws and courts of the home country. For example, China holds U.S. Treasury bills which are part of the debt of the U.S. government, but since the debt is denominated in dollars and subject to legal rules and adjudication in U.S. courts under U.S. law, it is considered domestic debt rather than external debt.

Restructuring of debt spreads losses through an economy and may cause previously solvent lenders to become insolvent since the value of the assets they own must be marked down. If their assets decline too much, they fall below their liabilities and the lender becomes insolvent. Debt crises can spread economic stagnation in other ways as well. In the 1990s, for example, Japanese firms and banks focused on paying off debt after the collapse of their real estate bubble in the late 1980s and early 1990s. This caused them to cut back on normal business spending and severely reduced the level of aggregate demand in the economy, leading to nearly a decade of stagnation. The euro crisis that began in 2011 has similar characteristics in that many businesses, including banks, are unwilling to lend and prefer to pay off the debts they accumulated after the collapse of the housing bubble and during the recession.

VULNERABILITIES, TRIGGERS, AND CONTAGION

LO 12.2   **Distinguish a crisis caused by economic imbalances from one caused by volatile capital flows.**

It is safe to say that every international financial crisis is unique in its origins and in the way it causes domestic economies to unravel. It is also safe to say that crises may be unexpected, but they rarely occur without antecedent areas of vulnerabilities. Banking, exchange rate, and debt crises are more likely when there are underlying weaknesses and vulnerabilities in the economy. These weaknesses do not necessarily lead to a crisis, but they make economies vulnerable to events that can trigger a crisis. Crisis triggers, such as a bank failure, or sudden speculation against a currency, are usually unpredictable; for this reason, attempts to predict crises tend to focus on the points of vulnerability and the probability that those points might lead to the onset and spread of a crisis.

In this section, two main types of vulnerabilities are considered. These are not the only possible ones, but they cover a wide range of situations that have contributed to economic weaknesses and, on occasion, turned into domestic and international crises. The first type of vulnerability is a result of definite and identifiable macroeconomic imbalances. For this type, the moment of crisis onset is unpredictable, but unless the underlying conditions are corrected, it is almost certain to occur eventually. The second type of vulnerability is brought on by volatile flows of financial capital that move out of a country quickly. These capital outflows are often preceded by a period of capital inflows and a buildup of foreign liabilities. A sudden change in investor expectations may be a triggering factor, and underlying fragility in the banking and financial sector may be present. Still, this type of crisis can be puzzling because in several recent cases it has affected countries with particularly strong international positions and stable macroeconomic policies.

Vulnerability: Economic Imbalances

Over the last few decades, a number of crises have been triggered by events that put severe pressure on existing macroeconomic imbalances. Macroeconomic imbalances can take various forms, including large budget deficits, large current account deficits, overvalued exchange rates, or unsustainable levels of private sector debt, such as in the housing market.

Historically, poor fiscal or monetary management have frequently played a role, as when governments allow large budget deficits or high rates of inflation. The need to finance budget deficits can make governments vulnerable to a change in the perceptions of lenders about their probability of being repaid, and inflation with a fixed exchange rate creates vulnerability through a real appreciation of the currency and a loss of competitiveness (see Chapter 10). Not all crises are caused by poor fiscal or monetary management, however, and many crises originate in the private sector where imbalances are caused by speculation in real estate, the stock market, or other asset.

The global crisis that began in 2007 has exhibited several of these sources of crisis, depending on the country and the time period. Beginning with the rise of house prices in the United States, the United Kingdom, Spain, and several other countries, private investors—including banks, insurance companies, pension funds, and individuals—had significant incentives to invest in real estate, driving prices to unsustainable levels. Investment was facilitated by global imbalances in which countries with high savings rates and large current account surpluses, such as China, Germany, and oil exporters, lent to the United States, the United Kingdom, Spain, and other countries with large current account deficits and significant investment opportunities. The result was an unsustainable increase in house prices and a housing bubble in many cities. When house prices began to fall, it put pressure on financial systems in countries where large financial institutions were using the home-loans they made as collateral to borrow heavily in short-term credit markets. The failure of U.S. investment bank Lehman Brothers occurred when it was no longer able to obtain short-term credit after its lenders rejected its collateral, triggering the most intense period of the financial crisis.

The first phase of the 2007–2009 crisis involved macroeconomic imbalances in current accounts, and savings and investment. These imbalances were not due to government policies in most cases but were the result of private sector decisions regarding spending, saving, and investment. The second phase began as tax revenues declined and social spending automatically increased as countries fell deeper into recession and government budgets came under pressure. During recessions, government income declines due to the fall in economic activity and the decline in income in the private economy. At the same time, income support programs, health care spending, and even pension expenditures rise unexpectedly as workers are laid off, lose their employer-sponsored health care, and (sometimes) retire early. The fall in tax collections and the rise in social spending constitute an automatic stabilizer since the changes are stimulatory and partially counteract the recession. Inevitably, however, they create a budget deficit, and in some cases the deficit becomes unsustainable.

The Latin American debt crisis (1982–1989) is an example of a crisis caused by unsustainable macroeconomic balances (see Chapter 15). In August, 1982, Mexico revealed that it was no longer able to service its external debt. This followed a decade of large scale borrowing to finance budget deficits and development projects. As the debt crisis spread to other Latin American economies, budget deficits, current account deficits, excessive money creation, and overvalued exchange rates added banking crises and exchange rate crises to the ongoing debt crisis. The crisis trigger in this case may have been the worldwide increase in interest rates that began in the United States, but as more countries were revealed to be insolvent after nearly a decade of high levels of borrowing, the crisis spread. The Latin American debt crisis is a case of **sovereign default**, since it was default by sovereign governments. It is a particularly painful episode in Latin American economic history, and is discussed more fully in Chapter 15.

Vulnerability: Volatile Capital Flows

Not all crises are the result of macroeconomic imbalances or unsustainable expansions in fiscal and monetary policies. National economies are increasingly vulnerable to the effects of technology that instantaneously shift vast sums of financial capital from one market to another. Together with the high degree of financial openness achieved in the last few decades, the contagion effects of crisis can spill across oceans and national borders. The best example of this kind of crisis is the one that hit some of the economies of East Asia in 1997 and 1998. While several economies had underlying weaknesses in their financial sectors, others such as Singapore, Hong Kong, and Taiwan were adversely affected, even without the same weaknesses.

The fundamental cause of this type of crisis is that financial capital is highly volatile, and technological advances have reinforced this volatility. The discovery of large emerging markets and the drive by financial investors in high-income countries to diversify their portfolios caused hundreds of billions of dollars to be invested throughout the world. Most savings stays in the country doing the saving, but an increasingly large volume of savings has entered international capital markets, where it moves relatively freely in response to interest rates, exchange rate expectations, and economic activity. This creates opportunities as well as problems. For example, portfolio managers often look at each other's actions for information about the direction of the market. Capital inflows can be a sign of economic strength and can generate more inflows, adding to the funds a country has to invest and generating more rapid growth. Capital outflows can also be a signal, however, and can intensify a small problem. What begins as a trickle of funds out of a country can be interpreted as bad news about underlying conditions and lead to an avalanche of capital flight. When that happens, international reserves disappear, exchange rates tumble, and the financial sector can suddenly look very weak.

A weak financial sector can also intensify the problems. A case in point is a banking sector that borrows internationally and lends locally. If the funds obtained in the international market are short-term and are used to fund long-term loans such as real estate, problems arise when the international loans must be repaid. As long as international lenders are willing to roll over the debt and extend new loans, everything moves along smoothly. As soon as the lenders believe that there is a problem with a borrowing bank, however, they refuse to roll over the debt, creating a liquidity problem if the bank's assets are tied up in real estate loans. In the short run, real estate is relatively illiquid and cannot be used to make a payment. When a number of banks are confronted with similar problems, their attempt to unload real estate depresses prices even further and undermines the solvency of the banking system since every bank with real estate investments is suddenly holding a portfolio of declining value.

This type of scenario is particularly troubling because it can go either way. That is, it may resolve itself without a crisis if international lenders are willing to extend additional credit while banks sell their long-term assets. Alternatively, if international investors expect a crisis and consequently are unwilling to give domestic banks the time they need to convert illiquid assets into liquid ones, then the crisis becomes a self-fulfilling prophecy. The belief in a crisis causes lenders to refuse to roll over the banking debts, and the banks, which are illiquid, become insolvent.

Several parts of this scenario are unsettling to economists and policymakers. First, there are multiple possible outcomes—or in economic terms, there are *multiple equilibria*—depending on the responses of international lenders. Second, one of the possible outcomes is a crisis, but the crisis is self-fulfilling. It is not predetermined, nor is it necessary. Third, the crisis affects banks that are fundamentally sound, but that have mismatches between the maturities of their debts and their assets. In other words, they are illiquid, but not insolvent.

These factors seem to imply that it should be possible to avoid this type of crisis. In part, it requires that banks pay closer attention to the maturity match between their debts and assets. In some cases, this requires a higher degree of supervision and regulation on the part of the banking authorities. International lenders, for their part, must be more informed about the activities of their borrowers. This requires greater information flows, the use of standard accounting practices, and overall greater transparency in domestic and international financial systems. Finally, once a crisis occurs, international agencies, such as the IMF, that are called in to make emergency loans need to be able to distinguish between insolvency and illiquidity. The distinction is more complex than it seems, but it is crucial, since the appropriate response will vary depending on the short- to medium-run prospects of the borrowing country.

How Crises Become International: Contagion

Most crises are domestic. Banking crises, currency crises, and debt crises nearly always begin in a national context and only some of them become international. Many crises, however, spill into other countries, and even if they do not become a global crisis, they nevertheless affect more than just the country where it originates. For example, the Mexican exchange rate crisis of 1994–1995 (see case study below) caused an outflow of capital from many middle income countries and contributed to a sharp recession in Argentina and other countries. Argentina recovered relatively quickly, but the episode illustrates how problems in one place are easily transmitted to another.

Some crises are contagious, in ways that are similar to diseases. Direct linkages between economies can sometimes spread a crisis that begins in one economy and turn it into an international crisis. For example, the crisis that began in 2007 in the United States with a decline in housing prices, spread fairly easily into Europe and Japan. Banks in those regions had purchased assets that ultimately depended on housing prices in the United States and when they began to fall, the value of assets based on them declined as well. Suddenly, the problems of United States were also the problems of Europe and Japan, including insolvent banks that had purchased assets based on housing prices.

Banking or other financial linkages may not be visible or known until a crisis begins, but ultimately they will be exposed if the crisis persists or is deep enough. Other forms of contagion may be less easily observed. For example, countries with no obvious linkages to a country in crisis may become entangled if the crisis country serves as "wake up call" to international investors and speculators. During the Asian Crisis of 1997–1998 (see case study below) for example, speculators successfully bet against Thailand's currency and then turned to similar countries in the region where they assumed there were similar problems. In some cases, their bets paid off, but in others they lost, as when they speculated against currencies that were backed by large reserves and were not overvalued.

The subprime crisis was a good example of an international crisis that developed as a result of contagion, but not all international crises are spread that way. Frequently, two or more countries face similar financial crises because they share a common set of economic fundamentals. For example, a long and steep decline in the prices of agricultural and mineral outputs between 1928 and 1931 was one of the factors that set in motion and sustained the worldwide Great Depression of the 1930s. Countries or regions with large agricultural or mining sectors saw declining prices for key commodities that eventually resulted in bankruptcies and banking crises. In this case, the spread of the crisis internationally was through the common set of economic conditions that many countries shared and not the result of direct contagion from one country to another. When commodity prices began to fall, it had similar effects in many countries simultaneously.

CASE STUDY

The Mexican Peso Crisis of 1994 and 1995

The collapse of the Mexican peso and the ensuing crisis that began at the end of 1994 had elements of a crisis caused by macroeconomic imbalances and one caused by volatile capital flows and financial sector weakness. On the one hand, there were definite signs of macroeconomic imbalances, including an overvalued real exchange rate and a large current account deficit. On the other hand, the Mexican government operated a relatively austere fiscal policy, and not counting foreign interest payments on its debt, the government budget was in

(continued)

surplus, not deficit. Similarly, inflation came down during the early 1990s and reached 7 percent overall in 1994, down from 22.7 percent in 1991. Between 1990 and 1993, Mexico experienced capital inflows of $91 billion, or an average of about $23 billion per year, the most of any developing country. The capital inflow was in the form of private portfolio investments ($61 billion), direct investments ($16.6 billion), and bank loans ($13.4 billion).

The administration of President Salinas (1988–1994) actively encouraged large inflows of foreign capital as a way to maintain investment rates far above the level that domestic Mexican savings could support. Recall from Chapter 9 the macroeconomic identity that private savings plus the government budget balance must equal domestic investment plus the current account balance:

$$S_p + (T - G) = I + CA$$

In 1994, Mexican savings of around 14 percent of gross domestic product (GDP) could not support investment of more than 20 percent of GDP unless there was an inflow of savings from the rest of the world. Mexico ran large current account deficits equal to 5 percent of GDP in 1991 and 6.5 percent in 1992 and 1993. The enormous inflow of foreign goods and services permitted more investment by providing capital goods that Mexico could not make itself, and by satisfying consumption through foreign goods and thereby allowing domestic factories to produce investment goods. This was the strategy of the Salinas government, and it seemed to be working. The North American Free Trade Agreement (NAFTA) between Canada, the United States, and Mexico took effect on January 1, 1994, and throughout the year U.S.–Mexican trade expanded by almost one-fourth (23.7 percent). NAFTA inspired confidence in Mexico's institutional stability and guaranteed access to the wealthy U.S. market for any goods made in Mexico.

During 1994, the world capital market began to shift toward a more conservative, risk-averse stance. In February 1994, interest rate movements in the United States and exchange rate movements around the world led to large losses for a number of banks and other investors. Portfolio managers began to reassess their investments and look for ways to reduce their exposure to risk. Political events also prompted investors to reassess their financial positions in Mexico. First, on January 1, 1994, at the moment NAFTA began implementation, subsistence farmers in the poorest Mexican state of Chiapas revolted against the federal government. Second, in March, the leading presidential candidate was assassinated while campaigning for office. While the lead-up to the signing and implementation of NAFTA had encouraged the view that Mexico was a safe, stable, and modernizing country, these events shocked investors into taking a closer look. Financial prudence seemed to call for reducing the level of exposure to Mexico, and many investors inside and outside the country sold their peso-denominated assets.

Less than three weeks after taking office in early December 1994, President Ernesto Zedillo finally agreed that the peso was overvalued and announced a 15 percent devaluation, from around 3.5 to 4 pesos per dollar. Ordinarily this measure might have been interpreted as a cautious and responsible move to address the problem of an overvalued currency. Unfortunately, currency traders and economists had expected a 20 to 30 percent devaluation, and President Zedillo's actions made it appear as if his administration did not understand the severity of the crisis. Consequently, rather than the calming effect he had hoped for, Zedillo's announcement of a 15 percent devaluation sent currency and financial markets into even greater turmoil. More capital fled the country, dollar reserves shrank, and the credibility of Mexico's exchange rate policies came under severe questioning.

Two days after announcing the devaluation, the government of Mexico announced that it would move to a floating exchange rate system. Although this was the right move, the damage had been done, and both foreign and domestic capital continued to leave the country. The currency continued to fall and by late December, it was over 5 pesos per dollar, and by the middle of March 1995, it was over 7 per dollar. This was a loss of more than 50 percent of its value compared to early December, 1994 (see Figure 12.1).

Zedillo addressed the short-run problems of the crisis by seeking financial support from the NAFTA partners and the IMF. Relief came in late January 1995, in the form of a line of credit and loans. Within weeks, currency markets were calmed down and the rate of capital flight slowed as the holders of peso-denominated assets began to relax in the knowledge that the government would be able to convert any amount of pesos to dollars. The peso regained some of its lost value, and by the end of April 1995, it was trading at six per dollar.

MyEconLab Real-time data

FIGURE 12.1   **Pesos per Dollar: December 1, 1994 to March 31, 1995**

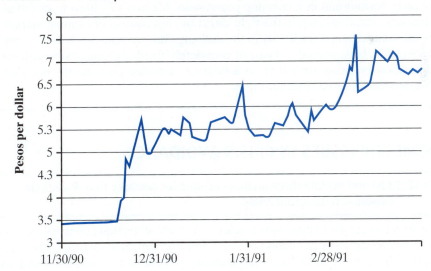

The peso lost over half its value between December 20, 1994, and March 9, 1995.

Source: Data from Federal Reserve Board, © James Gerber.

(*continued*)

The medium- and long-run problems were addressed with a package of **austerity** measures that cut government spending, increased taxes (T up, G down), and reduced consumption. The large current account deficit at the end of 1994 increased the vulnerability of Mexico's financial system to capital flight and had been partly responsible for the draining of dollar reserves. Expenditure reduction policies were therefore an appropriate step taken to address the crisis, because tax increases and government expenditure cuts would help reduce the current account deficit. Electricity prices and gasoline prices were raised (both were supplied through government-owned enterprises), and credit was restricted through steep increases in interest rates and new limits on bank lending. These measures reduced consumption and boosted saving, provided a greater pool of domestic funds for investment purposes, and decreased the country's dependence on foreign capital inflows. However, the fall in consumption and government expenditures brought a recession; Mexico's GDP fell by 6.2 percent in 1995, and more than 500,000 people lost their jobs.

Analysts are still digesting the lessons of the peso collapse, but a few things stand out. For Mexico, the policy of relying on large foreign inflows of world savings through a large financial account surplus (current account deficit) proved to be unstable. Too much of the foreign capital was invested in short-term portfolios rather than longer-term direct investment. This distribution is not inherently unsafe, but once the peso became overvalued, both foreign and domestic investors feared that a surprise devaluation would destroy the value of their assets, and they began to convert large numbers of pesos into dollars. In addition, the peso crisis demonstrated how hard it is to arrange an orderly devaluation in a crawling peg system. Mexico's 15 percent devaluation was a cautious step in the right direction, but instead of calming market fears, it undermined credibility in the exchange rate system. Since then, many economists have argued in favor of completely fixed exchange rates with no discretionary monetary policy, or a floating exchange rate like the one that Mexico has followed since the crisis.

DOMESTIC ISSUES IN CRISIS AVOIDANCE

LO 12.3 List and explain three measures countries can take to reduce their exposure to financial crises.

Not all crises are avoidable. Nevertheless, there are steps that countries can take to try to minimize the likelihood of crises and the damage they cause when they happen. In addition to the need to maintain credible and sustainable fiscal and monetary policies, governments must engage in active supervision and regulation of the financial system and provide timely information about key economic variables such as the central bank's holding of international reserves.

In these areas, the design of effective policies is relatively straightforward, but in other areas there is a wide array of expert opinion, and consensus remains elusive. Should countries bail out their banks if they fail, and what type of penalties should they impose if they do? Should they try to limit foreign capital inflows and outflows? Which type of exchange rate system is most stable? It is possible that in some areas there is no single optimal policy for avoiding a crisis and countries have a variety of equally viable options? In those cases, is it also possible that there are choices that are better for some countries, but not others, depending on the conditions inside the country?

Moral Hazard and Financial Sector Regulation

When a country's financial sector becomes dysfunctional, problems spread to the rest of the economy. Credit dries up, investment disappears, households worry about their lost savings, consumption falls, and the economy slides into recession. Hence, there is a big incentive to keep the financial sector operational, even if it means that governments have to spend revenues in order to keep the sector in working order.

This creates a dilemma for policymakers, since the knowledge that you will be bailed out if you fail usually leads people, including bankers, to take greater risks. If the costs of failure are removed, the calculation of risks versus rewards changes for financial institutions. Riskier investments usually offer greater returns in order to compensate for the risk. If some of the risk is removed because there is the possibility of a bailout when there is a failure, then firms will take on more risk in anticipation of more rewards. This is the problem of moral hazard. Examples of moral hazards in everyday life include the financial incentive to avoid giving out information about a used car you are selling, or divulging negative information about your health when buying life insurance. In these cases, individuals are able to transfer the risk of buying a bad car or insuring an unhealthy person to someone else who will pay the costs. Similarly, bailouts of financial firms give them the opportunity to transfer their risk to governments or taxpayers.

The problem of moral hazard is inescapable if there is a general policy of protecting the financial system from collapse. There is general agreement that one key to eliminating moral hazard in financial institutions is to increase **capital requirements** in order to raise the level of capital available in time of crisis. Capital includes items such as shareholders' equity, retained earnings, and bank reserves. Taken together they are the owners' investment in the bank. Several international agreements regulating bank capital levels, known collectively as the **Basel Accords**, have been signed, including Basel III, which was signed in 2010. In addition to tackling the problem of moral hazard, the Basel Accords also try to make banking systems more robust by setting new standards for bank supervision, information disclosure, and stress tests. The latter are designed to tell a bank in advance where its weaknesses are by subjecting it to different types of hypothetical negative shocks. Since the most recent of the Basel Accords (Basel III) was signed in 2010, it has not been tested by a new crisis, and there is disagreement as to its real effectiveness in helping to prevent another major financial crisis.

Exchange Rate Policy

Through the 1970s and 1980s, many countries adopted a crawling peg exchange rate system, often as part of an anti-inflation strategy. Recall from Chapter 10 that a crawling peg involves fixing the exchange rate to a major world currency such as the dollar or the euro, or to a basket of currencies that include the home country's major trading partners. The "crawling" part of the exchange rate involves regular—often daily—devaluations of a fixed amount. Pegs are usually intended to stabilize the real exchange rate in a country with higher inflation than its trading partners. If domestic inflation is higher than foreign inflation, nominal devaluation keeps the real exchange rate constant. Given the definition of the real rate as

$$R_r = R_n(P^*/P),$$

then if the change in P (domestic prices) is greater than the change in P^* (foreign prices), the nominal rate, R_n, must rise (devalue) in order to keep the real rate constant. Maintaining the peg requires the monetary authority to exercise discipline in the creation of new money and is anti-inflationary in that sense. In addition, countries frequently try to reinforce the anti-inflation tendency of the crawling peg by intentionally devaluing at a slower pace than the difference between home and foreign inflation. This creates real appreciation in the exchange rate, and is intended to act as a brake on domestic inflation as foreign goods steadily became cheaper in real terms, limiting the price increases that domestic producers were able to impose. The use of the exchange rate in this manner has mixed success in helping control inflation, but in a number of cases it has led to severe overvaluation of the real exchange rate and increased the country's vulnerability to a crisis.

Another way in which a crawling peg exchange rate system increases a country's vulnerability to crisis is that it is sometimes politically difficult to exit from the system if it becomes overvalued. When a government announces a change in the system, it runs the risk of losing its credibility. Both domestic and foreign economic agents accommodate the existing system, and a sudden large devaluation leads to economic losses and a loss of confidence in the country's policymakers. Consequently, it is common for countries to delay addressing the problem of overvaluation, and when the correction comes, it has to be larger. The end of Mexico's crawling peg in 1994 is a good example.

Capital Controls

Many economists hold that the free movement of capital is a desirable objective because it allows investors to send their financial capital wherever the return is highest, thereby raising world welfare by putting financial capital to its most valuable use. At the same time, capital mobility allows countries to invest more than is possible with their domestic savings alone, which again raises world welfare when there are valuable investment projects and insufficient savings to realize them. Others, however, claim that the benefits of complete capital mobility are based on theory, but are never fully demonstrated empirically. In addition, capital mobility generates very high costs in the form of macroeconomic crises, and these costs must be offset against any economic gain.

This issue is unsettled, and although economists agree that trade in goods and services raises a country's welfare, there is less agreement about the benefits of free capital movements. The sources of the disagreement not only cover the potential benefits of capital inflows versus the potential costs of sudden capital outflows, but also include debates over the actual ability of **capital controls** to prevent capital movements, whether controls on the movement of capital can stop a crisis once it begins, and whether it is better to limit inflows, outflows, or both.

Through much of the twentieth century, countries guarded against the problems of capital mobility by restricting its movement. This seems to imply that countries are able to prevent capital from crossing their borders, but what may have been true in 1970 is much more doubtful today. The growth of emerging stock markets and the implementation of technology to facilitate capital transfers have created both the incentive and the means for investors to send their capital abroad.

Ordinarily, capital flow restrictions are imposed by limiting transactions that are part of the financial account of the balance of payments. (See Chapter 9 for a discussion of the components of the balance of payments.) Capital movements to support transactions on the current account are usually permitted since they are necessary for trade. Consequently, one of the primary ways in which firms can get around capital account restrictions is to over-invoice imports. This allows them to make payments abroad that are larger than necessary for the purchase of imports. Alternatively, they can under-invoice exports so that the reported payments received are smaller than the actual payments, and the difference can be invested outside the country without reporting to authorities. While these techniques are common, and perhaps fraudulent, outright corruption in the form of bribes is also a possibility for getting money out of the country.

Whether these types of practices make controls on capital outflows completely ineffective is open to debate, but they clearly reduce the effectiveness of capital controls. For this reason, as a general rule, restrictions on inflows are seen as more workable than restrictions on outflows. Inflow restrictions can take a variety of forms, but they share the common goal of trying to reduce the inflow of volatile, short-run capital, which may add to the stock of liquid assets ready to flee the country.

Restrictions on capital inflows cannot stop a crisis once it begins, however. Consequently, there is an ongoing debate over the utility of imposing restrictions on capital outflows once a crisis starts. Since many crises include a speculative attack against the home country currency, some argue that a temporary limitation on capital outflows could help stop a crisis by artificially reducing the demand for foreign exchange. In theory, this would prop up the value of the domestic currency and eliminate expectations of a large decline in its value.

In the midst of the Asian crisis, Malaysia followed this policy in spite of a number of warnings that it would undermine investor confidence in Malaysian policies, cut them off from international capital markets, and do long-term damage to the economy. None of the dire predictions materialized, however, and Malaysia recovered from the crisis at about the same speed as Korea, which went the other way and eliminated some of its controls on capital flows. The fact that two different policies led to more or less similar outcomes is a measure of how much we do not know.

CASE STUDY

The Asian Crisis of 1997 and 1998

The Asian financial crisis began in Thailand in July 1997. From there, it spread to a number of other countries, including Malaysia, the Philippines, Indonesia, and South Korea. The outward symptoms of the crisis were fairly similar across countries: currency speculation and steep depreciations, capital flight, and financial and industrial sector bankruptcies. It is tempting to interpret these symptoms as signs of the region's weaknesses, but ironically, the causes are at least in part due to the region's great strengths.

Vulnerability 1: Large Current Account Deficits

The most severely affected countries all had large trade deficits. Table 12.1 shows current account deficits in 1996, the year before the crisis. For the five countries in the top panel, deficits averaged 5.2 percent of GDP in 1996. In Thailand, where the crisis began, the current account deficit was nearly 8 percent of GDP. The three countries in the bottom panel of Table 12.1 all felt reverberations from the crisis in spite of their small deficits (Hong Kong) or large surpluses (Singapore and Taiwan).

TABLE 12.1   Current Account Balances and Currency Depreciations

	Current Account Balance, 1996, Percent of GDP	Currency Depreciation in Dollars, 7/1/97 to 12/31/97
Countries with large deficits		
Indonesia	−3.4	−44.4
Malaysia	−4.9	−35.0
Philippines	−4.7	−33.9
South Korea	−4.9	−47.7
Thailand	−7.9	−48.7
Countries with small deficits or surpluses		
Hong Kong	−1.3	0.0
Singapore	+15.7	−15.0
Taiwan	+4.0	−14.8

Large current account deficits led to large depreciations. Nevertheless, some countries were hit with depreciations even when they had large surpluses.

Source: Data from Goldstein, Morris, *The Asian Financial Crisis: Causes, Cures, and Systemic Implications* Washington, DC: Institute for International Economics, June 1998, © James Gerber.

Large current account deficits necessarily imply large financial account borrowing, and the countries listed in the top half of Table 12.1 experienced large capital inflows. Foreign investors were more than willing to send their capital to East Asia, as the region had averaged about 5 percent growth per year in real GDP for the last thirty years, and there was no reason to believe that would change anytime soon. Furthermore, slow growth in Japan and Europe during much of the 1990s caused many international investors to scour the globe looking for higher returns, and the stable and dynamic economies of Southeast Asia stood out prominently. Low inflation, small budget deficits or consistent government surpluses, and the high rates of economic growth made them highly desirable places to invest and to loan funds.

Vulnerability 2: Overvalued Exchange Rates

Exchange rate policies in the region usually involved pegging to the dollar, so that as the dollar appreciated in the mid-1990s, it caused many exchange rates to appreciate along with it, resulting in a number of significant currency misalignments. The pegged exchange rates became harder and harder to sustain, partly because they made it more difficult for the pegged countries to export. According to some observers, this problem was exacerbated by China's devaluation of its fixed exchange rate in 1994 and the significant depreciation of the Japanese yen throughout the period of dollar appreciation. The movements in these two currencies made the exports of Thailand and several others less competitive.

Vulnerability 3: Weak Financial Sectors

The downturn in export revenues exposed several other weaknesses, including those in regulatory systems, corporate structures, and financial systems. Many countries in East Asia rely on corporate structures built around family ties and personal networks. This can have significant advantages for small and medium-size enterprises, but as firms grow, the lack of disclosure and transparency make it difficult for outside lenders to assess the microeconomic risks of lending. In addition, the lack of hard data and information make it difficult to implement the kinds of regulatory controls that all economies need for stability, especially in the financial sector. For example, many banks experienced the kind of mismatches between the maturities of their assets and liabilities described as a serious vulnerability earlier in the chapter. These firms took out short-term loans in international capital markets and used the money to finance real estate developments with long and risky payoffs.

Crisis Trigger and Contagion

The existence of several vulnerabilities does not make a crisis inevitable but they do make them more likely. When a sudden and unexpected event puts

(continued)

significant pressure on the vulnerable points, problems may develop. For example, the drop in computer chip prices reduced Thailand's export earnings and increased its current account deficit. That may have been manageable, but it also undermined investor confidence in Thailand's ability to keep its exchange rate pegged to the dollar. People began to expect a devaluation and did not want to be holding the Thai baht when it came. Furthermore, many of the loans to the Thai financial sector were short-term loans obtained in international capital markets, and required repayment in dollars. This raised the cost of a devaluation because Thai financial institutions earned revenue in baht, but owed a fixed amount of dollars. Any change in investor confidence could undermine the entire economy.

How the Thai crisis spread internationally is one of the less certain components of the overall crisis. One hypothesis is that Thailand served as a "wake-up call" for investors to examine more closely their holdings in other countries. Another hypothesis is that the Thai devaluation made exports from several neighboring countries less competitive and forced them to engage in competitive devaluations. Regardless, there was a contagion element in the Thai crisis, and it soon spread to countries as far away as Brazil and Russia.

Some of the consequences of the Asian crisis are easily visible in Table 12.2, which shows the growth rate of real GDP in 1998 and 1999. With the exceptions of Singapore and Taiwan, every country affected by the crisis experienced a

TABLE 12.2   Real GDP Growth

	1998	1999
Real GDP growth in countries with large current account deficits		
Indonesia	−13.2	+0.2
Malaysia	−7.5	+5.4
Philippines	−0.6	+3.3
South Korea	−6.7	+10.7
Thailand	−10.2	+4.2
Real GDP growth in countries with small current account deficits, or surpluses		
Hong Kong	−5.1	+3.0
Singapore	+0.4	+5.4
Taiwan	+4.6	+5.7

Many countries experienced deep depressions in 1998, but by the second quarter of 1999, virtually every crisis country had returned to positive growth.
Source: Data from Asian Development Bank, © James Gerber.

recession in 1998. Given their large trade surpluses and their ample international reserves, Singapore and Taiwan were able to focus on their domestic economies rather than trying to defend their currencies, thereby avoiding recessions. By the second quarter of 1999, every country had returned to positive growth.

The rapid recoveries shown in Table 12.2 caught most analysts by surprise, yet the flexibility and fundamental soundness of macroeconomic policies throughout East Asia facilitated swift recovery. Still, Table 12.2 does not tell the whole story since poverty rose significantly throughout the region. In addition, many emerging markets observed the crisis and decided that the best way to prevent a similar one in their own economy is to accumulate large stocks of international reserve currencies. Since 2001, China and others have done so, using their exports and export promotion policies as a means to obtain foreign reserves. In many respects, this is perhaps the most lasting and important legacy of the Asian Crisis of 1997–1998.

Crisis Management

Three issues in crisis management remain unresolved after this episode. First, did the IMF make a mistake in advising the borrowing countries to defend their currencies with interest rate hikes? Second, were there moral hazard elements present, perhaps as a result of the Mexican bailout in 1995? Third, are capital controls helpful as a temporary measure to stem a crisis?

The first issue is a specific instance of the dilemma of fixed exchange rates. Should countries try to protect their domestic economies, or must they defend their currencies? For countries with large trade surpluses and ample international reserves, defense of the domestic economy through lower interest rates seems feasible. The real question applies to the five countries with large current account deficits. Some critics of the IMF blame it for turning financial panics in those countries into full-blown depressions by counseling them to raise their interest rates. The critics charge that the IMF treated the crisis as if it were the same as the Latin American debt crisis of the 1980s, in which governments had large budget deficits and high rates of inflation. In East Asia, governments were running surpluses or small deficits, so there was no need to temporarily contract the economy with interest rate increases. Defenders of the IMF argue that interest rate hikes were necessary as a means to stop the slide in currency values.

A second issue relates to the moral hazard of bailing out a bank or corporation. Some critics allege that the IMF loans to Mexico set a precedent that taught lenders that their mistakes would be covered by loans from the IMF, and consequently the Asian crisis became more likely. The counterargument is that "bailouts" are not really bailouts in the full sense of the word because they do not protect investors from losses. Most investors in East Asia saw sizable reductions in the values of their portfolios, so they have plenty of reason to exercise caution when lending.

(continued)

A final unresolved issue is the problem of capital flight. Can it be stopped, at least in the short term, with controls on capital outflows? As noted in the previous discussion on capital controls, Malaysia imposed restrictions on the outflow of capital and Korea did not, yet both recovered from the crisis relatively quickly. In all likelihood, the optimal policy depends on a number of factors specific to each country. Further research is necessary to know which types of policies are most effective in which situations.

Domestic Policies for Crisis Management

It is relatively easy to prescribe a cure for financial crises that result from inconsistent macroeconomic policies. For example, if a crisis is triggered by a collapsing currency, which, in turn is the result of large government budget deficits financed by money expansion with a fixed or crawling peg exchange rate, then the prescription is relatively straightforward in economic terms: Cut the deficit, raise interest rates to help defend the currency, and, perhaps, let the currency float. In other words, the solution to a fiscal crisis brought on by macroeconomic imbalances is to correct the imbalances.

The problem is that the economic austerity of budget cuts and higher interest rates may not be politically feasible. In addition, several economic problems are often present. Tax systems in many countries are unenforceable, meaning that tax increases may not generate more revenue. The adoption of a floating exchange rate system may undermine the credibility of the government's commitment to fighting inflation, since financial sector interests often fear that it will remove the last bit of restraint over money creation and lead to hyperinflation. Governments may not be able to cut expenditures easily, since government employees may be unionized with multiyear contracts, may provide essential domestic services, or other elements of the budget may support powerful domestic interests.

The case of a crisis brought on by sudden capital flight in the context of relatively stable and credible macroeconomic policies is even more difficult to resolve. Given that this type of crisis may have multiple equilibria outcomes, depending on the direction taken by expectations, there is a powerful argument for addressing the problem of a collapsing currency through interest rate hikes, sales of reserves, and other actions that might help convince investors that the currency is strong. On the other hand, high interest rates and other actions to defend the currency are likely to intensify bankruptcies and other contractionary forces that develop during a crisis. Hence, defending a currency may push a small downturn into a full-blown depression.

In crises caused by either macroeconomic imbalances or sudden capital flows, there is a strong desire to avoid a recession. In the first type, however, both fiscal and monetary policies are usually overextended, and the crisis is partly a result of policies that are unsustainable and overly expansionary. In effect, this forecloses fiscal and monetary policies as tools to avoid the contractionary aspects of the crisis, and the only way out is usually through some sort of recession.

In the second case, however, fiscal and monetary imbalances may not be part of the initial problem, so the use of fiscal and monetary policies is not entirely ruled out. Governments face a dilemma in this position, however, in that expansionary policies include a reduction in interest rates, which can cause a further depreciation in the domestic currency. If domestic firms have debts that are denominated in dollars or another foreign currency, a depreciation implies a sudden increase in the size of their debts and spreads additional bankruptcies through the economy.

In effect, this implies that fiscal and monetary policies are limited if there is an international component to the crisis. It also creates a stark set of choices for handling the crisis. Either defend the currency with high interest rates and spread the recessionary effects of the crisis, or defend the domestic economy against contraction and intensify the problems of a collapsing currency. Much of the debate over the policies recommended by the IMF during the Asian Crisis of 1997 and 1998 (raise interest rates to try to stabilize the collapsing currencies) turned on precisely this point. Clearly, if there was an easy, nonrecessionary way to end a crisis, policymakers would use it.

REFORM OF THE INTERNATIONAL FINANCIAL ARCHITECTURE

LO 12.4 **Explain the need for reforms in the architecture of international finance and international financial institutions.**

LO 12.5 **Describe the main forces behind the global financial crisis that began in 2007.**

The frequency of international financial crises coupled with their high costs has generated a great deal of interest in finding the right policies for avoiding a crisis and for handling one if it begins. Taken as a whole, the discussion of new international policies for crisis avoidance and management is referred to as reforming the international financial architecture. In particular, a lot of attention is focused on the role of the IMF and the conditions it imposes as part of its loan packages.

A number of ideas for reforming the international financial architecture have been advanced in recent years. Private think tanks such as the Council on Foreign Relations, the Overseas Development Council, and the Centre for Economic Policy and Research in London have each published proposals, as have multilateral agencies such as the United Nations Conference on Trade and Development (UNCTAD) and government-appointed bodies such as the International Financial Institutions Advisory Commission of the U.S. Congress. In the aftermath of the crisis of 2007–2009, reform is also a major topic of discussion at international meetings of finance ministers and country leaders.

The proposals for international financial reform express a variety of conflicting viewpoints, but they agree that two issues are at the center of the discussion. The first is the role of an international lender of last resort and the rules governing its lending practices. A second issue is the type of conditions that such a lender might impose on its borrowers. In effect, both of these issues are questions about the role of the IMF and its current practices.

A Lender of Last Resort

Recall from Chapter 2 that a lender of last resort is a source of loanable funds after all commercial sources of lending have disappeared. In a national economy, this role is usually filled by the central bank. In the international economy, it is filled by the IMF, often with the support of high-income economies such as Canada, the EU, Japan, the United States, and others. As a lender of last resort, the IMF is often asked to intervene when countries reach a crisis point in their finances and cannot make payment on their international loans, or cannot convert their domestic currency into dollars or another foreign currency due to an insufficiency of international reserves.

Not everyone agrees that there should be a lender of last resort, and some observers worry about the moral hazard problems of such lending. This is particularly problematic as a crisis begins to develop and some firms are on the verge of collapse. The moral hazard problem can intensify since managers of failing firms have a large incentive to gamble on high-stakes, high-risk ventures that, if they pay off, will cover all their losses. In response, those who favor maintaining the IMF in its current role as an international lender of last resort stress the importance of financial sector regulation, including the elements outlined in the Basel Accords. If the owners of financial firms risk a substantial loss in the event of financial meltdown, they are less likely to take on excessive risk.

The final issue about the rules for IMF loans is the size of the loan. Countries pay a subscription, called a *quota*, to join the IMF. The size of the quota depends mainly on the size of the economy and its strength. The quota determines how much a country can borrow in a "normal" crisis, as well as how many votes the country has in setting IMF policy. Generally, countries can borrow up to 300 percent of their quota, but in extraordinary circumstances such as the Mexican peso crisis, the Asian crisis, or other crises with the potential to spread, the limits on country borrowing are determined more or less by the needs at the time, as well as the amounts available directly from other governments.

Although some countries have borrowed sums that are well above 300 percent of their quota, the limits on borrowing have not kept up with the growth in the size of national economies. Some argue that borrowing limits should be greatly expanded, while others propose differentiating between crises that have a high probability of spreading and those contained within a single country. In many cases, it may not be possible to determine the difference, but systemwide crises definitely have the potential to impose greater costs. Hence, there is a clear rationale for intervening with larger sums if it will stop a crisis faster. This seems to be a point on which most countries agree. At the 2009 meeting of the twenty largest economies, called the *G-20*, there was an agreement to treble the resources available to the IMF from U.S. $250 billion to U.S. $750 billion, for a total increase of U.S. $500 billion. In spite of its increased resources, however, the IMF has never had nor will it ever have sufficient funds to provide any more than moderate support for a large economy such as Italy or Spain. In the euro crisis that began in 2011 (unresolved as of this writing), the IMF partnered with the European Central Bank and a special fund created by the EU in order to assist some of the debtor countries.

Conditionality

The second issue surrounding the role of a lender of last resort such as the IMF is that of conditionality. IMF **conditionality** refers to the changes in economic policy that borrowing nations are required to make in order to receive IMF loans. Conditionality typically covers monetary and fiscal policies, exchange rate policies, and structural policies affecting the financial sector, international trade, and public enterprises. The IMF makes its loans in **tranches**, or installments on the total loan, with each additional tranche of the loan dependent on the completion of a set of reform targets. For example, a loan recipient may be required to develop a plan for privatization in order to receive the first tranche, have a workable plan to receive the second tranche, begin implementation for the third tranche, and so on.

Often these types of reforms generate significant opposition since they seem to override national sovereignty and generally impose contractionary macroeconomic policies. Some economists argue that conditionality requirements intensify the recessionary tendencies of a crisis, although there is a debate over whether countries recover faster with IMF assistance than without it. Until the early 1990s, the IMF focused its efforts on economic policy reforms in a way that more or less ignored their social consequences. Public outcry against the effects of conditionality on the vulnerable members of societies forced a closer look at the social impacts of policies, and the IMF has tried to make adjustments. Even so, there are still widespread complaints that IMF conditionality is too punitive and too contractionary, and a few countries in crisis have refused IMF assistance.

Before the 1970s, IMF conditionality focused primarily on correcting the immediate source of the problem that led to a crisis, and it avoided involvement with underlying economic issues, such as trade policy and privatization. This approach was criticized as short-sighted, and it was agreed that the Fund should involve itself beyond short-run economic policy. New loan programs were developed to provide money and technical assistance to countries that needed help in restructuring their economies. This shift involved the IMF in far more than crisis resolution, as it took on an active role in assisting in privatization, the design of social policies, trade policy reform, agricultural policies, environmental policies, and a number of other areas.

By the late 1990s, there was growing recognition that "mission creep" had become a problem and that the Fund had taken on responsibilities for which it is not suited, such as economic development in the long run. Economic development issues are better left to the World Bank, regional development banks, or other multilateral agencies such as the UN Development Program or the UN Conference on Trade and Development. Several of the proposals for reforming the international financial architecture envision a reduced role for the IMF in this area.

Two additional issues are worth mentioning as part of the reforms of the international financial architecture. First is the issue of a set of standards for transparency and data reporting in the financial sector. The purpose of greater transparency is to make a country's financial standing clearer to potential lenders. The issue of transparency and data reporting is moving forward with the Basel Accords and the IMF's standards for data reporting, called the **data dissemination standards**.

The second issue is the need to find ways to coordinate private sector involvement in times of crisis. Less progress has been made on this issue than on the data dissemination issue, and it continues to be a serious concern. When a country reaches a crisis, the insistence by numerous private creditors that they be paid first can make it more difficult to resolve a crisis. Hence, proposals have been put forward for **standstills**, in which the IMF officially recognizes the need for a country in crisis to stop interest and principal repayments on its debt temporarily. This would also impose a burden on the country's creditors and reduce the moral hazard element in their lending practices.

Conflict between private creditors over who deserves first repayment has often been an obstacle to resolving a crisis. Consequently, many analysts see the need for **collective action clauses** in all international bond loans. A collective action clause would require each lender to agree to a collective mediation between all lenders and the debtor in the event of a crisis. This prevents an uncooperative creditor from blocking a solution agreed to by a majority of the lenders. It would also promote a quicker resolution to a crisis caused by a borrowing country's insolvency.

Reform Urgency

In the aftermath of the Asian crisis, many reform proposals were circulated among academics, government officials, and the staff of multilateral organizations. The crisis drove home the points that international financial flows had grown dramatically over the previous decades, that many developing countries are now active participants in world finance, and that contagion effects can instantaneously spread a crisis from one country or region to another. Reform, beginning with a reconsideration of the role of the IMF, was at the top of everyone's agenda.

A decade after the Asian crisis began, the world was enveloped in a much broader and potentially deeper crisis. Yet, as the Asian crisis faded in memory, the urgency for reform diminished and not much had happened by the time the crisis in the U.S. housing market exploded in 2007. Reform is difficult, and without the urgency of a crisis it proved to be impossible. A relatively stable world economy after 1998, and the rise of issues such as terrorism, energy prices, climate change, and security, crowded out the issue of international financial reform. With the onset of a global financial crisis in 2007 and its conversion into a deep recession across most of the globe, the topic is once again timely and in the news.

CASE STUDY

The Global Crisis of 2007

The most recent financial crisis began in the United States in the fall of 2007. The first visible stage was called the *subprime crisis* in reference to housing loans made in the United States to borrowers with less-than-prime credit ratings. Many of these borrowers proved unable to manage the housing payments they had taken on, and many of the loans turned out to have clauses that made payment financially impossible for homeowners who could not refinance their loans within a year or two. When home prices started falling, refinancing became difficult or impossible for homeowners who now owed more than their houses were worth.

Problems in the housing sector quickly spread through the banking sector and into other parts of the financial services industry, such as insurance companies and investment banks, that had bought mortgage-backed assets. This would have posed serious problems for the United States under any circumstances, but at this stage the problem became global. Three critical factors or preconditions turned a national, U.S. problem into a global one. First, the world's financial markets had undergone a relatively steady transformation over several decades with the development of new and innovative financial products. The financial services industry of 2007 did not look at all like the industry it was in the 1960s or 1970s. Second, financial markets had become much more integrated. Open capital markets and flexible exchange rates created new global flows of financial capital that were not possible in earlier decades. These larger and more integrated capital flows were augmented by high rates of savings in a number of emerging markets, such as China, that had played virtually no role in global finance before the 1980s or 1990s. Third, a spirit of deregulation had captured the thinking of many economists, politicians, and regulators. This permitted new forms of very risky finance to develop without close supervision, and without consideration for the fact that some of the new forms of finance posed risks not only for the individual financial institutions using them, but to the entire economic system as well.

By early 2008, the subprime crisis had spread beyond the United States. One of the causes of its rapid contagion was the high level of innovation that occurred over the previous several decades. In the 1970s and 1980s, banks accepted deposits, which they lent to borrowers who wanted to buy homes. Beginning in the 1980s and increasingly through the 1990s into the twenty-first century, banks and other "non-bank financial entities" such as car financing firms, consumer credit firms, insurance companies, and others began to enter the market. Their strategy was not to profit from the interest they earned on the home loans, but to group a large number of loans together and sell shares in the entire package. This is known as **securitization**. It can be done not only to

(continued)

home loans but also to car loans, consumer credit loans, and a wide variety of other types of debt. If you buy a share in the securitized package, you receive a return based on the interest that the ultimate borrowers—home owners, car owners, credit card owners, and so on—pay to their lenders. The company that creates the securitized package of loans can, in turn, sell shares to another bank, a foreign-based insurance company, a foreign government, or virtually anyone willing and able to buy. Needless to say, if homeowners in the United States cannot pay what they owe, the owners of shares in the securitized package lose money.

The growing integration of global finance meant that these new products could be sold just about anywhere and finance crossed international boundaries with increasing ease. Pension funds in Wisconsin bought products that originated in Iceland, city governments in Germany bought securities based on Southern California real estate, and Hungarian home owners took out loans in Swiss francs from Swiss banks. Housing markets in many developed countries experienced a boom—finance was easy to obtain, prices were going up, and demand for new homes, either to live in or as investments, continued to increase. In the United States, home prices rose nearly 90 percent between 2000 and 2006, and the U.K., Spain, and a number of other markets experienced increases as great or even greater. Increases in home prices fed on themselves as they pulled more finance into the housing market. The growing international integration of financial services meant that capital for home loans could be moved from one country to another, and that the United States, Spain, Ireland, and other locations where there were rapid increases in home prices could continue to borrow to purchase even more homes.

New innovations in financial products and the growing integration of capital markets challenged regulators to keep up. With the growth of computer modeling and the application of advanced mathematics, many new financial products are complicated beyond nearly everyone's ability to understand, including the regulators and the corporate heads and risk managers of the companies that created them. Few, if any, regulators in the United States or elsewhere expressed concern, however. As explained by Alan Greenspan, the ex-chairman of the U.S. Federal Reserve Bank, most regulators were persuaded that financial firms would self-regulate since it is not in their interest to lend to someone who will default on his or her loan. His perspective reflected a much more general view that close regulation of financial markets was not in the national interest since regulators were likely to impose limits that reduced efficiency while favoring the objectives of the regulators over the interests of market participants. The thought that the global financial system was at risk was inconceivable to all but a few analysts. Almost no one believed that the most advanced countries of the world could stumble into a crisis that would lead to the near collapse of their economies.

Financial innovation, global financial integration, and financial deregulation can explain a lot of what happened. They do not tell us, however, why the crisis began in 2007 rather than earlier or later. As with many other crises, it is impossible to pinpoint an event that triggered the onset. There is one more factor, however, that played a very significant role and without which it is unlikely that there would have been the housing boom or the crisis. This factor is the large global savings imbalances that built up in the world financial system over the course of the first decade of the twenty-first century. To explain this, we need to briefly return to the Asian crisis of 1997–1998.

The Asian crisis caused a reaction among many developing countries, both in Asia and elsewhere. The countries that suffered the greatest crisis were those that lacked sufficient dollars, euro, yen, and other international reserves to defend their national currencies. Their solution was to accumulate a large supply of international reserves by increasing their savings and running large current account surpluses that they could use to purchase dollars, U.S. Treasury securities, and other secure, highly liquid financial assets. Large and important countries such as China began to increase their holdings of dollars, mostly in the form of short-term bonds, both government and private. Due to the sheer size of these accumulations, they began to play an important role in international finance. The savings held by governments are called **sovereign wealth funds**, but private entities also increased their savings.

Globally, current account balances must total to zero. If China and other countries run large current account surpluses in order to accumulate international reserves, their balancing counterparts are large-deficit countries. The country with the largest current account deficit, both over time and in all recent years, is the United States. Table 12.3 shows the five largest surplus countries and the five largest deficit countries between 2000 and 2007. The first column of numbers is the surplus or deficit for 2007, while the second column is the cumulative surplus or deficit from 2000 through 2007. The table shows that there are mainly, but not only, two kinds of surplus countries: Asian exporters and oil producers. Germany is an outlier, but is also one of the world's largest exporters. While five countries is not a lot to generalize from, the pattern holds, with some exceptions, if we look at all countries of the world together.

The importance of large imbalances is that they were a supply of savings that became available globally to countries such as the United States, where households and businesses wanted to borrow in order to maintain higher levels of current consumption and investment. Without the savings of China, Japan, Germany, and the others borrowing in the United States, the United Kingdom, Spain, and elsewhere would have been much more expensive countries to live in, and the bubble in housing markets would have been less likely. As a result, we probably would not have seen the boom in house prices, low interest rates, and the easy lending that took place in the high-deficit countries. Global imbalances should be added to the other three elements that made the crisis possible. They all were important, but if we can consider innovation, integration, and regulation to be microeconomic factors, then global savings and investment imbalances were the primary macroeconomic factor.

(continued)

TABLE 12.3   Current Account Deficits, 2000–2007 (Billions of U.S.$)

Country	Current Account Balances	
	2007	Cumulative, 2000–2007
Surplus countries		
China	371.8	973.8
Germany	252.9	768.9
Japan	244.0	1,175.0
Saudi Arabia	95.1	399.7
Russia	76.2	460.0
Deficit countries		
United States	−731.2	−4,660.1
Spain	−145.4	−494.1
United Kingdom	−78.8	−393.8
Australia	−57.7	−245.7
Italy	−51.0	−180.4

Source: Data from *World Development Indicators*, World bank, © James Gerber.

The policy implications of the crisis will be analyzed and debated for years. Each of the elements described in this case study has generated a set of questions with multiple answers and no consensus. For example, financial innovation has brought many benefits to economies by providing more sources of capital for investment and consumption and new mechanisms for insuring against risk. Yet, some new instruments may increase systemic risk if they are not carefully used. Is all financial innovation a good thing? Financial market regulation could, in theory, provide oversight, but what kind of regulation and by whom? Global financial integration has increased efficiency, but are all forms of integration equally desirable? These and other questions await a clear set of answers.

Summary

- International financial crises are generally characterized by financial disintermediation in the crisis country, a collapsing currency value, and a steep recession.
- One type of crisis is caused by severe macroeconomic imbalances, such as large budget deficits, hyperinflation, overvalued real exchange rates, and large current account deficits.

- Another type of crisis is the result of a speculative attack on a currency that prompts large outflows of financial capital and a run on the country's international reserves. This type of crisis can be self-fulfilling because economic agents that believe an attack on the currency is imminent will abandon the currency, which is equivalent to an attack on the currency.

- The Mexican peso crisis of 1994–1995 had elements of both types of crises, as did the Asian crisis of 1997–1998. However, several countries in East Asia were subjected to speculative attacks on their currencies even though their underlying macroeconomic fundamentals were very strong.

- Responding to a crisis is complicated by the problem of moral hazard. If a government or the IMF bails out the banks and other firms hit by crisis, it may encourage future risky behavior. The problem of moral hazard is particularly acute if the government has directed credit to specific enterprises for political or developmental purposes because directed credit either explicitly or implicitly includes a government guarantee.

- The Basel Accords, including Basel III, are a set of recommendations for internationally active banks and financial enterprises. They cover the supervision and regulation of enterprises, minimum capital requirements, and standards for information disclosure.

- Many economists believe that crawling peg exchange rates make countries more vulnerable to a crisis because they become overvalued more easily and there is no smooth way to abandon them when a crisis begins to brew.

- Capital controls on capital outflows are generally viewed as ineffective in the long run, although there is some debate about their temporary efficacy in times of crisis. Capital controls on the inflow of short-term financial capital have more supporters, but there is no consensus on their efficacy in avoiding crisis. Some research shows that they can help a country avoid a small crisis, but are less effective at avoiding a large crisis.

- The optimal response to a crisis depends on its causes. If it is caused by macroeconomic imbalances, then changes in macroeconomic policies are essential. If it is caused by sudden, unexplained capital flight, then the optimal response is less certain. Some economists, particularly those at the IMF, argue that stabilizing the currency with high interest rates will lead to a quicker recovery, even though this intensifies the contractionary elements of the crisis in the short run. Others favor expansionary fiscal and monetary policies to minimize the short-run effects of a recession.

- Reform of the international financial architecture includes a re-evaluation of the role of the IMF and other international agencies. A few favor abolishing the IMF as a lender of last resort, while most favor keeping it but reconsidering some of its policies. In particular, questions have been raised about the interest rates it charges on its loans, the length of the loan period, and the limits on the size of loans.

- The most contentious element of IMF lending policies is conditionality. In particular, there is widespread agreement that the IMF tries to support too many different types of reform and that it should refocus on its core competencies, which include financial sector reform, balance of payments assistance, and exchange rate policies. There is some discussion about whether it should require countries to prequalify before they are eligible for its lending programs.

- Other issues in the international financial reform discussion include standards for data dissemination and policies to create greater involvement of private creditors in working out the solutions to international financial crises when they occur.

- The crisis that began in 2007, had three microeconomic components and one macroeconomic one. Financial innovation, global financial integration, and a regulatory philosophy of "hands-off" or *laissez faire* each played a role. The primary macroeconomic cause was the presence of large global imbalances between high-savings and high-spending nations.

Vocabulary

austerity	exchange rate crisis
banking crisis	financial crisis
Basel Accords	intermediation
capital controls	international financial architecture
capital requirements	lender of last resort
collective action clauses	moral hazard
conditionality	securitization
contagion effects	sovereign default
data dissemination standards	sovereign wealth funds
debt crisis	standstills
disintermediation	tranches

Study Questions

All problems are assignable in MyEconLab

12.1 What is an international financial crisis, and what are the two main causes?

12.2 In the text, the point is made that the expectation of a crisis from volatile capital flows is sometimes a self-fulfilling crisis. How can a crisis develop as the self-fulfillment of the expectation of a crisis?

12.3 What are three things countries can do to minimize the probability of being hit by a severe international financial crisis?

12.4 Why are crises associated with severe recessions? Specifically, what happens during an international financial crisis to create a recession in the affected country or countries?

12.5 What type of exchange rate is associated with a higher probability of experiencing a crisis? Why?

12.6 In a crisis not caused by macroeconomic imbalances, economists are uncertain whether a country should try to guard against recession or try to defend its currency. Why are these mutually exclusive, and what are the pros and cons of each alternative?

12.7 Explain the moral hazard problems inherent in responding to a crisis.

12.8 Some people argue that U.S. loans to Mexico in 1995 led to the Asian crisis. Explain the logic of this argument.

12.9 Some countries impose capital controls as a means of preventing a crisis. Evaluate the pros and cons of this policy.

12.10 How has the role of the IMF come under scrutiny in the recent discussion of reforms in the international financial architecture?

PART **4** The United States in the World Economy

Regional Issues in the Global Economy

CHAPTER 13

The United States in the World Economy

Learning Objectives

After studying this chapter, students will be able to:

13.1 Identify major changes in U.S. economic relations that have led to bilateral and plurilateral agreements.

13.2 Evaluate the relative importance of the North American Free Trade Agreement, both for what it accomplished and as a model for subsequent agreements.

13.3 Explain when purchasing power parity estimates of income per person are superior to the alternatives, and when they are inferior.

13.4 State the reasons why Mexico and Canada sought free trade with the United States.

13.5 Differentiate free trade agreements from preferential trade agreements and give examples of each.

13.6 State why it is difficult to have precise estimates of job gains and losses due to trade, and give specific examples of how imports may create jobs and exports may occur after a loss of jobs.

INTRODUCTION: A CHANGING WORLD ECONOMY

The relationship of the United States to the world economy is shaped by its size, its wealth, and its role as a military super power. It is endowed with a wide range of resources, including abundant and fertile farmland, a relatively well educated population, and a disproportionate share of the world's top research universities, Nobel Prize winners, and venture capital. It is the third most populous country after China and India, and has either the largest economy in the world, or the second largest after China, depending on how it is measured.

Throughout most of the post-World War II era, the United States used its size, wealth, and military power to foster a set of international economic relations that encouraged a multilateral approach to international trade and finance and economic support for low- and middle-income countries. It provided technical and military assistance and engaged in direct military intervention when it was deemed necessary. With the collapse of the Berlin Wall in 1989 and the dissolution of the Soviet Union in 1991, the bipolar world of two superpowers and two economic systems suddenly disappeared.

Simultaneously, the global economic landscape was undergoing profound changes from the successes of middle-income emerging markets and the shift toward more open trade policies around the world. The transition to capitalism of formerly socialist economies; the worldwide preference for more open trade relations; and the economic success of countries from Botswana in Africa, to Chile in Latin America, to China in Asia are reshaping the world economy and the role of the United States.

BACKGROUND AND CONTEXT

LO 13.1 Identify major changes in U.S. economic relations that have led to bilateral and plurilateral agreements.

Given its large economy and population, U.S. trade with the rest of the world has been a smaller share of its gross domestic product (GDP) than in most other developed economies. Nevertheless, over the last fifty years, the trade share of GDP has more than tripled. Figure 13.1 shows the long ascent of the trade-to-GDP ratio as it climbed from under 10 percent in the 1960s to around 30 percent after 2010. Within the long upward trend, there are several short-run downturns in the series, each of them during and after a recession (1974–1975, 1980–1982, 2001, 2007–2009). Recessions cause a fall in imports due to the decline in income, and exports fall as well if other countries are also in recession.

FIGURE 13.1   The Trade-to-GDP Ratio for the United States, 1966–2014

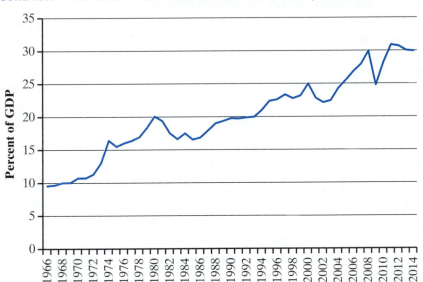

Over the last fifty years, trade in goods and services has more than tripled as a share of the U.S. GDP.

Source: Data from World bank, © James Gerber.

The top trading partners of the United States have not changed dramatically over the last several decades, with the major exception of China (Table 13.1). As recently as 1990, China was the eighth most important source of U.S. imports and the eighteenth most important market for U.S. exports. By 2007, it was the number one source of imports and the third most important export market. If the European Union (EU) is treated as one entity, then it moves into the second spot for both imports and exports, behind Canada (exports) and China (imports). The prominence of Canada and Mexico in Table 13.1 illustrates the relative importance of the North American Free Trade Agreement (NAFTA) partners, not only today, but over time as well, as both countries have been among the top five U.S. trade partners for several decades.

The goods and services that make up U.S. trade have not changed much either, although services have become more important. In 1980, services were approximately 20 percent of U.S. exports, and now they are close to 30 percent and continue to show strength, not the least of which is that they are an area in which the United States has a trade surplus. About 40 percent of service exports are travel and transportation services, while the remaining 60 percent are royalties, education, financial and insurance services, and business and professional services. Within the merchandise goods category (manufacturing, oil and minerals, and agricultural products), the United States is the world's second largest exporter of goods (behind China), and about three-fourths of those exports are manufactured goods, with the remaining one-fourth consisting of agricultural and mineral products, including oil and gas.

The Shifting Focus of U.S. Trade Relations

Throughout most of the post-World War II period, the United States was a strong supporter of multilateral trade opening as negotiated under the auspices of the General Agreement on Tariffs and Trade (GATT) trade rounds and then under the World Trade Organization (WTO). Support for open capital markets was less prominent until the 1980s, when it became another goal of U.S. policy. These positions were reinforced by the Cold War and the U.S. desire to ensure that developing nations joined the alliance of capitalist, democratic nations or, at a minimum, did not form strong ties with the Soviet Union.

TABLE 13.1   Leading U.S. Trade Partners, 1990 and 2015

	Top Five Trading Partners, in Order of Importance
Exports	
1990	Canada, Japan, Mexico, UK, and Germany
2015	Canada, Mexico, China, Japan, and UK
Imports	
1990	Canada, Japan, Mexico, Germany, and Taiwan
2015	China, Canada, Mexico, Japan, and Germany

Manufacturing in the United States

In what year did the United States produce its highest output of manufactured goods? When a large group is asked this question, the guesses range from the 1960s to the 1990s. The correct answer is usually "Last year." Figure 13.2 illustrates this by plotting on the left scale the real value added in manufacturing, 1950–2014. As the graph shows, there is a long-run upward trend in the value added of manufacturing output, which is interrupted by the occasional recession, most recently in 2007–2009.

The right scale shows manufacturing employment. Employment peaked in 1979 at 19,426,000 and began a long-run decline after that. In 1980, the United States entered a mild recession and then a more severe one in 1981–1982. Manufacturing employment recovered some of its losses in 1984 but continued its trend downward particularly after 2000.

Within the story of the growth of manufacturing output and manufacturing employment decline, there are two additional stories not directly shown in the graph. First, there is the story of manufacturing relocation within the United States. Traditional industrial states in the north central part of the United States, such as Ohio and Michigan, have seen many jobs leave for other parts of the country. Some jobs have gone overseas, but quite a few have also gone to Southern states such as South Carolina, Tennessee, and Texas. When

FIGURE 13.2   Real Value Added and Employment in Manufacturing, 1950–2014

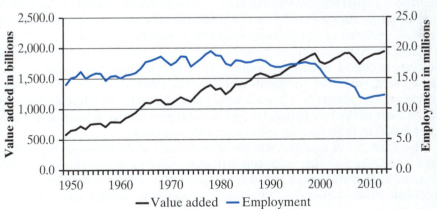

Since the late 1970s, manufacturing employment has declined, while manufacturing output has constantly risen except during recessions.

Source: U.S. Bureau of Economic Analysis; U.S. Bureau of Labor Statistics

(continued)

coupled with the overall decline in the total number of jobs, the plight of older manufacturing states has been grim. This has also contributed to the mistaken perception that the United States no longer has a vibrant manufacturing sector, but the story of Figure 13.2 is that the United States continues to produce a large and growing quantity of manufactured goods.

The second story is the rapid increase in productivity in the manufacturing sector. Fewer workers but more output means that each worker is producing more, and output per hour worked in manufacturing has increased at a very rapid rate. This has occurred in part through the application of new technologies and new processes, and while productivity growth speeds up and slows down, it is usually much more rapid in manufacturing than in services or agriculture. Hence, even as the United States produces more manufactured goods, fewer workers are involved.

Several factors have caused shifts in this stance. First, multilateral trade negotiations became more complicated as the GATT and then the WTO added new members. When the GATT was originally signed in 1947, it had twenty-three members, but by the time of the Uruguay Round (1986–1994), there were 128 signatories to the GATT. Currently there are 162 member countries in the WTO. The increase in membership has dramatically complicated negotiations.

Second, many quotas have been converted to tariffs, and tariffs in general have fallen dramatically (see Figure 6.4). Consequently, the new multilateral trade negotiations in the Doha Round are focused on much more difficult issues such as agricultural support systems, intellectual property, services trade, government procurement, and assistance for developing countries. These areas pose significant challenges, in part because they are not easily represented as reciprocal openings. If all countries cut their tariffs by 5 or 10 percent, it is easy to see a mutual gain; but if all countries agree to enforce intellectual property rights on an equal basis, it is hard to see the immediate benefits for countries with little or no intellectual property to defend. In addition, many of these new areas of negotiation are concerned with issues that are deeply embedded in national politics. For example, creating a level playing field in government procurement so that foreign firms can bid on contracts let by a national or sub-national government arouses resentment when domestic firms lose out in bidding to foreign ones.

Third, the end of the Cold War has removed one of the pressures that caused the United States to offer trade concessions to other countries. During the Cold War, the United States used access to its market as an incentive to keep countries from developing deeper ties to the Soviet Union. It frequently agreed to asymmetric opening of its markets without demanding equal access to foreign markets when the country in question was perceived to have geostrategic value in the Cold War. The United States also used its systems of quotas to reward nations for their cooperation by allowing them to sell more in the United States, particularly in the textile and apparel sectors, but also in agriculture. The demise of the USSR removed this need to compromise or to offer asymmetric access to the U.S. market.

These three factors have shifted the U.S. focus toward greater use of bilateral and plurilateral trade agreements. The United States is still supportive of the WTO and officially welcomes a successful conclusion of the Doha Round of negotiations that began in 2001, but multilateral agreements are no longer the only or even necessarily the main option. The movement toward bilateral solutions began in earnest in 1993 with the signing of the NAFTA and its implementation on January 1, 1994. While valuable in its own right, NAFTA also served the purpose of helping to push the multilateral system toward conclusion of the Uruguay Round of the GATT agreement by expanding trade policy to include bilateral agreements. This gave the United States additional leverage in multilateral negotiations, as it signaled that there are options beyond the GATT/WTO framework. In addition, from the perspective of the United States and many other countries that have signed a growing number of trade agreements, working within a bilateral or plurilateral framework entails easier negotiations than in the multilateral case and has the additional benefit of serving as a testing ground for new types of agreements. For example, the NAFTA agreement was the first to include labor and environmental standards.

The United States currently has free trade agreements (FTA) in force with twenty countries grouped into three strategic geographical regions: the Middle East and North Africa, the Pacific Basin, and the Americas. Most agreements are with small countries that account for a small share of U.S. merchandise trade, but Canada, Mexico, and Korea are major exceptions. Table 13.2 shows the agreements in force, their dates of implementation, and the total amount of merchandise goods traded in 2015.

The final two rows of Table 13.2 summarize size and relative importance of merchandise exports with free trade areas. Free Trade Agreement (FTA) countries are around 47 percent of U.S. exports and approximately 34 percent of imports. Proponents of FTAs make the argument that U.S. markets are relatively more open than many foreign markets. Given the relative openness of the U.S. market, bilateral and plurilateral FTAs that help open foreign markets promote U.S. exports relatively more than U.S. imports instead of causing a proportional increase in both. Consequently, U.S. exports to FTA partners are a larger share of total merchandise trade than U.S. imports from FTA partners.

This interpretation of Table 13.2 supports the idea that FTAs have been relatively good for the U.S. insofar as they have helped to open foreign markets. Similarly, many other countries have shifted toward signing bilateral and plurilateral agreements. Prior to 1990, twenty-seven FTAs were notified to the GATT. In the 1990s, another fifty-five were created, but since 2000, 217 agreements have been registered with the WTO. Some economists see the upsurge of bilateral and plurilateral agreements as one of the principal causes for the erosion of the Doha Round of the WTO, because they have diverted political attention toward bilateral or regional concerns and away from global ones. Theoretically, FTAs can be "stumbling blocks" that detract from multilateral agreements or "building blocks" that create more trade than they divert and that enable countries to try new types of agreements. The WTO has concluded that in practice, most are complementary to the multilateral trading system and not substitutes for it.

THE NAFTA MODEL

LO 13.2   **Evaluate the relative importance of the North American Free Trade Agreement, both for what it accomplished and as a model for subsequent agreements.**

LO 13.3   **Explain when purchasing power parity estimates of income per person are superior to the alternatives, and when they are inferior.**

LO 13.4   **State the reasons why Mexico and Canada sought free trade with the United States.**

Table 13.2 does not single out trade flows between the three NAFTA countries. Nevertheless, United States trade with Mexico and Canada, is a very large and important part of the country's overall trade, constituting 27 percent of U.S. exports and 24 percent of imports. Given NAFTA's importance, both in terms of the volume of trade and as a model that set the pattern for subsequent trade agreements, it is useful to look at it in more detail. We begin with some background on Canada and Mexico.

Demographic and Economic Characteristics of North America

Table 13.3 gives an idea of the size of the NAFTA region. Income per capita is measured in two ways: in U.S. dollars converted from Canadian dollars and Mexican pesos at market exchange rates, and in dollars measured in terms of

TABLE 13.2   Free-Trade Agreements and Merchandise Goods Trade, 2015

Regions and Countries	Exports (Millions)	Imports (Millions)
Middle East and North Africa		
Israel (1985), Bahrain (2006), Morocco (2006), Oman (2009), Jordan (2010)	20,176	28,764
Trans-Pacific		
Singapore (2004), Australia (2005), Korea (2012)	97,193	100,925
Americas		
Canada (1989), Mexico (1994), Chile (2004), Dominican Republic-Guatemala-Honduras-El Salvador-Nicaragua-Costa Rica (DR-CAFTA, 2006) Peru (2009), Panama (2011), Colombia (2012)	594,033	642,079
Total merchandise trade with FTAs	711,402	771,768
Share of total merchandise trade (%)	47.3	34.4

TABLE 13.3   Population and GDP for the NAFTA Region, 2015

Country	Population (Millions)	GDP (US$, Billions)	GDP per Capita (US$)	GDP per Capita (PPP)
Canada	35.8	1,552.4	43,332	45,553
Mexico	127.0	1,144.3	9,009	17,534
United States	321.6	17,947.0	55,805	55,805
Total	484.4	20,643.7	42,614	45,013

The NAFTA market is more than 484 million people and over 20.6 trillion in GDP.

Source: Data from International Monetary Fund, © James Gerber.

purchasing power parity (PPP). The PPP adjustment enables us to know internal purchasing power, which is defined as the amount an average income can buy inside the country where the income is earned when it is measured in terms of the cost of a similar basket in the United States. Income per capita at market exchange rates is the external purchasing power of an average income. The differences between internal and external purchasing power are more easily understood with an example. Looking at Table 13.3, an average Mexican income can buy goods and services in Mexico that would have a value of $17,534 in the United States. This is the internal purchasing power of an average Mexican income. The external purchasing power is $9,009, which is the value of the goods and services an average income can buy if it is spent in the United States. The numbers tell us that on average, goods and services cost more in the United States than in Mexico. The PPP concept adjusts for that fact and lets us make international comparisons of income based on similarly priced baskets of goods and services.

The PPP adjustment is necessary in order to compare actual living standards, while the market exchange rates income is useful to know something about the ability of people to buy goods and services in the world economy. The two numbers are not equal because exchange rates are rarely in long-run equilibrium and because non-traded goods vary in price across national boundaries. For example, labor-intensive goods and services are inherently less expensive in Mexico where there is a relatively abundant supply of unskilled and semi-skilled labor.

As shown in Table 13.3, the NAFTA region has more than 484 million people (2015) and over $20 trillion in combined GDP. This makes it slightly smaller in population than the 28 nations and 507 million people that make up the EU, and slightly larger than the EU's estimated 2015 combined GDP of US $16.2 trillion. With an average NAFTA-region GDP per capita (at market exchange rates) of over $42,000, it is a wealthy region by any standard.

Canada–U.S. Trade Relations

The United States and Canada have the largest bilateral trade relationship of any two countries in the world, with two-way merchandise goods and services trade in 2015 of more than $671 billion. This large sum is due to a shared border, a common historical background, and a similar culture, but it is also the result of three stages of integration over the last four and one-half decades. Beginning with the **Auto Pact** of 1965, followed by the **Canada-U.S. Free Trade Agreement (CUSTA)** in 1989, and the NAFTA agreement in 1994, Canada and the United States have taken advantage of their proximity to foster a set of mutually beneficial trade ties that focus on natural resources and intra-industry trade, particularly in the auto sector.

The Auto Pact of 1965 removed barriers to trade that previously forced the major U.S. firms to set up separate plants in Canada where they were unable to capture the full economies of scale essential to the car industry. By combining their production in the United States with their Canadian plants, General Motors, Chrysler, and Ford were able to produce for a single combined market. Before the agreement, Canadian plants produced solely for the Canadian market; after the agreement was implemented, they were suddenly more productive, as they could specialize in particular car models and increase their production runs to serve both the United States and the Canadian markets. Trade in both directions increased substantially, and productivity levels in Canadian plants, which were 30 percent below U.S. levels, rose dramatically.

By the 1980s, the car industry was integrated, but several new problems became apparent. Both the United States and Canada began to feel the rise of emerging markets in Asia, and Japan's inroads into the U.S. auto market, steel, and consumer electronics were troubling as this seemed to indicate a loss of competitiveness in many U.S. and Canadian firms. Furthermore, the United States began to use antidumping and countervailing duties more often along with a new set of quotas administered under voluntary export restraint (VER) agreements. The latter were not voluntary in practice but worked the same as quotas in limiting foreign imports to a set level. The most important affected industry was the Japanese car market.

From the perspective of Canada's leadership, growing U.S. protectionism and rising Asian manufacturing competitiveness were troubling signs because Canada is very dependent on the United States as an export market and as a source of imports. One solution to these pressures was to create FTA with the United States. This solution locked the United States into an international agreement that required it to keep its market open and, at the same time, put pressure on Canadian manufacturers to make changes to become more competitive.

The CUSTA was ratified in 1988 and implemented in 1989. CUSTA's impacts were more or less as expected. Between 1989 and 1994, Canadian exports to the United States grew 55 percent ($47 billion increase), while U.S. exports to Canada grew 46.6 percent ($36.5 billion increase). In percentage terms this growth is not quite as rapid as the period before and after the implementation of the Auto Pact, but given that trade was already at a high level in 1987, a 50 percent increase represents an enormous volume of trade.

The debate over U.S.–Canadian free trade was low key and dispassionate in the United States. In Canada, however, a heated public discussion erupted when it was announced that the United States and Canada were negotiating an agreement. The opponents of the trade agreement feared that (1) Canada might not be able to compete with U.S. firms, which had the advantages of economies of scale; (2) expanded trade might force Canada to jettison many of its social programs; and (3) Canadian culture might come to be dominated by the U.S. news, information, arts, and entertainment industries.

The issue of Canadian competitiveness was largely one about the need to gain economies of scale and to increase productivity through organizational or technological changes within firms. For the most part, the real issue for a high-income, industrialized country such as Canada is the length of time over which the changes can be expected to occur, and not whether firms are capable of competing.

The Canadian opponents of CUSTA also argued that it would erode Canada's social programs. For many citizens, Canada's more extensive social programs, such as universal health care and more developed income maintenance programs, are part of a national identity that make Canada unlike the United States. The opponents of CUSTA argued that the intensification of competition with the United States would undermine these social programs and dilute the difference between the two countries. They reasoned that social programs would be cut in order to reduce business taxes and make Canadian firms more competitive. Given that taxes are one component of business costs, and that in some cases, there are offsetting reductions in cost elsewhere, and it was incorrect to view a trade agreement with the United States as a threat to social programs. In the case of health care, for example, it makes more sense to argue that the United States' system is at a competitive disadvantage, because the cost of hiring workers is raised when they must be provided with health care benefits by their employer. In Canada, by contrast, health care coverage is universal and is paid for out of general government revenues and individual taxes.

The final and most contentious issue from the Canadian point of view was the possibility of U.S. cultural domination. A very wide spectrum of opinion, including both opponents and proponents of expanded free trade, argues that the combination of Canada's smaller population and its proximity to the United States will destroy its national identity if it allows completely free trade in the cultural industries. These industries include music in all of its venues, as well as radio, television, newspapers, publishing, magazines, drama, cinema, and painting. Under the rules of CUSTA, Canada is allowed to protect its national identity by imposing quantitative restrictions on imports of "cultural products." In most cases, the rules allow Canada to impose domestic content requirements on television, radio, and theater. For example, the content requirements make it illegal for a radio or TV station to play content originating in the United States twenty-four hours a day. Cable TV companies give preferences to Canadian-based TV networks, and there are national rules that favor Canadian theater companies, artists, and writers.

Mexican Economic Reforms

From the 1950s until the onset of a crisis in 1982, Mexican per capita growth averaged 3.3 percent per year in real terms, an impressive record that doubled living standards approximately every generation. This long boom in Mexico's growth occurred under a set of trade policies called **import substitution industrialization (ISI)** that target the development of manufacturing through support for industries that produce goods that substitute for imports. As the leading economic development strategy throughout much of the world from the end of World War II until the mid-1980s, ISI policies prescribed industrial policies for goods production, beginning with simple consumer goods such as food and beverage, textiles and apparel, furniture, and footwear; and advancing through more complex consumer goods such as household appliances; and into industrial goods such as generators, pumps, and conveyors. This was to be followed by the development of more sophisticated industrial goods as countries moved up the ladder of comparative advantage, gaining manufacturing experience and changing their endowment of capital and labor skills. The tools employed by ISI policy included industrial support policies of tax breaks, low-interest loans, subsidies, occasional nationalization, and high protectionist barriers.

A major weakness of ISI policies is that they discriminate against exports. They do this by raising the rate of return for firms that produce for the domestic market where they have high protectionist walls and can charge higher prices while facing little or no competition. This also hurt Mexico and other ISI economies in the long run because it reduced the incentive to innovate or make product improvements, given that there was limited competition. With higher rates of return in the production of import substitutes, labor and capital were drawn out of the export sectors and into production for the domestic market. Consequently, when a decade of poor macroeconomic management in the 1970s came to a head in the 1980s, Mexico found itself deeply in debt and with limited capacity to export.

The **debt crisis** that began in Mexico in August 1982 was the result of a series of factors. From Mexico, the debt crisis quickly spread to the rest of Latin America, where similar policies had resulted in poor macroeconomic management and the accumulation of a large amount of debt. This period came to be known as the **Lost Decade** and is discussed in more detail in Chapter 16 on Latin America. In Mexico, as in most countries, the underlying causes of the debt crisis were heavy borrowing from foreign banks, weak tax systems, and rising world interest rates that made debt service more expensive. Mexico had discovered new oil fields in the 1970s, and borrowing was encouraged by the belief that the price of oil would rise forever and along with it, the country's ability to service ever-increasing amounts of debt. When oil prices began to fall in the early 1980s, the Mexican government's oil revenue began to decline, just as its interest payments on the money it had borrowed were going up. These factors were intensified in their impacts on the Mexican economy by the fact that several decades of ISI policies had weakened the export sector (other than oil, which received special treatment). Weak export performance reduced the capacity to earn dollars that might be used to make payments on foreign debt. By August 1982, Mexico had exhausted its reserves of foreign currency and could no longer pay its debts. This triggered the onset of the debt crisis, which ultimately dragged on from 1982 until 1989.

The solution to the debt crisis required multiple policy changes. In the 1980s, Mexico privatized many firms that had been drains on the federal budget (938 were privatized between 1982 and 1992), brought its federal budget under control, reduced its restrictions on foreign direct investment in the country, and began to open its market to greater competition. In 1986, Mexico joined the GATT and in 1989, President Carlos Salinas proposed an FTA with the United States. Salinas had two goals in mind. First, he wanted to solidify his reforms in an international agreement. Before the political reforms that occurred in the late 1990s, Mexican presidents were granted extensive autonomy and authority. A more protectionist president could very well overturn the reforms that he and his predecessor (Miguel de la Madrid) had implemented; but if they were embedded in an international agreement, it would be much harder. Second, Salinas wanted to attract more foreign capital to increase the low domestic savings in Mexico. More foreign investment in Mexico would spur growth, while greater access to the large U.S. market would be an incentive for investors to build manufacturing plants in Mexico.

The North American Free Trade Agreement

NAFTA was ratified in 1993 and took effect on January 1, 1994. Trade flows increased significantly, but they had been growing before implementation, partly in anticipation of an agreement.

The first important feature of NAFTA is that most forms of trade barriers came down. Because the United States and Canada were relatively open economies with few trade barriers, most of the change came on the Mexican side. For example, between 1993 and 1996, average U.S. tariffs on Mexican goods fell from 2.07 to 0.65 percent. By contrast, Mexican tariffs on U.S. goods fell from 10 to 2.9 percent. These reductions in tariffs under NAFTA were a continuation of the reduction in trade barriers that began in the mid-1980s. Between 1982 and 1992, the percentage of Mexico's imports that required import licenses from the government declined from 100 to 11 percent, and tariffs fell from an average level of 27 to 13.1 percent. By 1994, Mexico's economy was substantially open to the world.

Some tariffs and investment restrictions on each country's cross border investment were eliminated immediately, but in many cases there was a variable period of phasing out tariffs and investment restrictions. The phase-out period for these remaining tariffs and investment restrictions varied from sector to sector. In cases where there was expected to be significant new competition, industries were given a longer period to prepare themselves because each country wants to avoid a sudden disruption of its economy even as it wants gains from trade.

A second feature of NAFTA is that it specifies North American content requirements for goods subject to free trade. To qualify for free trade or the reduced tariff provisions of the agreement, a specified percentage (usually 50 percent) of the value of the good must be made in North America. The purpose of local content requirements is to prevent non-NAFTA countries from using low tariffs in one NAFTA country to gain access to all three. Most trade economists dislike these provisions because they increase the likelihood of trade diversion. Production of inputs in lower-cost, nonmember countries could be reduced if firms move their operations to NAFTA countries in order to meet the content requirements—as happened in the apparel industry, for example. Firms moved from the Caribbean to Mexico, even though Mexico was not the lowest-cost producer. Mexico's exports to the United States paid zero tariffs, so goods produced there could sell for less than goods produced in lower-cost countries and subject to high tariffs when entering the United States. Nevertheless, content requirements were politically necessary in order to pass the agreement in Canada and the United States.

A third feature of NAFTA is that it set up three separate dispute resolution mechanisms, depending on the source of the disagreement. Individual chapters cover disputes related to dumping and anti-dumping duties; treatment of foreign investors by national policies, called **investor-state disputes**; and a third dispute resolution mechanism for general disputes. Each of these areas is separate from the consultation mechanisms for disputes over labor and environmental standards, which are a fourth significant feature of the agreement. NAFTA itself did not contain language regarding labor and environmental standards or concerns, but two side agreements were ratified and implemented at the same time as the trade agreement. These are the **North American Agreement on Labor Cooperation** and the **North American Agreement on Environmental Cooperation**. The labor and environmental side agreements, along with the investor-state dispute resolution mechanism, have served as frameworks for most of the subsequent FTAs negotiated by the United States. Each of these has its supporters and its detractors and will be considered in more detail in the following discussion of the new trade agreements signed by the United States.

Two NAFTA-Specific Issues

A number of highly contentious issues arose during the NAFTA debate, as alluded to in the previous section. Some of the issues are specific to NAFTA, and some apply to all or nearly all trade agreements. Labor and environmental standards, relations between foreign investors and national governments, and intellectual property rights enforcement are general controversies, but they are also issues where NAFTA has served as a model for the design of trade agreements with other nations (Table 13.2). These issues are discussed later in the chapter. Two specific issues that pose significant barriers to NAFTA's deepening are immigration and the ongoing drug violence in Mexico.

NAFTA did not provide any guidance on immigration policy. Because it is a free trade area and not a common market, there is no provision for the movement of labor, except some categories of business people, nor is there any discussion of such a provision. In most contexts, a free trade area without immigration provisions is the norm, but in the context of U.S.–Mexico relations, it is a problem. Over the last four decades, the flow from Mexico has been the largest wave of immigration from a single country to the United States in U.S. history. Mexican migrants in the United States numbered more than 11.7 million in 2014 and were 28 percent of all immigrants. Researchers estimate that just over one-half of the Mexican immigrant population is unauthorized to be in the United States. Migrants go to the United States for the usual reasons: jobs, income, and family reunification. They also leave Mexico for the United States for specific reasons: proximity, the 2,000-mile-long border that is impossible to close completely, and a lack of jobs and opportunity in their home country.

The unprecedented wave of migration has declined dramatically in recent years, as more Mexicans leave the United States than arrive. This trend began around 2005 or 2006 and has at least three factors behind it. One, the border has become harder and more dangerous to cross. Much of it is desert wilderness with extremely rugged conditions that are made more severe by the growth of drug violence and the targeting of migrants by criminal gangs and drug cartels. Two, the political and economic environment of the United States is more difficult. Jobs are harder to find since the recession of 2007–2009, and throughout the border region, anti-immigrant groups and politicians have created an aggressively unwelcoming political environment. Three, and most significant for the long term, the demography of Mexico is changing in ways that are reducing the number of potential migrants. In 1960, the average Mexican woman could expect to have 7.3 children during her lifetime. By 2009, the number had fallen to 2.4, barely above population replacement levels. The decline in childbirths leads, with a lag, to a decline in the growth rate of the young adult population and the number of potential migrants. In sum, between 2005 and 2010, the number of people born in Mexico and living in the United States did not increase, as new entrants fell to the same level as the number leaving the country.

A second issue of grave concern in the NAFTA region is the rise in drug violence in Mexico. This is a very contentious and tragic issue with no consensus on needed policy changes, but with a continuing loss of life, mostly in Mexico and mostly related to the violence of transporting and selling illegal drugs. This issue has far more than trade implications because it concerns law enforcement, medicine, public health, economic well-being, civil liberties, and other areas. Currently and for many years past, both in Mexico and the United States, the discourse is dominated by politics. In 1969, President Nixon declared a "national war on drugs," and nearly fifty years later, similar policies are in place, even as it is hard to show positive results from the war and as many tens of thousands of people have been murdered as a result of drug-related violence.

The violence in Mexico is a shared responsibility of the United States and Mexico because U.S. demand for illegal drugs generates the enormous profits for drug cartels that are used to corrupt Mexican judges, politicians, and police forces. There is no consensus on the solution to this dilemma. Classical arguments for legalization assert that making drugs illegal only forces them underground, where they are still available and provide profits to organized crime and incentives to use violence to settle disputes. Legalization proponents point to the problems of corruption, health and safety issues, and challenges to civil liberties as additional negative spillovers from the attempts by the authorities to enforce the laws. Counter-arguments are that addiction is likely to increase if drugs become more available or that it is immoral to condone drug usage by making it legal. While there is very little agreement, politicians in Mexico and the rest of Latin America are beginning to vocally challenge the U.S. lead in the war on drugs and have begun calling for new strategies—particularly ones that focus on demand reduction and the public health aspects of drugs instead of focusing solely on supply elimination.

CASE STUDY

Ejidos, Agriculture, and NAFTA in Mexico

The majority of Mexico's farmers work on a type of collective farm called **ejidos**. Ejido members can farm their individual pieces of land as independent farmers, planting whatever crops they choose, and their children can inherit the land, but they cannot sell the land and they cannot rent it out to someone else. In theory, they either farm it or lose it. The first ejidos were created about a decade after the Mexican Revolution (1910–1917) and continued to be formed until the constitutional reforms of 1992. Mexico's constitution put limits on the amount of land one person could own and gave landless agricultural laborers the right to petition the government for the excess land. The 1992 reforms stopped the creation of new ejidos and created a process for breaking up existing ones by turning them into private landholdings. The reforms do not require change, and most ejidos continue to operate the same as they did before the reforms, although some have been privatized and the land has been sold. At the same time that the government opened an avenue for buying and selling ejido lands, it cut many of the subsidies it had given to small farmers. In the long run, changes in the level of subsidies for small farmers have been more important than the new markets for ejido lands—and not always for the best.

According to the Mexican Census of Agriculture, in 2007 there were 31,518 ejidos, with 4,210,899 members (including people living on the communal lands of indigenous communities). This is approximately 72–73 percent of the labor force in agriculture in Mexico. On average, ejido farmers tend to own less valuable lands, have smaller individual plots of land than more commercially oriented farms, and produce a disproportionately small share of the nation's agricultural output. This is not to say that all ejido farmers are poor, but many of them lack access to markets, to capital, and to technical knowledge that would allow the members to earn a decent living.

In 1992, Mexico rewrote the section of its constitution that allowed for the creation of ejidos. The administration of Mexico's president, Carlos Salinas, argued that ejidos created disincentives for investment in agriculture, which kept productivity low and contributed to rural poverty. Some economists shared this view, but others were not so certain. The argument of the reformers was that the lack of complete ownership rights and ejidos' small plot sizes inhibited the use of machinery and other productivity-enhancing investments. Regardless of the analytical correctness or incorrectness of the causes of low productivity on ejidos, the vast majority of Mexico's poor people lived in rural areas and worked in agriculture, often as members of an ejido. In 1992, about 25 percent of the labor force was in agriculture, but it produced only 9 percent of GDP. One explicit purpose of the change in subsidies for small farmers and in ownership rights of ejido members was to reduce the size of the agricultural labor force by creating incentives to combine land holdings and to apply modern production technologies. In 1992, the undersecretary of agriculture stated that the goal was to reduce the share of labor in agriculture from 25 percent of the labor force to 15 percent.

Eighteen years later, in 2010, 13.1 percent of the labor force was in agriculture (compared to less than 2 percent in the United States and Canada). The highest levels of poverty continue to be concentrated in rural areas, and small-scale agriculture continues to struggle even as larger, more modern and productive farms do well. NAFTA opponents frequently blame the trade agreement for the difficult conditions on many ejidos and small farms, but Mexican agricultural policy plays a far larger role. Corn shows why. Corn is a dietary staple for many Mexicans and the main crop on many small farms. Under NAFTA, Mexico's import duties on corn were scheduled to be phased out over a fifteen-year period, but Mexico unilaterally cut tariffs ahead of schedule and increased imports from the United States, in part to lower the price of corn for animal feed, increase the size of the country's livestock herds, and expand the amount of animal protein in the diet of the average Mexican citizen. Mexico's larger and more commercial farmers expanded their corn production along with the growth in imports, and the total amount produced nationally increased. Nevertheless, small-scale farmers who operated at near-subsistence levels of production were badly hurt by this strategy because it lowered corn prices at the same point in time that the government cut subsidies to small farmers.

NAFTA allows each country to subsidize its farms as little or as much as it chooses. Mexico provided approximately US $8.4 billion in farm supports (subsidies) in 2014, but much of this went to farmers who were relatively better off. That level of subsidies is equal to 13.3 percent of the gross receipts of farmers. By way of comparison, in the United States, farm subsidies are 9.8 percent of farm receipts (see Table 7.3), according to the *Agricultural Outlook* of the Organization for Economic Co-operation and Development (OECD). The decision to downsize the agricultural sector was independent of the decision to sign a trade agreement with the United States and Canada, and clearly it did not take into account the plight of farmers who have few options other than a small plot of corn.

NEW AND OLD AGREEMENTS

LO 13.5 **Differentiate free trade agreements from preferential trade agreements and give examples of each.**

LO 13.6 **State why it is difficult to have precise estimates of job gains and losses due to trade, and give specific examples of how imports may create jobs and exports may occur after a loss of jobs.**

Table 13.2 shows the recent trade agreements, along with some older ones, that are in force. The United States is negotiating two additional agreements of some importance and has put into place a series of unilateral agreements that provide market access without demanding reciprocation, called **preferential agreements**. This type of agreement is enacted to support the development efforts of a set of countries, or for a specific political reason. Table 13.4 lists the two key FTAs that are still in negotiation as well as the preferential agreements in place.

The two FTAs listed in Table 13.4, particularly the Asia Pacific Economic Cooperation (APEC) economic forum, include a large number of countries.

TABLE 13.4   Key Trade Initiatives of the United States

Free Trade Agreements	Members	Goals
Trans-Pacific Partnership (TPP)	12	Free trade
Asia-Pacific Economic Cooperation (APEC)	21	Free trade in theory, but in practice an economic forum for addressing issues of concern
Transatlantic Trade and Investment Partnership (T-TIP)	29	Trade and investment liberalization

Preferential Agreements	Beneficiaries	Purpose
Generalized System of Preferences (GSP) (1976)	122	Duty-free access for many goods from 122 low- and middle-income countries
Caribbean Basin Initiative (CBI) (1983)	17	Duty-free access for most goods from 17 Caribbean nations
African Growth and Opportunity Act (AGOA) (2000)	39	Duty-free access for most goods from 40 sub-Saharan countries; eligibility varies with political conditions

The United States continues to seek new trade and investment agreements while unilaterally offering enhanced market access to many low- and middle-income countries.

Source: Office of the United States Trade Representative.

APEC spans the Pacific, from north to south and east to west, and includes some of the largest economies in the world, including China, Japan, South Korea, Mexico, Canada, and Australia. It differs from other FTAs in that it is not directed at creating an FTA among its members, but rather seeks to create free trade for all, members and nonmembers, within the Asia-Pacific region. In its original goals, it set 2010 as a target date for free trade for all its industrial economy members, and 2020 for the developing economies. The first target date was not met and has been scaled back as APEC has become a forum for discussing trade issues of concern. In part, it was lack of progress in APEC that caused the United States to join with a subset of APEC countries to pursue a FTA in the form of the Trans-Pacific Partnership (TPP).

In the agreements completed (Table 13.2) under negotiation, similar issues arise over and over. These include labor and environmental standards, investment, and job loss.

Labor and Environmental Standards

In nearly all the trade agreements signed since NAFTA (1994), the labor and environmental side agreements (North American Agreement on Labor Cooperation and North American Agreement on Environmental Cooperation) have served as a framework for adding labor and environmental clauses. The key principles of the labor and environmental side agreements to the NAFTA are that countries should enforce their own laws and that low or poorly enforced labor and environmental standards should not be used to attract trade or investment. Enforcement, for the most part, relies on consultations with parties levying a complaint of nonenforcement, and investigation by the home country government. The wording of the agreements is very specific and states that no investigation or enforcement may be performed by one country in the territory of another. Instead, the agreements attempt to create public awareness of noncompliance without setting specific standards or encroaching on the sovereignty of national governments.

In the newest of the proposed agreements, the Trans-Pacific Partnership, labor standards are part of the agreement, with a dispute resolution process and the possibility for imposing trade sanctions such as tariffs when standards are not met. The content of the labor standards reflect the core principles of the International Labour Organization's (ILO) Declaration on Fundamental Principles and Rights at Work and its follow-up (see Chapter 8):

1. Freedom of association and the effective recognition of the right to collective bargaining.
2. The elimination of all forms of forced or compulsory labor.
3. The effective abolition of child labor.
4. The elimination of discrimination with respect to employment and occupation.

The TPP is not the first agreement to incorporate labor standards directly rather than as a side agreement, but it is the first to offer the possibility of trade sanctions as a remedy for noncompliance and it is the first to specify the content of labor standards rather than leaving it up to individual countries to set their own standards. Note, however, that the specific content is rather general, and consequently, it would be incorrect to assume that standards are harmonized. For example, worker health and safety regulations, wages, and hours of work, will undoubtedly vary greatly across the members of the proposed TPP.

The environmental side agreement of the NAFTA established the framework for incorporating environmental clauses into subsequent FTAs. In many respects, it is parallel to the labor clause and is motivated by similar concerns that low environmental standards not be used to gain competitive advantages. As noted in Chapter 8, it is unrealistic to expect environmental standards, clean-up preferences, or resource commitments to be identical in countries with different income levels. Whereas some countries may prioritize the reduction of greenhouse gases, others may still be struggling to provide access to clean drinking water. The marginal benefits of one priority over another depend on the level of income and the state of the environment in each place. Consequently, the goal of the environmental side agreement to the NAFTA was, like the labor side agreement, to ensure that countries enforced their own laws and that they did not use low standards or poorly enforced standards as a means to attract investment or to lower costs of production.

The proposed TPP does not harmonize environmental standards. Rather it focuses on the enforcement of a number of international agreements, such as agreements on wildlife trafficking, protection of endangered species, and others, while also eliminating some subsidies to fishermen that have led to over-fishing. As with labor standards, its primary emphasis is on enforcement of each country's own standards, along with recognition of a number of multilateral commitments all countries have made, or must make.

Critics of the labor and environmental clauses come in two forms. Some economists think that trade agreements should not be about labor and the environment, and so these clauses do not belong in trade agreements. They think that including these clauses gives support to protectionists who will inevitably oppose increased trade flows by making arguments, whether based on fact or not, that the trade partner does not enforce its laws adequately. Another set of economists argue that the clauses are meaningless because there is no real enforcement mechanism. Countries are left to their own devices to determine whether laws are adequately enforced, and there is no clear consequence of nonenforcement.

These criticisms have resulted in the new approach that is being tried with the proposed TPP. The chief negotiator for the United States, called the U.S. Trade Representative (USTR), has insisted that basic labor standards be incorporated into the agreement and that countries must recognize and enforce environmental standards that have multilateral support, such as rules on wildlife trafficking and protection of endangered species. In addition, for the first time, trade sanctions would be allowed as a way to enforce standards.

It is fairly certain that NAFTA would not have been ratified by Congress without the inclusion of the labor and environment side agreements as a package deal. Members of Congress were nervous about the potential for jobs to migrate south, and they worried that Mexico's weaker enforcement of labor and environmental laws could be used to gain competitiveness. Since then, the strategy of including labor and environmental chapters directly in the trade agreements has helped gain Congressional support and has become the standard strategy for ensuring passage of new agreements. Whether the new approach of specifying in more detail the content of the standards and allowing for the possibility of trade sanctions as a punishment for noncompliance will help gain passage of the proposed TPP remains to be seen. Undoubtedly, any future agreement will have something similar.

Investor-State Relations

A majority of the FTAs in force have chapters on investment. In addition, the United States has forty-two **bilateral investment treaties (BIT)** with countries across the globe. These agreements, like the FTA chapters on investment, set out the rules governing cross-border investment, including the options for dispute resolution when an investor thinks they have been treated unfairly. The rules are set within a framework emphasizing national treatment for foreign investors with the intention of eliminating all distinctions between national and foreign investors. The rules also eliminate the use of most performance requirements for foreign investment (e.g., export requirement or local content use) and guarantee a uniform set of regulatory standards for foreign and domestic firms. As transportation and communication improvements have enabled more businesses to offshore some of their production processes, U.S. trade policy has sought to address the concerns they have about investing abroad. In a very general sense, the goal of these agreements is to create a higher level of certainty for investors with respect to their property rights if they invest in a country that has an agreement with the United States.

Again, NAFTA set a framework for investor-state rules by creating a dispute settlement process specifically for investors from one NAFTA country that invest in another NAFTA country. Chapter 11 of NAFTA sets out the rules, and is perhaps the most controversial part of the agreement. Specifically, Article 1110 states:

"No Party may directly or indirectly nationalize or expropriate an investment of an investor of another Party in its territory or *take a measure tantamount to nationalization or expropriation* of such an investment. . . ." (emphasis added)[*]

except for public purpose, on a nondiscriminatory basis, and with compensation. Critics of the NAFTA argue that undermines the sovereignty of nations by allowing private enterprises to sue governments that are seeking to protect their workers or their environment, or that implement regulations that they believe to be in the public interest. Since then, FTAs and BITs have introduced language referring

---

[*]NAFTA, Organization of American States

to "indirect nationalization" and added clauses to the effect that nothing in the agreement shall be interpreted to mean that environmental or other standards may not be upheld or implemented if they protect the public interest.

Critics of these agreements argue that the asymmetry between the United States and many developing countries necessarily creates an unlevel playing field in which U.S. corporations with extensive resources can bully developing countries' governments with the threat of lawsuits if they attempt to raise their regulatory standards. Again, the proposed TPP attempts to overcome the objections of critics by explicitly stating that nothing in the agreement can be interpreted as a limitation on the ability of countries to impose regulations to protect public health and safety or environmental quality.

Jobs and Trade Agreements

There are quite a few estimates of the job gains or losses caused by NAFTA and other trade agreements. Within five years of NAFTA's implementation, the estimates ranged from a net loss of 98,000 a year to a net gain of 42,000 a year. It is possible to estimate the number of workers needed to produce a given quantity of exports, and to estimate the number of jobs that would be created if imports were produced at home, but these values are not the same as job creation and destruction due to a trade agreement. For example, imports may supply a firm with capital or intermediate goods that make the firm more competitive and better able to survive; and exports may supply a foreign affiliate that has been recently off-shored by the home country firm. Hence, some imports create jobs, while some exports exist only because jobs at home have been moved abroad. Given these conceptual difficulties, actual estimates of the number of jobs gained or lost are closer to guesses. In addition, pro-trade think-tanks and scholars usually show job gains, while anti-trade think-tanks show job losses. In either case, however, neither side of the debate can show large job gains or losses in the United States due to trade agreements. Given that the United States creates more than 2 million net new jobs in an average (nonrecession) year, most estimates of job losses or gains due to the trade agreement are well below 5 percent of the measured total change.

Figure 13.3 illustrates this point by plotting gross job gains and gross job losses in the U.S. economy from March 1994, through March 2015. The values on the vertical axis are in thousands, making 8,000 equivalent to 8,000 thousand, or 8 million. Figures are annual totals, measured from March to March. Job gains include new establishments or expansions in existing ones, while job losses include layoffs and establishment closings. Whenever job losses exceed job gains, there is net job loss, and vice versa when gains are greater. First, note that the two major episodes of job losses are during the recessions of 2001 and 2007–2009. Second, the period immediately after the implementation of NAFTA is not one with net job losses, but on the contrary, corresponds to a period of strong net job gains. That does not prove that NAFTA created jobs, but it does show that if there were job losses, they were substantially outweighed by other factors, including the strong economic growth of the second half of the 1990s. The most important point of

FIGURE 13.3   **Gross Job Gains and Losses, 1994–2015**

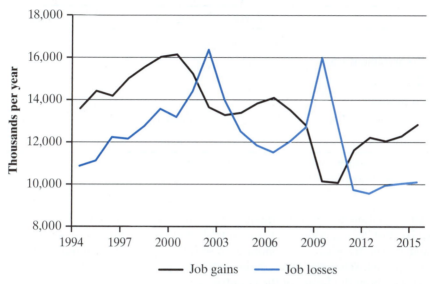

— Job gains   — Job losses

The U.S. economy creates between 10 and 16 million new jobs (gross) each year, while it loses slightly fewer in normal, nonrecession, years.

Source: Bureau of Labor Statistics

Figure 13.3 is that the U.S. economy is larger than most people realize and that it is very dynamic.

A second point that has often been overlooked in the evaluation of NAFTA and other trade agreements is that the United States has much less unbalanced trade with the countries that have signed FTAs. Table 13.5 shows U.S. merchandise exports, imports, and deficits for FTA countries and the rest of the world. Merchandise goods trade balances are much more favorable when countries sign an FTA because U.S. markets are already relatively open and tariff barriers are low, with the exceptions outlined in Chapter 7. When countries enter into an FTA, the required elimination of trade barriers is usually much greater outside the United States than it is inside. As foreign barriers decline, U.S. exports expand.

Anti-trade rhetoric usually assumes that trade deficits are encouraged by trade agreements, yet the data show otherwise. Anti-trade arguments also often assume that mercantilism is correct in its assertion that imports are harmful while exports are beneficial. Yet, consumers have more choices and businesses more competitive when they have access to imports. Nevertheless, it is important to try to understand the sources of anti-trade rhetoric. If FTAs are not the problem and if imports are beneficial, then why do so many people in the United States view international trade as harmful? There is no easy answer to this question and economists have not been able to reach a consensus as to the causes of anti-trade sentiments in the wider public. It may be partially related to the loss of manufacturing jobs, or to

TABLE 13.5   US Merchandise Goods Exports, Imports, and Deficits

	Exports	Imports	Deficits
FTAs			
Total (billions US$)	711.4	771.8	−60.6
Share (%)	47.3	34.4	8.2
Rest of world			
Total (billions US$)	793.2	1,469.9	−676.7
Share (%)	52.7	65.6	91.8

U.S. trade deficits are much smaller with countries that sign FTAs.

Source: See Table 13.2.

wage stagnation and growing inequality, or to the complaints of a vocal minority that has lost its livelihood as a result of trade and investment abroad. As Chapters 3 and 4 show, trade causes economies to shift their production and some workers are displaced. Whatever their causes, anti-trade perspectives reflect a deep set of concerns about the future of the country.

CASE STUDY

The African Growth and Opportunity Act

Preferential trade agreements cover a variety of schemes that admit imports either tariff free or with a reduced tariff. Most high-income countries and some developing countries use these schemes to support low- and middle-income countries by letting their goods bypass the normal tariff barriers. The most common scheme is called the **Generalized System of Preferences (GSP)**. The United States implemented the GSP in 1976 and currently offers tariff-free access to its market for a large percentage of goods coming from 122 developing countries.

In addition to the GSP, the United States offers two other preferential agreements: the **Caribbean Basin Initiative (CBI)**, and the **African Growth and Opportunity Act (AGOA)** (Table 13.4). Goods not covered under the GSP are covered in these additional preference schemes, although none of them cover all exports by the beneficiary countries. Each of these agreements has a political or economic objective. The CBI was implemented to diversify Caribbean exports and strengthen growth during a time of political unrest, guerilla warfare, and rising socialist parties in Central America and the AGOA is intended to promote export diversification and economic development in sub-Saharan Africa.

AGOA is the most recent of the agreements. Signed into U.S. law in 2000, it currently covers thirty-nine countries in sub-Saharan Africa and is the primary trade-promotion initiative of the U.S. government for Africa. It provides duty-free entry for 5,200 products, covering about 86 percent of products that the U.S. imports. Countries that qualify for duty-free access to the U.S. market under the AGOA include some of the poorest nations of sub-Saharan Africa, many with per capita incomes under $1,000 per person per year. The goal of the U.S. in offering enhanced market access on a unilateral basis is to encourage export diversification and promotion as a catalyst for economic development.

Duty-free access to the U.S. market is a significant benefit for sub-Saharan Africa and a few countries have taken advantage of the opportunity to increase exports, particularly in the automotive sector (car parts) and the relatively highly protected apparel sector. In spite of a few successes, more than one-half of all AGOA designated countries export less than $1 million in goods to the United States, and many of those with significant exports mostly sell oil, the most common export. The difficulties associated with diversifying out of oil are limited by two factors. First, a few goods that are sensitive to the United States are excluded. These are primarily agricultural products and include some key sectors. For example, cotton is an important product in several countries (see the case study on losing comparative advantage in Chapter 3), as are the excluded items peanuts and sugar. Secondly, distance matters, as it leads to higher transportation costs and less competitive pricing. Western African nations are not so far from the United States, given cheap ocean transportation, but East Africa is another matter. Furthermore, the disadvantage of distance is compounded for fourteen sub-Saharan African nations that are landlocked without direct access to the sea. (Africa has more landlocked nations than any other continent.)

As noted above, AGOA exports have grown since the implementation of the preferential scheme. Ideally, export growth would show a diversified set of manufactured goods and agricultural products, representing robust economic performance and new opportunities for these sub-Saharan nations. Yet, most of the growth has been in oil exports. Increased exploration and new discoveries have led to significant increases in oil exports to the United States from Angola, Chad, Equatorial Guinea, Gabon, and Nigeria. In 2015, 35.8 percent of U.S. imports from AGOA countries were oil and related products.

Summary

- The end of the Cold War and the rise of emerging markets have shifted U.S. efforts toward more bilateral and plurilateral trade agreements.
- Canada is the United States' closest ally and most important trading partner for reasons of language, cultural heritage, and proximity. Trade rela-

tions with Canada have developed through successive waves of agreements, beginning with the Auto Pact in 1965 and expanding through the Canada-United States Free Trade agreement in 1989 and the North American Free Trade Agreement in 1994.

- Mexico is the third most important trading partner with the United States, after Canada and China. Mexico's President Salinas proposed an FTA with the United States as a way to lock in his economic reforms and as a way to attract foreign capital for investment.

- NAFTA is the most important trade agreement for all three countries, with a much greater volume of trade than any other bilateral or plurilateral agreement signed by Canada, Mexico, or the United States.

- Canada sought protection for its cultural industries when it signed CUSTA, and Canadians debated the likely impact on their social policies. In the United States, CUSTA was not a topic of debate.

- The most contentious issues in the United States related to the signing of the NAFTA agreement were those of labor policy, environmental policy and enforcement, and migration.

- To date, the main impact of NAFTA has been to continue an ongoing trend toward increased trade. It is impossible to accurately measure the effects of NAFTA on jobs and wages, but most economists estimate a small, positive effect on job creation.

- NAFTA has served as a model for other trade agreements, particularly with the inclusion of labor and environmental clauses.

- The United States has signed FTAs with twenty countries (seventeen since 2000) and has negotiated forty-two bilateral investment agreements covering the rules for investment by foreigners. The purpose of the investment agreements is to create more secure property rights and to encourage foreign direct investment. In addition, it has created four preferential trade agreements worldwide and is negotiating two larger free trade areas in the Pacific region.

Vocabulary

African Growth and Opportunity Act (AGOA)

Auto Pact

bilateral investment treaty (BIT)

Canadian-U.S. Trade Agreement (CUSTA)

Caribbean Basin Initiative (CBI)

debt crisis

ejido

Generalized System of Preferences (GSP)

import substitution industrialization (ISI)

investor-state dispute

Lost Decade

North American Agreement on
Environmental Cooperation

North American Agreement on
Labor Cooperation

preferential agreements

purchasing power parity

Study Questions

All problems are assignable in MyEconLab.

13.1 What factors caused the United States to shift its focus from a more multi-lateral approach to a more bilateral and plurilateral one?

13.2 How has the trade-to-GDP ratio changed for the United States over the last several decades?

13.3 Why is the trade-to-GDP ratio for Canada greater than that for the United States?

13.4 Explain how an increase in U.S. and Canadian intraindustry trade altered the level of productivity in the affected Canadian sector.

13.5 What were Canada's motives for proposing and signing the Canadian–U.S. Free Trade Agreement?

13.6 What were the forces at work in the Mexican economy that led to the market reforms and market opening of the mid-1980s?

13.7 What were Mexico's motives for proposing and signing the NAFTA?

13.8 In what areas are there NAFTA side agreements? Discuss the pros and cons of these agreements.

13.9 Why has Mexican migration to the United States slowed?

13.10 What are preferential agreements and why are they used by the United States?

13.11 Explain why claims about job creation and job destruction due to NAFTA are likely to be misleading and inaccurate.

13.12 Explain how NAFTA served as a model for subsequent trade agreements.

CHAPTER 14

The European Union: Many Markets into One

Learning Objectives

After studying this chapter, students will be able to:

14.1 Describe the major institutions and treaty agreements of the EU.

14.2 Distinguish EU widening from EU deepening.

14.3 Explain the obstacles to regional integration agreements.

14.4 Give the economic rationale for each of the three waves of deepening of the EU.

14.5 State two theories as to why the single currency moved forward so quickly.

14.6 Analyze the EU's single currency program within the theoretical framework of an optimal currency area.

INTRODUCTION: THE EUROPEAN UNION

The **European Union (EU)** is an economic union of twenty-eight nations with over 500 million citizens and $16,220 billion in output. It is the largest, oldest, and most integrated of regional agreements. It helped put an end to over a century of wars on the European continent, and its incorporation of new members from Central Europe has reintegrated several countries whose historical and cultural ties to Western Europe had been cut. There are many lessons to be learned from the struggle of the EU to expand and deepen the economic ties of its member nations.

Since its inception in 1957, the EU has grown in numbers and increased the scope of its responsibilities. Originally, the EU was called the **European Economic Community (EEC),** membership was limited to six countries, and economic ties did not go beyond the formation of a free trade area. By the late 1960s, they had become a customs union and in the early 1970s, the EEC began to add new members. In 1979, the nine members of what was then called the **European Community (EC)** linked their exchange rates in a system designed to eliminate wide fluctuations among currencies. In the 1980s, the EC added three new members, making the total twelve countries, and in 1987 they signed the **Single European Act (SEA)** which signaled the creation of a common market. In 1992, the members signed the **Treaty on European Union,** which changed the name of the European Community to the European Union (EU) and led directly to the creation of the common currency, the euro, in 1999. Since 2004, thirteen new members have joined, including three newly independent nations that were part of the former Soviet Union, two countries that were formerly part of Yugoslavia, and seven ex-socialist countries in Central Europe.

None of these changes have been easy, and the problems of the single currency threaten to unravel many of the economic and political gains. In implementing the various integration initiatives, the member states have been forced to act pragmatically as internal and external events forced changes. The shift from fixed

European Union

Lambert Equal Area Projection

0   500   1000 Miles

Pearson Education

to floating exchange rates in the 1970s and 1980s, the fall of the Berlin Wall in 1989, the collapse of communism, the integration of world capital markets, the rise of environmental awareness, and the pressures on the single currency have shaped the EU's development. As economic and political changes have led to new arrangements and new responsibilities for EU institutions, the goal of a peaceful and integrated Europe has stayed on track. In this regard, the EU is a truly remarkable achievement, particularly when one considers the bloody history of twentieth-century Europe and the low expectations of most observers when the original documents were signed in 1957.

The EU is the most ambitious integration agreement in the world today. It has its own revenue and budget, a set of institutions for making laws and regulating areas of common interest, a common currency, and freedom of movement for people, money, goods, and services. Despite this profound integration, it has managed to protect the sovereignty of its member states and to avoid homogenization of cultures and linguistic regions. Indeed, integration in the larger sphere of nation-states has enabled a number of historical national identities to re-emerge and to claim greater autonomy in their political systems. Examples include the Catalans of Spain and the Welsh and Scots of the United Kingdom.

THE SIZE OF THE EUROPEAN MARKET

Before discussing the history or economics of economic integration in Western Europe, let us define the nations and groups that are important to get an idea of the size of the market. In terms of population, the EU is the largest integrated market in the world. By implication, the EU could play a major role in determining future international political arrangements, trade patterns and rules, and international economic relations in general.

Table 14.1 lists the members of the EU and their populations and incomes in 2015. Total gross domestic product (GDP) is given in dollars at market exchange rates, and in per capita terms at purchasing power parity equivalents. Several features of Table 14.1 are worth highlighting. First, not all Western European nations are members. Norway, which voted against joining in 1970 and 1995, and Switzerland are noticeably absent, along with a number of smaller Western European nations, including Iceland, Liechtenstein, San Marino, and Monaco. Second, the majority of nations in the EU are relatively small. The unification of Germany in the early 1990s created the largest country in the EU, but only six of the twenty-seven nations (France, Germany, Italy, Spain, Poland, and the United Kingdom) can be considered large, and none are as populous as the United States or Mexico. Third, the combined EU market is very similar to the size of the NAFTA market in terms of population and GDP. In 2015, the EU counted 507 million people, while the NAFTA nations counted 484

TABLE 14.1   Population and Income in the European Union, 2015

	Population	GDP (US$, Billions)	Average GDP per Capita (US$ PPP)
Original members (6)			
Belgium, France, Germany, Italy, Luxembourg, Netherlands	235.8	8,845	42,581
Entered 1973–1995 (9)			
Austria, Denmark, Finland, Greece, Ireland, Portugal, Spain, Sweden, United Kingdom*	166.9	6,073	38,878
Entered 2004–present (13)			
Bulgaria, Croatia, Cyprus, Czech Republic, Estonia, Hungary, Latvia, Lithuania, Malta, Poland, Romania, Slovak Republic, Slovenia	104.7	1,302	25,563
Totals (28)	507.4	16,220	37,852

* On June 23, 2016, the UK voted to exit the EU. The process of leaving will take two years and involve a wide range of negotiations to determine future relations between the UK and the EU.

The twenty-eight members of the European Union have income and population totals comparable to the NAFTA region.

Source: Data from International Monetary Fund, © James Gerber.

million; GDP comparisons were $16,220 billion in the EU and $20,643 billion in NAFTA.

THE EUROPEAN UNION AND ITS PREDECESSORS

LO 14.1 **Describe the major institutions and treaty agreements of the EU.**

The EEC was born on March 25, 1957, with the signing of the **Treaty of Rome** by the original six members. The treaty went into effect about nine months later, on January 1, 1958. The treaty remains the fundamental agreement, while more recent agreements, such as the Single European Act and the Treaty on European Union, also called the *Maastricht Treaty,* were passed as amendments to the original treaty. The six founding members include the Benelux countries (Belgium, Netherlands, and Luxembourg), France, West Germany, and Italy.

The Treaty of Rome

The EEC grew out of the reconstruction of Europe at the end of World War II. The goals of the founders of the EEC were to rebuild their destroyed economies and to prevent the destruction from happening again. The original vision of the founders of the EEC was for a political union that they hoped to create through economic integration. In 1950, Robert Schuman, the foreign minister of France, proposed an integration of European coal and steel industries. Coal and steel were chosen because they were large industrial activities that served as the backbone of military strength. Schuman's plan was to pool the industries of Germany and France, the two largest Western European antagonists, but Luxembourg, Belgium, the Netherlands, and Italy signed on as well. The **European Coal and Steel Community (ECSC)** Treaty was signed in 1951, and coal and steel trade between the six members grew by 129 percent in the first five years of the treaty.

The success of the ECSC led to early attempts at integration in political and military areas, but these efforts failed for political reasons. At that point, European leaders decided to focus their efforts on economic integration. In 1955, the six foreign ministers of the ECSC countries launched a round of talks to discuss the creation of the European Economic Community and **European Atomic Energy Community (EAEC or Euratom)**. The goal of the former was to create a single, integrated market for goods, services, labor, and capital. The latter sought jointly to develop nuclear energy for peaceful purposes. Two separate treaties were signed in 1957 in Rome, creating the EEC and Euratom.

Institutional Structure

The founders of the EEC debated the terms of their political affiliation. The key issue was and remains the degree of authority and power to grant the European institutions, and how much to reserve for national states. Officially, the EU is not a federation of states or provinces such as the United States or Canada, but a unique union of independent states that collaborate on transnational issues while maintaining sovereign authority on others.

In EU jargon, **subsidiarity** describes the relationship between national and EU areas of authority, and between national and EU institutions. Subsidiarity is the principle that the union will only have authority to tackle issues that are more effectively handled through international action than by individual nations acting alone. In some cases, these issues are easily defined, but in others they are not. Currently, the EU is responsible for trade policy, competition policy, environmental policy, regional development, research and technology development, and economic and monetary union. Areas that are less settled and more controversial include social policy—such as the social safety net and health care—and labor market policy—such as rules regarding working hours, safety, vacations, and wage rates.

There are three main governing bodies in the EU and several additional key institutions. The three governing bodies are the **European Commission**, the **Council of the European Union**, and the **European Parliament**. These three institutions represent the citizens of the EU and form the backbone of EU governance.

Table 14.2 shows the number of votes in each, as well as the range of votes granted the various countries, depending on their size.

EU Institutions and Finance   The executive body of the EU is the European Commission. Each country has one vote in the commission. The Commission elects one of its own members to serve as its president. The Commission's primary responsibility is to act as the guardian of the treaties, ensuring that they are faithfully and legally enforced. This role includes responsibility for creating the rules for implementing treaty articles and for EU budget appropriations. As the executive branch, the Commission has the sole right to initiate EU laws and the same right as the national governments to submit proposals.

The Council of the European Union is the primary legislative branch of the EU, a responsibility it shares with the European Parliament. Each country has between three (Malta) and twenty-nine (France, Germany, Italy, and the United Kingdom) votes. The Council enacts laws proposed by the commission and has more control over the budget than the Parliament or the commission. Its membership consists of ministers from each nation, with participation varying according to the topic under discussion. For example, labor ministers convene to discuss labor issues, and environmental ministers to discuss environmental legislation. Most legislative decisions require either unanimity among all countries or a **qualified majority**, which is at least 55 percent of countries (sixteen of twenty-eight) representing at least 65 percent of total EU population. (In addition to the Council of the European Union, the heads of state of EU countries, together with the president of the European Commission and the EU's foreign minister, comprise a similar sounding but different institution, known as the European Council. They usually meet four times a year to set the political direction of the EU.)

The European Parliament has 751 members, directly elected by the people for five-year terms and apportioned among the member states according to population. Members associate by political affiliation rather than national origin. The Parliament's three main responsibilities are the passing of laws (together with the Council), supervising other EU institutions, and passing the final budget. EU laws are usually a co-decision of the Council and Parliament, although the Council alone may make laws in certain areas. Passage of the annual budget of the EU requires approval of the Parliament. Over time, the role of the Parliament has probably changed more than that of any other institution. In its early years it was

TABLE 14.2   Votes in the Main EU Institutions

	Votes per Country		
	Total Votes	Minimum	Maximum
European Commission	28	1	1
Council of the European Union	352	3	29
European Parliament	751	6	96

primarily an advisory body with little real authority, but as the EU has grown it has taken on more authority.

The total budget of the EU in 2014 was €142.6 billion (approximately $156 billion) in commitments. This amounts to less than 1 percent of the gross national income of the member states—a very small amount of revenue by comparison to that of national governments that have total revenue equivalent to 30 to 50 percent or more of the nation's gross national income. The budget is financed by tariffs on goods entering the EU, an EU share of national value added taxes, and a payment from each member country based on the size of its economy. The last category is by far the largest, accounting for more than 70 percent of the total revenue collected by the EU.

The two largest expenditure categories of the EU are for agricultural support—both direct payments in the form of subsidies and indirect payments in the form of rural development—and **cohesion funds**. Agricultural support and rural development programs take approximately 43 percent of the budget. The other main category, cohesion funds, are used to support less developed regions within the EU, and are approximately one-half of the total budget. Economic support is given via funding for infrastructure development, including environmental projects such as water treatment and transportation projects.

DEEPENING AND WIDENING THE COMMUNITY IN THE 1970s AND 1980s

LO 14.2   Distinguish EU widening from EU deepening.

When Europeans speak of increasing the level of cooperation between member countries, they use the term *deepening*. Deepening refers to economic and noneconomic activities that cause increased levels of integration of the national economies. For example, the movement from a free market to a customs union, the harmonization of technical standards in industry, and the development of a common currency are deepening activities that increase interactions between the member states. On the other hand, when Europeans speak about extending the boundaries of the EU to include new members, they use the term *widening*. Between 1957, when the agreement was signed to create the EEC, and 1995, nine new members were added, bringing the total from six original members to fifteen. Since 2004, thirteen more members have been added. In the next section of this chapter we will look at the various stages of deepening.

Before the Euro

In 1979, the members of the EC began to link their currencies in an effort to prevent radical fluctuation in currency values. The EC wanted to prevent competitive devaluations, in which one country devalues in order to capture the export markets of another country. **Competitive devaluations** inevitably generate conflict and lead to a breakdown in cooperation, because the devaluing country is viewed as gaining exports and jobs at the expense of others. Nations sometimes find it difficult to resist devaluation, especially during recessions. This tactic is viewed as unfair, however, and in the medium to long term, it is usually ineffective because the nondevaluing countries are obliged to follow suit and retaliate with their own devaluations.

In addition to looking for a mechanism that might discourage competitive devaluations, the EC sought to remove some of the uncertainty and risk from trading and investing across national boundaries. While forward markets can be used to protect against exchange rate risk, they work only about six months into the future.

The goal was to create an environment in which trade and investment throughout the EC were determined by considerations of comparative advantage and efficient resource allocation rather than by changes in exchange rates. The result was the **European Monetary System (EMS)** and the **exchange rate mechanism (ERM)**. The formation of the EMS in 1979 was a significant deepening of the EC and served to prepare the way for the eventual introduction of a single currency. It was designed to prevent extreme currency fluctuations by tying each currency's value to the weighted average of the others. The group average, the **European currency unit (ECU)**, was used as a unit of account, but not as a means of payment.

The ERM is an example of a soft peg with an exchange rate band. Each currency in the band was fixed to the ECU, but was allowed to fluctuate several percentage points up or down. If a currency began to move out of the bandwidth, the central bank of the country was obligated to intervene by either buying its currency to prop it up, or by selling currency to push it down. In September 1992, for example, the United Kingdom spent an estimated $30 billion in just a few days of buying British pounds in a failed attempt to protect the currency from market speculators convinced that it was going to fall in value.

Given the ineffectiveness of market intervention in the face of a strong and determined market movement, most analysts predicted that the ERM would fail as a mechanism for maintaining stable European currency values. To most economists' surprise, the ERM effectively linked EC exchange rates for two decades. The ERM experienced several adjustments, but none of them threatened the functioning of the system until 1992.

Problems began in 1990 with Germany's decision to speed up its reunification with the German Democratic Republic (East Germany) after the fall of the Berlin Wall in November 1989. Economic conditions in East Germany were worse than expected, and it was soon apparent that the costs of building a productive economy would be enormous. Public infrastructure (roads, bridges, ports, utilities, schools, hospitals) was in worse shape than most people realized, and environmental pollution was significant. To build a prosperous economy in its eastern region, Germany had to raise the productivity levels of the people living there by making large investments in infrastructure and the environment. The unexpectedly large expenditures to raise the productivity of East Germany resulted in a very large fiscal stimulus to the German economy. Such large expenditures by both the government and private sectors were also expected to have an inflationary impact, and the Bundesbank (Germany's central bank) acted to counteract the increased probability of future inflation by raising interest rates. Germany, therefore, had an expansionary fiscal policy that was partially offset by a contractionary monetary policy.

High interest rates in Germany made German financial instruments more attractive and caused capital to flow into Germany from the other EC countries. This resulted in the selling of British pounds, French francs, and other currencies to buy German marks (and then German bonds) and caused the pound, the franc, and other currencies to fall in value. At first, the movement was within the 2.25 percent bandwidth, and most of the EC hoped that they would somehow muddle through without making any drastic changes in the ERM or the EMS.

One solution would have been for the countries with falling currencies to raise their interest rates to match Germany's. This would have stemmed the outflow of financial capital looking for better rates of return in Germany. Some of the countries—the United Kingdom, for example—were entering recessions in 1990 and 1991 and did not want to raise interest rates just as a recession was taking hold. Other countries—France, for example—were not yet entering the recessionary phase of their business cycle, but they had very high unemployment rates, and contractionary monetary policy was not desirable.

The dilemma faced by the EC countries is a good example of a recurring theme in the history of exchange rate systems. By tying their exchange rates to each other, the EC countries gave up a large measure of independence in their monetary policies. Because Germany was the largest country and the one with the most influential Central Bank, its monetary policy set the tone for the rest of the EC, and, at a time when many of the members wanted expansionary monetary policy, they were forced to adopt contractionary policies. The 1992 episode illustrates the recurrent tension between the appropriate external policies (exchange rate management) and the appropriate internal policies (full employment, reasonable growth, low inflation) when nations peg their exchange rates. Because the "right" policy choice for meeting the exchange rate problem was diametrically opposite to meeting the needs of the internal economy, EC members were left with a tough decision. They would have to honor their commitments to the ERM and make their unemployment and growth rates worse, or do the right thing for internal growth and watch the ERM fall apart. In the French case, an interest rate increase threw the country into recession, but France remained within the ERM. In Italy and the United Kingdom, the ERM was abandoned, and their currencies were allowed to freely float against other EC currencies. A third option was chosen by Spain, where the parity, or center of the band, was shifted. To lessen the probability of future repeats of this problem, the bandwidth everywhere was widened in 1993 from ± 2.25 percent to ± 15 percent.

THE SECOND WAVE OF DEEPENING: THE SINGLE EUROPEAN ACT

LO 14.3   Explain the obstacles to regional integration agreements.

Other than the creation of the EMS in 1979, the changes in the EC were minor through the 1970s and the first half of the 1980s. Low growth rates and high unemployment caused the European economies to appear stagnant and incapable of new dynamism; many in the United States began to refer to the European situation as "Eurosclerosis," signifying a permanent hardening of the arteries of commerce and industry. By the late 1980s, "Eurosclerosis" had turned into "Europhoria." While both terms were exaggerations, dramatic events had reshaped the EC in the intervening years. What was previously dismissed in the early 1980s as a hopeless case of bureaucratic inefficiency was now regarded as a dynamic, forward-looking, integrated regional economy. Europe seemed to be "on the move."

CASE STUDY

The Schengen Agreement

The Schengen Agreement was signed by five countries (Belgium, France, Germany, Luxembourg, and the Netherlands) in the town of Schengen, Luxembourg, in 1985. The purpose of the agreement was to eliminate all passport and customs controls at the common borders of the five nations. Given that they enjoyed free trade, and given the flow of people between the countries, the purpose of examining passports or checking customs paperwork seemed inefficient and unnecessary. Over the next few years, more members of the EU joined the agreement. When the SEA was implemented, the idea of a common market allowing free movement of people gave it added logic. By 1995, the agreement was extended to more countries and more areas of activity, including cooperation among police forces, drug enforcement agencies, and the sharing of criminal justice information. Originally, the Schengen Agreement and its subsequent extension were outside the legal framework of the EU, but in 1999, it was incorporated into EU law. Eventually non-EU countries, among them Switzerland, Lichtenstein, Iceland, and Norway, were allowed to participate.

The dismantling of border-control stations, including passport and customs inspections, undoubtedly has had a positive effect on EU efficiency because it reduces travel time for both goods and people. It also demonstrates a high degree of social trust among the member nations and contributes to goodwill and better relations. In effect, it shifts customs and passport controls to the perimeter of the EU, where non-EU citizens and goods first enter the region. While this is beneficial, several problems have arisen from the shifting of control to the perimeter.

First, Ireland and the United Kingdom have not accepted the dismantling of passport controls at the border because they fear the freedom of movement this will give terrorists. However, as members of the EU, they must extend the rights of all other EU citizens to travel freely and reside inside their borders, even as they maintain passport checks at the border. Second, the eventual extension of the Schengen Agreement to the thirteen new members since 2004 depends on those members' ability to demonstrate control over their own borders to the east, and on the development of a new EU data system for sharing information about individuals and lost or stolen objects.

(continued)

Countries on the eastern and southern peripheries of the EU have been severely challenged by the revolutions, wars, and crises in North Africa and the Middle East. Syrian, Somali, Libyan, Iraqi, and other refugees have migrated in large numbers to Turkey and eventually the EU, while terrorists have taken advantage of peripheral countries in order to gain entrance to the EU where, once they are inside, they are able to move more-or-less freely. These developments have created a political crisis for EU leadership, and have caused several countries to back away from their commitments under the Schengen Agreement. As of 2016, it is uncertain if the agreement will continue to operate, or how it might change if it does.

The Delors Report

Reshaping the European Community into the European Union got under way with the selection of the former French finance minister, Jacques Delors, to serve a five-year term as president of the EC. Delors was a compromise candidate, and no one expected unusual or dramatic changes in the EC under his stewardship. Delors's vision of the EC, however, was of a fully integrated union, and as president of the EC's executive branch he had a platform from which he could initiate significant change. His vision was shaped in part by the belief that the institutions of the EC could help return individual national economies to economic prosperity and by the desire to complete the task of building an economic and political union.

Delors's first step, and perhaps his most significant one, was to issue a report called "Completing the Internal Market," which detailed 300 specific changes necessary for the EC to move from a customs union to a common market and eventually an economic union. It laid out a timetable for completing the changes and implemented changes in voting on new policies that made it easier to pass legislation.

After some relatively minor changes in the **Delors Report**, it was adopted in its entirety in 1987 as the Single European Act (SEA), which came to be called, informally, the **Single Market Program (SMP)**. Of the 300 steps, or "directives," 279 were included in the SMP. Many of the twenty-one steps not included were considered too difficult to accomplish in the time period the EC gave itself, but were taken up as goals of the next round of deepening. For example, monetary union under a single currency was moved forward to the next round of deepening.

The date for implementation of the SMP was January 1, 1993. By the end of 1992, it was expected that the "**four freedoms**" (freedom of movement for goods, services, capital, and labor) spelled out in the SMP would be instituted and, as a result, the EC would be at the common market level of economic integration. By the end of 1992, nearly all the directives had been implemented, along with two additional initiatives. One additional measure was to strengthen the EC's competition policy so that mergers could not lead to increased market power by individual firms. The second initiative came on the heels of the admission of Spain and Portugal to the EC in 1986 and called for a strengthening of regional policies designed to reduce the differences in income between the wealthier states and new entrants.

The steps taken to implement the SMP can be broadly divided into three areas: (1) the elimination of physical barriers, such as passport and customs controls at the borders between member countries; (2) the elimination of technical barriers, such as differences in product and safety standards; and (3) the elimination of fiscal barriers, such as differences in taxes, subsidies, and public procurement. Each of these poses its own benefits and challenges and will be discussed in more detail. First, we will consider the gains that the EC hoped to reap from the elimination of these barriers.

Forecasts of the Gains from the Single European Act

The two primary means by which economic gains were expected to be realized were an increase in competition and economies of scale. A reduction in barriers at the border was expected to expand trade between member states by bringing down transportation costs, including wait times and other obstacles associated with shipping goods across national boundaries. In theory, removing barriers at the borders of markets that are segmented into separate national markets will enable them to become more integrated and will increase competition. Furthermore, the harmonization of standards and regulations reduces the costs of operating internationally. In the case of imperfectly competitive markets, where goods prices are above marginal costs, the mark-up charged by firms would come down as more competitive pressures are applied. Economies of scale can have similar effects as firms find it easier to operate across national boundaries, expand production, and reduce their costs by taking advantage of internal scale economies.

The predictions for the impacts of the SMP are testable. Economists and EC commissioners predicted that there would be more trade, lower price mark-ups, increased concentration of firms due to the ability to take advantage of scale economies, and increased price convergence. In nearly all cases, the predicted effects were realized by the actual effects. For example, trade among EC partners rose from 61.2 percent of the total trade of member states to 67.9 percent between 1985 and 1995. The percent of total output in each industry that is produced by the four largest firms rose in most industrial sectors. The share of world mergers and acquisitions that took place in Europe rose dramatically between 1985–1987 and 1991–1993. In the end, it is estimated that between 300,000 and 900,000 more jobs were created, and GDP in 1994 was 1.1 to 1.5 percent greater than it would have been without the measures taken to implement the SEA and the SMP.

Increased competition and economies of scale both led to more GDP and employment, but perhaps the most positive aspect of the changes was the convergence in income levels. Figure 14.1 shows GDP per person (measured in PPP terms) for Greece, Ireland, Portugal, and Spain. All of these countries were members of the EC before the SMP was negotiated and signed, and each had incomes below the average of the twelve members. In all but the Greek case, per capita

FIGURE 14.1   GDP per Person (PPP) as a Percentage of the EC-12 Average

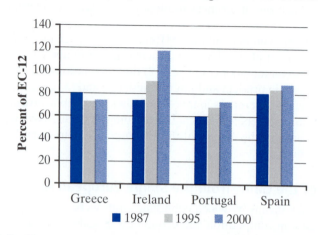

The least well-off countries experienced income convergence to the EC-12 average after the beginning of the SMP, with the exception of Greece.

Source: Data from IMF, *World Economic Outlook Database,* © James Gerber.

income rose toward the EC average, and in the Irish case, income was above average by 1997. It is impossible to prove that convergence was a direct result of the SMP, but there is strong evidence that it played a significant role.

Problems in the Implementation of the SEA

One of the most interesting lessons of the SMP is that it is still difficult to reduce barriers to trade and investment even when the citizens, businesses, and governments of the involved countries are united in their desire to do so. According to all the polls, the SMP enjoyed very broad support throughout the EC. Still, from the time when it was first proposed in 1985 until its final implementation in 1993, there were very difficult negotiations among the member countries.

The Effects of Restructuring   As we saw in Chapter 3, when a national economy goes from a relatively closed position to a relatively open one, economic restructuring takes place. The less efficient firms are squeezed out, and the more efficient ones grow; overall economic welfare expands as countries concentrate on what they do best, which inevitably means abandoning some industries and expanding others. In the case of the EC, it was forecast that almost all manufacturing industries would see shrinkage in the number of firms. The most extreme case was the footwear industry, which was predicted to lose 207 of its 739 firms.

The auto industry is an example of an economic interest that fought to prevent the full realization of the goals of the SMP. Car prices vary throughout the EU due to a lack of harmonization of national technical standards, documentation requirements, and rates of taxation. Ordinarily, price differences would present an opportunity for consumers and distributors to move cars from the low-price countries to the high-price ones and, in the process, bring about a reduction in price differences. The auto industry is covered by a separate set of tax laws, however, that require buyers to pay the tax rate of the country where they register the car, not where they buy the car. This effectively discourages buyers from crossing national borders to search out the best deal on car prices and helps maintain the status quo in automobile production.

One significant reason why there have not been more exceptions to the dropping of trade barriers is that the EU has a broad array of programs to address the problems of structural change. Some of these programs are funded out of the EU budget, and others are national in origin. Programs include the EU's Regional Development Funds, which can be used to address problems of structural unemployment, and the member nations' income maintenance, education, and retraining funds. The latter vary across the member countries, but in general they reduce the costs to individuals and communities of unemployment and structural change by providing a generous social safety net for laid-off workers.

Harmonization of Technical Standards   A second major obstacle to the creation of the four freedoms was the problem of harmonizing standards. These include everything from building codes, industrial equipment, consumer safety, and health standards, to university degrees and worker qualifications. The EU estimated that there were more than 100,000 technical standards that required harmonization in order to realize the benefits of a completely integrated market. Many of the technical standards involved rules that directly touch upon cultural identities. Nowhere was this more true than in the case of food processing. For example, there were discussions around the allowable level of bacteria in French cheese, the type of wheat required to make Italian pasta, the ingredients of German beer, and the oatmeal content of English bangers (breakfast sausages). In the end, the EU recognized that complete harmonization of standards would generate significant hostility and that the work required to agree on a set of common standards was beyond its capacity. Consequently, a combination of harmonization and mutual recognition of standards was adopted. In particularly sensitive cases, mutual recognition is the rule, but individual nations are allowed to keep their own national production requirements. For example, German beer must be certified as having been made according to the German standards, but Germany must allow all brands of beers to be sold within its borders.

As the discussion in Chapter 8 noted, standards do not have to be the same in order to create a single market, but the gains in economic efficiency that come from sharing the same standard can be significant. Shared standards permit manufacturers to produce to one standard and to capture important economies of scale in the process. These economies also pass outside the EU, because U.S. or Japanese manufacturers share the benefits of being able to produce to one set of standards as well.

Value-Added Taxes   A third difficulty standing in the way of completely realizing the four freedoms is the issue of value-added taxes (VAT). These taxes function essentially like sales taxes and are levied by each of the EU members but at a wide variety of rates and coverage. When the SEA was first proposed in 1987, there were significant differences in the dependence of the member governments of the EU on value-added taxes, ranging from 19 to 35 percent of total government revenue. The EC studied the United States to determine the effects of different rates of sales taxation on states sharing common borders and found that once the difference in sales taxes exceeded 5 percent, the higher tax state lost revenues, sales, and jobs to the neighboring lower tax state. In other words, a 5 percent difference was enough to cause consumers to cross state boundaries to make purchases.

VAT rates proved impossible to completely harmonize because they go to the heart of national political philosophy. High-tax countries expect the state to play a relatively greater role in national economic life, while low-tax countries are closer to the laissez-faire end of the political economy spectrum. The level of VAT, and the degree to which the national government depends on them, are in large part determined by the political philosophy of the nation. These philosophical attitudes, in turn, are shaped by economics as well as complex historical, cultural, and social factors.

The attempt to harmonize VAT was stymied by the inability to agree on a single rate. What was accomplished, however, was the creation of minimum and maximum rates that were set at 15 and 25 percent. Because the difference still exceeds the 5 percent differential that is the threshold at which high-tax countries lose revenue and sales, a number of controls were established to prevent revenue loss, even though these controls prevent the complete realization of the four freedoms.

Public Procurement   Public procurement is the purchase of goods and services by governments or government-owned enterprises, such as state-run television companies, utilities, or hospitals. Most nations tend to use procurement processes that discriminate in favor of nationally owned suppliers, although there are limits on their ability to do so if they belong to the World Trade Organization (WTO).

Since 1970, the EU has attempted to eliminate discrimination in public procurement, but this has proved difficult. It is a problem particularly in the areas of telecommunications, pharmaceuticals, railway equipment, and electrical equipment. These are often the areas of economic activity where governments have state-owned enterprises or national firms that are considered critical to national prosperity and therefore receive significant support, including government's purchase of output.

CASE STUDY

The Erasmus+ Program and Higher Education

It is easy to forget that during the first part of the twentieth century, the European continent was engulfed in one of the most brutal and violent periods in human history. Wars, depression, and genocide marked the history of every country until the end of World War II. How then did the countries that comprise the EU manage to deepen their ties and to form an economic union? The answer is multidimensional and would take volumes, but one thing we know is that the EU built political, social, professional, and commercial networks across national borders. The process of building networks is ongoing, and student mobility is a fundamental component.

The most prominent effort is the **Erasmus+ Program**. Erasmus+ began in 1987 as the Erasmus Program with the mission to promote student mobility in higher education through travel grants. In 2014, it combined a number of separate programs to become Erasmus+. It kept its focus on higher education and student mobility but has added support for joint master's degrees, vocational and professional training, promotion of EU studies around the world, and collaboration and support for sports. Erasmus+ university students receive a mobility grant that helps defray the cost of studying abroad, while units, courses, and curriculum are coordinated across different universities in order to reduce bureaucratic barriers to study abroad.

With an annual budget of around €2 billion ($2.2 billion), Erasmus has served as a base for higher education innovation and reform. It was key to the development of the Bologna Process, which is an agreement among the twenty-eight EU countries, joined by twenty-one non-EU members, to form a Higher Education Area. Bologna created common structures for higher education around three degrees: bachelor's, master's, and doctorate. It has also created a common set of unit requirements for degrees and harmonized the recognition of credits. Bologna's intent is to reduce the variability in higher education degrees by creating a common set of standards that will ensure quality.

The objectives of these programs are to increase student mobility, foster language acquisition, train individuals for different vocations, reduce youth unemployment, and increase the sophistication and international understanding of EU citizens. In the long run, the goal is to develop international networks among business people, intellectuals, government workers, and other educated labor.

THE THIRD WAVE OF DEEPENING: THE MAASTRICHT TREATY

LO 14.4 Give the economic rationale for each of the three waves of deepening of the EU.

LO 14.5 State two theories as to why the single currency moved forward so quickly.

LO 14.6 Analyze the EU's single currency program within the theoretical framework of an optimal currency area.

By 1989, planning for the implementation of the SMP was well under way. Europe had seen several years of economic expansion, and the excitement of the SMP seemed to signal that the time was right to consider some of the directives proposed in the Delors Report that had been set aside because they were seen as too complex to accomplish quickly. In 1990, the EC convened an Intergovernmental Conference on Economic and Monetary Union. The purpose of the conference was to bring together the leaders of the twelve nations to discuss the steps necessary to create a monetary union under a single currency. There were other issues on the agenda, but this was the one that attracted the most interest inside and outside the EU.

The Intergovernmental Conference continued through most of 1991. The final draft of the proposed agreement, called the *Treaty on European Union,* was completed in December in the Dutch town of Maastricht and became known as the **Maastricht Treaty**. Many of the provisions in the agreement were technical and put more control over health, education, cultural, and consumer safety issues in the hands of the EC. Most importantly, it defined the steps for achieving a common currency under the control of a **European Central Bank (ECB)** by 1999.

Achieving a single currency required each country to give up its ability to set its own monetary policy and instead accept whatever contractionary or expansionary policy the European Central Bank chooses. This is one of the most controversial features of the Maastricht Treaty. The controversy stems from the fact that there are economic risks associated with voluntarily giving up one of the few tools that governments have to counteract recessions. If, for example, Germany is booming, but Spain is in an economic slump, there is no common monetary policy that will be suitable to both countries. Germany would need a contractionary policy to cool off the economy and to prevent the ignition of inflation, while Spain would need an expansionary policy to create employment and growth. These controversies led to a public reception for the Maastricht Treaty very different from that for the SMP. Whereas citizens, businesses, and governments were solidly behind the SMP, support for the Maastricht Treaty was much more tentative.

Monetary Union and the Euro

The timetable for monetary union under a single currency was scheduled to occur in three separate stages. Stage one began in 1990 with the lifting of controls on the movement of financial capital within the EU. Stage two began in 1994 with the creation of the European Monetary Institute, based in Frankfurt, Germany. The institute was charged with the responsibility for coordinating the move to monetary union and gradually took on elements of a supranational central bank. The third stage began in 1999 with the phased-in introduction of the **euro** and the European Central Bank.

During stages one and two, nations were expected to bring their monetary and fiscal policies into harmony so that the introduction of the euro would not happen under wildly different sets of monetary and fiscal policies. To judge whether individual national policies were in agreement, the EU developed a set of **convergence criteria**. Table 14.3 lists the specific monetary and fiscal variables that must be met to join the single currency and the target ranges for each.

TABLE 14.3   Convergence Criteria for Monetary Union

Goals	Targets
1. Stabilize exchange rates	Maintain currency within the ERM band
2. Control inflation	Reduce it to less than 1.5 percent above the average of the three lowest rates
3. Harmonize long-term interest rates	Bring to within 2 percent of the average of the three lowest rates
4. Reduce government deficits	Make less than 3 percent of national GDP
5. Reduce government debt	Make less than 60 percent of national GDP

These five goals were designed to harmonize fiscal and monetary policies in preparation for the single currency.

Initially, nations were expected to meet all five goals for monetary union. The experience of the first half of the 1990s, however, indicated that no nation, except perhaps Luxembourg, could consistently maintain each of these targets and that some countries would never meet them. For example, Italian and Belgian central government debts were well over 100 percent of their annual GDP, and there was no way to change this in the span of a few years. Some economists questioned why these particular criteria were chosen in the first place, because a country that can maintain its interest rates, debts, deficits, inflation, and exchange rates in the target range is already doing what the EU hopes to achieve with monetary union. In other words, meeting the convergence criteria was an indicator that the nation can do what monetary union does but without actually giving up its currency. Why, then, should countries surrender control over monetary policy, and why should they give up their national currency, particularly because there are hidden costs?

Costs and Benefits of Monetary Union

There is no doubt that there are benefits to having one currency in a market as large as the EU's. For example, the average cost of currency conversion for travelers is 2.5 percent of the amount converted. A trip from Portugal to Sweden, with stops along the way, can quickly eat up a sizable portion of one's vacation money. Businesses fare much better, however, and if they buy in quantities greater than the equivalent of US$5 million, then the costs are a much smaller 0.05 percent, or $5,000 to convert $10 million. One estimate combining tourists and businesses puts the total costs of currency conversion at 0.4 percent of the EU's GDP. This is not a trivial sum, but it is not huge, either. The 0.4 percent figure could be higher, however, given the costs of maintaining separate accounting systems and separate money management processes for the different currencies.

A second reason for desiring monetary union is to reduce the effects of exchange-rate uncertainty on trade and investment. Because orders for goods are often placed long before delivery occurs, traders face a good deal of uncertainty about their earnings (if they export) and their payments (if they import). A single currency eliminates this uncertainty in the same way, for example, that California manufacturers can always be certain of the value of payments they will receive when they ship goods to New York. Recall from Chapter 10 that traders and investors can protect themselves from currency fluctuations with forward markets. Therefore, it should not be surprising that there is not much evidence that the elimination of currency fluctuations through a monetary union will increase cross-border trade and investment. On the other hand, tests of this idea are difficult because there are few examples of monetary unions.

Given these considerations, the benefits of a single currency appeared to be uncertain. The same could not be said for the potential costs. A single currency does not allow individual nations to pursue an independent monetary policy, in the same way that the state of New York cannot have a monetary policy that differs from that of California or the rest of the United States. It may be optimal to have a single currency and to eliminate the costs of currency conversion and other transaction costs, as long as the regions in the single currency area have synchronized business cycles and mobile labor forces. Synchronization of business cycles means that a single monetary policy might be appropriate. A mobile labor force guarantees that if some regions are not well synchronized, labor will move from the shrinking region to the expanding one, making the business cycles move together. If, however, the business cycles are not synchronized and labor is relatively immobile, then a single monetary policy will be right for some areas but wrong for others. Business cycles in Europe have never been synchronized, although the convergence criteria were partly designed with this goal in mind. In addition, the SMP's guarantee of freedom for labor mobility does not seem to have created significantly more continent-wide labor mobility given language and cultural differences.

Another major cost to joining a currency union is that countries lose their ability to use the exchange rate as a buffer against external shocks. This cost is particularly apparent, and severe, for some EU members in the wake of the 2007–2009 financial crisis. Without an ability to devalue or depreciate, countries with large current account deficits and/or with severe recessions are not able to depreciate their currencies to restore demand for their exports. Normally, the options for remedying a recession caused by a lack of demand are increased spending by households, businesses, government, or some combination of the three. Alternatively, countries can devalue to decrease domestic prices and increase their exports. In the case of Greece, Italy, Spain, Portugal, and Ireland, a deep recession after the financial crisis meant that households and businesses were not spending. Governments, which had large deficits that opened in the wake of the financial crisis, were also unable to spend, so the only option for increasing demand was through exports. Because domestic prices made these countries' goods uncompetitive in world markets, they were forced to adopt policies that reduced their domestic prices. This is called an *internal devaluation* and, unfortunately, can be done only through further cuts in demand, which allow prices to fall but worsen the recession. The euro crisis was the result, as discussed later in the chapter.

Given that currency unions can have large potential costs and that the EU is not an optimal currency area, it is curious that seventeen of twenty-seven member governments agreed to join the euro project. Any explanation must take into account political forces as well as economic ones.

The Political Economy of the Euro

Why did monetary union push ahead, given that the SMP was not complete and that the EU is not an optimal currency area? Undoubtedly, there are many reasons, some more valid than others. One explanation is that EU leaders believed that the potential gains were large and that the potential costs would lessen as countries became more integrated. Another explanation is that EU leaders were swept up in the excitement of the SMP and wanted to push further integration. A third explanation is that German reunification caused anxiety in some European capitals and this was a strategy to tie Germany ever more deeply into a pan-European project.

All of these explanations have their adherents, but one of the most widely voiced explanations is that the single currency became necessary after the removal of capital controls that took place under the SMP. Before 1990, many countries had controls on the movement of foreign exchange into their country. Regulatory measures such as taxes on foreign currency holdings, or on assets denominated in foreign currencies, and limitations on the uses of foreign currencies were widespread. The removal of these controls made it easier to speculate in foreign currency markets. One outcome of the removal of capital controls was the turmoil of 1992, when speculators became convinced that a number of currencies in the ERM would ultimately have to be devalued, prompting them to sell off large quantities of the currencies. During the sell-off, Portugal, Ireland, and Spain all devalued; Italy temporarily suspended participation in the ERM; and the United Kingdom dropped out permanently. Ultimately, the British pound fell by 25 percent from the speculative attacks. Soon after it left the ERM, there were several cases of firms that announced their intentions to close plants inside ERM countries and move to the United Kingdom where the depreciated pound reduced production costs. Philips Electronics, the giant Dutch firm, for example, closed plants in Holland, and SC Johnson and the Hoover Company closed French plants, all in order to open new plants in the United Kingdom where French and Dutch currencies bought more land, labor, buildings, and machinery.

Political friction increases and cooperation decreases when one country loses jobs to another as a result of currency depreciations. The desire to reduce these types of frictions is the reason why the EMS, with its ERM, was created in 1979. Consequently, it is the reason why many believed that a flexible exchange rate system was not an option. Although floating exchange rates have the advantage of permitting the greatest amount of flexibility in a nation's monetary and exchange rate policies, the EU's economic integration plans have closed the door on the use of flexible exchange rate systems.

Given that flexible rates are ruled out, it seems logical to ask why the EU did not choose to institute a system of fixed exchange rates. In fact, the ERM acted somewhat like a fixed exchange rate system because it tied each country's currency to a weighted average of the other currencies. Exchange rates were not completely fixed, however, and there were bands that the currencies tried to stay within. The EU's problem with a fixed exchange rate system is that it lacked the ability to keep the currencies within their bands, let alone to completely fix them. International currency markets know that there are definite limits to the resolve and the resources of member countries trying to defend their currencies. The EU partially solved this by changing the bandwidths from ± 2.25 percent to ± 15 percent, but this did nothing about the serious pressure against a currency that the United Kingdom and Italy experienced in 1992. If a country is not willing to defend its fixed rates when the costs grow high, then fixed rates are not really "fixed."

CASE STUDY

The Financial Crisis of 2007–2009 and the Euro

In their masterful work on the economics of financial crises, *This Time Is Different*, Carmen Reinhart and Kenneth Rogoff define four types of financial crises: banking crises, debt crises, currency crises, and inflation crises. The crisis of 2007–2009 was a banking crisis, both in the United States and in Europe, but in the European case, it evolved into a debt crisis. This is not uncommon, as banking crises and recessions often go hand-in-hand, and recessions depress tax collections and increase government spending on social support programs, health care, and pensions. Reinhart and Rogoff find that unemployment after a severe banking crisis rises 7 percentage points, on average, and GDP declines 9.3 percent from its peak to its lowest point during the recession. When income falls that much, government budgets move into deficit as fewer taxes are collected while government expenditures increase to support the unemployed and early retirements.

The euro area is no different from other regions that undergo a crisis, except that the individual countries do not have their own currencies and do not have a fiscal union. The five euro-crisis countries of Greece, Ireland, Portugal, Spain, and Italy all experienced increases in their budget deficits during the crisis. Figure 14.2 shows the average budget deficit or surplus, as a percent of GDP, from 2000 to 2006 and from 2007 to 2011. The first date is before the crisis and the second date is after. France and Germany are included because they are big countries and neither is considered risky. Germany, in particular, is the yardstick used to measure other countries' performances.

The rise in deficits added to the debt levels of these countries. Figure 14.3 shows the changing levels of debt, measured in relation to GDP. Irish debt was less than half of Germany's when measured as a share of GDP until it exploded as a result of the banking crisis and the government's decision to take responsibility for the bad debt held by private banks. Spain's debt is still significantly below Germany's and was trending down until the crisis. Portugal's debt level was well below Germany's until 2007 and the onset of the crisis. Greece and Italy both had significantly higher debt levels, but both showed no significant

FIGURE 14.2 **Average Budget Deficits as a Percent of GDP**

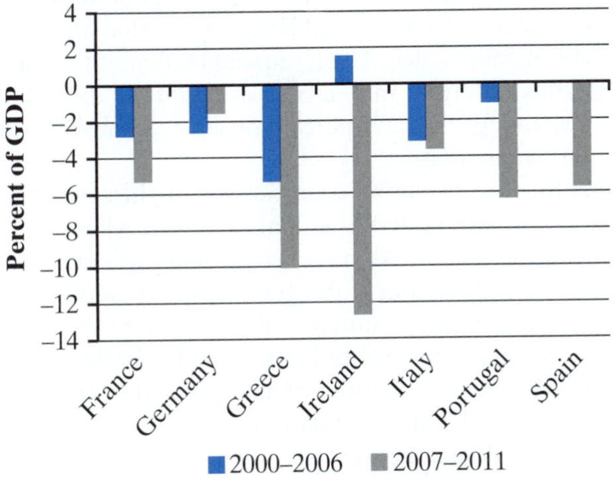

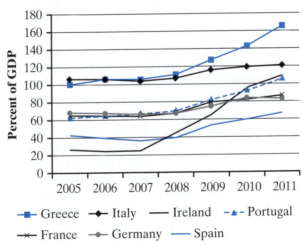

With the exception of Greece, none of the euro-crisis countries had large budget deficits before the financial crisis of 2007–2009.

Source: Data from IMF, *World Economic Outlook Database,* © James Gerber.

FIGURE 14.3 **Gross Debt as a Percentage of GDP**

With the exceptions of Greece and Italy, the euro-crisis countries had debt levels at or below German levels.

Source: Data from IMF, *World Economic Outlook Database,* © James Gerber.

(continued)

trend until 2008 when they began to increase. By 2009, at the depth of the recession caused by the banking crisis, both had higher debt levels that were expanding unsustainably. Reinhart and Rogoff show that after a banking crisis and the recession it causes, debt levels expand 86 percent within three years, on average. By this criterion, the euro-crisis countries did relatively better, with debt that expanded "only" 75 percent on average, most of which is due to Ireland's 212 percent increase.

The problem for the euro-crisis countries is straightforward. First, the collapse of a real estate bubble led to a banking crisis, which, in turn, led to a recession. The recession depressed tax revenue and expanded social spending, causing an increase in government budget deficits. In addition, governments were called on to bailout their banks in order to prevent the spread of the crisis to the rest of the Eurozone where France, the Netherlands, Germany, and other countries owned large quantities of bonds issued by the euro-crisis countries. In a recession, fiscal and monetary policies should become expansionary in order to stimulate demand and to try to restore growth. The politics and economics of the single currency, however, put this option out of reach. First, governments had deficits that exceeded the agreed limit of 3 percent of GDP, and debt above 60 percent. Second, their economies are so depressed that bond markets are reluctant to lend except at relatively high interest rates, which only add to the debt burden. Third, governments were called on to bailout banks, putting even greater strains on government budgets and undermining further the confidence of investors in government debt. In effect, governments depended on the banks to buy their bonds which they needed to sell in order to bailout the banks. Some economists refer to this as a doom-loop—insolvent banks buying government debt so governments can bailout the insolvent banks. These conditions make fiscal policy unavailable and create the possibility of a **sovereign default**, or a government default on its debt.

In a sovereign nation with its own currency, the central bank can purchase the government debt with the creation of new money. That is, the central bank becomes the lender of last resort. In the Eurozone, however, there is no lender of last resort. This is not an oversight but was an intentional part of the design of the European Central Bank (ECB), which manages the euro. Designers of the euro feared that a lender of last resort would create a moral hazard for undisciplined governments if they thought central bank loans could be used to avoid budget cuts. Hence, the ECB was created with explicit "no bailout clause" which prohibits direct lending to governments in deficit. In 2012, the President of the ECB announced that he would do "whatever it takes" to solve the crisis in the Eurozone. Many observers interpreted this as a commitment to use the ECB indirectly as a lender of last resort, and pressures on the indebted governments temporarily lessened. In the long run, however, the absence of an official lender of last resort is a serious liability.

In other countries where similar conditions have prevailed, part of a solution has been to devalue the currency. For example, Latin American economies in the 1980s had a decade-long debt crisis in which governments could not borrow and monetary policy became ineffective after it was used too expansively. Countries could devalue their currencies, however, and this was one measure that helped restore competitiveness. The euro countries do not have this option, but they were encouraged to create an internal devaluation, which consists of falling domestic prices.

Recall the formula for the real exchange rate from Chapter 10: $R_r = R_n \times (P^*/P)$, where R_r is the real rate, R_n is the nominal rate, P^* is the index of foreign prices, and P is the index of domestic prices. Because R_n cannot change for Greece or the other crisis countries, the only way to gain competitiveness is if P falls or P^* rises. A rise in P^* would mean that the stronger countries like Germany would have to have higher inflation, but German policy makers prefer to avoid that at all costs. That leaves a fall in domestic prices as the only option for gaining competitiveness, restoring demand, and returning to growth. The problem, however, is that a fall in domestic prices requires a deep recession. The costs of a recession in terms of lost output, high unemployment, and destroyed lives is a great burden plus it is not clear that the strategy works.

The internal devaluation policies are part of a package that is labeled *austerity economics* and is often contrasted with an alternative, called *growth economics*. The debate is over the timing of policy measures. Economists agree that the crisis countries need to restore fiscal balance by addressing their budget deficits and that they need economic growth. But do they opt for growth first—even if it widens the deficits—and where do they get the financing for expansionary fiscal policies; or do they restore balance first, and then tackle the growth problem with the hope that fiscal balance will generate confidence and bring investment and badly needed resources for financing the debt?

In the long run, discussion is focused on the need for more integration via the creation of a fiscal union. The United States is a currency union, as well, but it is also a fiscal union. Individuals pay taxes to the federal government, which provides infrastructure spending, social security, support for the unemployed, healthcare, and other benefits. When one state is in recession, its citizens still get their social security checks and federal transportation funding is still distributed even if the state budget is cut drastically. Some poorer states such as New Mexico, Mississippi, Alaska, Louisiana, and others receive far more in federal expenditures than they pay in taxes. The EU, in contrast, has no such mechanism for automatically redistributing significant proportions of income from rich countries to poor ones. In effect, each country in the EU has its own budget and its own expenditures, and the pooling of resources is limited because the EU budget is very small relative to the size of the national economies. When a recession strikes, there is no outside source of funding that helps maintain expenditures and demand for goods and services. A fiscal union would create the possibility for transfers from rich to poor countries, but the terms of the union are under debate, and the loss of national sovereignty that would be required is a serious obstacle for many citizens.

WIDENING THE EUROPEAN UNION

After the achievement of monetary union, one of the most pressing problems facing the EU was the timetable and conditions under which new members would be added.

New Members

Ten countries joined the EU in 2004, two more in 2007, and Croatia joined in 2013. Several additional countries, including Turkey, are considered candidates and have started negotiations for membership. Membership requires a stable democratic government, market-based economies, and formal adoption of the EU's body of laws and regulations, known as the *acquis communautaire*.

For prospective members, many of the gains from trade have already been realized because most countries have free trade agreements (FTA) with the EU, and some participate in the Schengen Agreement allowing free movement. Membership, however, confers some additional benefits such as voice in EU governance, a more secure set of property rights, and perhaps additional investment and trade from the adoption of EU laws. As with any new integration agreement, there are some areas that are more difficult to resolve.

First, the EU budget contains a shrinking, but still extensive, set of farm support programs. Direct payments to farmers are about 30 percent of the EU budget, with another 11 percent for rural development. Much of this amount is administered under the **Common Agricultural Program (CAP)**, which provides farmers with about 18.4 percent of their gross revenue (see the case study on agricultural subsidies in Chapter 7, Table 7.3). Inclusion of new countries such as Turkey, with its large farm sector, is a difficult issue because the EU cannot offer the same level of support, and the creation of a two-tier system raises objections that new members do not have the same rights as existing ones.

Second, EU governance structures were not designed for twenty-eight members, and additional ones only adds to the pressure to change the voting system. Voting, democracy, and governance are tied up with the third issue, which is the wide gap between the poorest and the richest members. The original six members of the EEC were more-or-less equal in their incomes, their level of institutional development, their security of property rights, and the rule of law. As the EU has expanded, however, it has inevitably drawn in members at different levels of economic and political development. Formerly socialist economies such as Bulgaria and Romania had to make up a great distance between their legal institutions and the EU, and income gaps between the richest and poorest exacerbate the sense of social and economic distance between member countries, undermining the sense of solidarity and unity that the EU tries to create. In a similar vein, and as an illustration, the gap between the United States and Canada is small on most accounts, while the gap between the United States and Mexico is much greater and diminishes social trust between the two countries.

In the case of the EU, Bulgaria's per capita income (purchasing power parity definition) is about 40 percent of Germany's and Turkey's is only slightly higher at 43 percent. These differences are not insurmountable, but they create a variety of economic pressures on migration and institutional support payments, as well as social pressures related to trying to integrate countries at very different levels of economic development. The EU recognized this problem in its earlier efforts of widening and created regional funds and cohesion funds to try to ameliorate the differences and to close the gaps between less well-off members, such as Ireland and Portugal, and better off members, such as Sweden, France, and Germany. These efforts were mostly successful, but as the EU considers adding more members, the pressures on the EU budget will grow.

CASE STUDY

Spain's Switch from Emigration to Immigration

Spain's period of highest emigration was from 1881 to 1930, when approximately 4.3 million people left. In 1910, its population was just under 20 million, so a loss of 4.3 million people was significant. The decade with the highest out-migration was 1910 to 1920, when 1.3 million people, or well over 5 percent of the population, left.

Emigration was slowed by the world depression of the 1930s and World War II, but it began again in earnest after 1950. Unlike the earlier migrations, when the majority of migrants went to the Americas, increasing numbers headed for other countries in Central and Western Europe. In particular, France, Germany, and Switzerland were major recipients of Spanish citizens.

By the time Spain joined the EU in 1986, changes in the Spanish economy were reducing the supply-push forces that cause emigration. In 1950, Spain's work force was nearly 50 percent agricultural, but by 1970 agriculture's share of the labor force had fallen to less than 25 percent. With more industry came higher productivity and a shrinking wage gap with France, Germany, and even Switzerland. By the early 1990s, Spain's economic success was turning it into a net attractor of migrants rather than a net sender. As a result, in the second half of the 1990s, immigration to Spain was accelerating, particularly from North Africa, South America, and Western Europe. Well-off Europeans discovered Spain's Mediterranean coast, while Colombians, Ecuadorians, Moroccans, and Mauritanians came for jobs and wages that were significantly higher than what they could earn at home. By 2015, more than 1.2 million Spaniards lived outside Spain, but 5.9 million immigrants from other countries lived in Spain. Immigrants to Spain come from traditional senders such as Ecuador, Colombia, Peru, and other South American countries, but also from new EU entrants Romania and Bulgaria, North Africa (especially Morocco), and high-income Western European countries such as Germany, Great Britain, and France.

(continued)

Immigration creates a reaction in most countries where the numbers of immigrants are large. The U.S.–Mexican case is famous, but there are numerous others. Mexico itself resists immigration from Guatemalans on its southern border, while Costa Ricans appreciate the hard work of Nicaraguans who come to pick the coffee crop, but they complain about their behavior and use of social services. Germans have a long love–hate relationship with Turks, the French with Algerian immigrants, and so on around the globe. Spain's policy has been relatively accommodating toward immigrants, including six amnesties for undocumented workers since 1990. Its last amnesty occurred in 2005 and offered legal status to more than 700,000 foreigners. At the same time, Spain increased its program of border enforcement, which is aimed primarily at deterring Africans. It also built walls around Ceuta and Melilla, which are two Spanish territories located inside Morocco, and stepped up its coastal patrols.

Migration policies are fraught with uncertain side effects, but one of the most frequent consequences of increased enforcement at the border is a displacement of immigrants to alternative points of entry. In the Spanish case, the walls around Ceuta and Melilla, together with increased vigilance along the coast, resulted in migrants moving their point of departure from Morocco to Western Sahara, a disputed territory on Morocco's southern border. From there, migrants could reach the Canary Islands, which is Spanish territory. When Spain increased its patrols off the coast of Western Sahara, migrants moved their departure points south to Mauritania, and then farther south to Senegal when Spain began to target Mauritania.

It is difficult to name a country that has not gone through a period of high rates of out-migration at some point in its development. Europeans went to the Americas, U.S. citizens went west into what was Mexico and the frontier, Koreans spread around the globe, and the Japanese went to North and South America. Spain's period of high emigration appeared to be over for good by the 1990s, but the financial crisis of 2007–2009 and its development into a debt crisis and deep recession have begun to generate a new wave. Young people, particularly those with skills and college degrees who cannot find work in a country where over half of all people under twenty-five are unemployed (estimates are between 53.2 and 57.9 percent in 2014), have begun to leave. In all likelihood, this is a temporary shift due to a deep recession, but it could go on for a while.

THE DEMOGRAPHIC CHALLENGE OF THE FUTURE

As the EU looks toward the future, a number of challenges are visible. In the short to medium run, it must continue to create convergence in income and living standards between its poorest and its most well-off members, while finding a way to end the lingering crisis in some Eurozone countries. Over the medium run, it must also prepare for further widening, in particular for the possible accession of

Turkey, a large nation with per capita income levels about 40 percent (purchasing power parity) of the EU average. Finally, in the long run, it must adapt its economies and social support systems to prepare for a much older population.

One of the primary determinants of social spending in virtually all countries is the age structure of the population. As populations age, they need more health care, more pensions, and more long-term care. Each of these entails increases in public spending, and given that older citizens regularly vote, democracies usually respond to their demands. A small part of increased spending on services for the elderly will be offset by decreases in educational spending and unemployment benefits, as a smaller share of the total population will need schooling or experience involuntary unemployment. These savings, however, will not begin to offset the increases in social spending associated with an aging population. According to estimates carried out by the European Commission, if current policies are left in place, the average EU government will have to increase the public sector by 10 percent simply to maintain its existing programs at their current levels.

Table 14.4 shows a projection of EU population (twenty-eight countries) through 2050. By then, the percent of the population of people aged sixty-five and over is expected to reach nearly 28 percent of the total, up from 18.8 percent in 2015. The ability of governments to manage a much larger population of retired people will be constrained by the fact that after 2011, the working-age population began to decline, soon to be followed by the total number of people working. Fewer workers will put downward pressure on the rate of economic growth and constrain the development of new resources for supporting an aging population. At the same time, the number of available workers to support the production of social services needed by the aging population will be both relatively and absolutely smaller.

Migration can play a role at the margin to ameliorate the changes, but it is unlikely that migration alone will have a major impact. Simply to return the estimated 2050 working age population (15–64) to its 2015 estimates would require the immigration of more than 46 million people, or about 9 percent of the predicted

TABLE 14.4   Population Forecast, 2010–2040: Twenty-Seven Members of the European Union

	Population, 2015 (Millions)	Percent, 2015	Population, 2050 (Millions)	Percent, 2050
Total	513.9*	100.0	507.2	100.0
By age category				
Ages 0–15	79.6	15.5	72.6	14.3
Ages 15–64	337.9	65.8	291.5	57.5
Ages 65+	96.5	18.8	143.1	28.2

Population in the European Union will stop growing around 2029–2030, and will see a significant increase in its elderly population.

Source: Data from U.S. Census Bureau,© James Gerber.

2050 population. And this still would not compensate for the absolute increase in the number of people 65 and over. Nevertheless, given the potential for EU expansion beyond its current members along with the migration pressures emanating from North Africa and elsewhere, any assumption about the capacity of the EU to absorb migrants may turn out to be false.

The Commission of the EU has begun to analyze trends and to recommend changes to pension and health care systems. For example, several countries have begun to experiment with linking pensions to changes in life expectancy, and to encourage workers to postpone retirement. Demographic changes are clearly visible and well understood; whether or not the EU and the national governments respond will depend on the flexibility and adaptability of their electorates.

Summary

- The twenty-eight-member EU was created in several stages. The earliest stage involved agreements over open trade for coal and steel (ECSC), followed by cooperation over the peaceful development of nuclear energy (Euratom) and a free-trade agreement.

- The main institutions of the European Union (EU) are the European Commission, the Council of the European Union, and the European Parliament. The roles of these institutions have evolved.

- The Treaty of Rome was signed in 1957 and was put into effect in 1958, creating a six-country, free-trade area that was phased in gradually over the next ten years.

- The next wave of deepening was the creation of the European Monetary System (EMS) and the Exchange Rate Mechanism in 1979, linking exchange rates.

- Following the EMS, the Single European Act was passed, creating a common market by 1993. While preparations were taking place for the implementation of the Single Market Program (SMP), the Treaty on EU was signed in 1991 and approved by the national governments in late 1993.

- The Treaty on European Union created a common currency. In preparation, a set of convergence criteria was developed with targets for interest rates, inflation, government spending, and government debt.

- While the EU was undergoing its several rounds of deepening integration, it was also widening membership to nearly all of Western Europe. Between 1958 and 1995, it expanded from the original six members to fifteen. In 2004, ten more countries joined, followed by three more from 2007–2013.

- Eastward expansion of the EU created problems in the areas of agricultural policy, governance, and income differences.

Vocabulary

acquis communautaire

cohesion funds

Common Agricultural Policy (CAP)

competitive devaluation

convergence criteria

Council of the European Union

Delors Report

Erasmus Program

euro

European Atomic Energy Community (EAEC or Euratom)

European Central Bank

European Coal and Steel Community (ECSC)

European Commission

European Community (EC)

European Currency Unit (ECU)

European Economic Community (EEC)

European Monetary System (EMS)

European Parliament

European Union (EU)

exchange rate mechanism (ERM)

four freedoms

Maastricht Treaty

qualified majority

Single European Act (SEA)

Single Market Program (SMP)

sovereign default

subsidiarity

Treaty of Rome

Treaty on European Union

Study Questions

All problems are assignable in MyEconLab.

14.1 What were the three main stages of deepening that occurred in the European Community after the Treaty of Rome was passed?

14.2 What are the three main institutions of the EU, and what are their responsibilities?

14.3 The SEA is a case in which it was difficult to create an agreement, despite the fact that there was near unanimity in support of an agreement. If everyone wanted the agreement, why was it hard to negotiate?

14.4 How did the EU expect to create gains from trade with the implementation of the SEA?

14.5 A sudden sharp increase in the demand for the German mark almost destroyed the Exchange Rate Mechanism in 1992. Explain how a rise in the demand for a currency can jeopardize a target zone or exchange rate band.

14.6 Discuss the pros and cons of the single currency.

14.7 What problems arose from the admission of twelve new members between 2004 and 2007?

14.8 How does the European Union, compare and contrast to the North American Free Trade Agreement (NAFTA) region in size, institutional structure, and depth of integration?

15 Trade and Policy Reform in Latin America

Learning Objectives

After studying this chapter, students will be able to:

15.1 Describe the strengths, weaknesses, and reasons for import substitution industrialization.

15.2 Explain the strategy and performance of economic populism.

15.3 Give the main reasons for the Debt Crisis of the 1980s and analyze its relationship to ISI.

15.4 Discuss the goals of economic policy reforms that began in the later 1980s.

15.5 Explain why some Latin American leaders have become impatient with economic policy reforms.

INTRODUCTION: DEFINING A "LATIN AMERICAN" ECONOMY

Latin America stretches from Tijuana on the U.S.–Mexico border to Cape Horn at the southern tip of South America. Within this vast geographic area lies such a diversity of languages and cultures that any definition of Latin America must have exceptions and contradictions. For example, *Merriam-Webster's Collegiate Dictionary* defines the region as Spanish America and Brazil, a standard view that leaves out a few small countries in Central and South America (Belize, Suriname, Guyana, and French Guiana) and the island nations of the Caribbean that were outside the region of Spanish and Portuguese settlement. *Webster's* second definition—all of the Americas south of the United States—is more inclusive but purely geographical. Perhaps it is less important to give a precise definition than it is to recognize the variety of physical geographies, cultures, and income levels that coexist within any definition. In fact, the variety is so great that it is worth asking whether these nations can truly constitute a single world region. In other words, what is the "Latin American" experience, and how does it allow us to group together nations as different as Argentina, with its European culture and relative prosperity, and Guatemala, with its indigenous culture and rural poverty?

The diversity within Latin America should make us careful not to overgeneralize. Nevertheless, there are several common themes shared by all, or nearly all, the nations in the region. First, there are common historical threads, beginning with the fact that many of these nations share a heritage of Spanish and Portuguese colonization and a common linguistic base. In some countries, however, the languages of indigenous people are important as well. A second part of their shared histories is that many Latin American countries gained their national independence from Spain and Portugal during the nationalist revolutions of the early and middle nineteenth century. This differentiates their experiences from the colonial ones of Africa and Asia, and implies that the national identities of Latin Americans are perhaps deeper than in other parts of the developing world.

During the first wave of globalization in the late nineteenth century, many countries were connected to the world economy through exports of agricultural and mineral commodities. Then, in the 1930s, the Great Depression caused many nations to shift their policies away from an outward-looking export orientation toward an inward-looking, targeted industrial strategy. At the same time, state-led industrialization began to encourage more manufacturing along with a new strategy that came to be known as *import substitution industrialization*. More recently, most nations were borrowers in the 1970s, and suffered through a prolonged debt crisis in the 1980s. From that point forward, the region began a wide-ranging set of economic policy reforms, similar in scope to the transformation of Central and Eastern Europe after the collapse of communism. Finally, in the twenty-first century, several countries have grown impatient with the economic reforms of the 1990s and have turned toward more interventionist policies, with more reliance on the state to direct and support the economy.

In this chapter, we examine the origins and extent of the economic crisis that hit Latin America in the 1980s and analyze the responses. Before we examine the crisis of the 1980s and the economic reforms of the late 1980s and 1990s, we must first step back and look at the long-run performance of the economies of Latin America. Then, when the severe problems of the 1980s are viewed in context, it is easier to understand the policy shifts of the 1990s and after.

POPULATION, INCOME, AND ECONOMIC GROWTH

Table 15.1 is a snapshot of the current levels of income and population. Nations are grouped according to their membership in important regional trade agreements, and per person totals are weighed by the population size of the individual nations in the group. In 2014, more than 590 people lived in the eighteen countries included in Table 15.1 and they produced gross domestic product (GDP) equivalent to $5,850 billion U.S. dollars. Individual countries ranged in population from under 4 million (Panama and Uruguay) to more than 200 million (Brazil), while incomes varied from under $5,000 per person in the least well-off countries (Honduras and Nicaragua) to more than $20,000 per person in the most well-off (Argentina, Chile, Uruguay, and Panama). If Table 15.1 included data for all the individual countries, four countries would account for over 70 percent of the total population and nearly 80 percent of GDP. In order of population size, they are Brazil, Mexico, Colombia, and Argentina. Indeed, Brazil and Mexico together are more than 55 percent of the population and 63 percent of the GDP.

For long stretches of the twentieth century, Latin America was one of the fastest-growing regions of the world. In particular, from 1900 to 1960, the region's real GDP per capita grew as fast as or faster than that of Europe, the United States, or Asia. Individual experiences varied, but most countries saw adequate to excellent growth along with rising living standards. After World War II, most countries in Latin America experienced good rates of growth, as did most regions in the world, and the two largest countries, Brazil and Mexico, had remarkable increases in their per capita income levels. Circumstances began to change as world economic growth slowed in the 1970s, and Latin American experiences became more varied. Some countries grew faster in the 1970s and some grew slower, but nearly all relied more heavily on government expenditures to stimulate growth. The undoing of this period was the onset of the Latin American debt crisis (1982–1989), which is described later in the chapter. The Debt Crisis turned the 1980s into a **Lost Decade**, sovereign debt problems were compounded by negative growth, banking crises, currency crises, and hyperinflation. The Debt Crisis of the 1980s brought an

TABLE 15.1   Population and GDP for Latin America and the Caribbean, 2014

Region	Population (Millions)	GDP (US$ Billions)	GDP per Capita (US$ PPP)
Central American Common Market			
Costa Rica, El Salvador, Guatemala, Honduras, Nicaragua	41.5	164.9	7,512
Common Market of the South (Mercosur)			
Argentina, Bolivia, Brazil, Paraguay, Uruguay, Venezuela	297.5	3,333.8	16,742
Pacific Alliance			
Chile, Colombia, Mexico, Peru	222.3	2,137.3	16,079
Other countries			
Dominican Republic	9.8	64.0	14,014
Ecuador	16.0	100.9	11,324
Panama	3.9	49.2	20,779
Total	591.0	5,850.1	15,680

Source: Data from International Monetary Fund, © James Gerber.

end to nearly fifty years of economic policy, as one country after another tried bold new experiments in their search for a way to restore economic growth.

IMPORT SUBSTITUTION INDUSTRIALIZATION

LO 15.1 Describe the strengths, weaknesses, and reasons for import substitution industrialization.

Economic policy reforms began in the 1980s as a response to that decade's Debt Crisis. They brought the demise of a state-led economic development strategy that had been in place since the 1930s in most countries and they brought the rise of more market-oriented policies. Prior to the economic reforms, countries were private market economies, but they used a heavy dose of state intervention to determine key elements of policy, such as the allocation of credit, investment decisions, and trade patterns. The most important part of this strategy occurred in the trade arena, where countries adopted the economic development strategy known as **import substitution industrialization (ISI)**. After World War II, the theory of ISI was grafted onto a broader state-led development strategy and every country in Latin America, as well as many outside the region, adopted ISI policies. In Latin America, ISI policies were brought to an end in the 1980s and 1990s as countries moved away from state-led development strategies and began to look for ways to harness market forces to promote economic development. This shift from state-to-market was encouraged by a variety of factors, including the long Debt Crisis of the 1980s and a worldwide shift toward greater reliance on market forces.

Origins and Goals of ISI

From the second half of the nineteenth century until the middle of the twentieth century, most of Latin America relied on exports of agricultural commodities (sugar, bananas, coffee, cotton, and grains) and minerals (petroleum, silver, copper, and tin) to earn foreign revenue. These export sectors were often developed or controlled by foreign capital and had few economic linkages to the domestic economy, functioning instead as foreign enclaves within the nation. In cases where the export sector was domestically owned, it usually brought wealth to a relatively small number of people and added greatly to the inequality of power and money pervasive in Latin American society.

World War I and the Great Depression of the 1930s disrupted the flow of Latin American exports and severely reduced export earnings. World War II partially reversed this trend, as many countries turned to Latin America for the minerals and foodstuffs they could no longer make at home due to the war, but at war's end there was another drop in demand for Latin America's commodities. In the late 1940s, a young Argentine economist, Raul Prebisch, and a German exile, Hans Singer, developed a theory to explain the loss of foreign exchange earnings. In their view, the fall in demand for Latin American commodities was not solely due to the end of the war, but was also a long-run tendency for the prices of primary commodities to fall. Singer and Prebisch argued that coffee, tin, copper, bananas, and other primary commodity exports would inevitably experience price declines relative to the prices paid for manufactured goods.

In trade analysis, the ratio of average export prices to average import prices is called the **terms of trade (TOT)**:

$$TOT = (\text{Index of export prices})/(\text{Index of import prices})$$

Latin America exported raw materials and imported finished goods, so the Prebisch-Singer prediction was that the terms of trade for the region would decline. For obvious reasons, this view was labeled **export pessimism**.

The reasoning behind export pessimism included both statistical studies and economic theory. Statistical analysis showed raw material prices falling over periods as long as several decades. More recent analysis shows that while prices may fall for extended periods of time, there is no long-run trend up or down. Economic theory holds that as incomes rise, people spend a smaller share of their overall income on foodstuffs and other raw-material-based goods such as textiles and apparel, and they spend more on manufactured items. Consequently, the demand for raw materials declines in relation to the demand for manufactured goods. Note, however, that this effect does not necessarily lead to a decline in the terms of trade for raw material producers, as productivity increases in manufacturing can overwhelm increases in demand and push down the real prices of manufactured goods.

Export pessimism formed the basis of orthodox economic policy from roughly the 1950s through the 1970s. As the head of the United Nations' **Economic Commission on Latin America (ECLA, or CEPAL** in Spanish), Prebisch guided economic policies throughout Latin America and reinforced a shift that had begun with the destruction of trade in the 1930s. The loss of markets during the Great Depression temporarily forced Latin America away from dependence on raw material exports and toward industrial development through the production of manufactured goods that substitute for imports—hence, the name *import substitution industrialization (ISI)*. Ironically, domestic production of manufactured import substitutes required the importation of large quantities of capital goods (machinery and parts), and in order to earn the revenues needed to buy these imports, most nations continued to depend on raw material exports in the decades after World War II. Primary commodities still make up a significant share of today's exports from Latin America, and countries have benefitted greatly from China's strong demand for raw materials and foodstuffs, and also suffered as Chinese growth began to slow.

ISI is a form of industrial policy that focuses on those industries that produce substitutes for imported goods. According to Prebisch and Singer, the inevitable decline in the terms of trade for primary commodities means that the biggest constraint on industrial development is the shortage of foreign exchange. Lower export prices mean that countries find it harder and harder to earn the foreign exchange they need in order to buy the machinery and other capital goods they cannot produce themselves. One of the most important roles of import substitution is to reduce the need for foreign exchange used to buy goods that could be made at home.

ISI theorists argued that a country should begin by producing inexpensive and relatively simple consumer items, such as toys, clothing, food products (e.g., beverages and canned goods), and furniture. Gradually, the focus of industrial targeting should move on to more complex consumer goods (e.g., appliances and autos) and intermediate industrial goods (e.g., pumps, generators, basic metals). In the third stage, complex industrial goods would be produced (e.g., chemicals, electronic equipment, machine tools).

Source: Pearson Education

Criticisms of ISI

The economic tools for implementing ISI are the same as those for industrial policies discussed in Chapter 5. These include a variety of different types of government support, from subsidies of all kinds to trade protection and monopoly power in the domestic market. In retrospect, ISI generated a number of unintended consequences that caused inefficiencies and wasted resources. Among the many criticisms that have been leveled at ISI are the following: (1) governments misallocated resources when they became too involved in production decisions; (2) exchange rates were often overvalued; (3) policy was overly biased in favor of urban areas; (4) income inequality worsened; and (5) ISI fostered widespread rent seeking.

Foremost among the problems of ISI are those related to an overconfident belief in the ability of the state to direct resources efficiently into their best uses. In the 1950s and 1960s, it was often assumed that **market failures** were far more common in developing nations than in industrial ones, and that one of the main goals of any state should be to correct these through selective and careful state intervention in the economy. In this context, ISI can be interpreted as a set of policies in which government uses its economic and political power to improve on the market.

Many economists think that ISI overestimates the technical ability of government officials to identify market failures and their solutions (see Chapter 5's discussion of industrial policies). It also assumes that government officials are selfless individuals who ignore political considerations and focus only on economic efficiency and what is best for the nation as a whole. This model of political decision making caused an under-emphasis on problems related to the implementation of economic policies, such as corruption and the lobbying power of economic elites. It also failed to take into account the slow accumulation of special provisions, favors, and economic inefficiencies that built up over time when policies were heavily influenced by politics. This was magnified by the inequality in wealth and income throughout Latin America, where powerful interest groups were able to use ISI policies to their own benefit rather than in the national interest.

A second problem of ISI was the persistence of overvalued exchange rates. Overvaluation was a deliberate policy in some countries, while in others it was a chronic problem stemming from the maintenance of a fixed exchange rate under conditions of higher inflation than those in the countries' trading partners. As a deliberate policy, overvaluation of the exchange rate accomplished several goals. In particular, it made it easier for the targeted industries to obtain the imported capital goods they needed. It also helped to maintain political alliances between the urban working classes and the political parties in power by providing access to relatively less expensive foreign goods. When governments were forced to depreciate in the 1980s and 1990s, they often lost the political support of the urban classes.

Although overvalued exchange rates had some benefits, they also had costs. Most importantly, they made it difficult to export because they raised the foreign price of domestic goods. This hurt the agricultural and traditional export sectors, directed capital away from agriculture, and contributed to low productivity and income in rural areas.. Overvalued exchange rates also hurt industries that did not produce substitutes for imports because they made it less profitable to export. They also made foreign machinery less expensive and caused industrial investment to be too capital intensive and insufficiently labor intensive. Consequently, industry did not create enough new jobs to absorb the growing urban labor force. Furthermore, because most industry is located in urban areas, government investments in infrastructure improvements—such as transportation, communication, and water—were heavily targeted toward cities and their environs. As a result, subsistence farmers and their families did not benefit from, or contribute to, national economic development, and Latin America continued to have the highest levels of inequality of any region in the world.

In addition to a persistent tendency toward overvalued exchange rates, ISI trade and competition policies were heavily protectionist and often favored the creation of domestic monopolies. The lack of foreign and domestic competition meant that manufacturing was often inefficient, uncompetitive, and inwardly focused. With profits from a protected domestic market, many producers had no incentives to invest in modern equipment, further reinforcing the lack of competitiveness of their products. It is ironic that as a consequence of ISI many countries became more vulnerable to economic shocks that originated outside of Latin America. This was precisely the opposite effect from the one that motivated ISI in the first place.

A final problem of ISI is the development of widespread rent-seeking behavior. When governments intervene in the planning and directing of industrial development, they give government officials a wide range of valuable privileges to distribute. These include the many subsidies and licenses that are a part of ISI policies. For example, in order to protect the domestic market and to ensure access to needed imports, governments often required import licenses. At the same time and in order to make imports less costly, they provided foreign exchange to importers at subsidized prices. When government policy creates something of value, such as the license to import or a subsidy to buy foreign exchange, the private sector will spend resources to obtain it. In the absence of strong institutions to ensure the independence of the bureaucracy—and, often, even when strong institutions are present—bribes and corruption become a part of the decision making. Ultimately, some decisions are made for the wrong reasons, and economic waste is the result.

CASE STUDY

ISI in Mexico

The Mexican constitution of 1917 established the power and the responsibility of the federal government to intervene in the economy in order to act as the leading agent of economic growth and as the referee of social conflict. This role was not institutionalized inside the Mexican government until the Mexican revolution was consolidated in the 1930s under the presidency of Lázaro Cárdenas.

In order to lead and direct economic growth, government could legitimately claim the need to be powerful—otherwise, powerful social classes could resist the government's directives and initiatives, particularly those with distributional goals or consequences. Therefore, economic policy served not only to meet the needs of the country for economic growth and a fairer distribution but also to increase the political power of government. Mexico nationalized its oil industries in 1938, and throughout the twentieth century a number of sectors were nationalized and turned into state-run monopolies (telephones, airlines, banks, railroads, and mineral development companies). The use of the government budget in this manner guaranteed access to investment funds, while monopoly markets ensured that the favored firms would succeed, at least within the nation.

The government also offered loans and loan guarantees to many firms in targeted industries. Loans and loan guarantees helped firms obtain capital at interest rates that were below market rates. Similarly, the government sold foreign exchange at artificially low prices to targeted firms that needed to buy imports. Mexican exporters were required to convert their foreign exchange earnings into pesos at an overvalued peso rate—too few pesos per dollar—which made exporting relatively less profitable; the government then sold the cheaply acquired foreign exchange to targeted industries. In effect, exporters were subsidizing the development of the targeted industries.

Unlike many ISI nations, Mexico limited foreign investment. Like most ISI nations, however, when investment was permitted (e.g., autos), performance requirements were placed on the foreign firms. A common requirement was that the foreign firm balance its foreign exchange requirements so that each peso of imports was matched by a peso of export earnings. Further interventions occurred in the area of commercial policy where import licenses limited many types of imports. Recall that import licenses are essentially quotas. By the 1970s about 60 percent of all imports were subject to licensing.

From 1950 to 1973, Mexico's real GDP per capita grew at the rate of 3.1 percent per year. By comparison, the United States grew 2.2 percent per year; the fourteen largest Organization for Economic Co-Operation and Development (OECD) nations grew 3.5 percent per year; and growth in the six largest Latin American economies was 2.5 percent. At the same time that the economy was undergoing relatively rapid economic growth, industrialization was changing the structure of the economy. Mexico's manufacturing sector expanded from 21.5 percent of GDP to 29.4 percent. Overall, import substitution may have had many problems, but it cannot be called a failure. Judged by the economic growth of its partners, or by its own growth before or after, Mexico attained very healthy rates of growth. In part, ISI was relatively more successful in Mexico than it was other parts of Latin America because it is a large country, where producers can obtain economies of scale. Brazil, for example, had similar or even greater successes.

Growth began to slow in the 1970s, as it did in many parts of the world. One widely shared view is that Mexico's growth began to stall because the country was running out of easy targets for industrial development. Light manufacturing and simple consumer goods industries were relatively easy to start, and the conversion of a part of the nation's economy from subsistence agriculture to

(*continued*)

simple manufacturing made growth rates look good. The next stages required more sophisticated manufacturing, however, and were relatively harder to start growing. According to this view, Mexico ran out of simple industries to start and inevitably had a harder time producing more sophisticated goods that were further from its comparative advantage.

In spite of rapid economic growth during the 1950s and 1960s, poverty and income inequality continued. Large numbers of Mexicans, many of them indigenous people living in rural areas, did not participate in the growth of the economy. This is evidenced by the fact that in the 1980s a large part of agriculture was still at a subsistence level, using 26 percent of the nation's labor force to produce just 9 percent of the nation's GDP. The urban bias in Mexico's development strategy turned Mexico City into one of the largest metropolises in the world, with more than fifteen million people in the greater metropolitan area by the late 1980s. The sensational growth and crowding of people and industry into the basin that holds Mexico City resulted in serious pollution problems.

The relationship of ISI to the debt crisis of the 1980s is complicated, but most economists think that poor macroeconomic management and external shocks stemming from the collapse of oil prices and rising interest rates played a far larger role than ISI. Certainly, ISI policies expanded the role of the federal government in economic activity and increased government expenditures and borrowing during the 1970s. Nevertheless, overall economic growth remained fairly robust until the mid-1970s. One view is that the easy gains of ISI were gone by the 1970s, and in order to keep growth on track, Mexican presidents used their power over public finances to increase expenditures dramatically. At first the government argued that it could easily afford to borrow in foreign capital markets because the nation became a major oil exporter in 1978 and had high potential oil export earnings. Ultimately, the government's fiscal policies generated enormous public sector deficits, fears of devaluation, and capital flight. By 1982, a year after the price of oil fell, the nation had run out of international reserves and could no longer service its international debt. If the government had not resorted to unsustainable macroeconomic policies, it is less likely that the country would have fallen into the debt crisis in 1982 and subsequently rejected its ISI policies by the late 1980s.

MACROECONOMIC INSTABILITY AND ECONOMIC POPULISM

LO 15.2   Explain the strategy and performance of economic populism.

Many economists are convinced that while ISI policies are suboptimal, they had less of a direct effect in creating the economic crisis of the 1980s than misguided macroeconomic policies. The reasons are relatively straightforward. ISI policies involve trade barriers and government support for selected industries. Collectively, these policies may lower a nation's income by a few percentage points, but they rarely lead to a full-blown economic crisis. Faulty macroeconomic policies, on the other hand, often lead to hyperinflation, depression, and balance of payments crises. In addition, while most of Latin America used ISI policies from the 1950s through the 1980s, economic growth remained at fairly high levels for most countries until the early 1980s when growth turned negative in nearly all countries. While it is possible that the 1980s crisis was the culmination of several decades of ISI policies, it is certain that the crisis was directly linked to the faulty macroeconomic policies of the late 1970s and early 1980s.

Populism in Latin America

Many Latin America specialists blame the faulty macroeconomic policies of the region on populist or economic populist political movements that use economic tools to obtain support from labor and domestically oriented business, or to isolate rural elites and foreign interests. Examples of populist leaders abound: in Argentina, Juan Perón (1946–1955 and 1973–1976) and Raúl Alfonsín (early 1980s); in Brazil, Getúlio Vargas (1951–1954), João Goulart (1961–1964), and José Sarney (1985–1990); in Chile, Carlos Ibáñez (1952–1958) and Salvador Allende (1970–1973); in Peru, Fernando Belaúnde Terry (1963–1968), Juan Velasco Alvarado (1968–1975), and Alan García (1985–1990); in Mexico, Luis Echeverría (1970–1976) and José Lopez Portillo (1976–1982); in Venezuela, Hugo Chavez (1998–2013). Populist movements in Latin America share nationalistic ideologies and a focus on economic growth and income redistribution. Before the 1970s, populist tendencies did not cause large macroeconomic imbalances and government budgets were more likely to be balanced or near balance, inflation was controlled, and trade deficits did not exist or they were manageable. Beginning in the 1970s, however, a new breed of populists began to take power. This group, often called economic populists, was more likely to use expansionary fiscal and monetary policies without regard for the importance of inflation risks, budget deficits, and foreign exchange constraints. They were much more aggressive in using government spending to promote growth, and much less cautious in avoiding the pitfalls of too much spending.

Economic populism is usually triggered by three initial conditions. First, there is a deep dissatisfaction with the status quo, usually as a result of slow growth or recession. Second, policymakers reject the traditional constraints on macro policy. Budget deficits financed through printing money are justified by the existence of high unemployment and idle factories, which offer room for expansion without inflation. Third, policymakers promise to raise wages while freezing prices and to restructure the economy by expanding the domestic production of imported goods, thereby lessening the need for foreign exchange. In the words of one analyst, the policies call for "reactivating, redistributing, and restructuring" the economy.

Early in the populist regime, there is a vindication of the policies. The economic stimulus of government expenditures and newly created money leads to rising growth rates and rising wages. Soon, however, bottlenecks begin to appear. For example, construction firms run out of particular inputs, such as cement or specialized steel products, and manufacturing firms cannot find the parts they need to repair their machinery. Prices begin to rise, and the budget deficit grows. In the next stage, inflation begins an extreme acceleration, and shortages become pervasive throughout the economy. The budget falls into serious deficit as policies become unsustainable, and wage increases cease keeping up with inflation. In the final stage, countries experience massive capital flight as fears of a devaluation develop. The flight of capital out of the country depresses investment and further depresses real wages.

In the end, real wages are often lower than before the cycle began, and there is an international intervention under the sponsorship of the IMF, which is designed to stop the high inflation and end a balance of payments crisis. Typically, the IMF oversees the implementation of stabilization and structural reform policies that call for serious budget cuts, a slowdown in the growth of the money supply, a reduction in trade barriers, and in general, greater reliance on market mechanisms and less government intervention. While these stages of the populist cycle are an idealization, they capture the essence of the populist experience as it has occurred in many Latin nations.

CASE STUDY

Economic Populism in Peru, 1985–1990

Alan García became president of Peru for the first time in July, 1985. After leaving in disgrace in 1990 he spent several years reforming his image and was re-elected in 2006, serving until 2011. His first presidency is a textbook case of the problems of economic populism, while his second presidency is widely regarded as successful. Before his first election in 1985 and as part of the fallout from the debt crisis, the country suffered through a serious recession in 1983. By 1985, it was on the mend, and García began a program to raise real wages in order to stimulate demand and redistribute income ("reactivate, redistribute, restructure"). In 1986 and 1987, the economy responded to the stimulus of higher consumption with robust growth and without inflation. The lack of inflation was due to the presence of idle factory capacity and unemployed workers. By mid-1987, however, some essential imported inputs became scarce and began to act as bottlenecks on further increases in production. Consequently, inflation rekindled. The exchange rate was a crawling peg that was periodically devalued, but because inflationary price increases were greater than the exchange rate devaluations, there was an inevitable appreciation in the real exchange rate and a significant increase in the current account deficit. Table 15.2 illustrates the course of the major macroeconomic variables and real wages during García's presidency.

Rising budget deficits, trade deficits, and inflation should have been enough to cause a cautious government to reign in expenditures; but instead, García responded by nationalizing the property of the financial services sector (banks and insurance companies) and expanding credit subsidies for favored groups in the agricultural and industrial sectors. In 1988, the government tried to tackle the problem of inflation through devaluations and price freezes, but in order to protect incomes and to bring relative prices into agreement, it simultaneously permitted selected price increases and compensating wage increases.

By 1990, the economy reached the deepest point in its recession. In July, a

TABLE 15.2   Economic Indicators during the García Administration

	1984	1985	1986	1987	1988	1989	1990
GDP growth	4.8	2.3	9.2	8.5	−8.3	−11.7	−5.1
Real wage (% change)	−8.0	−8.4	26.6	6.1	−23.1	−46.7	−14.4
Deficit/GDP	6.7	3.4	5.7	7.9	8.1	8.5	5.9
Inflation (%)	110	163	78	86	667	3339	7482
Current account balance (millions of US$)	−221	−137	−1077	−1481	−1091	396	−766

Source: Data from Inter-American Development Bank, *Economic and Social Progress in Latin America,* © James Gerber.

new government took office and implemented a relatively orthodox stabilization program of fiscal and monetary austerity to end inflation and curb the budget deficit. By then, however, real wages were well below the level they had attained when the previous government took power in 1985.

THE DEBT CRISIS OF THE 1980s

LO 15.3   Give the main reasons for the Debt Crisis of the 1980s and analyze its relationship to ISI.

In August 1982, Mexico announced that it lacked the international reserves it needed to pay the interest and principal due on its foreign debt. Mexico was not the first country to declare its inability to service its debt, but it was the biggest up to that point. Its announcement soon led to the realization that a number of other countries, including most of Latin America, were in similar circumstances. Thus began the Lost Decade.

Proximate Causes of the Debt Crisis

In Mexico's case, the collapse of oil prices in 1981 undermined its ability to earn the revenue it needed to service its debt. The problem was compounded by the fact that a significant portion of its debt was owed in dollars at variable interest rates and that efforts to combat inflation in the United States and elsewhere had resulted in a higher level of world interest rates. Consequently, interest payments on Mexico's debt rose at the same time that the nation's ability to earn dollars shrank.

The collapse of oil prices in 1981 and the rise in world interest rates were not the only external shocks to the economies of Latin America. In 1981–1982, the world's industrial economies entered a deep recession that reduced world demand and prices for many of the raw materials produced in Latin America and elsewhere. In Mexico's case, oil was the critical commodity, but a number of other primary commodity exports experienced a similar decline in their world price.

The price decline for Latin America's exports and the rise in interest rates were significant parts of the mix of events that led up to the debt crisis. These external economic shocks probably would not have caused a generalized debt crisis without some additional factors, however. Historically, debt crises are often triggered by a set of external shocks and are preceded by an acceleration of international lending. In Latin America's case, the lending occurred between 1974 and 1982. Added to these two factors was the complicating problem of mismanagement of national macroeconomic policies in the late 1970s and early 1980s.

During the 1970s, financial institutions in London, New York, and elsewhere were awash in money that they were eager to lend. The rise in oil prices in 1973 and 1974, and again in 1979, led to an enormous expansion of bank deposits by the oil-rich nations of the world. Banks aggressively sought new borrowers beginning in 1974. For Latin America and the Caribbean, long-term, publicly guaranteed debt rose more than sevenfold between 1973 and 1983. The sudden acceleration in commercial bank lending and the rise in the amount of debt made the economies vulnerable to a sudden and unforeseen economic shock.

Table 15.3 shows the size of the debt for some of the most heavily indebted countries after the first year of the crisis. The second column of numbers expresses the debt in net terms (gross debt minus debt owed by foreigners) as a percentage of GDP. The third column shows the net interest payments owed as a percentage of exports of goods and services. This is a useful indicator because nations ultimately have to pay the interest on their international debts out of the revenues they earn from their exports. What we see is that between 10 and 63 percent of the revenue earned by exports went to pay interest and, consequently, was unavailable for purchasing imports or for investing domestically.

Responses to the Debt Crisis

Initially, most analysts in the United States and in international financial institutions such as the IMF perceived the debt crisis to be a temporary, short-run liquidity problem. Under this assumption, the reasonable response is to increase capital flows to Latin America and other indebted regions so that they would have the financial resources to service their debts and stimulate higher rates of economic growth that enables countries to outgrow their debt.

From the standpoint of U.S. policy, the key to growth was viewed as increased investment, which was possible only if capital flows into the region were restored. The first policy proposal along these lines was that of U.S. Treasury Secretary

TABLE 15.3   Debt Indicators at the Onset of the Debt Crisis, 1983

Country	Gross External Debt (Millions of US$)	Net External Debt as a Percentage of GDP	Net Interest Payments as a Percentage of Exports
Argentina	43,634	75.3	62.8
Bolivia	3,328	141.9	38.5
Brazil	92,961	48.3	38.7
Chile	17,315	87.6	32.9
Colombia	10,306	25.1	18.8
Costa Rica	3,646	137.8	45.4
Mexico	86,081	63.8	32.1
Peru	10,712	52.4	20.1
Venezuela	32,158	38.8	9.6

A large percentage of the exports of indebted countries went to pay interest on their debts.

Source: Data from World Debt Tables, 1987; *International Debt Reexamined* 1995, World Bank © James Gerber.

James Baker in 1985. The **Baker Plan** tried to organize a renewed lending program by commercial banks. The problem was that most banks that had Latin American loans in their portfolios were trying to reduce their exposure to the region, not increase it. Consequently, few resources were forthcoming under this plan.

Without capital flows from developed country banks, the choices were not attractive. Outright default and disavowal of the debt would cut off most of a nation's trade and investment linkages. The consequences for investment and growth would be risky and potentially disastrous, depending on the reaction of the United States and other governments. On the other hand, if they continued to make interest payments and principal repayment, huge trade surpluses would be required to earn the revenue they needed to pay for imports plus interest on the debt.

Interest payment on the debt owed to foreigners enters the current account as a debit in the category of primary income paid abroad, as discussed in Chapter 9. Consequently, interest payments severely increased the current account deficits of many countries. Recall the fundamental accounting balance of an open economy,

$$S_p + T - G = I + CA,$$

where S_p is private savings, $T - G$ is government (public) savings, I is investment, and CA is the current account balance. Without financial capital inflows to finance their current account deficits, countries must eliminate the deficit through a combination of increased exports and reduced imports. The policies that accomplish this are expenditure switching and expenditure reducing policies. Recall from Chapter 11 that expenditure switching policies such as devaluations of the currency turn the demand for foreign goods into a demand for domestic goods and raise CA directly. Expenditure reducing policies, such as tax increases and cuts in government spending, raise $T - G$ and, indirectly, reduce consumption, investment, and imports. The net effect of expenditure reducing policies is often a recession in which the demand for domestic and imported goods falls due to a fall in domestic income.

To accumulate the resources they needed for their interest payments, governments were forced to follow contractionary policies that caused deep recessions throughout the region. Between 1982 and 1986, the average rate of growth of real per capita GDP was −1.8 percent per year in Latin America and the Caribbean.

By 1987, it was apparent to analysts throughout the world that restoring capital flows was not enough. There was a need for deep reform in the economies of Latin America. First, it was observed that the faulty macroeconomic policies of the region consistently left aggregate national expenditure above national income and that the likelihood of a return to growth was small as long as the gap between the two remained. Second, in their attempt to keep government expenditures higher than warranted, many countries had resorted to printing money, which resulted in high and increasing rates of inflation. Third, the burden of the debt itself was becoming apparent to everyone inside and outside Latin America. After the interest and principal payments were made, insufficient export earnings remained for domestic investment and consumption, and growth was stunted. By 1988–1989, both creditors and multilateral lending agencies such as the IMF were in agreement that debt relief was in everyone's interest.

The growing consensus on the need for debt relief led to the **Brady Plan** in 1989, named after the secretary of the treasury, Nicholas Brady. Essentially, the Brady Plan gave something to everyone. Creditors were expected to restructure some of the old debt into longer-term debt with a lower interest rate and to make some additional new loans. The multilateral lending agencies, such as the IMF, were expected to provide additional loans on concessional terms (below market interest rates) and borrowers were required to provide evidence of their willingness to begin serious economic reform before any new loans would be forthcoming. The Brady Plan did not end the debt crisis, but it was a significant step toward greater stability in the region. Countries that renegotiated their debt with the Brady Plan package were perceived by the international financial community to have greater credibility and sounder finances. Consequently, after 1989 capital flows began to return to Latin America but this time not in the form of bank loans. Rather, savers and investors in the United States, Europe, and Asia began to increase their direct investment in Latin America, as well as their holdings of various financial assets, such as stocks and bonds issued by private companies doing business there. While large inflows of capital can create problems if they reverse and flow out, they were the additional savings and investment that the region needed to return to its historical levels of growth.

From the vantage point of the twenty-first century, the most lasting effects of the debt crisis—other than the forgone output due to the recessions of the 1980s—are the deep economic reforms that have taken place in country after country. These reforms are key to explaining the return of capital flows to Latin America. Reforms vary by country, both in kind and degree, but they mark a historical shift away from the protectionist and interventionist policies of ISI and economic populism and toward more open and market-oriented policies.

NEOLIBERAL POLICY REFORM
AND THE WASHINGTON CONSENSUS

LO 15.4   Discuss the goals of economic policy reforms that began in the late 1980s.

LO 15.5   Explain why some Latin American leaders have become impatient with economic policy reforms.

By the late 1980s, most countries in Latin America had started a series of economic policy reforms that began to alter the fundamental relationships between business and government and between their national economy and the world. After 1989, the reforms intensified and became more general. In most cases, the reforms consisted of three separate, but interrelated, features. First, and with varying degrees of success, governments implemented stabilization plans to stop inflation and to control their budget deficits. Second, most countries began privatizing the government-owned parts of their economies, such as manufacturing enterprises, financial and other services, mining operations, tourism, and utility companies. Third, trade policies became more open and less discriminatory against exports.

Throughout Latin America, this package of reforms has come to be known as the **neoliberal model or neoliberalism** because it represents a partial return to classic nineteenth-century European liberalism, which favored free markets and minimal government intervention in the economy. In addition to being labeled as neoliberalism, these reforms also came to be known as the **Washington Consensus** on policy reform. Both the neoliberal agenda and the Washington Consensus were considered policy prescriptions for reform of government finances and management of the economy. Neither, however, was offered as a manual for economic development, although that is how each came to be seen and used. By the early 1990s, growth had returned to most of Latin America, but it remained relatively slow, and disappointment with these policies began to set in after the mid-1990s. Before we look at the reaction that reform disappointment created, it is first useful to discuss the reforms in more detail.

Stabilization Policies to Control Inflation

Many countries sought to avoid the recessionary consequences of the onset of the debt crisis by increasing government spending. The only way to finance government spending, however, was through the printing of more money because tax systems were inadequate and government borrowing abilities were limited by the debt crisis. The reckless printing of money to finance government spending drove a number of nations into periods of hyperinflation, as detailed in Table 15.4.

The solution to the hyperinflation experienced by Argentina, Bolivia, Brazil, and Peru is simple to prescribe: Cut government spending and stop printing money. The implementation of this prescription was difficult, however. In the short run, if price increases outstrip wage increases, as is often the case in a period

TABLE 15.4   Inflation Rates, 1982–1992

Country	Inflation (in Percentage)		
	Average 1982–1987	Average 1987–1992	Highest 1982–1992
Argentina	316	447	4924 (1989)
Bolivia	776	16	8170 (1985)
Brazil	158	851	1862 (1989)
Chile	21	19	27 (1990)
Colombia	21	27	32 (1990)
Mexico	73	48	159 (1987)
Peru	103	733	7650 (1990)
Venezuela	10	40	81 (1989)

High rates of inflation were a common problem of the 1980s.

Source: Data from *Crisis and Reform in Latin America,*1995, by Edwards, Sebastian © James Gerber.

of disinflation, then the burden of bringing down the rate of inflation falls mainly on wage earners who experience a fall in their real wages. Consequently, anti-inflation policies create economic hardship and alienate the political support of many wage earners, making governments unpopular with a large share of the population.

A further complication was the lack of agreement over the causes of inflation. Some argued that it was caused by inertia because everyone expected future inflation to be high. This caused producers to raise prices in anticipation of higher future input costs. The problem of inflation developing a momentum of its own, and a lack of empirical information about the depth of this problem, led to two different policy prescriptions for controlling inflation: the orthodox model and the heterodox model.

The **orthodox model** minimizes government involvement in the economy. Consequently, its anti-inflation prescription is straightforward—cut government spending, reform the tax system to increase compliance and revenues, and limit the creation of new money. The heterodox model calls for the same actions plus the freezing of wages and prices. In the **heterodox model**, inflationary expectations are so embedded in economic decision making that price increases will continue even if government spending and new money creation cease. In practice, heterodox plans often ignored the budget deficits that were part of the problem.

Between 1986 and 1992, Brazil implemented five separate heterodox stabilization plans to end inflation, and none of them worked. Similarly, heterodox plans in Argentina and Peru in 1985 succeeded for approximately a year, but then failed as inflation returned with a vengeance. Nevertheless, Brazil and Mexico each ultimately controlled inflation using heterodox methods.

An issue that continued to plague many nations was the problem of inconsistency between inflation stabilization and exchange rate policy. Mexico's experience is a good example of the problem and stems from the fact that the exchange rate is a powerful weapon in the fight against inflation. Mexico fixed its peso to the dollar in the mid-1980s as part of its anti-inflation strategy. Argentina and Brazil did the same under their stabilization plans of 1991 and 1994, respectively. Domestic producers that competed with U.S. goods were forced to avoid price increases so they would remain competitive. Furthermore, prices did not increase on imports of U.S.-made capital goods, which were essential to Mexican industry, thereby helping to hold down Mexican prices for finished manufactured goods. Because Mexico's inflation was still slightly higher than U.S. inflation, the peso became overvalued over a period of time. Ultimately, this contributed to a serious trade imbalance and the collapse of the peso in December 1994, followed by a deep recession in 1995. Since 1994, Mexico has let the peso float against the dollar and has stopped trying to use the exchange rate as an anchor against the current of inflation. Argentina's struggle to control inflation and its use of the exchange rate are discussed in the case study in Chapter 11.

Structural Reform and Open Trade

Stabilization policies to control inflation and curtail large budget deficits are usually one part of a package that also includes **structural reform policies**. One way to keep the two types of policies separate is to recognize that stabilization generally focuses on macroeconomic policies—for example, inflation and government budgets—while structural reform tends to be more microeconomic, dealing with issues of resource allocation. Structural reform policies include the privatization of government-owned enterprises, the deregulation and redesign of the regulatory environment of over-regulated industries such as financial services, and the reform of trade policy.

The many initiatives to privatize and reform the regulatory environments of the economies of Latin America are quite remarkable, but this section will focus on the most impressive area of structural reform to date: the economic integration of the region with the world economy. Before the onset of the debt crisis, the economies of Latin America had the most restricted trade systems of all the nations in the noncommunist world. In many countries, the debt crisis reinforced the belief that isolation from the world economy was the only way to protect a nation from shocks that originated in the external environment.

In the 1970s, Chile broke with this tradition and began to reform its trade policies. Mexico and Bolivia followed in 1985 and 1986, and by 1987–1988, it was apparent throughout Latin America that trade had to be more open if economic growth was to be restored. In the late 1980s and early 1990s, nearly all the countries of Latin America began reducing both the level of tariffs and nontariff barriers (NTBs) and the variability of tariff rates across industries and goods. Table 15.5 shows the changes in tariffs that occurred between the mid-1980s, when the reforms began, and the early 1990s and beyond. As large as the tariff reductions were, the effect of the elimination of NTBs such as quotas and import licensing requirements was even more dramatic, as many countries eliminated all or nearly all these barriers. By the early 1990s, most of the tariff and nontariff changes had been implemented, and countries began to turn to alternative forms of market opening.

TABLE 15.5   Average Tariff Rates, in Percents, Selected Countries

	1985	1992	2010
Argentina	28	14	11
Brazil	80	23	13
Chile	36	11	5
Colombia	83	12	11
Mexico	34	14	7
Peru	64	18	5
Venezuela	30	17	13

Latin American countries have dramatically reduced their trade barriers, including tariff rates. Most of the opening occurred between 1985 and 1995.

Sources: Data from *Crisis and Reform in Latin America by Sebastian Edwards,*; World Bank, *World Development Indicators.*, © James Gerber.

The three main goals of trade reform were to reduce the anti-export bias of trade policies that favored production for domestic markets over production for foreign markets, to raise the growth rate of productivity, and to make consumers better off by lowering the real cost of traded goods. In response to the changes in trade policy, the growth rate of exports picked up in most countries, while nontraditional exports increased dramatically. Furthermore, productivity rose in a majority of countries for which there is data. The productivity increase is at least partly the result of trade opening due to the impact of technology transfers, the improved investment climate, and the pressures on local firms to remain competitive.

CASE STUDY

Regional Trade Blocs in Latin America

Latin America has many regional trade agreements and some of the oldest. The first wave of agreements were signed in the 1960s as Prebisch and others began to recognize that ISI strategies eliminated the possibility for economies of scale and productivity increases that come with it. As long as production was limited to the home market, firms in many sectors would not be large enough to invest in research and development and to compete internationally. The solution was to encourage regional trade agreements such as the Central American Common Market (1961), the Caribbean Free Trade Association (1966, now called the *Caribbean Community and Common Market*) and the Andean Pact (1969, now called the Andean Community of Nations). The goals of these agreements are shown in Table 15.6. While the agreements conferred commercial advantages on firms located in member countries, they did not significantly alter trade patterns nor did they increase the flow of trade within the regions. Countries

TABLE 15.6 Selected Regional Trade Blocs

Trade Bloc	Year	Members	Goals
Andean Community of Nations	1969	Bolivia, Colombia, Ecuador, Peru	Customs union
Caribbean Community (CARICOM)	1973	Antigua and Barbuda, the Bahamas, Barbados, Belize, Dominica, Grenada, Guyana, Haiti, Jamaica, Montserrat, St. Kitts and Nevis, Saint Lucia, St. Vincent and the Grenadines, Suriname, Trinidad and Tobago	Customs union
Central American Common Market	1961	Costa Rica, El Salvador, Guatemala, Honduras, Nicaragua	Customs union
Dominican Republic-Central America Free Trade Agreement (DR-CAFTA)	2005	Costa Rica, Dominican Republic, El Salvador, Guatemala, Honduras, Nicaragua, United States	Free-trade area
Common Market of the South (MERCOSUR)	1991	Argentina, Bolivia, Brazil, Paraguay, Uruguay, Venezuela	Customs union
North American Free Trade Agreement (NAFTA)	1994	Canada, Mexico, United States	Free-trade area
Pacific Alliance	2011	Chile, Colombia, Peru, Mexico	Free-trade area

resisted pressures to lower their tariffs, and momentum toward freer trade within trade blocs quickly dissipated. By the 1980s, the agreements were on paper only and were having scant effects on member countries.

With the onset of trade reforms in the mid-to-late 1980s, regional trade agreements once again became popular. Mexico took the lead with its announcement in 1989 that it was pursuing a free-trade agreement (FTA) with the United States. In addition to economies of scale, trade agreements seemed to hold the promise of attracting foreign investment as well as increasing market access and possibly diversifying trade partners. From the 1990s forward, a large number of agreements have been implemented as countries revitalized old agreements, signed new plurilateral agreements, and also created a large number of bilateral FTAs with countries inside and outside Latin America. For example, Mexico signed FTAs with eleven countries and regions, including Japan and the EU, and is part of two other plurilateral agreements, including NAFTA. Chile is part of the Pacific Alliance, and has agreements in force with twenty other countries and regions, including the

EU, the United States, and China. A complete list is available through the OAS's Foreign Trade Information System, http://www.sice.org.

The Next Generation of Reforms

The Washington Consensus overlaps with stabilization policies and structural reforms, and they are commonly mixed together under the label of neoliberalism. Neoliberalism and the Washington Consensus are negative terms throughout most of Latin America, primarily because the reforms of the last two decades have created uncertainty and change, but they have not begun to fulfill expectations of growth and prosperity. That is, the narrowly defined Washington Consensus may have helped some countries to end hyperinflation or runaway budget deficits, but it has not solved some of the region's most pressing and fundamental long-term problems. Inadequate growth rates, dramatic inequality, and vulnerability to macroeconomic crises and volatility continue to plague most of the countries of the region. After the reforms of the 1980s and 1990s, economic growth rates increased, but were still too low to offer much encouragement, and rates of poverty and levels of inequality hardly changed. Analysts in the mid-1990s began to talk about "reforming the reforms" and a "second generation of reforms," while popular frustration over the lack of material improvement in many countries led to widespread disillusionment with the reforms. Several countries (Brazil, Venezuela, Bolivia, Ecuador, Nicaragua) elected leaders who promised an end to the reforms or to at least moderate them, and while the new policies have varied, there is generally a much stronger element of nationalism and a reduction in market-friendly policies. Some leaders, like Hugo Chavez in Venezuela (1999–2013), called for the creation of a socialist bloc in Latin America and a complete repudiation of the last two decades of reforms.

More moderate reformers have begun to develop a second generation of reforms that take into account the region's institutions, and that address the problems of social and economic inequality. The reformers' goals are to develop more inclusionary economic systems by creating opportunities for excluded groups, to make countries less prone to macroeconomic crises, and to create greater flexibility by addressing some of the legal and institutional rigidities. For example, many small firms and individual-owned businesses or homes are located on property for which owners do not have a formal title. This situation makes it impossible for them to use their assets as collateral for loans, or to participate in the formal financial system. In effect, it limits growth by disallowing the full economic participation of a large share of small-scale entrepreneurs. To address this problem, bureaucratic processes must be redesigned and simplified, while legal and judicial structures must be reorganized to meet the needs of small businesses and individuals rather than large companies and powerful political interests. Similarly, bankruptcy laws that encourage risk taking, competition policies that break up monopolies, and financial sector supervision that limits unnecessary or unwanted risk are all areas that need work.

Mechanisms for addressing Latin America's highly unequal distribution of income are also on the agenda. In many countries, a long history of exclusion has blocked economic opportunity for particular groups, including indigenous people, African Americans, and isolated subsistence farmers. Although conditions vary greatly, most countries share an income distribution that is among the least equal of any region of the world. The mechanisms for addressing inequality are a greater emphasis on primary education and health care for children, as well as a set of social policies called **conditional cash transfers (CCT)**. CCT began in Brazil and Mexico and have been adopted in more than seventeen countries. These programs vary somewhat in their size and administration, but in each case, households are given a small monthly cash grant that is contingent on their children's school attendance and often also requires regular health check-ups and vaccinations. The thinking behind the programs is that families are more likely to send their children to school if there is a financial incentive, and the incentive has the added bonus of replacing any lost wages that might result from attending school rather than working. Early research into program effectiveness shows that there has been an increase in primary school attendance and a slight decrease in economic inequality.

Over the last twenty years, a few countries, including Mexico and Chile, have become among the most open and outward-oriented countries anywhere. In a relatively short period, Latin America has undergone a historical shift from a relatively closed, inward-looking region in which national governments led economic development strategies, to a relatively open, market-oriented region. This shift has required fundamental changes in economic policy and in the thinking of politicians and citizens. In many respects, the region had no choice because the previous strategy of ISI was unable to ease the debt crisis of the 1980s. So far, the results of these reforms are disappointing, but they highlight the need for reformers to consider more than economics alone as they struggle to find the sources of economic development in a more integrated world environment.

CASE STUDY

The Chilean Model

Chile suffered through a brutal dictatorship in the 1970s and 1980s. General Augusto Pinochet came to power in 1973 after a military coup that overthrew the democratically elected Salvador Allende. Pinochet tortured and jailed an unknown number of Chilean citizens, and tortured and killed an estimated 2000–3000 more. He was an extreme nationalist who knew little about economics and preferred advisors who had no affiliation with previous governments. After the failure of his first economic advisor, he selected an ambitious group of Chilean academics who were outside the country's political establishment and who had received training at the University of Chicago. The University of Chicago was known for its free-market ideology, and Pinochet's economic advisors came to be known as the Chicago Boys.

The Chicago Boys quickly ended Chile's import substitution policies. They rapidly privatized banks, copper companies, and other firms that had been nationalized. They cut tariffs steeply, ended most import licensing requirements,

(*continued*)

and opened the Chilean economy to the world. Agricultural subsidies were cut and government supports were dismantled. The economy, which had been in crisis, began to grow two years after Pinochet gained power and after a disastrous recession in 1975. But the growth was illusory, and when a worldwide recession started in the early 1980s, Chile's economy collapsed. Banks were renationalized, and many of the trade reforms were turned back.

After two more years of crisis, the economy began to recover in 1984. This time, the Chicago Boys practiced a more pragmatic style of policymaking and growth remained strong through the remainder of the 1980s. By 1990, Pinochet was gone and democracy had been restored. A coalition of center and left parties, called Concertación, came to power and remained in office until 2010. During Concertación's twenty years in office, the presidency alternated between centrist Christian Democrats and leftist Socialists, but economic policy remained relatively constant. Ricardo Lagos, the Socialist Concertación president from 2000 to 2006, explained,

I do believe . . . that to have sound economic policies is not something of the right-wing or the left-wing parties. It's simply sound economic policies—now (that) took some time to learn.[*]

Under the Chicago Boys and the brutal dictator Pinochet, and under Socialist and center-right (Christian Democrat) members of Concertación, Chile implemented a broad spectrum of market reforms. These governments introduced school vouchers that subsidize students, not schools. They established a system of individual retirement accounts that workers manage like a mutual fund account. They built infrastructure such as roads, but if the government's budget was stretched too thin, they made them toll roads and got the private sector to construct them. They implemented a uniform tariff that is the same on all goods so it does not divert investment away from one sector and toward another, and they slowly reduced the tariff over time.

The governments that came after the Pinochet dictatorship kept many of the same market-oriented policies, even when the Socialists controlled the presidency. They added a series of new initiatives, however, to provide greater social justice. Health care was expanded, along with retirement funds for people who were too poor to have built up an individual account, and infrastructure spending was increased to connect the country and to increase mobility of goods, services, and people. Poverty rates fell, incomes rose, and Chile became a model for many other countries. Lagos explained the government's perspective in the following way:

It's one thing to say, "Look, we have a market economy." It's a different story to say, "I don't want to have a market society." I think it is really the big issue today in the world. It's true we are living in a global world where the market is allocating resources, but where to allocate resources in the area of public goods and services is something that remains in the domain of the citizen.[*]

---

[*]Quote by Ricardo Lagos
[*]Quote by Ricardo Lagos

Summary

- Latin America was one of the fastest-growing regions of the world throughout most of the twentieth century. Growth came crashing to a halt in the 1980s, however, and only began to return in the late 1980s and early 1990s.

- Until the recent reforms, Latin American economic growth has focused on inward development rather than outward orientation. Productivity in subsistence agriculture has lagged behind overall growth, leading to much higher rates of poverty in rural areas than in urban ones.

- The primary development strategy of Latin America was adopted in the 1930s, 1940s, and 1950s. It came to be called *import substitution industrialization* (ISI) and focused on the inwardly oriented development of industries that could produce goods that would substitute for imports. This model of development was favored because it was thought that Latin America would suffer ever-declining terms of trade for its primary commodity exports, and that ISI would reduce the need for foreign exchange and imports, thereby making the region less vulnerable to economic shocks from outside.

- Economic growth under ISI was adequate, but ultimately it led to an inefficient manufacturing sector, excessive rent seeking, a persistent tendency toward overvalued exchange rates, and too great a concentration of resources on the urban sector.

- ISI policies were often made worse by the tendencies of many countries to elect or support economic populists. Populists favored economic growth and redistribution while, in the extreme, they ignored economic constraints such as government budgets and foreign exchange shortages.

- Populist policies generated macroeconomic instability, which often led to hyperinflation and falling real wages.

- The debt crisis that began in 1982 affected every country of the region, even those without high levels of debt or debt problems. As a result of the crisis, it became extremely difficult to borrow internationally.

- The main causes of the debt crisis were the increases in lending during the 1970s and the external shocks of interest rate hikes and primary commodity price decreases, especially oil. The faulty macroeconomic policies of many Latin American governments during the late 1970s and early 1980s made them more vulnerable to the shocks.

- The debt crisis resulted in negative growth throughout the region for most of the period from 1982 through 1987. By 1987–1988, the need for significant reforms in economic policy was apparent to almost all governments.

- From the mid-1980s through the present, the governments of Latin America have engaged in serious reforms of economic policy. The reforms have first tried to create macroeconomic stability through controlling inflation and reducing budget deficits. Stabilization policies have been followed by structural reforms that have opened trade, privatized, and reduced and re-designed the regulatory environment.

■ Growth has returned to most of Latin America, but dissatisfaction with the economic reforms is widespread. Job creation is less than desired, inequality persists, and economic growth is below the rate necessary to significantly reduce poverty.

Vocabulary

Baker Plan

Brady Plan

conditional cash transfers (CCT)

Economic Commission on Latin America (ECLA, or CEPAL in Spanish)

economic populism

export pessimism

heterodox model

import substitution industrialization (ISI)

Lost Decade

market failure

neoliberal model or neoliberalism

orthodox model

structural reform policies

terms of trade (TOT)

Washington Consensus

Study Questions

All problems are assignable in MyEconLab.

15.1 What were the main characteristics of economic growth in Latin America from the end of World War II until the debt crisis of the 1980s?

15.2 What is import substitution industrialization (ISI)? Explain its goals and methods.

15.3 What are the main criticisms of ISI? Did ISI fail?

15.4 Describe a typical cycle of economic populism. Why does it often leave its supporters worse off than before the cycle began?

15.5 Explain how economic populist policies usually lead to overvalued exchange rates and large trade deficits.

15.6 What were the proximate causes of the debt crisis? How did the United States and other industrial countries respond?

15.7 Why did the Latin American debt crisis of the 1980s cause recessions in each country?

15.8 What is the difference between stabilization policies and structural adjustment policies? Give examples of each.

15.9 What is neoliberalism? Why do some people consider it a negative term?

15.10 What was the content of Latin American trade reforms of the late 1980s and 1990s? How do the actions taken relate to the desired goals?

CHAPTER 16

Export-Oriented Growth in East Asia

Learning Objectives

After studying this chapter, students will be able to:

16.1 List four general characteristics of success in the export-oriented East Asian economies.

16.2 Describe how the institutional environment supported economic growth.

16.3 Analyze the degree of openness in the export-oriented East Asian economies.

16.4 Explain the pros and cons of the idea that industrial policies mattered to East Asian success.

16.5 Evaluate the impact of export promotion policies and the debate over their applicability to other world regions.

16.6 Define total factor productivity and explain why economists use it to understand whether growth in East Asia is similar to growth elsewhere.

INTRODUCTION: HIGH-GROWTH ASIAN ECONOMIES

One of the most interesting and important economic stories of the last fifty years is the success of several Asian economies. In Chapter 17 we will look more closely at two economic giants, China and India, but in this chapter the focus is on a set of very diverse countries that experienced rapid economic growth over several decades after World War II. Hong Kong, Korea, Taiwan, and Singapore, have reached World Bank classification status as high-income, while Malaysia, Thailand, and Vietnam, began their periods of rapid growth somewhat later and are still classified as middle-income. Rounding out this group is Japan, the first of the high-growth East Asian economies and a significant influence on the economic policies of the others. This is a very diverse group with many differences. Not all of them are sovereign nations, for example, as Hong Kong is a Special Administrative Region of China. Several are former colonies of Britain (Hong Kong, Malaysia, Singapore) or Japan (Korea), and although most were solidly capitalist, Vietnam is formerly socialist and, like China, retains some elements of socialism. What they share, beyond their decades of rapid economic growth, is an out- ward-looking export orientation. In the 1980s, the World Bank called attention to their successes by including them in a group of eight economies it labeled High Performance

Asian Economies (which also included Indonesia but omitted Vietnam because it had just begun its transition from socialism to capitalism); subsets were called the Little Dragons, or the Four Tigers. Their impact on world markets through their capacity to export and their high growth rates made them a focus of economic attention before Chinese growth began to reshape the world economy, and stood in contrast to other world regions where growth was mediocre at best. Their economic successes were a testimony to the idea that low-income and middle-income

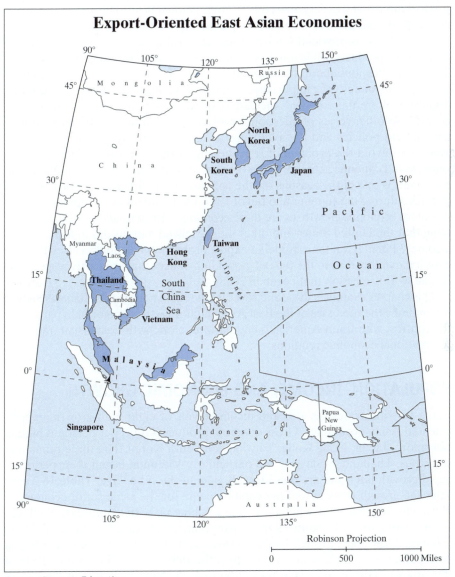

Export-Oriented East Asian Economies

Robinson Projection

0   500   1000 Miles

Source: Pearson Education

countries are capable of eliminating poverty and generating growth sufficient to become high-income, industrial societies.

Economists agree on several facts about these high-growth Asian economies. First, they were careful to maintain stable macroeconomic environments and had fewer recessions and financial crises than were common in most other regions of the world. Second, they had strong and credible commitments to sharing the benefits of economic growth, in part through expanded access to health care, education, and housing. These policies and others enabled them to develop a skilled, highly literate workforce that was very attractive to multinational firms. Third, they promoted their exports, but they remained more open to imports than most other developing countries. Exports provided foreign exchange earnings and forced firms to make competitive products, while imports brought new technologies and new products.

Several questions about the economic success of these countries remain unanswered. For example, the importance of industrial policies, or industrial targeting is unclear. Were these policies incidental, or were they instrumental in creating growth? Another series of questions revolves around the use of interventionist government policies and the avoidance of rent seeking. Specifically, did these economies avoid the problem of rent seeking in the various government interventions in economic activity? Some economists argue that they did not avoid it, and that it is one of the reasons for the collapse of the financial sector in several countries during the summer and fall of 1997. Do their successes represent a new model for economic growth, or are these economies doing fundamentally the same thing that the United States and other industrialized nations did to achieve high incomes? Finally, can their model of export promotion be adopted elsewhere, or does it inevitably lead to the type of global imbalances that are partly responsible for the world recession that began in 2008?

This chapter examines these and several other questions as it explains the issues surrounding the successes of the East Asian high-growth economies. In particular, the contrast with Latin America is emphasized, along with East Asian trade and international economic relations.

POPULATION, INCOME, AND ECONOMIC GROWTH

Table 16.1 illustrates the size and income levels of eight high-growth, export-oriented Asian economies. Gross domestic product (GDP) per person is high in Singapore, Japan, Hong Kong, Taiwan, and South Korea. The three remaining countries, Thailand, Malaysia, and particularly Vietnam, began their period of rapid growth later and are considerably behind the other five. Table 16.2 contains the growth rates in real per capita income for the same set of economies. Between 1980 and 2000, while they were catching up with countries in the high-income categories, all countries grew faster than the average for middle and high income. After 2000, growth began to slow, particularly in Japan which began to experience a unique set of problems in the 1990s. According to the "Rule of 72," if a variable (income, for example) grows at the rate X, then it doubles in

TABLE 16.1   Population and GDP for the Export-Oriented East Asian Economies, 2015

	Population (Millions)	GDP (US$, Billions)	GDP per Capita (US$, PPP)
Hong Kong SAR	7.3	309.9	56,701
Japan	126.9	4,123.3	38,054
Korea	50.6	1,376.9	36,511
Malaysia	31.0	296.2	26,315
Singapore	5.5	292.7	85,253
Taiwan	23.5	523.6	46,783
Thailand	68.8	395.3	16,097
Vietnam	91.7	191.5	6,024

High-growth Asian economies have different income levels depending on the length of time they have experienced rapid economic growth.

Source: Data from International Monetary Fund, *World Economic Outlook Database*. © James Gerber.

TABLE 16.2   Average Annual Growth in Real GDP per Capita, 1980–2015

	Income-level	1980–2000	2000–2015
Hong Kong SAR	High	3.9	3.1
Japan	High	2.4	0.7
Korea	High	7.3	3.4
Malaysia	Middle	3.8	2.9
Singapore	High	4.7	3.0
Taiwan	High	5.4	3.3
Thailand	Middle	4.7	3.3
Vietnam	Middle	4.8	5.3
Average growth in countries with income levels:			
High		2.1	1.1
Medium		2.1	4.6
Low		−0.9	2.8

* 1990–2000

The high-growth East Asian economies outperformed low-, middle-, and high-income countries from 1980–2000, although growth began to slow down in most countries after 2000, or sooner in the case of Japan.

Source: Data from International Monetary Fund, *World Economic Outlook Database*. © James Gerber.

approximately $72/X$ years. In other words, Korea's 7.3 percent annual rate of growth between 1980 and 2000 implies that its per capita real GDP doubled in just under ten years (72/7.3).

A Note on Hong Kong

On July 1, 1997, Great Britain officially returned the colony of Hong Kong to China after more than 150 years of British rule. China has pledged itself to follow the policy of "one country, two systems" in its relations with Hong Kong. In practical terms, this means that China will allow Hong Kong to keep its own currency, will limit migration between Hong Kong and the mainland, and will generally try to preserve Hong Kong's current system. Statistics for Hong Kong and China are treated separately.

GENERAL CHARACTERISTICS OF GROWTH

LO 16.1 **List four general characteristics of success in the export-oriented East Asian economies.**

Recall from Chapter 15 that from the end of World War II until the mid- to late 1980s, economic growth in Latin America was characterized by high levels of inequality, periods of macroeconomic instability, and an inward orientation. The contrast with the export-oriented Asian economies could not be more striking, because their growth included much lower and sometimes falling levels of inequality, generally sound macroeconomic fundamentals, and the promotion of exports. It is worth looking at each of the elements in more detail.

Shared Growth

One of the most remarkable features of growth in the export-oriented Asian economies is that it was frequently accompanied by falling income inequality. This feature is even more remarkable when it is realized that inequality in income and wealth was already relatively low at the start of the period of high growth. Until relatively recently, economists thought that economic development led to rising inequality, followed eventually by a decline. This idea came from the 1950s work of Simon Kuznets and led to the idea of a Kuznets Curve which was an inverted U, with GDP per person on the horizontal axis and inequality on the vertical. Kuznets acknowledged that his data was limited primarily to the United States, the United Kingdom, and a few German territories, and was somewhat tentative about his conclusions, but his followers adopted the Kuznets Curve as a central truth about the relationship of inequality and GDP. The diversity of East Asian economies, along with their later start in the growth process and their policy differences from Europe and North America led to a relationship between economic growth and income inequality that was completely different from the one hypothesized by Kuznets because it showed a decline in inequality as GDP per person increased.

The conditions that led to greater income equality were rooted in the unique historical experiences of each country. Nevertheless, each of the Asian economies had a similar set of highly visible wealth-sharing mechanisms. Specifically, these included land reform, free public education, free basic health care, and significant investments in rural infrastructure, such as clean water systems, transportation, and communication systems. These policies did not equalize incomes, but they provided people with the tools they needed to raise their individual incomes and gave hope for the future. This had several positive effects. For example, when purchasing power is spread more widely through a society, it increases the opportunities for small- and medium-scale entrepreneurs that produce for the local market. The experience gained in meeting local demand helps small firms develop into larger enterprises and may carry over into numerous other activities. In addition, rising incomes across a broad spectrum of socioeconomic groups raise hopes for future improvements and encourage cooperation among the different classes of society while conferring legitimacy on the ruling governments. Both factors contribute to political stability as well as willingness by the business elites to commit to long-term investments.

Rapid Accumulation of Physical and Human Capital

Rising levels of equality were closely tied to very rapid rates of accumulation of physical and human capital. Rapid accumulation of physical capital is synonymous with high levels of investment. Investment, in turn, depended on high savings rates. The level of savings in the export-oriented Asian economies is considerably higher than in many other parts of the world. The explanations for the high savings are varied. In part, it is a result of the rapid **demographic transition** from high birth and death rates to low birth and death rates experienced by those nations after World War II. Countries that have completed a demographic transition have fewer children below working age and a larger percentage of the population engaged in economically productive work. Hence, they tend to have higher savings rates because a smaller share of the population is dependent on the savings of others for their care.

Savings rates were also boosted by the stable macroeconomic environment of low inflation, but it is likely that the most important underlying factor in the creation of high savings was the rapid rate of income growth. That is, savings and income growth are interdependent, and these economies seemed to have created a "virtuous cycle" in which rapid income growth caused high savings. Savings led to high rates of investment, which fed back into a second round of income growth and high savings.

Investment in people was as important as the accumulation of physical capital. One of the key features of educational policy is that public investment in education was focused on the primary and secondary levels. Educational dollars go further at this level, and the social impact is much greater per dollar spent than at the university level. These investments raised literacy rates dramatically and laid the foundation for a skilled workforce capable of tackling increasingly sophisticated forms of production. In effect, the continuous rise in human capital endowments constituted an ongoing shift in the comparative advantages of those nations so that new investments could continually push into new product lines.

Rapid Growth of Manufactured Exports

Each of the eight countries in Table 16.1 actively and successfully promoted exports, although several began development pushes with import substitution policies. Import substitution industrialization (ISI) policies, however, were quickly replaced with an emphasis on export promotion. The timing of the switch from ISI to export promotion varied by country. Japan began promoting exports in the late 1950s and early 1960s; the Four Tigers (Hong Kong, Korea, Singapore, and Taiwan) started in the late 1960s; and the newly industrializing economies (Malaysia, Thailand, and Vietnam) began in the early 1980s and 1990s.

Table 16.3 shows the results of the export push. By 2015, the eight export economies accounted for over 16 percent of world merchandise exports even though they had just over 10 percent of world GDP. These totals represented a significant growth in their share of merchandise exports precisely during the years that exports overall were rapidly growing Table 16.3 shows comparisons with the United States, Germany (another export-oriented economy), and China. China's strategy of export promotion has been similar, although its share of world merchandise exports is less than its share of world GDP, mostly because it is such a large economy that, like the United States and Japan, it depends less on trade. China's impact on the world economy through its export promotion policies has probably been greater, however, than the impacts of any of the other individual countries in Table 16.3, precisely because it is so large in absolute terms.

In part, the success of export promotion was the result of education policies that favored primary and secondary schooling. These policies created widespread literacy and an adaptable and easily trained labor force. In addition, each of the export economies in Tables 16.1–16.3 pursued various export promotion policies. For example, Japan and the Four Tigers made export financing credit readily available; they required export targets for firms that wished to receive favorable credit terms or tax benefits; and they provided tariff-free access to imports of capital equipment used to manufacture exports. Policies in the other countries were somewhat less interventionist and relied to a greater extent on attracting direct foreign investment in export activities.

The connection between export promotion and high rates of growth is an area of some controversy in economics. Several possible connections are explored in greater detail later in the chapter. A second controversy is the possibility of other nations using similar export promotion strategies and their potential to generate trade conflicts.

TABLE 16.3   **The Share of East Asian Exporters in World Merchandise Exports and GDP, 2015**

Country	Share of World:	
	Merchandise Exports	GDP
East Asian exporters		
Hong Kong	2.8	0.4
Japan	3.6	5.9
Korea	3	1.8
Malaysia	1.2	0.4
Singapore	2.2	0.4
Taiwan	1.6	0.7
Thailand	1.2	0.5
Vietnam	0.8	0.2
Total	16.4	10.3
Comparisons		
United States	8.5	22.3
Germany	7.9	5
China	12.3	13.3

Export promotion policies in the East Asian export economies resulted in a disproportionately high share of total world merchandise exports.

Source: Data from World Bank, *World Development Indicators,* © James Gerber.

Stable Macroeconomic Environments

The fourth and final characteristic of the East Asian export economies is the maintenance of stable macroeconomic environments. Chapter 15 argued that one of the persistent problems of Latin America has been the frequent re-occurrence of macroeconomic crises. This is not to imply that there were no crises in East Asia, as even before the Asian Crisis of 1997–1998, there were recessions and crises, but when they occurred, policy responses were usually quick and appropriate. Overall, macroeconomic stability was a high priority, and countries worked to ensure that inflation was controlled, government debts were well managed, and external debt was monitored and quickly resolved when a crisis threatened. In general, macroeconomic policy has been characterized as "pragmatic and flexible."

On average, budget deficits and foreign debt were not dramatically smaller than in other regions of the world, although there was a significant amount of varia-tion across countries. The difference in the export-oriented economies, however, is that with the exception of the 1997–1998 crisis, deficits and debts remained manageable. High growth rates helped ease the constraints imposed by a given level of debt, partly because the high levels of exports earned the foreign assets necessary for debt servicing.

The commitment to low inflation helped keep real interest rates stable and enabled firms to take a longer-run view of their investments. In addition, low inflation helped avoid severe real appreciations in the exchange rate. Low inflation also meant that variations in the real exchange rate, the real interest rate, and the inflation rate were relatively low. In turn, this helped to foster a greater security in the minds of investors.

THE INSTITUTIONAL ENVIRONMENT

LO 16.2 **Describe how the institutional environment supported economic growth.**

LO 16.3 **Analyze the degree of openness in the export-oriented East Asian economies.**

Economic success stems from an ability to mobilize and allocate resources. In the export-oriented Asian economies, large flows of savings were generated; they were channeled into the financial system; and they were lent to business enterprises that used them productively. Simultaneously, governments emphasized education and universal literacy. Ultimately, an efficient mobilization and allocation of resources is based on the decisions of individuals and businesses that own resources. To ensure that individuals and businesses use their resources in the most productive manner, governments must create rules that foster efficient outcomes. In this regard, the institutional environments of countries are essential to their success.

Several components of the institutional environment are critical insofar as they help to make government policy credible. In particular, property rights are relatively secure and free from the threat of nationalization. Bureaucracies are generally competent, individuals and businesses are free to make contracts that will be enforced, access to information is widespread, and regulations tend to be clear and well publicized. Of course, there are exceptions to each of these features, depending on the time and place, but in general they characterize the institutional environments of the Asian economies under consideration.

These characteristics should not be confused with the characteristics of open, democratic societies. The fact that several of the successful Asian economies have a mixed record when it comes to support for democratic institutions, raises issues about the relationship between authoritarian rule and economic growth. Does democracy support or hinder growth? The answer to this question is complex and beyond the scope of this text. Nevertheless, it should be noted that many authoritarian governments have failed in their bid to mobilize and allocate resources. These regimes may be as likely to prey upon society as they are to foster its

CASE STUDY

Worldwide Governance Indicators

Economists and political science have long recognized the importance of institutions, both for economic development and for a complete and fulfilling life. Institutions, in this view, are the rules of the game, as discussed briefly in Chapter 2. Governance indicators are quantitative measures of the effectiveness, fairness, and quality of government in the exercise of its authority. The Worldwide Governance Indicators (WGI) project measures governance institutions in six dimensions for 215 separate economies. The indicators allow governments to benchmark against leaders and to chart progress over time.

The six dimensions included in the WGI are:

1. Rule of law: The confidence of individuals and businesses in the fairness and impartiality of the law, police, and the courts.
2. Control of corruption: The ability of governments to prevent the use of state power for individual gain.
3. Voice and accountability: The ability of citizens to participate in government and to express themselves freely.
4. Government effectiveness: A measure of the quality of public services and the civil service.
5. Political stability and the absence of violence/terrorism: A measure of the absence of political instability, violence, and terrorism.
6. Regulatory quality: A measure of government's ability to implement effective and necessary regulations.

Quantitative indicators for each of the six dimensions are captured through data sources provided by surveys of households and firms, suppliers of business information, reports from private non-governmental organizations and think tanks, and publicly available multilateral and government information. The comparisons are broad estimates of the differences between countries and general changes over time.

Table 16.4 shows some of the indicators for the Asian export economies. The numbers represent the percentile for each country when it is ranked in a particular dimension against all 215 countries. Therefore, Korea's score of 87 in the "Government Effectiveness" category can be interpreted to mean that 87 percent of countries score worse, 13 percent score better. As shown, all eight countries except the poorest, Vietnam, do much better than average in controlling corruption, maintaining the rule of law, implementing quality regulations, and achieving a high overall level of government effectiveness. The scores not shown, voice and accountability and political stability/absence of violence, are lower in every case, and below world averages in the middle-income countries (Malaysia, Thailand, and Vietnam; Malaysia is slightly above average in the political stability category).

(continued)

TABLE 16.4   Comparative Measures of Governance, 2014

Country	Control of Corruption	Rule of Law	Regulatory Quality	Government Effectiveness
High income				
Hong Kong	92	94	100	98
Japan	93	89	84	97
Korea	70	81	84	87
Singapore	97	95	100	100
Taiwan	77	86	89	88
Middle income				
Malaysia	68	75	76	84
Thailand	42	51	62	66
Vietnam	38	45	30	52

Most of the export economies score above average in most measures of institutional quality; high-income countries consistently score higher than middle-income countries.

Source: Data from *The Worldwide Governance Indicators*: Methodology and Analytical Issues, by Kaufman, D., A. Kray, and M. Mastruzzi © James Gerber.

The pattern of differences shown in Table 16.4 raises a central question about institutional quality and its impact on the economy: Do good institutions create more economic growth, or does economic growth create better institutions? For example, does Singapore have good governance because it is relatively well-off, or is it well-off because it has good governance? Which is cause and which is effect? Undoubtedly there is some mutual interaction and while causation runs in both directions, the strength of the interaction cannot be determined by looking at the data alone. What we can say, is that the most successful economies also have very high-quality governance indicators and, generally speaking, the higher the income level, the better the governance in most dimensions.

economic development. However, the Asian economies in this chapter fostered growth rather than the enrichment of a small elite at the expense of the majority.

A second issue that arises from the general lack of traditionally defined democratic rights is the relevancy of the experience these countries to other regions of the world, such as Latin America. Some social scientists argue that the context of authoritarian rule makes the Asian economies irrelevant to Latin American nations, where policy reform took place within an institutional setting that allows far more dissent. Generally speaking, there does not seem to be a correlation between the type of government (democratic or authoritarian) and the ability to put good policies into place.

Fiscal Discipline and Business–Government Relations

As noted in the previous case study, not all of the eight economies score above world averages in the "Voice and Accountability" category. Nevertheless, whether they are fully democratic or not, governments must create stable macroeconomic environments in order for economic growth to succeed. The characteristic of macroeconomic stability has already been mentioned, but it is worth revisiting because of its central importance. The maintenance of a stable macroeconomic environment requires fiscal discipline and an acceptance of the resource constraints that limit government actions. Budget deficits and foreign debt must be kept manageable, and the real exchange rate must be relatively stable. The benefits of accepting these limitations are that it increases the credibility of government policy and builds the private sector's confidence. The result is more investment and less capital flight.

Stable macroeconomic policies are necessary for growth, but they are no guarantee. For example, macroeconomic stability does not address the very significant problem in all developing countries of the coordination of interdependent investment projects. The coordination problem results from the fact that many private sector investments are interdependent. That is, their profitability depends on the simultaneous or prior creation of a complementary investment. The same often holds true for private sector/public sector investments. For example, profitable investment

CASE STUDY

Doing Business in the Export Oriented Asian Economies

In 1989, Peruvian economist Hernando de Soto published *The Other Path,* a brilliant work that argued against cumbersome, complex, and unnecessary business regulations in developing countries. De Soto made his case with a simple, yet powerful, experiment: He hired a small team of researchers in Lima, Peru, to work full time at obtaining a business license for a small apparel manufacturing firm. The researchers spent the equivalent of 289 days of full-time work by an individual—nearly ten months—and paid an amount equal to thirty-two times a monthly minimum wage to obtain the signatures and permits required to register their business officially. Then they duplicated this experiment in a number of other developing countries to show that Peru is not atypical. Ultimately, these barriers constrain the economic growth of national economies by limiting the growth of small business.

De Soto's work found its way onto a larger stage at the World Bank where his ideas were built into an ongoing research project and an online database comparing the ease of doing business in 189 countries. The Doing Business Web site (http://www.doingbusiness.org) issues an annual report on the ease

(continued)

of doing business. In all, there are ten different dimensions, each of which is composed of four indicator variables and five or six indices that measure the indicator variables. Each country is ranked on each of the ten dimensions:

1. Ease of starting a business.
2. Dealing with construction permits.
3. Getting electricity.
4. Registering property.
5. Getting credit.
6. Protecting investors.
7. Paying taxes.
8. Trading across borders.
9. Enforcing contracts.
10. Resolving insolvency.

The overall rankings are a combination of scores on each of these ten. Table 16.5 shows comparisons for the Asian export oriented economies. Five are in the top twenty and seven are top fifty. Only Vietnam ranks in the middle of the 189 countries in the sample.

The ease of doing business is one factor that explains the high performance of this group of Asian economies, although some countries may succeed without scoring very high in this area. China, for example, ranked number 84 of 189 in 2015, yet its growth is exceptionally rapid and foreign investors are extremely active in the country. In China's case, size matters and investors go to China in spite of the difficulties of doing business there. None of the economies in Table 16.5 has that advantage, except perhaps Japan.

TABLE 16.5   **Rankings on the Ease of Doing Business Index, 2015**

Country	World ranking
Singapore	1
Hong Kong	5
Korea	4
Taiwan	11
Malaysia	18
Japan	34
Thailand	49
Vietnam	90

One key to the successes of the East Asian export economies is the ease of doing business.

Source: From International Finance Corporation and the World Bank, *Doing Business*, © 2015 The World Bank.

in warehousing facilities at a seaport depends on prior investment in sufficient port infrastructure to provide an adequate flow of goods through the warehouses. Yet the port and related transportation linkages may not be worthwhile unless there is a simultaneous investment or a guarantee of future investment in the warehouses.

The coordination of interdependent investment activities is difficult in a purely free-market framework. The difficulty stems from the fact that the flow of information is not sufficient to let all investors know of each other's intentions. Six of the eight countries in this chapter surmounted this problem through the creation of **deliberation councils**, a set of quasi-legislative bodies that bring together representatives from the private and the public sectors. In effect, deliberation councils coordinate the information flow between businesses and policymakers.

Individual councils are usually created to deal with a limited set of issues involving one industry or a particular set of policy issues, such as the government budget. By bringing together government officials and affected business groups, the councils reduce the cost of acquiring information about new policies, provide a forum for bargaining over policies, instill greater investor confidence, and raise the level of credibility of the government's policies. More than perhaps any other function, however, deliberation councils serve as a vehicle for the business elites to have a strong voice in the setting of government policy and thereby ensure their cooperation in the overall economic strategy.

For example, Japan has used deliberation councils extensively. This involves a feedback process in which the first step is for officials to call a hearing and invite comments from various interested parties on a proposed policy or industrial strategy. Based on the information they collect, a draft report is issued that is then forwarded for discussion to a council made up of industry representatives, academics, journalists, consumer advocates, labor leaders, former bureaucrats, financial specialists, and politicians. Representation is not proportional in any sense, nor are representatives elected. Based on the feedback from the council, officials change the draft plan and issue a final document that details the steps that will be taken, such as policy changes or new policy initiatives. The final action is essentially a public relations campaign to sell the plan to the wider public.

Avoiding Rent Seeking

Economic policy in the East Asian export economies has been relatively interventionist. That is, the laissez-faire ideology of letting markets determine outcomes has not been followed. Hong Kong is an exception, but even there, the government has directed and actively participated in the creation of extensive public housing. In the next section, we examine some of the issues related to the effectiveness and extent of government intervention in the economy. Whether extensive or not, however, one of the biggest puzzles surrounding these economies was the degree to which most countries were able to avoid the costs and inefficiencies associated with private sector rent seeking.

When governments intervene to help specific industries or to channel resources in a particular direction, they create benefits that are of value to someone. Generally speaking, when private interests perceive the possibility of obtaining something of value from government (for instance, credit subsidies, import protection, and business licenses) they will devote scarce resources to obtaining those benefits. The result, as discussed in several earlier chapters, is wasteful rent seeking. Government policies created numerous benefits of value to specific industries, yet in spite of this there was relatively little rent seeking by those interests. To be sure, rent seeking still occurs, and there is significant variation across the economies. Nevertheless, there is less overall rent seeking than in many other societies, as evidenced indirectly by measures of governance shown in the prior case study.

It is unlikely that there is a single, simple explanation for this lack of rent-seeking behavior, but the deliberation councils probably played a key role. By providing a policy forum in which various interests can make their views known and have a chance to argue in favor of policies that are particularly beneficial, the need to hire lobbyists is reduced. Furthermore, given that industrial and business interests meet with government officials as a group rather than single interests by themselves, there is greater transparency and less worry about what competing interests may be doing behind the scenes.

In addition to the role played by deliberation councils, some analysts point to the fact that whenever governments offer something of value, they usually attach performance requirements. For example, firms receiving credit subsidies or import protection are usually required to meet specific targets—often export targets—or else the subsidies are taken away. What is remarkable, and not clearly understood, is how governments are able to enforce the performance requirements they lay down. Many nations outside East Asia, including many Latin American governments, have used performance requirements as incentive mechanisms, but often they have proven to be unenforceable. That is, when firms in Latin America have not met their production or export targets, governments have often been unable to withdraw the special considerations they are providing to the noncompliant firms.

Two key elements that have played a role in enforceability are the presence of a well-educated bureaucracy along with its insulation from the political process. In most of the export-oriented economies, civil service careers are highly respected and well paid. Consequently, bureaucrats are well educated and competent. In addition to ability, their insulation from the political process gives them the room to make decisions based on merit rather than on the basis of special interests.

A final explanation for the relative lack of rent seeking is the commitment to shared growth that we saw at the beginning of the chapter. The fact that business elites are convinced that they will share the benefits of economic growth reduces the pressure for them to seek added benefits through the manipulation of the political process. In effect, greater equality reduces the number of individuals and groups that feel left out of the growth process and eliminates the underlying cause of much rent seeking.

CASE STUDY

Were East Asian Economies Open?

High-growth Asian economies relied on their export sectors for a substantial part of their growth. They actively promoted exports in various ways and to varying degrees, and there is a consensus among economists that manufactured exports played a key role in their economic development. Export promotion is not the same thing as an open economy, however, and there is disagreement about their trade policies and the extent of their openness.

It would seem easy to settle the debate simply by looking at tariff rates and quotas. Unfortunately, these are inadequate measures of trade policy, particularly if a country has significant nontariff measures that it uses to block imports. For example, the U.S. auto industry argued for years that red tape and unnecessary safety inspections made their cars uncompetitive in Japanese markets. This may or may not have been the case; U.S. cars were not designed for Japan, and the Japanese marketing and distribution systems are fundamentally different from those in the United States. Did U.S. cars fare poorly because the playing field was tilted to favor Japanese brands, or was the playing field level and U.S. automakers had products that were less competitive?

It is possible that high-growth Asian economies promoted their exports and severely restricted imports to protect domestic markets. In that case, their policies were not market-oriented, but instead reflected a high degree of government intervention with the purpose of determining outcomes selected by planners and government officials. In this view, some East Asian economies followed the policies of mercantilism and viewed exports as the path to wealth creation and imports as destructive to their wealth and prosperity (see Chapter 3). Alternatively, East Asian economies did not set tough constraints on imports, but followed relatively open export promotion policies that contributed to rapid economic growth, more or less in line with market-based incentives.

This is an important debate. Some of the countries examined in this chapter were among the first since World War II to go from developing to developed, or low and middle income to high income. If mercantilism is the key to their success, it would be an important empirical case against the paradigm of comparative advantage and the gains from trade.

Table 16.6 contrasts imports and exports for high-growth East Asian countries with those of the main Latin American economies. Imports and exports include goods and services and are measured relative to the size of each country's GDP. Data is provided for two years. In 1980, most of the East Asian economies were practicing export promotion policies, and Latin America had weak export sectors and relatively closed economies.

Between 1980 and 2014, every country except Singapore increased its imports relative to its GDP, and most countries increased the relative share of exports in

(continued)

its GDP. Beginning in the late 1980s, most Latin American economies started to become more open to trade as they began to dismantle their import substitutions policies and started to sign regional free trade agreements. Nevertheless, Latin America trades much less than the high export East Asian economies. The partial exception is Japan, which as a large country has a smaller trade-to-GDP ratio than any of the other Asian economies in Table 16.6.

East Asian economies apparently did not close their import sectors, but rather imported quite a large amount of goods and services. While they used selective protection for targeted industries, in general the data do not support the idea that they were relatively closed to imports. This is entirely consistent with theoretical models showing that protectionism often hurts exports by causing the currency to appreciate as a result of a lack of demand for foreign goods, and due to the higher returns that protectionism creates for the production of import substitutes. In other words, just as Latin America's depressed imports went hand-in-hand with its depressed exports in 1980, East Asia's high level of exports went hand-in-hand with a relatively high level of imports.

TABLE 16.6   Imports and Exports as a Share of GDP

	Imports		Exports	
	1980	2014	1980	2014
East Asian Exporters				
Hong Kong, China	89.4	219.6	88.9	219.6
Japan	14.5	20.8	13.6	17.7
Korea, Republic	40.0	45.3	32.1	50.6
Malaysia	54.3	64.6	56.7	73.8
Singapore	209.0	163.2	202.1	187.6
Taiwan	52.6	60.4	24.1	70.1
Thailand	30.4	62.6	51.4	69.2
Vietnam		83.1		86.4
Latin America				
Argentina	6.5	14.5	5.1	14.8
Brazil	11.3	13.9	9.0	11.2
Colombia	15.6	21.4	16.2	16.0
Mexico	13.0	33.5	10.7	32.4
Peru	19.4	23.9	22.4	22.4
Venezuela	21.8	29.5*	28.8	24.7*

East Asian economies promoted exports but also absorbed large quantities of imports.

THE ROLE OF INDUSTRIAL POLICIES

LO 16.4 Explain the pros and cons of the idea that industrial policies mattered to East Asian success.

The most influential study of export-oriented Asian economies is the World Bank's policy research report entitled *The East Asian Miracle: Economic Growth and Public Policy*. The World Bank's research team concluded that government interventions were common in three areas: (1) targeting of specific industries, that is, industrial policies narrowly defined; (2) directed credit; and (3) export promotion. In this section, we examine the debate over the effectiveness of industrial policies and offer a word of caution about the use of directed credit.

Targeting Specific Industries

Recall from Chapter 5 that industrial policies can be defined in broad or narrow terms. The broad definition is policies that alter a nation's endowment in a way that does not favor particular industries. For example, we have already seen that the East Asian success story involves high rates of primary and secondary schooling that altered the characteristics of the labor force, and high rates of savings and investment that created the infrastructure and capital goods necessary to enter more sophisticated lines of manufacturing.

The narrow definition of industrial policies is the targeted development of specific industries. In effect, targeted industrial policies attempt to change the comparative advantage of a nation through the alteration of its industrial structure. These policies channel resources to favored industries and are often criticized as being "government bureaucrats picking winners and losers."[*]

With the exception of Hong Kong, each of the countries has had, or still has some form of targeted industrial policy. These policies were strongest in Japan, Korea, and Taiwan (the "northern tier"), but were significant in the other countries as well. In Japan, the focus has been on steel, autos, textiles, shipbuilding, aluminum, electronics, and semiconductors, among others. The height of Korean policies was between 1973–1979 with the Heavy and Chemical Industries (HCI) program, which targeted steel, shipbuilding, petrochemicals, and other heavy industries. While lacking the same clear focus as Japan and Korea, Taiwan's programs have provided research institutes, science parks, and basic infrastructure for a variety of industries and seem to have targeted the development of import substitutes.

Malaysian policies took off in the early 1980s with the Look East policy, which emulated Korea's and Japan's industrial development. Malaysia created the Heavy Industries Corporation of Malaysia (HICOM) to develop steel, nonferrous metals, machinery, paper and paper products, and petrochemicals; but it ran into financial constraints in the late 1980s when many of the firms under HICOM proved to be unprofitable and required government bailouts. Since then, Malaysia has privatized many firms and reduced the degree of state control in others. Thailand did

---

[*]From Ethanol industry buys a top seed and three key politicians by Mark tapscott, The Washington Examiner © MediaDC.

not make systematic efforts such as Japan and Korea did, but the Thai Board of Investment promoted industries that it deemed to have the potential for technological learning. Singapore's policies have focused largely on encouraging technology transfer from firms in industrial nations through the promotion of foreign direct investment. Vietnam did not begin its transition to a market-oriented economy until approximately 1989, but it has focused on attracting foreign direct investment to supply it with technology and manufacturing capacity, and has begun to copy Korea's development of large conglomerates in targeted sectors. Vietnam, unlike Korea, however, has retained state ownership of many of the conglomerates.

The tools that nations use to promote specific industries include the instruments of trade policies. Restrictions on imports, through licensing, quotas or tariffs, and export subsidies were all used. In many cases, protection from foreign competition enabled firms to earn high profits in domestic markets, which compensated for the losses they suffered in foreign markets. In addition to trade policy, countries used numerous other mechanisms to channel resources to targeted industries. Directed credit was one of the most important tools, because even when it was small in size, it signaled the private sector that government policy favored the industry receiving the funds. This official stamp of approval was an important device for encouraging private lending to new and potentially risky industries. Other tools included subsidies; market information especially with respect to foreign markets, infrastructure construction, and research and development funds.

There are two essential elements to these policies that make them different from most other national attempts to promote specific industries. First, resources were usually only provided as long as the companies receiving them met specific export targets. If the targets were not met, the resources (protection, credit, and so on) were withdrawn. Export targets are argued to be a better criterion than profits because many firms had monopolies or significant market power in their domestic markets; hence, profitability may be unrelated to efficiency. Second, governments placed macroeconomic stability above industrial policies. If they began to experience fiscal problems caused by the industrial promotion programs, they scaled them back or abandoned them.

The World Bank view of these programs is that they were insulated from purely political influences so that industrial targeting decisions were based on technical analysis rather than politics. The collapse of the financial sectors in many countries in 1997 and 1998 has called this assumption into question. For example, government use of directed credit programs appears to be one of the main causes of the financial crisis. Government involvement in credit allocation forced financial institutions to make unsound loans. In turn, the failure to apply business criteria led to a mountain of bad debt, which ultimately sank many banks and whole financial sectors.

Did Industrial Policies Work?

The role of industrial policies in the story of East Asian growth is controversial. Ideally, we would like to know the answers to two simple questions. First, did they work? A successful policy would be one that increases the overall rate of

GDP growth or the rate of productivity growth. Second, if they worked, were they important? That is, was their contribution to economic growth significant enough to be considered one of the reasons for economic success?

With respect to the question of whether they made a positive contribution to growth, opinion ranges from "no effect" to "positive effect." The reason for the lack of consensus on this important issue is that, in general, it is difficult to measure the effects of policy interventions on growth rates. There are conceptual disagreements about the measurements that should be made, and few countries have data of sufficient quality. In the World Bank's view, "reasoned judgments" must be used to settle the issue. Unfortunately, the paucity of data, together with disagreements over measurement techniques, results in the use of qualitative judgments of the sort that inevitably lead researchers to confirm the opinions that they began with.

In spite of these obstacles to assessing industrial policies, the variety of opinions among researchers can be characterized as falling into two camps. One camp is represented by the World Bank's research. In its view, some government interventions fostered economic growth (export promotion and directed credit), but in general industrial policies did not. They assert that industrial policies usually targeted the same industries that market forces were developing and, therefore, were unnecessary. In the cases where the "wrong" industries were targeted, pragmatic and flexible policymakers managed to quickly change policies before any damage was done to the rest of the economy.

The World Bank's analysis rests on two pieces of evidence. First, it compares the growth rates of productivity in the targeted and nontargeted sectors in the three countries with sufficient data (Japan, Korea, and Taiwan). In general, it finds that productivity change in the promoted sectors was high but no higher than in the rest of the economy. Possible exceptions to its general finding are Japan's chemical and metalworking industries and Korea's chemical industry. Second, it examines the change over time in the industrial structure of the countries. If industrial policies worked, they should have led to a different pattern of industrial growth than the pattern caused by a change in factor endowments. The World Bank concluded that industrial policies were at most marginally effective, because the sector-by-sector growth pattern is as expected, given the national endowments of labor and the high savings and investment rates.

Critiques of the World Bank's findings usually rest on two points. First, the fact that productivity growth was generally no faster in promoted sectors is irrelevant, according to the critics. The important issue is what the growth rates would have been without promotion. It is conceivable that without industrial policies, growth in the targeted industries would have been much slower than with the policies. Second, the critics point out that the World Bank analysis is overly general. In their view, it is based on industry groupings that are too broad to uncover the details of selective targeting. For example, some components of the textile industry were heavily promoted in both Japan and Korea in the early period of their industrial policies. Therefore, it is not surprising that textiles overall have experienced a rapid increase in productivity and that they remain a larger than expected component of Japanese and Korean industry.

At present, there is no way to resolve this debate. Consequently, there are various opinions about the relevance of industrial policies for developing countries in general. To the extent that there is an agreement, most analysts share the view that if industrial policies are to be successful, they should have three key characteristics. Countries must have (1) clear performance criteria such as export targets, (2) institutional mechanisms to monitor compliance and enforce compliance, and (3) low costs so that nontargeted sectors do not suffer.

CASE STUDY

HCI in Korea

Most observers agree that Korean industrial policies have at least partially succeeded. The most enthusiastic observers argue that they have accelerated the rate of overall growth without creating offsetting inefficiencies elsewhere in the economy. Less optimistic observers concede success in generating exports and in changing the industrial structure of the country, but they offset many of those gains with the huge financial costs of the Heavy and Chemical Industries (HCI) promotion in the 1970s.

Korea's industrial promotion drive began a few years after the Korean War in the early 1960s. Early efforts at industrial targeting focused on key industrial materials such as cement, fertilizer, and petroleum refining. The government typically supported large-scale conglomerates, called *chaebol*, which were given monopolies in the domestic market. Trade policy in the form of an aggressive promotion of exports along with high levels of protection was the main tool for targeting industries, but directed credit and tax breaks were important as well.

Industrial targeting evolved into the Heavy and Chemical Industries program, which was at its most active from 1973 to 1979. HCI targeted six specific industrial groups—steel, petrochemicals, nonferrous metals for enhanced self-sufficiency, shipbuilding, electronics, and machinery (especially earth-moving equipment and autos)—for export. The tools used to promote these industries were the same as previously described, but with a different emphasis. By the mid-1970s, trade policy had become somewhat more liberal, although most industries still received significant protection. Greater emphasis was placed on subsidies, directed credit through loans at below-market interest rates, and special tax exemptions.

The cost of promotion during the HCI period was significant. Direct funds provided to targeted industries were around 5 percent of the overall budget, and tax exemptions amounted to about 3 percent of total tax revenues. In 1977, around 45 percent of the banking system's total provision of domestic credit went to the targeted industries. Gradually, bottlenecks and large debts began to accumulate.

By 1979, when the second oil crisis hit, inflation was high, the exchange rate had appreciated, causing exports to falter, and the targeted industries had significant idle capacity. In addition, the labor-intensive sectors, which had not been targeted, were starved for credits, and bad debts and financial insolvencies were growing in the HCI sector.

Policymakers quickly switched course. HCI promotion was curtailed, the currency was devalued, and financial market and import liberalization were hastened. One of the main efforts of policymakers in the 1980s was to restructure a number of the distressed industries that were over promoted in the 1970s. The cost to the government budget has been significant, as it has been forced to bail out bankrupt firms and dispose of nonperforming loans.

Was HCI promotion worth it? It is impossible to answer this question definitively because we can never know what would have happened under an alternative set of policies. During the height of the HCI program and its immediate aftermath, Korea's growth rate dipped slightly (from the mid-1970s through the mid-1980s), but the change was slight and growth overall remained extremely high. Korea achieved classification as a high-income nation, a feat that only Japan and the city-states of Singapore and Hong Kong accomplished in the twentieth century.

Source: Based on World Bank, *The East Asian Miracle*; Industrial Policy in an Export-Propelled Economy: Lessons from South Korea's Experience", in *The Journal of Economic Perspectives*, Summer 1990 © James gerber.

THE ROLE OF MANUFACTURED EXPORTS

LO 16.5   Evaluate the impact of export promotion policies and the debate over their applicability to other world regions.

The promotion of manufactured exports played a significant role in the industrial strategies of most of the countries examined in this chapter. The lone exception is Hong Kong that attained a high level of trade not by manufacturing products itself, but by acting as a major port for trade with China and East Asia. The promotion of manufactured exports were largely successful, and the exports of each country grew even faster than its GDP. Given these facts, it is reasonable to assume that there might be a connection between the two. That is, a number of studies of the East Asia and other regions have shown that higher rates of growth of exports are correlated with higher rates of growth of GDP. What is the mechanism that causes this?

The Connections between Growth and Exports

It is true by definition that exports are part of the GDP, so growth in exports would seem to be simply a part of overall GDP growth. If production of exports crowds out production for domestic consumption, then export growth may not increase GDP. In effect, the idea that export growth causes faster GDP growth is an assertion that export growth causes the overall capacity of the economy to grow faster than it would have if production was focused on goods for the domestic market.

If production focused on exports results in greater overall growth, then there must be something in the production process or its links to the rest of the economy that is absent from domestically focused production. One possibility is that because exports are produced for the world market, economies of scale come into play in a way that is absent when firms produce for a small domestic market. Larger firms often have lower average costs because they can spread their fixed costs for capital and machinery over a larger volume of output. Another possible reason why exports might foster growth is that as firms produce for a world market, there are added incentives to increase research and the development of new products. Economies of scale may make it worthwhile, and the need to keep up with foreign competition may make it necessary.

Other connections between export growth and GDP growth are possible as well. Exports may speed up the adoption and mastery of international best practices. Firms that operate in global markets are not protected from competition. In fact, they are going up against the world's best, and the competitive pressures may force firms to stay abreast of the latest developments in their product area and production process. Measurement of this possible effect can be complicated by the existence of export promotion policies because an exporter does not have to be among the world's best if it receives subsidies (for example, direct payment or access to low-interest loans or tax breaks). Firms can be competitive due to subsidies received at home, which may reduce the pressures to compete based on efficiency or quality. Successful export promotion programs, such as those in Korea, are well aware of this problem, and because their goal is to develop firms capable of head-to-head international competition without special breaks, they carefully monitor the programs to ensure that the subsidies granted to the exporters do not become the reason for competitive success abroad. In addition, successful export programs gradually reduce the subsidies they offer as firms become internationally competitive. Note, however, that since 1995, the international rules for subsidies have tightened considerably, and it is much harder for countries to provide direct support for industries within the World Trade Organization (WTO) framework.

Production of exports has several other potential advantages. Exports make possible the purchase of imports. Developing countries are not usually on the technology frontier, and the creation of an efficient manufacturing enterprise is often dependent on imports of machinery and other capital goods. A scarcity of exports impairs a country's ability to purchase imports, with the result that firms are unable to obtain the imported inputs they need in order to raise their efficiency. A related advantage of exports is that the need to meet export targets caused export-oriented economies to encourage inward foreign direct investment (FDI) and the acquisition of new technology. One way to overcome the backwardness of domestic manufacturing is to encourage foreign firms to invest. Most of the Asian export economies welcomed FDI and Singapore and Vietnam went so far as to build industrial policies around it. At the same time that FDI was encouraged, several countries also sought to provide incentives for the foreign firm to license its technology to potential domestic rivals. This was a particularly common strategy in Japan (and currently in China), where the incentive of access to the large Japanese market was sufficient to encourage many firms to sign technology licensing agreements.

The ability to import capital and modern technology is seen by some as the most critical ingredient in policies that successfully close the gap between developing and developed countries. Export promotion can encourage the acquisition of new technologies because in order to succeed, governments must allow access to whatever imports firms need to become efficient. Most of the governments selectively protected their domestic markets, but they also adjusted their policies so that exporters were given access to needed imports. In general, they used less protection than other developing areas.

Is Export Promotion a Good Model for Other Regions?

The export promotion model has succeeded so well in East Asia that, inevitably, it is being prescribed for other developing areas. In Latin America, for example, the economic crisis of the 1980s, together with the very visible counterexample of East Asia, has propelled many nations into similar types of policies. A serious question is whether other areas can duplicate the export successes of the Asian export economies.

If developing countries around the world begin to emphasize export promotion policies, an issue arises as to whether the world's industrial nations can absorb the exports of a series of newly industrializing countries. Some analysts view the large trade imbalances of the early 2000s as a contributor to the vulnerabilities that ultimately led to the financial crisis in 2007 and a global recession in 2008. If all of the world's low- and middle-income countries, along with some high income ones, attempt to export their way to prosperity without purchasing a similar quantity of imports, export surpluses will have to be matched by deficits somewhere else in the system. In the long run, this is not sustainable, and in the short and medium runs, it runs the risk of political confrontations and trade wars.

Perhaps the greatest obstacle for countries that wish to replicate the export promotion policies of the Asian exporters is the Uruguay Round of the General Agreement on Tariffs and Trade (GATT). Under the rules that went into effect in 1994, developing countries must eliminate any subsidies that are contingent on export performance. (See the case study on WTO rules in Chapter 5.) Extremely poor countries with per capita GDP less than $1,000 are exempted. Essentially, the new GATT rules eliminate the possibility that developing countries can use the same tools—credit subsidies, tax breaks, direct payments—that have been used previously. The only exceptions are the poorest countries, which do not export manufactured goods in any quantity.

CASE STUDY

Asian Trade Blocs

The first edition of this text (1994) began this case study as follows: "Asia is the one region of the world without significant trade blocs." Since then, and more particularly since 2000, that has changed dramatically. Table 16.7 shows the progression in Asia of the signing of trade agreements.

Before the growth of trade agreements in the 1990s, the **Association of Southeast Asian Nations (ASEAN)** was the most notable example of an Asian cooperation agreement. Founded in 1967 with five members (Indonesia, Malaysia, Philippines, Singapore, and Thailand), it added five more countries (Brunei Darussalam, Vietnam, Lao PDR, Myanmar, and Cambodia) between 1984 and 1999. ASEAN's initial mission was political and security cooperation, but it has expanded into trade and economic arenas. In 1992, it created the ASEAN Free Trade Area (AFTA), which was implemented over a fifteen-year span.

New agreements began to take shape in the 1990s, especially after the Asian Crisis of 1997–1998. Political and business leaders in East Asia decided that their economies and regulatory agencies were not prepared to handle the increase in trade and investment flows, and that they could not rely on the advice of the International Monetary Fund (IMF) or other multilateral agencies. Stronger bilateral and regional relations were accepted as a means for building greater regional stability. New agreements were proposed, negotiated, and eventually signed. These agreements take many forms, both with respect to their regional coverage and their scope. Some are bilateral and intraregional, such as the Japan-Singapore Economic Partnership Agreement, while others are between one country and an existing group, such as the ASEAN-China Comprehensive Economic Cooperation Agreement. Others are bilateral, but interregional, such as the Japan-Mexico Free Trade Agreement, or the Korea-Chile Free Trade Agreement.

TABLE 16.7   Free Trade Areas in Asia and Oceania

Year	Under Negotiation	Concluded	Proposed
1975	0	1	0
1991	0	7	1
2000	6	45	3
2016	69	151	67

The number of trade blocs in Asia increased dramatically after the Asian Crisis of 1997–1998.

Source: Data from Asian Development Bank, Asia Regional Integration Center, © James Gerber.

Nor are trade agreements the only form of regional cooperation that emerged after the crisis of 1997–1998. ASEAN opened negotiations with China, Korea, and Japan to increase regional cooperation and share technical expertise in managing exchange rate risk, bond financing, and other financial matters. Information on the integration efforts within Asia, and between Asian and non-Asian economies is readily available on the website of the Asian Regional Integration Center (aric .adb.org), a unit of the Asian Development Bank (ADB, www.adb.org). The Asian Development Bank was created in 1966, long before the Asian Crisis of 1997–1998 and currently has sixty-seven member countries. It is one of many regional development banks around the world that are financed by its member countries with the mission to promote sound economics and economic growth and to provide technical and financial assistance. The ADB is complemented by the newly created Asian Infrastructure Investment Bank (www.aiib.org) that started up in 2015 with fifty-seven member countries, after two years of Chinese efforts. The mission of the AIIB is similar to that of the ADB, although it hopes to be more flexible, faster, and greener in providing finance, technical assistance, and infrastructure development. (See the case study in Chapter 2).

IS THERE AN ASIAN MODEL OF ECONOMIC GROWTH?

LO 16.6 Define total factor productivity and explain why economists use it to understand whether growth in East Asia is similar to growth elsewhere.

The East Asian "miracle" has given rise to a large number of studies that seek to explain rapid growth in the East Asian export economies and China. While the issue may appear academic, it has become one of the more interesting and heated debates in recent popular economics. Proponents of laissez-faire economics have used the relative openness of the East Asian economies, their use of private markets, and their strong macroeconomic fundamentals to argue for government policies that are less activist. Proponents of a more activist government have pointed to selective interventions, such as export promotion, industrial policies, and deliberation councils, to argue in favor of a larger government role in the economy. Some Asian politicians have pointed to their restrictions on civil and political liberties as laying a foundation for order and the avoidance of chaos.

Is there an Asian model of the economy? That is, have the Asian exporters managed to achieve their extraordinary growth rates through policies that are fundamentally different from traditional policies that rely more heavily on market forces alone? At stake are the paths followed by today's low- and middle-income economies and the future role of government policy in the industrial countries. Naturally, with a question so controversial, there are various answers and opinions. Recent work, however, seems to be pointing toward a robust set of conclusions.

Before we look at those conclusions, however, we must briefly review the idea of growth accounting. Recall that labor productivity is defined as output per worker: Q/L, where Q is output and L is labor, usually measure by the number of hours of work. Labor productivity is equivalent to the coefficients we used in Chapters 3 and 4 when the Ricardian and Heckscher-Ohlin trade models were presented. East Asian growth is remarkable for its growth in per capita income and its growth in labor productivity. In essence, labor productivity growth led to increases in the amount of output per person.

Any given rate of growth of labor productivity can be broken down into the share that is due to more capital and the share that is due to more skills or education. In the economics literature, such an exercise is called *growth accounting*. When growth accounts are constructed for a country or a region, there is always some share of the growth in labor productivity that cannot be explained by the amount of additional capital or education. This share is a measure of the effects of using the available inputs more efficiently. That is, if growth cannot be explained by increased capital or education, it must be due to a more productive use of the available inputs. For example, the organization of production may have changed so that people are working more efficiently, or the quality of technology may have changed so that each unit of capital and labor input produces more units of output, or greater scale economies are available.

Another name for productivity that is not explained by capital or education is **total factor productivity (TFP)**. TFP growth reflects changes in output that are unrelated to changes in capital or labor inputs but that are related to new technologies, innovation, and organizational improvements. According to most estimates, over the long run a majority of per capita income growth in high-income countries has resulted from increases in total factor productivity.

Growth accounting may seem a long way from the debate on East Asia, but it is actually very relevant. Economists can decompose the overall growth of labor productivity into the part that is due to more capital, the part that is due to more education, and finally, the part that is the result of TFP growth. The results show that the vast majority of labor productivity growth is due to increased capital accumulation. In effect, labor productivity grows because each worker has more machinery and other forms of physical capital at their disposal. The rapid capital accumulation in the East Asian export economies resulted from the very high rates of savings and investment in these economies, which is one of their most notable features. And, consistent with the pattern in the United States and other industrial nations over the same period, TFP growth explains a smaller share of overall growth. The relative importance of capital accumulation versus TFP growth supports the idea that East Asian export economies are similar in their sources of growth to other nations that have achieved high levels of income. If they had much higher rates of TFP growth as their source of overall economic growth, then it would have supported the idea that they had discovered a new growth formula, that their forms of organization or perhaps some unknown cultural factor, gave them an edge in the economic growth race.

While this research says that there is no "East Asian Miracle," it does not reduce the remarkable nature of the growth process in that part of the world. Instead of painting a picture of an entirely new growth process, however, the research on high-growth, export-oriented East Asian economies illustrates clearly how hard work, forgone consumption, and high savings which is productively invested, can change a nation's standard of living in less than a generation.

Summary

- The major characteristics of economic growth in the export-oriented Asian economies are (1) increasing equality, (2) rapid accumulation of savings and high rates of investment, (3) rapid increases in levels of schooling, (4) rapid growth of manufactured exports, and (5) stable macroeconomic environments.

- The institutional environment is instrumental in creating confidence in policymakers. The policymaking bureaucracy tends to be insulated from the push and pull of the political system. This leads some to decry the lack of representation of the population in policy decisions, but it allows decisions to be made on technical merit rather than political expediency. The voice of business and industry, and to a lesser extent other groups such as consumers, is often heard through consultative bodies known as *deliberation councils*. Deliberation councils are a mechanism for the private sector and government policymakers to exchange information and discuss policies.

- One of the key elements of policy is a stable macroeconomic environment, including inflation control, moderate budget deficits, manageable foreign debt, and credible exchange rates. While these key macroeconomic variables differ across countries, they were usually sustainable.

- With the exception of Hong Kong, each of the Asian export economies followed industrial policies that targeted the development of particular industries. These policies were most focused in the "northern tier" of Japan, Korea, and Taiwan. The effects of these policies are difficult to measure, and there is a long and contentious debate about their efficacy.

- Each country promoted manufactured exports, again with the exception of Hong Kong, which is a large port serving China and East Asia. These policies largely succeeded, although the mechanisms that link export growth to faster GDP growth are still uncertain.

- Recent empirical work shows that the main contributor to economic growth in the export economies is the extremely rapid accumulation of physical capital. Consequently, the argument that they have pioneered a model that leads to more rapid total factor productivity growth appears false, and the keys to growth should be looked for in the policies that raise savings and investment.

Vocabulary

Association of Southeast Asian
Nations (ASEAN)

deliberation councils

demographic transition

Ease of doing business index

total factor productivity (TFP)

Worldwide Governance Indicators

Study Questions

All problems are assignable in MyEconLab

16.1 Contrast the characteristics of economic growth in the East Asian export economies with Latin America's growth.

16.2 How can passage through a demographic transition lead to high savings and investment rates?

16.3 What are the characteristics of East Asian institutional environments that contributed to rapid economic growth?

16.4 Economists are divided over the effectiveness of East Asian industrial policies. Provide a balanced assessment of the issues relevant to understanding the role of industrial policies in fostering growth. Do you think one point of view is better than another? Why?

16.5 How might manufactured exports contribute to economic growth?

16.6 Is there a uniquely Asian model of economic growth? What are the issues, and how might we go about answering that question?

CHAPTER

17 China and India in the World Economy

Learning Objectives
After studying this chapter, students will be able to:
17.1 State why China and India are considered disruptive to the world's economic status quo.
17.2 Describe the demographic trends in China and India.
17.3 Relate the economic reforms that occurred in China and India.
17.4 Compare and contrast the transition from socialism to capitalism in China and Russia.
17.5 Compare and contrast Indian and Chinese economic growth.
17.6 Use a gravity model to explain Chinese and Indian trade patterns.
17.7 Discuss the impact of Chinese manufacturing on industrial economies such as the United States.

INTRODUCTION: NEW CHALLENGES

LO 17.1 State why China and India are considered disruptive to the world's economic status quo.

When measured in current dollars, China and India are the second and tenth largest economies in the world (2015). In population, they are first and second with a combined total of over 2.6 billion people, or more than one-third of the world. In part, their importance is a result of their size, but it is also due to their relatively sudden emergence onto the world stage as active traders, investors, and consumers. Until the late 1970s, China was relatively isolated from world markets, partly as a result of its extreme nationalism under its communist system, and partly as a result of its political isolation during most of the Cold War. India participated far more in international economic affairs, but its nationalism, together with its extreme poverty and very low growth rates limited its economic interactions with other countries. In 1978, China began a series of economic reforms that brought it into the world economy, and in 1991, India's economic reforms generated more rapid growth and encouraged more interactions outside its borders. Beyond their size, it is this dramatic and somewhat sudden shift away from relative isolation of more than one-third of humanity that has called the world's attention to these two large nations.

Accommodating China and India in the world trading system is a challenge. India's economy was highly regulated before the reforms of the early 1990s, albeit less than China's. Indian reforms focused on privatizing state-owned industries, increasing efficiency, reducing red tape, and making its businesses more competitive. As it has grown, its size and competitiveness in some sectors, such as information technology and services, biotechnology, and others, have disrupted existing markets. Chinese reforms went much deeper and involved a transition away from socialism and public ownership of most of its economy, toward capitalism and more extensive private ownership. Many more firms in China than in India remain state-owned, and pose challenges for the global trading system given that state subsidies, government procurement rules, and intellectual property rights are less clearly defined when the state is the owner and when prices do not necessarily reflect market conditions. China's enormous size, as the second largest economy in the world, together with its aggressive foreign investment and trade policies, and its historically unprecedented rate of growth, have caused it to be more disruptive of the status quo as it has become integrated with world markets.

India and China were world powers in the past; China has reclaimed that position and India is moving in the same direction. History tells us that when world powers emerge, it usually creates economic, political, and military challenges for other nations and leads to a period filled with transitions and tensions. This chapter surveys the most important economic issues associated with the sudden impact on the world economy of the emergence of China and India.

DEMOGRAPHIC AND ECONOMIC CHARACTERISTICS

LO 17.2 Describe the demographic trends in China and India.

LO 17.3 Relate the economic reforms that occurred in China and India.

LO 17.4 Compare and contrast the transition from socialism to capitalism in China and Russia.

Table 17.1 shows population, GDP in current U.S. dollars, and GDP per person in purchasing power parity terms. The population totals for China and India are well above one-third of the world total, while output is nearly one-fourth when measured in PPP. Their weight in the world economy is relatively recent, unless we count back several centuries when they were a much larger share of a much less integrated world. As recently as 1950, however, estimates put their share of world GDP in the range of 8 to 9 percent. As the world economy grew in the second half of the twentieth century, they grew faster than most other countries and their shares of the total increased. Figure 17.1 compares the average annual

TABLE 17.1   Population and Income in China and India, 2015

	Population (Millions)	GDP (US$, Billions)	GDP per Capita (US$ PPP)
China	1,374	10,983	14,107
India	1,293	2,091	6,162

China and India have over one-third of the world's population and almost one-fourth of world GDP measured in terms of purchasing power parity.

Source: Data from International Monetary Fund, World Economic Outlook Database. © James Gerber.

FIGURE 17.1   Average Annual Growth of GDP, 1991–2014

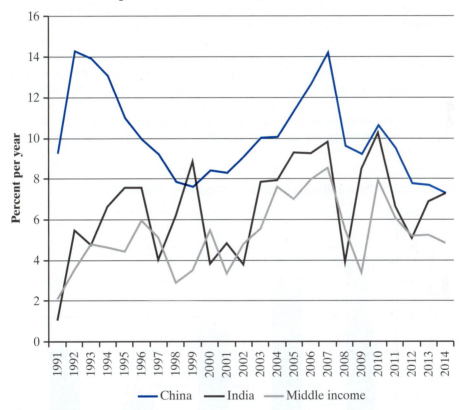

China's GDP has doubled every 7 years since 1991, while India's took 11 years. The average for middle income countries was 14 years.

Source: Data from *World Development Indicators*, World bank, © James Gerber.

growth over 25 years in China, India, and countries that are middle income by the World Bank's definition (income per capita of approximately $1,000 to $13,000). The data begin after the initiation of Chinese reforms (1978) and at the beginning of major Indian economic reforms (1991).

China's growth, in particular, has been unprecedented in world history. With growth rates that frequently exceeded 10 percent per year, often by a large margin, it has moved hundreds of millions of individuals and families out of poverty and has closed a significant part of the gap in per capita income between itself and the world's high income countries. And while India's growth rate has neither been as spectacular nor historically unprecedented, it has managed to grow faster than most middle income countries. This too is remarkable given that its growth rate prior to the 1990s was relatively low, and given that the comparison group, middle income countries, are usually the fastest growing economies in the world. The growth rates for China and India from 1991 to 2014 imply that Chinese GDP doubled every 7 years and Indian GDP every 11 years.

Figure 17.2 looks back in history to show the importance of China and India in the world economy prior to the industrial revolution. Many economic historians date the "great divergence" between East and West as beginning around 1820, when Western Europe and North America began to industrialize ahead of most other regions of the world. Prior to then, cities in China and elsewhere were as modern and prosperous as anything in Europe or the Americas. The industrial revolution led to an earlier adoption of new technologies in the first places it occurred and generated higher levels of productivity, increased incomes, and ultimately greater military power. Long periods of colonial rule in India and many

FIGURE 17.2 **China and India in the World Economy, 1700–2003**

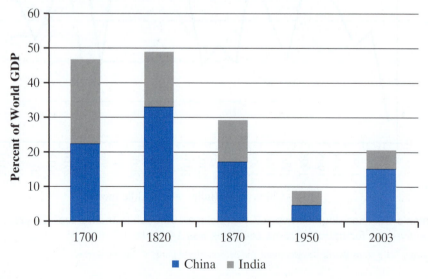

China and India produced a significant share of world GDP before the industrial revolution but rapidly fell behind after about 1820.

Source: Data from *Contours of the H World Economy*, by Angus Maddison, © James Gerber.

decades of military intervention in China by the West, compounded the effects of lagging industrial development and helped create a widening gap between incomes in China and India on the one hand, and Western Europe and North America on the other. By 1870, China and India were rapidly losing ground to the new industrial economies. By 1950, they were less than 10 percent of world GDP, after having been nearly 50 percent in 1820. In China's case, there was essentially no growth from 1820 to 1950. India fared somewhat better, growing at one-half of 1 percent per year, a rate sufficiently slow to ensure that India fell behind the industrializing economies of the West.

Since 1950, both countries but especially China have increased their share of world's GDP by growing faster than other countries. Most of the increase in their share has occurred since the implementation of economic reforms, after the 1970s. The consequences of higher growth have been significant, both for the world economy and for the citizens of those two nations. In 1981, more than 88 percent of China's population lived in extreme poverty (defined as less than $1.90 a day, in 2011 purchasing power parity dollars), while 53 percent of India's population (1983) lived in similar circumstances. By 2010–2011, extreme poverty had fallen to just above 11 percent in China and 21 percent in India. Large reductions in extreme poverty in countries as populous as China and India translate into hundreds of millions of people rescued from lives of deprivation and limited opportunity.

While poverty has fallen, a middle class has appeared in both countries. Given their large populations, even a small middle class represents purchasing power on a scale large enough to influence world demand. The sizes of the middle classes are not well-defined but consider a simple hypothetical situation. According to the World Bank, in 2010–2011, the 10 percent of the population with highest incomes received about 30 percent of total income in both countries. Given China's spectacular growth over the last several decades and the higher incomes it has generated, this group is much better off, on average, in China than in India. For the top 10 percent, sharing 30 percent of total income represents an average of approximately $26,000 in China and $5,500 in India (in U.S. dollars). The Chinese income of $26,000 per person puts them in the same category as Greece or Portugal, and just below Spain. The main difference is that 10 percent of China's population represents more than 137 million people, or the equivalent of more than twice the size of France, or the United Kingdom, or Italy. The impact on world demand and supply is considerable when so many new consumers and producers are added to the world economy.

The future growth of China and India will partly depend on their changing populations. Figure 17.3 shows past and estimated future populations in both countries. Around 2030, China's population growth is expected to start a long-run, slow decline. At about the same time, India is projected to pass China as the world's most populous country, and to continue its growth into the foreseeable future. Chinese limits on the number of children families may have, together with its rapid economic development and increased economic opportunities, particularly for women, have reduced rates of childbirth and increased the average age of

FIGURE 17.3 **Population, 1950-2050, in Millions**

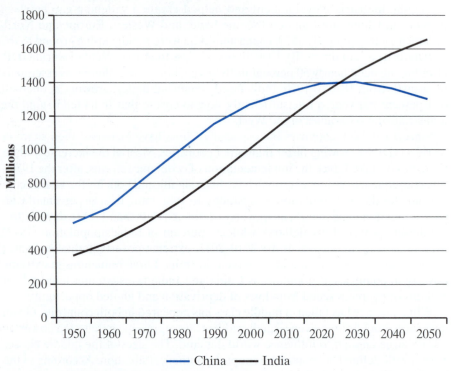

India is projected to pass China around 2030 as the world's most populous country; Chinese population growth will begin a slow decline around the same time.

Source: Data from U.S. Census Bureau, *International Statistics Database,* © James Gerber.

the population. Between 2030 and 2040, population growth will fall below replacement levels and begin to exert a strong influence on economic growth as fewer young adults enter the labor force and an increasing share of the population enters old age. India's population is projected to continue growing, although more rapid economic development and increased economic opportunities for women could alter its trajectory.

Economic Reform in China and India

Economic reform of China's communist system began in 1978. Under communism, every aspect of China's economy was controlled by the state. Private enterprise did not exist, and the basic decisions that every economy makes about what to produce, how to produce it, and who should receive it were made from the top down by government planners and Communist Party politicians. China had limited contact with outsiders, and the emphasis of its economic policy was self-sufficiency in all goods and services.

India's reforms began in the 1980s and then gathered momentum in 1991 when the government was forced to respond to a balance of payment crises. India's economic system was best characterized as socialist, with a mix of state ownership and control together with private enterprise. Most large industrial enterprises were completely state-owned, however, and the Indian system of regulation meant that all firms had to obtain permits for even minor changes. If a firm wanted to expand, if it wanted to change its product lines, or even if it wanted to change its board of directors, first it had to obtain a permit from the government.

After the reforms, both countries are more market oriented and more active participants in the international economy. The remarkable degree of economic opening is observable in their individual trade-to-GDP ratios, which increased dramatically (see Table 17.2). China's ratio peaked in 2006, prior to the financial crisis, at 65 percent, before falling back to 41.5 percent. Meanwhile, India's ratio has increased beyond the level of China's and trade continues to grow in importance. As large countries, we expect the trade-to-GDP ratio to be less than it is for smaller countries that must depend on international trade to a greater extent. Nevertheless, both countries have emphasized international economic integration through trade and investment as part of their reform strategies.

The Reform Process in China

A country's decision to undertake large-scale economic reform can come from many directions. As we saw in Chapter 15, reforms in a number of Latin American countries were a result of the debt crisis of the 1980s. In China's case there was no immediate crisis, but rather a long period of instability and disappointment with the results achieved under communism. The leader of Chinese economic reforms, **Deng Xiaoping**, put it in terms of a choice between distributing poverty under the old system and distributing wealth under a new system.

There was no master plan for Chinese reforms, but rather a gradual, steady dismantling of the controls exercised by the state and the Communist Party. Deng Xiaoping is famously reported to have described the reforms as analogous to "feeling the stones to cross the river." You advance one foot, see if it holds, then advance another. The slow and steady pace of reform was dictated in part by a lack of experience and information about how to proceed but also by the fear of a reaction from the hard-line, conservative anti-reformers.

TABLE 17.2   Trade-to-GDP Ratios for China and India

	1970	2000	2014
China	5.0	39.4	41.5
India	7.5	26.4	48.7

Trade has become more important to both China and India.

Source: Data from *World Development Indicators*, World bank, © James Gerber.

The first changes were confined to agriculture and involved loosening the constraints on peasant producers by allowing them more control and ownership of individual plots of land. Peasants were allowed to sell their product in markets and were soon increasing the quantity of foodstuff available. Foreign trade under the old system was controlled by twelve **foreign trading corporations (FTC)**, which were attached to the various branches of government. All exports and imports went through the FTC and were strictly regulated with no consideration given to comparative advantage. The reforms gradually opened trade, first through the creation of additional FTC and then through a series of steps that removed price controls and ended export subsidies. To limit the initial impact of reforms on the domestic economy and to prevent a political backlash, China created a number of **Special Economic Zones (SEZ)**, which were modeled on the concept of export processing zones (EPZ). Recall from the case study of Mexican manufacturing in Chapter 5 that an EPZ allows duty-free imports, usually under the condition that they are processed and re-exported, often after having been incorporated into another product. SEZ went further by giving provincial and local authorities wide latitude to experiment with radically different economic and trade policies. Incentives were given to form joint ventures with foreign producers who came to the SEZ to set up production facilities. Between 1979 and 1988, China created five SEZ, all of which successfully attracted foreign investment (particularly from Taiwan, Hong Kong, and the overseas Chinese business communities), generated a large flow of exports, and helped raised the rate of economic growth. The SEZ created a demonstration effect for the rest of China, and other regions began to push for similar policies.

China also applied to join the General Agreement on Tariffs and Trade (GATT) in 1986. Membership requires a country to describe all trade and economic policies that may affect GATT agreements and to open bilateral negotiations with individual members over any issues of concern. Negotiations were difficult and lasted until China joined the WTO in 2001. The protracted period of negotiations probably kept the reform process moving forward and ultimately resulted in a strong Chinese commitment to an open economy, both for trade and for investment.

Indian Economic Reforms

Indian reforms began gradually in the 1980s and speeded up considerably after the 1991 crisis. Three forces played significant roles in preparing Indian policymakers for the necessary changes. First, India's primary trade partner, the USSR, suffered a number of setbacks through the 1980s and finally dissolved itself in 1991. India had partially modeled its economic policies on the USSR, and its demise laid bare the failure of its economy to produce prosperity. Second, the success of several East Asian countries was important. In 1960, South Korean and Indian income per capita were about the same, but by 1990, Korea was entering the ranks of the developed world, while India remained stuck at low levels of income. When **Manmohan Singh**, the finance minister who carried out many of the reforms, visited Korea in 1987, he was shocked to see how far behind India had fallen. Third in the list of forces was a financial crisis that developed as a result of heavy borrowing by the government. When the Gulf War (1991) drove up oil prices and cut off the flow of remittances from Indian workers in the Gulf States, the country was left with inadequate foreign reserves and an inability to finance its debt.

The changes in economic policy that followed touched on a number of areas, including the permitting process. India's regulation of its economy was based on a system of permits that stifled innovation and creativity with their extensive, complicated, and inefficient rules. Permits were intended to prevent the creation of powerful interests that might undermine democracy and promote inequality. Yet, their unintended consequence was that they fostered inefficiency, and by protecting Indian businesses from competition, both domestic and foreign, they thereby allowed them to operate without regard for product quality or firm efficiency. Many of the larger firms were state-owned, and, as in the Chinese and Russian cases, the state-owned sector of the economy operated without the imperative of profitability. Firms could lose money for years and still continue in business since, as state-owned, they had no hard budget constraints. Losses were covered by the government budget, even as it meant a drain on government revenue and fewer resources for important public projects such as safe drinking water, highways and ports, rural education, and other needs. Privatization was the second set of reforms begun after the crisis of 1991.

A final critical area that began to receive attention from the reformers was international trade and investment. Indian trade policy was based on the idea of import substitution industrialization (see Chapter 5), the same as Latin America and other developing regions after World War II. Domestic firms received high levels of protection, exports were implicitly discouraged, and self-sufficiency was the goal. India's famous Ambassador car is an example. Protected from foreign imports, it remained essentially the same for nearly 40 years. Why go through the expense of changing the product line if there is a captive market? In addition to dismantling many of the restrictions on trade, India also began to dismantle the restrictions on inward foreign investment.

Shifting Comparative Advantages

Both China and India have undergone profound changes in the last several decades. The breadth and depth of the reforms constitute a definitive break in their historical trajectories and are shifts from low-growth, relatively closed economies, to higher growth and relatively open ones. The two countries are at different stages of this transformation, however, and further changes are required if they hope to close the income gaps with high income countries.

China's remarkable transformation of its economy was partly accomplished by the movement of large numbers of people from the countryside to the city and from agriculture to manufacturing. This shift in location and activities resulted in a decline in low value-added production in agriculture and its replacement with higher value-added production in low-skilled manufacturing. The change in employment was consistent with China's comparative advantage given its abundant supplies of unskilled labor, and led to dramatic increases in income. Workers in labor-intensive manufacturing still had relatively low marginal products and the low wages that implies, but their marginal products and wages were much higher than in agriculture. China supported this shift with a variety of policies encouraging investment in manufacturing and infrastructure, industrial policies such as subsidies for key sectors and state-owned enterprises, and fewer restrictions on trade and foreign investment.

China's next transformation requires it to build a high-consumption economy. Its current success has depended on extremely high rates of investment. New cities were built, together with high-speed trains and highways, power plants, steel mills, car factories, and all the other facilities that helped turn the country into the largest exporter of manufactured goods in the world. Yet its ability to keep growing by increasing its level of investment has come to a close. China is currently investing over 45 percent of its annual GDP when most advanced economies annually invest 15 to 25 percent. At some point, the payoff from additional investments begins to decline and over capacity becomes endemic. China has reached a saturation point in many industries, such as steel, where its capacity to produce far exceeds its ability to export or to absorb the output into the domestic economy. Too much investment is a different problem from too little, but it is still a problem and represents a waste of resources. The long term macroeconomic challenge is to shift those expenditures toward consumption, leading to a higher standard of living today, rather than in the future. The short-term problem is the mountain of private and public debt that was taken on as investors built factories and housing that turned into excess capacity which has no ability to generate needed revenue.

India, by contrast, has not yet moved as large a proportion of its population out of low value added agriculture and into manufacturing. It continues to have a large majority of its population residing in rural areas (69 percent in 2010) and working in agriculture (51 percent) where productivity is low and poverty remains a serious problem. For India to follow China in the transformation of employment away from agriculture and into low-skilled, labor-intensive manufacturing it must overcome many obstacles, including its lack of infrastructure in the form of transportation and utilities, limited education, and the obstacles of complex, unreliable, institutions.

Neither China nor India score well in the Doing Business Index which measures the ease of starting and running a business, nor in measures of governance (see Chapter 16). Consequently, markets are more limited than they might be, and large amounts of labor and many small businesses remain in the informal sector where it is harder for them to obtain capital and develop into large enterprises. This is particularly true in India where a complicated bureaucracy is filled with red tape and regulations to the extent that it ranks 130th out of 189 countries in its ease of doing business. China does somewhat better, but still ranks in the middle, scoring 84th out of 189. Neither country comes close to the export-oriented economies of East Asia. In the long run, institutional development is as important as other forms of development.

CASE STUDY

Why Did the USSR Collapse and China Succeed?

In contrast to the Russian experience, the Chinese economy did not decline at all during its transition from communism to capitalism. Although its reforms were begun in 1978, until the mid-1980s they mainly affected the agricultural sector. Since China had such a large share of its population in rural areas, the positive effects on food output and rural incomes were significant. Primarily, the agricultural reforms let families and villages take individual responsibility for meeting their production quotas and allowed them to consume or sell whatever amount they produced above the quota. Villages and communes were allowed to disband the collectivist system of production, and individual incentives began to rule the efforts and decision making of producers.

In the mid-1980s, China extended its market-based reforms to a number of SEZ, Economic and Technology Development Zones (ETDZ), High Technology Development Zones (HTDZ), and other special developmental areas, located mostly along the coast. The rules of each type of zone varied, but in general they allowed far more independent, profit-oriented, market-based decision making. The SEZ, in particular, were encouraged to experiment with new forms of economic organization and to develop joint ventures by attracting foreign investment. These areas began to account for the bulk of Chinese growth, exports, and foreign investment.

China's transition strategy is considered a gradualist strategy because it did not attempt to reform the entire economic structure all at once. Rather, it used a **dual track strategy**, which localized reforms to certain areas or sectors (e.g., agriculture) while maintaining traditional, central planning structures in the remainder of the economy. Slowly, subsidized prices were raised to the market level and the mandatory production targets were reduced to a small share of the total output or zero. By the early to mid-1990s, more than 90 percent of retail prices and 80 to 90 percent of agricultural and intermediate goods prices were decontrolled. China has been much slower to privatize its state-owned sector.

Many observers argue that the gradual implementation of reforms in a slow but steady sequence removed the pressure to instantaneously develop new institutions and economic relations. By adopting a dual track approach, China allowed the market economy to develop alongside the centrally planned economy and to gradually take over more and more of its functions. Perhaps

(*continued*)

even more importantly than avoiding an economic downturn, it gave the Chinese people time to adjust their expectations to fit a market-based system and reduced the shock of change.

The proponents of rapid reform see China as a special case. First, central planning was less extensive in China, with the result that its economy was less distorted and less over concentrated on heavy industry. Second, and most importantly, China's economy is much more agricultural. In 1978, when China began its reforms, 71 percent of the labor force was in agriculture. The figure for Russia in 1990 at the beginning of its transition was 13 percent. China's heavier concentration in agriculture gives it a large rural labor force with very low productivity. If these workers leave the countryside, the resulting loss of output is small, while the offsetting productivity gains from employment in urban and village industrial enterprises are significant. Hence, China can move labor from agriculture into the new enterprises, but Russia had to take labor out of heavy industry to staff the new enterprises.

Janos Kornai, the eminent Hungarian economist and perceptive observer of the transition, summarized the debate in the following terms:

> *Some developments are rapid, others slow. Some call for a one-stroke intervention while many others come about through incremental changes. . . . The emphasis has to be on consolidation, stability, and sustainability, not on breaking speed records*[1] (Finance and Development, September 2000).

[1]From Making the Transition to Private Ownership by János Kornai ,Finance and Development Magazine, © 2000 International Monetary Fund.

CHINA AND INDIA IN THE WORLD ECONOMY

LO 17.5 Compare and contrast Indian and Chinese economic growth.

LO 17.6 Use a gravity model to explain Chinese and Indian trade patterns.

LO 17.7 Discuss the impact of Chinese manufacturing on industrial economies such as the United States.

India and China have influenced the direction of world trade and investment. As they have become more integrated with the rest of the world, multinational businesses have quickly moved to establish production and distribution networks inside both countries and Chinese and Indian firms have begun to invest outside their home markets. Between 1990 and 2014, China and India's share of inward foreign direct investment grew from 1.8 percent of the world total to 13.2 percent. The majority was directed toward China, but India received the third largest total of any Asian economy, after China and Singapore. Similarly, trade flows have grown significantly. This is most notable in the case of China, which has begun to have a very significant impact on world trade and investment patterns, but India also has increased its share of both merchandise goods and services trade.

Figure 17.4 shows the growth of China and India's share of world exports of goods and services, 1990 to 2015. As shown, the majority of their growth is due to the increase in Chinese exports, primarily goods, but services as well. The Indian economy, which is about one-fifth the size of China's, lags behind China in its growth of merchandise goods exports and its share of the world total, but it has nearly as large a share of world services exports, reflecting strengths in information technologies, business services, and other high-skilled services.

Chinese and Indian Trade Patterns

China's transformation has turned it into the world's largest exporter of merchandise goods and the 5th largest exporter of services. India's economic transformation has not progressed as far as China's, and it still has half of its labor force in agriculture, and a majority of its population in rural areas. Nevertheless, it is the 19th largest exporter of merchandise goods and the 8th largest exporter of services.

Chinese and Indian trade is with an overlapping set of trade partners that reflect their proximity to large markets and energy suppliers. The **gravity model** of international trade uses just two variables to predict which countries trade with each other: distance and GDP. The model hypothesizes that, all else equal,

FIGURE 17.4   **Share of World Exports, 1990–2015**

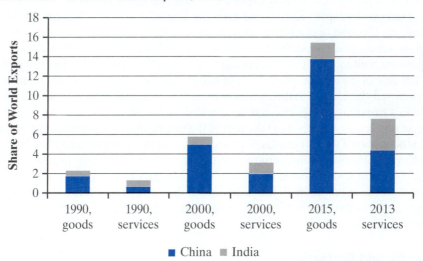

China and India have significantly increased their share of world exports.

Source: Data from UNCTAD, "Total trade and share," and "Exports and imports of total services.", © James Gerber.

countries will trade more if they are closer to each other and therefore have lower transportation costs, and if their GDP is larger so that they are a larger market. The model is called a gravity model because it resembles Newton's Law of Universal Gravitation which asserts that the gravitational pull between two bodies is proportional to their individual mass and to their distance. In the gravity model of trade, distance is considered directly and the metaphor for physical mass is market size, or GDP. The gravity model predicts that China and India will trade more with larger economies, and especially ones that are close by. This is a good approximation of the trade pattern of the two countries.

China's top five export markets are the United States, the European Union, Hong Kong, Japan, and Korea. Its top import sources are similar, with Taiwan replacing Hong Kong. This pattern is embedded in Chinese production, as made clear in the discussion below of China's trade balances and its impact on global manufacturing. India's top export markets are nearly the same, except China figures prominently as does the oil-rich United Arab Emirates. Indian imports are primarily from China, the EU, and the relatively close oil-producing countries, Saudi Arabia and the United Arab Emirates.

The gravity model is particularly useful for thinking about China's export and import markets. The United States, the European Union, and Japan are obviously large markets for their exports given their size and their wealth. Similarly, those countries export to China because it is large too, and in the case of Japan and Korea, because they are relatively close. The fact that China has a number of large ports on its east coast also makes it a convenient trading partner for many countries. Proximity and GDP explain a significant part of the trade patterns.

China's role as the largest exporter of manufactured goods is enhanced by its proximity to Japan, Korea, and even the United States which is reachable by relatively low-cost ocean transport. Recall from Chapter 4's discussion of United States–China trade, and the case study of the iPhone 3G manufacturing, that China plays an integral part in a production system that is spread across the globe. In the case of the iPhone, production of components was done in Germany, Korea, Japan, and the United States, and assembly into the final product was in China. China's proximity to specialized design and high-technology manufacturing in Japan and Korea enables it to take part in the production chain of high-technology products, even if its own production capacity is not yet as sophisticated as Japan's or Korea's. Participation in production chains of high-technology products is not the only form China's trade takes, but it is a key part of its overall trade pattern and its trade relations with more advanced industrial economies. Proximity to large markets that are rich in technology and sophisticated, well-off, consumers encourages this pattern.

Tariffs and Protection

As noted, India lags China in the development of a large manufacturing sector, and in its export of manufactures. India is more rural, and has not yet experienced the mass migration of agricultural laborers into the cities on the scale that China and other industrializing countries have. Consequently, agriculture remains a core part of its production. Given that agriculture is not particularly efficient in India, and that many farmers struggle with little or no capital, the Indian government protects them from foreign competition with high tariffs and extensive quotas. In general, both China and India have relatively low tariffs and relatively open markets, but Indian agriculture is an exception. Table 17.3 shows average tariff rates applied by both countries and for agricultural and nonagricultural products. Tariff rates vary by product, and the averages in Table 17.3 are weighted by the relative importance of the individual goods that are tariffed.

Agriculture in India is protected because it is relatively inefficient, yet it occupies over one-half of the total labor force (2010). The nation's long-run growth requires it to transform agriculture into a leaner sector with fewer workers and higher levels of productivity. In most countries, China included, that process has entailed large migrations from the countryside to the city. Workers give up low productivity agriculture and engage in manufacturing and urban services which are still low productivity by the standards of high-income countries, but much higher than in the countryside they left. This process leads to the development of a low skill, labor-intensive manufacturing sector which is an important step on the way to industrial development.

Undoubtedly, India would raise income levels faster if it engaged in this transformation. The cost of such a transformation, however, is an extreme amount of dislocation of communities, families, and individuals, along with a complete change in lifestyles, cultures, and habits. As a democracy, India cannot force economic changes in the way that authoritarian regimes can. Forcing families and individuals off the land, either through direct action or extreme neglect, is painful and is not a policy that democracies can easily practice. Hence, high tariffs in agriculture may be economically inefficient because they help keep people in agriculture, but tariffs provide some protection to rural workers who are unable to leave the land, albeit at the cost of higher food prices.

Current Account Balances

China's growth and, in particular, its dynamic, competitive, manufacturing sector has a range of effects on other countries. On the one hand, it has created a large

TABLE 17.3   Applied Tariffs, China and India, 2014

	Agriculture	Non-agriculture
China	13.0	4.0
India	45.0	4.5

Import tariffs are relatively low in both China and India, except for agricultural imports by India.

Source: Data from World Trade Organization, *Tariff Profiles*, © James Gerber.

demand for imports and has benefitted economies as diverse as African exporters of minerals, Argentine and Brazilian producers of soybeans, and German machinery manufacturers. On the other hand, the rise of Chinese manufacturing is correlated in time with the decline of manufacturing employment in the United States and Western Europe. We do not know with certainty if China's rising manufacturing sector is responsible for the decline in manufacturing in the United States and elsewhere, but some analysts have pointed out that cities and communities that compete directly with Chinese exports have not fared well in recent years, and that this is directly a result of Chinese exports.

That is one possibility. However, it is uncertain what might have happened to manufacturing in the United States and elsewhere if China had remained isolated. Setting aside the human tragedy and the deep poverty such isolation implies, the question that cannot be answered is whether manufacturing employment in high-income countries would have declined more slowly, or not at all, if China had not grown so fast. Some of the forces shaping the economies of advanced industrial nations are completely independent of China. Technological advances in manufacturing such as the increasing use of automated processes and robotics would probably have proceeded anyway. Telecommunications and transportation advances, which enable firms to locate parts of their production in different countries, would also have occurred. Consequently, it is not certain what would have been the course of manufacturing in advanced economies if China had not entered the picture.

In addition to its enormous productive capacity, China is a huge market for goods and services produced outside the country. It is, in fact the second largest importer of both goods and services. Nevertheless, as shown in Figure 17.5, China has consistently run trade surpluses since at least 2000, often by a large margin. Trade surpluses reflect its focus on exports and investment-driven growth, and its desire to build large foreign exchange reserves after the Asian Crisis of 1997–1998. Persistent large trade surpluses have heightened trade tensions in the world economy. Some observers argue that China accomplishes the trade surpluses by manipulating its currency and keeping it undervalued. More careful analysis can show that China's currency may have been undervalued against the dollar in the first part of the 2000s, but that has not been the case since 2006 or 2007. In other words, currency manipulation is not the source of its competitiveness. Furthermore, China is not the only country that has adopted a strategy of trade surpluses and export-oriented growth. German trade surpluses are frequently as large as Chinese, and sometimes larger. Both Germany and Japan have adopted export-oriented growth strategies, as have a number of smaller economies, including those discussed in Chapter 16. Hence, China is not unique in its policy of large trade surpluses. Nevertheless, the task of accommodating China and its very large current account surpluses poses a challenge for the world economy.

FIGURE 17.5   Current Account Balances, 2000–2015

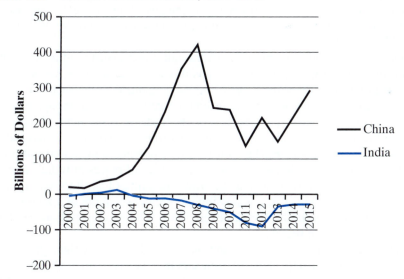

China has had large current account surpluses since the early 2000s.

Source: Data from IMF, *World Economic Outlook Database,* © James Gerber.

Looking Forward

Chapter 4's case study on Chinese exports to the United States give some idea of the direction China's trade is moving. Table 4.4 lists the top ten exports of China to the United States. Among them are low-technology items, such as apparel, footwear, toys, and furniture, and a few high-technology items, such as cell phones, telecommunications equipment, computers, and computer accessories. In this chapter and in Chapter 4 it was emphasized that China is not yet as large a producer of high-technology products as its exports make it seem since those products are often assembled in China from technical components made elsewhere. Nevertheless, it is clear that the country is engaged in extensive industrial upgrading and that more and more sophisticated products are coming. One indicator of this trend is the number of patents issued. In 2013, China's patent office granted 143,535 patents to residents of the country. The United States, in contrast, issued 133,593 to its residents (Japan issued 225,571). China is also spending large sums on its infrastructure, including universities.

Industrial upgrading in China is supported by the ability of its large market to attract a significant share of the world's foreign direct investment. From 2005 to 2014, it pulled in 7.7 percent of total world FDI, on average each year. By contrast, the United States received 13.7 percent on average, each year. China has aggressively required foreign investors to license their technologies to Chinese producers and to take on Chinese partners, so that new technology and methods are made available to Chinese firms. Over time, we should expect to see a growing and increasingly sophisticated manufacturing capacity that moves well beyond assembly operations.

India has attracted large amounts of foreign direct investment as well, albeit not on the scale of China. In addition, as discussed, it has been less successful in the creation of a low-skilled, labor-intensive manufacturing sector. In recent years, however, Indian trade has captured the world's attention though its ability to participate in the growing area of services trade. Several factors account for this, not the least of which is the fact that English is spoken by educated Indians. In addition, India's leadership has consistently emphasized higher education and technology, and although there is a severe shortage of places in India's universities, its leading institutions, such as the India Institute of Technology (IIT), are among the world's best. There is possibly no greater example of a sector in any country that has benefited from the advent of the telecommunications revolution than India's high-tech sector.

A closer examination of Chinese and Indian service exports highlights this fact and points to another important difference in the two economies. China's service exports are larger than India's, although not by as much as its goods exports. More important is the composition of each country's service exports. China has a deficit in services, which primarily comprise transportation and travel services (shipping and business and personal travel). India has a surplus in services, which primarily comprise information services and other business services, two high-growth areas.

India's computer and information services and other business services include medical consultations, data entry, legal briefs, and myriad other activities that are now sometimes performed at a distance and then sent over the Internet to the final user of the information. As described in Chapter 4, the outsourcing of services depends on the telecommunications revolution, including the Internet, video conferencing, satellite communications, and the software to take advantage of the services offered. In the past, most services were consumed at the point of production, but as technology allows a separation of production from consumption or use, services have begun to be outsourced in the same way that manufacturing has been for decades.

A key question for India is whether it can skip industrialization and jump ahead into a predominantly services economy. That is, can its relatively strong services exports serve as a replacement for the development of an extensive manufacturing sector? Might it pioneer a new development model that does not first require industrialization with low-skill, labor-intensive manufacturing, but instead jumps right into a high-skilled services economy? It seems unlikely. First, India is not abundant in high-skilled, highly educated labor that is needed in high-skilled services. This is not to say that it does not have excellent engineers, software programmers and developers, medical doctors, and other highly trained individuals, but they are not its abundant factor. Nor will they become relatively abundant any time soon, given the shortage of universities and other educational facilities.

Hence, services trade will continue to be important and will likely continue to grow, but it will not become the core of the Indian economy.

FOUR ISSUES

There are numerous challenges to existing trade patterns and trade relations posed by the integration of China and India into the world trading system. We will look at four such challenges: Indian services, Chinese manufacturing, the demand for resources, and China's challenge to multilateral institutions.

Services

Services such as shipping have been traded for decades, as shipping companies hire crews around the world and register their vessels in the most convenient location, selling their services to firms wherever they are in need. Business services and information services, however, are relatively new to international trade since they can be traded only if technology and infrastructure can pass large amounts of information across long distances at low costs. Since the mid-1990s, this has been possible, and trade in information and computer services has taken off. The outsourcing of services from high-income industrial economies to India is a new arena for the application of comparative advantage.

As with all economic changes, some people benefit and some are hurt. It is clear, however, that there are net benefits overall for national economies. Consider the case of the United States. As the hardware for computer and information technology (IT) has become less expensive, IT services and software and not hardware are taking the majority share of total IT spending by U.S. businesses. Outsourcing reduces the price of IT services and software, makes business-specific applications cheaper to purchase, and allows businesses to achieve higher levels of productivity at a lower cost. It is another case of comparative advantage–based trade, the same as described in Chapters 3 and 4. In this case, India's comparative advantage allows it to trade with the United States and other high-income countries and to contribute to the increase in their productivity while at the same time creating good-paying jobs and advancing its own economy.

Those who oppose this form of trade fear that all computer and IT work will end up in developing countries. This seems highly unlikely. For example, the U.S. Bureau of Labor Statistics projects significant job growth in the United States in IT-related occupations. These new workers and many already in the IT services sector will not continue to do the same thing, however, as the comparative advantage of the United States is shifting within the IT field. While demand for computer programmers may decline, database administrators, hardware and software engineers, systems analysts, and a host of other occupations are expected to grow.

Manufacturing

China's emergence as an export platform and as a high-volume manufacturer of consumer goods challenges existing trade patterns and manufacturing trends. The challenge to middle-income markets that compete directly with China, such as Mexico, Brazil, Malaysia, and Thailand, is to reduce their dependency on low wages as the primary source of their comparative advantage. The challenge appears in the form of intense competitive pressures from low-cost goods produced in China, but the nature of the challenge is beginning to change. Chinese manufacturing wages have been low, but they are rapidly rising. In some cases, electronics and other production has begun to migrate to lower-age countries such as Vietnam, Indonesia, and Thailand. Nevertheless, the competitive pressure of low-wage manufacturing in China is not likely to disappear anytime soon and countries that compete on the basis of labor costs alone are unlikely to succeed. For example, Mexico's export processing zone lost a large share of its apparel sector when China entered the WTO. Mexico's geographic advantage next to the U.S. market was nullified for products that do not need a rapid turnaround between order and delivery. The effect on some of the manufacturing in high-income countries is similar, such as apparel in the United States and Italy. Furthermore, as China expands its exports of more sophisticated products such as cars, the competitive pressure are spreading into other sectors of manufacturing.

China has several sources of comparative advantage in manufacturing. Its abundance of low-wage, low-skilled labor has already been mentioned, as has its large domestic market. One way to look at China is as a large economy that confers the advantage of scale economies when producing for the domestic market. Coupled with overall growth and expansion of its middle class, the demand for manufactured goods is increasing rapidly and will continue to absorb a larger share of Chinese output. A third advantage is China's coastal areas, which have potentially convenient logistics for trading internationally. China continues to invest heavily in its port facilities and coastal infrastructure in an effort to develop its geographic advantages.

There are also a few institutional disadvantages that reduce China's competitiveness. One is the overall business climate, as mentioned already. A related disadvantage is China's inability to enforce intellectual property rights. This was the main point of contention between the United States and China in its accession to the WTO, and it continues to be a major issue in China's relations with its trading partners. Some firms routinely resist making investments in China for fear that their products will be copied, and firms that do invest often limit themselves to product lines that do not contain trade secrets. China meets WTO standards, but its enforcement is ineffective. Chinese firms frequently reverse engineer products, produce a knock-off at a fraction of the price of the imported good since no royalties are paid, and expand across the domestic market. Many observers believe that China's enforcement will not become effective until China itself has significant intellectual property to protect.

Resources

China's rapid growth has increased its appetite for natural resources. For resource producers in Latin America, including Brazil, and in Africa, this has been a boon since China is below the world's per capita average in all major natural resources except coal. Copper, oil, iron ore, and other minerals have experienced spikes in their world prices, which are in part related to Chinese demand. Simultaneously, a number of developing countries have been able to sign long-term agreements that will provide them with investment for exploration and supply contracts for the delivery of their resources. China's substantial export earnings are available for purchasing the resources it will need as it continues its development.

The fact that China buys its resources from other developing countries does not guarantee that the countries selling the resources will spend the money well. And sudden shifts in Chinese growth rates can have a large effect on countries that sell resources. For example, China's stated goal of reducing its growth rate from 10 percent per year to around 7 percent per year has a significant effect on its demand for commodities and their prices. Countries such as Brazil, Argentina, and Chile that export large quantities of raw materials to China must adjust to a sudden change in the prices they earn.

Multilateral Institutions

As noted in Chapters 2 and 16, China has created the Asian Infrastructure Investment Bank (AIIB). This was the outcome of a series of efforts to provide alternative financing and monetary support to other developing countries, particularly but not only those in Asia. China has made significant investments in Africa and Latin America as well. There are a variety of motives for these efforts. On the one hand, China is interested in securing access to raw materials and infrastructure development assistance in Africa, Latin America, and developing Asia can be useful for that purpose. In addition, Chinese leaders are interested in gaining political and economic influence beyond their own borders that is commensurate with its new status as a world power. China's long relative isolation from the end of World War II up until the 1970s and 1980s meant that it did not actively participate in the creation of many multilateral institutions nor in their operation. That left it without a strong say in the policies of the IMF, World Bank, and the WTO. As China's economy has grown and become more central to world trade and payments, it is natural that its government would want a larger say in the operation of multilateral institutions, and that if that is not possible to the extent desired, that it might seek to establish new alternatives.

The AIIB is the first significant alternative multilateral institution created by China (see Chapter 2). It is too new to judge its effectiveness in fulfilling the tasks it has set itself. Regardless, China is likely to keep pushing for greater recognition and authority that is commensurate with its economic status and power. It has, for example, persuaded the IMF to accept its currency, the yuan, as a reserve currency that can be used to settle international payments, and it is clearly aiming at eventually gaining some of the status and uses currently held by the U.S. dollar. The role of yuan in international trade and payments will evolve, along with other Chinese initiatives to establish its position in international economic affairs.

Unresolved Issues

The integration of China and India in the world trading system poses a number of problems, some of which have been discussed. Two that have not been touched on are the impact of both countries on the world's environmental systems, and the increasingly contentious issue of state ownership of manufacturing enterprises that trade across borders.

Environmental Pressures   Rapid growth in two countries with more than one-third of the world's population puts pressure on the environment. China's development has been partly at the expense of its natural capital of water, air, and soil, and its population suffers from toxic contamination of its cities, and many parts of its countryside. China's per capita energy consumption is well below that of the United States, but it consumes more energy per unit of GDP produced. Given its large coal deposits (its one abundant natural resource), it has become reliant on an energy source that generates a high level of green house gases. Much of the same is true of India, although its democracy allows for more pushback from citizens when they are subjected to environmental degradation.

Both countries acknowledge the problems of the environment. Nevertheless, in the discussion of global warming, India points out that the world's rich economies used the environment in destructive ways in order to reach their current levels of high income. Asking middle-income countries such as India and China to make sacrifices in energy consumption and GDP growth for the sake of future genera-tions is, in their view, somewhat hypocritical. Better, India argues, for the world's rich countries to make sacrifices, particularly since they generated the majority of green house gases.

China and India both continue to generate large amounts of greenhouse gases, even as they attempt to transition to alternative energy sources. China, in particular, has made large investments in solar power, but the size of both their economies and the still developing technology of solar implies that the transition to clean energy is not happening soon. China's extremely rapid growth has also increased the intensity of many other forms of pollution and has challenged the ability of its environmental controls to keep up with its economic growth. Conse-quently, environmental challenges continue to increase, often in alarming ways that affect the safety of food systems, drinking water, and other basic elements of everyday life. Both China and India will have to address these issues if they are going to have a secure future.

State Capitalism   China and India use the powers of the state to shape economic outcomes in a way that suits their national development goals. Market forces are important, but when a market outcome is thought to be harmful or less benefi-cial to national interests, states intervene. In China, where this process is most developed, state-owned enterprises (SOE) control a large share of the economy, particularly in industries thought to be important to future economic development. India has fewer state-owned enterprises after the reforms of the 1990s, but it still has quite a few.

WTO rules allow state-owned enterprises, but they require countries to treat them at arm's length and as if they were private. Direct links from government to enterprise are to be minimized, and SOE are not allowed to be subsidized or given special treatment. In practice, it is hard to tell when a SOE is receiving subsidies in the form of tax breaks, easy access to credit, favorable legislation, or some other type of preference that is not a direct payment. This has created significant trade tensions with the United States and the European Union, where it is viewed as an unfair trade practice. The United States has reacted by levying both anti-dumping duties and countervailing duties on Chinese products, and has begun to include rules on state-owned enterprises in proposed trade agreements, such as the Trans-Pacific Partnership (see Chapter 13).

This issue overlaps the issue of unbalanced trade since subsidized industries are potentially more competitive. Given that Indian trade balances tend to run toward deficits, their state-owned enterprises are less likely to face opposition from other countries. China, by contrast, uses its SOE as a primary tool for implementing its policies, and together with its large surpluses, it is more vulnerable to complaints of unfair trade practices.

The Choices Ahead

As China and India, and other large middle-income countries, grow economically, there are political reactions to their participation in world markets. Negotiations for China's accession to the WTO led to a series of bilateral agreements between China and its trading partners that allow voluntary export restraints and other measures to block Chinese exports if they threaten firms in importing countries. The U.S. Congress introduced, and then retracted under political pressure, a measure that would label China's previous exchange rate management system as an unfair trade advantage. Although China altered its exchange rate system for its own reasons, there continue to be calls in the United States to punish China for what some politicians claim is blatant currency manipulation to achieve commercial advantages. If those voices were ever to be successful, it would legitimize blocking some Chinese exports from entering the United States. Similar measures have not been proposed for India, although the outsourcing by firms of their IT work has led to calls for the re-examination of policies that may be encouraging firms to go abroad. In the end, however, measures against China and India become difficult to enforce because for every firm hurt by Chinese or Indian imports, others are helped by the low prices and availability of their goods and services. Hence, trade measures to stem trade flows will hurt businesses and consumers that depend on the imports.

If Chinese success in particular is frightening to some politicians, businesses, and workers, Chinese failure should be seen as an even greater threat. For example, the country is unlikely to begin to make serious headway in addressing its environmental problems unless it has political stability and some degree of economic prosperity. The switch to cleaner energy sources is highly unlikely if the country is struggling against economic failure or political instability. The same holds for its ability to address the problems of water and air pollution, missing urban infrastructure, and other remediation needed to counter the effects of rapid economic growth.

China and especially India still have large numbers of people living in poverty or not far above. While conditions have significantly improved for many, not everyone has benefited from growth, and many who have are falling farther and farther behind the new economic elites in both countries. In China this has led to growing dissatisfaction and rising protest. India's democratic system creates more legitimate means for changing leaders who do not deliver, whereas China's growing inequality is seen by many as a potential threat to the current system. A failure of its economic project would undoubtedly worsen economic inequality and lead to greater social unrest.

Summary

- India and China are the two most populous countries in the world. By the early 2000s, they had over 20 percent of world GDP. Their high rates of economic growth have brought increased prosperity to many people, and significantly reduced rates of poverty, although many people remain poor.

- Indian economic growth lags Chinese. China has moved large numbers of workers out of the countryside and agriculture and into low-wage, low-skilled manufacturing. India has not yet experienced a similar transformation and more than half its labor force remains in agriculture where productivity is low and poverty is high.

- Both countries undertook extensive economic reforms. China began in 1978 and India in the 1980s, but more strongly in 1991. The reforms led to much higher growth rates in both countries.

- China is one of the few formerly communist countries that did not suffer a loss of output during its transition to the market economy. This is partly a result of a more cautious approach to reforms, but also because of its large agricultural sector. When it began its reforms, about 70 percent of its labor force was in agriculture, much of it very low productivity. A loss of workers to that sector did not result in a decline in output.

- Institutions remain relatively weak in both countries. China scores in the middle of 189 countries while India is in the bottom third in the Doing Business Index. Both are below average in most of the dimensions considered by the Worldwide Governance Index.

- China and India have had a very rapid growth of imports and exports. China's manufacturing sector is extremely competitive and relies on technology imports. Its exports are mostly low-technology goods or high-technology goods assembled in China from imported parts, although this is changing and strong industrial upgrading is taking place. Exports of Indian business services and computer and information services have taken off since the middle of the 1990s. This type of trade in services represents a new area of trade but is another application of the theory of comparative advantage.

- Trade and growth in China and India pose several challenges for other countries. China's manufacturing sector has a strong comparative advantage in the production of goods that need abundant supplies of low-wage labor, while India's production of business services and computer and information services is supported by its English-speaking engineers and technicians.

- China's and India's growth has levied a toll on both society and the environment. Particularly in China, where water, air, and soil resources are degrading rapidly.

Vocabulary

Deng Xiaoping

dual track strategy

foreign trading corporation (FTC)

gravity model of trade

Manmohan Singh

Special Economic Zones (SEZ)

state capitalism

Study Questions

All problems are assignable in MyEconLab Real-time data

17.1. Compare the role of agriculture in China and India.

17.2. Describe the process of Chinese reforms from their beginning in 1978 up until China's accession to the WTO.

17.3. What were the factors that led to economic reform in India, and what were the main elements of the reforms?

17.4. Use the gravity model of trade to explain why China trades with Korea, Japan, the United States, the European Union, Hong Kong, and Taiwan.

17.5. China is a middle-income country with abundant supplies of low-skilled labor. How does it manage to export high-technology products? Does it have a comparative advantage in high-technology goods?

17.6. What are the sources of China's comparative advantage and how does that show up in the goods it trades?

17.7. What are the factors that make India competitive in business services and computer and information services? Do these factors give it a comparative advantage or do they reflect some other source of competitiveness?

17.8. Why has India not been able to develop a large low-wage, low-skilled manufacturing sector? Can it skip this stage of development and go directly to services economy that exports high value-added services?

17.9. Chinese growth has created a great deal of controversy and discussion outside China. What are some of the major concerns of countries that trade with China?

GLOSSARY

Absolute productivity advantage, or absolute advantage. A country has an absolute productivity advantage in a good if its labor productivity is higher; that is, it is able to produce more output with an hour of labor than its trading partner can.

Acquis communautaire. The European Union rules governing technical standards, environmental and technical inspections, banking supervision, public accounts, statistical reporting requirements, and other elements of EU law.

Adjustment process. Usually refers to the changes in a country's current account that occur as a result of a fall in the value of its currency.

African Growth and Opportunity Act (AGOA). A preferential agreement offered by the United States to countries in sub-Saharan Africa giving them improved access to the U.S. market for their exports.

Aggregate demand (AD). The sum of household consumption, business investment, government spending on final goods and services, and net exports.

Aggregate supply (AS). The total output of an economy.

Andean Trade Preference Act (ATPA). A preferential agreement offered by the United States to countries in the Andean region of South America giving them improved access to the U.S. market for their exports.

Antidumping duty (ADD). A tariff levied on imports in retaliation for selling below fair value. *See also* Fair value.

Appreciation. An increase in a currency's value under a floating exchange rate system. *See also* Revaluation.

Asia Pacific Economic Cooperation (APEC). A group of Pacific-region nations founded in 1989 for the purpose of creating free trade among all its members by 2020. APEC includes the United States, Japan, and China, among others. APEC's goal is not a free-trade area; instead, it is to get all members to commit to free trade and open investment flows as a part of their trade policies toward all nations.

Asian Infrastructure Investment Bank (AIIB). A multilateral development bank founded by China and 56 other countries with the purpose of providing investment funds for infrastructure projects in Asia.

Association of Southeast Asian Nations (ASEAN). ASEAN is a community of ten nations with a security component, an economic component, and a socio-cultural component. It was founded in 1967 and has set the date of 2020 for the achievement of a free-trade area.

Austerity. Usually refers to the cuts in government spending and increases in taxes that are implemented to reduce or eliminate a government budget deficit.

Autarky. The complete absence of foreign trade; total self-sufficiency of a national economy.

Auto Pact. The 1965 agreement between the United States and Canada that created free trade in the automotive sector.

Baker Plan. The first U.S. plan (1985) to assist indebted nations during the debt crisis of the 1980s.

Banking crisis. A common feature of international financial crises; a banking crisis occurs when banks fail and disintermediation spreads.

Basel Accords. A set of recommended "best practices" designed to help countries avoid banking and financial crises. The accords emphasize capital requirements, supervisory review, and information disclosure.

Bilateral investment treaty (BIT). An agreement between two countries that specifies the rules for cross-border investment.

Brady Plan. A 1989 plan of U.S. Treasury Secretary Nicholas Brady intended to help indebted developing countries. Unlike previous plans, the Brady Plan offered a modest amount of debt relief.

Bretton Woods Conference. A small town in New Hampshire that was, in July 1944, the site of talks establishing the international financial and economic order after World War II. The International Monetary Fund and the World Bank emerged from the Bretton Woods Conference.

Bretton Woods exchange rate system. The exchange rate system that emerged from the Bretton Woods Conference at the end of World War II. *See also* Smithsonian Agreement.

BRICs. Brazil, Russia, India, and China. The term was first used by Jim O'Neill at Goldman Sachs in 2001 to single out four large economies with the potential to dramatically alter world trade and payments.

Canadian-U.S. Trade Agreement (CUSTA). A 1989 free trade agreement between the United States and Canada, and a precursor of NAFTA.

Capital account. A record of the transactions in highly specialized financial assets and liabilities between the residents of a nation and the rest of the world.

Capital controls. National controls on the inflow and/ or outflow of funds.

Capital requirements. Requirements that owners of financial institutions invest a percentage of their own capital so that all losses are personal losses to shareholders and other bank owners, as well as to depositors.

Caribbean Basin Initiative (CBI). Is the name for a set of preferential agreements offered by the United States to countries in the Caribbean region giving them preferential access to the U.S. market for their exports.

Cohesion funds. Cohesion funds are a type of EU funding used to support regional development. They are directed toward less developed regions, particularly new members with incomes below the EU average. The funds pay for infrastructure development and environmental projects such as water treatment and transportation projects.

Collective action clauses. A requirement that each international lender agrees to collective mediation between all lenders and the debtor in the event of an international crisis.

Common Agricultural Policy (CAP). The system of support payments and other forms of assistance that is the main agricultural program of the European Union.

Common external tariff. The policy of customs unions in which the members adopt the same tariffs toward nonmembers.

Common market. A regional trade agreement whose member nations allow the free movement of inputs as well as outputs, and who share a common external tariff toward nonmembers.

Comparative productivity advantage, or comparative advantage. Achieved in a good when a country has lower opportunity costs of producing the good than those of its trading partners.

Competitive advantage. The ability to sell a good at the lowest price. Competitive advantage may be the result of high productivity and a comparative advantage. Alternatively, it may be the result of government subsidies for inefficient industries.

Competitive devaluation. A devaluation or depreciation in a currency with the intent to gain export markets.

Conditional cash transfers (CCT). A social policy that offers small monthly stipends to families in return for various socially desirable actions by the family; for example, that the children attend school and/or receive prescribed vaccinations and health check-ups.

Conditionality. *See* IMF conditionally.

Consumer surplus. The difference between the value of a good to consumers and the price they have to pay. Graphically it is the area under the demand curve and above the price line. *See also* Producer surplus.

Consumption possibilities curve (CPC). The CPC shows the ratio at which goods can be exchanged when trade occurs. The slope of the CPC is the trade price of one good in terms of another.

Contagion effects. The spread of a crisis from one country to another. This may happen through trade flows, through currency and exchange rate movements, or through a change in the perceptions of foreign investors.

Contractionary fiscal policy. Tax increases and/or cuts in government spending.

Contractionary monetary policy. A cut in the money supply and a rise in interest rates.

Convergence criteria. The five indicators of readiness to begin the single currency in the European Union: stable exchange rates, low inflation, harmonization of long-term interest rates, reduction of government deficits, and reduction of government debt.

Core labor standards. Eight core labor rights developed and advocated by the ILO and embodied in eight ILO conventions. They cover areas such as freedom from coercion, minimum work age, freedom to bargain collectively, and others.

Council of the European Union. The chief legislative body of the European Union.

Countervailing duty (CVD). A tariff on imports that is levied in retaliation against foreign subsidies. *See also* Subsidy.

Covered interest arbitrage. Interest rate arbitrage that includes the signing of a forward currency contract to sell the foreign currency when the foreign assets mature. *See also* Interest rate arbitrage.

Crawling peg. A system in which a country fixes its currency to another currency (or a basket of currencies) and makes regular periodic adjustments in the nominal exchange rate in order to offset or control movement in the real exchange rate.

Currency board. A government board that strictly regulates the creation of new money.

Current account. A record of transactions in goods, services, investment income, and unilateral transfers between the residents of a country and the rest of the world.

Current account balance. The broadest measure of a nation's commerce with the rest of the world.

Customs union. An agreement among two or more member countries to engage in free trade with each other and to share a common external tariff toward nonmembers.

Data dissemination standards. The IMF's standards for reporting macroeconomic data.

Deadweight loss. A pure economic loss with no corresponding gains elsewhere in the economy. *See also* Efficiency loss.

Debt crisis. A financial crisis brought on by unsustainable levels of debt. The debt may be either privately or publicly owed.

Debt service. Principal repayment and interest payments that are made in order to pay off a debt.

Deep integration. Economic integration beyond removal of barriers at each country's border. Deep integration requires changes in domestic laws and regulations that sometimes inadvertently restrict trade.

Deliberation councils. Quasi-legislative bodies that combine representatives from industry with government and that have the purpose of discussing government policy and private sector investment. Japan, Korea, Malaysia, Singapore, and Thailand use deliberation councils.

Delors Report. Named after the president of the European Commission during the 1980s, the report contained three hundred steps that the European Union needed to follow in order to become a common market. The report was adopted in 1987 and led to the creation of a common market under the Single European Act.

Demand-pull. *See* Demand-pull factors.

Demand-pull factors. Economic conditions in the receiving country that "pull" in migrants. *See also* Supply-push factors.

Demographic transition. The shift from high birth rates and high death rates (characteristic of nearly all pre-industrial societies) to low birth rates and low death rates (characteristic of high-income, industrial societies).

Deng Xiaoping. Chinese leader who began China's reforms in 1978.

Depreciation. A decrease in a currency's value under a floating exchange rate system. *See also* Devaluation.

Derived demand. Demand for a good or service that is derived from the demand for something else. For example, the demand for labor is derived from the demand for goods and services.

Disintermediation. A failure on the part of the banking system that prevents savings from being channeled into investment.

Doha Development Agenda. The name for the trade negotiations that began in 2000 under the auspices of the World Trade Organization.

Doha Round. The current WTO round of trade negotiations. *See* Doha Development Agenda.

Dollarization. The use of the dollar in place of a country's domestic currency. Technically, dollarization can refer to the use of any currency that is not the country's own.

Dual track strategy. China's strategy for transitioning from communism to capitalism is known as a dual track strategy because it localized market reforms to certain geographical areas or economic sectors (e.g., agriculture) while maintaining government planning for the remainder of the economy.

Dumping. Selling in a foreign market at less than fair value. *See also* Fair value.

Economic Commission on Latin America (ECLA, or CEPAL in Spanish). The United Nation's agency that oversees UN activity and information gathering in Latin America.

Economic populism. Economic policies emphasizing growth and redistribution that simultaneously de-emphasize (or deny the importance of) inflation risks, deficit finance, external constraints (i.e., trade and exchange rate issues), and the reactions of economic agents.

Economic restructuring. A movement from one point to another along a country's production possibility curve.

Economic union. The most complete form of economic integration, these unions are common markets that also harmonize many standards while having the same or substantially similar fiscal and monetary policies. Economic unions may include a common currency.

Economies of scale. A decline in average cost while the number of units produced increases.

Effective rate of protection. Effective rates of protection consider levels of protection on intermediate inputs as well as the nominal tariff levied on the protected good. Effective rates are measured as the percentage change in the domestic value added after tariffs on the intermediate and final goods are levied. *See also* Nominal rates of protection.

Efficiency loss. A form of deadweight loss that refers to the loss of income or output that occurs when a nation produces a good at a cost higher than the world price.

Ejido. A Mexican system of collective farms.

Erasmus+ Program. A EU program for student and faculty mobility at the university level.

Escape clause relief. Temporary tariff protection granted to an industry that experiences a sudden and harmful surge in imports.

Euro. The new currency of the European Union. Formally introduced as the unit of account in 1999, the euro appeared in January 2002.

European Atomic Energy Community (EAEC or Euratom). An agreement concurrent with the Treaty of Rome that committed the six countries to the peaceful and cooperative development of nuclear energy.

European Central Bank. The central bank for the euro area countries.

European Coal and Steel Community (ECSC). A 1951 agreement among the six countries that eventually formed the EEC, creating free trade in the coal and steel industries.

European Commission. The executive branch of the European Union.

European Community (EC). The name for the European Union before the signing of the Maastricht Treaty and the creation of the economic union.

European currency unit (ECU). A monetary unit of account that was used in the European Union before the introduction of the euro; the ECU was not a currency and was not used in transactions.

European Economic Community (EEC). The original name for the community founded by the Treaty of Rome. The EEC eventually became the EC, and then the EU.

European Monetary System (EMS). An exchange rate system started in 1979 that linked the currencies of each of the members of the EC. The EMS was replaced in 1999 by the euro.

European Parliament. A quasi-advisory body of the European Union. The parliament is the only directly elected government body in the European Union, and it has been moving toward becoming a true legislature.

European Union (EU). Twenty-seven western European nations that are an economic union.

Exchange rate. The price of one currency expressed in terms of a second currency. Exchange rates may be measured in real or nominal terms.

Exchange rate crisis. A collapse of a country's currency.

Exchange rate mechanism (ERM). The system adopted by the EC when it used the EMS. The ERM was a target zone exchange rate that allowed some limited flexibility in an otherwise fixed set of exchange rates.

Exchange rate risk. Risk that occurs when an individual or firm holds assets that are denominated in a foreign currency. The risk is the potential for unexpected losses (or gains) due to unforeseen fluctuations in the value of the foreign currency.

Expansionary fiscal policy. Tax cuts and/or increases in government spending.

Expansionary monetary policy. Increases in the money supply and cuts in interest rates.

Expenditure reducing policy. Policies that reduce the overall level of domestic expenditure. These are appropriate for addressing the problem of a trade deficit, and they include cuts in government expenditures and/or increases in taxes.

Expenditure switching. *See* Expenditure switching policy.

Expenditure switching policy. Policies designed to shift the expenditures of domestic residents. If the problem is a trade deficit, they should shift toward domestically produced goods; if the problem is a trade surplus, they should shift toward foreign goods. Examples of these policies are changes in the exchange rate and changes in tariffs and quotas.

Export pessimism. The views of Argentine economist Raul Prebisch and his followers, who believed that real prices received by Latin American countries for their exports would fall over time.

Export processing zone (EPZ). A geographical region in which firms are free from tariffs as long as they export the goods that are made from imports. Rules and regulations governing EPZs vary by country, but all of them are aimed at encouraging exports, often through encouragement given to investment.

External debt. Debt that is owed to agents outside a country's national boundaries.

External economies of scale. Scale economies that are external to a firm, but internal to an industry. Consequently, all the firms in an industry experience declining average costs as the size of the industry increases.

Externality. A divergence between social and private returns.

Factor abundance, factor scarcity. These are relative

terms because, strictly speaking, all factors are scarce. Relative factor abundance implies that an economy has more of a particular factor in relation to some other factor and by comparison to another economy. Relative factor scarcity implies the opposite.

Fair value. A standard for determining whether dumping is occurring. Generally, in the United States fair value is the average price in the exporter's home market or the average price in third-country markets. Definitions vary by country, making fair value a source of disagreement.

Financial account. The part of the balance of payments that tracks capital flows between a national economy and the rest of the world.

Financial crisis. Usually involves a banking crisis and may also entail an exchange rate crisis. A financial crisis results in disintermediation and a slowdown in economic activity that may be severe.

Fiscal policy. Policies related to government expenditures and taxation.

Fixed exchange rate system. An exchange rate that is fixed and unchanging relative to some other currency or group of currencies.

Flexible (floating) exchange rate system. When supply and demand for foreign exchange determine the value of a nation's money.

Foreign affiliate. A foreign-based operation that is owned by a firm in the home country.

Foreign direct investment (FDI). The purchase of physical assets such as real estate or businesses by a foreign company or individual. It can be outward (citizens or businesses in the home country purchase assets in a foreign country) or inward (foreigners purchase assets in the home country). *See also* Foreign portfolio investment.

Foreign exchange reserves. Assets held by the national monetary authority that can be used to settle international payments. Dollars, euros, yen, and monetary gold are examples of reserves.

Foreign portfolio investment. The purchase of financial assets such as stocks, bonds, bank accounts, or related financial instruments. As with FDI, it can be inward or outward.

Foreign trading corporation (FTC). Before reform, all foreign trade in China was controlled by twelve enterprises attached to various branches of government. These enterprises were called *foreign trade corporations.*

Forward exchange rate. The exchange rate in a forward market.

Forward market. Market in which buyers and sellers agree on a quantity and a price for a foreign exchange or other transaction that takes place in

(usually) 30, 90, or 180 days from the time the contract is signed. *See also* Spot markets.

Four Freedoms. The freedom of movement of goods, services, capital, and labor. These were the key elements of the Single European Act of 1993 and changed the European Community from a customs union into a common market.

Four Tigers. Hong Kong, Korea, Singapore, and Taiwan. Their economic growth began shortly after Japan's post–World War II development. They are classified by the World Bank as either high-income or upper-middle-income economies. (The Four Tigers are sometimes called the *Four Dragons* or the *Little Dragons.) See also* High-performance Asian economies and Newly industrializing economies.

Free riding. Occurs when a person lets others pay for a good or service, or lets them do the work when he or she knows that he or she cannot be excluded from consumption of the good or from the benefits of the work.

Free-trade area. A preferential trade agreement in which countries permit the free movement of outputs (goods and services) across their borders as long as the outputs originate in one of the member countries.

Gains from trade. The increase in consumption made possible by specialization and trade.

General Agreement on Tariffs and Trade (GATT). The main international agreement covering the rules of trade in most, but not all, goods. The GATT's origins can be traced to negotiations that took place in 1946, after World War II.

General Agreement on Trade in Services (GATS). An attempt to extend the rules and principles of the GATT to trade in services. GATS was one of the outcomes of the Uruguay Round.

Generalized System of Preferences (GSP). A set of preferences given by some high-income countries to low- and middle-income countries. The GSP provides low income countries with preferential access at reduced tariff rates to high-income markets.

Gold standard. A fixed exchange rate system that uses gold as its standard of value.

Goods and services. Goods and services are the components of international trade and the two main components of the current account.

Gross domestic product (GDP). The market value of all final goods and services produced in a year inside a nation.

Gross national product (GNP). The market value of all final goods and services produced by the residents of a nation, regardless of where the production takes place. GNP equals GDP minus income paid to foreigners plus income received from abroad.

Hard peg. An exchange rate system with a completely fixed currency value. *See* Soft peg.

Harmonization of standards. Harmonization of standards occurs when two or more countries negotiate a common standard or policy. Harmonization can occur with respect to safety standards, technical standards, environmental standards, legal standards, certification, or any requirement set forth by national policies. *See also* Mutual recognition of standards.

Heckscher-Ohlin (HO) trade theory. A trade theory that predicts the goods and services that countries export and import. The theorem states that countries will export goods that require the intensive use of relatively abundant factors to produce, and import goods that require relatively scarce factors to produce.

Hedging. Eliminating risk (e.g., exchange rate risk can be eliminated, or hedged, by signing a forward contract).

Heterodox model. A heterodox stabilization policy is designed to cure inflation by the following: cutting government spending, limiting the creation of new money, reforming the tax system, and freezing wages and prices. *See also* Orthodox stabilization policies.

High-income, upper-middle-income, lower-middle-income, and low-income countries. Categories used by the World Bank to classify countries by their level of per capita income. The criteria for categories change over time. Currently, low income is less than $1,006 per year, lower-middle income is $1,006 to $3,975 per year, upper-middle income is $3,976 to $12,276 per year, and high income is above $12.276 per year.

IMF conditionality. The changes in economic policy that borrowing nations are required to make in order to receive International Monetary Fund loans. The changes usually involve policies that reduce or eliminate a severe trade deficit and/or a central government budget deficit. In practical terms, they involve reduced expenditures by the government and by the private sector (to reduce imports) and increased taxes. *See also* International Monetary Fund.

Import substitution industrialization (ISI). An economic development strategy that emphasizes the domestic production of goods that substitute for imports. ISI policies decrease imports and exports.

Industrial policy. A policy designed to create new industries or to provide support for existing ones.

Infant industry. A young industry. An argument for tariff protection is often made based on the belief that a particular industry is incapable of competing at present but that it will soon grow into a mature and competitive industry that no longer needs protection.

Informal economy. The part of a national or local economy that is unmeasured, untaxed, and unregulated.

Institution. A set of rules of behavior. Institutions set limits, or constraints, on social, political, and economic interaction. An institution may be informal (e.g., manners, taboos, or customs) or formal (e.g., constitutions or laws).

Intellectual property rights. Intellectual property is divided into copyrights and related rights for literary and artistic work, and industrial property rights for trademarks, patents, industrial designs, geographical indications, and the layout of integrated circuits.

Interest parity. The notion that the interest rate differential between two countries is approximately equal to the percentage difference between the forward and spot exchange rates.

Interest rate arbitrage. The transfer of funds from one financial asset and currency to another to take advantage of higher interest rates. *See also* Covered interest arbitrage.

Interindustry trade. Trade that involves exports and imports of goods that are produced in different industries, for example, when the United States exports cars and imports sugar cane.

Intermediate inputs. Parts and materials that are incorporated into a final good such as a consumer good or investment good.

Intermediation. The role of banks as institutions that concentrate savings from many sources and lend the money to investors.

Internal economies of scale. The idea that an individual firm experiences a decline in its average cost of production as it increases the number of units produced.

International financial architecture. The complex of institutions, international organizations, governments, and private economic agents that make up the international financial system.

International investment position. The value of all foreign assets owned by a nation's residents, businesses, and government, minus the value of all domestic assets owned by foreigners.

International Labour Organization (ILO). The international organization charged with responsibilities for researching international labor conditions and providing technical assistance in the area of labor conditions and standards.

International Monetary Fund (IMF). One of the original Bretton Woods institutions, the IMF's responsibilities include helping member countries that suffer from instability or problems with their balance of payments. It also provides technical expertise in international financial relations.

Intrafirm trade. International trade between two or more divisions of the same company that are located in different countries.

Intraindustry trade. Exports and imports of the same category of goods and/or services.

Investment income. A subcomponent of the current account; income received or paid abroad.

Investor-state dispute. A dispute between a foreign enterprise and the government where the enterprise is located.

J-curve. A currency depreciation often results in a worsening of the trade deficit in the short run and an improvement in the long run.

Labor argument. The argument for trade protection based on the false belief that high-wage countries will be harmed by imports from low-wage countries.

Labor productivity. The amount of output per unit of labor input.

Large country case. A country that purchases a significant share of the world's output of a particular good may improve its welfare by imposing a tariff that causes import prices to fall.

Lender of last resort. In international economics, a place where nations can borrow after all sources of commercial lending have dried up. Today, the IMF (International Monetary Fund) fills this role.

Lost Decade. The period of recession in Latin America brought on by the region-wide debt crisis beginning in August 1982. There is no official date ending the Lost Decade, but 1989 is a useful benchmark, since it coincided with a new strategy for handling the crisis.

Maastricht Treaty. Sometimes called the *Treaty on Economic and Monetary Union*. Ratified in 1991 by the members of the European Union, its most visible provision includes the single currency program that began in 1999. It creates an economic union among the members of the European Union.

Magnification effect. The idea that a rise or decline in goods prices has a larger effect in the same direction on the income of the factor used intensively in its production.

Manmohan Singh. Indian leader responsible for initiating economic reforms in 1991.

Maquiladora. Mexican manufacturing firms, mostly along the U.S.-Mexico border, that receive special tax breaks.

Market failure. A situation in which markets do not produce the most beneficial economic outcome. Market failure has numerous causes, including externalities and monopolistic or oligopolistic market structures.

Mercantilism. The economic system that arose in western Europe in the 1500s, during the period in which modern nation states were emerging from feudal monarchies. Mercantilism has been called the politics and economics of nation building because it stressed the need for nations to run trade surpluses to obtain revenues for armies and national construction projects. Mercantilists favored granting monopoly rights to individuals and companies, they shunned competition, and they viewed exports as positive and imports as negative. Today, the term *mercantilism* is sometimes used to describe the policies of nations that promote their exports while keeping their markets relatively closed to imports.

Merchandise trade balance. Exports of goods minus imports of goods.

MERCOSUR. The Mercado Común del Sur, or Common Market of the South, is the largest regional trade grouping in South America. It includes four countries: Brazil, Argentina, Uruguay, and Paraguay.

Monetary policy. National macroeconomic policies related to the money supply and interest.

Monopolistic competition. Competition between differentiated products, combining elements of perfect competition and monopoly.

Moral hazard. A financial incentive to withhold information, take on excessive risk, or behave in a manner that generates significant social costs.

Most-favored nation (MFN) status. The idea that every member of the World Trade Organization (WTO) is required to treat each of its trading partners as well as it treats its most favored trading partner. In effect, MFN prohibits one country from discriminating against another.

Multilateralism. An approach to trade and investment issues that involves large numbers of countries. Multilateralism stands for the belief that market openings should benefit all nations. Multilateral institutions include the World Trade Organization, the World Bank, and the International Monetary Fund.

Multiplier effect. The macroeconomic concept that a change in spending has an impact on the national product, which is ultimately larger than the original spending change.

Mutual recognition of standards. An alternative to the harmonization of standards. Under a mutual recognition system, countries keep different standards while agreeing to recognize and accept each other's standards within their national jurisdictions.

National income and product accounts (NIPA). A set of accounts for a nation showing the components of GDP. These have both an income view and a product view. In theory, they are equivalent, as total income in an economy must equal the total value of output produced.

National treatment. The idea that foreign firms operating inside a nation should not be treated differently from domestic firms.

Neoliberal model or neoliberalism. Market fundamentalism that became common throughout Latin America in the late 1980s and 1990s.

New Trade Theory. A new approach to modeling international trade that began in the 1980s. New trade theory drops the assumption of constant or decreasing returns to scale (increasing costs) and introduces economies of scale that are either internal to the firm or external to the firm but internal to the industry.

Newly industrializing economies (NIE). The most recent wave of rapidly growing and industrializing developing nations. There are a number of these economies in Latin America (e.g., Argentina, Brazil, Chile, and Mexico) as well as in East Asia (the HPAE, Indonesia, Malaysia, and Thailand).

Nominal exchange rate. The price of a unit of foreign exchange. *See also* Real exchange rate.

Nominal rate of protection. The amount of a tariff (or the tariff equivalent of a quota) expressed as a percentage of the good's price. *See also* Effective rate of protection.

Nominal tariff. The tax on imports of a particular good, expressed in either percentages or absolute amounts. *See also* Effective rates of protection.

Nondiminishable. A good or service that is not reduced by consumption. For example, listening to a radio broadcast does not reduce its availability to others.

Nondiscrimination. The notion that national laws should not treat foreign firms differently from domestic firms.

Nonexcludable. When people who do not pay for a good or service cannot be excluded from its consumption. National defense is an example.

Nonrival. *See* Nondiminishable.

Nontariff barrier (NTB). Any trade barrier that is not a tariff. Most important are quotas, which are physical limits on the quantity of permitted imports. Nontariff barriers include red tape and

regulations, rules requiring governments to purchase from domestic producers, and a large number of other practices that indirectly limit imports.

Nontariff measure. Nontariff measures are nontariff barriers that are not quotas. They include red tape or cumbersome and unevenly applied rules. In general, the term refers to any regulatory or policy rules other than tariffs and quotas that reduce the physical quantity of imports or exports.

Nontransparent. Not easily interpreted or understood. For example, some countries use red tape and bureaucratic rules to block imports.

North American Agreement on Environmental Cooperation. The environmental "side agreement" to the NAFTA.

North American Agreement on Labor Cooperation. The labor "side agreement" to the NAFTA.

North American Free-Trade Agreement (NAFTA). The free-trade area formed by Canada, Mexico, and the United States. NAFTA began in 1994.

Odious debt. Debt that is contracted by a country with an unrepresentative government and that is used in ways that do not benefit the people of the nation.

Official reserve assets. Assets held by governments for use in settling international debts. Official resource assets consist primarily of key foreign currencies.

Off-shoring. The movement of some or all of a firm's activities to a foreign country.

OLI theory. A model of the determinants of foreign direct investment that is based on the key variables Ownership-Location-Internalization.

Oligopoly. A market with so few producers that each firm can influence the market price.

Open market operations. The main tool of monetary policy, consisting of the buying and selling of government debt (bills, notes, and bonds) in order to influence bank reserves and interest rates.

Opportunity cost. The value of the best forgone alternative to the activity actually chosen.

Optimal currency area. A region of fixed exchange rates or a single currency. A currency area is optimal in the sense that it is precisely the right geographical size to capture the benefits of fixed rates without incurring the costs.

Orthodox model. An orthodox stabilization policy is designed to cure inflation by the following: cutting government spending, limiting the creation of new money, and reforming the tax system. *See also* Heterodox.

Outsourcing. Outsourcing is the shifting of procurement from within a firm to outside a firm. It is often used to refer to services that are purchased abroad, such as the procurement of business services in India by a firm based in Europe or the United States.

Partial trade agreement. An agreement that covers only some goods and/or services and is less than a free-trade agreement.

Pegged exchange rate. A form of fixed exchange rate. *See* Crawling peg.

Pollution havens. Countries that compete for investment by advertising their low environmental standards.

Preferential agreement. A trade agreement in which one side makes unilateral concessions to the other; used by high-income countries to grant preferential access to developing countries.

Private returns. The value of all private benefits minus all private costs, properly adjusted to take into account that some costs and benefits are in the future and must be discounted to show their value in today's dollars. *See also* Social returns.

Producer surplus. The difference between the minimum price a producer would accept to produce a given quantity and the price it actually receives. Graphically it is the area under the price line and above the supply curve. *See also* Consumer surplus.

Product cycle. The idea that manufactured goods go through a cycle of heavy research and development requiring experimentation in the product and the manufacturing process, followed by stabilization of design and production, and a final stage of complete standardization.

Product differentiation. Two products that serve similar purposes but that are different in one or more dimensions. Most consumer goods are differentiated products.

Production possibilities curve (PPC). This curve shows the maximum amount of output possible, given the available supply of inputs. It also shows the trade-off that a country must make if it wishes to increase the output of one of its goods.

Public goods. Goods that share two characteristics: nonexcludability and nonrivalry or nondiminishability. If they are excludable but nondiminishable goods, they are sometimes called *collective goods*.

Purchasing power parity. An adjustment to exchange rates or incomes designed to keep constant the real purchasing power of money when converted from one currency to another.

Qualified majority. Most EU legislation passed by the European Union Council of Ministers requires a qualified majority, equivalent to about 72 percent of the total votes cast.

Quota. A numerical limit on the volume of imports.

Quota rents. The excess profits earned by foreign producers (and sometimes domestic distributors of foreign products) in an export market. Quota rents occur whenever a quota causes a price increase in the market receiving the exports.

Race to the bottom. Downward pressure on labor, environmental, or other standards that comes about through price competition.

Real exchange rate. The inflation-adjusted nominal rate. The real rate is useful for examining changes in the relative purchasing power of foreign currencies over time.

Regional trade agreement (RTA). Agreements between two or more countries, each offering the others preferential access to its markets. RTAs provide varying degrees of access and variable amounts of deep integration.

Relative price. The price of one good in terms of another good. It is similar to a money price, which expresses the price in terms of dollars and cents, but relative price is in terms of the quantity of the first good that must be given up in order to buy a second good.

Rent seeking. Any activity by firms, individuals, or special interests that is designed to alter the distribution of income to their favor. Political lobbying, legal challenges, and bribery are common forms of rent-seeking behaviors, which use resources (labor and capital) but do not add to national output. For this reason, rent seeking is a net loss to the nation.

Resource curse. The economic and/or political problems caused by an abundance of one valuable natural resource such as petroleum.

Revaluation. An increase in the value of a currency under a fixed exchange rate system. *See also* Appreciation.

Section 301. A clause in U.S. trade legislation that requires the United States Trade Representative to take action against any nation that persistently engages in what the United States considers unfair trade practices. *See also* Special 301.

Securitization. The bundling of a group of assets so as to sell shares in the bundle.

Separate standards. Environmental, labor, or other standards that are unique to each country.

Shallow integration. The elimination or reduction of tariffs, quotas, and other border-related barriers (such as customs procedures) that restrict the flow of goods across borders. *See also* Deep integration.

Single European Act (SEA). The act that created a common market among the members of the European Community. The SEA was implemented in 1993.

Single Market Program (SMP). A reference to the set of changes initiated by the SEA.

Smithsonian Agreement. This 1971 agreement by major industrialized countries to devalue the gold content of the dollar was the beginning of the end for the Bretton Woods exchange rate system.

Social networks. Members of a migrant's family or village that provide support in the migrant's new location.

Social returns. Social returns include private returns, but they add costs and benefits to the elements of society that are not taken into consideration in the private returns. For example, a firm that generates pollution that it does not have to clean up imposes costs on society, which causes social returns to be lower than private returns.

Soft peg. An exchange rate system that is fixed but that allows some fluctuation within a set range or that is periodically adjusted to reduce changes in the real exchange rate. *See* Hard peg.

Sovereign default. Debt default by a national government.

Sovereign wealth funds. Assets held by a central government that are available for settlement of international claims.

Sovereignty. Freedom from outside intervention, or self-determination.

Special 301. A part of U.S. trade law requiring the United States Trade Representative to monitor property rights enforcement around the globe.

Special drawing right (SDR). The unit of account and artificial currency used by the International Monetary Fund (IMF). The SDR is a weighted average of several currencies and serves as an official reserve asset.

Special economic zones (SEZ). A special region in China in which local officials are encouraged to experiment with new economic policies. SEZs are designed to encourage foreign investment and exports.

Specific factors model. A trade model that allows for mobile and immobile factors of production.

Spot market. Market transactions that are concluded at the same time the price is agreed upon. In the currency spot market there is usually a day's lag before the currency is actually delivered. *See also* Forward markets.

Stabilization policies. National macroeconomic policies designed to cure inflation and reduce a government deficit. Stabilization policies are usually a first step in compliance with IMF conditionally during a macroeconomic crisis. *See also* Structural adjustment policies, Orthodox stabilization policies, and Heterodox.

Standstills. An agreement between international creditors and debtors to allow a temporary halt to the payment of interest and principal on previous loans.

State capitalism. A form of economic organization in which the national government takes an active role in shaping market outcomes to ensure they serve the national interest.

Statistical discrepancy. The sum of the current, capital, and financial accounts (multiplied by minus one).

Sterilization. Sterilization refers to the actions by a central bank to counteract the money supply effects of an inflow of foreign currency. Without sterilization, foreign currency inflows will expand the domestic money supply as recipients of foreign funds convert them to domestic money. With sterilization, the central bank removes excess money from the economy with open market operations.

Stolper-Samuelson theorem. A corollary of the Heckscher-Ohlin Theory stating that changes in import or export prices lead to a change in the same direction of the income of factors used intensively in production of the imported or exported good.

Structural adjustment policies. Policies that are designed to increase the role of market forces in a national economy. Structural adjustment policies are mainly microeconomic in nature and include privatization, deregulation, and trade reform. *See also* Stabilization policies.

Structural reform policies. A set of reform policies designed to make economies more efficient. These usually include the freeing of prices (ending of price subsidies), liberalization of trade, privatization, and the removal of interest rate controls, among others.

Subsidiarity. The principle that the authority of the European Union to involve itself in individual national affairs is limited to issues that are transnational in scope. In current practice, this includes environmental policies, regional policies, research and technology development, and economic and monetary union.

Subsidies. Government assistance for industry. The Uruguay Round of the GATT defined subsidies as direct loans or transfers, preferential tax treatments, a direct supply of goods, or income and price supports.

Subsidies and Countervailing Measures (SCM). An agreement to limit subsidies that also specified when countervailing measures were allowed that emerged from the Uruguay Round of GATT negotiations.

Sudden stop. The sudden cessation of capital inflows that had been used to finance a current account deficit.

Supply-push. *See* Supply-push factors.

Supply-push factors. The factors that "push" migrants out of their home country. *See also* Demand-pull factors.

Tariffs. Taxes imposed on imports. Tariffs raise the price to the domestic consumer and reduce the quantity demanded.

Technology transfer. The spread of technological information and capacity from one country to another.

Terms of trade (TOT). The average price of a country's exports divided by the average price of imports: TOT = (index of export prices)/(index of import prices). A decline in the terms of trade means that each unit of exports buys a smaller amount of imports.

Total factor productivity (TFP). A measurement of the quantity of output per unit of input. Increases in TFP mean that overall productivity has improved and that a given level of inputs will create more output; hence, technology or enterprise organization must have improved.

Trade adjustment assistance (TAA). Government programs that offer temporary assistance to workers who lose jobs because of foreign trade or their firms moving abroad.

Trade balance. Net exports, that is, the difference between exports of goods and services and imports of goods and services.

Trade bloc. A preferential trade area; a group of nations that reduces or eliminates barriers between themselves while maintaining higher tariffs and other barriers to trade against non-member, third-party countries.

Trade creation. The opposite of trade diversion. Trade creation occurs when trade policies cause a shift in production from a higher-cost producer (often a domestic one) to a lower-cost producer.

Trade deficit. A negative merchandise trade balance; the deficit may or may not include measurement of services trade.

Trade diversion. The opposite of trade creation. Trade diversion occurs when trade policies cause a shift in production and imports from a lower-cost producer to a higher-cost producer.

Trade-Related Aspects of Intellectual Property Rights (TRIPS). An agreement that emerged from the Uruguay Round of the GATT. It requires increased enforcement of intellectual property.

Trade-Related Investment Measures (TRIMS). An agreement that emerged from the Uruguay Round of the GATT that emphasizes national treatment and nondiscrimination in the treatment of foreign investors.

Trade rounds. Multilateral negotiating rounds under the auspices of the GATT or the WTO.

Trade-to-GDP ratio. The ratio of exports plus imports to GDP; often used as an indicator of the relative importance of international trade in an national economy.

Tranches. Parts of an IMF loan that are made in several installments.

Transaction costs. The costs of gathering market information, arranging a market agreement, and enforcing the agreement. Transaction costs include legal, marketing, and insurance costs, as well as quality checks, advertising, distribution, and after-sales service costs.

Transboundary and non-transboundary environmental impacts. Environmental externalities that do or do not cross international borders.

Transition economies. Countries that are in the process of moving from bureaucratically controlled economies to market-based economies. Transition economies include most of the countries that adopted socialist or communist ideologies during the twentieth century.

Transparent. Describes any trade barrier that is clearly defined as a barrier. Tariffs have the most transparency (are the most transparent) because they are usually clearly specified and published in each country's tariff code. Any disguised or hidden trade barriers cause a country's trade policy to be nontransparent.

Treaty of Rome. The funding document of the European Economic Community (EEC), the Treaty of Rome was signed by six nations in 1957 and went into force in 1958. The EEC has since become the European Union and includes fifteen members, but the Treaty of Rome remains its core legal document.

Treaty on European Union. Also known as the *Maastricht Treaty,* it is the agreement that deepened EU integration from a common market to an economic union.

Unilateral transfers. A component of the current account that measures the grants from one country to another.

Uruguay Round. The last concluded round of tariff negotiations within the GATT framework, the Uruguay Round began in 1986 in Punta del Este, Uruguay, concluded in 1993, and was ratified in 1994. Among other accomplishments, it created the World Trade Organization.

Value added. The price of a good minus the value of intermediate inputs used to produce it. Value added measures the contribution of capital and labor at a given stage of production.

Voluntary export restraint (VER). An agreement between nations in which the exporting nation voluntarily agrees to limit its exports in order to reduce competition in the importing country.

Washington Consensus. A set of policies prescribed for developing countries by the U.S. government, the International Monetary Fund and World Bank, and the unofficial community of think tanks centered in Washington, DC. In general, the policies favor the use of market forces over government direction as an allocative mechanism.

World Bank. A Bretton Woods institution, originally charged with the responsibility for providing financial and technical assistance to the war-torn economies of Europe. In the 1950s, the World Bank began to shift its focus to developing countries.

World Trade Organization (WTO). An umbrella organization created by the Uruguay Round of the GATT talks, the WTO houses the GATT and many other agreements. It is the main international body through which multilateral trade talks take place.

Zero sum. The costs and benefits of an activity cancel each other (equal zero).

INDEX